PAGE 28

ON THE ROAD

and insider tips

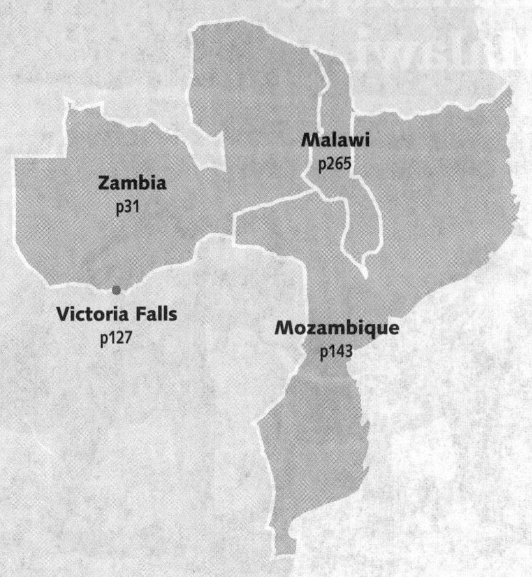

THIS EDITION WRITTEN AND RESEARCHED BY

Mary Fitzpatrick

Michael Grosberg, Trent Holden,

Kate Morgan, Nick Ray, Richard Waters

welcome to Zambia, Mozambique & Malawi

Wildlife

Zambia's wildlife-filled plains are legendary, from South Luangwa National Park in the southeast to Kafue National Park in the west. With their remoteness, species diversity and fine network of camps, the country's protected areas offer outstanding wildlife watching for those willing to meet the challenge of getting there and around. While Mozambique and Malawi aren't typically 'Big Five' destinations, they do offer rewarding wildlife watching, especially Mozambique's Gorongosa National Park (which is also a prime birding destination) and Malawi's Liwonde National Park, with its hippos and crocs.

Waterfalls

Thundering Victoria Falls is one of the continent's iconic images, the Seventh Natural Wonder of the World and a Unesco World Heritage Site. Whether you raft the rapids or stand on the spray-misted sidelines, the wildness, power and magnificence of the falls are unforgettable.

Landscapes

From the mist-covered peaks of Malawi's Mt Mulanje to the azure sea surrounding Mozambique's Bazaruto and Quirimbas Archipelagos, and the tracts of bush bordering the Zambezi River in southern Zambia, the diverse landscapes of these countries will captivate you at every turn.

Zambia's wildlife and waterfalls, Malawi's lake and mountains, Mozambique's islands and beaches. Each country has its own personality. Focus on exploring one, or sample a bit of all three.

(left) Elephants in South Luangwa National Park (p52), Zambia
(below) A dhow in the Bazaruto Archipelago (p186), Mozambique

Beaches

Mozambique's curvy coastline is one of Africa's longest and most alluring, from the windswept dunes of Ponta d'Ouro to the languid archipelagos and palm-fringed beaches of the far north. There are countless islands, including magical Mozambique Island and enchanting Ibo. The country's history and culture are tied to the sea, and most visitors spend their time along the coast, travelling from one wonderful beach or island to the next. Inland, the golden sands of Lake Malawi, with their backdrop of lush mountains rising up from the lakeshore, are a firm fixture in southern African travel itineraries.

Cultures

Wherever you go, immerse yourself in the everyday beauty, realities and vibrancy of African life and take advantage of opportunities for community-based tourism. In English-speaking Zambia and Malawi, local culture is often readily accessible. In Mozambique, Maputo's excellent dance, theatre and cultural scenes provide a good jumping-off point. In the end, it will be encounters with Zambians, Mozambicans and Malawians that will make your visit to the region so memorable.

›Zambia, Mozambique & Malawi

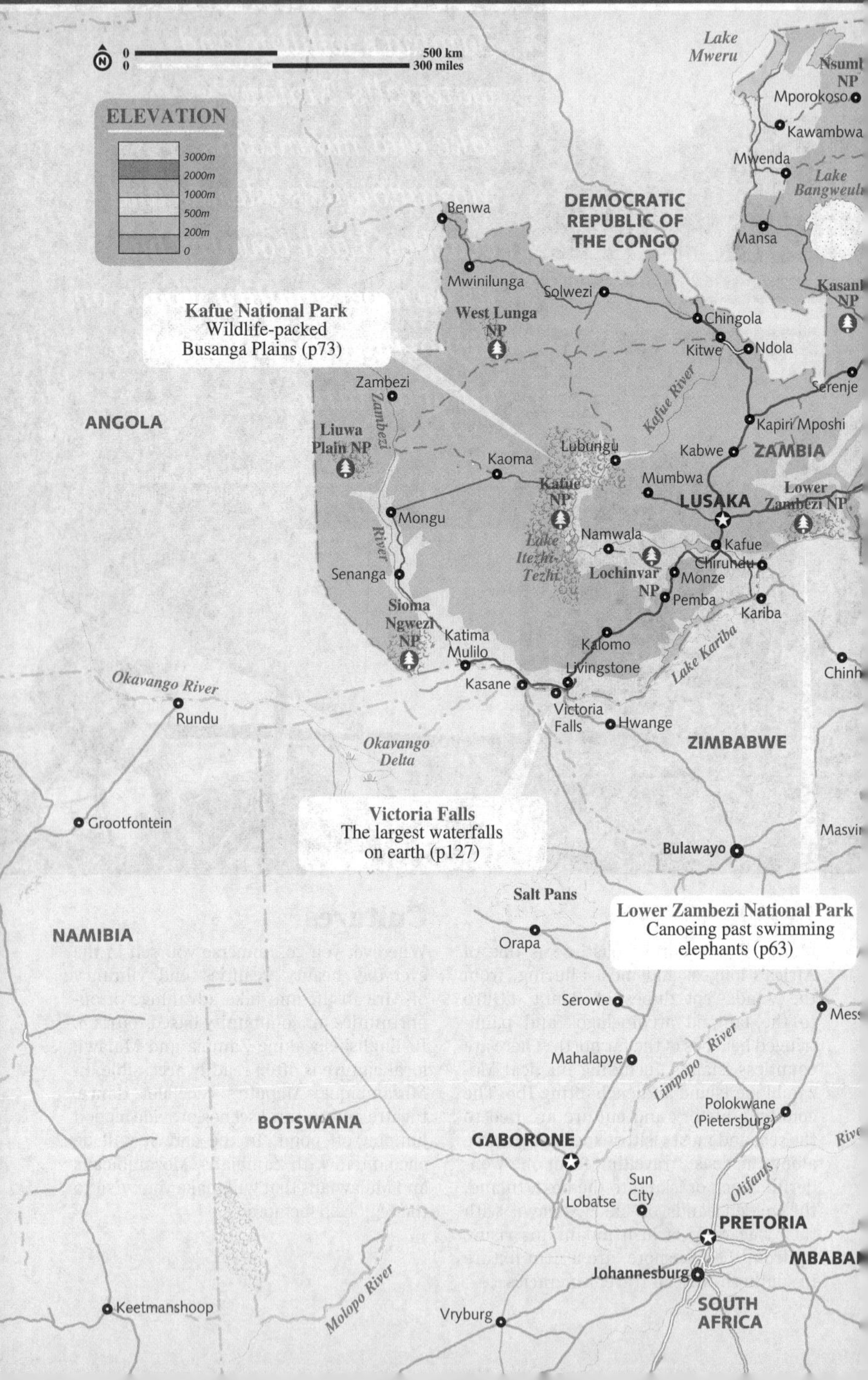

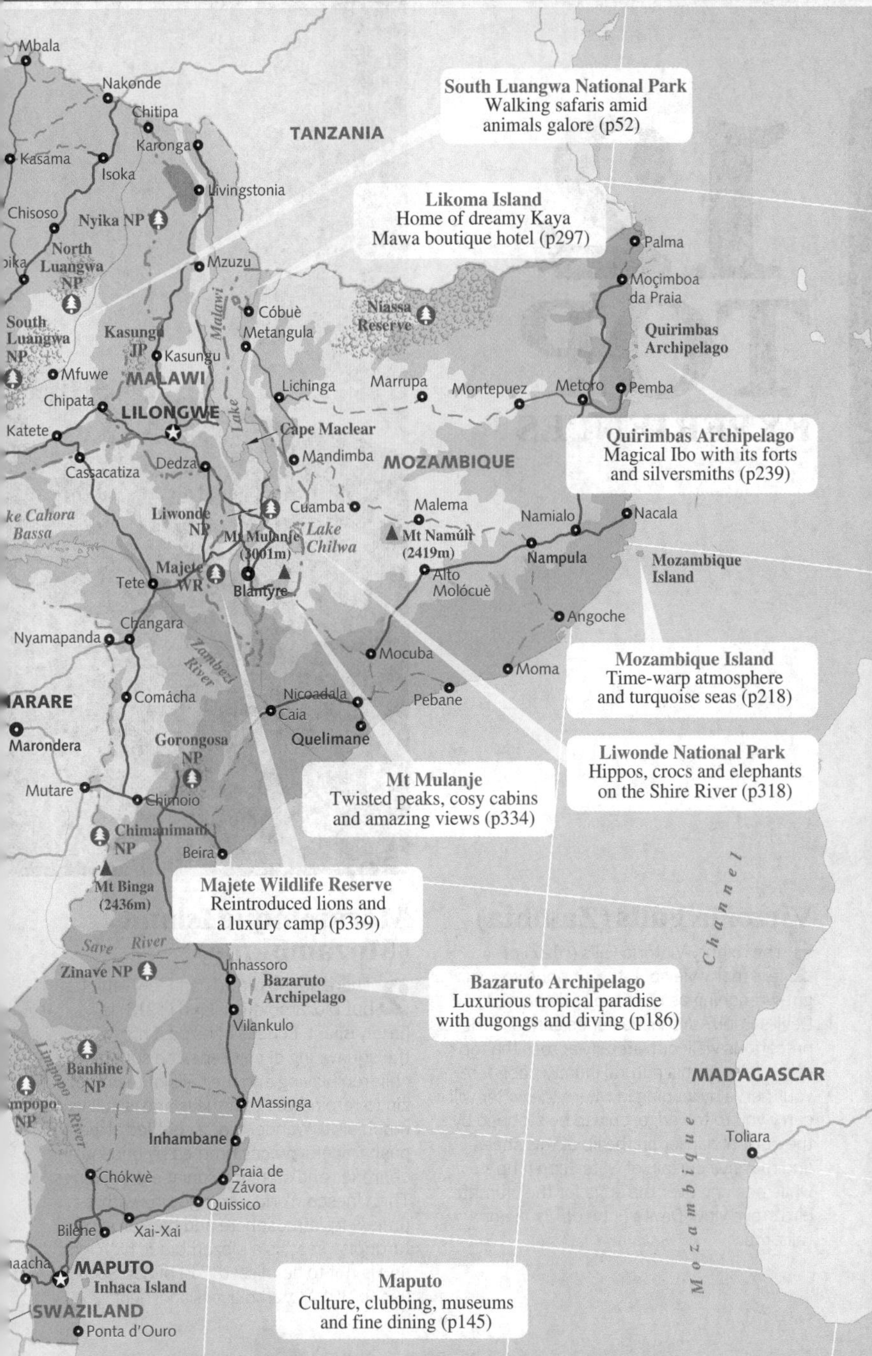
South Luangwa National Park
Walking safaris amid animals galore (p52)
Likoma Island
Home of dreamy Kaya Mawa boutique hotel (p297)
Quirimbas Archipelago
Magical Ibo with its forts and silversmiths (p239)
Mozambique Island
Time-warp atmosphere and turquoise seas (p218)
Liwonde National Park
Hippos, crocs and elephants on the Shire River (p318)
Mt Mulanje
Twisted peaks, cosy cabins and amazing views (p334)
Majete Wildlife Reserve
Reintroduced lions and a luxury camp (p339)
Bazaruto Archipelago
Luxurious tropical paradise with dugongs and diving (p186)
Maputo
Culture, clubbing, museums and fine dining (p145)
TANZANIA
MALAWI
LILONGWE
MOZAMBIQUE
MADAGASCAR
SWAZILAND
MAPUTO
Mozambique Channel
Mbala
Nakonde
Chitipa
Karonga
Kasama
Isoka
Livingstonia
Chisoso
Nyika NP
North Luangwa NP
Mzuzu
South Luangwa NP
Mfuwe
Kasungu JP
Kasungu
Chipata
Katete
Cassacatiza
Dedza
Lake Malawi
Cóbuè
Metangula
Niassa Reserve
Lichinga
Marrupa
Montepuez
Metoro
Pemba
Palma
Moçimboa da Praia
Quirimbas Archipelago
Cape Maclear
Mandimba
Cuamba
Malema
Namialo
Nacala
Nampula
Mozambique Island
Lake Cahora Bassa
Liwonde NP
Mt Mulanje (3001m)
Lake Chilwa
Mt Namúli (2419m)
Alto Molócuè
Majete WR
Tete
Blantyre
Angoche
Changara
Nyamapanda
Zambezi River
Mocuba
Moma
Pebane
Comácha
Nicoadala
Caia
Quelimane
HARARE
Marondera
Gorongosa NP
Mutare
Chimoio
Chimanimani NP
Beira
Mt Binga (2436m)
Save River
Zinave NP
Inhassoro
Bazaruto Archipelago
Vilankulo
Banhine NP
Limpopo River
Limpopo NP
Massinga
Inhambane
Toliara
Chókwè
Praia de Závora
Quissico
Bilene
Xai-Xai
Inhaca Island
Ponta d'Ouro

12 TOP EXPERIENCES

Victoria Falls (Zambia)

1 The mighty Victoria Falls (p127) offers many viewpoints, but none so gut-wrenching as from the aptly named Devil's Pool. Adrenaline fiends can take the precarious walk out, literally across the top of the falls, to this natural infinity pool. Test your nerve by leaping in where the water will carry you to the edge, only to be stopped by the natural barrier on the lip of this sheer and massive curtain of water. Lap it up while peeking over the edge for the ultimate bird's-eye view. Devil's Pool (p132), Victoria Falls, top

Mozambique Island (Mozambique)

2 There are no crowds and few vehicles, but Mozambique Island (p218) is hardly silent. Echoes of its past mix with the squawking of chickens, the sounds of children playing and the calls of the muezzin to remind you that the island is still very much alive. Wander along cobbled streets, past graceful *praças* rimmed by once-grand churches and stately colonial-era buildings. This Unesco World Heritage site, with its time-warp atmosphere and backdrop of turquoise seas, is a Mozambique highlight, and is not to be missed. Fort of São Sebastião (p219), Mozambique Island, right

1

YVETTE CARDOZO / GETTY IMAGES ©

2

OLIVER STREWE / GETTY IMAGES ©

Lower Zambezi National Park (Zambia)

3 Floating down one of Africa's great rivers – Zimbabwe's sandy banks on one side, Zambia's Lower Zambezi National Park (p63) on the other – can be a mesmerising experience. It's a front-row seat to a menagerie: pods of hippos surface with warning calls, crocodiles scuttle through grass, elephants slosh their way between islands, the odd impala churns through the water fleeing a predator and fierce tigerfish tempt anglers. Whether going by canoe or motorised boat, you'll be hypnotised by the languidly flowing river and pastel-hued sunsets.

South Luangwa National Park (Zambia)

4 On a walking safari, stroll through the bush single file with a rifle-carrying scout in the lead. No engine sounds break the music of the bush, and no barriers stand between you and the wildlife. Listen to animals scurrying in the underbrush as you focus on the little things, such as traditional medicinal uses of local plants or tracking animal dung spoor. Pause in the shade of an acacia tree, gaze over the wide plains filled with munching grazers and immerse yourself in the magnificent wildness that is South Luangwa National Park (p52).

3

4

ARIADNE VAN ZANDBERGEN / GETTY IMAGES ©

PER-GUNNAR OSTBY / GETTY IMAGES ©

GARY COOK / ALAMY ©

Liwonde Vational Park 'Malawi)

5 Set in dry savannah and woodland, this small eserve (p318) punches way ibove its weight with staggering populations of eleohants (500), hippos (1900) ınd almost two thousand rocs. Stay in the beguilingly omantic Mvuu Camp beside he Shire River, listening to assing elephants and snufing hippos as you fall asleep ı your cosy cabana. Then et up early and enjoy a dawn 'alk and boat ride past some ery territorial hippos. Bring ut your inner Indiana Jones.

Likoma Island (Malawi)

6 A visit to Likoma Island (p297) – on a turquoise stretch of Lake Malawi within a stone's throw of Mozambique – is unforgettable: think Caribbean-like waters, friendly locals, rustling palm trees and a sense that everything can wait until tomorrow. Once you've seen the extraordinary St Peter's Cathedral, get down to chilling in the country's nicest hostel, Mango Drift. Alternatively, stay at the heavenly Kaya Mawa, on a crescent beach with powder-fine sand, and perfectly calibrated staff and rooms designed around the island's natural rock formations. Kaya Mawa (p297), Likoma Island, top right

Bazaruto Archipelago (Mozambique)

7 Brilliant hues of turquoise and jade, laced with shimmering white sand in the banks, dolphins cavorting in the swells and dugongs grazing in the shallows, graceful sand dunes, pink flamingos, shoals of fish, brilliant corals and swaying palm trees – this is the Bazaruto Archipelago (p186), a world-class marine park and the quintessential tropical paradise for anyone seeking a getaway. Stay for a while in one of the handful of luxury lodges or sail over from the mainland for a day on a dhow. Either way, you'll undoubtedly wish your visit was longer.

MIKE D KOCK / GETTY IMAGES ©

Quirimbas Archipelago (Mozambique)

8 Idyllic islands strewn across azure seas, dense mangrove channels opening onto pristine patches of soft, white sand, dhows silhouetted against the horizon and magical Ibo Island, with its silversmiths, fort and crumbling mansions – the remote Quirimbas Archipelago (p239) is a time and place apart, accessed with difficulty, and left behind with regret. Whether you dive and snorkel amid the corals and fish, wander Ibo's sandy lanes, relax in a luxury lodge or explore on a dhow, the archipelago never fails to enchant. Reef at Vamizi Island (p242), Quirimbas Archipelago, above left

Maputo (Mozambique)

9 Maputo (p145) is Mozambique's pulse point, its economic centre, cultural heart and historical treasure trove, with an intoxicating vibe and a stunning setting overlooking Maputo Bay. Wide jacaranda- and flame-tree-lined streets flow from the quieter upper part of town down into the bustling, low-lying baixa. Shady sidewalk cafes offer an ideal spot to watch the passing scene, and the city's pulsating nightlife, good shopping, rewarding museums and fine array of restaurants all beckon, making any visit here a pleasure. A Maputo market, top right

Kafue National Park (Zambia)

10 Imagine a small, extremely diverse country, but with animals substituted for people – this is western Zambia's Kafue National Park (p73). On the Busanga Plains in the north, the vistas open up to the horizon, with herds of grazer congregating as far as you can see. The park's south feels worlds away, with mysterious riverine landscapes, jungle-clad islands, fast moving rapids and meandering channels. North or south, there are few visitors in this land where the wild things roam. Cheetah, bottom right

Mt Mulanje (Malawi)

11 At an elevation of 3002 m, the Mulanje massif (p334) is a vision of rolling rasslands intersected by forest ravines. It's lso a paradise for trekkers and climbers, with everal climbable peaks and a series of cabaas for overnight stays during longer hikes. magine montane forest acroak with frogs, ocky outcrops and clear mountain streams or refilling your bottle. This is among the nost dramatic scenery in the country. But, be varned, you have to earn it. The only way up s on foot. Hiking on Mt Mulanje, top

Majete Wildlife Reserve (Malawi)

12 The new star in the Malawian firmament is lovely Majete Wildlife Reserve (p339), 700 sq km of riverine valleys and *miombo* woodlands situated in the Rift Valley close to Blantyre. Sip sundowners under the watchful eyes of hippos and crocs in the meandering Shire River, dodge buffaloes and elephants and ensconce yourself in luxurious boutique-style digs at wonderful Mkulumadzi Camp. Majete – a conservation model for others to follow – is also home to Malawi's first reintroduced lion pride. Sable antelope, bottom

11

DAVID ELSE / GETTY IMAGES ©

12

JOHN WARBURTON-LEE / GETTY IMAGES ©

need to know

Currencies

» **Zambia** Zambian kwacha (ZMW)

» **Mozambique** New Mozambican Metical (Mtc)

» **Malawi** Malawian kwacha (MK)

Languages

» **Zambia** English, African languages

» **Mozambique** Portuguese, African languages

» **Malawi** English, African languages

When to Go

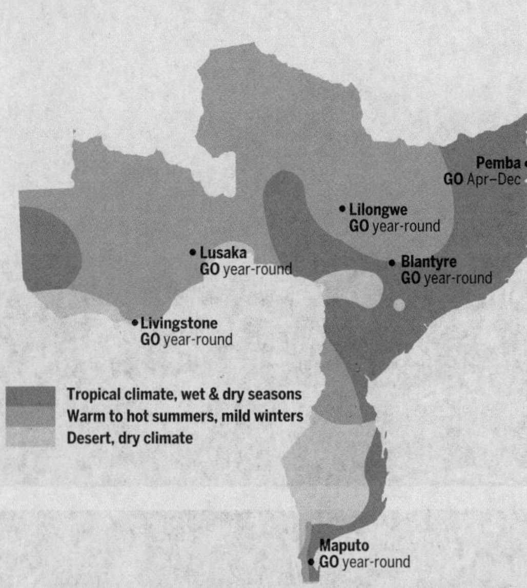

High Season
(Jun–Oct)

» Weather throughout is cooler and dry.

» August can be very crowded and pricier.

» Animal-spotting is easiest from August to October, due to sparse foliage and animals congregating around dwindling water sources.

Shoulder Season
(Apr–May, Nov–Dec)

» Ideal for travel, with green landscapes, but watch for muddy, impassable roads before the rains have dried out.

» Peak-season prices from mid-December to mid-January and at Easter.

Low Season
(Jan–Mar)

» Heavy rains make secondary roads muddy and some areas inaccessible.

» It seldom rains all day, every day; landscapes are lush and green.

Your Daily Budget

Malawi tends to be cheaper, Zambia and Mozambique pricier.

Budget Less Than
US$50

» Room in basic budget guesthouse US$15-30.

» Ask about low-season and children's discounts.

» Local-style meals are tasty and cheap.

Midrange
US$50-200

» Double room in a mid-range hotel US$50-150.

» Meals in Western-style restaurants.

» Extra for safaris and vehicle rental.

Top End
US$200-$500-plus

» Upmarket hotel room from US$150.

» All-inclusive safari packages from US$200 per person per day.

Money

» ATMs are found in cities and major towns; most take Visa, some also take MasterCard. Credit cards are not widely accepted for payment, and often incur a surcharge.

Visas

» Single-entry visas, where required, are available at major international airports and at many land borders (though not at land borders with Tanzania).

Mobile phones

» Local SIM cards can be used in (unlocked) European and Australian phones; others must be set to roaming. Starter packs and top-up vouchers are widely available.

Driving

» Drive on the left in all three countries.

Websites

» **BBC News – Africa** (www.bbc.co.uk/news/world/Africa) Keeping a finger on southern Africa's pulse.

» **Club of Mozambique** (www.clubofmozambique.com) Heaps of tourism info and news.

» **Integrated Regional Information Network** (www.irinnews.org) Regional humanitarian news.

» **Lonely Planet** (www.lonelyplanet.com) Destination info, hotels, forum and more.

» **Zambezi Traveller** (www.zambezitraveller.com) For destinations along the Zambezi.

Exchange Rates

Australia	A$1	ZMW5.56	Mtc31	MK369
Canada	C$1	ZMW5.32	Mtc30	MK355
Japan	¥100	ZMW5.86	Mtc33	MK392
New Zealand	NZ$1	ZMW4.46	Mtc25	MK294
UK	UK£1	ZMW8.43	Mtc48	MK559
US	US$1	ZMW5.34	Mtc30	MK350

For current exchange rates, see www.xe.com.

Important Numbers

In all three countries, mobile numbers are six digits plus a four-digit provider code. There are no central police or other emergency numbers.

	Zam	Moz	Mal
Country code	☎+260	☎+258	☎+265
International access code	☎00	☎00	☎00

Arriving in Zambia, Mozambique & Malawi

» **Kenneth Kaunda International Airport, Lusaka (Zambia)**
Taxis to centre (ZMW110-150)

» **Maputo International Airport, Maputo (Mozambique)**
Taxis to centre (Mtc400-500)

» **Kamuzu International Airport, Lilongwe (Malawi)**
Taxis to centre (MK4000); Airport bus to central hotels (MK1000)

What to Bring

Binoculars and a field guide Essential for wildlife watching and birding.

Torch (flashlight) You'll be without electricity in the bush

Mosquito repellent, net and prophylaxis Always sleep under a net; follow your doctor's recommendations regarding malaria prophylaxis

Travel insurance Be sure emergency medical air evacuation (at least to Johannesburg) is included; also check diving and other 'dangerous activities' coverage

Wind- and waterproof jacket For chilly, damp highland areas

Yellow fever vaccination certificate Required for crossing many land borders

Shore shoes For beach walking

Visa card For accessing cash at ATMs

Portuguese phrasebook Useful if you'll be visiting Mozambique

if you like...

Wildlife

Southern Africa abounds with wildlife, and Zambia, Mozambique and Malawi reflect this. Zambia is the big wildlife-watching drawcard, but Mozambique and Malawi each have their own attractions as well.

South Luangwa National Park Wildlife, wonderful scenery and walking safaris (p52)

Kafue National Park A vast wilderness known especially for its wildlife-packed Serengeti-like grasslands (p73)

Lower Zambezi National Park Canoe safaris, riverine vistas, swimming elephants and fantastic scenery (p63)

Gorongosa National Park Antelopes, bushwalks, elephants, and a sublime setting (p194)

Niassa Reserve Awash in elephants, sable antelopes, buffaloes and zebras, but dense bush makes sightings challenging (p232)

Liwonde National Park Crocs, hippos and elephants in an enchanting river setting (p318)

Kasanka National Park Swamplands and sitatungas are some of this park's most attractive features (p91)

Majete Wildlife Reserve Reintroduced lions in one of Malawi's best reserves (p339)

Beaches

The region's best beaches are in Mozambique, where you'll find fine white sand, dunes, palms and a languid ambience. Inland, Lake Malawi's tranquil shoreline has been drawing travellers for decades.

Tofo A lovely arc of white sand with azure waters, surfing and diving opportunities with manta rays and whale sharks (p176)

Chidenguele High, vegetated dunes back a long, wide beach that stretches into the horizon in both directions (p171)

Pomene A stunning estuarine setting and rewarding birding are among the draws at this often-overlooked spot found on the southern Mozambique coast (p180)

Ponta d'Ouro Mozambique's southernmost tip features a long, dune-fringed beach with reliable surf and the chance to spot dolphins (p165)

Lake Malawi Cape Maclear, with its golden sands and exclusive Mumbo Island, is just one of many enjoyable spots along the Lake Malawi shoreline (p309)

Chilling Out

Whether it is laid-back backpacker vibes, upmarket island-lodge pampering or bush camp chic, Zambia, Mozambique and Malawi have chilling out down to a fine art.

Nkwichi Lodge Spend a night here, or three, revelling in the remoteness, snorkelling in crystal-clear waters and kayaking past quiet coves (p232)

Bazaruto Archipelago Lodges Take your pick – all are lovely patches of luxury amid the stunning, natural setting of Bazaruto Archipelago National Park (p187)

Shiwa Ng'andu For something out of the ordinary, try this peaceful country manor and the nearby Kapishya Hot Springs (p96)

Lake Kariba Spend a few low-key days at this beautiful artificial lake enjoying sunset cruises and walks along the dam wall (p67)

Likoma Island This jewel in Lake Malawi has sublime crescent bays, views across the water to Mozambique and a delightfully slow pace (p297)

Nkhata Bay Chill out in a reed hut on the beach at one of Malawi's classic relaxation destinations (p291)

JOHN WARBURTON-LEE / GETTY IMAGES ©

» A pride of lions in Kafue National Park (p73), Zambia

History & Culture

Early Bantu-speaking migrants, later influxes from Arabia, India and the Orient and European colonialists – all have left their mark on the region's history and cultures.

Mozambique Island Step back through the centuries in this historical treasure trove and cultural melting pot (p219)

Ibo Island With its fortress, silversmiths and crumbling colonial-era mansions, Ibo Island is caught in an enchanting time warp (p240)

Livingstonia Stroll around the old stone buildings for a glimpse into Malawi's fascinating colonial-era past (p283)

Maputo Whether taking a walking tour through lively Mafalala neighbourhood, exploring the bustling baixa or watching for revolutionary-themed murals, Mozambique capital's history comes alive at every turn (p145)

Kungoni Centre of Culture & Art Malawian history and culture come alive here, especially in the vibrant murals of the Chamare Museum (p307)

Kuomboka The logistics can be challenging, but it's worth trying to catch this annual ceremony of the Lozi people of western Zambia (p80)

Landscapes & Nature

In all three countries, diversity and beauty will surround you.

Mutinondo Wilderness Mutinondo offers wide vistas and soul-stirring landscapes dotted with huge purple-hued inselbergs and laced with meandering rivers (p94)

Inhambane This province's long coastline is known for its stunning beaches, its flamingos and water birds and its picturesque dhows (p173)

Victoria Falls Thundering Victoria Falls is one of the most breath-taking natural spectacles on earth (p127)

Mt Mulanje This towering hulk of twisted granite – Malawi's 'Island in the Sky – rises up majestically from the surrounding plains, and offers lovely scenery and easy access (p334)

Viphya Plateau Sweeping valleys and cool forests are the highlights of this stunning highland area (p299)

Nyika Plateau Enjoy Nyika Plateau's grasslands and wildflowers on foot, by bike or on horseback (p285)

Ngonye Falls This 1km-wide chain of waterfalls, rapids and rocky islands is remote, and stunningly beautiful (p82)

Adventure & Off-Beat Travel

Few regions are so ideally suited to adventure travel as this one. In Zambia, almost anywhere outside of Lusaka is remote, while northern Mozambique is one of the continent's last travel frontiers. Malawi is tamer, but with some off-beat gems.

Northern Mozambique Sail by dhow past remote islands or venture into trackless bush in the interior (p212)

Chimanimani Mountains Get to know local culture while hiking through lush, seldom-visited forest areas (p200)

Kalambo Falls Hike to the top of Africa's second-highest single-drop waterfall (p100)

Vwaza Marsh Wildlife Reserve Off Malawi's mainstream tourist track, this intriguing reserve is awash with buffaloes, elephants and hippos (p288)

Liuwa Plain National Park These remote grasslands host vast herds of wildebeest and exceptionally large and numerous hyenas (p80)

Mt Gorongosa Steeped in local lore and wonderful for birdwatchers, Mt Gorongosa is also an off-the-beaten-track hiking destination (p195)

month by month

Top Events

1. **Kusefya Pangwena**, August (Zambia)
2. **Lake of Stars Music Festival**, October (Malawi)
3. **Mt Mulanje Porters Race**, July (Malawi)
4. **Timbilas Festival**, August (Mozambique)
5. **Marrabenta Festival**, February (Mozambique)

January

January throughout the region is warm, wet and ideal for birding. Despite the humidity and the rains, the early part of the month still sees many visitors enjoying the New Year's peak-season holiday period.

February

The rains are now in full force, with the occasional tropical storm and high humidity along the coast. Secondary roads are muddy, and getting around away from main roads can be a challenge.

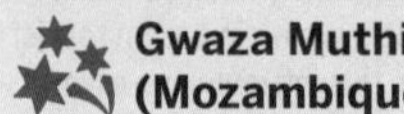

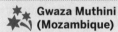

Gwaza Muthini (Mozambique)

This celebration in Marracuene (25km north of Maputo) in early February commemorates the colonial resistors who lost their lives in the 1895 Battle of Marracuene. It also marks the start of the season of *ukanhi*, a traditional brew made from the fruit of the *canhoeiro* tree.

Marrabenta Festival (Mozambique)

To hear *marrabenta* – Mozambique's national music – at its best, don't miss the annual Marrabenta Festival. It's held mostly in Maputo, but also in Beira, Inhambane and several other locations. The timing is set to coincide with Marracuene's Gwaza Muthini commemorations. See ccfmoz.com.

N'cwala (Zambia)

The Ngoni people hold this thanksgiving or 'first fruits' festival in late February near Chipata in eastern Zambia. There's plenty of food, dance and music for celebrating the approaching end of the rainy season and to pray for a successful harvest.

April

The long rains are finally tapering off, with green landscapes everywhere and still-muddy roads. Visitor numbers increase in connection with the Easter holidays. Birding is at its best, and Victoria Falls are swathed in spray.

Kuomboka (Zambia)

Kuomboka is celebrated by the Lozi people of western Zambia at the end of the rainy season to mark the journey of their *litunga* (king) from his compound on the Zambezi flood plains to higher ground. Dates vary.

May

Cooler, drier weather throughout the region makes May a delightful time to travel, although secondary roads may still be difficult to negotiate in some areas.

Maputo International Music Festival (Mozambique)

This festival – held as much to celebrate the charms of Maputo, as to celebrate music itself – consists of a series of concerts by classical and contemporary musicians at various venues around the city. See www.maputomusic.com.

June

The entire region is now settling in to enjoy the cool, dry weather. June is generally a comfortable, uncrowded time to travel, although the sea along the southernmost coast can be windy and choppy.

Ibo Island Day (Mozambique)

June 24th marks the feast of St John the Baptist, which is celebrated (more recently as 'Ibo Island Day') with great gusto on Ibo Island in Mozambique's Quirimbas Archipelago. Events include traditional music and dance, and dhow races.

July

Prime wildlife-watching season is just around the corner, with the weather continuing to be cool and dry. Travel season is also entering full swing. Humpback whales have reached Mozambican waters on their migration up from Antarctica.

Lake Malawi International Yachting Marathon (Malawi)

This five-day sailing extravaganza on Lake Malawi – claimed by promoters to be one of the longest freshwater sailing competitions in the world – covers about 500km, from Mangochi in the south to Nkhata Bay in the north.

Mt Mulanje Porters Race (Malawi)

Originally only for Mt Mulanje porters, this 25km rocky run across rivers and gorges to the 2500m high Chambe Plateau now has an international following. Hikers typically take around 12 to 13 hours for the route; the runners do it in two to three.

August

Humpback whales are now readily spotted along much of the Mozambican coast. Although dolphins are seen year-round, August tends to be particularly favourable for sightings. Along the coast, hotels fill up, with peak-season prices.

Timbilas Festival (Mozambique)

Watch Chopi musicians play intricate rhythms on large marimbas, often in orchestras consisting of 20 or more instruments, plus singers and dancers. While the festival is not always well organised, the musical tradition is fascinating. It's held in the southern Mozambique town of Quissico. See www.amizava.org.

Kusefya Pangwena (Zambia)

At Kusefya Pangwena, northern Zambia's Bemba people celebrate their 1830s victory over the marauding Ngoni with a programme of music, drama and dance. The festival is held near Kasama over four days in August.

September

Clear, dry weather, minimal foliage and dwindling rivers make September one of the best months for wildlife watching, as animals congregate around scarce water sources.

Dockanema (Mozambique)

This festival showcases documentary films from the southern Africa region and from other Lusophone countries, and is a real highlight for both history and cinematography buffs. Maputo is the place to be, with many free screenings and discussion forums. See www.dockanema.org.

National Arts & Crafts Fair (Mozambique)

The low-key National Arts & Crafts Fair, held in Maputo's small *fortaleza* (fort), celebrates artisanry of all types. Both browsers and buyers are welcome. Months and dates vary; see www.cedarte.org.mz for an update.

October

Prime wildlife-watching season continues into dry, warm October, with water sources scarce and wildlife plentiful. It's an ideal time to travel – very hot in the interior, but still moderate along the coast, with jacarandas abloom.

Lake of Stars International Music Festival (Malawi)

One of the region's largest spectacles, this three-day music festival features live acts from around Africa and from the UK. It's held in various places on the lake shore, with proceeds benefitting charity. See www.lakeofstars.org.

November

November marks the end of the dry season and the start of the hottest weather before the rains arrive. With the start of the rains come muddy roads, as well as calving season for many animals.

December

Along the coast, changing winds have brought calmer seas. Whale shark sightings tend to be particularly good now, during the height of summer. Diving conditions are also optimal, with calmer seas and warmer temperatures.

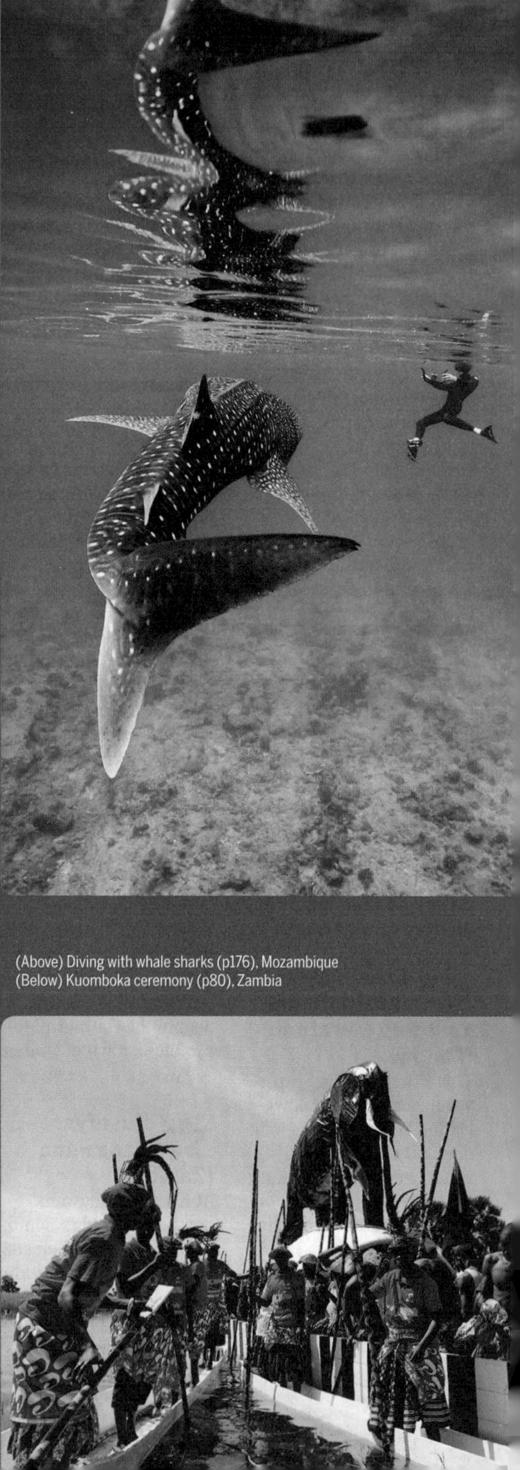

(Above) Diving with whale sharks (p176), Mozambique
(Below) Kuomboka ceremony (p80), Zambia

itineraries

Whether you've got six days or 60, these itineraries provide a starting point for the trip of a lifetime. Want more inspiration? Head online to lonelyplanet.com/thorntree to chat with other travellers.

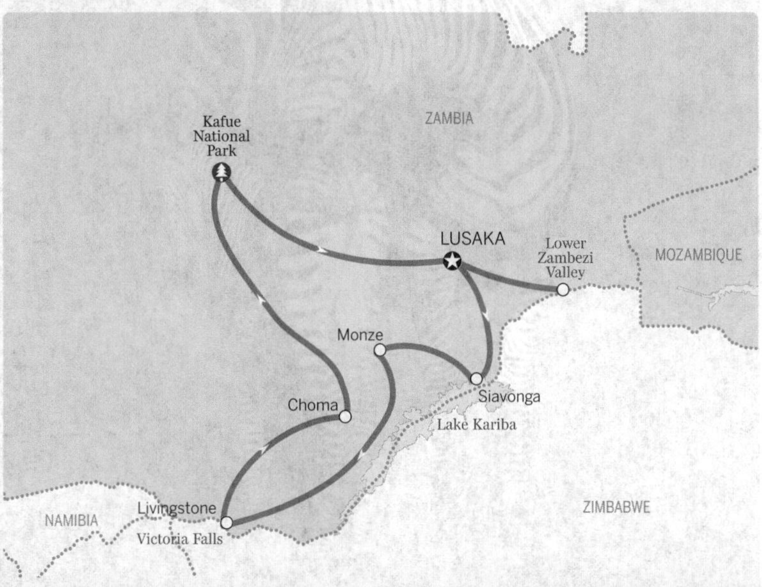

Two Weeks

Wildlife & Waterfalls

This itinerary takes in several of the region's highlights: wildlife, the majestic Victoria Falls and Lake Kariba, one of Africa's largest artificial lakes. Start in **Lusaka**, Zambia's gateway and an amenable place to get acquainted with local life. Once settled, head down to **Siavonga** on sparkling, scenic **Lake Kariba** and relax on a boat cruise. From Siavonga, retrace your steps northwest towards Kafue junction, and then head southwest to the small town of **Monze**, with its attractive nearby campsite.

The next stop is the historic town of **Livingstone**, gateway to thundering **Victoria Falls**, which have spray that can be seen from 50km away. Among the many diversions: serene canoe trips on top of the falls or rafting along the churning Zambezi down below. Once you have had a chance to appreciate the falls' magnificence, retrace your steps to the busy market town of **Choma**, and from there travel northwest to **Kafue National Park**, with excellent birding and abundant wildlife, especially on the grasslands of the Busanga Plains. Spend as much time here as possible before returning to Lusaka. With another week, you could include a detour to the lovely, wildlife-filled **Lower Zambezi Valley**.

ARIADNE VAN ZANDBERGEN / GETTY IMAGES ©

» (above) Zebras, South Luangwa National Park (p52), Zambia
» (left) The shores of Lake Malawi at Livingstonia (p283), Malawi

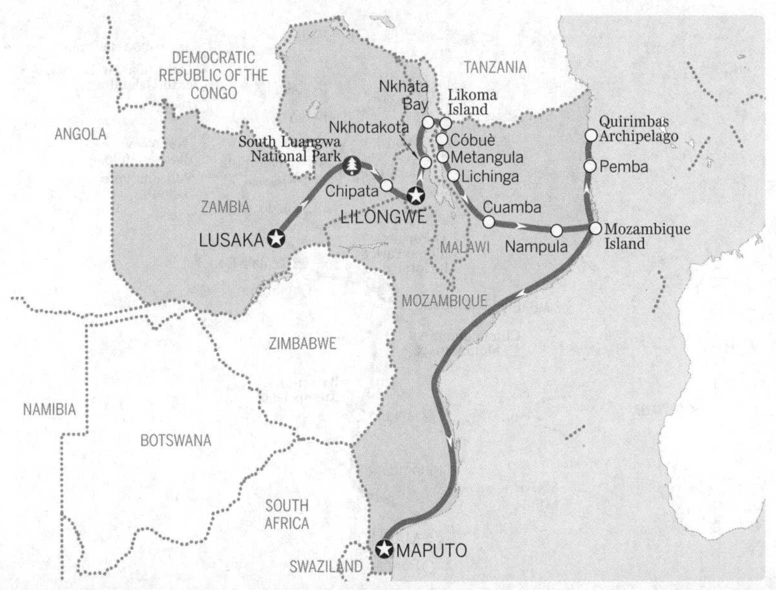

Six Weeks

Zambia, Mozambique & Malawi Sampler

Exploring all three countries in a single trip makes for an excellent journey. Start in **Lusaka**, getting your bearings and becoming acquainted with this low-key capital. Allow time also to appreciate its restaurants and its nightlife before taking a flight (or enduring two days of torturous bus and minibus connections) to **South Luangwa National Park**. This is Zambia's premier park, with an incredible density of animals. Plan on at least three days here, including time for night drives, daytime wildlife drives and a walking safari or two before continuing towards the Malawi border. Continue on via the busy but amenable town of **Chipata** to the Zambia–Malawi border, from where it is just a short jaunt to sleepy **Lilongwe**. Lilongwe merits a day or two, perhaps visiting the renowned Dedza Pottery or hiking through the cool forests of the Ntchisi Forest Reserve, before heading north to Lake Malawi, passing through historic **Nkhotakota**. A possible detour en route is to Nkhotakota Wildlife Reserve where, with luck, you may see elephants, antelopes and even lions.

Once at the lake, **Nkhata Bay**, with its chilled vibe and many water-based activities, is the perfect place to relax. From here, make your way to **Likoma Island** to explore the lake's crystal waters, visit the historic cathedral and enjoy the laid-back island pace. From Likoma, it is straightforward to continue over to **Cóbuè**, a short sail away on Mozambique's wild northwestern lake coast. Once in Cóbuè, you could continue by pre-arranged charter boat to lovely Nkwichi Lodge, or make your way southwards towards **Metangula** and on to **Lichinga**. Spend a day or two in Lichinga, with its jacarandas and cool temperatures, before travelling to **Cuamba**, starting point for the classic 10-hour train ride east to **Nampula**. Nampula, in turn, is the jumping off point for magical **Mozambique Island**, a Unesco World Heritage Site and Africa highlight, with its cobbled streets, colonial-era architecture and constant backdrop of turquoise seas. You'll likely want to linger at least two or three days here, perhaps longer, before heading north to **Pemba** and the wonderful **Quirimbas Archipelago**, or south towards **Maputo**.

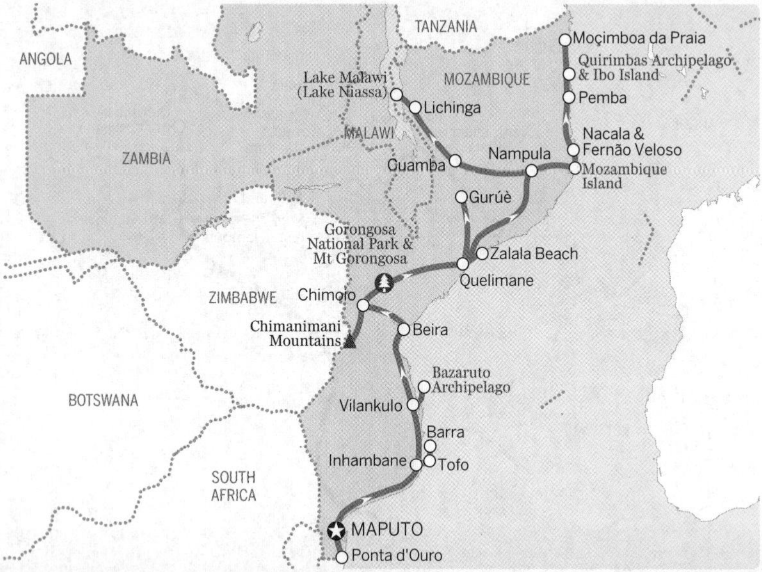

ANGOLA
TANZANIA
Moçimboa da Praia
Quirimbas Archipelago & Ibo Island
Lake Malawi (Lake Niassa)
MOZAMBIQUE
Lichinga
Pemba
MALAWI
Nacala & Fernão Veloso
ZAMBIA
Nampula
Cuamba
Mozambique Island
Gurúè
Gorongosa National Park & Mt Gorongosa
Zalala Beach
Quelimane
ZIMBABWE
Chimoio
Chimanimani Mountains
Beira
Bazaruto Archipelago
BOTSWANA
Vilankulo
Barra
Inhambane
Tofo
SOUTH AFRICA
MAPUTO
Ponta d'Ouro

Two Months
Mozambique Grand Tour

To explore Mozambique from south to north (north to south works just as well) in a grand overland tour, allow at least two months. With more limited time, it's easy enough to choose sections from the following itinerary, perhaps taking a flight or two to break up the longer stretches.

Starting in the far south, spend time enjoying the wonderful beach at **Ponta d'Ouro** before continuing on to the lively, culture-packed capital of **Maputo**. Here, the many museums, sidewalk cafes, restaurants and craft shops will keep you busy for at least several days.

Continue northwards to **Inhambane**, with its flamingos, dhows and wonderful nearby beaches, including those at **Tofo** and **Barra**. Further north, **Vilankulo** is an amenable spot for a day or three. It is also the springboard to the **Bazaruto Archipelago**, with its diving and upmarket lodges.

From Vilankulo, continue north by bus to **Beira**, spending a day or two in this old port city before heading west to **Chimoio**, the best base for organising hiking in the **Chimanimani Mountains**. Allow four days or more, including transport, for the excursion. Once back in Chimoio, make your way northeastwards to lovely **Gorongosa National Park** and some more hiking and birding on **Mt Gorongosa**.

The overland route continues north via **Quelimane** (nearby **Zalala Beach** makes a good detour) and **Nampula** to **Mozambique Island**, where it is easy to spend at least two or three days taking in the sights. Possible diversions en route include to scenic **Gurúè**, with its cool climate, jacarandas, tea plantations and hiking, and to the area around **Nacala** for relaxing and diving at Nuarro lodge or in the **Fernão Veloso** area.

Continue north to **Pemba** or nearby beaches before travelling to the **Quirimbas Archipelago**. All the islands are lovely, with **Ibo** a highlight. Sail back to the mainland, and continue northwards to **Moçimboa da Praia** – a pleasant stop for a day or three – and on into Tanzania. Alternatively, after visiting Mozambique Island, take the train west from Nampula to **Cuamba** and then continue on to **Lichinga**, **Lake Niassa** and into Malawi.

» (above) Cathedral of Nossa Senhora de Fátima, Nampula (p213), Mozambique
» (left) The beach at Tofo (p176), Mozambique

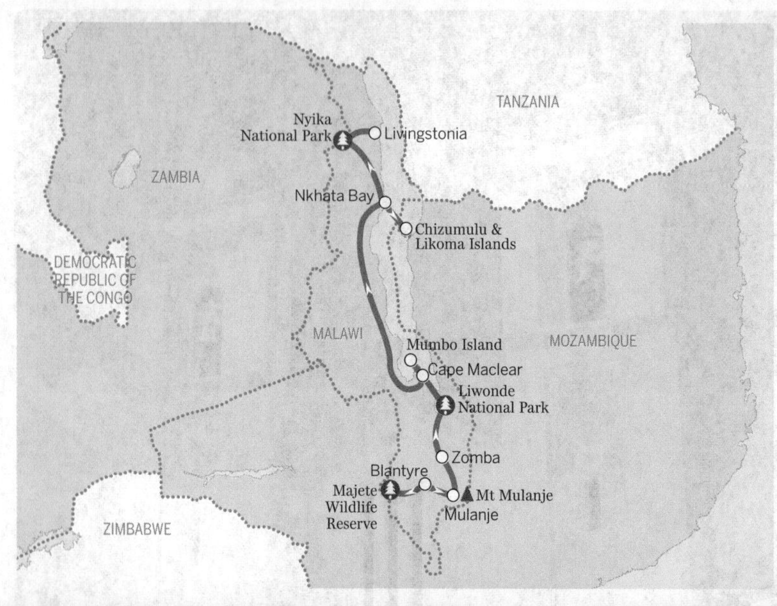

Three to Four Weeks

Malawi Odyssey

Whether you start in the north or south, this is the ultimate Malawi journey, taking in mountains, wilderness, historical riches and the lake with its beaches. It is best done in a month, to allow time for side trips, but you could squeeze it into three weeks in a pinch.

Fly first into **Blantyre** and spend a day or so getting acclimatised. Time and budget permitting, you could make an easy detour southwest to **Majete Wildlife Reserve** for several days of pampered wildlife watching before continuing southwards to **Mulanje** for a three-day hike across **Mt Mulanje**, the country's highest peak. Recover by spending time in an old planter's house on one of Mulanje's many tea estates before continuing on to the colonial gem of **Zomba**. Here, enjoy a day or two of gentle walking on the misty Zomba Plateau, perhaps finding time for a riding lesson as well.

From Zomba make your way northwards to nearby **Liwonde National Park**, its lovely scenery dominated by the wide, meandering Shire River. There are hippos and crocs aplenty, as well as various antelope species, zebras and the chance for both canoe and walking safaris. After you've had your fill, head for the lake and the small resort village of **Cape Maclear**. Budget at least three days here, with an overnight visit to **Mumbo Island** in Lake Malawi National Marine Park and time kayaking and swimming with the brilliantly coloured fish.

From Cape Maclear make your way up the lakeshore to **Nkhata Bay**, Malawi's other famous lakeshore resort. Here, you can snorkel, kayak or even take a course at a local dive school. From Nkhata Bay you could detour to **Chizumulu and Likoma Islands**, or continue northwards to lovely **Nyika National Park**, the country's largest, where you can explore wild, flower-carpeted grasslands, reminiscent of the Yorkshire Moors, on foot or on horseback. Finally, it's time to delve into history at **Livingstonia**, a quiet hilltop town that provides a glimpse into Malawi's colonial-era past. From Livingstonia, continue northwards into Tanzania (and from there into Zambia), or retrace your steps southwards, perhaps continuing on into Mozambique or Zambia.

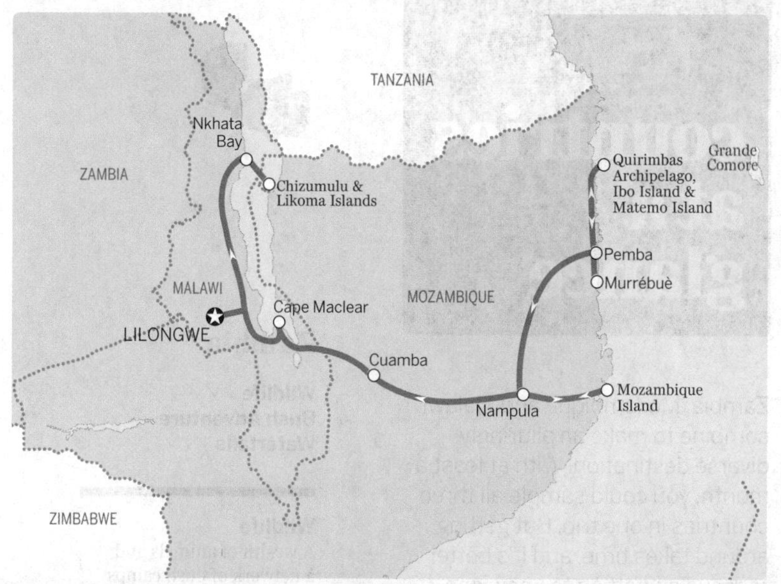

Three Weeks

Beaches & Islands

Mozambique has some of the most enticing coastline on the continent. Combine exploration of its northern highlights with visits to Lake Malawi's alluring islands and inland beaches for an adventurous but relaxing itinerary.

The beach town of **Pemba**, in northern Mozambique, makes a good starting point. Spend a few days here getting acclimated and enjoying the vibe. Don't miss nearby **Murrébuè**, with its kite-surfing, quiet, white sand and turquoise-hued ocean vistas. Next, set off for enchanting **Ibo Island**, a regional highlight, with its massive star-shaped fort, its silversmiths and its crumbling colonial-era mansions. After exploring and enjoying the island's pace, charter a dhow for several days to explore **Matemo** or one of the other nearby islands in the **Quirimbas Archipelago**. Once you manage to tear yourself away from the charms of the Quirimbas islands, turn southwards – the most straightforward route will take you via Pemba – to the crowded regional hub of **Nampula**. If you arrive early enough in Nampula, it is possible to avoid overnighting here, continuing the same day on to magical **Mozambique Island**. Plan at least several days exploring this Unesco World Heritage Site, with its time-warp atmosphere, historical treasures, cultural riches, sea breezes and wonderfully low-key pace.

Once back on the mainland, you will need to pass through Nampula for an overnight, before catching the train west to **Cuamba**. The ride is not anywhere near the coast, but it is scenic, and offers fascinating glimpses into local life. After an overnight in Cuamba (where the train arrives late afternoon), continue into Malawi via either the Entre Lagos or Mandimba border posts, and then travel straight on to lovely **Lake Malawi**. **Cape Maclear** makes a convenient first stop, with many options for snorkelling, kayaking and relaxing.

From Cape Maclear, the route turns northwards to the scenic beachside outpost of **Nkhata Bay**, with its fine selection of lodges, kayaking, swimming and diving. From Nkhata Bay, it is possible to detour to beautiful **Chizumulu and Likoma Islands**, where the highlights are the scenery, local life, the relaxed pace and Likoma's historic cathedral. Once you've had your fill, travel southwards to **Lilongwe** and a flight home.

countries at a glance

Zambia, Mozambique and Malawi combine to make an alluringly diverse destination. With at least a month, you could sample all three countries in one trip. But getting around takes time, and it's better to focus on getting to know one or two areas in depth, rather than trying to take in too much on one visit.

For wildlife, Zambia tops the list, with vast tracts of animal-filled bush. Majestic Victoria Falls is another major draw, and one of the continent's highlights. For culture, Malawi is one of the most accessible destinations. It's also the easiest introduction to southern Africa for first-time visitors. Mozambique offers outstanding beaches, idyllic islands and – in the north – the chance for real adventure travel.

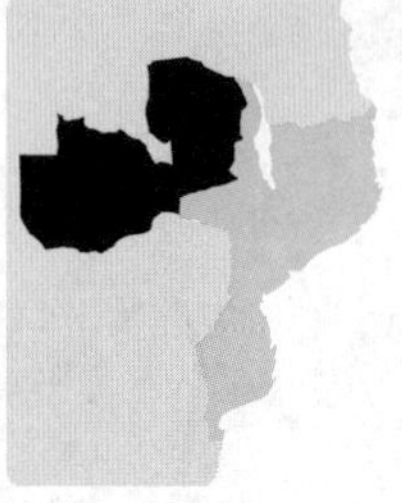

Zambia

Wildlife ✓✓✓
Bush Adventure ✓✓✓
Waterfalls ✓✓✓

Wildlife

A wealth of animals and a network of bush camps make Zambia one of southern Africa's most alluring wildlife-watching destinations. South Luangwa National Park is the highlight, but there are many more including Kafue and Lower Zambezi National Park.

Bush Adventure

Outside Lusaka almost everywhere in Zambia is bush. While the country can be difficult to get around, this remoteness is one of Zambia's main draws. Once you're out in the wild, the logistical hassles fade away as the raw beauty of Zambia's landscapes takes over.

Waterfalls

The world's largest waterfall assaults the senses: get drenched by the spray, fill your ears with its roar and feast your eyes on its magnificence. Whether you raft the rapids, cruise the Zambezi or stand awestruck on the sidelines, Victoria Falls is one of Africa's unforgettable destinations.

p32

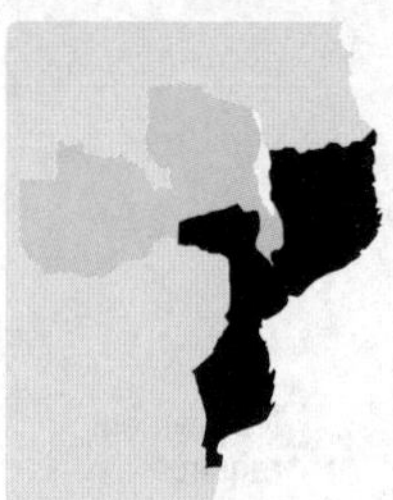

Mozambique

Beaches & Islands ✓✓✓
Culture ✓✓
Bush Adventure ✓✓✓

Beaches & Islands
From the pounding surf and windswept dunes of Ponta d'Ouro to the turquoise waters and powdery white sand of the Quirimbas Archipelago, Mozambique has some of the continent's best beaches. Fringing the coastline are alluring archipelagos and magical islands, with Mozambique Island at the top of the list.

Culture
After being suppressed during the war days, Mozambique's colourful cultures are now coming back with full force. One of the best places to sample this vibrancy is Maputo, with its array of dance, theatre and other cultural offerings.

Bush Adventure
Northern Mozambique is one of the continent's last adventure frontiers, with unspoiled beaches and islands and vast expanses of bush. Sail on a dhow to magical islands, relax on pristine beaches or track wildlife in the interior. Adventure is everywhere.

p144

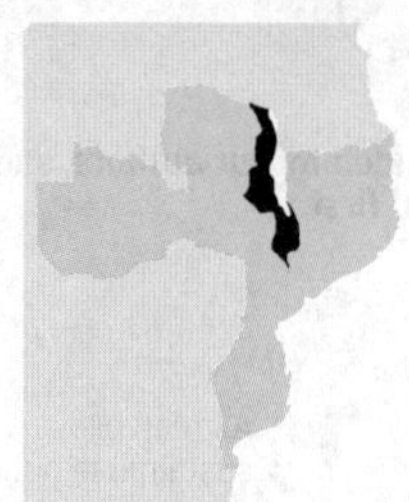

Malawi

Wildlife ✓
Inland Beaches ✓✓✓
Landscapes ✓✓✓

Wildlife
With several reserves managed by solid operators, Malawi now has lions, as well as representatives of the rest of the 'Big Five'. Add to this some fine safari lodges and the country merits packing your binoculars.

Inland Beaches
Lake Malawi offers relaxing beaches and wonderfully scenic mountain-backed panoramas. Cape Maclear – a legendary backpacker hangout – is one of the most popular spots to appreciate the lake. Likoma Island is another, and there are many more.

Landscapes
From the forests and valleys of the Viphya Plateau to the wildflowers and grasslands of the Nyika Plateau and the coves, beaches and hillsides fringing Lake Malawi, Malawi's landscapes are stunning. They are also easily accessible, thanks to a decent road network and good transport links.

p266

❯ **Every listing is recommended by our authors, and their favourite places are listed first.**

❯ **Look out for these icons:**

Our author's top recommendation

A green or sustainable option

No payment required

See the Index for a full list of destinations covered in this book.

On the Road

Zambia

TOM COCKREM / GETTY IMAGES ©

Zambia

☎260 / POP 13 MILLION

Includes »

Best Places to Stay

» Busanga Plains Camp (p76)

» Zungulila Bushcamp (p58)

» Chongwe River Camp (p64)

Best Off-the-Beaten-Path

» Shiwa Ng'andu (p96)

» Liuwa Plain National Park (p80)

» Bangweulu Wetlands (p93)

» Chimfunshi Wildlife Orphanage (p87)

Why Go?

Get out into the bush where animals, both predators and prey, wander through unfenced camps, where night-time means swapping stories around the fire and where the human footprint is nowhere to be seen. The rewards of travelling in Zambia are those of exploring remote, mesmerising wilderness as full of an astonishing diversity of wildlife as any part of Southern Africa. Where one day you can canoe down a wide, placid river and the next raft through the raging rapids near world-famous Victoria Falls.

Though landlocked, three great rivers, the Kafue, the Luangwa and the Zambezi, flow through Zambia, defining both its geography and the rhythms of life for many of its people. For the independent traveller, however, Zambia is a logistical challenge, because of its sheer size, dilapidated road network and upmarket facilities. For those who do venture here, the relative lack of crowds means an even more satisfying journey.

When to Go

Lusaka

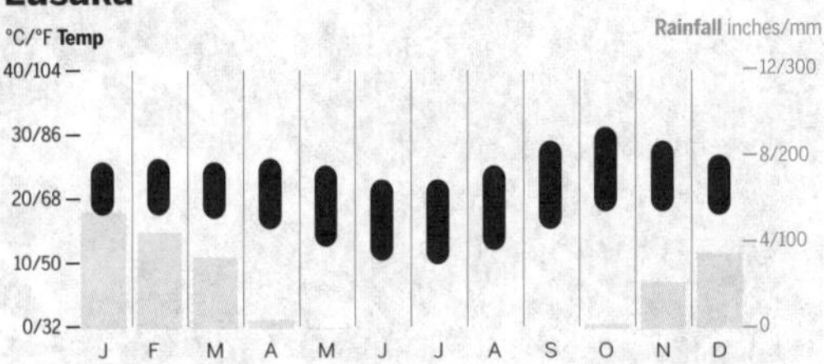

Late May–early Oct The dry season offers prime wildlife viewing; tourist high season.

Jun–Aug Generally dry, with cooler temperatures and sometimes frosty nights.

Dec–Apr The landscape is vibrant and blooming during the rainy or 'emerald' season.

LUSAKA

☎0211 / POP 1.4 MILLION / ELEV 1300M

All roads lead to Lusaka, the geographic, commercial and metaphorical heart of the country. However, Zambia's capital and largest urban zone, with its mishmash of dusty tree-lined streets, bustling African markets, Soviet-looking high-rise blocks and modern commerce, doesn't easily justify exploration by the casual visitor. There are no real attractions, grand monuments to drool over or historical treasures to unearth. Lusaka, like the rest of the country, is not well-equipped for independent tourism and you'll likely find more travellers in Zambia who, besides a short stopover in its airport, have bypassed the city. However, for some, the city's genuine African feel, cosmopolitan populace, quality restaurants and accommodation – at least as far as top-end hotels go – is reason enough to spend a night or two. If you feel like letting loose, expat bars and the home-grown nightclub scene will see you through to the wee hours.

ZAMBIA FAST FACTS

» **Area** 752,614 sq km

» **Capital** Lusaka

» **Famous for** National parks, safari walks, top-notch wildlife viewing and Victoria Falls

» **Languages** English, Bemba, Lozi, Nyanja and Tonga

» **Money** Zambian kwacha (ZMW)

Information

The main commercial thoroughfare, or at least that of the 'old' central business district, is Cairo Rd, lined with basic shops, fast-food outlets, banks and offices (the burnt-out Society House, something of an embarrassing landmark, is to be redeveloped into a hotel and mall complex by summer 2014). To the north and south are major traffic roundabouts. West of Cairo Rd are small shops selling everything from maize meal to auto parts and then the crowded and chaotic city markets. North and northwest of here is the industrial area, and beyond that are the poorer suburbs, generally called 'the compounds' (read 'townships'). East of Cairo Rd, across the railway line and near the train station, is the Inter-City Bus Station. Further east are the wide jacaranda-lined streets of the smarter residential suburbs and the area officially called Embassy Triangle (not surprisingly, home to many embassies and high commissions). Further east and north, around Manda Hill and Arcades Shopping Centres, is where many visitors end up spending the bulk of their time; a good number of corporate offices have relocated out this way continuing the gradual emptying of the central business district.

Sights & Activities

Taking a walk down Cairo Rd (during the day) is interesting if only to experience the hustle and bustle of Zambia's modern commercial district. The streets are often packed and it might be best walking down the central strip; just be careful crossing the road to get there.

Munda Wanga Environmental Park ZOO

(☎0211-278614; www.mundawanga.com; Kafue Rd, Chilanga; adult/child ZMW25/15; ⏲8am-5pm Mon-Thu, to 6pm Fri-Sun) Munda Wanga Environmental Park rehabilitates all sorts of animals for re-entry into the wild, including rarely seen pangolins and owls used for black magic (there's also a breeding program for genets and cerval cats). The park features plenty of regional fauna, including cheetahs, lions, banded mongoose, wild dogs, jackals, warthogs and baboons; feeding time is at 2pm Friday to Sunday (Fridays when crowds of schoolchildren are in attendance might best be avoided). The park is shabby in parts with slightly dilapidated enclosures, but the animals seem well cared for and it's perhaps the first and only exposure to wildlife for Zambians in Lusaka. But the lovely **botanical gardens**, with nearly 500 species of plants and one of the few places in the city suitable for a picnic, is at least as much of a reason to visit.

There's also renewable energy environmental education centre, a pool and kids' playground, plus a bar/restaurant (croc or beef burgers ZMW12). Munda Wanga is about 16km south of central Lusaka and accessible by any minibus heading towards Chilanga or Kafue from the Kalima Towers Bus Station or South End Roundabout (near the downtown Spar supermarket).

National Museum MUSEUM

(Map p38; Nasser Rd; adult/child ZMW20/12; ⏲9am-4.30pm) This big square box of a building resembling a Soviet-era Moscow ministry is not much more than a shell of a museum. The decade-long plan to renovate the upstairs galleries to include exhibitions on urban culture and Zambian history seems to be in a permanent state of suspension leaving a rather

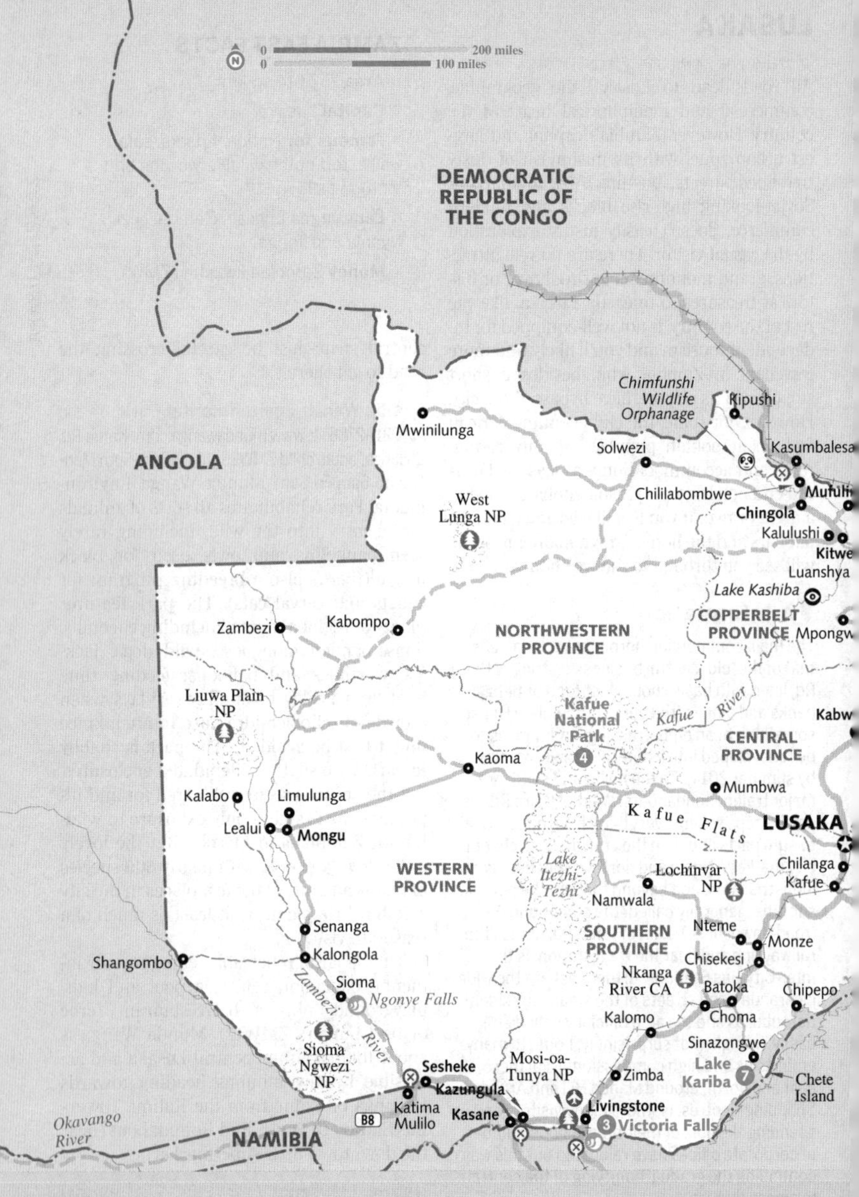

Zambia Highlights

1 Bushwalking like a detective following the tracks of wild animals in **South Luangwa National Park** (p52)

2 Paddling a canoe down the **Zambezi River** (p63) past pods of hippos, menacing-looking crocs and thirsty elephants

3 Rafting, bungee jumping or getting your adrenaline going in any one of the adventures available at **Victoria Falls** (p127)

4 Spotting leopards in **Kafue National Park** (p73), a behemoth wilderness area

where wildlife dreams unfold amid stunning landscapes

5 Spying on the elusive, semi-aquatic sitatungas from a tree-hide in **Kasanka National Park** (p91)

6 Taking a step back in time and a leap to another continent at **Shiwa Ng'andu**, (p96) a remarkably well-preserved English manor estate

7 Kicking back at **Lake Kariba** (p67), and watching a storm roll in over the jagged peaks of Zimbabwe across the waters

Greater Lusaka

decrepit hodgepodge of cultural, ethnographic and archaeological artefacts. Some of the textual descriptions related to witchcraft and initiation ceremonies are interesting at least. Contemporary Zambian paintings and sculpture are displayed downstairs. There's a basic cafeteria on sight and access to the museum is off Independence Ave.

The **Freedom Statue** (Map p38; Independence Ave), just around the corner from the museum, is dedicated to freedom fighters and those who lost their lives in the struggle for Zambia's independence. The depiction of a man breaking his chains symbolises the country's break with colonial bondage and was erected to celebrate Zambia's independence in 1964. It's a popular place for celebrations on Africa Freedom Day (25 May).

Lusaka City Market MARKET

(Map p38; Los Angeles Rd, New City Market; ⏲7am-7pm) Fronted by the chaotic and congested eponymously named bus station as well as a veritable Maginot Line of sidewalk vendors, reaching the entrance to the **Lusaka City Market** is an achievement in and of itself. Unfortunately, while large, lively and packed to the rafters, the clothing and housewares sold in the warren of stalls aren't of much interest to the average traveller.

Near Lusaka City Market, **Soweto Market** (New City Market; Map p38) is the largest market in Lusaka (and Zambia). This is one place where you are most likely to be relieved of your valuables – so you might as well exercise caution and not bring any. The sheer scale of the market, essentially a densely packed shanty town spilling out into the surrounding streets in a haphazard fashion, and the amount of goods on offer and people buzzing around can be overwhelming – consider a visit on a Sunday when things are a little quieter. Immediately to the west of the market, separated only by a dusty road-cum-parking lot full of cars soon meant for

Greater Lusaka

the scrap heap, is the **New Soweto Market**, a dull and only partly occupied building with numbered stalls under a covered roof.

Kalimba Reptile Park PARK, ZOO
(☎0211-213272; off District Rd; adult/child ZMW25/15; ⊙9am-6pm) A bit of a trek northeast from town, Kalimba Reptile Park (often simply referred to as the 'Croc Park') is not only a crocodile and snake zoo but a pleasant place to grab a beer and a crocodile sandwich, though you'll need a 4WD to get here. There's also a swimming pool, fishing pond, crazy golf and a children's playground. Go east on the Great East Road 13km from Arcades Shopping Centre, then make a left at the Caltex petrol station; take the potholed and rutted road to the end (11km).

FREE **Namwandwe Gallery** GALLERY
(Map p36; ☎0977 796443; Leopards Hill Rd; admission free; ⊙9am-4.30pm Tue-Fri, to noon Sat & Sun) Home to the impressive private collection of businessman and patron of the arts John Kapotwe, some of the best contemporary Zambian and African art (paintings, sculptures, masks and fabrics), both of established and up-and-coming artists, can be found at this private home-cum-gallery about 15km southeast of the city centre. A return taxi from the city costs at least ZMW100, depending on waiting time.

Public Swimming Pool SWIMMING
(Map p38; off Nangwenya Rd; admission ZMW8; ⊙10am-6pm Tue-Sun) The spotlessly clean Olympic-sized public swimming pool is surrounded by a pleasant shaded area and is a great place to relax and unwind.

Sleeping

Lusaka's sleeping options are pretty spread out, although if you're looking for a backpackers there are several within a few blocks of one another. In central Lusaka

Lusaka

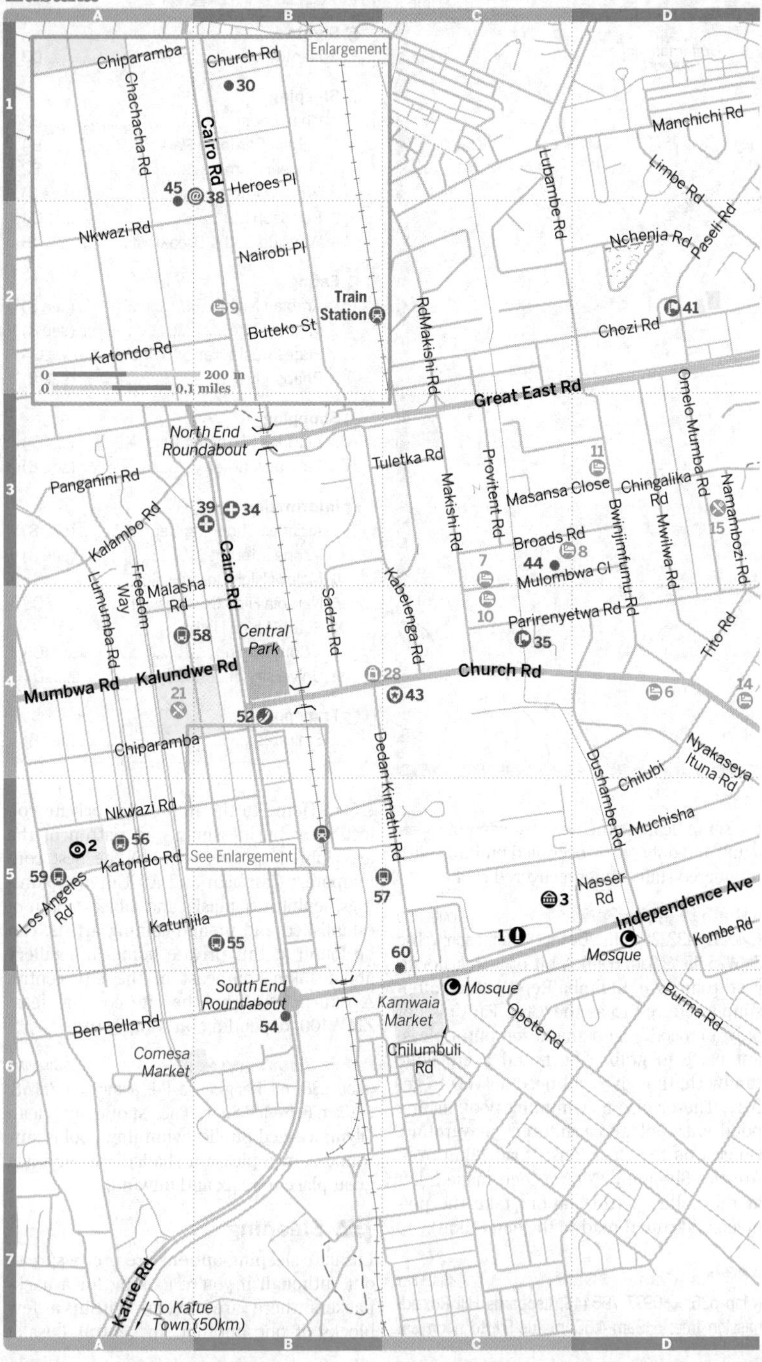

Enlargement
Chiparamba
Church Rd
Chachacha Rd
Cairo Rd
Heroes Pl
Nkwazi Rd
Nairobi Pl
Train Station
Buteko St
Katondo Rd
200 m
0.1 miles
Manchichi Rd
Limbe Rd
Lubambe Rd
Nchenja Rd
Paseli Rd
Chozi Rd
RdMakishi Rd
Great East Rd
Omelo Mumba Rd
North End Roundabout
Tuletka Rd
Makishi Rd
Provitent Rd
Masansa Close
Chingalika Rd
Namambozi Rd
Panganini Rd
Kalambo Rd
Broads Rd
Mulombwa Cl
Bwinjimfumu Rd
Mwilwa Rd
Freedom Way
Malasha Rd
Lumumba Rd
Sadzu Rd
Kabelenga Rd
Parirenyetwa Rd
Tito Rd
Central Park
Mumbwa Rd
Kalundwe Rd
Church Rd
Chiparamba
Dedan Kimathi Rd
Dushambe Rd
Chilubi
Nyakaseya Ituna Rd
Nkwazi Rd
Muchisha
Katondo Rd
See Enlargement
Los Angeles Rd
Nasser Rd
Independence Ave
Katunjila
Kombe Rd
Mosque
South End Roundabout
Mosque
Burma Rd
Kamwaia Market
Obote Rd
Ben Bella Rd
Chilumbuli Rd
Comesa Market
Kafue Rd
To Kafue Town (50km)

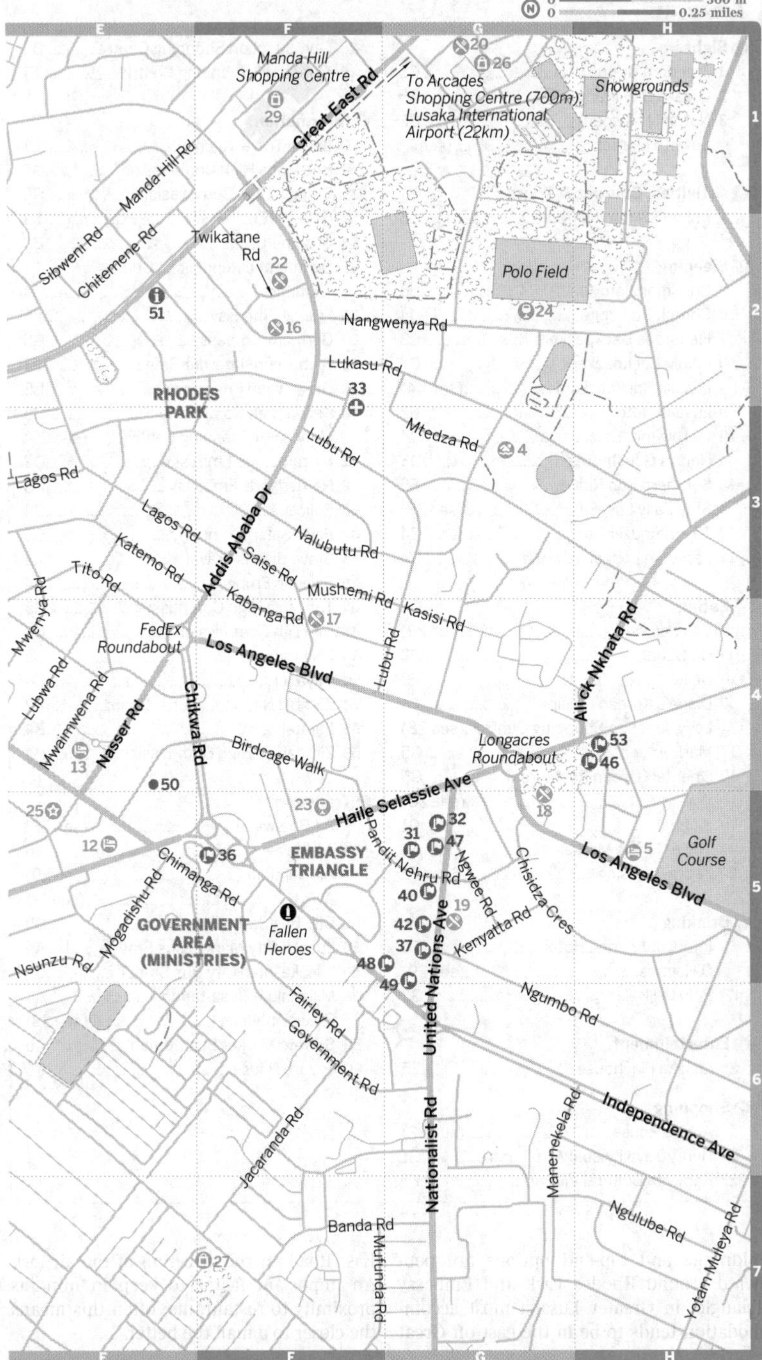

0 500 m
0 0.25 miles
Manda Hill Shopping Centre
Great East Rd
To Arcades Shopping Centre (700m); Lusaka International Airport (22km)
Showgrounds
Manda Hill Rd
Sibweni Rd
Chitemene Rd
Twikatane Rd
Polo Field
Nangwenya Rd
Lukasu Rd
RHODES PARK
Mtedza Rd
Lubu Rd
Lagos Rd
Addis Ababa Dr
Nalubutu Rd
Katemo Rd
Saise Rd
Tito Rd
Mwenya Rd
Kabanga Rd
Mushemi Rd
Kasisi Rd
FedEx Roundabout
Los Angeles Blvd
Lubu Rd
Alick Nkhata Rd
Lubwa Rd
Mwaimwena Rd
Nasser Rd
Chikwa Rd
Birdcage Walk
Longacres Roundabout
Haile Selassie Ave
Golf Course
Chimanga Rd
Pandit Nehru Rd
EMBASSY TRIANGLE
Ngwee Rd
Chisidza Cres
Los Angeles Blvd
Mogadishu Rd
GOVERNMENT AREA (MINISTRIES)
Fallen Heroes
Kenyatta Rd
United Nations Ave
Nsunzu Rd
Ngumbo Rd
Fairley Rd
Government Rd
Independence Ave
Jacaranda Rd
Nationalist Rd
Manenekela Rd
Ngulube Rd
Banda Rd
Mufunda Rd
Yotam Muleya Rd

Lusaka

Sights

1 Freedom Statue C5
2 Lusaka City Market A5
3 National Museum C5
Soweto Market .... (see 2)

Activities, Courses & Tours

4 Public Swimming Pool G3

Sleeping

5 Chrismar Hotel H5
6 Church Rd Lodge D4
7 Flintstone Backpackers C3
8 Kalulu Backpackers C3
Lusaka Backpackers .... (see 44)
9 Lusaka Hotel B2
10 Marble Inn C4
11 Nena's Guesthouse D3
12 Southern Sun Ridgeway E5
Stay Easy Lusaka .... (see 28)
13 Taj Pamodzi Hotel E4
14 Zamcom Lodge D4

Eating

Chicago's .... (see 29)
15 Chit Chat D3
16 Deli F2
17 Diane's Korean Cuisine F4
Levy Junction Shopping Centre .. (see 28)
18 Marlin G5
19 Oriental Garden Restaurant G5
Portico .... (see 20)
20 Sichuan G1
21 Town Centre Market A4
22 Zebra Crossing F2

Drinking

23 InterContinental Hotel F5
O'Hagans .... (see 29)
24 Polo Grill G2

Entertainment

25 Lusaka Playhouse E5

Shopping

Ababa House .... (see 22)
26 Henry Tayali Visual Arts Centre G1
27 Kabwata Cultural Village F7
28 Levy Junction Shopping Centre B4
29 Manda Hill Shopping Centre F1

Information

30 Bimm Travel Agency B1
31 Botswana High Commission G5
32 Canada High Commission G5
33 Care for Business F3
34 Corpmed B3
35 Democratic Republic of Congo Embassy C4
36 France Embassy F5
37 Germany Embassy G5
38 Global.com Internet Cafe B1
39 Greenwood Pharmacy B3
40 Kenya High Commission G5
Manda Hill Shopping Centre .... (see 29)
41 Mozambique Embassy D2
42 Netherlands Embassy G5
43 Police C4
44 River Safari Company C3
45 Steve Blagus Travel A2
46 Sweden Embassy H4
47 Tanzania High Commission G5
48 UK High Commission G5
49 US Embassy G5
50 Voyagers E4
51 Zambia National Tourist Board E2
52 Zamtel B4
53 Zimbabwe High Commission H4

Transport

Air Botswana .... (see 23)
54 Air Malawi B6
Air Namibia .... (see 29)
Avis .... (see 12)
55 City Bus Station B5
56 Lusaka City Market Bus Station A5
57 Lusaka Inter-City Bus Station C5
58 Millennium Bus Station A4
Precision Air .... (see 23)
59 Soweto Market Bus Station A5
60 Tazara House C5

midrange and top-end options are peppered around Rhodes Park and Embassy Triangle; in Greater Lusaka most accommodation tends to be in the east off Great East Road, in the direction of the airport. An important factor to keep in mind is proximity to restaurants; often this means the closer to a mall the better.

CENTRAL LUSAKA

Southern Sun Ridgeway HOTEL $$$
(Map p38; ☎0211-251666; www.southernsun.com; cnr Church Rd & Independence Ave; s/d incl breakfast ZMW1,445/1,602; ❄📶🏊) Deservedly popular with in-the-know expats and a coterie of international business and government types, the Southern Sun is a no-brainer for those seeking an affordable low-key, comfortable city centre option. Adrian Penny, the experienced South African GM, runs the operation like a tight ship, quick to respond and cater to guests' every need. Rooms are tastefully done in muted tones; those in the 'weaver' block wing are the most newly renovated (all are due to be refurbished by the summer of 2013). Past the foyer is an inviting outdoor sitting area surrounding a fishpond and **Musuku**, a restaurant serving possibly the best breakfast and dinner buffet in the city. A pub, small gym, large outdoor pool area and free wi-fi round out the offerings. Conveniently on the premises are a Barclays Bank, offices for South African Airways and Proflight.

Taj Pamodzi Hotel HOTEL $$$
(Map p38; ☎0211-254455; www.tajhotels.com; Church Rd; s/d incl breakfast from US$300/325; ❄@📶🏊) An oasis of luxury and tranquility with fastidiously trained staff, the Taj is a welcoming cushion for travellers transitioning between the bush and home. Featuring plush bedding and top-quality amenities, from the slippers to skin-care products, rooms at the Taj are a step-up from others in a similar category in Lusaka. Views from the top-floor balconies of the sprawling city below are incomparable.

A lavish breakfast buffet is served in one of the hotel's restaurants – the other, **Steaks & Grills**, does candlelit dinner outside with live music most nights – and drinks can be had at the bar accompanied by the tinkling keys of a piano. Guests have access to the full service gym – racquetball anyone? – and spa out back next to a lovely pool and patio area.

Stay Easy Lusaka HOTEL $$
(Map p38; ☎0211-372000; www.tsogosunhotels.com; cnr Church & Kabalenga Rds, Levy Junction; r incl breakfast ZMW500; ❄@📶🏊) Only in Lusaka would a mall parking lot be considered an ideal location for a hotel. Part of a South African hotel group along with the Southern Sun, this smart boutique-style property is not only within shouting distance of Levy Junction's restaurants, banks and cinema but it's also a short walk to Inter-City Bus Station and Cairo Rd.

Rooms are small (as are the wall-mounted flat-screen TVs) but comfortable, and you can decamp to the backyard patio pool area or breakfast dining room for more elbow room during the day. Free wi-fi is a bonus.

Radisson Blu HOTEL $$$
(Map p36; ☎0211-368900; www.radissonblu.com/hotel-lusaka; Great East Road; r from ZMW7500; ❄📶🏊) The newest addition to the city's top-end hotel scene might be mistaken for an alien mothership. A large domed building fronts this development directly across the street from Arcades Shopping Centre (crossing the Great East Road here, though, is like playing a game of Frogger). Modern and sleek throughout with polished marble and shiny mirrored details, the Radisson's slight feeling of anonymity is more than offset by the resort-style pool area, possibly the nicest gym in town and an excellent on-site Italian restaurant.

Bongwe Barn GUESTHOUSE $$
(☎0977 762096; www.bongwesafaris.com; 305 Ngwezi Rd, Roma; s/d with shared bathroom ZMW175/250, s/d with private bathroom ZMW250/350; 📶🏊) In a quiet suburban neighborhood 2½km north (and slightly west) from Arcades Shopping Centre, Bongwe's seven rooms offer a secure and social – if so inclined – refuge. Owned and operated by Alec and Emma, a charming and knowledgeable couple who run budget-minded safaris to their camp just outside Kafue proper (Lower Zambezi trips are in the planning stage). Alec's sister is to take over, which might lead to an expansion and other changes.

Simply furnished rooms line a single hallway with a stocked kitchen (coffee and toast and scones for breakfast) and living room at one end. Out back is a small pool and members-only bar (guests of course are considered members) with a TV tuned to international sporting events, pool table and menu of hearty steaks and other fare.

Protea Hotel Lusaka HOTEL $$$
(Map p36; ☎0211-254664; www.proteahotels.com/lusaka; Great East Road, Arcades Shopping Centre; r US$215; ❄📶🏊) With direct access to Arcades Shopping Centre, this Protea is comfortable and convenient, though it might feel rather interchangeable with wherever you are flying into Zambia from – it's part of a large South African chain with a Cairo Rd

location and others elsewhere in the country. The spacious wood-floored rooms come with the standard bells and whistles; the pool, however, is small and in an uninviting 2nd floor outdoor enclosure.

Lusaka Backpackers BACKPACKERS $
(Map p38; ☎0977 805483; www.lusakabackpackers.com; 161 Mulombwa Cl; dm ZMW75, r with/without bathroom ZMW250/150; @ ☎ ≋) With few alternatives, this deservedly popular place (formerly Chachacha) is the obvious choice for those on a budget in Lusaka. The centrepiece of activity – and a good place for meeting other independent travellers – is the patio area out front with a small pool and bar, which can get lively and loud, especially on weekends.

The backyard accommodation options are better all-round than those up front: a mixed dorm is nicer and quieter than the smaller and barer ones up front; there are two basic safari tents; the simply furnished A-frame double and 'log cabin' are probably the most pleasant. Other facilities include a restaurant (serving basic meals); a tub for doing laundry; a communal, dilapidated kitchen and baggage storage. Organises trips to Kafue National Park, Lower Zambezi National Park, South Luangwa National Park and Livingstone. Airport transfer available.

Chrismar Hotel HOTEL $$
(Map p38; ☎0211-253036; www.chrismarhotels.com; Los Angeles Blvd; r incl breakfast from ZMW500; ❄ @ ☎ ≋) Something of an oasis (except when there's a wedding or conference on, and on some weekend afternoons) located on a large grassy property away from the dusty city centre streets, Chrismar remains a good midrange option even if some of the rooms are calling for attention. Go for one of the colorfully painted 'African' style rooms rather than the older standard hotel-style ones with carpeting and bland furnishings.

The Cattleman's Grill (p45) restaurant and bar are popular with expats and there's a good gym and shaded pool area.

Zamcom Lodge HOTEL $
(Map p38; ☎0211-253503; doreen@zamcom.ac.zm; Church Rd; r ZMW250; ❄ ☎) Although it looks like a school built in the '70s or earlier, this small motel-style complex has simple spick-and-span rooms. There's a shady courtyard/car park with resident turkeys strutting their stuff out the front. Conferences and wedding receptions aren't uncommon on weekends so it's best to check with reception beforehand as these can be loud and raucous affairs.

Nena's Guesthouse GUESTHOUSE $$
(Map p38; ☎0211-239541; www.nenaguesthouse.co.zm; 126 Masansa Cl, Rhodes Park; s/d incl breakfast ZMW250/300; ❄ ≋) Friendly Nena's has four clean but rundown rooms, so peruse more than one if possible (keeping in mind that some have a shower, others a bath). There's an on-site restaurant, a leafy patio and pool area and it's well located in the Rhodes Park district, not far to Cairo Rd and Levy Junction Shopping Centre.

Church Rd Lodge MOTEL $$
(Map p38; ☎0211-255302; shaazam@microlink.zm; 1012 Church Rd; r ZMW350; ❄ ☎) A small compound not really geared for foreign travellers but nevertheless a secure and well-kept spot within walking distance of Levy Junction Shopping Centre and Cairo Rd – that is if you don't mind walking the narrow dirt shoulder of busy Church Rd. There are seven rooms in total but the two out back are a slight step up from the others; all have flat-screen TVs and there's a small lawn and bar in front.

Marble Inn MOTEL $$
(Map p38; ☎0211-230617; marbleinn.lusaka@gmail.com; Makanta Cl; r ZMW260; P) This low-slung building, similar to an American roadside motel, has good-sized, simply decorated, clean rooms. Other than parking, there's not much in the way of amenities, and although it's down a quiet suburban-like street, noise from the next-door backpackers is potentially an issue.

Lusaka Hotel HOTEL $$
(Map p38; ☎0211-229049; www.lusakahotel.com; cnr Cairo & Katondo Rds; s/d from ZMW295/315, d with air-con ZMW365; ❄ ≋) Given its central location on maddening Cairo Rd, this longest-standing of Lusaka hotels has a surprisingly serene entry set back from the road, with the sound (and sight) of water trickling through a lush little swamp as you approach reception. The respite ends there, however, and a consistent flow of people means service is lacklustre and impersonal.

Other than old photos and paintings along the main stairway, there's little character or attention in the rooms, which feel institutional and in need of some dramatic upkeep or complete renovation.

Flintstone Backpackers BACKPACKERS $
(Map p38; ☎0212-21060; www.flintstonebackpackers.com; Makanta Cl; dm ZMW50, r with/without bathroom ZMW250/150) Formerly Kuomboka

ON THE ROAD TO CAIRO

Lusaka started life as a dusty railway siding and storage depot on the new line that empire-builder Cecil Rhodes was constructing from South Africa. This was the first stage of his grand design for a Cape Town to Cairo railway that would pass through British territory all the way. The nearest village to the siding was called Lusaakas, after the name of its chief, and the title was simplified to Lusaka and attached to this point on the railway.

In the 1920s copper was discovered in the highlands north of Lusaka, and the railway became important for transporting goods to Southern Rhodesia (in present-day Zimbabwe), South Africa and the industrial markets of Europe and America. At Lusaka, a small station was built, and nearby a few shops were established to serve settlers farming in the surrounding area. Then came some houses, a ramshackle hotel and even a main street, running parallel to the railway line.

By the 1930s Lusaka had developed into a sizeable town, and in 1935 the capital was moved here from Livingstone, to take advantage of Lusaka's central position. The railway never reached Egypt, but Rhodes' dream was remembered when the name of the main street was formally changed to Cairo Rd – the name it still has today.

Backpackers, this labyrinthine place has plain but serviceable private rooms and darkened dorms with low ceilings; each of the three has ten beds. A small bar area and pool table are about all that's available in terms of public space. Meals can be provided.

Kalulu Backpackers BACKPACKERS **$**
(Map p38; 0211-231486; www.backpacklusaka.com; 20 Broads Rd; dm ZMW50, r without bathroom ZMW150;) A budget option in a city without many. Rooms are very basic and existing rooms are in need of attention; construction to add several more in the back was ongoing at the time of our visit. The bar and lounge area in the front were more inviting.

GREATER LUSAKA

Pioneer Camp CAMPSITE, CHALET **$$**
(Map p36; 0966 432700; www.pioneercampzambia.com; Palabana Rd, off Great East Road; campsite per person ZMW35, r ZMW300;) An isolated 25-acre camp, surrounded by bird-rich woodland, Pioneer is the accommodation of choice for many expats living outside Lusaka, especially those with a flight out of the country in the morning. Most of the widely dispersed and simply furnished thatch-roofed chalets have flagstone floors, small verandahs and large bathrooms. The well-kept facilities for campers are up front next to the small plunge pool and comfortable bar, lounge and restaurant (mains ZMW70) area, where the free wi-fi reception works best.

It's signposted 5km south of Great East Road; if you don't have a car, a transfer from the airport or city centre should run to around ZMW150.

Eight Reedbuck Hotel HOTEL **$$$**
(0211-264788; www.tribehotels.co.zm; 8 Reedbuck Rd, Kabulonga; s/d incl breakfast ZMW1155/1292;) Boutique with a twist of African kitsch best sums up the design scheme of the rooms in this walled-off compound in a suburb southeast of the centre. Individually decorated with various Zambian tribal identities in mind, all have the somewhat off-putting plush carpeting of a downstairs rec room. Bathrooms have great claw-footed tubs and showers illuminated by sunlight through glass ceilings. Public chill-out spaces include a Miami-like lounge pool area.

Kilimanjaro Country Lodge LODGE **$$**
(0211-255830; www.kilimanjarozambia.com; Leopards Hill Rd; s/d incl breakfast ZMW540/648;) A good out-of-town option – especially for groups and families – around 7½km east of the city centre, Kilimanjaro consists of several well-kept, low-slung buildings on a manicured lawn. The 10 rooms are spacious and simply furnished and management is responsive to any requests. A perk is free laundry for guests staying more than a night. Another eight rooms and a pool were in the works at the time of our visit.

The curio-filled garden restaurant here has a large menu (mains ZMW45) including wraps, pasta, burgers, salads and excellent coffee and a mouthwatering selection of desserts; it has a playground for children and mini pony rides as well.

Eureka Camping Park CAMPGROUND, CHALET **$**
(Map p36; 0211-272351; www.eurekacamp.com; Kafue Rd; campsite per person ZMW35, dm

ZMW105, chalet from ZMW290;) The grassy campsite here, shaded by big trees, is popular with overlanding groups. The security is good, while the swimming pool and bar (which sells snacks) are nice touches. Chalets are cool and comfortable and modelled on the traditional thatch hut. Firewood is for sale and there is an abutting walkable safari area with animals that don't want to eat you. It's about 12km south of the city centre. Minibuses from the City Bus Station or South End Roundabout go past the gate.

Wayside Bed & Breakfast GUESTHOUSE **$$**
(Map p36; 0211-273439; www.wayside-guesthouse.com; 39 Makeni Rd, Makeni; s/d incl breakfast ZMW500/550;) This upmarket and peaceful guesthouse is one of the best in Lusaka, with only a handful of snug ensuite rooms. It used to be a farm and today the sizeable grounds are devoted to the owners' love of gardening, and really are magnificent (and ever-growing); it's a place where you can wander well away from other guests. Three rooms in a separate cottage have air conditioning and there's a lounge with TV and comfortable couches. Located around 4½km southwest of the Kafue Roundabout on Cairo Rd.

Chita Lodge LODGE **$$**
(Map p36; 0211-293779; www.chita.co.zm; 25 Chakeluka Rd; r incl breakfast ZMW450;) This lodge, set in beautifully landscaped grounds, has paintings and sculptures adorning the walls and passageways. It has 10 sumptuous rooms: eight doubles and two family rooms, which come with bath and shower. If you want to stay here book ahead as it caters for lots of conferences. Airport transfer is ZMW100 for the bus, one way, making it a great deal for groups.

Eating

The better places tend to congregate either inside or fairly close to the three main shopping centres: **Arcades** (Map p36; Great East Road), **Levy Junction** (Map p38; cnr Church & Kabalenga Rds) or **Manda Hill** (Map p38; Great East Road), where you'll find a handful of quality independent restaurants and a wide range of mostly South African fast-food and chains. Manda Hill probably has the best selection including a Nando's, Steer's, Mugg & Bean, Debonair's Pizza, Curry in a Hurry and My Asia, the last two fast-food Indian and Asian eateries respectively. All three shopping centres have massive, modern grocery stores, though easily the fanciest is the Whole Foods–equivalent Food Lover's Market at Levy Junction replete with a sushi bar and gourmet freshly prepared foods. It can be a bit weird going to a shopping centre for a candlelit dinner, but what the setting lacks in ambience is usually made up for in the quality of the cuisine. Other options are scattered around the suburbs, especially around Embassy Triangle and Rhodes Park.

For local meals, the food stalls at the **Town Centre Market** (Map p38; Chachacha Rd) serve cheap local food, but the scavenging dogs roaming the piles of rubbish are not a sight for the squeamish. Sausages and steaks are grilled before your eyes and served with a generous portion of veg and *nshima* (maize porridge) for around ZMW10. Cleaner food stalls are scattered elsewhere around the city.

Rhapsody's INTERNATIONAL **$$$**
(Map p36; Great East Road, Arcades Shopping Centre; mains ZMW55-110;) This is one of the best places to eat in Lusaka; mind you, it can take a while to get used to fine dining Zambian-style – in a shopping centre with a nice view of the parking lot. But don't let that bother you as the food is excellent. It has huge eating areas, inside and outside under an industrial-style roof, and the international menu does everything from steaks to Thai chicken, salads and even nasi goreng.

There are also lots of seafood dishes but you should try the chicken Espetada, a delicious Portuguese-inspired chicken dish – the presentation will have you playing hangman in minutes.

TOP CHOICE **Design House Cafe** INTERNATIONAL, ORGANIC **$$**
(Leopards Hill Rd, Sugarbush Farm; mains ZMW35-60; 8am-5pm Tue-Sat, 9am-4pm Sun) This picture-postcard idyllic cafe is worth every kwacha of the journey it takes to get here. Chill out for an afternoon at one of the picnic tables munching on homemade bread and pastries, salads made with vegetables from the organic garden and expertly prepared sandwiches, pasta and meat dishes as well as a glass of wine. Every Sunday from noon to 3pm there is a special roast rump of beef and Yorkshire pudding meal – reservations are recommended. Past the turnoff for Kilimanjaro Lodge on the same premises as the also-highly-recommended shop Jackal & Hide.

Chicago's STEAKHOUSE $$
(Map p38; Great East Road, Manda Hill Shopping Centre; mains ZMW45-115; ⊙lunch & dinner) This theme restaurant – think Al Capone and gangsters – located on the mall's 2nd floor is a night-time haunt of Lusaka's young, prosperous and stylish. While the service can be a little desultory and the background noise renders conversations a challenge, the buzzing atmosphere is rare enough to warrant a visit or two. The large menu specialises in steaks and seafood though the quality is akin to, well, a theme restaurant.

Deli CAFE, BAKERY $
(Map p38; Lunzua Rd, Rhodes Park; mains ZMW25; ⊙7am-6pm Mon-Fri, 9am-2pm Sat;) Boasting the best barista in Lusaka (the winner of an international competition) as well as an enviable garden setting, the Deli is a good place to plant yourself for a few hours. The sophisticated kitchen turns out all-day breakfast-like eggs and French toast, specialty sandwiches like Asian pork meatball and classics like pastrami, wood-fired pizzas and homemade ice cream. The turnoff from Addis Ababa Dr isn't clearly marked; look for the 'Inzy Advertizing Co' sign.

Plates Restaurant & Wine Bar INTERNATIONAL $$$
(Map p36; 0211-841015; Acacia Park, Great East Road; mains ZMW60-95; ⊙noon-10pm Mon-Thu, to midnight Fri & Sat) In a modern office park with nice outdoor seating next to Arcades Shopping Centre, Plates is quickly becoming regarded as one of the city's best restaurants. A CIA-trained chef (not *that* CIA, the Culinary Institute of America) prepares sophisticated dishes (the menu changes monthly) like almond crusted bream, Kansas barbecue-style ribs, plus good burgers and wraps.

Mint Lounge INTERNATIONAL $$
(Map p36; Acacia Park, Great East Road; mains ZMW45-85; ⊙10am-10pm Mon-Fri, 9am-11pm Sat & Sun;) Look for this place, with a small, stylish dining room and pleasant outdoor seating, in the inner courtyard of Acacia Office Park. There's an impressive selection of Western-style creations such as tortilla wraps or freshly made open sandwiches for lunch and omelettes for breakfast as well as pasta, steaks and specials like prawn risotto for dinner. Good coffee, smoothies and dessert pancakes round out the offerings.

Next door within Arcades Shopping Centre, in a darkened corridor just outside the entrance to the Protea Hotel, is another somewhat less inviting brightly lit location.

Diane's Korean Cuisine KOREAN $$
(Map p38; 5018 Saise Rd; mains ZMW30-65; ⊙11.30am-2.30pm & 7-11pm) Hidden behind a wall with only 'Korean Cuisine' painted in fading, hard-to-read letters and the parking lot of a low-slung house, Diane's has a bare-bones backyard garden and small dining room. It does however have an excellent selection of Asian foods (a variety of hotpots) with an emphasis on Korean dishes, including *bulgogi* and a superb cook-at-the-table barbecue.

Portico ITALIAN $$
(Map p38; 0211-250111; off Nangwenya Rd, Showgrounds; mains ZMW55-85; ⊙closed Mon) Italian owned and operated, this restaurant located on the Showgrounds serves arguably the best pizza in Lusaka. Somewhat quirkily decorated, it's nevertheless authentically Italian in terms of its coffee, wines and well-trained chefs. Live music on weekends and Wednesday nights.

Oriental Garden Restaurant CHINESE, INDIAN $$
(Map p38; United Nations Ave; mains ZMW25-65; ⊙lunch & dinner;) Forget the Chinese and grill dishes at the back of the menu and stick to the specialty – Indian. There's a small bar-terrace area (with a pool for diners in need of a refreshing dip?) and a spacious indoor dining room, offering excellent service. Good veggie options are on the menu, such as a tasty masala kofta.

Cattleman's Grill STEAKHOUSE $$
(Los Angeles Blvd, Chrismar Hotel; mains ZMW30-70; ⊙lunch & dinner) As the name suggests, this is a meat-centric place, pride of of place going to the flame-grilled barbecue selections. It's a good place to mix with Lusaka expats as well as visiting business types, in a relaxed atmosphere outdoors under a high thatch roof next to the pool at the Chrismar Hotel. Live music will often accompany your meal.

Marlin STEAKHOUSE $$
(Map p38; 0211-252206; Los Angeles Blvd, Longacres Roundabout; mains ZMW50-70; ⊙lunch & dinner Mon-Sat) Housed in the colonial-era Lusaka Club with decor that probably hasn't been touched since the '60s, this wood-panelled favourite serves some of the best steak in Lusaka. While it does serve gargantuan portions of every cut of meat under

the sun, most guests come for the aged fillet with mushroom or pepper sauce. Reservations are strongly recommended.

Arabian Nights MIDDLE EASTERN, PAKISTANI $$$
(Map p36; Great East Road, Arcades Shopping Centre; mains ZMW70-95; ⏲lunch & dinner Mon-Sat) With fairly kitschy exotic Middle Eastern decor – imagine what a heavy-handed set designer of Disney's *Aladin* would do to a darkened room – this place nevertheless serves a head-spinning variety of quality dishes including kudu and impala steaks; Pakistani is the mainstay. Try the Kenyan coriander lamb, Parmesan meatballs or Pakistani barbecue. Middle Eastern spiciness is combined with Zambian friendliness.

Sichuan CHINESE $$
(Map p38; off Nangwenya Rd, Showgrounds; mains ZMW35-65; ⏲lunch & dinner Mon-Sat, dinner Sun;) One of the better Chinese restaurants in Lusaka, bizarrely situated at the back of a warehouse at the Showgrounds. Despite this, there's a nice ambience, and authentically prepared dishes come out of the kitchen in record time.

Zebra Crossing CAFE, SANDWICHES $$
(Map p38; cnr Addis Ababa Dr & Twikatane Rd, Ababa House; sandwiches ZMW48; ⏲9am-5pm Mon-Fri, 8am-2.30pm Sat;) At this small boutique you can eat at shaded tables overlooking a garden surrounded by woodcarvings and African artwork. You can tuck into carrot-and-marmalade muffins, wraps and sandwiches. It's a pleasant stop to refuel after a browse through the curio shop and art and handicrafts gallery; Mukambi Safari Lodge (p75) in Kaufe has a booking office here.

Chit Chat CAFE, INTERNATIONAL $$
(Map p38; 5A Omelo Mumba Rd; mains ZMW30-60; ⏲9am-4pm Mon, 8.30am-midnight Tue-Sat, hours vary Sun;) This informal garden restaurant features an eclectic menu with burgers, tortilla wraps, pastas and steaks, as well as Mexican dishes and a variety of breakfasts. It's on a lovely tree-shaded street – the rusting children's playground equipment surely would not pass a safety inspection – and a good place to hang out for a few hours or catch a football or rugby match on the bar TV.

Drinking & Entertainment

Bars and restaurants aren't allowed to sell alcohol after 11pm (nightclubs after 2am); the selling of alcohol is prohibited everywhere Sunday.

Lusaka nightclubs like **Roma House** (609 Zambezi Rd) near Bongwe Barn play international house music on Friday and Saturday nights; Club 101 in Arcades Shopping Centre, next to the indoor entrance to the Protea Hotel, occasionally has foam parties; and Vegas and the Lounge in Northmead are safe spots to let your hair down. The pub at the **InterContinental Hotel** (Map p38; ☎0211-250000; www.ichotelsgroup.com; Haile Selassie Ave;) is good for watching English Premier League and rugby on the telly, as is O'Hagan's, though it's less conveniently located in Kabulonga. Most of the hotels, from backpackers to the top-end places, have their own bars.

Levy Junction and Manda Hill Shopping Centres have stylish and state-of-the-art Fresh View Cinemas and Ster-Kinekor is at Arcades (tickets from ZMW16).

The busy casino at Arcades Shopping Centre is one of the most popular in the city, especially with Chinese businessmen and visitors.

Rhapsody's BAR
(Great East Road, Arcades Shopping Centre) This place, combined with a large restaurant, is an upmarket option for a drink. The large open-air space includes a bar and a good selection of South African wines and spirits. It's mainly frequented by well-to-do Zambians, expats and NGO workers. Live music is on tap Tuesdays from 9pm onwards.

Polo Grill BAR
(Map p38; 2374 Nangwenya Rd; ⏲8am-midnight) A large, open-air bar under an enormous thatch roof overlooking a huge, well-kept polo field (where you can occasionally catch a live match). It's all rather incongruous for Lusaka, but an exceedingly pleasant place to knock back a few Mosis and catch some live music.

O'Hagans PUB
(Map p38; Great East Road, Manda Hill Shopping Centre) This South African chain pub, popular with South Africans and Brits, is ideal if you like fake Irish pubs and a more Western drinking experience. There are decent beers and a great outdoor terrace, even if it does overlook a car park.

Lusaka Playhouse THEATRE
(Map p38; cnr Church & Nasser Rds; tickets ZMW20-50) From time to time local performers put on a good show. Check signs outside to see what's playing.

Shopping

If you're looking for a cheap, local souvenir, consider a *chitenje* from a local shop or one of the markets. This is the brightly patterned cotton cloth that you'll see all over the place, often wrapped around local women to hold their bubs in place. You should be able to pick one up for roughly ZMW50.

The swish **Levy Junction** (Map p38; cnr Church & Kabalenga Rds), **Manda Hill** (Map p38; Great East Road) and **Arcades** (Map p36; Great East Road) shopping centres (the latter is the oldest and least swish) are easy to reach by minibus from along Cairo Rd or from the Millennium Bus Station, or by taxi (around ZMW25). As well as banks, bookshops, internet cafes, furniture stores, restaurants and fast-food outlets, the shopping centres boast huge supermarkets.

Jackal & Hide LEATHER GOODS
(www.jackalandhide.net; Leopards Hill Rd) For extremely high-quality leather goods, especially purses, travel bags and accessories, head to this spot, which shares an idyllic location with a highly recommended cafe on Sugarbush Farm east of Kabulonga, around 15km from the city centre.

Sunday Market MARKET
(Map p36; Great East Road, Arcades Shopping Centre; ⏲9am-6pm Sun) This weekly market, held in the parking lot at the Arcades Shopping Centre, features Lusaka's best range of handicrafts, especially wood carvings, curios made from malachite and African prints. Bargaining is expected though it's a relaxed low-pressure affair.

Kabwata Cultural Village HANDICRAFTS
(Map p38; Burma Rd; ⏲9am-5pm) You'll find a scruffy collection of thatch-roofed huts and stalls selling carvings, baskets, masks, drums, fabrics and more at this place southeast of the city centre. Prices are cheap because you can buy directly from the workers who live here.

Ababa House ARTS & CRAFTS
(Map p38; cnr Addis Ababa Dr & Twikatane Rd; ⏲9am-5pm Mon-Fri, to 2pm Sat) A smart boutique full of imaginative creations made for Western tastes from Zambian and Zimbabwean artists, furniture-makers and weavers. Chocoholics can visit a shop selling handmade Belgian chocolates.

FREE **Henry Tayali Visual Arts Centre** ARTS & CRAFTS
(Map p38; ☎0211-254440; Showgrounds; ⏲9am-5pm Mon-Fri, 10am-2.30pm Sat) Check out Henry Tayali Visual Arts Centre if you're in the mood for buying local contemporary art. Ask about the studio nearby for working artists – come here on weekdays only.

Information

Dangers & Annoyances

Like most African cities, pickpockets take advantage of crowds, so be alert in the markets and bus stations and along the busy streets immediately west of Cairo Rd. Don't flash a mobile phone around and don't carry a bag. Take only the cash you need in your pockets. Soweto Market in particular is notorious for robbery and pickpockets (if in a car, wind windows up and lock doors); there is a township nearby with a very bad reputation. At night, most streets are dark and often empty, so even if you're on a tight budget, take a taxi.

The suburb of Rhodes Park, between Cairo Rd and Embassy Triangle, which is quite upmarket during the week, takes on a sleazy twist at weekends when prostitutes display their wares at night, especially along Mwilwa Rd.

Emergency

Ambulance (☎994)

Police (Map p38; ☎991; Church Rd)

Specialty Emergency Services (☎0211-273302; www.ses-zambia.com) For evacuations. Has bases in Lusaka, Livingstone and Kitwe but operates throughout the country. Also has ambulances and in-patient care.

Internet Access

Wireless internet is available at many cafes, restaurants and hotels. Look for the 'I Spot' sign. The quality of connections vary and ZMW5 will buy you a 30-minute voucher often only good for that particular location. All three of the large malls have internet cafes and there are a couple along Cairo Rd; however, these seem to come and go with some frequency.

Global.com Internet Cafe (Map p38; 2nd fl, cnr Cairo & Nkwazi Rds; per half hour ZMW4.5; ⏲7.30am-9pm)

I-Zone Internet (Map p36; Great East Road, Arcades Shopping Centre; per half hour ZMW6; ⏲9am-9pm) Reliable, fast internet access, plus wireless facility.

Medical Services

If you fall sick you should have no problems getting an appointment at one of Lusaka's well-equipped private clinics – ask your hotel or embassy. Good pharmacies are at Arcades, Levy Junction and Manda Hill shopping centres.

Care for Business (Map p38; ☎0211-256731; Addis Ababa Rd) Private medical clinic.

Corpmed (Map p38; ☎0211-222612; Cairo Rd) Located behind Barclays Bank. Has a doctor on duty 24 hours and is probably the city's best-equipped facility. Also runs its own ambulance service.

Greenwood Pharmacy (Map p38; ☎0211-227811; 680 Cairo Rd)

Hilltop Hospital (☎0211-263407; Kabulonga Rd, Ibex Hill)

Money

Banks (Barclays Bank, FNB, Indo-Zambian Bank, Standard Chartered Bank and Zanaco) with ATMs and bureaux de change are located in Arcades, Levy Junction and Manda Hill shopping centres, along Cairo Rd and elsewhere in Lusaka, such as on Haile Selassie Ave.

Telephone & Fax

A dozen telephone booths (using tokens and phonecards) can be found outside the post office. 'Phone shops' and 'fax bureaux' are dotted along Cairo Rd.

Zamtel (Map p38; cnr Cairo & Church Rds) International calls can be made and faxes sent at the telephone office upstairs from the main post office.

Tourist Information

Zambia National Tourist Board (Map p38; ☎0211-229087; www.zambiatourism.com; 1st fl, Petroda House, Great East Road; ⏲8am-1pm & 2-5pm Mon-Fri, 9am-noon Sat) Information and maps of Luska are limited.

Travel Agencies

Bimm Travel Agency (Map p38; ☎0211-234372; www.bimmtourszambia.com; Shop 3, Luangwa House, Cairo Rd) Located just south of the post office, this agency is reliable and locally run. It can also arrange car hire.

Bush Buzz (Map p38; ☎0211-256992; www.bush-buzz.com; 4169 Nangwenya Rd) Organises trips to Kafue, Lower Zambezi and South Luangwa National Parks and Livingstone.

Steve Blagus Travel (Map p38; ☎0211-227739; www.sbltravel.com; 24 Nkwazi Rd; ⏲8am-4pm Mon-Fri, 8-11.30am Sat) The agency for Amex and a dozen upmarket lodges/camps; also organises regional and domestic tours.

Travel Shop (☎0211-255559; www.travelshopzambia.com; Great East Road, Arcades Shopping Centre) An agency for lodges/camps, tours and safari companies and sells discounted air tickets. Another branch is at Manda Hill Shopping Centre.

Voyagers (Map p38; ☎0211-253064; www.voyagerszambia.com; Suez Rd) Perhaps the most popular agency in Zambia (other offices in Ndola, Chingola and Kitwe), it arranges flights, hotel reservations and partners with Europcar for car hire.

Getting There & Away

Air

There's a departure tax of ZMW156 per person applicable to all international flights. Before you make your way to the relevant counter to pay, check with your airline, as it's often included in the price of your ticket. You *will* have to pay the ZMW58 tax at the counter (just outside and to the right of the entrance to the domestic lounge) for all domestic departures.

The humble international airport has slim pickings as far as services are concerned. There's a coffee stand in the main hall, or if you have time on your hands, make your way upstairs to the Copper Chimney Restaurant or the Nsonga Walala Cocktail Lounge. Once through security for international flights the only eating option is a very basic bar selling reheated burgers, hot dogs and pies (ZMW25); a couple of shops sell a poor selection of over-priced curios. Several ATMs, a bureau de change, Europcar and Avis rental car offices and Airtel and MTN mobile-phone company offices are in the hallway immediately outside the arrivals area.

Bus & Minibus

DOMESTIC From in front of the massive and chaotic **Lusaka City Market Bus Station** (Map p38; Lumumba Rd) buses and minibuses leave for nearby towns such as Kafue (ZMW25, one hour, 10 to 15 daily), Chirundu (ZMW30, 2½ hours, five to seven daily), Siavonga (ZMW70, three hours, three to five daily) and Luangwa Bridge (ZMW85, four hours, one or two daily) and destinations are more or less signposted.

Public transport, especially minibuses, to nearby towns also leaves from the **Soweto Market Bus Station** (Map p38; Los Angeles Rd), but here *nothing* is signposted and you're better off avoiding it.

To add to the confusion, minibuses to places not far south of Lusaka also leave from the **City Bus Station** (Map p38; off Chachacha Rd), also called the Kulima Towers Station. So it's possible to get to Kafue, Chirundu and Siavonga from here too. Minibuses heading to the north (eg the Manda Hill Shopping Centre) depart from the **Millennium Bus Station** (Map p38; Malasha Rd).

All long-distance public buses (and most private ones) use the larger though still somewhat confusing and disorderly **Lusaka Inter-City Bus Station** (Map p38; Dedan Kimathi Rd), where there is a left-luggage office and inquiries counter. A range of buses from different companies cover most tourist destinations (all leaving from this bus station unless otherwise stated) – we've quoted the highest prices because they represent the best companies, with the most comfortable buses (two-storey with reclining seats) and are generally only between ZMW10 and ZMW20 higher in price (and well worth the extra). It's certainly worth double-checking the schedules and booking your tickets one or two days before you leave.

Heading southwest, as you'd expect, there are lots of buses to Livingstone (ordinary/business class ZMW90/115, six to seven hours, at least seven daily), but we'd recommend travelling business class (one or two morning departures) with either **Mazahandu Family** (☎0978 05064) or **Shalom bus** (☎0977 176989) services. It's best to purchase the ticket the day before or phone ahead of time to get seat details.

Travelling east, many companies operate services to Chipata, the road link for South Luangwa or Malawi (ZMW130, seven hours); Johabie has departures at around 5am, 6am, 7am & 2pm and is the most recommended.

Heading west, catch an 8am Juldan or Shalom bus through Kafue National Park and onto Mongu (ZMW160, seven hours); for Kafue camps just off the highway it's ZMW100 and three hours.

Juldan, Power Tools and Mazandhu Family buses, among others, go to Copperbelt destinations such as Ndola (ZMW65, four hours, five daily), Kitwe (ZMW70, five hours, five daily) and Solwezi (ZMW110, two daily); Kapiri Mposhi (ZMW50, 2½ hours, five daily) is also reached along this route.

Tracking northeast, Germins and Juldan are two of the better companies, making a beeline for Kasama (ZMW130, 14 hours, four daily) and Mpulungu (ZMW150, 18 hours, four daily).

INTERNATIONAL All buses mentioned here (unless stated otherwise) leave from the Lusaka Inter-City Bus Station.

To Botswana, Zambia-Botswana has buses to Gaborone (ZMW180, 22 hours, three weekly) via Kasane and Francistown; Mazandhu Family has a 5am departure for the border at Kazngula.

For South Africa, Intercape (ZMW400, 6am & noon daily) and Shalom (ZMW380, 6am Tue & Wed) have buses that head to Johannesburg (18 hours, more or less) via Livingstone, Harare, Masvingo and Pretoria. Juldan is less recommended.

To Zimbabwe, take any bus going to South Africa, or Pioneer, Zupco or First Class buses go directly to Harare (ZMW120, nine hours, one daily each).

For Malawi, there's no direct service to Blantyre, but there are three services a week to Lilongwe (ZMW150, 12 hours, 5am), where you can change buses; try Kobs Transport.

AIRPORT ADVICE

Queues for immigration at Lusaka's international airport can be long whatever your arrival time; however, they can be exceptionally long and frustratingly slow late at night and early in the morning when few officers are on hand. With that in mind, it's best to use the bathroom before disembarking from the plane, and do your best to get as close to the front of the line as possible and join the much shorter queues earmarked for Zambian residents and SADC card holders or the one for diplomats. Be polite when feigning ignorance and you'll likely have no problems. Insure that you have US$50 in cash for the entry visa – change is sometimes not available. Somewhat incongruously, a fingerprint scanner is used to identify visitors.

Zambia-Tanzania and Takwa Bus Services both make the run to Dar es Salaam (ZMW250, 27 hours, six weekly), Tanzania, but services can be haphazard (and the train is a more interesting and adventurous experience). For the pathologically masochistic, you can even board Nairobi- and Kamapla (Uganda)-bound buses.

Hitching

Although we can't necessarily recommend hitching, many locals do it and it is a chance to socialise with Zambians from all walks of life. There are several recognised places to wait for lifts: for Eastern Zambia, including Chipata, wait just beyond the airport turn-off; for places to the south, go to the Chirundu–Livingstone junction 10km past Kafue town; for the north, try at the junction north of Kapiri Mposhi.

Train

The *Zambezi Express* travelling to Livingstone (economy class ZMW40, 14 hours), via Choma, leaves Lusaka at 11.50pm on Monday and Friday but has no 1st or sleeper class. Tickets are available from the reservations office inside the **train station** (btwn Cairo Rd & Dedan Kimathi Rd). Get there early and be prepared for hustle and bustle. Slow, 'ordinary' trains to Ndola (standard class ZMW25, 12 hours), via Kapiri Mposhi (ZMW17, eight hours), depart Tuesday and Saturday at 1.20pm.

The Tazara train runs between Kapiri Mposhi and Dar es Salaam (Tanzania).

Getting Around

To/From the Airport

The international airport is about 20km northeast of the city centre. Taxis to and from the airport to central Lusaka cost anywhere from ZMW110 to ZMW150. There's no airport bus but the upmarket hotels send minibuses (usually for a fee) to meet international flights, so you may be able to arrange a ride into town with the minibus driver (for a negotiable fee).

Car & Motorcycle

The roads can get extremely clogged around Lusaka at peak traffic times, and you should always be alert on the road as accidents are not infrequent. Speed limits are enforced in and around the city. Do not park your vehicle on the streets unless you have someone to keep an eye on it for you; hotels, restaurants and shopping centres all have guarded car parks. If you drive around at night you increase the risk of an accident or carjacking; after dark leave the car at your hotel and take a taxi.

Several international car rental companies have counters at the airport, including Avis (p125) and Europcar/Voyagers (p125). **Benmark Transways & Car Hire** (☎0211-292192), which can be booked through Lusaka Backpackers, rents cars for within Lusaka for ZMW300 or for outside for ZMW400 to ZMW500 per day.

If you want a car and driver to help get you around Lusaka, you're better off hiring a taxi for the day, although travel agencies do offer this service. One of the official blue taxis should charge around ZMW300 to ZMW350 for a day, but an unofficial taxi would be cheaper.

For car rental to take out outside Lusaka and around the national parks see p125.

Public Transport

Local minibuses run along Lusaka's main roads, but there are no route numbers or destination signs, so the system is difficult to work out. There is a confusing array of bus and minibus stations.

Otherwise, it is possible to flag down a minibus along a route. For instance, from the South End Roundabout, the 'Kabulonga' minibus goes along Independence Ave to Longacres Roundabout and then heads back towards the city along Los Angeles Blvd and Church Rd; the 'Chakunkula' or 'Chelston' minibus shuttles down Kafue Rd to Kafue town; and the 'Chilanga' minibus heads to Chilanga, via Kafue Rd. The standard fare is ZMW2 to ZMW3.

Taxi

Official taxis can be identified by the numbers painted on the doors and their colour (light blue but hundreds of unofficial taxis also cruise the streets (you'll hear them honk their horn as they go past you on the street, looking for business). Some unofficial taxis are really decrepit vehicles so have a good look before jumping in one. Generally they'll be ZMW5 to ZMW10 cheaper for a single journey within the city.

Official taxis can be hailed along the street or found at ranks near the main hotels and markets. Fares are negotiable, but, as a guide, ZMW30 will get you between Cairo Rd and Manda Hill Shopping Centre during the day in an official taxi. If you're unsure, official taxis should carry a price list for journeys around the city; always agree on the fare before setting out.

EASTERN ZAMBIA

☎0216

Eastern Zambia contains a couple of the country's wilderness gems. It's a sparsely populated region with one long highway, the Great East Road, meandering out to the border with Malawi and onto Lilongwe. South Luangwa and North Luangwa National Parks complement each other beautifully: stunning South Luangwa is the most 'set-up' park for tourism in Zambia, as well as one of the best in the region for wildlife-watching and the best park for budget tourists in Zambia; while North Luangwa is wild, difficult to access – usually by private charter flights – and spectacular for exploring on foot.

The Great East Road: From Lusaka to Chipata

The Great East Road crosses the Luangwa River on a large suspension bridge about halfway between Lusaka and Chipata; there's a permanent security checkpoint manned by the army. In the nearby settlement of Luangwa Bridge, about 3km south of the main road on the western side of the muddy river, is the **Bridge Camp** (☎0977 197456; www.bridgecampzambia.com; Feira Rd; campsite per person ZMW40, chalets per person ZMW85-205; ☒) with comfortable simple stone chalets.

Another 180km east of here, nondescript little Petauke is where people with rugged 4WDs, plenty of time, GPS and trustworthy local advice can turn off to reach South Luangwa. Apart from that, there's **Chimwemwe Lodge** (campsite ZMW50, s/d ZMW300/350). Don't expect much in terms of service and the chalets are dated, but it's an option if you want to break up a journey and there's a restaurant (mains ZMW35); camping is also an option.

BLUE LAGOON NATIONAL PARK

On the north side of the Kafue Flats, small **Blue Lagoon** (admission US$5, plus US$15 per vehicle) was one of many national parks abandoned in the 1980s, then overlooked through the 1990s. It was owned by the Critchleys, a conservationist farming couple. For years it was then used by the Zambian military; animals were handy for target practice, then ended up in the soldiers' canteen. Today, the park is open to visitors but you need your own vehicle, there are no real facilities (ad hoc camping is the only sleeping option) and the wildlife is understandably skittish – so close to the capital, it's sometimes referred to as 'Lusaka's larder'. There's talk of future rehabilitation attempts. One unusual sight is the huge river pythons which are attracted by the large numbers of *lechwe* and birds (these include pelicans, storks, and black and white squadrons).

To get here, take the Mumbwa–Mongu road from Lusaka, and turn left at the sign for Nampundwe Konkola Coppermine, about 28km from Lusaka. Along this road you'll see a sign on the left: 'Blue Lagoon National Park'. Drive a further 7km to find the entrance gate, and then it's into the park until you reach the old farmhouse. A 4WD with high clearance is highly recommended to reach and get around the park (around two hours in total from Lusaka).

About 90km from Chipata and 500km from Lusaka, **Katete** is a small town just south of the Great East Road. On the main road, 4km west of Katete, **Tikondane Community Centre** (☎0216-252122; tikoeducation@gmail.com; campsite per person ZMW25, dm ZMW30, s/d from ZMW60/75), next to St Francis Hospital, is a grassroots initiative that works with local villages. Among its many activities, it focuses on adult and child education, agricultural initiatives, and trains home-based carers for AIDS victims. Tikondane also accepts volunteers to work at their centre and on their projects (two weeks minimum). Elke-Kroeger Radcliffe is the passionate and committed volunteer director.

If you're interested in experiencing village life or just want a break from the road, consider a stay at the friendly Community Centre's Guest House. The rooms are small and simple; meals, such as chicken and *nshima* (ZMW30), are provided and internet access is available. You can visit the school, hospital community projects, take a guided walk up a nearby mountain or see a traditional dance performed – either Chinamwali (girls initiation dance) or the mens' Ghost Dance.

Chipata

POP 320,000

The primary commercial and urban centre in this district, Chipata is a traffic-clogged town in a valley surrounded by a fertile agricultural region. For travellers, it's simply a stop on the way to South Luangwa National Park or Malawi, which is only 30km away. There are a few decent accommodation options, petrol stations, banks with ATMs and a large Spar supermarket to stock up on food and other supplies.

Sleeping

Mama Rula's CAMPGROUND, HOTEL $$

(☎0977 790226; www.mamarulas.com; campsite per person ZMW35, s/d incl breakfast ZMW248/315; @≋) Owned and operated by Andrea, a friendly South African (she also happens to own the Spar supermarket and will fill guests' grocery lists upon request), and her family, this long-running operation is in a leafy compound around 4km out of Chipata along the road to Mfuwe. Simply furnished rooms with mosquito nets are in a low-slung building by the pool; out back is a huge grassy garden campground popular with overland groups and nearby are small but clean cheaper rooms with shared bathroom facilities. (Tired of wildlife? Five dogs and two cats wander the property.) Meals (T-bone steaks or schnitzel with chips and salad ZMW90) are served in the large dining room or more informal bar festooned with pennants and flags; there's also a lantern-lit lapa with a firepit. Transport to and from Chipata airport can be provided.

Deans Hill View Lodge CAMPGROUND, LODGE $

(☎0216-221673; www.deanshillview.com; campsite per person ZMW25, r without bathroom per person ZMW50) This small lodge run by a friendly British expat is perched at the top of a hill with great views of the valley and Chipata below. There's little to distinguish the rooms, which are very simple, and the shared ablutions are generally kept clean; camping is out on a nice big sloping garden. Meals are served in a small dining area. Coming from Lusaka, take the first right after the welcome arch, just before the Total petrol station.

Protea Hotel Chipata HOTEL $$
(in Lusaka 0211-254605; www.proteahotels.com/chipata; Great East Road; r incl breakfast ZMW585;) Compared to other choices in town, this Protea, up to the standard of others in the chain, is absolutely luxurious. A rather grand lobby and rooms with hardwood floors, an outdoor pool with lounge chairs and a somewhat formal dining room can feel like quite a jolt after a long drive or stay in the bush.

Katuta Lodge LODGE $$
(0216-221210; www.katutalodge.com; s/d ZMW 120/150;) This sprawling compound set on nicely landscaped grounds is the closest accommodation in Chipata for the run to Mfuwe. There's a range of spacious rooms with varying degrees of luxury (such as cane couches, fridges and cable TV), though not a whole lot of character as might be expected from a place marketing itself as a conference facility.

Getting There & Away

Of the handful of bus companies offering services to Lusaka, Johabie (ZMW130, seven hours, 5am, 6am, 8am & 2pm) is easily the most recommended. Touts from competing companies can be very aggressive in trying to steer you, or rather manhandle you, towards their waiting vehicle. Really, only the 5am departure leaves on time but it's best to arrive an hour early to guarantee a seat. Always choose the bus closest to being filled, otherwise you might have a long, uncomfortable wait.

The main bus station, also the departure point for minibuses to Mfuwe (around ZMW150, 3½ hours, 11pm) for South Luangwa National Park, is located in the tangle of streets about 1.5km north of the town centre. A taxi, official or otherwise, to Mfuwe (ZMW450, three plus hours) is a better option, especially as the minibuses arrive in Mfuwe around 3.30am.

Minibuses for the Malawi border depart from the BP petrol station on the main drag in town; otherwise, a taxi should run at around ZMW80 (30 minutes). Once you've passed through Zambian customs, it's a few minutes' walk to the Malawian entry post. From the border crossing you can catch a shared taxi to nearby Mchinji (MK300) before getting a minibus all the way to Lilongwe.

South Luangwa National Park

For scenery, variety and density of animals, accessibility and choice of accommodation, **South Luangwa** (admission per person/non-Zambian registered vehicle US$25/15, Zambian-registered vehicle ZMW15; 6am-6pm) is the best park in Zambia and one of the most majestic in Africa. Impalas, pukus, waterbuck giraffe and buffaloes wander on the wide-open plains; leopards, of which there are many in the park, hunt in the dense woodlands; herds of elephants wade through the marshes; and hippos munch serenely on Nile cabbage in the Luangwa River. The bird life is also tremendous: about 400 species have been recorded – large birds like snake eagles, bateleurs and ground hornbills are normally easy to spot. The quality of the park is reflected in the quality of its guides – the highest in Zambia. The local professional guide association sets standards, and anyone who shows you around this park should have passed a set of tough examinations.

The focal point is **Mfuwe**, an uninspiring though more prosperous than average village with shops as well as a petrol station and market. Around 1.8km further along is **Mfuwe Gate**, the main entrance to the park, where a bridge crosses the Luangwa River. A little before the gate are turn-off signs for a handful of lodges and camps. The area around the gate can get quite busy with vehicles in the high season but only because it probably has the highest concentration of wildlife in the park. But compared to the rush-hour, rally-style safaris in South Africa's Kruger National Park, for example, it's positively peaceful. (Note that lots of wild animals in this area make walking around at night *very* dangerous.)

Away from Mfuwe, in the northern and southern parts of the park, the camps and lodges enjoy a quieter and more exclusive atmosphere. The animals may be less used to vehicles and slightly harder to find, but there are fewer visitors in these areas and watching the wildlife here is immensely rewarding. In all, only around one eighth of the park is 'operated in' while the remainder sees few if any visitors.

Much of the park is inaccessible because of rains between November and April (especially February and March), so many lodges close at this time.

If you're in either Zambia or Malawi, on a budget and looking for ways to see South Luangwa without breaking the bank, consider organising an all-inclusive safari, which will also sort out those challenging transport logistics. Recommended budget operators with accommodation in tents are: **River Safari Company** (Map p38; www.riversafaricompany.com; 161 Mulombwa Cl, Lusaka; 3/4 day safari per person US$545/695), which is run out of Lusaka Backpackers, and **Jackalberry Safaris** (www.jackalberrysafaris.net; 3-/4-/5-day safari per person US$425/545/645) in Zambia; and Land & Lake Safaris (p126) and **Kiboko Safaris** (www.kiboko-safaris.com; 4 day safari per person US$515), both of which operate from Lilongwe, Malawi.

FLORA & FAUNA

The wide Luangwa River is the lifeblood of the park. It rises in the far northeast of Zambia, near the border with Malawi, and flows southward for 800km through the broad Luangwa Valley – an offshoot of the Great Rift Valley, which cuts through East and Southern Africa. It flows all year, and gets very shallow in the dry season (May to October) when vast midstream sandbanks are exposed – usually covered in groups of hippos or crocodiles basking in the sun. Steep exposed banks mean animals prefer to drink at the park's numerous oxbow lagoons, formed as the river continually changes its course, and this is where wildlife viewing is often best, especially as the smaller water holes run dry.

Vegetation ranges from open grassy plains to the strips of woodland along the river bank, dominated by large trees including ebony, mahogany, leadwood and winterthorn, sometimes growing in beautiful groves. As you move away from the river onto higher ground, the woodland gets denser and finding animals takes more patience.

Not that you'll ever be disappointed by Luangwa's wildlife. The park is famous for its herds of buffaloes, which are particularly large and dramatic when they congregate in the dry season and march en masse to the river to drink. Elephant numbers are also very healthy, even though ivory poaching in the 1980s had a dramatic effect on the population. Elephants are not at all skittish as they are very used to human activity and wildlife vehicles, especially around Mfuwe. This park is also a great place to see lions and leopards (especially on night drives), and local specialities include Cookson's wildebeest (an unusual light-coloured subspecies) and the endemic Thornicroft's giraffe, distinguished from other giraffes by a dark neck pattern.

South Luangwa National Park

South Luangwa National Park

Activities, Courses & Tours

	Bush-Spa	(see 9)

Sleeping

1	Bilimungwe	A3
2	Chamilandu	A3
3	Croc Valley	A1
4	Flatdogs Camp	A1
5	Kafunta	A2
6	Kaingo Camp	B1
7	Kapani Lodge	A1
8	Kawaza Village	B2
	Marula Lodge	(see 13)
9	Mfuwe Lodge	A1
10	Nkwali	A1
11	Nsefu	B2
12	Tafika	B1
13	Track & Trail River Camp	A1
14	Wildlife Camp	A1

Shopping

15	Tribal Textiles	B2

NORMAN CARR & SOUTH LUANGWA

The history of South Luangwa National Park is inextricably linked with the story of Norman Carr, a leading wildlife figure whose influence and contribution to conservation has been felt throughout Africa.

One year after the North and South Luangwa Game Reserves were created in 1938 to protect and control wildlife populations, Carr became a ranger there. With the full backing of the area's traditional leader, Carr created Chief Nsefu's Private Game Reserve in 1950 and opened it to the public. Until this time reserves had been for animals only. All visitor fees were paid directly to the chief, thus benefiting the wildlife and the local community.

Carr was years ahead of his time in other fields, too: he built Nsefu Camp, the first tourist camp in Zambia, and developed walking safaris. In the following decades, other wildlife reserves were created, more tourists came to Luangwa parks and more camps were built along the river.

In 1972 Nsefu and several wildlife reserves were combined to form the South Luangwa National Park, but poaching of elephants and rhinos soon became an increasing problem. So, in 1980 Carr and several others formed the Save the Rhino Trust, which helped the government parks department to deter poachers.

In 1986 Carr opened yet another camp, Kapani Lodge, and continued operating safaris from this base. He retired from 'active service' in the early 1990s, and died in 1997, aged 84.

Even the zebras here are unusual; called Crawshay's zebras, their stripes are thin, numerous and extend down to the hooves, under the belly, with no shadow stripe – they are an intermediate form between the 'standard' East African form and the extra-stripy subspecies in Mozambique.

There's a stunning variety of 'plains game'; the numerous antelope species include bushbuck, waterbuck, kudu, impala and puku. Roan antelopes, hartebeests and reedbucks are all here, but encountered less often.

Luangwa's population of wild dogs, one of the rarest animals in Zambia (and Africa) seems to be on the increase, especially around the Mfuwe area from November to January; there has been a resurgence in numbers around the Nsefu sector as well. An organisation that works to protect and rehabilitate wild dog populations is the **Zambia Carnivore Programme** (www.zambiacarnivores.org) – healthy packs require huge areas to roam for their nomadic lifestyles, and it is trying to open up a viable corridor for the dogs between South Luangwa and the Lower Zambezi National Parks.

The birdlife in South Luangwa is also tremendous. As small lagoons dry out, fish writhe in the shallows and birds mass together as 'fishing parties.' Pelicans and yellow-billed storks stuff themselves silly, and become so heavy they can't fly. Herons, spoonbills and marabou storks join the fun, while grasses and seeds around the lagoons attract a moving coloured carpet of queleas and Lilian's lovebirds. Other ornithological highlights are the stately crowned cranes and the unfeasibly colourful Carmine bee-eaters, whose migration here every August is one of the world's great wildlife spectacles – some visitors come just to see these flocks of beautiful birds busy nesting in the sandy river banks.

Activities

All lodges/camps run excellent day or night **wildlife drives** (called 'game drives' in Zambia) and some have **walking safaris** (June to November). These activities are included in the rates charged by the upmarket places, while the cheaper lodges/camps can organise things with little notice. A three-hour morning or evening wildlife drive normally costs around ZMW210, and the evening drive in particular offers the chance to spot an elusive leopard and shy nocturnal creatures such as a genet or a cerval. You also have to pay **park fees** (ZMW156) on top of this, but only once every 24 hours, so you can have an evening drive on one day and a morning drive on the next. A walking safari (ZMW260) is perhaps the best way of all to experience the park, offering the chance to break out of the confines of the vehicle and experience the African bush first hand with an expert guide and a rifle-carrying ZAWA scout. Expect most attention to be paid to animal tracks, what their dung reveals and the medicinal uses of various plants.

For something entirely different, **SEKA** (Sensitisation and Education through Kunda arts; www.seka-educational-theatre.com) is a local NGO that organises and conducts performances for the local Kunda people on important issues such as poaching, AIDS/HIV, malaria etc –pressing issues in the community. Have a look on their website, and ask your lodge about any performances going on while you're in the area.

Bush-Spa MASSAGE

(☎0216-246123; www.bush-spa.com; 1hr massage ZMW380; ⊙8am-4.30pm daily) All those bumpy hours in 4WDs can wear the body down. For an absolutely decadent experience of relief, head to this beautifully designed Balinese-style spa built over a hippo pond. The owner Nathalie Zanoli, originally from the Netherlands, not only has trained her staff to give massages of the absolutely highest quality but has consciously set out to employ local Zambian women, who are usually excluded from livelihoods in the tourism industry. The extensive menu of services include a variety of treatment techniques, facials and body wraps. 'House calls' to area lodges can also be arranged.

Sleeping & Eating

Most lodges/camps in South Luangwa are along the banks of the river or at an oxbow lagoon. All of the lodges/camps deep in the park are all-inclusive and at the very top end in terms of price (park fees for these camps, ZMW309 per person per night, are also included). Some companies offer walking safaris for a few days from one bush camp to the next (p57) as well as what's often referred to as 'fly camping': nights are spent camping out under the stars with nothing more than a mosquito net separating you from the sights, sounds and smells of the bush, and which is usually the highlight of any trip.

Most travellers will end up choosing from the places just outside the park boundary. These range from budget camping to top-end lodges; however, you don't pay admission fees until you actually enter the park. Note that some lodges/camps open only in the high season (April to November), but those in and around Mfuwe are open all year. Places that open in the low (or 'green' or 'emerald') season offer substantial discounts – often up to 40%. Keep the following in mind: on the plus side there are few visitors, newly born animals, stunning colors and the possibility to see the Luangwa River by boat, however the grass is high, walking safaris are for the most part unavailable, many tracks are impassable and you might not see that much wildlife.

Any rates listed here are per person during the high season; single supplements usually cost 30% more. All-inclusive rates include accommodation, meals, snacks, laundry, activities such as wildlife drives, and park fees. Transfers from Mfuwe airport, local alcohol and house wine are also usually included, but double-check when booking – you might be surprised by how quickly all those gin and tonics add up. None of the lodges or camps described here are fenced which means loud grunting hippos and their like might disturb your sleep and mean you'll need an escort at night.

Only to be considered as an option of the very last resort are the two extremely unpleasant and basic guesthouses (Chiwayu and Cobra) in the village, both no cheaper than a few Mfuwe area camps.

All the lodges/camps and camping grounds provide meals – from simple snacks to creative haute cuisine at the top-end places. Flatdogs Camp probably has the best food of the 'drop-in' lodge restaurants. Highly recommended by area expats and one of the few places to eat in the village is friendly **Dophil Restaurant** (mains ZMW25; ⊙5am-10pm). The owner/chef Dorika prepares samosas, spring rolls, T-bones with *nshima* and pizza, served at a few outdoor tables under a thatch roof. If coming from the airport it's on the left hand side of the road just after the Matizye Bridge.

AROUND MFUWE GATE

Mfuwe Lodge LODGE $$$

(☎0216-245041; www.bushcampcompany.com; per person per night all-inclusive US$450; ⊙year-round;) Laid out along an enviable stretch of a well-trafficked oxbow lagoon only 2km from the Mfuwe Gate, this lodge, one of the largest, is also certainly one of the nicest and most well run. The 18 separate cottages (12 face the lagoon and six the hippo pool) are imaginatively designed with private verandahs (and hanging wicker 'basket chairs') and colourful bathrooms with big windows.

From the back porch of the suites or from the huge outdoor deck with a restaurant, bar and swimmming pool it's like having front row seats to, well, The Lion King. Giraffe

WORTH A TRIP

KAWAZA VILLAGE

This **enterprise** (www.kawazavillage.co.uk; day visits ZMW181, s incl full board ZMW362) run by the local Kunda people gives tourists the opportunity to visit a real rural Zambian village while helping the local community. Four *rondavel* (round, traditional-style hut; each sleeps two) with open-air reed showers and long-drop toilets are reserved for visitors, who are encouraged to take part in village life such as learning how to cook *nshima* (maize porridge), attending local church services and visiting local schools. Other activities include visits to the local healer or to the chief's palace, and bushwalking. Traditional meals are eaten in the chitenge (a thatched, open-sided shelter with traditional wooden chairs and reed mats); and evenings are filled with dancing, drumming and storytelling around the fire. Transfers can be arranged from camps around Mfuwe village; if you have your own wheels, inquire as to the state of the track to the village before heading off.

and buffalo wander about below, unconcerned by people polishing off a dessert of banana toffee pie with a biscuit crust after a candlelit dinner. You can settle into one of the leather armchairs in the old colonial-style library with your wildlife guide, checking off the various species you spotted on the morning drive. Or you might be lucky to be in residence when elephants Wonky Tusky and Winston (one of her sons) plod their way through the lobby to eat from a huge mango tree. Every room has solar panels for water and all food waste goes to the worm farm to be converted to compost and delivered to area farmers. Besides operating as the base for its own six bush camps in the southern section of the park, it's also the site of the recommended Bush-Spa (p55).

Flatdogs Camp TENTED CAMP **$$**
(☎0216-246038; www.flatdogscamp.com; safari tent from ZMW240, chalet ZMW405; @☒) This large, leafy property along a kilometre of riverfront is one of the best of the midrange options. Eleven safari tents of varying features – all are well-kept and have outdoor showers – are at the end of snaking pathways. Groups of four can consider the 'tree house,' which has two open-air bedrooms overlooking a flood plain frequented by all manner of wildlife (a telescope is on hand for star gazing). Four enormous chalets, basically two-story homes, have mosaic-tiled bathrooms and self-catering facilities – good for families or small groups (they sleep six).

No longer the go-to-spot for wild expat bacchanals with people literally hanging from the rafters, Flatdogs bar is still a welcoming spot with a good choice of cocktails and wine. The restaurant, one of the only places with an à la carte menu open to nonguests, has a variety of Zambian and international fare like chicken mango curry and *nshima* with vegetables, and a chalkboard full of daily specials (mains ZMW60). Wildlife drives and walking safaris are offered at affordable rates and all-inclusive packages are available.

Kapani Lodge LODGE **$$$**
(☎0216-246015; www.normancarrsafaris.com; all-inclusive per person ZMW2440) Known as one of the camps Norman Carr built, and intertwined with this pioneer's reputation, Kapani is set about 4km southwest of Mfuwe Gate overlooking a beautiful oxbow lagoon frequented by munching hippos and glorious birdlife. The 10 fairly ordinary thatch and stucco cottages are simply furnished and meals are taken on a large wooden deck that hangs over the river.

There's a relaxed vibe and the guiding is of top quality; the majority of guests spend only a night or two here, choosing to shuttle between the company's four smaller rustic bush camps in the north of the park. It's open all year and runs discounted 'Rivers & Rainbows' safaris from the end of January through March; an uncommon chance to boat on the Luangwa River.

For those with deep pockets, Norman Carr Safaris is opening a luxury lodge (all-inclusive rooom rates will likely be around US$1000 per person) called Chizombo on the nearby site of Carr's original camp.

Kafunta LODGE **$$$**
(☎0216-246046; www.luangwa.com; all-inclusive per person ZMW2330; ☒) Kafunta has a nice set-up with a vast bar–dining area built around a mango tree offering a wonderful open view of the river and adjacent flood plains. The open-air deck to the front is great for wildlife viewing, and it's the perfect spot for a candlelit dinner. Apart from a swimming pool

there's also a hot tub, which is filled from a local hot spring – not a bad spot to relax while you feast on the views. The accommodation itself is unusual: thatch wooden chalets built on stilts with four-poster beds and white-tiled bathrooms. It provides airy digs but makes you feel somewhat disconnected from the land.

It's located about 1.5km from the Nkwali pontoon and 9km southwest of Mfuwe. Further south in the park is its sister camp, **Island Bushcamp**.

Croc Valley CAMPGROUND $

(☎0216-246074; www.crocvalley.com; campsite per person ZMW52, r without bathroom ZMW78, safari tent from ZMW180; ❄) This sprawling, continually expanding compound is set under a tangle of trees lining the riverbank. Because of all the ongoing development it's difficult to sort out the range of accommodation – it's extensive. The campground is popular with independent travellers; 'backpacker rooms' with shared, clean toilets and showers, stone walls, mosquito nets and floor fans are quite a good deal; safari tents of varying levels of luxury and cost run the gamut from air-conditioned semi-permanent structures with private 'butler' service and separate bar and pool area (per person ZMW416) to more standard ones with open-air, thatch-walled bathrooms.

There's a big bar (with its own menu of burgers and chips and the like), now the spot for rowdy expat gatherings, and a restaurant with nightly three-course meals on offer for those paying full-board (all-inclusive rates are offered), not to mention plenty of hammocks and shaded chill-out spots. Wildlife drives (ZMW208) and walking safaris (ZMW260) can be arranged, as can trips to a traditional healer in the village; in the dry season, you can play beach volleyball on the river bed.

Track & Trail River Camp CHALET, CAMPGROUND $$

(☎in Lusaka 0211-246020; www.trackandtrailrivercamp.com; campsite per person ZMW53, full-board chalet/safari tent $190/170; ❄) Set on a riverfront property about 400m east of Mfuwe Gate, and within walking distance of two boardering camps, are four fairly luxurious chalets sleeping up to four, each with a deck overlooking the river. There are also five large safari tents raised on concrete platforms with open-air bathrooms, some a bit further back in the bush, and the camping grounds shaded by a giant African fig are just lovely. An above-ground pool has an elevated deck with lounge chairs overlooking the river. The bar and restaurant are built around a lime tree so, unsurprisingly, lime cocktails are its speciality and the food is excellent. There's also a 'wellness

BUSH CAMP COMPANIES

Only a handful of companies offer lodging within the park proper, primarily in what are generally referred to as 'bush camps'. Despite the misleading name, these are very comfortable, ranging from simple thatch-roofed chalets to stylishly furnished tents with gold-plated faucets and plunge pools. Most have only three to five rooms and offer customised itineraries that take guests to multiple camps by vehicle or on foot.

The three major companies, all with 'base lodges' near the Mfuwe Gate, are the following:

Bushcamp Company (www.bushcampcompany.com) Sophisticated and expertly managed by its founder Andy Hogg. Operates six uniquely designed camps (Bilimungwe, Chamilandu, Chindeni, Kapamba, Kuyenda and Zungulila), which are all in the southern section of the park, as well as its base Mfuwe Lodge (p55).

Norman Carr Safaris Operates five somewhat more rustic camps (Kakuli, Kapani, Luwi, Mchenja and Nsolo) in the northern section of the park as well as its base at Kapani Lodge (p56).

Robin Pope Safaris (p126) With its base at Nkwali (p58) not far south of Mfuwe Gate, Robin Pope Safaris operates three camps (Luangwa River Camp, Nsefu and Tena Tena).

The other companies in the park are the highly recommended Remote Africa (Chikoko, Crocodile and Tafika) in the northern section run by John and Carol Coppinger, Sanctuary Retreats (Chichele, Puku Ridge and Zebra Plains), Shenton Safaris (Mwamba and Kaingo) and Wilderness (Kalamu Lagoon).

area' where you can indulge in an aromatherapy massage and other such treats.

Wildlife Camp CAMPGROUND **$**
(☎0216-246026; www.wildlifecamp-zambia.com; campsite/safari-tent/chalet US$10/40/60; 🏊) This spacious, secluded spot about 5km southwest of Mfuwe village is popular with both overland groups and independent travellers. There are nine simple stone and thatch chalets (two with basic kitchenettes), five airy tented ones and a big, open area for campers with its own bar and pool area perfect sundowner views. A restaurant serves up standard international fare (mains ZMW80). Wildlife drives and walks are available in the park and in the area around the camp, which is rich in wildlife (and outside the park, so you don't pay fees). There's also a bush camp, which makes a great overnight safari walking option (US$220 per person, all-inclusive).

Marula Lodge BACKPACKERS, LODGE **$**
(☎0216-246073; www.marulalodgezambia.com; r with/without bathroom per person ZMW206/51, tents per person ZMW51; 📶🏊) Occupying a stretch of riverfront alongside several other properties, Marula offers a few options for budget travellers. These include two barebones backpacker rooms with shared bathrooms and locker space just outside, three small tents and several simple rooms with private bathrooms. There's a self-catering kitchen, a restaurant with an à la carte menu serving up spaghetti, chicken (mains ZMW70) and the like, and an inviting swimming pool.

SOUTHERN CAMPS

Zungulila BUSH CAMP **$$$**
(☎0216-245041; www.bushcampcompany.com; per person per night all-inclusive US$600; ⏱Jun-Dec) Imagine a *Vogue* photo shoot with an *Out of Africa* theme and you'll have the sophisticated design aesthetic of this camp. Spacious safari tents evoke colonial-era fantasies with copper-plated facuets and Middle Eastern rugs; each has its own sun deck with tiny circular plunge pool and outdoor shower. The furnishings, including piles of refurbished antique suitcases in the open-sided lounge area pavilion, are ready for the trendiest NYC loft. Zungulila's decadent signature treats are the sundowners had barefoot in folding chairs in the shallow river.

Chamilandu BUSH CAMP **$$$**
(☎0216-245041; www.bushcampcompany.com; per person per night all-inclusive US$600; ⏱mid-Jun–Nov) A night-time arrival at Chamilandu is a magical experience – a lantern-lit dinner table is set out under the stars and staff in chef's whites are lined up to cook your Mongolian barbecue (just one of the dinner specials often served). Sunrise offers another revelation when the true brilliance of the camps' design comes to light. Utterly exposed to the elements, the elevated chalets have no fourth wall, only three sides of expert carpentry work; you'll never want to spend more time in a bathroom.

Bilimungwe BUSH CAMP **$$$**
(☎0216-245041; www.bushcampcompany.com; per person per night all-inclusive US$600; ⏱end of Apr-start of Jan) Four enormous and charming wood, bamboo and thatch chalets – the bathrooms themselves can house a family – surround a stunningly beautiful watering hole; equally sizeable terraces (with a second shower) put you at arms-length from the elephants who come to drink.

NORTHERN CAMPS

Tafika BUSH CAMP **$$$**
(www.remoteafrica.com; per person per night all-inclusive US$660-800) The largest of the three Remote Africa camps, Tafika's six comfortable thatch-roofed chalets have hot water showers heated by wood-fired boilers. Food is top flight as is the guiding, and hosts John and Carol Coppinger are gracious and extremely informative hosts. Besides the usual driving and walking safaris, you can also cycle through the park or to the nearby village of Mkasanga, where nearly a third of the adults are employed by Remote Africa. And to get an exciting and new perspective on things, get strapped into the microlight, basically a hanglider with a motor, for a truly bird's-eye view.

Nkwali LODGE **$$$**
(www.robinpopesafaris.net; per person all-inclusive US$540; ⏱year-round; 🏊) A long-standing, classic Luangwa lodge, Nkwali has just six small cottages with delightful open-air bathrooms. They're all very comfortable but with no unnecessary frills, which gives a feel of the bush – rustic but also quite classy. If you're after privacy the two-bedroom Safari House has traditional African decor and a private guide, hostess and chef! The bar-restaurant, built around an ebony tree, overlooks the river and a small water hole

WHAT TO BRING

Clothes suitable for safari don't need to be specialised or expensive. It's colour that matters. Nothing bright that can easily be spotted by wildlife and no black or very dark colours, which will attract tsetse flies. Go with greens and light browns (no camouflage) and a combination of shorts for very hot days and long, lightweight trousers for walking in the bush as well as cities and towns where dress is generally conservative.

Also bring binoculars, camera, of course, wide-brimmed hat, sunglasses, high-ankle walking shoes, headlamp or small torch and a squashable bag like a duffel (large, heavy and solid suitcases are harder to fit in the luggage compartments of small planes).

And cash, either in US$ or ZMW for tipping guides (Zanaco has an ATM at the BP petrol station in Mfuwe village if you run low).

that attracts wildlife right into the camp. It is located in the Lupande GMA overlooking the park, incorporating acacia and ebony woods, making it a favourite spot for elephants and giraffes. Walking safaris are conducted throughout the year.

Kaingo Camp BUSH CAMP **$$$**
(www.kaingo.com; per person per night US$700; mid-May–Oct) Run by highly respected safari guide Derek Shenton, in the northern part of the park, Kaingo is relaxed, understated and exclusive with five delightful cottages surrounded by bush overlooking the Luangwa River. The honeymoon suite has a huge skylight – ideal for bedtime star-gazing – and a private section of river bank, complete with hammocks and outside bathtub. A highlight is the camp's three hides, popular with photographers. Other attractions include excellent food, a floating deck for eye-to-eye views of the hippos, and wildlife walks through the enchanting grove of ebony trees just a short distance from the camp.

Nsefu BUSH CAMP **$$$**
(www.robinpopesafaris.net; per person all-inclusive US$640) Luangwa's first tourist camp (now protected as a historic monument) has an excellent location smack bang in the middle of the Nsefu sector on an open plain awash with wildlife and with hot springs nearby. The *rondavels* (round, traditional-style huts) retain a 1950s atmosphere (along with the rest of the camp), complete with brass taps in the bathrooms and a wind-up gramophone (that works) in the bar – which is perfectly placed for sunrise *and* sunset. Inside, *rondavels* are stylishly furnished and good-sized windows provide river views.

Luwi BUSH CAMP **$$$**
(www.normancarrsafaris.com; per person per night all-inclusive US$605) The entire front side of the thatch huts at this classic and especially serene bush camp cleverly pivot to open directly onto the ground level of a grassy field; lounge away in large, plush beds during the afternoon siesta for a front row seat of elephants feeding only metres away. Amply shaded by African teak and mahogany trees.

Mchenja BUSH CAMP **$$$**
(www.normancarrsafaris.com; per person per night all-inclusive US$665) This is the least rustic of the Carr bush camps. The most noteworthy design features of Mchenja, other than the plunge pool, are the claw-footed bathtubs partially open to the outside through mesh in the safari tents. It's about a 1½-hour drive north of Mfuwe Gate and an 8km walk along the river to Kakuli, another Carr camp, which is open during the 'emerald season.'

Shopping

Tribal Textiles HANDICRAFTS
(0216-245137; www.tribaltextiles.co.zm; 7am-4.30pm) Along the road between Mfuwe village and the airport is a large enterprise that employs a team of local artists to produce, among other things, bags, wall hangings, bed linens and sarongs, much of which are sold abroad. Tribal Textiles have some striking original designs and it's quite a refined place for a shop or to take a short (free) tour around the factory. Local craftspeople outside in the car park sell animal carvings, jewellery and other handicrafts. It's a relaxed place to browse with no hassle, but the range is limited.

Getting There & Away

Air

Most people reach South Luangwa by air. Mfuwe airport is about 20km southeast of Mfuwe Gate and served by **Proflight** (0211-271032; www.proflight-zambia.com), with several daily flights from Lusaka (ranges from ZMW810 to ZMW1500 one way). There are also regular daily flights to/from Livingstone. **Bush & Lake Aviation** (www.bla.mw) and **Nyassa Air Taxi** (www.nyassa.mw) fly from Lilongwe (Malawi) to Mfuwe. There's a bureau de change in the little terminal, Barclays Bank and Zanaco ATMs and a cafe by the parking lot where you can grab a coffee and meal while waiting for your flight. Almost every lodge meets clients at the airport (the charge is often included in the room rates). Otherwise, a taxi to locations near the Mfuwe gate should run around ZMW80.

The airfare is fairly reasonable when you consider the alternative: two wasted days on uncomfortable buses and minibuses, which may end up costing you about ZMW500 anyway (with bus or taxi fares, food and accommodation). Many travellers who endure the road trip from Lusaka bite the bullet, find the credit card and buy a flight out of Mfuwe back to Lusaka. (For a chance at a discounted Proflight stand-by fare of around ZMW500, turn up at the Mfuwe airport anywhere from one to three hours prior to departure.)

Road

South Luangwa is accessible from Chipata via a three plus–hour drive over an extremely rough dirt road; work to improve this road has been ongoing for several years and the hope is that teams tarring out from Chipata and Mfuwe will eventually meet in the middle. Many projected completion dates have come and gone but once finished (local wags remain skeptical) it will likely increase the number of visitors to South Luangwa for better or worse.

BUS & HITCHING

Several crowded minibuses leave from the BP station in Mfuwe village for Chipata (around ZMW150, luggage supplement ZMW10 to 20, 3½hours). Unfortunately, they depart around 7.30pm meaning a late-night arrival.

A shared taxi (around ZMW450 for the entire taxi, around ZMW250 for the front seat for solo travellers) is a more convenient though pricier alternative. If you arrive at the BP station early in the morning, say before 7am, you have a good chance of joining a carload of Zambians or possibly other travellers. Any later and you'll likely have to negotiate with a driver (simply ask around or stand by the side of the road) and you might end up having to pay the bulk of the fare. Set conditions in advance otherwise the driver will likely stop frequently packing in other passengers to supplement his earnings.

Hitching is another option. You might find other foreign travellers with their own vehicle willing to give you a ride or a truck heading south. Be sure to start early at the BP station in Mfuwe.

Arriving in Mfuwe village, it's about one to two kilometres to several camps and it might be possible to hitch, but do *not* walk at night – local wildlife roams freely. Try offering some extra kwacha to the minibus driver to take you closer to your accommodation or to Mfuwe Gate. A taxi from the village to one of the lodges near the gate only a few kilometres away will cost anywhere from ZMW30 to 100.

CAR

To get to Mfuwe Gate and the surrounding camps from Chipata you should have a 4WD, high-clearance vehicle; broken-down compacts and sedans do ply the route, however. In the dry season the dirt road is poor and the drive takes about three hours. In the wet season, the drive can take all day (or be impassable), so seek advice before setting off. In September 2012 the road was still in a pretty bad way in places. Check locally before you make the trip as conditions may be significantly improved by the time this book is published.

Getting Around

For independent drivers, South Luangwa is probably the easiest park to access (with the exception of Kafue) and to drive around. A limited section of all-weather gravel roads are in excellent condition near Mfuwe Gate (there's a vehicle charge of ZMW79 in addition to the per person per day park fees) and then lots of smaller tracks. You should be able to pick up a very basic map at the gate. The bush opens up off the side of the roads (even early after the rainy season in May), making wildlife spotting fairly easy, especially along the river.

If you're not staying at an all-inclusive place and you want to arrange a 4x4 (up to nine people; around ZMW635 per 24hrs) for wildlife viewing or to explore villages in the area contact Ben Koobs, the owner of **Personal Touch** (☎0216-246123; www.tptouch.com).

North Luangwa National Park

This **park** (admission US$20, vehicle US$15; ⏰6am-6pm) is large, wild and spectacular, but nowhere near as developed or set-up for tourism as its southern counterpart. The big draw of North Luangwa is its walking safaris, where you can get up close to the wildlife in a truly remote wilderness.

The bush in North Luangwa is dense in places, so the animals are slightly harder to see, and there are very few tracks for vehicles, so the emphasis is firmly on walking. The range of wildlife is similar to South Luangwa's, except there are no giraffes, and the park is particularly famous for its huge buffalo herds (sometimes up to 1000-strong), which in turn attract large numbers of lions and hyenas. While all the black rhino in the valley were wiped out by the late 1980s (Zambia once had one of the largest populations of black rhino in the world), over the last decade nearly 30 have been introduced to a specially protected area of the park thanks in large part to the **Frankfurt Zoological Society** (www.zgf.de), the conservation group working with ZAWA to protect the park.

North Luangwa's eastern boundary is the Luangwa River, but the heart of the park is the Mwaleshi River – a permanent watercourse and vital supply for wildlife. Dotted along the river, specialised camps and lodges cater for enthusiasts and aficionados. These are open only in the dry season, usually June through the end of October, as access is very restricted in the rains.

It's important to note that most of the southern part of the park has been set aside as a wilderness area. There are not many roads and only three smallish camps that mainly run walking safaris. The only way to access this part of the park is to arrange your stay with one of these operators. However, to the north is a zone that allows wider self-drive access with one main track and several smaller tracks running off it. Note though that you'll need to have a fully-equipped 4WD vehicle to attempt this.

Sleeping

Mwaleshi Camp BUSH CAMP $$$

(☎0216-246185; www.remoteafrica.com; all-inclusive per person ZMW2900) A top-notch operation, at once luxurious, in terms of care from the staff, and relaxed bush camp with accommodation in four charmingly simple chalets made from reeds and thatch with open-roofed bathrooms. Walking is the main activity and that's a fortunate thing once you've tasted their excellent food. Spotted hyenas are commonly seen in this area as are buffaloes and, of course, lions. The spectacular Mwaleshi Falls is another highlight. Most guests on organised tours fly in and out of the national park on chartered planes.

Buffalo Camp BUSH CAMP $$$

(☎0976 970444; www.shiwasafaris.com; all-inclusive per person ZMW1700) Located in the south of the park, Buffalo Camp is a quiet, secluded place run by Mark Harvey, grandson of Stewart Gore Browne of Shiwa Ng'andu, where he was raised. It's good value (and unusually welcomes children) and the six traditional-style thatch-roofed chalets overlook the river. Book ahead for the 'self-catering rates' (ZMW500 per person excluding park rates and bed levy), normally only available when there's a paucity of guests on the all-inclusive package. Transfers for those without vehicles are usually possible from Kapishya Lodge or Mpika (maximum four people).

PITSTOP

Despite the relative proximity of North and South Luangwa National Parks, driving between them is long and hard, and it will take over 11 hours if you were to try the trip in one go. However, most who venture this route stop after around six hours in small Luambe National Park and spend a night or more at the **Luangwa Wilderness Lodge** (www.luangwawilderness.com; campsite per person ZMW53, full board s/d US$245/360; all-inclusive s/d US$440/700), only 3km off the roadway on the Luangwa River. It's another five hours or so from here to Buffalo camp in North Luangwa.

Kutandala Camp BUSH CAMP $$$

(www.kutandala.com; all-inclusive s/d ZMW2800/3600) The hospitality is first rate at this small bush camp with its three chalets, each with a nice big verandah fronting the Mwaleshi River. A four- to five-night stay gives the opportunity for a thorough exploration of the area on foot, and the camp only caters for six guests at a time so solitude is not hard to find. The food is expertly prepared, all the more remarkable considering the camp's isolation. A makeshift library is well stocked with wildlife and natural history books.

Getting There & Away

There is no public transportation. Most guests fly in and out on expensive charter flights arranged by their lodge (typical price per person from Mfuwe to one of the airstrips is ZMW1000 one-way); the result is that only several hundred people visit the park each year.

If you are coming to the park independently remember that you need to be well set-up with a fully-equipped, high-clearance 4WD, and your accommodation prebooked. Also, get advice regarding the state of the roads into the park and make sure you've got maps that cover the area (and GPS); they should be supplemented by a map of the park, usually available at Mano Gate and detailing where you're allowed to drive.

Coming from the north of North Luangwa by car, you can reach Mano Gate from the Great North Road near the village of Luana, about 60km north of Mpika – it's well signposted. The road can be rough, rarely travelled and drops steeply down the Muchinga Escarpment into the Luangwa Valley.

SOUTHERN ZAMBIA

This region is a real highlight of Zambia with some wonderful natural attractions. There are national parks, with the Lower Zambezi in particular highly regarded for both its wildlife (especially elephants) and its scenic landscape. The area is also home to the remote Lochinvar National Park, a World Heritage Wetland Site with pristine wetlands well worth a visit. Then there's the massive Lake Kariba, with Siavonga's sandy beaches and Chikanka Island (smack in the middle of the lake) providing fascinating views of the night sky and a glimpse of the 60 elephants that make their way between the islands. If you're lucky enough to see a storm roll in over the steely waters from Zimbabwe, it'll be an experience you'll long remember. Siavonga itself offers the chance to experience the more rural side of the country, including an opportunity to go on a traditional village tour.

Southern Zambia covers the area southwest down to Livingstone, south to Lake Kariba and southeast to incorporate the Lower Zambezi National Park.

Chirundu

☎0211

This dusty and bedraggled border town is on the main road between Lusaka and Harare. The only reason to stay here is if you're going on to Zimbabwe or planning to explore the Lower Zambezi National Park. Other than a few shops and bars, as well as a Barclays Bank with ATM and a number of moneychangers, there's little else to note. What's more, the roads are permanently clogged with snaking queues of heavy-duty trucks, all heading for, or coming from, the Zimbabwean border.

There is no petrol station in town. Gwabi Lodge has a couple of fuel pumps, but there is a limited supply so it's safer to stock up in Lusaka or Kafue. If all else fails, there are always a few people selling black-market fuel in the street.

Sleeping

Zambezi Breezers CAMPGROUND **$$**
(☎0979 279468; zambezibreezers@gmail.com; campsite per person ZMW50, r without bathroom ZMW190, s/d chalet incl breakfast ZMW375/650; 🏊) Especially popular with backpackers and overland trucks, Breezers, only 6km from Chirundu, can take on a party atmosphere when busy. There's a variety of accommodation options including a wide lawn for camping along the riverbank. There are also six simple and clean tented chalets with small decks. If you're on a budget, consider a block room, really nothing more than a concrete box with beds.

A pool table, basic but cavernous bar area and riverside deck encourage socialising. Other activities on offer are boat trips (ZMW50 per hour or ZMW200 per half day, plus petrol), and River Horse Safaris, which operates out of Breezers, can organise recommended multiday canoeing trips on the Zambezi. The à la carte restaurant serves dinner mains (ZMW60) of basic chicken, better burgers and steaks.

Gwabi Lodge CAMPGROUND, CHALET **$$**
(☎0211-515078; www.gwabiriverlodge.com; campsite per person ZMW50, s/d chalets incl breakfast ZMW425/660; @🛜🏊) This long-running lodge, which sees mostly weekending Lusakans, is set on large leafy grounds 12km east of Chirundu. There's a well-equipped camping ground (tents can be rented) and nine solid chalets with stone floors and TVs (four new chalets were in the works). With a lovely elevated outlook over the Kafue River, 6km from the confluence with the Zambezi, the decking in front of the à la carte restaurant is a great spot to observe birds and wallowing hippos. Fishing is definitely the draw or just having a poke around on a boat (per hour ZMW100, plus fuel), although overnight canoe safaris can be arranged.

Getting There & Away

Minibuses leave regularly for Chirundu from Lusaka (ZMW30, 3½ hours, five to seven daily). To reach Siavonga (on Lake Kariba) from Chirundu, catch a minibus towards Lusaka, get off at the obvious turn-off to Siavonga and wait for something else to come along.

Lower Zambezi Valley

One of the country's premier wildlife viewing areas includes the Chiawa GMA as well as the Lower Zambezi National Park, covering 4200 sq km along the northwestern bank of the Zambezi River. Several smaller rivers flow through the park itself, which is centered around a beautiful flood plain alongside the Zambezi, dotted with acacias and other large trees, and flanked by a steep escarpment on the northern side, covered with thick *miombo* woodland.

On the Zambezi are several islands. Some are large rocky outcrops covered in old trees, which feature in the writings of explorers such as Livingstone and Selous. Others are nothing more than temporary sandbanks with grass and low bush. Along the riverside grow the largest trees – jackleberry, mahogany and winterthorn. On the opposite bank, in Zimbabwe, is Mana Pools National Park, and together the parks constitute one of Africa's finest wildlife areas.

The best wildlife viewing is on the flood plain and along the river itself, so **boat rides** are a major feature of all camps and lodges; doing a boat trip down the river (about ZMW150) is certainly a rewarding activity and it won't be long before you're lulled into the majesty of the Zambezi. The elephant population was ravaged by poaching until the early 1990s, but thanks to the efforts of **Conservation Lower Zambezi** (www.conservationlowerzambezi.org), an organisation funded by the area's lodges and private grants, they are making a strong comeback now, with the surrounding Chiwa Game Management Area particularly dense with elephants. However, despite regular antipoaching flights (keep your eyes open for a Cessna 172 Reims Rocket passing overhead at about 300ft) and regular ZAWA patrols, two dozen elephants were killed in 2011; in the same year another 40 or so died from a naturally occurring anthrax outbreak (in addition to 150 hippos and a large number of buffalo).

Other mammal species include puku, impala, zebra, buffalo, bushbuck, leopard, lion and cheetah, and more than 400 bird species have been recorded, including the unusual African skimmer and narina trogon. There are also plenty of water birds such as plovers and egrets on the reed islands. Seeing elephants swim across the river, or hundreds of colourful bee-eaters nesting in the steep sandy banks, could be the highlight of your trip. The best time to visit is May to October; however, temperatures average around 40°C – and have been recorded as high as 55°C – in the latter half of October.

The main entrance is at **Chongwe Gate** along the southwestern boundary (park fee ZMW132). The southwestern sector of the park is the easiest to reach and the most scenic, and has excellent wildlife viewing, so as you might expect, it's a popular area. As you go further into the central part of the park the surroundings become wilder and more open and there's more chance of having the place to yourself. Although the park is technically open all year, access is impossible in the rainy season and most lodges are closed down from at least mid-December to the end of February.

The eastern part of the park is different in character as here the hills are close to the Zambezi and there's virtually no flood plain. The park's eastern boundary is the dramatic Mpata Gorge where the steep hillsides plunge straight into the river, and the only access is by boat. There are gates along the northern and eastern boundaries for hardy travellers.

Sights & Activities

One of the best ways to see the Lower Zambezi is by **canoe safari**. Drifting silently past the riverbank you can get surprisingly close to birds and animals without disturbing them. Nothing beats getting eye-to-eye with a drinking buffalo, or watching dainty bushbuck tiptoe towards the river's edge. Excitement comes as you negotiate a herd of grunting hippos or hear a sudden 'plop' as a croc you hadn't even noticed slips into the water nearby.

Most of the camps and lodges have canoes so you can go out with a river guide for a few hours. Longer safaris are even more enjoyable; ask your lodge what is available.

The best time for **tiger fishing** (strictly catch and release) is September to December but still possible other months. Rods, reels and even bait can be supplied by all the lodges and camps.

Sleeping

There is a line of lodges running through the Chiawa GMA before the Chongwe Gate,

Lower Zambezi National Park

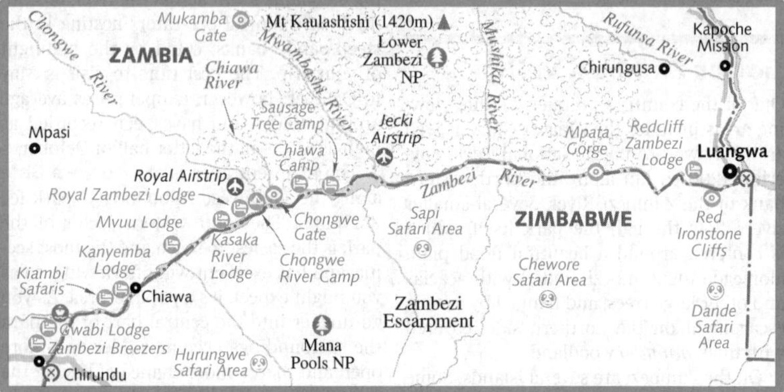

a few in the park itself (all at the very the top end in terms of price) and one to the east of the park boundary (only really accessible to self-drivers). Knowing the distances of the lodges from Chirundu should assist independent drivers in getting around.

Rates listed are usually per person during the high season (April to October) staying in twins/doubles unless mentioned otherwise; single supplements are usually 30% extra. (The rates for camping are also per person.) Also, add on transfers if you haven't got your own wheels. Most lodges offer wildlife-viewing activities by boat or by safari vehicle and are not fenced. Keep in mind, however, that while theoretically on offer, most of the lodges in the GMA, especially those closer to Chirundu than to Chongwe Gate, don't take their wildlife drives in the park proper.

The **community campsite** a few kilometres before Chongwe Gate was bought by a private developer; it was basically abandoned when we passed through, though it might be worth inquiring about.

IN THE GMA

TOP CHOICE **Chongwe River Camp** TENTED CAMP **$$$**

(☎0211-286 808; www.chongwe.com; s/d all-inclusive US$900/1400; ⏲Apr-Nov; 📶🏊) Right on the Chongwe River that marks the boundary between the GMA and the national park, and overlooking the river crossing to Chongwe Gate, this camp has an enviable position with plenty of game around the camp but without the park fees. The confluence of the Zambezi is within view and a menagerie of wildlife graze on a spit of grassland with the park's escarpment in the background – an absolutely Edenic view.

The tented chalets, well spaced along the edge of the river, have plush bedding, shaded verandahs and charming open-air bathrooms. It's a laid-back place with a small fenced-in pool, nightly bonfires and large lantern-lit communal dining table. All-day wildlife drives into the park are available as are canoe-drive combinations and walking safaris.

Chongwe also has other accommodation options, including the luxurious open-air **Albida** and **Cassia Suites**; the latter is especially well-suited for honeymooners. Nearby is the spectacularly anomalous two-storey **Chongwe River House** (sleeps eight), commonly referred to as 'the Flintstones' house because of its curving stone shape, gnarly exposed timber and ceilings made from rocks and wood.

Tsika Island is Chongwe's own very rustic adobe and thatch bush camp further upriver; hot water for showers is supplied by buckets suspended high above on poles to catch sunlight.

Royal Zambezi Lodge CHALET **$$$**

(☎0211-840682; www.royalzambezilodge.com; per person all-inclusive US$650; ⏲year-round; 📶🏊) The epitome of luxury bush mixed with a colonial-era viba, Royal is only a short drive to the eponymously named airstrip and Chongwe Gate. Despite its understated opulence – think brass fixtures, claw-footed tubs and private day beds on decks overlooking the river – it's unpretentious and friendly.

In addition, there's a full-service spa (the only one on the Zambezi) and a bar built around the trunk of a sausage tree next to a small pool, essentially in the river; rest your elbows on the edge and you might see a hippo glide by only a few feet away. Kids and families are welcome and there are discounts in the 'green' season when rains tend to be heavy and quick; although wildlife drives might be impossible, canoe trips are still on and there are few visitors around.

Kanyemba Lodge CHALET **$$$**
(☎0977 755720; www.kanyemba.com; full board around US$330; ❄) This lodge has phenomenal river views and proximity to big wildlife, as well as authentic, homemade Italian food and a cappuccino machine that's ready to roll 24 hours a day – Riccardo, the owner, is a charming and knowledgeable Italian-Zambian. The spacious, round chalets are stylishly furnished with carved wooden pieces from their own workshop and stone floored bathrooms with rainwater showers; shrubbery between neighbouring chalets means privacy is valued.

In an attic-like space above the open-air dining area is a charming little library and lounge, and the pool with riverfront deck is ideal for those long 'between activities' afternoons. Take a guided canoe safari, try your luck at tiger fishing or down G&Ts on a sundowner cruise. If you don't have your own wheels, take a bus to Chirundu and someone will collect you there.

If you're after more seclusion, Kanyemba has its own rustic bush camp (shower heads are stuck onto the branches and trees protrude into the bathrooms) in a secluded corner of the island just across the water from the lodge – you're sure to see loads of animals, especially elephants and hippos, outside your door.

Kasaka River Lodge TENTED CAMP **$$$**
(☎0211-256202; www.kasakariverlodge.com; safari tent all-inclusive per person ZMW2090) The sister property to Chongwe River Camp, this place is perched high above the Zambezi only 4km from the park entrance. On one side are eight fairly luxurious tented chalets with charming outdoor bathrooms set on a manicured lawn with a small pool where a particularly frisky hippo is known to visit. On the other 'bush' side is the honeymoon suite with Ottoman-style bed and open-air bath and a family- (children are welcome here) or group-oriented two-bedroom thatch-roofed home with its own viewing deck and fire pit.

In between, built under several large trees where monkeys and baboons scamper, is the dining and bar area; just below is another small 'library' deck, best used for kicking back and watching the river flow by. Cultural visits to a local community and local schools are a good way to break up the wildlife viewing.

Kiambi Safari CAMPGROUND **$$**
(☎0977 186106; www.kiambi.co.za; campsite per person ZMW52, chalet per person incl full board from ZMW420; ❄📶❄) This well-run operation at the confluence of the Zambezi and Kafue Rivers has a smattering of different, relatively affordable accommodation options. Wood-floored tented chalets are comfy with attached outdoor bathrooms and small private porch areas. The spacious air-con chalets are good if the humidity is getting a bit much though the TV and concrete might strike a dissonant note. Well-equipped, self-catering cottages can sleep six and are a great choice for families. Campers maybe get the best deal of all with their own fire pit, swimming pool, a separate bar (with pool table and TV) and upstairs viewing platform. And don't worry if you've forgotten a tent; they'll provide one with bedding for an extra ZMW42.

If you're not on an all-inclusive deal, note that meals are set choice (ZMW115 for dinner). Canoeing, fishing, wildlife viewing cruises and fishing are on offer as well as three-night canoe safaris (ZMW820 per person per day including all meals, tent and bedding). Pick-up by boat from Chirundu is ZK580 per boat return. This place is one of the few in the area to stay open all year (inquire about discounts from December to March).

Mvuu Lodge CAMPGROUND **$$$**
(☎in South Africa 012-660 5369; www.mvuulodge.com; campsite per person ZMW115, safari tent per person from ZMW1155) A large, leafy property with an informal vibe, Mvuu is built on the edge of the tree-lined riverbank. Comfortable elevated safari tents with balconies are on either side of a casual lounge and dining area. The communal campfire encourages guests to share their tales of leopard and lion sightings.

Each site in the campground, the furthest one into the GMA, has its own outdoor stone shower and toilet, fire pit (firewood is provided), concrete cooking table and sink; self-caterers can use the lodge kitchen's fridge.

INSIDE THE PARK

Sausage Tree Camp CHALET $$$
(☎0211-845204; www.sausagetreecamp.com; d per person incl full board US$895; ⊙May–mid-Nov;) Overlooking the Zambezi, deep inside the national park, Sausage Tree is wonderfully unconventional. Traditional safari decor is rejected in favour of cool and elegant Bedouin-style tents, each in a private clearing, with minimalist furniture, cream fabrics and vast open-air bathrooms, which continue the North African theme. Each tent has a discreet *muchinda* (butler; which means service is incredibly personalised), while other features are the library tent with couches and cushions, and the airy dining tent with a Paris-trained chef – despite the exclusivity, socialising, especially at meals, is encouraged.

Chiawa Camp CHALET $$$
(☎0211-261588; www.chiawa.com; per person all-inclusive US$895; ⊙Apr-Oct) In a spectacular position at the confluence of the Chiawa and Zambezi Rivers, inside the park, this luxurious lodge was one of the first in the Lower Zambezi. As a pioneer in this area, the owner Grant Cummings knows the park intimately and his expertise is highly regarded. The large walk-in tents feature pine-clad private bathrooms. The bar-lounge has an upstairs deck with majestic views over the river and there's a viewing platform high up in the trees.

The food is top notch and for the romantics among you (and honeymooners), candlelit private tables can be set up in the bush, on a boat, or, when the full moon is out, on a sand bar in the middle of the river.

Chiawa's sister camp, **Old Mindoro**, is a classic old-school safari bush camp unlike anything else in the park and receives raves from visitors we spoke with.

EAST OF THE PARK

Redcliff Zambezi Lodge TENTED CAMP $$$
(☎0979 844377; www.redcliff-lodge.com; per person all-inclusive US$275;) This lodge is east of the park, about 20km upstream from Luangwa town on the Mozambican border. Accommodation is in tented chalets, which are simply furnished with indigenous teak and are spaced along the bank of the Zambezi. Fishing (especially for tiger fish) is a major feature here or you can take boat trips to Mpata Gorge or to the towering red ironstone cliffs that give the lodge its name – they are absolutely stunning at sunset. Access is by boat or plane from Luangwa, which in turn can be reached via a turn-off (and very bad road) from the Great East Road. Charter flights from Lusaka or Livingstone are also possible.

ℹ Getting There & Away

Air

Proflight (www.proflight-zambia.com) has twice daily flights (in the high season) on four-, eight- and 16-seater planes between Lusaka and Royal Airstrip (30 minutes; in the GMA just a few kilometres west of Chongwe Gate) and Jeki Airstrip (40 minutes; in the heart of the park); both cost around ZMW820 one-way. Almost every guest staying at one of the top-end lodges in the park flies into and out of Jeki, while Royal is very convenient for the lodges near Chongwe Gate. All include transfers from the airstrip, which for the fitness-minded is the only safe place to get in a run free of predators.

Road & Water

There's no public transport to Chongwe Gate, nor anything to the eastern and northern boundaries, and hitching is very difficult. Most people visit the park on an organised tour, and/or stay at a lodge that offers wildlife drives and boat rides as part of the deal. The lodges also arrange transfers from Lusaka – generally a minivan to Chirundu and then boat to the lodge (rates and travel times vary depending on the distance from Chirundu).

Uncomfortable minibuses run from the City Bus Station in Lusaka to Chirundu; departures run throughout the morning, however, you will have to sort out transport from town to your accommodation.

If you have your own vehicle (you'll need a high-clearance 4WD), head down to Chirundu. As you enter the town, you are looking for a left-hand turn to Gwabi Lodge and from there head into the GMA and on to the Chongwe Gate into the Lower Zambezi (all the same route).

There are also tracks via the north for those heading to the eastern side of the park but these are far less used: there's an approach road accessed from the Great East Road, 100km east of Lusaka, that will take you to Mukanga Gate; and there's a track from Leopards Hill in Lusaka, which is earmarked for improvement though this could be many years in the future. Seek local advice before attempting either of these routes.

For budget travellers, ask at Bongwe Barn and Lusaka Backpackers in Lusaka or Jollyboys in Livingstone for deals on budget safaris into the Lower Zambezi.

ℹ Getting Around

Remember that you'll need a well-equipped 4WD to access and get around the park. You must drive slowly in the GMA area and the park itself – watch especially for elephants along the roadside at all times. There are several loops inside the park for wildlife viewing, but these change from year to year, especially after the rainy season, so pick up a guide at any of the gates.

Not far from Gwabi Lodge in the GMA is a pontoon (6am to 6pm), which you'll need to take to cross a river; it costs ZMW40 for a Zambian registered vehicle, or ZMW100 for a non-Zambian-registered vehicle, while foot passengers go free.

One adventurous way to visit the park is by canoe along the Zambezi. Most lodges offer two- or three-day canoe trips, with stops at seasonal camps along the river or makeshift camps on midstream islands.

Lake Kariba

Beyond Victoria Falls, the Zambezi River flows through the Batoka Gorge then enters the waters of Lake Kariba. Formed behind the massive Kariba Dam, this is one of the largest artificial lakes in Africa. The lake is enormous and spectacular with the silhouettes of jagged Zimbabwean peaks far across its shimmering waters. The Zambian side of Lake Kariba is not *nearly* as developed or as popular as the southern and eastern shores in Zimbabwe. On the Zimbabwean side are national parks and wildlife areas, and some tourist development, while the Zambian side remains remote and rarely reached by visitors. For those who make it here, this remoteness is the very attraction.

The main base for activities on and around the lakeshore is Siavonga, which is a small town with accommodation set up mainly for the business market, although tourist facilities do exist. Sinazongwe, almost halfway between Livingstone and Siavonga, is even less set up for tourism. Only 17km away across the water, closer to Zimbabwe (150m away) than Zambia, is Chete (27 sq km), the largest island on the lake. It has lions, leopards, elands, waterbucks, bushbucks, impalas and kudus, and of course hippos and crocs, an astonishing variety of birds but no roads or accommodation at the time of writing.

THE CURSE OF KARIBA

Kariba Dam was constructed at the head of Kariba Gorge, and both are named after a huge rock buttress called Kariba, which the local Tonga people believe is the home of their river god – fish-headed and serpent-tailed Nyaminyami. When the Tonga learnt that the new lake would flood Nyaminyami's residence they were understandably angry, but when they found out their own homes and ancestral lands would also be submerged it was the last straw, and they called on their god to step in and destroy the white man's interference.

Did the god deliver? Oh yes. In July 1957, about a year into the dam's construction, a torrential storm on the Upper Zambezi sent flood waters roaring through the work site, breaching the temporary 'coffer' dam and damaging equipment. The following March there was an even greater flood – the sort expected only once in 1000 years, and never two years running – again destroying the coffer dam and causing major damage, as well as washing away a bridge that had been constructed downstream.

The engineers may have had a grudging respect for Nyaminyami by this time (they did increase the number of spillway gates from four to six), but the building continued and the dam was officially opened in 1960. Meanwhile, the justifiably disgruntled Tonga were forced to leave their homeland.

But Nyaminyami still had a final trick up his sleeve. No sooner had the lake begun to fill, than a destructive floating weed called Salvinia molesta began choking the lake's surface. A native of South America, its arrival in Kariba remains a mystery, but the Tonga no doubt assumed divine intervention. At one stage, a third of Lake Kariba was covered in this green carpet, rendering boating impossible and threatening to block the dam's outflow.

Finally, for reasons still not fully understood, the weed started to disappear, but other problems continued: in the early 1990s, a drought caused water levels to drop so low that there wasn't enough to generate power. The rains returned and through 2000 and 2001 the lake was mostly full again, but with rumours of earth tremors and cracks in the concrete, and concern over the dam's long-term strength and design, not to mention another dam proposed at Batoka Gorge below Victoria Falls, it remains to be seen whether Nyaminyami will rise in wrath again.

WORTH A TRIP

VISITING THE DAM WALL

A visit to the dam wall with your own wheels is quite straightforward. Head down to the Zambian border crossing; it's a few kilometres from the wall. Enter the immigration building (on the right-hand side down some stairs as you face the border gate). Tell them that you just want to visit the wall and that you are coming back to Zambia and not going onto Zimbabwe. They will give you a stamped pass to the dam wall and ask you to leave some ID behind (driving licence or passport are OK). At the gate, show them your pass and you'll be let through. From here it's a short drive or walk to the wall. Once there, park your car, and walk out over the wall; the views are spectacular, and it's well worth the trip – particularly if you admire gargantuan engineering projects. You should be allowed to take pictures of the wall but not the power station. Remember that the authorities don't like cameras around here and have a fear of terrorism or sabotage to the dam. So, do what they tell you, but be firm about reminding them that it's only a picture of the wall you want. On the way back, surrender your pass at the border gate, and don't forget to pick up your ID from immigration.

History

Lake Kariba was formed in the 1960s, its waters held back by the massive Kariba Dam, built to provide electricity for Northern and Southern Rhodesia (later Zambia and Zimbabwe) and as a symbol of the Central African Federation in the days before independence. Today, Kariba measures 280km long by 12km to 32km wide, with an area of over 5500 sq km, making it one of the largest artificial lakes in the world. Underground power stations on both sides of the dam produce over 1200 megawatts between them.

As well as being a source of power, Lake Kariba is an important commercial fishing centre. Small sardine-like fish called *kapenta* were introduced from Lake Tanganyika, and they thrived in the new mineral-rich waters. During the 1970s and 1980s the fishing industry flourished, with many '*kapenta* rigs' (floating pontoons) on the lake. Lights were used to attract the fish at night; the fish were then scooped up in large square nets on booms. In recent years, overfishing has led to a decline in catches, but some rigs still operate, and you'll often see their lights twinkling on the horizon.

The fishing industry was always part of the plan, so while the dam was being constructed, vegetation in the valley was cleared by bulldozers pulling battleship chains through the bush, tearing down everything in their path. The chains were held off the ground by huge steel balls – three of which are now on display in Choma Museum (p71). When the dam was complete, the waters rose faster than expected and covered huge areas of woodland before the trees could be cleared. Scuba divers today tell stories of enchanted forests under the water – swathes of large trees, still with every leaf and twig intact, frozen in time – a poignant reminder of the valley now covered by the lake.

SIAVONGA

☎0211

Siavonga, the main town and resort along the Zambian side of Lake Kariba, has a location to be envied. Set among hills and verdant greenery, just a few kilometres from the massive Kariba Dam, views of the lake pop up from many vantage points, especially from the lodges. Built up primarily in the 1960s and '70s, it can at times appear as if no architects, builders or designers have visited since. Set up mainly for the conference/business market and wealthy urban Zambians (especially from Lusaka) who tear down here towing their sleek boats and stay in their vacation bungalows, independent travellers without their own wheels might not find enough upside to offset the challenges of a visit. The accommodation, though relatively affordable, is spread out with just a market, a few shops, a bakery, Zanaco bank with ATM, post office and little else. But for those seeking down time at the closest 'beach vacation' to Lusaka, you can kick back or experience water activities available such as canoeing through Zambezi Gorge, as well as a civilised sunset cruise to the dam wall. Just don't even think of putting your big toe in the water – crocs lurk around the lake shore.

Activities

The lodges organise activities in and around the lake, including boat trips to the dam wall (price depends on boat size and ranges from ZMW135 to ZMW530), **sunset cruises** (per person ZMW75), **fishing trips**, longer distance motoring around to Lottery Bay (ZMW1550) and one-day to four-night **canoe safaris** on the Zambezi where you'll canoe through the gorgeous Zambezi Gorge (these must be booked in advance). You have a choice of standard safari where everything is done for you, or DIY with everything supplied. A DIY safari works out to be roughly ZMW500 per day per person (food included).

Sleeping & Eating

The lodges are spread out along a series of coves and headlands, some several kilometres from one another and the 'town centre.' There's not much reason to stay at one of the guesthouses in the town proper since there's no direct lake access.

Eagles Rest CAMPGROUND, CHALET **$$**

(0211-511168; www.eaglesrestresort.com; camp site per person ZMW50, s/d incl breakfast ZMW400/550;) A great change of pace from all those crack-of-dawn safari wake-up calls is a lazy weekend at this laid-back beachfront resort. With its own little sandy area (swimming not recommended, of course), pool and the only campsite around town, Eagles Rest is easily the best set-up for independent travellers. Large, spacious chalets have stone floors and great decking outside with patio furniture overlooking the lake. The camping ground is nice and grassy and well landscaped, and the ablutions are reasonably looked after; tents (ZMW50) and matresses (ZMW25) are available for rent. The owners are knowlegeable about the local area and experienced in organising lake-based activities, everything from wake boarding, tubing, fishing and canoeing; their houseboat *Bateuleur* (which sleeps 12) is available for rental March to November.

Lake Kariba Inns HOTEL **$$**

(0211-253768; www.karibainns.com; s/d from ZMW305/420;) Lush gardens, great lake views and relatively luxurious rooms, that is, at least an attempt to bring the decor into the modern era, make this a good choice for those who don't mind sharing space with conference attendees (the upside is a good gym, and for those who have spent too much time in the bush, a hair salon). The restaurant is a grandiose affair, ablaze with African carvings and decoration, overlooking the pool area, which is itself perched high above the lake, as are the verandahs in many of the rooms. Lunch and dinner buffets are ZMW75 each and full-board deals are available.

Lake Safari Lodge LODGE **$$**

(0211-511148; www.lake-safari.com; s/d incl breakfast from ZMW400/500;) Slightly upmarket and nicely situated with an elevated position on the shore, it's the longest-standing lodge in town though definitely geared towards groups and conferences. The large rooms, though certainly lacking in charm, come with cable TV and bland stylings catering to the tastes of urban-weary Zambians. There are lovely landscaped outdoor areas under palm trees, including a nice pool area, giving the whole set-up a tropical vibe.

Getting There & Away

Drivers should be aware of road conditions on the way to Siavonga. Minibuses from Lusaka (ZMW70, three hours, three to five daily) leave when bursting to capacity for Siavonga and the nearby border. Alternatively, get a bus towards Chirundu and get dropped off at the Siavonga turn-off; from here take a local pick-up (ZMW15) the rest of the way. From the makeshift bus stop in Siavonga, you can easily walk to Leisure Bay Lodge or Lake Safari Lodge. Leaving Siavonga, minibuses depart from near the market. There are no official taxis in Siavonga, but there are plenty of unoffical ones or your hotel can arrange a car to the border; otherwise, minibuses head here as well.

AROUND SIAVONGA

West of Siavonga are a number of alternative lake accommodation options. They provide solitude and a more personalised way to experience a stay by the lake. Take the turn-off to the west about 2km north of Siavonga. The track is very rough and a 4WD is recommended (in the dry season a high-clearance 2WD would probably suffice).

Sleeping

Village Point CAMPGROUND, CHALET **$$**

(0979 278676; www.village-point.com; campsite per person ZMW30, tent hire ZMW40, chalet per person incl full board ZMW300;) This small property in a pretty bush setting on a peninsula in Lotri Bay, 40km west of Siavonga, is ideal for washing away urban grit and everyday concerns. Very comfortable thatch chalets have an upper storey open to the lake and the breeze, and couples should note the open-air bathtubs strategically located for sunsets; less expensive beds are available in basic huts. You can fill your days with a local village tour, fishing, walks or just plain lazing about.

Sandy Beach Safari Lodge CAMPGROUND, CHALET **$$**
(☎0967 860739; www.sandybeachzambia.com; campsite per person ZMW30, chalet ZMW190/250;) A quiet, secluded camp around 13km from the Siavonga turn-off, it does indeed have a wonderful sandy beach – as long as the lake waters aren't too high. The relaxed owner Herman the German gives the place a laid-back vibe, and a plethora of activities are on offer such as windsurfing, abseiling and canoeing.

Butete Bay CAMPGROUND **$$**
(☎0977 713752; campsite per person/chalet ZMW45/200) Located overlooking a bay further on from Sandy Beach, this is a basic camp oft frequented by groups. In addition to camping there are three very simple thatch chalets. Meals can be provided but most self-cater. Fishing, bush walks and visits to local villages are all on offer.

SINAZONGWE

☎0213

Near the southwestern end of Lake Kariba and far from its cousin on the water at the other end of the lake, Sinazongwe is a small Zambian town used by *kapenta* fisherman as an outpost. The centre of town is actually up on a hill away from the lake's edge and the whole area has little tourism footprint.

Sleeping & Eating

Lakeview Lodge LODGE **$$**
(☎0976 667752; www.keview-zambia.com; campsite per person ZMW50, s/d incl breakfast ZMW250/470;) A kilometre from town and easy to find is Lakeview Lodge, where simple chalets with ceiling fans have a secluded terrace overlooking the lake and verdant grounds. There's also a pool, small beach area and a *braai* (barbecue). Meals are ZMW40 and you can hire a boat to Chikanka or Chete Island. This is a good spot to chill out for a few days.

Kariba Bush Club
(☎0979 493980; www.karibabushclub.com; campsite per person ZMW50, dm ZMW110, r ZMW192;) About 60km from Sinazongwe, but with an excellent array of accommodation options, is Kariba Bush Club, a beautifully landscaped site. Traditional buildings have dorm accommodation as well as very tastefully furnished double, twin and family rooms and thatch-roofed chalets; there are also two wonderfully comfortable guesthouses for groups with DSTV, brilliant locations and gobsmacking views. You can self-cater or meals are available, including local specialities such as crocodile curry and lake bream. Activities include walking safaris on the private islands (you can camp or stay in a safari tent on Maaze Island 20 minutes away by speed boat). To get to the club, take the road to Maamba from Batoka on the main Lusaka–Livingstone Highway – about 2km before Maamba take the dirt road to the left and follow the signs.

Getting There & Away

Ask in Choma for minibuses that can take you to Sinazongwe. By car, head to Batoka, just north of Choma. From here take the turn-off to Maamba. After about 50km look for the turn-off to Sinazongwe; the town is a short distance down this dirt road.

CHIKANKA ISLAND

This beautiful private island (actually an archipelago of three islands since a rise in water levels), 18km from Sinazongwe, is mostly wooded, with impalas, kudus, zebras, bushbucks and the occasional elephant dropping in. Crocs and hippos patrol the shores so don't even think about taking a dip. To spend a night or two in one of the stone-and-thatch A-frame chalets or campgrounds at **Chikanka Island Camp** (☎0976 667752; www.lakeview-zambia.com; campsite per person ZMW50, s/d incl breakfast ZMW250/475, chalet all-inclusive ZMW350/450;) catch a boat (ZMW400, up to eight people) from its mainland sister lodge, Lakeview (p70). Fishing, canoe trips and wildlife walks can all be arranged but mother nature provides great early morning views looking out towards Zimbabwe.

Choma

☎0213 / POP 40,000

This busy market town, the capital of the Southern Province, is strung out along the highway 188km northeast of Livingstone. Most visitors zip through on their way to Lusaka or Livingstone, but Choma is a convenient stopover or staging post for trips to Lake Kariba and even to the southern section of Kafue National Park. Other than the museum there's not much to distinguish the town, but it has all of the facilities and services travellers need including a Spar supermarket, banks with ATMs, internet, a couple of petrol stations and an every expanding range of accommodation.

Sights

Choma Museum & Crafts Centre MUSEUM

(adult/child ZMW10/5; 9am-5pm) Based in a former school dating from the 1920s east of the centre along the highway, the museum's exhibits concentrate on the Tonga people, most of whom were forcibly displaced by the construction of the Kariba Dam. There are displays on the traditional life of Tonga women and men, including Possession Dances, and craftwork with some lovely beadwork exhibited. There's also lots of info on Zambia's Southern Province, including interesting old black-and-white photos, an art gallery with exceptionally good carvings, and a craft centre selling basketry, crafts, textiles and carvings.

Sleeping & Eating

Leon's Lodge LODGE $$

(0978 666008; r ZMW180-200, chalet ZMW250-350) Despite the two enormous stone carved lions out front, Leon's, just off the main street (clearly signposted), is welcoming rather than grandiose. The rooms are clean and large, with satellite TV and fridge, and the thatch-roofed chalets are a step up in luxury. There's a small bar and restaurant on-site and a tiny outdoor circular bar area.

Gwembe Safari Lodge CHALET $$

(0213-220169; www.gwembesafaris.com; campsite per person ZMW30, s/d without bathroom incl breakfast ZMW180/260) There's a lovely shaded area at this lodge, complete with thick grass, tables and chairs and a *braai*. When tour groups aren't around, the large camping area and clean chalets make a peaceful place for the night. The lodge is signposted 1km southwest of town and is a further 2km north off the tar road.

Kozo Lodge & Lituwa Fast Foods CHALET $$

(0977 619665; www.kozolodge.co.zm; s/d ZMW200/300) About 7km south of Choma this large fast-food outlet (mains ZMW15 to ZMW35), designed as a stop for tour groups, does lots of chicken combinations including its speciality, *kozo* (smoked) chicken. Loud pop music blares outside or you can enjoy a real coffee indoors. Around back is Kozo Lodge, which has chalets with fridges, fans and somewhat limited satellite TV, but being this far south of town, they are quiet and convenient for getting on the road the next morning; deluxe versions come with Jacuzzi.

Getting There & Away

All daily buses and trains between Livingstone and Lusaka stop at Choma. The bus to either Lusaka or Livingstone is ZMW50 or ZMW65 and there are many departures every day.

Nkanga River Conservation Area

This rudimentary conservation area (admission ZMW30) covers a few local farms and is a tourism venture aimed squarely at birdwatchers but welcoming everyone. It protects many different varieties of antelope, too, including eland, sable, wildebeest and kudu. It's an excellent area for birdwatching with an excess of 400 species recorded, including Chaplin's barbet, Zambia's only endemic species.

The turn-off to Nkanga River is about 3km north of Choma, and then it's about 20km on a decent gravel road to **Masuku Lodge** (0977 760756; www.masukulodgezambia.com; s/d incl breakfast ZMW447/500), a birdwatcher's paradise with six spacious *rondavels* in beautiful shaded grounds. You'll probably be greeted by a horde of friendly, motley pooches on arrival.

Lochinvar National Park & Around

This small, 410 sq km **park** (admission US$10, vehicle US$15; 6am-6pm), northwest of Monze, consists of grassland, low wooded hills and the seasonally flooded Chunga Lagoon – all part of a huge World Heritage Wetland Site called the Kafue Flats. You may see buffaloes, wildebeests, zebras, kudus and some of the 30,000 Kafue lechwes residing in the park. Bushbucks, oribis, hippos, jackals, reedbucks and common waterbucks are also here. Lochinvar is also a haven for birdlife, with more than 400 species recorded. Its mudbanks and shallows are a treat for wading birds. An excellent selection of wetland birds (including wattled cranes) occur near the ranger post along the edge of Chunga Lagoon.

For history and geology fans, **Gwisho Hot Springs** is the site of a Stone Age settlement, today surrounded by palms and

MWANACHINGWALA CONSERVATION AREA

This conservation area protects an area of wetlands on the Kafue Flats about 25km north of Mazabuka, a fairly large, spread-out town and the epicentre of the surrounding farming district. At the time of research there were no facilities in the park for visitors so you really need your own vehicle and to be prepared to drive in and out the same day (Mazabuka has a number of guesthouses and lodges). It consists of land donated by the local community and some private farms in the area and attracts a wealth of birdlife, especially water birds, as well as being home to the semi-aquatic Kafue lechwe and sitatunga antelopes. You can walk, fish or possibly hire a boat to explore some of the lagoons. Information is supposedly available at the Mwanachingwala Conservation Area office in the municipal offices in Mazabuka; however, it may not be staffed.

Access is in the dry season only by 4WD: head south from Mazabuka towards Livingstone for about 5km, take a right onto Ghana Rd, then a few kilometres along it's another right to Etebe School. Another 4km or so takes you to a turn-off to a fishing camp; now you're on the flats.

lush vegetation with steaming water far too hot to swim in. Nearby Sebanzi Hill was the site of an Iron Age settlement inhabited last century. Keep an eye out for an enormous baobab tree with a hollow trunk big enough for a small number of people to sleep in. The tree apparently had special powers that would protect travellers passing by from animals.

Lochinvar was virtually abandoned in the 1980s; since then various developers have come and gone. Provided you bring all your own gear, you should be able to camp – ask the scouts at the gate for the latest on viable campsites within the park. Remember that facilities will be poor, and don't forget to bring your own food.

The best option for sleeping in the area with one of the nicer campgrounds in Zambia is **Moorings Campsite** (☎0977 521352; www.mooringscampsite.com; campsites ZMW35, s/d chalets ZMW175/250), located on an old farm 11km north of Monze. It's a lovely secluded spot with plenty of grass and open-walled thatch huts with *braais*. There's plenty of shade, and a large bar area with a stone floor where simple meals are available. Day visitors can picnic here (ZMW5/2.50 adult/child) and proceeds are used to support an on-site clinic and the Malambo Women's Centre.

The network of tracks around the park is still mostly overgrown, with only the track from the gate to Chunga Lagoon reliably open. By car from Monze, take the dirt road towards Namwala. After 15km, just past Nteme village, turn right and continue north along the narrow dirt road for 13km. Near Kembe village, turn left (west) and grind along the road for another 13km to the park gate. A 4WD with high clearance is recommended for getting to and around the park, though you may get stuck if you don't also have a winch.

WESTERN ZAMBIA

☎0217

Western Zambia is at the bottom of some travellers' itineraries and at the top of others': if you're after easy access, lots of other tourists and well-known attractions then you should look elsewhere. This western area is dominated by two huge rivers, the Kafue and the upper waters of the Zambezi, and the woodlands of central Zambia thin out here as the soil becomes sandy – this area is an extension of the Kalahari Desert in neighbouring Namibia.

Kafue National Park is the biggest single park in Africa, and is truly magnificent with all the big mammals, great birdwatching, and a thousand different landscapes that include river systems offering the chance to float past a leopard stretched out on the shore, a fish eagle perched imperiously on a branch above the water or a 500-strong buffalo herd lapping noisily at its cool waters. It's the only place in the country where you can track lions on foot and have a great chance of finding them.

Other highlights are thundering waterfalls and tremendous views of flood plains; a chance to experience even more remote wilderness areas such as Liuwa Plain National Park, which sees few visitors but is a majestic patch of Africa; an exploration of Barotseland, home of the Lozi people and site of the colourful Kuomboka, which is Zambia's best-known traditional ceremony; and easy access to Botswana and Namibia with world-class national parks such as Chobe to explore.

Kafue National Park

This stunning park (per person/vehicle US$15/15; ⏲6am-6pm) is about 200km west of Lusaka and is a real highlight of Zambia. Covering more than 22,500 sq km (nearly the size of Belgium), it's the largest park in the country and one of the biggest in the world (ZAWA has only one scout for every 400 sq km). This is the only major park in Zambia that's easily accessible by car, with a handful of camps just off the highway.

The main road between Lusaka and Mongu runs through the park, dividing it into northern and southern sectors. (You don't pay the park fee of ZMW105 per person per day if in transit; self-drivers pay another ZMW79 per vehicle per day.) There's an incredible amount of animals to be seen just from the main road – wildlife watching doesn't get much easier than this! There are several gates, but three main ones: Nalusanga Gate, along the eastern boundary, for the northern sector; Musa Gate, near the New Kalala Camp, for the southern sector; and Tateyoyo Gate for either sector if you're coming from the west. Rangers are also stationed at the two park headquarters: one at Chunga Camp and another 8km south of Musa Gate.

FLORA & FAUNA

Kafue is classic wildlife country. In the northern sector, the Kafue River and its main tributaries – the Lufupa and Lunga – are fantastic for boat rides to see hippos in great grunting profusion, as well as crocodiles. The forest along the water's edge conceals birds such as Pel's fishing owls and purple-crested louries, while you can't miss the African fish eagles perched on top of palm trees. Away from the rivers, open *miombo* woodlands and *dambos* (grassy, swampy areas) allow you to spot animals more easily, especially the common antelope species such as waterbuck, puku and impala, and the graceful kudu and sable antelope. This area is one of the best places in Zambia (maybe even in Africa) to see leopards – they are regularly spotted on night drives.

To the far north is Kafue's top highlight, the Busanga Plains, a vast tract of Serengeti-style grassland, covered by huge herds of near-endemic red *lechwes* and more solitary grazers such as roan antelopes and oribis. (Note that this area is accessible only between mid-July and November.) Attracted by rich pickings, lions (which climb the local sycamore figs to keep cool and away from the flies, and swim through deep pools in the swamps during the wet season) and hyenas are plentiful, and during the dry season there are buffaloes, zebras and wildebeest herds that move onto the plain from the surrounding areas. Cheetah spottings picks up during September after wildebeests birth their young. There are also at least two packs of wild dogs.

In the southern sector of the park, the vegetation is more dense, and early in the season the grass is very high, making animals harder to locate, although the thick woodland around Ngoma is the best place to see elephants. Lake Itezhi-Tezhi, a vast

DRIVING IN WESTERN ZAMBIA

The road from Livingstone to Sesheke is in very good condition and sees little traffic; it's tar all the way, and about 200km in distance. From Sesheke north to Mongu, you need to check road conditions before you set off. As of late 2012, nearly 60% of the 220km had been paved. From Sesheke to Sitoti it's paved in parts only (targeted completion date is mid 2013). But it's the 23km stretch of road between the Sitoti pontoon ferry and Senanga (the bridge at Kalongola that will replace the ferry should be finished by mid-2014 if not earlier) that is questionable. During the floods (January to the end of May) it's underwater and so the ferry shuts down. The road is in good condition the remainder of the way from Senanga to Mongu.

Along the Great West Road, the stretch from Lusaka to Nasalunga Gate (Kafue National Park) is excellent, and it's also in very good condition through the park (beware of a series of speed bumps). From the western gate (Tateyoyo) to Kaoma road conditions worsen considerably, so keep your speed down; it's bumpy: there are dips and hiding-in-the-shadows potholes. The road then, from Kaoma to Mongu, is quite good, with few potholes.

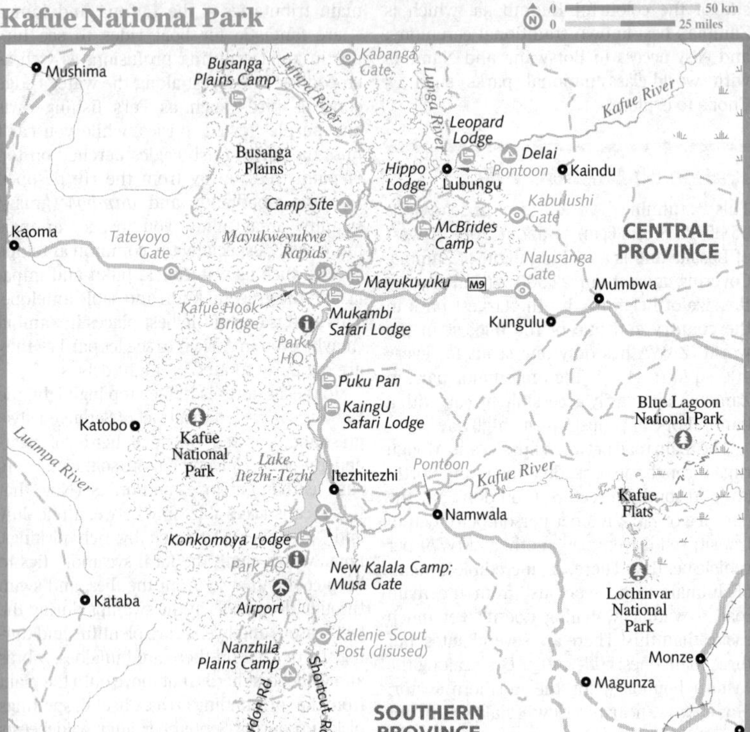

expanse of water, is both tranquil and beautiful, especially at sunset. In the far south, the Nanzhila Plains support an abundance of red lechwes, while other species include oribi, roan and sable antelope, hartebeest, wildebeest and puku. Large buffalo herds are sometimes seen, and there are lions and leopards around. The southern sector is less visited (not that the north is crowded); you're unlikely to see another vehicle all day.

For birdlovers, Kafue is a dream; the wide range of habitats means that over 400 species have been recorded. The south of the park is the best place for spotting Chaplin's barbet – Zambia's only endemic species – and the equally rare black-cheeked lovebird.

Staying a few days in Kafue allows you to explore different habitats and to experience the great diversity of wildlife that this beautiful park has to offer.

Activities

All camps and lodges can arrange wildlife-viewing drives (also called game drives in Zambia) in open-top cars. Night drives, in vehicles armed with powerful spotlights, can be especially exciting as lions and leopards are often most active at night. Walking safaris (also called game walks) are available too, but you can't walk in the park without an armed scout (ranger). Activities are included with accommodation at top-end lodges, or are available as extras at budget/midrange places. It's worth noting that the evenings in Kafue can be surprisingly cold from May until September, and you'll need a coat, a hat and gloves for the night drives.

Multiday walking safaris with nights spent in the bush, commonly referred to as 'fly camping' in Zambia, are available with **Jeffery & McKeith Safaris** (☎0976-215426; www.jmsafaris-zambia.com; 3 nights per person all-inclusive US$1200). Run by two young, but experienced and extremely passionate, wildlife guides, trips can include a night or several at Musekese, a bush camp with four safari tents overlooking a *dambo*.

Sleeping

There are numerous campsites and lodges/camps offered in and around the park. Several lodges/camps are just outside the park boundaries, which means that you don't have to pay admission fees until you actually visit the park. An additional 'bed levy' (ZMW53) that is charged to tourists is usually included in the rates for the upmarket lodges, but elsewhere the levy is added to your accommodation bill (unless you're just camping).

JUST OFF THE LUSAKA–MONGU HIGHWAY

TOP CHOICE **Mukambi Safari Lodge** CHALET $$$
(☎0974 424013; www.mukambi.com; per person incl full board ZMW1422; ⏲year-round; 📶❄) Easily the most accessible of the Kafue lodges and easy to reach from Lusaka, Mukambi makes a great base to explore the park. Tastefully designed *rondavels* with Adirondack-style chairs on each front porch are set back from the riverfront on a lawn with a manicuring assist by Basil, the sometime resident hippo. A few luxurious 'tents,' reserved for Busanga Plains Camp guests, have flowing white drapery, solid-wood furnishings and private back decks overlooking the river with their own outdoor claw-footed tubs!

The pool is ideal for relaxing between morning and afternoon activities and the beautifully designed dining area has a 2nd-floor lounge, a great spot for contemplating sunsets – that is, if you're not out on a sunset cruise on the motorised pontoon boat, which covers a placid stretch of the river. Hot water is delivered to rooms for early morning coffee before wildlife drives are taken across the river. As it's outside the national park there are no park fees associated with a stay here. Ask about camping which is soon to be available nearby. And it might be interesting to check out the Dutch reality TV series 'Van Amstelveen naar Afrika,' which chronicled the owner and his family's travails in building Mukambi and its sister camp in the Busanga Plains.

Head west along the main road from Lusaka until about 10km before Kafue Hook Bridge (or 82km from Nalusanga Gate) and look for the signposted turn-off to the south.

BUDGET SAFARIS INTO KAFUE

For a budget safari into the park, check with Lusaka Backpackers (p42) and Bongwe Barn (p41) in Lusaka and **Jolly Boys Backpackers** (☎324229; www.backpackzambia.com; 34 Kanyanta Rd; campsite/dm/r ZMW40/50/205; @📶❄) in Livingstone.

Mayukuyuku CAMPGROUND, TENTED CAMP $$
(www.kafuecamps.com; campsite per person ZMW78, full board US$150; ⏲year-round) A rustic bush camp, small and personal, in a gorgeous spot on the river with a well-landscaped camping area and four tastefully furnished thatch-roofed safari tents. Each of the latter have hammocks, chairs and table out front and great outdoor bathrooms (even campers get open-air toilets and showers). If you don't have your own gear, you can even rent tents (ZMW78/130 small/large tent). It's possible to self-cater, have meals prepared with advance notice (dinner ZMW150) or to stay full board, or even on an all-inclusive deal in a safari tent (accommodation, meals, wildlife drives and walks, park fees and laundry are included); a six-night package is US$1800 per person.

Mayukuyuku is accessible by 2WD and is only 5km off the main highway on decent gravel; the camp does pick-ups (ZMW160 per vehicle) from the nearby bus stop (jump off from any Lusaka–Mongu bus or minibus) or transfers from Lusaka (ZMW2650 round trip).

NORTHERN SECTOR

Other than one highly recommended property, Wilderness Safari Company (Busanga Bushcamp, Lufupa Bushcamp, Shumba Camp) has a monopoly on accommodation in the Busanga Plains (guests are ferried in by a charter flight and a short hop on a helicopter), perhaps the most beautiful part of the park. Several other lodges/camps are in the center and northeastern section and one, Delai Camp, is outside the park proper in the Mushingashi Conservancy, a GMA/hunting concession owned by the son of the assassinated Lebanese Prime Minister, Rafik Hariri; patrolled with almost military efficiency, poaching here is rare and wildlife thrives.

To get to these camps by road, you pass through the small bustling town of Mumbwa (the Zambian air force is based nearby), your last chance to refuel. The discovery of rich mineral deposits around Hippo and McBrides might threaten the area's preservation.

TOP CHOICE **Busanga Plains Camp** TENTED CAMP **$$$**
(www.mukambi.com; all-inclusive per person ZMW3409; ⌚Jul-Oct) The approach to this bucolic oasis, basically an island just 7km from the park's northern border, is made all the more dramatic by the wooden walkway over a prairie of 'floating grass.' Being served a glass of juice and handed a face towel ain't bad either. The pièce de résistance of each of the four simply but comfortably outfitted safari tents is the outdoor bathroom with bucket shower (hot water is provided with a little notice). An air of informality and intimacy is encouraged by fireside pre-dinner drinks and meals taken communally in the thatch-roofed lounge area. The six-hour transport (160km) from Mukambi is basically an extended wildlife viewing drive; a box lunch is served at the halfway point. You're likely to see a tremendous variety of animals; the only caveat is that tsetse flies can be a nuisance. Most visitors spend time at Mukambi on either end of their journey here.

Delai BUSH CAMP **$$**
(☎0977 762096; www.bongwesafaris.com; 3 night all-inclusive per person incl transport from Lusaka US$1100) Located in the wildlife-rich Mushingashi Conservancy just outside the northeastern border of Kafue proper, this rustic camp is run by Alec and Emma of Bongwe Barn (p41) in Lusaka (all guests here are on all-inclusive multiday trips). Basic thatch-roofed chalets are on a hillside overlooking a stunning bend in the river, a setting evocative of the American west if it weren't for the occassional hippo or lion or even leopard wandering through. In part because of the lack of electricity and its isolation, a stay of several nights here is to be cherished and feels truly like a refuge from the wider world, which couldn't feel further away. The food served for the communal-style meals is delicious and the portions huge. Alec, a long-time safari guide, is a knowledgeable and entertaining host when in residence. Morning and night-time wildlife drives rival those of anywhere else in Kafue. It's about a four-hour drive in an air-conditioned minivan from Lusaka. It also offers a 'self drive' option for US$190 per person per night, which includes three meals and one activity per day.

McBrides Camp CHALET, CAMPGROUND **$$$**
(☎0977 414871; www.mcbridescamp.com; campsite per person ZMW155, chalet per person ZMW1200) Situated at the confluence of the Mushingashi and Kafue Rivers, this genuine bush camp is cleverly built around wildlife paths, assuring the regular presence of wild visitors. The seven chalets are spacious and simple, and are built of thatch and wood. The campsite is the budget alternative and is simple, shady and has two clean ablution blocks; meals in the main lodge are available (dinner ZMW102). The other side of the river is where walking safaris are conducted. This is a wild part of the park and you've a good chance of spotting lots of wildlife, but owners Chris and Charlotte's passion is lions. Chris has written three books on them (with the *White Lions of Timbavati* the only one still easily available) and is a fountain of knowledge.

Hippo Lodge CHALET **$$$**
(☎in Lusaka 0211-295398; www.hippolodge.com; chalets all-inclusive per person around US$420; ⌚year-round) This long-running, owner-operated place has loads of character and beautiful riverine views. Individual stone chalets, with quirky features like impala antlers for toilet paper holders and tree branches as key design features of the bathrooms, are spaced well apart (from the honeymoon chalet you can watch the river ripple past as you rejuvenate weary bones).

Alternatively, basic but comfortable safari tents are more of a budget option and the riverfront bar and restaurant are great places to kick back and revel in the setting. The standard fare for one-way transport from Lusaka is around ZMW1250 (up to four people).

Leopard Lodge CHALET **$$$**
(☎in South Africa 027-82 553 8767; www.leopard-lodge.com; per person all-inclusive ZMW1600) Situated on the Kafue River, in a GMA at the edge of the park, Leopard Lodge is a small, secluded camp in an enviable location about 4km from one of Zambia's best hot springs. There are stunning views from the hill behind the camp, and this is where lions come to mate, usually in May. The six brick, thatch-roofed chalets are very comfortable with cotton linen and ceiling fans.

There's a bar and restaurant on-site, although private lunches and dinners in the bush are the way to go, and a picnic on a river island is a highlight. Boat trips and fishing trips feature alongside walking safaris and game drives.

SOUTHERN SECTOR

Places in the Southern sector are outside the park and south of the main road between Lusaka and Mongu.

To get to Puku Pan and KaingU, you have two options. First, passable only from June to November, is a very rough, though scenic, dirt track that mostly hugs the eastern bank of the river (the tsetse flies here are horrendous so only venture this way if you have air-conditioning and can close the windows), or the 'good' (longer in terms of kilometres) road that turns off the Lusaka–Mongu Highway around the village of Kachereko. From here, you head south for 46km and then west for another 36km to the river. This road (work paving it should begin in mid 2013) also heads all the way to to Lake Itezhi-Tezhi and the accommodation there.

TOP CHOICE KaingU Safari Lodge CAMPGROUND, CHALET $$$
(in Lusaka 0211-256992; www.kaingu-lodge.com; campsite per person ZMW127, full board & two activities ZMW1905; year-round;) Experienced African travellers will especially love this remote camp set on a magical stretch of the Kafue River – broad but filled with lush islands among the rapids, providing lots of nooks and crannies to explore (pathways lead to a *dambo* hide and a few croc-free bathing spots), with delightful birdwatching. The four tastefully furnished Meru-style tents raised on rosewood platforms with stone bathrooms overlook the river and have large decks to enjoy the view. Families can opt for the large high-ceilinged two-bedroom chalet with its own kitchen, living room and outdoor shower.

There are also three campsites, each with its own well-kept thatch ablution and *braai* facilities. Before, all wildlife drives were in the GMA, but now they can be done across the river in the park; however, it's the river that's the highlight and two-day to week-long fly-camping canoe (large inflatable ones) safaris are offered.

For those not paying all-inclusive rates, activities are ZMW127. Contact KaingU for driving directions from the Lusaka–Mongu Highway. Charter flights can land at Chunga, the nearby airstrip.

Puku Pan Safari Lodge CAMPGROUND, CHALET $$
(in Lusaka 0211-266927; www.pukupansafarilodge.com; campsites per person ZMW156, chalets incl full board & one activity per person ZMW1090; year-round) A low-key, no-frills Zambian-managed compound beautifully situated overlooking the hippo- and croc-filled river. The eight somewhat rustic mud and thatch cottages have verandahs and the campgrounds have hot showers and clean ablutions blocks. Out back overlooking the swamps and the hunting concession that surrounds the property is a boma viewing area with wicker chairs and a hammock. Walking safaris (ZMW106) and boat trips (ZMW132) are available as well as the usual wildlife drives.

For independent drivers, take the road to Itezhitezhi, which is clearly signposted; after 50km you'll need to sign in at the Mwengagwa scout post, and a couple of kilometres after that there's a clearly marked turn-off to the lodge. Then it's about another 40km through woodlands and past an airstrip before you reach the lodge. Transfers from Lusaka (ZMW260) and pick-ups from the highway near Mukambi (ZMW518) are available; prices are per vehicle.

Nanzhila Plains Camp CHALET $$$
(0977 212302; www.nanzhila.com; campsite per person ZMW100, chalet per person incl full board ZMW900; Jun-Oct) In the very southern section of the park this isolated camp is beautifully situated on a large *dambo*. Four thatch and two Meru-style safari tents are very comfortably furnished. This area, once depleted of wildlife, has seen its return, including sables, roans, kudus, hartebeests, wildbeests, cheetahs and several lions, after conservation work done by this camp in conjunction with ZAWA and the Nature Conservancy. It is accessed from the Dundumwezi Gate or is a two-hour drive south from Lake Itezhi-Tezhi.

Konkamoya Lodge CHALET $$$
(www.konkamoya.com; all-inclusive per person ZMW1820; mid-Jun–mid-Nov) Easily the best accommodation on the southern shores of Lake Itezhi-Tezhi, Konkamoya has five enormous and luxurious safari tents with wicker furniture raised on wooden platforms and stunning lake-facing views. Morning and afternoon walks and wildlife drives are part of the daily schedule.

New Kalala Camp CAMPGROUND, CHALET $$
(0213-263179; www.newkalala.com; campsite per person ZMW76, s/d ZMW457/711, s/d incl full board

ZMW607/1016; ❄️🚭) Just outside the park boundary, this old-school place has large, bland chalets in a rocky setting overlooking beautiful Lake Itezhi-Tezhi. There's a bar and a restaurant serving breakfast (ZMW30) and other meals (around ZMW70). The campsite is separate from the lodge in a patch of shady trees. Fishing, boat rides, wildlife drives and village visits can all be arranged.

Getting There & Away

Some guests of the top-end lodges/camps fly in on chartered planes (this includes all guests of Wilderness Safari properties in the northern part of the park).

For drivers, the main route is along the road between Lusaka and Mongu. It's about 200km from Lusaka to Nalusanga Gate, and then 30km west of Nalusanga Gate a road leads southwest towards Lake Itezhi-Tezhi. The road is in very bad condition, with a small part graded only. The rest is terrible – it's only accessible by a 4WD with high clearance. Note the tsetse flies are bad down here, too – so air-con is a big comfort. Just past Itezhitezhi village is Musa Gate, from where the road crosses Lake Itezhi-Tezhi to the New Kalala Camp.

Head west along the main road from Lusaka until about 10km before Kafue Hook Bridge (or 82km from Nalusanga Gate) and look for the signposted turn-off to the south. Heading west along the main road from Lusaka, you'll find a main track leading into the northern sector of the park on the western side of Kafue Hook Bridge.

There's no public transport in the park, but you could easily catch a Mongu-bound Juldan or Shalom bus from Lusaka (ZMW100, three hours, 8am) to the highway stop near Mukambi Safari Lodge (contact Mukambi for pick up; only a couple hundred metres away wildlife roams free) or Mayukuyuku (arrange pick-up from the highway for a fee). For a ride back to Lusaka, wait out by Hook Bridge or the stop by Mukambi between 11am and 11.30am.

Alternatively, take the slow daily bus, or one of the more regular minibuses from Lusaka to Itezhitezhi village (ZMW75, six hours). From the village bus stop wait around for a lift (because of the number of wild animals it's not safe to hike).

Kaoma

Kaoma is a busy little town about 80km west of Kafue National Park. It's a good place to fill up with petrol (two stations) and not a bad spot to break a journey from Lusaka out to the far west of Zambia. **Kaoma Cheshire Orphanage Guesthouse** (☎0977 221782; r per person ZMW55, chalet per person ZMW100) is a simple, basic set-up that's clean and friendly. It overlooks the Luena Valley and has some gorgeous views, especially early in the morning; your patronage supports a local orphanage. There are clean twin rooms with shared bathrooms or ensuite chalets available. If you give them notice a simple dinner can be prepared (ZMW15) and breakfast is available in the morning; you can also self-cater.

Mongu

The largest town in Barotseland, and the capital of the Western Province, is on high ground overlooking the flat and seemingly endless Liuwa Plain. This is a low-key town with plenty of activity on the streets but little to draw travellers outside of the annual **Kuomboka ceremony** when thousands flock here and room prices skyrocket. The town is quite spread out with no real centre and the highlight is the spectacular panoramic view over the flood plains. From a harbour on the southwestern outskirts of town, an 8km canal runs westwards to meet a tributary of the Zambezi. The river port is a settlement of reed and thatch buildings, where local fishermen sell their catch, and it's a good spot for people-watching as longboats glide down the river transporting people and goods to nearby villages.

There are a few internet cafes around town.

Sights & Activities

Mumwa Craft Association MARKET

(Lusaka Rd) A visit here is well worth your time. Proceeds from sales of expertly made basketry and woodcarvings – at low prices – are ploughed back into the local communities that produce them. Located next to the Total petrol station on the road to Lusaka.

Visiting the Palaces

The village of **Limulunga** is 15km north of Mongu. Here, you can see the palace of the *litunga* (the king of the Lozi). It's a large traditional house occupied by the *litunga* from around April to June when his main residence at Lealui is flooded. You cannot go inside, and photos are not allowed. Of more interest is the **Nayuma Museum** (admission ZMW5; ⏲8am-5pm daily), with its colony of bats in the roof, and exhibits about the Lozi, *litunga* and Kuomboka including a large model of the *nalikwanda* boat used in the ceremony. There are also some fascinating

BAROTSELAND

For many Zambians, the Western Province is Barotseland – the kingdom of the Lozi people who settled the fertile flood plains of the Upper Zambezi, and established a stable system of rule and administration, under the power of a paramount chief or king, called the *litunga*.

In the early 19th century the effects of the *difaqane* (forced migration) disrupted Lozi culture. Barotseland was occupied by the Makololo people for around 40 years, but the Lozi regained control in the mid-19th century and reinstated the *litunga*. At around the same time the explorer Livingstone came through, blazing the trail for other Europeans, including George Westbeech, a trader who settled and became an adviser to the *litunga*.

During the 'Scramble for Africa' of the 1880s, Portugal wanted the Upper Zambezi region to link the colonies of Angola and Mozambique, but the British South Africa Company had designs on the mineral rights in the area. The incumbent *litunga,* whose name was Lewanika, felt threatened by the neighbouring Matabele people, so he requested British support, and in 1900 Barotseland became a British protectorate. It was later incorporated into the colony of Northern Rhodesia, despite Lozi hopes that they might retain some autonomy.

When Zambia became independent in 1964, the new government of Kenneth Kaunda maintained control over Barotseland, further fuelling Lozi bitterness and separatist aspirations. After the change of government in 1992, President Chiluba declined to address the Barotseland issue, and through the late 1990s, the Lozi people found themselves supporting the main opposition party – the UNIP, led, ironically, by Kenneth Kaunda.

A new *litunga,* Lubosi Imwiko II, came to the throne in 2000. The Lozi independence issue remains unresolved and calls for self-rule continue.

shots of royal pageantry, Zambian-style, in a black-and-white photo exhibition titled, 'A Retrospective in the Forties' by Max Gluckman. Otherwise, various artefacts and cultural exhibits including a potted history of snuffing are pretty old and dusty, but there are some interesting pictures of the historical line of the Lozi *litungas*. Minibuses run between Mongu and Limulunga throughout the day.

The village of **Lealui**, on the flood plain 15km northwest of Mongu, is the site of the *litunga's* main palace; he lives here for most of the year (July to March), when the waters are low. The palace is a large single-storey Lozi house, built with traditional materials (wood, reeds, mud and thatch) and meticulously maintained. Around the palace are smaller houses for the *litunga's* wives and family, and a tall reed fence surrounds the whole compound. It's not easy to reach, but the journey by boat (along a canal from Mongu to a branch of the Zambezi, then upstream to Lealui) is spectacular, passing local villages and plenty of birdlife. Avoid visiting at weekends when *litunga's kotu* (court) is closed, because you need permission from his *indunas* (advisors) to get a close look at the palace and even to take photos – and the *kotu* is only open from Monday to Friday.

Public longboats between Mongu harbour and Lealui (ZMW10, one hour) leave once or twice a day. Alternatively, charter a boat to Lealui for about ZMW500 return, which could take six people: the price includes fuel and is usually negotiable. There are many more options for boats around the time of the Kuomboka festival; then it's possible to get a ride for around ZMW70 per person if you ask around. Make inquiries at the shed on the left as you enter the harbour. Buses do the trip in the late months of the dry season.

Sleeping & Eating

Standard Zambian fare like chicken with *nshima* is available from most accommodation places and basic restaurants in town.

Greenview Guesthouse CAMPGROUND, GUESTHOUSE **$$**
(☎0217-221029; www.limagarden.com; Limulunga Rd; campsite per person ZMW25, r from ZMW225; ❄) Located next to the church, chalets here sleep two people and are fantastic value; newer ones come with air-conditioning, shiny tiled floors and DSTV. Spacious inside and set in nice, grassy grounds with views of the flood plains, they may well be the best deal in Mongu. It belongs to the new Apostolic church

KUOMBOKA CEREMONY

The Kuomboka (literally, 'to move to dry ground') is probably one of the last great Southern African ceremonies. It is celebrated by the Lozi people of western Zambia, and marks the ceremonial journey of the *litunga* (the Lozi king) from his dry-season palace at Lealui, near Mongu, to his wet-season palace on higher ground at Limulunga. It usually takes place in late March or early April, and sometimes ties in with Easter. The dates are not fixed, however; they're dependent on the rains. In fact, the Kuomboka does not happen every year and is not infrequently cancelled because of insuficient flood waters; the 2012 ceremony was called off because it's against Lozi tradition to hold the Kuombaka under a full moon.

In 1933, a palace was built by Litunga Yeta III on permanently dry ground at the edge of the plain at a place called Limulunga. Although the Kuomboka was already a long-standing tradition, it was Yeta III who first made the move from Lealui to Limulunga a major ceremony.

Central to the ceremony is the royal barge, the *nalikwanda*, a huge wooden canoe, painted with black-and-white stripes, that carries the *litunga*. It is considered a great honour to be one of the hundred or so paddlers on the *nalikwanda*, and each paddler wears a head-dress of a scarlet beret with a piece of a lion's mane and a knee-length skirt of animal skins. Drums also play a leading role in the ceremony. The most important are the three royal war drums, *kanaona*, *munanga* and *mundili*, each more than one-metre wide and said to be at least 170 years old.

The journey from Lealui to Limulunga takes about six hours. The *litunga* begins the day in traditional dress, but during the journey changes into the full uniform of a British admiral, complete with regalia and ostrich-plumed hat. The uniform was presented to the *litunga* in 1902 by the British King, Edward VII, in recognition of the treaties signed between the Lozi and Queen Victoria.

next door, so partying is probably not a great idea. To find it, head up the road to Limulunga and keep an eye out for the sign on the left.

Mongu Lodge LODGE $
(☎0217-221501; Mwanawina St; s/d incl breakfast ZMW160/220; ❄) In a nice, quiet location not far from the post office, this business-style lodge attracts Zambian business folk. Rooms are small and some could do with more light and functioning TVs; there's a pleasant outdoor bar and small restaurant.

Country Lodge LODGE $
(☎0977 427777; countrylodge@iconnect.zm; 3066 Independence Ave; r incl breakfast ZMW175; ❄📶) Close to the centre of town, this modern and well-run place sees its fair share of conferences and weddings and the like. The rooms are plainly decorated but come with amenities like satellite TV and nice modern bathrooms. There's a bar and restaurant on-site.

ℹ Getting There & Away

The public bus station is on the southeastern edge of town, behind the Catholic church. Juldan and Shalom are the most recommended of the bus companies servicing the Lusaka to Mongu route (ZMW150, eight hours).

A daily bus operates between Livingstone and Mongu (ZMW125, 10 hours) via Sesheke, Kalongola and Senanga, but you might want to break up the journey in Senanga; minibuses and pick-ups leave on a fill-up-and-go basis from here (ZMW25, 2½ hours).

Liuwa Plain National Park

About 100km northwest of Mongu, **Liuwa Plain National Park** (☎0977 158733; liuwa@africanparks.co.zm; per person per day US$40; campsite per person US$10, scout per day US$10) is 3600 sq km of true wilderness on the Angolan border. A remote and rarely visited wild grassland area (one distinctive landmark, the 'lone palm,' can be seen from 40km away), it's where vast numbers of wildebeests and other grazing species such as lechwes, zebras, tsessebes and buffaloes gather at the beginning of the wet season (November). Although their gathering is often called a migration, it's more of a meander, but the wall-to-wall herds are nonetheless spectacular. Roan antelope, wild dogs, cheetahs and especially large and well-fed hyenas in particularly high numbers can be found in the park. Birdwatching is also a highlight with water birds such as wattled and crowned cranes, marabou, saddle-billed storks, herons, pelicans and egrets, among others, making an appearance when the pans fill with water. In 2009, two male lions from Kafue were introduced in order to mate with Liuwa's lone female. Although unsuccessful, two Kafue lionesses were then brought to Liuwa to mate with the two males; while one of the lionesses was killed in September 2010, efforts continue.

Although it became a national park in 1972, for years the park was in decline with no government funds to rehabilitate it. However, an organisation called **African Parks** (www.african-parks.org), which assists African governments in funding conservation projects, signed a lease agreement in 2004, and now manages the welfare and facilities of the park.

Liuwa Plain is accessible from June to December but the best time to go is November, just after the rains start (the later the better). Make sure you leave before the flood waters rise, however, or you'll be stuck for months.

Getting here independently, via the park headquarters at Kalabo, is restricted to well-equipped and completely self-contained vehicles and is a real expedition, hence the small visitor numbers (only 25 vehicles are allowed in at any one time; and a GPS is advisable). One of the only companies to offer all-inclusive organised trips is the highly recommended **Robin Pope Safaris** (www.robinpopesafaris.net); a trip out to Liuwa Plains will cost about ZMW17,200 for four nights.

Sleeping

There are three campsites in the park – **Kwale**, **Lyangu** and **Katoyana** – that are open to independent travellers and run by the local community in partnership with African Parks. Remember that you must be totally self-sufficient, including bringing all your food for yourself and your guide. Each campsite can take up to five vehicles and is situated among the densest game areas in the park along the wildebeest migration path. Campsites have cold-water showers, flush toilets and a craftshop with local souvenirs. Guided walks, boat trips and even traditional fishing trips can be organised here.

Robin Pope Safaris has improved and developed the Matamanene campsite, the only semi-permanent Meru tent-style development in the park. There's an airstrip nearby used by guests of RPS's four- and five-day Liuwa trips.

African Parks is encouraging the development of another semi-permanent camp by 2014.

Getting There & Around

Access to Liuwa Plain National Park is restricted to the dry season and even then you should seek information about the state of the roads from Mongu through to the park before attempting the run.

It's about a 70km drive from Mongu northwest to Kalabo. The road from Mongu to the ferry across the Zambezi River is rough and for 4WD vehicles only. From here the road improves but access depends largely on the severity of the rainy season so it is best to contact the national park for up-to-date information. From Kalabo, you need to cross another river via a pontoon (per vehicle ZMW40). From that point it's 12km to the park boundary.

Despite a network of tracks, Liuwa is serious 4WD territory; a lot of the tracks are very sandy, wet or both. Although the trackless, featureless, endless plains appear benign, it's also very easy to get lost. Taking a scout with you is highly recommended and also financially assists the national park; this can be organised at the park headquarters.

Senanga

If you're coming from Lusaka, Senanga has a real 'end of the line' feel – although the main street can be surprisingly lively, especially in the evening, and the views of the Zambezi are beautiful. It is the best place to break up a journey between Mongu and Ngonye (Sioma) Falls or Sesheke.

The best accommodation option is **Senanga Safaris** (☎0217-230156; campsite per person ZMW30, d incl breakfast US$60). It offers comfortable *rondavels* with splendid views over the Zambezi plains – spoiled only by the giant satellite TV dish in the garden. The bar sells cold beer and the restaurant serves expensive meals. Several cheaper restaurants are dotted along the main street nearby. Be warned that you may have difficulty getting accommodation when it hosts an annual fishing competition over a few days in the dry season.

Minibuses and pick-ups run between Senanga and Mongu (ZMW25, 2½ hours) several times a day. About 30km south of Senanga, the pontoon ferry (passengers free, 2/4WD vehicles ZMW100/150) across the

Zambezi to the tiny settlement of Kalongola (marked as Sitoti on some maps, but this is a separate village about 5km south of Kalongola) on the west bank of the river is being replaced by a bridge, which is likely to be finished by early 2013. From here, a recently tarred road continues south towards Sesheke and Namibia.

Sioma & Ngonye Falls

The village of Sioma is about 60km southeast of Kalongola. It has a large mission, a row of shops, and that's about it. The only reason to come here is **Ngonye Falls** (Sioma Falls; admission free; ⌚24hr), a 1km-wide chain of waterfalls, rapids and rocky islands cutting across the Zambezi River. It's beautiful and very impressive and would be a major attraction if it wasn't so difficult to reach. Imagine something almost as majestic as Victoria Falls, but with almost no other person (local or foreign) in sight.

If you can, stop at the National Parks & Wildlife Service office near the falls, where you can receive advice on the best way to visit and they can point out a local **campsite** (US$10). You should be able to engage an official guide here. While it's easy to get a view of the falls, getting a really good view is much harder as you need to get out onto an island in front of the falls – ask at the National Parks office if there are any boats that might take you there.

Situated 8km south of Ngonye Falls, **Maziba Bay Lodge** (☎0927-11 234 1747; www.mutemwa.com/maziba.htm; all-inclusive per person US$320) has large wooden chalets with bathrooms and comfortable furnishings, overlooking an idyllic sandy beach on the Zambezi. Bookings are necessary for the chalets, but campers can just turn up; no large trucks are permitted. This place organises visits for its guests to the falls.

The falls are less than 1km east of the main road, about 10km south of Sioma. For drivers, access is not difficult; otherwise, hitch a ride and ask to be dropped by the turn-off (look for the 'Wildlife Department' sign).

Sesheke

Sesheke consists of two towns on either side of the Zambezi River linked by a bridge. It is 200km upstream from Livingstone (virtually opposite the Namibian town of Katima Mulilo) – and it makes a handy gateway to Barotseland if you're coming from the southeast. The major part of town is on the eastern side of the river, before you cross the bridge. There's not much to actually see or do here and it's really used as a transit point between Zambia and Namibia. The smaller section of town, on the western side of the river, is centred around the Zambian border crossing, with the Namibian border a few hundred metres down the road.

Small buses link Sesheke with Natakindi Rd in Livingstone (ZMW55, two hours, two daily), usually in the morning, and minibuses also make this journey. Occasional minibuses also link Sesheke with Katima Mulilo.

Sleeping

Brenda's Best & Baobab Bar CAMPGROUND, CHALET $
(☎0979 011917; campsite per person ZMW30, chalets ZMW150-250) This is the best place to stay in Sesheke. It is friendly, and offers airy thatch-roofed double-story chalets and a bar built around a massive baobab. The grassed area along the riverfront with bench seating makes a lovely place to camp: watch for hippos and monitor lizards. The entrance to Brenda's (which is well hidden from the

EXCURSION INTO BOTSWANA & NAMIBIA

Both Botswana and Namibia are short drives away if you're in the southwest of Zambia, and both make excellent excursions, even for a few days, although a week or longer would be ideal. The two countries are also easily accessible from Livingstone.

Kasane in northeastern Botswana – about 12km from Kazungula, the Zambian border crossing – is the northern gateway to one of the country's gems: magnificent Chobe National Park. Having your own vehicle here is very handy for accessing Chobe.

Across the border in Namibia is the far-flung town of Katima Mulilo in the spindly northeastern appendage called the Caprivi Strip, an area with some unique off-the-beaten-path wildlife areas: hidden gems such as Mudumu, Mamili and Bwabwata National Parks. The latter is the easiest and quickest to access.

main drag) is 200m on the western side of the church on the main street, down an unmarked road towards the river.

Sisheke Lodge LODGE $$
(☎0211-481086; s/d incl breakfast ZMW180/200) A functional and practical place with basic rooms with a TV, fridge and fan. Meals can be provided in the small dining room and self-caterers can use the kitchen. Coming into town from the north, look for it near the fuel station on the left.

Sioma Ngwezi National Park

This undeveloped, very remote and rarely visited 500 sq km **national park** (per person/vehicle per day US$5/15) is one to watch for future developments given its proximity to Livingstone and with plans for the Kavango Zambezi Transfrontier Park (KAZA) slowly moving forward. It's in the southwestern corner of Zambia, bordering Angola and the Caprivi Strip in Namibia; it's also only 50km from Botswana. The park is dry, quite flat and forested with *miombo* and acacia woodland with areas of teak forest. It's unfenced and there is free movement of animals between the park and the surrounding Game Management Area (GMA). The park has a history of cross-border poaching problems and wildlife is scarce, although elephants still do occur in reasonable numbers. There are few roads and no permanent settlements. If you want to visit, it's worth contacting **Mutemwa Lodge** (☎0927-11 234 1747; www.mutemwa.com), located not far from the park, which sometimes runs safaris here.

An independent trip is possible but very difficult – you need to be completely self-sufficient and have a fully equipped 4WD. Begin by heading to Sioma and picking up a scout from the National Parks & Wildlife Service office.

THE COPPERBELT

Not on the radar for most visitors unless they happen to be mining consultants, the Copperbelt Province is the industrial heartland of Zambia and the main population centre outside of Lusaka. The region is home to the unique attraction of Chimfunshi Wildlife Orphanage, the largest chimpanzee sanctuary in the world.

DRIVING IN THE COPPERBELT

The Copperbelt is one of the best regions in the country for driving, which is understandable given the importance of the copper industry. The road from Lusaka to Ndola is in excellent condition, but the traffic can be slow around Kapiri Mposhi. The dual carriageway between Ndola and Kitwe is perhaps the best in the country.

The world copper market slumped during the 1970s, so vast opencast mining companies cut back production, creating high unemployment in the area. The cost of copper and cobalt went through the roof in the early 21st century and this has once more seen the region prosper as Zambia records impressive economic growth.

Kabwe

This is a dusty but well-laid-out service centre about 150km north of Lusaka. It makes a good stop for lunch if you're driving between Lusaka and the Copperbelt.

Fig Tree Cafe CAFE $
(☎0977 872966; Great North Road, 4km south of Kabwe; mains ZK10,000-35,000; ⏰6am-6pm) Providing a welcome break from the road, the Fig Tree Cafe, set in manicured gardens, has breezy outdoor benches or comfy indoor seating. It does burgers, toasted sandwiches, tea, coffee and cold drinks. There's even a selection of homemade cakes and shakes, plus swings and trampolines for kiddies. Fig Tree is well signposted.

Kapiri Mposhi

☎0215

This uninspiring transit town, about 200km north of Lusaka, is at the southern end of the Tazara railway from Dar es Salaam (Tanzania) and at the fork in the roads to Lusaka, the Copperbelt and Northern Zambia.

Coming from Tanzania, there's a passport check before exiting the station, then from outside the station there's a mad rush for buses to Lusaka and elsewhere. Thieves and pickpockets thrive in the crowds and confusion, so stay alert.

Buses and minibuses from Lusaka (ZK40,000, three hours) leave regularly and are a quicker and more convenient option than the irregular local trains.

Ndola

0212 / POP 500,000

Ndola, the capital of the Copperbelt Province, is a prosperous little city that provides relief from the pace and pollution of its larger cousin, Lusaka. In comparison it is clean and well tended with no real evidence of its industrial base, although genuine visitor attractions are thin on the ground.

Sights

Copperbelt Museum MUSEUM
(0212-617450; Buteko Ave; adult/child ZMW25/10; 9am-4.30pm) The Copperbelt Museum showcases the local industry and downstairs there are billboards with displays on Zambia's mining history, gemstones and the processing of copper. Upstairs is more interesting with artefacts used in witchcraft, personal ornaments, smoking and snuffing paraphernalia, and musical instruments such as talking drums. At the entrance there is a well-stocked craft shop.

Mupapa Slave Tree HISTORIC SITE
(Makoli Ave) A short walk from the Copperbelt Museum, the old Mupapa Slave Tree is of great historical importance. The shade from this ancient pod mahogany tree was used as a meeting place by Swahili slave-traders. It's a bit neglected nowadays but can easily be spotted by the steel fence surrounding its girth.

Sleeping

New Ambassador Hotel HOTEL $$
(0212-374396; President Ave; r ZMW140-550) 'New' is rather optimistic given the creaky state of the corridors but the Ambassador provides reasonable value for its spacious rooms. Ensuite rooms include a full English breakfast and are better than those that share a bathroom.

New Savoy Hotel HOTEL $$$
(0212-611097; savoy@zamnet.zm; Buteko Ave; r incl breakfast ZMW500-1100;) It's a bit of a hulking concrete block from the outside and the 154 rooms add up to the largest hotel in the Copperbelt; yet inside the Savoy is upholding standards well: old-fashioned, true, but without a certain charm.

Eating

TOP CHOICE **Michelangelo** ITALIAN $$
(0212-620325; 126 Broadway; mains ZMW35-65; breakfast,lunch & dinner;) *The* dining destination in Ndola, there is a mock Italianate interior and an attractive cafe-terrace under a designer awning. Pizzas are impressively authentic and the menu includes homemade pasta and ground coffee. There is also a small boutique hotel attached. On Sundays it is only open to hotel guests and local residents.

Danny's Restaurant INDIAN $$
(0212-621828; President Ave; mains ZMW30-50; lunch & dinner) It doesn't look very inviting but the food at this Indian favourite has an excellent reputation. Try the lamb *saag waala* (lamb in a decadently rich gravy).

WORTH A TRIP

DAG HAMMARSKJÖLD MEMORIAL

Located just off the Ndola to Kitwe road is the **Dag Hammarskjöld Memorial** (adult/child US$15/7; 8.30am-4.30pm), a national monument and World Heritage Site that commemorates the UN secretary-general whose plane crashed here in the 1960s during a peace mission to the Democratic Republic of the Congo. It's a simple plinth with memorial stones from different countries and organisations, topped by a globe and surrounded by a circle of trees in the shape of a plane. The caretaker-guide brings the place to life as he presents a vivid account of the plane crash while introducing the attached **museum**. Whether the plane was shot down or mechanical failure was to blame remains unclear. The new national monument entry charges are a little high for the experience on offer.

To get here, travel about 10km from Ndola on the main highway towards Kitwe and turn north (signposted), following a minor gravel road for about 7km to reach the memorial.

Ndola

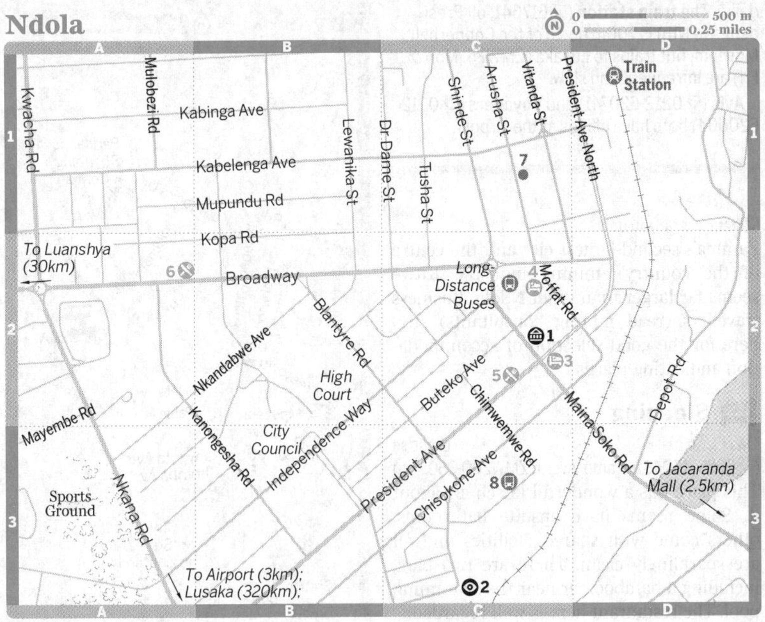

Jacaranda Mall FOOD COURT **$**
(Great North Road, 3km from Ndola; ZMW5-50; ⌚7am-10pm) Jacaranda Mall is straight out of Lusaka; it's a huge shopping complex on the edge of Ndola complete with a Pick & Pay Supermarket as well as the usual South African chains like Steers, Debonairs and Nando's. Best of all is homegrown *Gigibonitas*, a little gelato parlour turning out delicious homemade ice-cream in a dozen or more flavours.

Information

Mixed Doubles Internet Cafe (Buteko Ave; ⌚8am-8pm Mon-Sat, 8am-6pm Sun) Wireless service and internet access. Located above a bar next to the Copperbelt Museum.

Voyagers (☎0977 860647; Arusha St; ⌚8am-1pm & 2-5pm Mon-Fri, 9am-noon Sat) The reliable Voyagers can organise car rental and other travel arrangements.

Getting There & Away

Ndola is about 325km north of Lusaka. **Proflight Zambia** (☎0211-271032; www.proflight-zambia.com) flies daily between Lusaka and Ndola (from US$60 one way). **South African Airlink** (☎0211-254350; www.saairlink.co.za) has daily flights to Johannesburg from US$400 one way, and **Kenya Airways** (☎0212-620709; www.kenya-airways.com) has daily flights to Nairobi from US$600 one way. The airport is 3.5km south of the public bus station.

From the **public bus station** (the southern end of Chimwemwe Rd), three blocks south of Buteko Ave, minibuses and buses run every few minutes to Kitwe (ZMW15, 45 minutes). Long-distance buses depart from the stand next to the Broadway–Maina Soko roundabout and run to Lusaka (ZMW65, four hours, around 10 buses

Ndola

Sights
1 Copperbelt Museum C2
2 Mupapa Slave Tree C3

Sleeping
3 New Ambassador Hotel C2
4 New Savoy Hotel C2

Eating
5 Danny's Restaurant C2
6 Michelangelo A2

Information
Mixed Doubles Internet Cafe .... (see 1)
7 Voyagers C1

Transport
8 Public Bus Station C3
Voyagers .... (see 7)

daily). The **train station** (☎617641; off President Ave Nth) is 700m north of the Copperbelt Museum, but trains to Lusaka (ZMW25, Mon & Fri) are infrequent and slow.

Avis (☎0212-620741) and **Voyagers** (☎0212-620604) both have offices at the airport.

Kitwe

☎0212 / POP 700,000

Zambia's second-largest city and the centre of the country's mining industry, Kitwe seems far larger than quiet Ndola. Business travellers (read mining consultants) stop here for the good selection of accommodation and eating places.

Sleeping

Dazi Lodge LODGE **$$**
(☎0955 460487; Pamo Ave; r ZMW200-350; 🏊) This place has a wonderful kitsch air about it. Some rooms have ensuite bathrooms, others come with shared facilities and all are sparklingly clean. There are two bars, including a bamboo bar near the swimming pool. The restaurant here is well regarded.

Hotel Edinburgh HOTEL **$$$**
(☎0212-222444; makwaram@edinburgh.co.zm; cnr Independence & Obote Aves; r ZMW480-975; ❄@📶) Hotel Edinburgh has a Scottish theme and central location; try to get a room on or close to the 5th floor, which offers terrific views and heaps of light from large windows. The bar includes a 1st-floor patio for sundowners.

TOP CHOICE **Mukwa Lodge** LODGE **$$$**
(☎0212-224266; www.mukwalodge.co.zm; 26 Mpezeni Ave; s/d incl breakfast ZMW585/690; ❄@📶🏊) This lodge has gorgeous rooms with stone floors, which are beautifully furnished, and the bathrooms are as good as any in Zambia. It's a delightful place to stay that's well worth the indulgence. The Courtyard Cafe here is an excellent international restaurant open to nonguests.

Eating & Drinking

Mona Lisa INTERNATIONAL **$$**
(☎0212-229677; Freedom Ave, Parklands Shopping Centre; pizza & pasta ZMW35-50, other mains ZMW75) A popular spot for a drink, this place is also the place for pizza and pasta, as well as steaks and grills. It's a cross between a sports bar and an eatery.

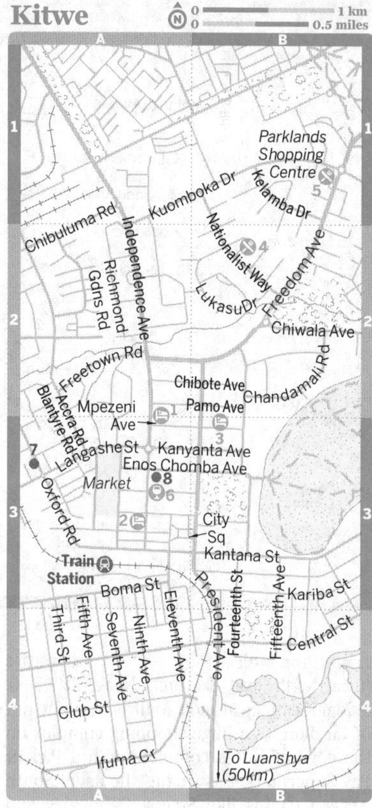

Kitwe

Sleeping
1 Dazi Lodge A2
2 Hotel Edinburgh A3
3 Mukwa Lodge B3

Eating
4 Heer B2
5 Mona Lisa B1

Drinking
6 Cosy Jo's A3

Transport
7 Public Bus Station A3
8 Voyagers A3

Heer INTERNATIONAL **$$$**
(☎0212-229530; 11 Mushita Cl; mains ZMW60-95; ⊙noon-2.30pm & 6-10.30pm; ❄📶) Formerly Arabian Nights, this is one of the top restau-

rants in the region, featuring subcontinental curries, European dishes and sizeable cuts of meat. It doubles as a salubrious place for a drink, but add 18% sales tax and 10% service to the bill. It's off Nationalist Way with a sign 'Heer LTD' on the gate.

Cosy Jo's BAR
(☎0212-221180; Kabengele Ave; ⏰5pm-late, closed Mon) Kitwe's nightlife is surprisingly low-key compared to the capital, but Cosy Jo's is the place to be at night. It is a huge garden bar and draws a large crowd for chilled Mosi Lager and African tunes.

Getting There & Away

Kitwe is about 60km northwest of Ndola. The **public bus station** is situated 500m west of Independence Ave, and the **train station** (☎0212-223078) is at the southern end of Independence Ave. Frequent minibuses and buses run to Lusaka (ZMW70, five hours), Ndola (ZMW15, 45 minutes) and Chingola (ZMW15, 30 minutes).

Voyagers (☎0212-617062; Enos Chomba Ave) is very helpful and can arrange car hire and other travel arrangements.

Chingola

☎0212

Chingola is essentially a huge mine with a settlement wrapped around it. On the Solwezi Rd it is possible to see the enormous, open-pit mine; the giant dumper trucks mean it is crucial to obey the red lights here. It is the closest town to Chimfunshi Wildlife Orphanage and has a decent range of accommodation.

There are petrol stations on Kabundi St as well as Dondou Bureau de Change. Shoprite supermarket is on Kwacha St, and a Stanbic with an ATM is on Independence Dr.

Sleeping & Eating

New Hibiscus Guest House GUESTHOUSE $$
(☎0212-313635; hibiscus@copperbeltlodging.com; 33 Katutwa Rd; r per person incl breakfast US$70, full board US$100;) Traditional B&B is served up at this homy, English-style guesthouse. Decent rooms come with ensuite and the hospitality includes a good old-fashioned welcome.

Protea Hotel HOTEL $$$
(☎0212-310624; www.proteahotels.com; Kabundi St; s/d US$149/165;) The accommodation is set around a swimming pool with manicured grass verges at this branch of the ubiquitous chain. Rooms sparkle with modern amenities, including an enormous shower head in the ensuites.

Nchanga Golf Club INTERNATIONAL $$
(www.nchangagolfclub.org; Mpuka Rd; mains ZMW20-50; ⏰breakfast, lunch & dinner) Overlooking the manicured grounds of the golf course, the outdoor tables here are a relaxing place to sit. For lunch and dinner the limited menu includes a couple of stir-fry options, pasta dishes or steak.

Mona Lisa ITALIAN $$
(Kabundi St; pizza & pasta ZMW35-50; ⏰lunch & dinner) This branch of the Copperbelt pizza chain has a more African feel with plenty of locals taking advantage of the cheap bar. Authentic wood-fired pizzas are the international draw.

Getting There & Away

Chingola is 50km northwest of Kitwe. The **bus station** (13th St) is in the centre of town. There are frequent buses and minibuses to Kitwe (ZMW15, 30 minutes). Buses also run to Solwezi.

Chimfunshi Wildlife Orphanage

On a farm deep in the African bush, about 70km northwest of Chingola, is this impressive **chimpanzee sanctuary** (www.chimfunshi.org.za; day visit adult/child project area ZMW50/25; ⏰9am-3pm). It's home to around 120 adult and young chimps, most of which have been confiscated from poachers and traders in the neighbouring Democratic Republic of Congo or other parts of Africa. It's the largest sanctuary of its kind in the world. This is not a natural wildlife experience, but it's still a unique and fascinating opportunity to observe the chimps as they feed, play and socialise. It is undoubtedly the standout highlight in the Copperbelt region.

The sanctuary was started by Sheila and David Siddle on their farm; Sheila and her daughter still run the orphanage here. Visiting the sanctuary provides much-needed income and your entry fees go directly to helping it remain financially viable. *Please do not visit if you're sick, as the chimps can easily die of a simple disease like the flu.* Visitors can come to the sanctuary for the day and spend some time at the orphanage where there are chimps being rehabilitated and other wildlife such as a beloved hippo.

The highlight, though, is observing the chimps feeding in their wild enclosures in the project area; the best time to visit is at their 1.30pm feed when they are out in the open (not in the concrete blocks they enter for their morning feed). Bring a packed lunch and drinks; there's also a *braai* (barbeque) area available.

It is possible to stay overnight at the **campsite** (per person ZMW75) or in the **self-catering cottage** (per person US$25, whole cottage US$200) at the education centre, which has 10 beds, self-catering facilities and bed linen.

A very special way to experience Chimfunshi is to do a chimpanzee bush walk (US$100) with some of the younger chimps. Listen closely to the guide and don't take anything the chimps can easily grab.

It is also possible to volunteer at Chimfunshi for a minimum of 14 days and a maximum of 90 days. Contact Chimfunshi directly for more details or sign up through the African Impact (www.africanimpact.com) website. Volunteers get involved in all facets of the project, including fencing, cleaning out the chimps' feeding areas and helping out at feeding times.

By car, there is a new road that starts about 55km from Chingola and it is well signposted. It's about 20km off the main road straight to the project area. Contact the project in advance and staff can arrange a one-way transfer from Chingola for ZMW100 to coincide with a supply run. Although buses between Chingola and Solwezi can drop passengers at the turn-off, it is generally easier to visit Chimfunshi with a private vehicle.

NORTHERN ZAMBIA

Those with a spirit of adventure and who love wild, open spaces will be at home in Zambia's untamed north. True, it can be difficult to get around as the distances are vast and the tracks often rough once you leave the main road, but this is all part of the experience.

Topping the list of attractions are Kasanka National Park, where you can camp by the side of a river and watch sitatungas splashing in the swamps at dawn from high up in a mahogany tree; Mutinondo Wilderness, a vast area of whaleback hills, rivers and valleys so untouched you feel almost like you have been transported to a prehistoric era; and striking Shiwa Ng'andu, a grand English mansion buried deep in the Zambian bush with a relaxing hot springs on tap.

Northern Zambia starts after the 'Pedicle,' the slice of DRC territory that juts sharply into Zambia, almost splitting it in two. From here onwards the old Great North Road shoots its way straight up to Tanzania, passing national parks, vast wilderness areas and waterfalls along the way. With your own vehicle there's a lot to be discovered here, but it can be a challenge using public transport as most of the headline acts lie beyond the highway.

THE CHIMPS OF CHIMFUNSHI

The Chimfunshi Wildlife Orphanage was founded in the early 1980s by cattle farmers David and Sheila Siddle. The whole thing was an accident: Sheila was well known for nursing sick calves, so an orphan chimpanzee confiscated from poachers in the neighbouring Democratic Republic of Congo (DRC; formerly Zaïre) was brought to her for help. The young chimp recovered, word got around, and over the following years increasing numbers of chimps rescued from poachers, zoos and circuses all over the world were brought to Chimfunshi. Many were sick, traumatised and unused to the company of other chimps.

Meanwhile, the farm became a sanctuary, the cattle were sold and the Siddles forgot all ideas of retirement. Along the way, they also became experts in chimpanzee behaviour and rehabilitation techniques. Contrary to the advice of primatologists, chimps from different backgrounds (eg the jungle of Cameroon, a zoo in Russia and the private house of an Arab millionaire) were placed together in enclosures. This proved successful, as many chimps settled down happily and formed cohesive family groups.

It was not possible or safe to release the chimps back into the wild, so to cope with the growing numbers the sanctuary expanded. Two 200-hectare enclosures of natural forest and grassland – the largest of their type in the world – were established in April 2000, giving groups of 20 to 30 chimps huge areas of secure 'virtual wilderness' where human contact is kept to a minimum.

Mkushi

☎0215

Deep in the heart of farming country, this prosperous small town serves as the 'big smoke' for surrounding farms and villages. Located just 1km north of the Great North Road, it is a handy stop-off point for travellers who are heading to or from northern Zambia and need to stock up on provisions or use an ATM.

Sleeping & Eating

Forest Inn CHALET **$$**
(☎0215-362003; www.forestinn-zambia.com; Great North Road; camping per person ZMW30, s/d chalets ZMW200/380) Located on the Great North Road, Forest Inn has a pretty setting, with leafy gardens dotted with funky wire sculptures. Comfortable chalets have stone floors and local artwork. There's also a campsite with hot showers, a dining area, barbecues, plenty of electric lights and power points. Birdwatchers will be kept happy with birding trails and nature walks in the surrounding forest. Forest Inn is 30km south of Mkushi and 65km from Kapiri Mposhi; it is well signposted.

The restaurant at the Forest Inn is excellent, making it a good rest stop on a long drive. Meals (ZMW15 to ZMW65) include burgers, grills and pasta dishes.

Shalom Lodge LODGE **$**
(☎0966 694764; r ZMW80-250) Rooms here range from basic singles with shared bathroom to spacious brick chalets, so ask to see a selection. The friendly owner seems to have a penchant for animal statues. There's also a good bar and restaurant here. It's behind Chibefwe Upper Basic School and signposted from the main road.

Getting There & Away

There are regular buses to Lusaka (ZMW70, four hours), Mpika (ZMW70, four hours) and Kasama (ZMW110, six hours) from the bus station in Mkushi town.

Serenje

☎0215

Serenje is a relatively uninspiring town spread out around the Great North Road. The only reason for travellers to pass through is for a convenient refuelling stop on the way to more exciting destinations.

DRIVING IN NORTHERN ZAMBIA

The road network in Northern Zambia has dramatically improved in recent years with the resurfacing of the old Great North Road, or M1, right up to Mpulungu. There is barely a pothole in sight on the main roads, but some of the most popular attractions are located along graded dirt tracks. With careful driving it is just about manageable in a 2WD, although a high-clearance pick-up is preferable. A 4WD is necessary for travel overland to Nsumbu National Park in the far northeast, overland travel to the Bangweulu Wetlands or transfers into North Luangwa National Park from Shiwa Ng'andu or Mpika.

There are two main hubs in the town: the turn-off at the junction, which has a petrol station, a couple of shops and a few basic restaurants; and the town centre, 3km north of the Great North Road, which has a bank, a market, a bus station and some lodgings.

Sleeping & Eating

Mapontela Inn GUESTHOUSE **$**
(☎0215-382026; r ZMW175-235) This charming guesthouse is the lodging of choice in Serenje. Opening out onto the leafy courtyard are a number of bright, homy rooms with fans and spotless bathrooms. The attached restaurant (meals ZMW15 to ZMW25) has a patio overlooking the street and serves tasty staples.

Siga Siga Resthouse GUESTHOUSE **$**
(☎0215-382362; d with shared bathroom ZMW60) This is a useful option for bus travel as it's right by the junction with the Great North Road. Rooms here are pretty basic and share passable bathrooms; on the plus side there are a couple of reasonable places to eat nearby, including the Siga Siga Restaurant and (are you seeing the pattern here?) the Siga Siga Supermarket.

Getting There & Away

All buses between Lusaka (ZMW80, five hours) and Kasama (ZMW90, five hours) pass through Serenje. Most of the big buses stop beside the petrol station at the junction with the Great North Road, while minibuses stop in town.

WATERFALL COLLECTING

Northern Zambia is packed full of rivers and sweeping hills. Put these together and you get an incredible array of waterfalls. The following list is organised roughly clockwise. For more inspiration see *Waterfalls of Zambia* by François d'Elbee; it's a large-format book with evocative descriptions and a collection of stunning photos.

It has to be said that this is mainly an undertaking for drivers, as nearly all the falls are off the main routes, away from public transport, but for backpackers, Chisimba and Kalambo waterfalls are reachable. Fortunately, these are among the most impressive.

Most waterfalls are protected as heritage sites or National Monuments, and even at the most remote locations a caretaker may appear from the bush to collect a fee. With National Monument fees now set at an ambitious US$15 per person, plus US$15 for a vehicle, waterfall visits have become an expensive proposition. At some waterfalls, camping is permitted (US$10), although facilities are usually limited to a long-drop toilet.

Kundalila Falls

These are the most southerly falls, about 15km south of the Great North Road, between Serenje and Mpika. Here, the Lukusashi River tumbles about 60m, almost diagonally over steeply tilting rock strata, before rushing away down a narrow ravine. There's a campsite here.

Ntumbachusi Falls

About 15km west of Kawambwa, between Mansa and Lake Mweru, Ntumbachusi is a small but very picturesque waterfall, with little cascades and pools upstream and down. Camping is possible.

Lumangwe Falls

Often called 'mini Victoria Falls,' Lumangwe does indeed look like a smaller version of the famous Zambezi waterfalls. However, it's a surprisingly large (30m high and 100m wide) curtain of water, broken into several separate streams by rocks and miniature islands at the lip of the falls. Camping is possible.

Kabweluma Falls

About 8km downstream from Lumangwe via a beautiful walk, Kabweluma is actually three separate waterfalls. The highest is a small, perfectly formed horseshoe, and the lowest is a more gently angled cascade flowing over grass and moss-covered rocks. The caretaker at Lumangwe can act as a guide.

Kundabwika Falls

On the Kalungwishi River about 40km downstream from Kabweluma Falls, Kundabwika Falls is reached from the road between Mporokoso and Lake Mweru. The river flows through a gorge over two small falls then plummets over the main waterfall, which is about 25m high, before thundering off down the gorge again.

Kalambo Falls

By far the highest falls in Zambia, and the second highest in Africa, the Kalambo Falls (p100) can be reached by road from Mbala or by boat from Mpulungu.

Chishimba Falls

Chishimba is a series of three waterfalls, shaped into a wide curtain of water pounding over rocks in a thickly wooded amphitheatre. Camping is permitted nearby and buses and minibuses run daily between Kasama and Mporokoso, passing close to the falls.

Kasanka National Park

☎0214

One of Zambia's least-known wilderness areas and a real highlight of a visit to this part of the country is the privately managed **Kasanka National Park** (www.kasanka.com; admission US$10; ⏲6am-6pm). At just 390 sq km it's pretty small compared to most African parks, it doesn't have a huge range of facilities and it sees very few visitors – and this is what makes it special. There are no queues of jeeps to get a look at a leopard here; instead, you'll discover great tracts of *miombo* woodland, evergreen thicket, open grassland and rivers fringed with emerald forest, all by yourself.

Kasanka is perhaps most famous for its swampland though, and this is the terrain to see the park's shy and retiring star, the sitatunga, a semi-aquatic antelope distinguished by its long splayed hooves and oily coat. Kasanka is arguably the only national park in the world to offer guaranteed sightings of the sitatunga. Other common antelope species include bushbuck, duiker, reedbuck and puku. Between July and October you'll most likely see sable antelopes and hartebeests, and may also be treated to a glimpse of roan antelopes. Hippos and crocodiles inhabit the lakes and rivers here and there's a small population of elephants, though these aren't as commonly seen. Night time brings out jackals, civets and porcupines, and during the months of November and December, the park is home to more than eight *million* migratory fruit bats – the biggest mammal gathering anywhere in the world – which can blanket the sky for several minutes at dusk. Bird spotters will also love Kasanka. There are 463 species here, including the wattled crane, Ross's turaco, Bohm's bee-eater and Pel's fishing owl.

Kasanka is a privately managed national park, run by the Kasanka Trust. Revenue is reinvested in the park, and the trust is also involved in conservation and local community projects.

Sights & Activities

A trip to Kasanka isn't complete without viewing the park from the heights of the **Fibwe Hide**, a 15-minute drive from Wasa Lodge. It's not for those with vertigo. You ascend 20m up an old mahogany tree via a rickety wooden ladder to a platform where you can sit and watch the swamps below. Come at dawn and dusk for the best chance of spotting sitatungas. It's also a good spot for birdwatching, or, in season, for watching the hordes of fruit bats heading off from the nearby trees to feed.

Game drives can be arranged at the main lodge for wildlife viewing in comfort. Drives cost ZMW140 per person (minimum two people). They also arrange walking safaris, anything from a one-hour jaunt near the camp to a five-day extravaganza with an armed ranger, camping out in the bush.

Finally, gliding along the Luwombwa River in a canoe (ZMW40 per person) or a motorboat (ZMW140 per person) surrounded by bustling forest on either side is a wonderful way to get a different look at the park, and see crocodiles, otters and even the rare blue monkey. Fishing on the river can also be arranged.

Just inside the camp is a **conservation centre** that it is worth passing through on the way in or out of Kasanka. It is mostly used as an educational centre for local children, and also runs re-education programs for poachers, but there's a small museum that's open to all and it is particularly interesting for children. There's a display of animal skulls, information on the birds and bats of Kasanka, interactive wildlife Q&As and there are weighing and measuring stations where you can compare your height and bulk to that of the park's larger beasts. There's no fee to enter the centre but donations are appreciated.

The Kasanka team also runs excellent tours of northern Zambia, using vehicles or planes, linking the park with visits to the Bangweulu Wetlands, Shiwa Ng'andu and North Luangwa National Park. This is well worth considering if you want to cover this area in a limited period; rates depend on group size, duration and interests.

Sleeping

There are two campsites in Kasanka where you'll be surrounded by the noise of animals, the stars and little else. **Pontoon Campsite** (per person US$10) and **Kabwe Campsite** (per person US$10) both look out over the Kasanka River. They are located around 10–12km from the main Wasa Lodge and come equipped with long-drop toilets and bucket showers (staff will prepare hot water for you if you let them know in advance). Pontoon is shaded by large mahogany trees and blue monkeys sometimes pass through. Kabwe is an open campground with views over the floodplain where sitatunga wander by.

Conservation Centre CAMPGROUND $
(campsite per person US$10, r per person US$30) Just inside the park is a small conservation centre with a campsite as well as basic twin rooms in thatched chalets. There's a shared bathroom for every pair of rooms. School groups often book these out, but if they're empty then visitors are welcome to stay. It's convenient but lacks the atmosphere or the views of the other places inside the park.

Wasa Lodge LODGE $$$
(☎873 76 2067957; www.kasanka.com; self-catering chalets per person US$50; full board incl all activities per person US$360) This place doubles as the park headquarters. Accommodation consists of thatched bungalows in two sizes. Larger chalets are airy and cool with wide balconies and lovely stone showers. The real advantage of a stay here is the setting. The lodge overlooks Lake Wasa and you can look out over the swamp and spot hippos and puku and sometimes even sitatungas. There are several vantage points, including stone benches on the lakeshore, a small hide in the trees and the deck of the large bar and dining area.

If you don't want the full-board option you can bring your own supplies and the camp staff will cook for you.

Luwombwa Lodge LODGE $$$
(☎873 76 2067957; www.kasanka.com; self-catering chalets per person US$50; full board incl all activities per person US$360) This lodge is on the western side of the park and is popular for fishing as it sits on the banks of the Luwombwa River. There is a choice between smaller and older chalets with shared facilities or larger family-style affairs with more space and balconies with a view. Luwombwa is likely to be closed during the wet season.

Getting There & Away

From Lusaka, take a bus (ZMW110) in the direction of Mansa, or take any bus from Lusaka to Serenje and change onto a minibus (ZMW35) for Mansa. After turning off the Great North Road, ask the driver to drop you at Kasanka National Park (near Mulembo village), not at Kasanka village, which is much further away. From the gate to Wasa Lodge is 12km; you can radio Wasa Lodge for a lift. It is also possible to charter a taxi from Serenje directly to Wasa Lodge; ZMW150 is a good price to aim for, but ZMW200 might be more realistic.

If you have your own vehicle, continue north along the Great North Road from Serenje for 36km, then turn left onto the road towards Mansa. It's then 55km on a good road to the Kasanka entrance gate, clearly signposted on the left. There is no fuel available in the park so stock up at Serenje.

There are two airstrips in the park and charter flights are available through **Skytrails Charters** (☎216 245268; www.skytrailszambia.com), which is based there. For further information and prices contact **Kasanka Trust** (www.kasanka.com).

Around Kasanka

☎0214

Drivers with a 4WD with high clearance may like to take the 'back route' from Kasanka direct to the Great North Road, which winds past several attractions.

History buffs can go in search of the **David Livingstone Memorial**, a simple stone memorial topped with a cross, which honours the famous explorer's death here in 1873 while he was searching for the source of the Nile. The local villagers buried Livingstone's heart under a mupundu tree before his body was sent home to the mother country, and the memorial marks the spot, although the tree is no longer there. To get here, pass the Kasanka National Park gate and continue 11km to the Livingstone Memorial turn-off, which will be on your right. Take the first left, from where it's another 25km to the memorial. The road is pretty bad, however, so it is really only for dedicated Livingstone buffs.

This route also winds past beautiful little **Lake Waka-Waka**, with its glassy, croc-free waters (though always check the situation locally before jumping in) encircled by *miombo* woodland. Accommodation is in the form of a small community **campsite** (per person US$5) with basic bucket showers, barbecues and long-drop toilets. Local villagers can provide clean water. To get here, pass the Kasanka gates and take the turn-off to the Livingstone Memorial, but this time continue straight on for 35km, leaving the Livingstone Memorial road on your left.

Sleeping

Nakapalayo Tourism Project CAMPGROUND $
(www.kasanka.com; campsites incl village tour & entertainment per person US$20, huts incl village tour & entertainment per person US$40, huts incl village tour, entertainment & meals per person US$60) In between Kasanka National Park and the Bangweulu Wetlands is the Nakapalayo Tourism Project, a community initiative that

LAVUSHI MANDA NATIONAL PARK

The wildlife population of Lavushi Manda National Park, originally created to protect the black rhino population, was decimated by poaching in the bad old years. Located to the east of Kasanka National Park, it borders the Bangweulu Wetlands and offers a dramatic rocky landscape rising to 1800m. The World Bank is funding the park's recovery in partnership with the Kasanka Trust (www.kasanka.com). Two campsites are planned, as well as multiday hikes to remote waterfalls.

allows tourists to experience life in a real Zambian village. Visitors can camp or stay in huts with double beds and mosquito nets. Activities revolve around village life and include learning how to pound cassava, meeting local healers and bush walks to learn about traditional uses for plants and trees. Meals are local fare, eaten with the villagers. Day visits are also available for US$20 per person. To get here, continue just past Lake Waka-Waka, where the road will fork. Take the left-hand fork and continue for 35km to Chiundaponde, where the project is located.

Bangweulu Wetlands

☎0214

The Bangweulu Wetlands is a watery wilderness of lakes, seasonally flooded grasslands, swamp and unspoiled *miombo* woodland that lies 50km to the north of Kasanka. This rarely visited part of Zambia is the only place in Africa to see major numbers of black *lechwes* (antelopes with long, curved antlers). There are estimated to be some 100,000 here, enough to rival the great wildebeest migrations of the Serengeti, and the endless sound of thousands of lechwe hooves clattering and splashing through the marshes could be one of the standout images of Zambia. The wetlands are also home to the swamp-dwelling sitatunga and many other antelope species, including oribi, tsessebe, bushbuck and reedbuck. Attracted by rich pickings, jackals are often seen and hyenas often heard at night, and, when the floodwaters have receded, herds of elephants and buffaloes venture here.

Bangweulu is also known for its birds. Some 400 species have been noted, and a particular highlight for twitchers is the strange and rare shoebill stork. Cruising silently through the papyrus and lilies in a dugout canoe searching for this elusive evolutionary misfit is a magical experience. Other birds found here include crowned hornbill, swamp flycatcher, Denham's bustard, herons, ibis and storks, plus 15% of the world's wattled cranes, and when the floodwaters are high, huge numbers of water birds, including flamingos and geese, migrate here from elsewhere in Africa.

The best time to see the lechwe herds is from June to July as the waters have begun receding, leaving vast plains of fresh green grass. September to November is great for general birdwatching, though you may not see shoebills at this time. The best time to see shoebills is when the water levels are still high but starting to recede, from March to April. After the waters have retreated you can still see shoebills on canoe trips up until August.

The wetlands are surrounded by small villages living mainly by subsistence fishing and hunting. The running of the Game Management Area (GMA) was passed to the African Parks Network (www.african-parks.org) in 2008, though Shoebill Island Camp is still managed by the Kasanka Trust.

Sleeping

Nsobe Camp CAMPGROUND $

(www.african-parks.org; campsite per person US$10) This is a basic campsite with *braai* area, bucket showers, long-drop toilets and a couple of thatched cooking shelters. It is now under the management of African Parks.

Shoebill Island Camp CAMPGROUND $$$

(www.kasanka.com; tents per person US$50, tents incl meals & activities per person US$360) This camp rests in the heart of the wetlands and is splendidly positioned on a tiny permanent island with only birds, hippos, lechwes and the occasional passing fishermen for company. Booking is essential. Guests stay in safari tents and there's a dining area and lookout point. Most activities revolve around dugout canoes, but drives are also on offer in the drier areas and in the surrounding woodlands.

When there's not enough water for the canoes, it is possible to take a guided walk over the spongy floating reed beds. The camp aims to stay open year round but is sometimes inaccessible from January to April.

THE SHOEBILL STORK

One of the rarest birds in Africa, the shoebill stork (*Balaeniceps rex*) is found only in the Bangweulu Wetlands, in some parts of Uganda, and possibly in Sudan and the Democratic Republic of the Congo (formerly Zaïre). This bird has a body pretty much like that of any other large stork (about 1m high), but its bill (or beak), as its name implies, is bizarrely shaped like a shoe, more like a clog in fact. Another name for this species is the whale-headed stork and that's even nearer the mark. Technically, it's not even a stork, as it's nearest relative is thought to be the pelican. Whatever, for ornithologists it's a big tick on the list. These weird birds can usually be seen perched high on palm trees or wading through the reeds searching for fish. They are extremely shy, and fly surprisingly well for such top-heavy giants, so seeking them out takes silence and patience.

Getting There & Away

The only way into the wetlands is by vehicle and chartered plane. Dirt roads lead here from Kasanka via Lake Waka-Waka and the Nakapalayo Tourism Project. The Chikuni ranger post and Nsobe Camp are 65km on from Nakapalayo, and from here it's another 10km to Shoebill Island Camp if it's dry. In the wet, you'll have to travel this last stretch by boat. You will definitely need a fully equipped 4WD to attempt this trip as the going is tough. Set off from Kasanka in the early morning in order to reach Bangweulu before it gets dark. The Kasanka team can provide a detailed information sheet about getting to the wetlands.

There is an airstrip 3km from Shoebill Island Camp and charters are available to both Kasanka and Bangweulu through **Skytrails Charters** (☎216 245268; www.skytrailszambia.com), based in Lusaka.

Samfya

☎0214

Perched on the western shore of Lake Bangweulu, about 10km east of the main road between Mansa and Serenje, is Samfya, a small and dusty trading centre with little going for it except for its excellent position on the western shores of this beautiful lake. In the local language *bangweulu* means 'where the water meets the sky' and if you watch the lake at sunset, when the lake and hazy clouds both turn the same shade of blue, it's not hard to see why. Just outside town is a long strip of white-sand beach set by startling blue waters. Don't jump in here, though, unless you fancy wrestling with crocodiles.

Sleeping

Samfya Beach Hotel HOTEL $

(campsite per person ZMW50, r ZMW150) Sitting on Cabana Beach, this place has a pretty good location but the rooms are small with basic bathrooms. Camping is an affordable option for those with a tent. Take the first turning on the left in town and it's about 2km north of the centre.

Bangweulu Bay Lodge LODGE $$$

(☎Lusaka 0211-266927; www.bangweulubaylodge.com; r from US$150-180 per person) Located on the shores of Lake Bangweulu, this new lodge offers three smart guest chalets with views over the beach and blue waters beyond. Bathrooms include hot water and the resort has solar power throughout. Activities on tap include Hobie Cat sailing, boat trips and wildlife spotting in the area.

Getting There & Away

Samfya is regularly served by minibuses from Serenje (ZMW70, four to five hours). Buses from Lusaka (ZMW120, 10 hours) may drop you in town or at the junction 10km away, from where local pick-ups shuttle passengers to and fro.

Mutinondo Wilderness

☎0214

This is one of the most stunning places in northern Zambia. Mutinondo is a beautiful 10,000-hectare wilderness littered with whaleback hills or *inselbergs*; huge, sweeping hulks of stone in varying shades of black, purple, green and brown. The landscape here feels unspoiled and ancient. Scramble to the top of one of those great granite beasts (and they do look like they could be giant animals who've been asleep for so long they've sunk back into the earth) and it is easy to imagine a time when Stone Age hunters wandered the endless valleys, woodland and rivers below.

Mammal sightings are rare here, although there are plenty of tree squirrels, klipspringers and other antelopes (roan, sable, reedbuck and bushbuck) lurking around out of sight. Mutinondo is an important birding destination and there are about 320 species here including plenty of rare specimens that are difficult to find outside the country. Notable are the Ross's turaco, Anchieta's sunbird and the bar-winged weaver. The bar at the Mayense Camp lodge has a list of all the bird species recorded so far at Mutinondo.

Sights & Activities

Maps are available at the Mayense Camp lodge for the vast number of wilderness trails (more than 60km of them) around the area. It's beautiful walking country and it is easy to pass the time here just gently soaking it up. For groups of six or more, guided hiking and camping experiences are also available, including a six-day hike with game scouts, tents and meals, which includes a striking waterfall on the escarpment. Contact the lodge about one month in advance for this sort of wilderness experience.

The network of rivers and waterfalls at Mutinondo are incredibly clear and calm, safe to swim in (and to drink), and lazily swimming upstream and listening to the sounds of nature all around is a wonderful way to spend a day. Canoes are also available.

During the mushroom-friendly rainy season (December to March), it is possible to go in search of the largest edible mushroom in the world, and the area also contains rock art and Iron Age workings.

Sleeping

TOP CHOICE **Mayense Camp** LODGE $$$

(www.mutinondozambia.com; s/d per person incl meals & activities from ZMW600/550) It's tough to design accommodation that fits in with the splendour of this setting but the Mutinondo team has succeeded. Built into the hillside are a handful of individually designed chalets, which, while not luxurious, are beautiful in their simplicity and blend in seamlessly with their natural environment. Honeymoon 'Mulombwa' is built into the granite rocks, with a huge handmade bath with a view. 'Musase' is suitable for families with enough beds to sleep four. All have outstanding views and the majority are open to the elements so it feels as if you're sleeping out in the middle of the wild. The friendly and hospitable owners are keen to protect the environment and the camps here use a number of alternative sources of energy such as solar panels, a wind generator and sun stoves. The food cooked here uses as much locally-sourced produce as possible and campers at other sites can enjoy hearty home-cooked meals at the main Mayense Camp (breakfast ZMW70, packed lunch ZMW30, three-course dinner ZMW120).

Mayense Campsite CAMPGROUND $

(campsite per person ZMW70, chalet per person ZMW100) This is a fantastic campsite, a user-friendly spot to pitch a tent. Each pitch has cooking areas and bird-proof cupboards to protect supplies. The large, open-air showers (constructed out of sustainable materials) have plenty of space and hot water. The sinks have framed pieces of information to read while you brush your teeth, and the eco-toilets have magazines to browse and strategically placed viewing slots with views over the bush.

Kankonde CAMPGROUND $

(campsite per person ZMW80, tent with bedding per person ZMW130) Around 10km from the main camp (Mayense), this basic bush campsite sits alongside the Mutinondo River. It's a beautiful spot but you'll have to be fully self-sufficient, although there is a caretaker on hand to assist.

Getting There & Away

The turn-off to Mutinondo is 164km past Serenje heading north on the Great North Road. It's signposted to the right; Mutinondo is 25km down a 2WD-friendly track. Travelling by bus from Lusaka, ask for a ticket to Kalonje Railway Station (ZMW110, six hours). Road transfers for a maximum of five people can be arranged from the Great North Road turnoff (ZMW180). There's also an airstrip for charters.

Mpika

☎0214

Mpika is a busy crossroads on the Great North Road. The old road (M1) runs north to Kasama and Mpulungu, while the newer road (T2) runs northeast to the Tanzanian border at Nakonde. It's actually a tale of three towns, with the old colonial-era town east of the highway, the 'Tazara' town near the train station southwest of the highway and a new town stretching along the road. It is a good supply stop, with several petrol stations, a Barclays Bank ATM, plus several well-stocked shops and a large market in the town centre.

Sleeping & Eating

TOP CHOICE **Bayama's Lodge, Pub & Grill** LODGE $

(☎0977 410839; www.bayama.de; Plot 5434; r ZMW80-170; 📶) Bayama's Lodge is a real gem for a backwater like Mpika. Under German-Zambian ownership, it is just off the Great North Road and offers budget rooms with bathroom for ZMW80 or larger chalet rooms from ZMW150. The best feature is a lively bar-restaurant with all mains at ZMW25, including a huge T-bone and homemade pizzas. The bar has cold beer, Zambian tunes and a popular pool table. It also doubles as an unoffical tourist information office.

CIMS Restaurant INTERNATIONAL $

(☎0214-370058; mains ZMW15-30; ⏲24hr) Located in the middle of the new town is this large restaurant and cafe. Decent meals of *nshima*, chips and rice with pork, beef or chicken are available and are popular with long-haul residents. There's a cake stall in the corner selling cupcakes, bread and ice cream.

Getting There & Away

Buses and minibuses stop at the junction where the Kasama road and the Great North Road divide. Destinations include Lusaka (ZMW115, eight hours) and Kasama (ZMW75, two hours). There are also daily services to Nakonde (ZMW80, six hours) on the Tanzanian border, but the buses usually pass through around midnight on their way from Lusaka.

Mpika's huge and impressive Tazara train station is about 7km southwest of the town centre, and is reachable by minibus when trains are due.

Around Mpika

Nachikufu Cave CAVE

(admission per person US$15, per car US$15; campsite per person US$10; ⏲daily) Keen fans of precolonial art may want to see the rock art at Nachikufu Cave, a heritage site signposted 2km west of the Great North Road, 56km south of Mpika and 180km north of Serenje. The paintings here were discovered in 1948 and are estimated to be up to 15,000 years old. Sadly most of the paintings are worn away or have been defaced.

Nsalu Cave CAVE

(admission per person US$15, per car US$15; campsite per person US$10; ⏲daily) The paintings here are thought to be at least 20,000 years old, much older than those at Nachikufu Cave. Instead of the stick figures and animals usually associated with San paintings there are abstract patterns, lines and outlines. As with the paintings at Nachikufu Cave, these paintings have been vandalised and neglected in the past, but Zambia's Heritage Department is involved in the cave's protection and things have improved somewhat with many of the paintings now visible. The cave is signposted on the stretch of the Great North Road between Serenje and Mpika, about 60km north of Serenje. After the turn-off it's another 20km to the cave.

Shiwa Ng'andu

☎0214

Deep in the northern Zambian wilderness sits Shiwa Ng'andu, a grand country estate and labour of love of eccentric British aristocrat Sir Stewart Gore-Brown. The estate's crowning glory is **Shiwa Ng'andu manor house**, which is a glorious brick mansion. Driving up to the house through farm buildings, settlements and workers' houses it almost feels like an old feudal domain: there's a whole community built around it, including a school and a hospital, and many of the people now working at Shiwa Ng'andu are the children and grandchildren of Sir Stewart's original staff. Today, Gore-Brown's grandchildren live on and manage the estate, which is a working farm.

Sights & Activities

Shiwa House HISTORIC SITE

(www.shiwangandu.com; tours US$20; ⏲tours 9-11am Mon-Sat, closed to nonguests Sun) Shiwa House itself is the main draw here and visitors can take a guided **tour**. The great house is full of old family heirlooms, photographs and stories, and standing out on the perfectly manicured lawns you could almost forget that you're in Southern Africa and imagine instead that you're at a 1920s garden party on an English summer's day.

Guided tours of the estate, in a car or on foot, are also possible (though you are also free to wander) and on the estate are 27 species of mammal, including puku, kudu, zebra and wildebeest, although animal lovers should be aware it doubles as a game lodge.

Shiwa is also an important birdwatching area with about 380 species recorded here, including long-toed fluff tails, palm-nut vultures, and, by the lake, pygmy geese, herons and kingfishers.

Kapishya Hot Springs HOT SPRINGS
(nonguests US$5) Kapishya Hot Springs is about 20km west of Shiwa House but still on the Shiwa Ng'andu estate. The setting is marvellous, the blue-green steaming lagoon of bath-hot water surrounded by thick palms. If staying at Kapishya Lodge, then you can use the springs for free. From the lodge, walking, fishing and canoeing trips are also offered, as well as trips to Buffalo Camp in North Luangwa National Park.

Sleeping

TOP CHOICE **Kapishya Hot Springs Lodge** LODGE $$
(☎0211-229261; www.shiwasafaris.com; campsite/chalet per person US$10/60, d incl breakfast and dinner per person US$110;) This is a beautiful spot. The chalets are light and spacious, with wide wooden decks complete with fireplaces and views down over the river and the gardens. Excellent meals (full breakfast ZMW100, packed lunch ZMW50, three-course dinner ZMW150) are available as co-owner Mel is a self-taught chef, inspired by her extensive wanderings in the Far East. There's also a lovely campsite here with free firewood, hot showers and barbecue areas. The owners have recently added a spa on the banks of the river.

Shiwa House HISTORIC HOTEL $$$
(☎0211-229261; www.shiwasafaris.com; d per person incl full board from US$350) This old place is suitably attired for a grand old English manor, with fireplaces, four-poster beds, oil paintings and big old roll-top baths. There's a glorious guest sitting room looking out onto the front lawn, which is even more atmospheric at night when lit by candles and a

THE SHIWA STORY

In 1914, a young British colonial officer called Stewart Gore-Brown was helping establish the border between Rhodesia and the Belgian Congo, when he stumbled across a lake that the local Bemba people called Shiwa Ng'andu or the place of the royal crocodiles. For years he'd harboured dreams of his own kingdom in Africa, and with characteristic verve he decided Shiwa Ng'andu was the ideal spot, swiftly buying about 10,000 hectares from the local chief and returning to the spot after the end of WWI to build his little piece of England in the bush.

The heart of the estate was the great mansion of Shiwa House, made from materials found locally, or transported on foot by porters from the nearest town of Ndola, an eye-watering 300km and three weeks' walk away. Items such as chairs and tables were made locally in an antique style, but essentials such as grand pianos and fine wines were shipped from London. The house sat overlooking the lake, complete with manicured lawns and servants clad in white gloves and pillbox hats. Around the house grew an estate, which included workers' houses for 2000 employees, schools and a post office.

All of this upkeep was expensive and Gore-Brown tried many money-making schemes, including growing flowers from which to extract and export oils for perfume, but none ultimately succeeded, and Shiwa was continually bankrolled by his wealthy aunt in Britain.

Gore-Brown was a stickler for discipline in his attempts to create a utopian fiefdom, and his violent temper was legendary. Beatings measured out on hapless workers earned him the nickname Chipembere (Rhinoceros). But unusually for the time, he believed in African independence. Gore-Brown became a well-known figure in Northern Rhodesia and in Britain. He was knighted by George VI and was close friends with early nationalists including Kenneth Kaunda, Zambia's first president. When he died in 1967 he was, uniquely for a white colonist, given a full state funeral and is buried on the hill overlooking the lake at Shiwa.

Through the 1980s, Gore-Brown's daughter and son-in-law continued struggling to run the estate, and were actively involved in the campaign against poachers, especially in nearby North Luangwa National Park. In 1992 they were mysteriously murdered, allegedly because they knew too much about senior government figures connected to the illicit ivory trade. Shiwa House stood empty for several years, and rapidly disintegrated, but in 2001 Gore-Brown's grandsons began a major renovation and opened the house to visitors again.

Stewart Gore-Brown's story is described (or perhaps romanticised) in *The Africa House* by Christina Lamb.

crackling fire. Tasty dinners are taken in the rather splendid dining room. The hosts (the grandchildren of Sir Stewart Gore-Brown) are happy to chat and to give you personal tours of the house. Guests can browse the Gore-Brown archives, a fascinating collection of Sir Stewart's journals, letters and old photographs.

Getting There & Away

To reach Shiwa House, head along the highway by bus (or car) from Mpika for about 90km towards Chisoso. Look for the signpost to the west, from where a 20km dirt road leads to the house. Kapishya Hot Springs and the lodge are a further 20km along this track.

You can also get to Shiwa from the Mpika to Kasama road, this time look for the signpost pointing east and it's then 42km down the dirt track to Kapishya. There is no public transport along this last section but vehicle transfers are available from the Great North Road turn-off for US$40 per vehicle (maximum four people). Transfers are also available between Kapishya and Shiwa House for US$30 per vehicle.

Kasama

☎0214

Kasama is the capital of the Northern Province and the cultural centre of the Bemba people. With its wide, leafy streets and handsome, old, tin-roofed colonial houses, it is the most appealing of the northern towns. There's a laid-back, friendly vibe here, a number of good guesthouses, decent shops and good bus connections. Kasama's environs are home to ancient rock art and a beautiful waterfall.

Sleeping

Sahelen Lodge LODGE $

(☎0977 815190; s/d with shared bathroom ZMW65/75, s/d with bathroom ZMW85/90) The colours are garish and the garden is overflowing with stork statues, but inside the rooms are a calmer shade and are cool and spacious. It's about 800m out of town on Luwingu Rd, in the direction of Chishimba Falls. Look for the signpost to the right.

TOP CHOICE **Thorn Tree Guesthouse** GUESTHOUSE $$

(☎0214-221615; www.thorntreesafaris.com; 612 Zambia Rdnge; s/d ZMW230/290, family from ZMW350; wi-fi) The Thorn Tree is family-run, homy and very popular so book ahead to avoid disappointment. Rooms are either in the main house sharing spic and span facilities or in larger family rooms, including a three-room cottage for ZMW410. There's a bar and a restaurant serving fresh farm produce. The family also runs a safari company specialising in tours of the little-visited northern region. It is well signposted from the centre of town.

Eating

Kasama will be a welcome change to people who've been travelling in the north for a while. There's a large Shoprite here with everything a self-caterer could ask for, as well as a very good market.

JB Hotel INTERNATIONAL $

(Golf Rd; mains ZMW20-40) The JB Hotel has a good restaurant at the rear which serves local dishes such as *nshima* and chicken as well as more exotic dishes like sea bream curry and chicken schnitzel. There's a verandah bar outside.

Information

There are Zambia National Commercial, Finance, and Barclays Banks with ATMs in town as well as an internet cafe (8am-5pm Mon-Fri, 8am-noon Sat) on Luwingu Rd. **Thorn Tree Safaris** (www.thorntreesafaris.com), based at Thorn Tree Guesthouse, organises tailor-made trips all around Zambia's northern region.

Getting There & Away

Buses and minibuses leave for Lusaka (ZMW130, 10 hours) daily. Buses go via Mpika (ZMW75, two hours) and Serenje (ZMW95, four hours). Northbound buses go to Mbala (ZMW35, two hours) and Mpulungu (ZMW40, three hours). Cheaper local minibuses run to Mpulungu, Mbala and Mpika.

The Tazara train station is 6km south of the town centre. The express train to Nakonde (for the Tanzanian and Malawian border) and Dar Es Salaam (1st class ZMW196) leaves in the small hours of Friday night/Saturday morning. Trains to Mpika (ZMW35) and Kapiri Mposhi (ZMW87) pass through on Tuesday night.

Around Kasama

☎0214

About 35km west of Kasama are the stunning **Chishimba Falls** (adult/child US$15/7, campsite per person US$10), a series of three waterfalls: two natural and one formed by a small hydro-electric power station. The main falls are the furthest from the entrance and are an impressive torrent of water tum-

THE ROCK ART OF KASAMA

Archaeologists rate the **Kasama rock art** (admission adult/child US$15/7, campsite per person US$10) as one of the largest and most significant collections of ancient art in Southern Africa, although it has to be said that in terms of quality, pictures found in Zimbabwe or Namibia are easier for casual visitors to appreciate.

The works are attributed to Stone Age hunter-gatherers (sometimes known as Twa) and are up to 2000 years old. Many are abstract designs but some of the finest pictographs show human figures and animals, often capturing a remarkable sense of fluidity and movement, despite being stylised with huge bodies and minute limbs.

The paintings (about 700 in all) are in caves and overhangs spread over a very wide area of bush about 7km east of Kasama, on the road towards Isoka. The most famous site is called Sumina, and here you scramble up a steep path and squeeze between boulders to reach a well-preserved picture of a hunter chasing a lion and a buffalo. At the Mwela site, the pictures are mainly geometric patterns: spirals, circles, 'ladders' and rows of dots, although one picture shows an antelope and four figures, supposedly in a trance. The Mwankole site has a mix of designs, including a group of dancing people, plus the famous (and remarkably lifelike) penis image. Other patterns have been likened to female genitalia, leading archaeologists to propose that these paintings were connected to fertility rites, while the dots and stipple may symbolise hope for good rains.

Without a vehicle, the easiest way to reach the paintings area is by taxi (about ZMW35 each way, plus waiting time). About 4.5km from Kasama is a signpost for 'Mwela Rocks National Monument' with an entry kiosk and guides to escort visitors.

bling into a deep canyon, thought to be inhabited by spirits. There are walkways and thatched picnic spots all around the site as well as a campsite near the entrance. To get here, take the Luwingu Rd west of Kasama. After 25km there is a gravel road to the right heading to Mporokoso. The falls are signposted 10km down this track. Minibuses headed for Mporokoso can drop passengers at the turn-off to the falls, where it's about a 1km walk to the car park.

Mbala

☎0214

Once the colonial centre of Abercorn, this sleepy town sits on the periphery of the Great Rift Valley. From here the road drops about 1000m from the highest settlement in Zambia down to Lake Tanganyika and Mpulungu, the lowest town in the country. Today, the only reason to visit is the Moto Moto Museum, or as a stop-off point for Kalambo Falls. In practical terms, there's a Barclays Bank ATM, a post office, a fuel station and some general stores.

Sights & Activities

Moto Moto Museum MUSEUM

(admission ZMW15; 9am-4.45pm) This museum is well worth a visit if you're in the area. It has a large and diverse collection, much of which details the cultural life and history of the Bemba people. Items on display here include old Bemba drums, traditional musical instruments and an array of smoking paraphernalia. Particularly noteworthy is an exhibition detailing how young Bemba women were traditionally initiated into adulthood. It includes a life-size, walk-in example of an initiation hut, and small articles on the wall explain the initiation process.

The only drawback is that it's quite dark so exhibits are not displayed at their best and some are without sufficient explanation. Better set out is the new gallery opposite the gift shop/reception. It covers everything from the lives of hunter-gatherers to the early economic activities of the Bantu, and Zambia during the slave trade. There's also a display on rock art, including a map pointing out the country's key sights.

The gift shop sells baskets, sculptures and masks. To get here, follow the road north out of town for about 500m and turn left just before the prison. The museum is about 3km from the main road.

Sleeping & Eating

Makungo Guest House GUESTHOUSE $

(Old Great North Road; r ZMW60) Rooms here are clean and good value and are centred on a courtyard that also doubles as a minibus garage. The guesthouse is about 100m off the main road; take the turning opposite the fuel station.

Lake Chila Lodge LODGE $

(☎0977 795241; lakechilalodge@yahoo.com; Lake Chila; r ZMW150) The most atmospheric place to stay in Mbala, this welcoming lodge is located on the shores of Lake Chila, about 2km from town. Rooms are set in spacious chalets with satellite TV and hot showers. The lodge has a lively little bar-restaurant (mains ZMW20-40), which makes for a good rest stop on a road trip.

Getting There & Away

Minibuses owned by the Makungo Guest House run a couple of times a day to Kasama (ZMW35, two hours) and Mpulungu (ZMW15, 50 minutes), leaving from the main street. Long-distance buses serve Lusaka (ZMW140, twelve hours), Mpika (ZMW90, four to five hours) and Kasama (ZMW35, two hours) and most depart around lunchtime.

Kalambo Falls

☎0214

About 40km northwest of Mbala, along the border between Zambia and Tanzania, is the 221m-high **Kalambo Falls** (adult/child/car US$15/7/15, campsite US$10). Twice as high but nowhere near as expansive as Victoria Falls, Kalambo is the second-highest single-drop waterfall in Africa (the highest being Tugela Falls in South Africa). From spectacular viewpoints near the top of the falls, you can see the Kalambo River plummeting off a steep V-shaped cliff cut into the Rift Valley escarpment down into a deep valley, which then winds towards Lake Tanganyika. There is a campsite here, with stunning views out over the Great Rift Valley. Facilities are basic, with only a long-drop toilet available, but there is a caretaker.

The best way for travellers without a car to get here is from Mpulungu. A thrice-weekly taxi boat service (ZMW25) stops at villages east of Mpulungu. It moves quite slowly and makes plenty of stops so just getting to the base of the falls can take all day. Avoid arriving in the dark as it's two to three hours walking uphill to the viewpoint near the top of Kalambo Falls (and the campsite). It's also possible to hire a private boat from Mpulungu harbour, which will cost around ZMW700 per day including fuel. Ask around at the market near the lake in Mpulungu.

Another alternative is to stay in one of the lakeshore lodges near the falls, from where you could hike to the falls or visit on an organised boat trip.

Travel by road is possible but only with a 4WD as the road is in very poor condition, with plenty of deep sandy stretches. Some taxis may be willing to tackle the road and will charge about ZMW400.

Mpulungu

☎0214

Resting at the foot of mighty Lake Tanganyika, Mpulungu is a crossroads between Eastern, Central and Southern Africa. As Zambia's only international port, it's the terminal for the ferry across the lake to Tanzania. It's also a busy commercial fishing port and several fisheries are based here, some of them exporting tropical fish to aquariums around the world. The streets are fairly lively and busy, especially at night, but there is no real reason to come here unless travelling north to Nsumbu National Park and Ndole Bay or northeast to Tanzania. Although it's always very hot, don't be tempted to swim in the lake in this area because there are a few crocs.

Sights & Activities

Niamkolo Church CHURCH

Check out Niamkolo Church, a five-minute walk up the hill from Nkupi Lodge. It's an old stone ruin that you can walk inside and around. It was built in 1895 and 1896 by the London Missionary Society, who had arrived in the town some ten years earlier to establish a mission. It was abandoned in 1908 when the missionaries all got sleeping sickness and moved away from the lakeshore.

Sleeping & Eating

Nkupi Lodge LODGE $

(☎0214-455166; nkupilodge@hotmail.com; campsite per person ZMW40, dm ZMW75, rondavel from ZMW125) The best place for independent travellers, this shady campsite and lodge is a short walk out of town near the lake and has plenty of space for tents as well as a number of spacious *rondavels*. Showers and toilets are spotless and there's plenty of hot water. There's also a self-catering kitchen and a bar, or food can be prepared with plenty of notice. The friendly owners Charity and Dinesh can arrange onward transport to Tanzania.

GETTING TO TANZANIA

The MV *Liemba*, a hulking ex-German warship, leaves from Mpulungu harbour every second Friday, arriving in Kigoma (Tanzania) on Sunday. Fares for foreigners travelling in 1st, 2nd and economy class are US$95, US$85 and US$65, respectively. Visas can be issued on the ferry and cost US$50 single-entry.

Great Lakes LODGE $

(☎0977 173874; chalets ZMW150) Sharing large grounds with Great Lakes Products are a few large thatched *rondavels*, which are spacious and comfortable if a little sparse. There is a view of the lake from here but there's nowhere to sit and enjoy the scenery. There's a decent restaurant (mains ZMW20 to ZMW30).

Waterfront Bar BAR $

(Lake Tanganyika; ⏲4pm- late) Mpulungu's newest bar, it has a fantastic setting on the shore of Lake Tanganyika. The food menu is limited to barbecued chicken or sausages, but it is a great spot for a cold beer and draws a local crowd most nights.

Getting There & Away

Long distance buses link Mpulungu with Lusaka (ZMW150, 16 hours) via Kasama (ZMW40, three hours) and Mpika (ZMW100, six hours). Minibuses also depart from near the BP petrol station in Mpulungu for Mbala (ZMW15, 40 minutes).

Around Mpulungu

☎0214

Along Lake Tanganyika are some attractive lodges that can only be reached by boat. They can arrange to pick up guests from Mpulungu harbour.

Sleeping

Isanga Bay Lodge LODGE $$$

(☎0966 46991; www.isangabay.com; campsite per person US$15, full-board chalets per person US$130) For a beautiful place to stay, try Isanga Bay Lodge. It's the perfect place to make like Robinson Crusoe for a few days. There are breezy thatched and wood chalets right on the beach, with small terraces and fabulous views of the lake, as well as smaller stone *rondavels* in the gardens. Food is good and includes lots of fish pulled freshly from the lake.

For the active there's beach volleyball, snorkelling, fishing and kayaking, plus trips can be arranged to Kalambo Falls (per person US$15). Transfers can be arranged from Mpulungu for US$105 per round trip. It's a 30-minute boat ride. Road access is only possible by high-clearance 4WD.

Mishembe Bay LODGE $$$

(☎contact via Thorn Tree Safaris 0214-221615; www.thorntreesafaris.com; full board per person US$150) Another beachside option is Mishembe Bay. Run by Thorn Tree Safaris, which is based in Kasama, this rustic lodge has reed chalets set on wooden platforms overlooking the bay. The price includes tasty meals baked in their bush oven. Booking ahead is essential and transfers (ZMW500 return) are available from Mpulungu, which is a half-hour boat ride away.

Nsumbu National Park

☎0214

Hugging the southern shores of Lake Tanganyika, little visited **Nsumbu National Park** (admission US$10; ⏲6am-6pm) is a beautiful 2020 sq km of hilly grassland and escarpment, interrupted by rivers and wetlands. Back in the 1970s, this was one of the leading national parks in Africa with the largest density of rhino on the continent, and Kasaba Bay was like the St Tropez of Zambia, with the jetset flying in from South Africa and beyond. Like other remote parks in Zambia, Nsumbu was virtually abandoned in the 1980s and 1990s and poaching seriously depleted wildlife stocks here; however, conditions have improved over the past decade. Poaching has come under control, and animal numbers have increased, in part thanks to a buffer zone created by two Game Management Areas that adjoin the park.

Herds of elephants and buffaloes are seen here once again, often coming to the lake to drink. There are also plenty of antelope, including roans and sable antelopes, waterbucks and sitatungas. All of these animals attract predators and these days lions and hyenas can often be heard at night. In the lake itself are hippos as well as some of the largest crocodiles in Africa. For anglers, Lake Tanganyika offers top-class sport: Nile perch, tigerfish and *nkupi* (yellow belly) are plentiful, while golden perch and giant tigerfish are all found in the waters.

LAKE TANGANYIKA

Spreading over a massive 34,000 sq km, and reaching 4700ft deep, cavernous Lake Tanganyika is the second-deepest lake in the world and contains about 15% of the earth's freshwater. Believed to be up to 15 million years old and lying in the Great Rift Valley, the shores of the lake reach Tanzania, Burundi, the Democratic Republic of the Congo and Zambia. The climate here is always very hot, especially at the end of the dry season. This makes a swim very tempting, but there are a few crocodiles and hippos around, as well as the poisonous Tanganyika water cobra, so seek local advice before plunging in.

Other notable inhabitants of Lake Tanganyika are the many species of colourful cichlid fish (p302), which specialist operators catch and breed for export to aquariums all over the world. There are more than 350 species here, most of which are endemic and many are similar to those found in Lake Malawi. Snorkelling and diving can be good here because of the plentiful brightly coloured fish; for professional scuba equipment and lessons contact Ndole Bay Lodge (p102).

Fishing is also popular on the lake, especially around Nsumbu National Park, which is well-known for its excellent angling. The best time of year to get a good catch is November to March, and Zambia's annual National Fishing Competition is held every Spring.

For more on the lake and its inhabitants, visit the Conservation Lake Tanganyika website (www.conservationtanganyika.org).

There is decent birdwatching here, too, with some 300 species recorded, including red bishop and Pel's fishing owl.

Sleeping

TOP CHOICE Ndole Bay Lodge LODGE $$
(☎088-2165 2077; www.ndolebaylodge.com; campsite per person US$11, chalets with full board per person from US$100;) Set on a pretty beach just outside Nsumbu National Park, this lodge has several spacious chalets dotted around the grounds, all made from natural local materials. The newest rooms are stunning and include beautiful furnishings and a huge attached bathroom with Balinese-style outdoor showers. There is also a campsite right under the trees on the sandy beach and a large communal area right by the beach with plenty of comfy chairs and hammocks. The restaurant includes plenty of fresh Lake Tanganyika fish on the menu.

All kinds of activities are on offer here including snorkelling, water-skiing, bush walks and fishing trips. Ndole Bay also has a PADI dive centre where you can take half-day discover scuba diving courses as well as a PADI open-water course. For trips further afield try a sailing trip up Lake Tanganyika in a wooden dhow, including fishing and diving on the side. The friendly hosts also offer rainforest and waterfall walking safaris in Nsumbu National Park, including overnight expeditions, and private beach dining for incurable romantics.

Nkamba Bay Lodge LODGE $$$
(☎027 73 690 2992; www.nkambabaylodge.com; full board incl activities per person from US$180-400;) This exclusive private lodge is the only accommodation operating within Nsumbu National Park itself. It's set in a gorgeous, pristine cove, and has nine luxurious and spacious chalets, decorated with African prints and art. The chalets all have bathrooms and balconies overlooking either the lake or the bush. There's also a small swimming pool with views of the lake (you can't swim in the lake here because of crocodiles and hippos, the latter of which sometimes wander around the lodge at night).

Food here is excellent and plentiful and, for romantics, dinner is candlelit. Game drives, birdwatching and fishing are the main activities, but canoe trips or walks in the surrounding rainforest are also available.

Getting There & Away

Each lodge will arrange transfers for guests from the airstrip in the national park, or across the lake from Mpulungu. Kasaba Bay is the usual airstrip of choice but was under renovation at the time of writing. **Proflight Commuter Services** (☎0211-271032; www.proflight-zambia.com) offers charter flights to Kasaba Bay on a five-seater plane from US$3000 for the plane one-way or US$5000 or more for a round trip. Once Kasaba Bay airport is refurbished, scheduled services may eventually resume.

Local passenger boats (ZMW60 one-way) chug up and down the lake heading north to Nsumbu on Thursday and Friday and heading south to Mpulungu on Monday and Wednesday. They leave when full, stop anywhere and everywhere, and are fairly unprotected if the lake winds change suddenly. Boat charters to either lodge start from US$250 one-way for a slow boat (six hours) to US$500 for a fast boat (two hours).

Hardy overlanders can drive, but aim to come from the southwest, where the roads are in better condition. There are good roads up to Mporokoso, followed by a rough dirt road to Nsumbu, which requires a 4WD. A new road is nearing completion from Mbala direct to Nsumbu, but the Lukwesa Bridge is yet to be completed. When finished this will make the national park and lodges accessible in less than three hours from Mbala. Check with the lodges for up-to-date information.

UNDERSTAND ZAMBIA

Zambia Today

In September 2011, Michael Sata, nicknamed 'King Cobra', and his party the Patriotic Front (PF) won national elections, to become only the fifth president in Zambia's post-independence history. The tables have turned on the two major opposition parties – the Movement for Multiparty Democracy (MMD; Frederick Chiluba, Levy Mwanawasa and Rupiah Banda's party) and the United National Independence Party (UNIP; the party of Kenneth Kaunda) – who now face a familiar strain of authoritarianism in the form of the PF's hostility to a free press and a series of laws introduced with little consultation.

There's an undercurrent of worry in the country that Sata's rhetoric and certain of his decisions – as well as his continued support of Robert Mugabe in Zimbabwe – augur a move towards a more centralised economy and a less democratic government. After Sata's inauguration, he sacked and replaced all of the Supreme Court judges with new, hand-picked ones. He was widely criticised in local and international media after snubbing former US President George W Bush and his wife Laura, who were visiting Zambia in July 2012 promoting health and anti-poverty initiatives. And in a disturbing move for conservationists, he ordered the release of hundreds of prisoners, including many doing time for poaching.

The populist strain in Sata's policy can be observed in his decision to revalue the country's currency. Motivated more by symbolism than economics, this move also girds a sincere focus on redirecting the country's wealth to the majority of Zambians who are poor. Also to this end, he announced a significant increase in the minimum wage in September 2012, and his administration continues to encourage Zambian participation and ownership in the tourism industry.

Another prominent issue surrounds the influence of Chinese investment in the mining sector. During Sata's presidential campaign he argued against Chinese involvement, citing concerns about workers' rights and pay. Perhaps unsurprisingly since, his administration has been more welcoming. Conflict between Zambian mine workers and Chinese management has sporadically spilled over into violence, and tensions over the business practices and the benefits of China's influence continue to press on the government.

Economy

Poverty continues to plague Zambia despite the economy having experienced strong and steady growth in the early part of the 21st century, including 6.5% GDP growth in 2011. An estimated 64% of the population live on US$1 per day or less, and nearly the same percentage is considered 'economically active.' The country is still very dependent on world prices of its minerals (copper and cobalt). Knocking Zambia off its feet in the early '70s, the whim of the market then brought about huge gains in wealth early in the new millennium as world copper prices rose steadily. The full privatisation of the industry in 2001 also led to an increase in output and revenue.

However, the government didn't take advantage of the boom time to diversify the economy, and in 2009, the global financial crisis had a serious impact. Foreign investors pulled out of mines, Zambians who had enjoyed a brief period of prosperity were out of work, consumer spending plummeted and there were concerns the country couldn't cope with a collapse of copper prices. As well being subject to the whims of global markets, the country's fortunes are also at the mercy of natural disasters, especially flooding that destroys crop yields.

In the years since there has been significant foreign investment in the mines

HIV & AIDS

Zambia has one of the world's highest HIV and AIDS rates. Around 14% of adults are infected, and although access to anti-retroviral therapy (ART) has improved and lowered the death rate, the disease has claimed enough lives that life expectancy hovers around 52 years (a significant improvement nevertheless from over a decade ago, when it was 42 years). According to a UN report issued in 2012, an estimated 72% of 480,000 Zambians were receiving ART (though significantly, only one in four children in need were receiving treatment).

AIDS hasn't just devastated households and communities, the loss of healthy workers, especially at planting and harvesting time, means the economy and national development have been weakened as well. Children orphaned by parents who have died as a result of AIDS (nearly 700,000) have swelled the population of 'street kids' living in roadside sewers and on central reservations in urban centres.

(especially from China), and South African-owned businesses are sprouting rapidly in towns across the country. Other important sources of revenue are manufacturing and agriculture. Despite foreign investment, the economy is still fragile, especially because the highly automated mining industry can't solve the unemployment crisis. In addition, it's widely acknowledged that companies misreport their production numbers in order to minimise their taxable income. But possibly equally important is the fact that potential entrepreneurs can't borrow money because of excessively high interest rates within Zambia.

In July 2011 President Michael Sata declared a significant increase in the monthly minimum wage – from the equivalent of US$30 to US$105 for maids and household servants and from US$50 to US$220 for non-unionised shopworkers. Some business owners question the precipitousness of the decision and claim that the new wages are out of step with their ability to meet payroll. The troubling increase in costs of staple food products and transport has also been linked to the raise.

In July 2012, in an attempt to strengthen the currency and arguably as a symbolic nationalistic gesture, Sata rendered the kwacha the sole legal tender. Equally important, he announced its revaluing so that as of 1 January 2013 three zeros would be lopped off all figures, so that, for example, ZK20,000 becomes ZMW20. There would be a six-month transitional period, in part of an attempt to bring money outside the system back in, as well as to ensure that every ATM in the country would issue the new currency expressed as 'ZMW'.

History

The first of the 'modern' (eg still found today) ethnic groups of Zambia to arrive were the Tonga and Ila peoples (sometimes combined as the Tonga-Ila), who migrated from the Congo area in the late 15th century. By 1550 they had occupied the Zambezi Valley and plateau areas north of where Lake Kariba is now – and which is still their homeland today. Next to arrive were the Chewa. Between the 14th and 16th centuries they followed a long and circuitous route via Lakes Mweru, Tanganyika and Malawi before founding a powerful kingdom covering much of present-day eastern Zambia, as well as parts of Malawi and Mozambique. Today, the Chewa are still the largest group in eastern Zambia.

The Bemba (most notably the ruling Ngandu clan) had migrated from Congo by crossing the Luapula River into northern Zambia by around 1700. Meanwhile, the Lamba people migrated to the area of the Copperbelt in about 1650. At around the same time, the related Lala settled in the region around Serenje.

Meanwhile, in western Zambia, the Lozi people established a dynasty and the basis of a solid political entity that still exists. The Lozi's ancestors may have migrated from what is now Angola as early as AD 450.

Early 19th Century

In the early 19th century, the fearsome reputation of the newly powerful and highly disciplined warrior army under the command of Shaka Zulu in KwaZulu Natal (South Africa) led to a domino effect of groups who lived in his path fleeing elsewhere and in turn displacing other groups. This included the Ngoni, who fled to Malawi and Zambia, as well as the Makololo who moved into southern Zambia, around the towns of Kalomo and Monze, and who were eventually forced further west into southwest Zambia, where they displaced more Tonga people.

Also around this time, the slave trade, which had existed for many centuries, increased considerably. Swahili-Arabs, who dominated the trade on the east coast of Africa, pushed into the interior; many people from Zambia were captured and taken across Lake Malawi and through Mozambique or Tanzania to be sold in the slave markets of Zanzibar.

The Colonial Era

In 1855 David Livingstone, the Scottish explorer, journeyed through large swathes of Zambia, including the Lower Zambezi where he came upon a magnificent waterfall, never before seen by a European. He dubbed it 'Victoria Falls' in homage to royalty back home. On a subsequent trip in 1873, Livingstone died while searching for the source of the Nile in northern Zambia. His heart was buried under a tree near the spot where he died, in Chief Chitambo's village, southeast of Lake Bangweulu in Zambia.

Twelve years later, claims made by European powers over African territory were settled at the Berlin Conference and the continent was split into colonies and spheres of influence – Britain claimed Rhodesia (Zambia and Zimbabwe) and Malawi.

This 'new' territory did not escape the notice of entrepreneur Cecil John Rhodes, who was already establishing mines and a vast business empire in South Africa. Rhodes' British South Africa Company (BSAC) laid claim to the area in the early 1890s and was backed by the British Government in 1895 to help combat slavery and prevent further Portuguese expansion in the region.

Two separate territories were originally created – North-Western Rhodesia and North-Eastern Rhodesia – but these were combined in 1911 to become Northern Rhodesia. In 1907, Livingstone became the capital. At around the same time, vast deposits of copper were discovered in the area now called the Copperbelt. The indigenous people had mined there for centuries, but now large European-style, opencast pits were dug, and these, combined with the influx of European settlers, drove them from their land. Yet the main source of mine labour was Africans, who needed to earn money to pay the new 'hut tax' – a tax imposed on each household by British colonial authorities in an attempt to make their colonies independent of the British treasury.

In 1924 the colony was put under direct British control, and in 1935, the capital was moved to Lusaka. To make themselves less dependent on colonial rule, settlers soon pushed for closer ties with Southern Rhodesia and Nyasaland (Malawi), but various interruptions (such as WWII) meant the Federation of Rhodesia and Nyasaland did not come about until 1953.

Independence & Kaunda

The United National Independence Party (UNIP) was founded in Zambia in the late 1950s by Dr Kenneth Kaunda, who spoke out against the Federation on the grounds that it promoted the rights of white settlers to the detriment of the indigenous African population. UNIP was an offshoot of the previously banned Zambia African National Congress (ZANC) which itself became a splinter group when its members decided not to participate in elections held in 1958 since only a small sliver of the African population was allowed to vote. As other African countries gained independence, Zambian nationalists opposed the colonial forces through a short but successful campaign of civil disobedience in 1961 called the Chachacha Rebellion.

The Federation was dissolved in 1963 and universal elections were held the following year. Northern Rhodesia was no more and the country's name was changed to Zambia, with Kaunda as its president. While the British government had profited enormously from Northern Rhodesia, the colonialists chose to divert a large portion of this wealth towards the development of Southern Rhodesia (now Zimbabwe), to the detriment of the north.

After gaining independence, Zambia inherited a British-style multiparty political system. Kaunda, as leader of the majority UNIP, became the new republic's first president. The other main party was the African National Congress (ANC), led by Harry Nkumbula. But Kaunda disliked opposition. In one swift move during 1972, he disbanded the Zambian ANC, created the 'second republic,' declared UNIP the sole legal party and made himself the only presidential candidate.

Consequently, Kaunda remained in power for the next 27 years. His rule was based upon 'humanism' – his own mix of Marxism and traditional African values. The civil service was increased, and nearly all private businesses (including the copper mines) were nationalised. But corruption and mismanagement, exacerbated by a fall in world copper prices, doomed Zambia to become one of the poorest countries in the world by the end of the 1970s. The economy continued to flounder while Zambia's trade routes to the coast through neighbouring countries (eg Zimbabwe and Mozambique) were closed in retaliation for Kaunda's support for several liberation movements in the region.

By the early 1980s two important events occurred that had the potential to significantly improve Zambia's economy: Rhodesia gained independence (and had become Zimbabwe), which allowed Kaunda to take his country off a war footing; and the Tazara railway to Dar es Salaam (Tanzania) was completed, giving Zambia unencumbered access to the coast. Yet the economy remained on the brink of collapse: foreign exchange reserves were almost exhausted; serious shortages of food, fuel and other basic commodities were common; and unemployment and crime rates rose sharply.

In 1986, an attempt was made to diversify the economy and improve the country's balance of payments. Zambia received economic aid from the International Monetary Fund (IMF), but the IMF conditions were severe and included cutting basic food subsidies. Subsequent price rises led to countrywide riots in which many people were killed. Kaunda was forced to restore subsidies.

The winds of change blowing through Africa during the late 1980s, coupled with Zambia's disastrous domestic situation, meant something had to give. Following another round of violent street protests against increased food prices in 1990, which quickly transformed into a general demand for the return of multiparty politics, Kaunda was forced to accede to public opinion.

Kaunda announced a snap referendum in late 1990, but as protests grew more vocal, he was forced to legalise opposition parties and announce full presidential and parliamentary elections for October 1991. Not surprisingly, UNIP (and Kaunda) were resoundingly defeated by the Movement for Multiparty Democracy (MMD), led by Frederick Chiluba, a former trade union leader. Kaunda stepped down without complaint, which may have saved Zambia from descending into anarchy.

The 1990s

President Chiluba moved quickly to encourage loans and investment from the IMF and World Bank. Exchange controls were liberalised to attract investors, particularly from South Africa, but tough austerity measures were also introduced. Once again, food prices soared. The civil service was rationalised, state industries privatised or simply closed, and thousands of people lost their jobs.

By the mid-1990s, the government's failure to bring about any perceptible improvements to the economy and the standard of living in Zambia allowed Kaunda to confidently re-enter the political arena. He attracted strong support and soon became the UNIP leader. Leading up to the 1996 elections, the MMD panicked and passed a law forbidding anyone with foreign parents to enter politics (Kaunda's parents were from Malawi). Despite intercessions from Western aid donors and world leaders like Nelson Mandela – not to mention accusations that Chiluba's parents were from the Democratic Republic of the Congo (Zaïre) – the law was not repealed. The UNIP withdrew all its candidates in protest and many voters boycotted the election. Consequently, Chiluba and the MMD easily won, and the result was grudgingly accepted by most Zambians.

In the 21st Century

The political shenanigans continued unabated at the start of the new millennium: in mid-2001, Vice-President Christon Tembo was expelled from parliament by Chiluba, so he formed an opposition party – the Forum for Democratic Development (FDD). Later, Paul Tembo, a former MMD national secretary, joined the FDD but was assassinated the day before he was due to front a tribunal about alleged MMD corruption.

Chiluba was unable to run for a third presidential term in December 2001 (though he badly wanted to change the constitution so he could). He anointed his former vice-president, Levy Mwanawasa, as his successor, but Mwanawasa only just beat a coalition of opposition parties known as the United Party for National Development (UPND). Again, allegations from international observers about the MMD rigging the results and buying votes fell on deaf ears. To Chiluba's horror, Mwanawasa stripped his predecessor of immunity from prosecution and proceeded to launch an anti-corruption drive, which targeted the former president. In August 2009, after a long-running trial, Chiluba was cleared of embezzling US$500,000 by Zambia's High Court. His wife, however, was not so lucky, having been given a jail term earlier in the year for receiving stolen funds while her husband was in office. In a separate case in 2007, the High Court in Britain ruled Chiluba and four of his aides conspired to rob Zambia of about US$46 million, but it remains to be seen whether this judgement will be enforced within Zambia.

Although Zambia remains a poor country, its economy experienced strong growth in the early part of the 21st century with GDP growth at around 6%. However, the country is still very dependent on the world prices of its minerals (copper and cobalt).

As well as combating global markets, natural disasters have played a significant role in the country's fortunes. Although a bumper harvest was recorded in 2007, floods in 2008/09 were declared a national disaster and killed dozens of people – the Zambezi River, which flooded much of Western Zambia, was said to be at its highest level in 60 years, and crops were severely affected.

Hardly publicised is Zambia's role as a host to refugees from political and ethnic conflicts in neighboring countries and others in the region, including Angola, Rwanda, Burundi, the DRC and Somalia. In 2012, there were still over 40,000 refugees, primarily in the Meheba and Mayukawayukwa camps in the northwestern province. Thousands of Angolans and Rwandans who had been residing in the camps for years, many born there, were repatriated by the United Nations High Comission for Refugees in 2011, and plans are for a further reduction in numbers in 2012 and 2013.

Zambian Way of Life

Almost half of all Zambians live in urban centres, crowding into housing compounds, where water shortages and overstretched sewage systems cause all sorts of health problems. Most unskilled city labourers work six to seven days per week, with their families sometimes living on less than US$1 per day. Still, a small middle class and expats frequent high-end shops and cinemas in Lusaka's malls and the music industry is thriving, in part because ordinary Zambians can listen and share music on their Bluetooth mobile phones. Meanwhile in rural Zambia, life hasn't changed much – subsistence farmers still eke out a living at the whim of a crop's success or failure and traditional religions mixed with Christian beliefs and village hierarchies are the mainstays of life. (Interestingly, the production of Christian-themed music videos, usually with a chorus of 'church ladies,' is a big business in Lusaka.)

People

The population of Zambia is made up of between 70 and 80 different ethnic groups (the final count varies according to your definition of ethnicity, but the Zambian government officially recognises 73 groups). Despite these numbers there is considerable homogeneity among the tribes of Zambia. This is partly due to a long history of people moving around the country, settling new areas or looking for work, and also because after independence president Kaunda fostered national unity, while still recognising the disparate languages and cultures. Intermarriage among the officially recognised groups is also common, and Zambia is justifiably proud of its relative lack of ethnic problems.

The vast majority (99%) of Zambians are indigenous Africans. The final 1% are Zambian citizens of Indian or European origin (mostly involved in business, commerce, farming and the tourist industry). Many white and Asian families have lived here for generations – although race relations are still sometimes a little strained.

RELIGION

Around 75% of Zambians are Christians. The majority are members of one of the hundreds of Protestant churches but in addition, there are Catholics and those who follow homegrown Christian denominations, including large branches of the African Zion churches. Many of these people also follow traditional animist belief systems. There is also a significant Muslim population.

ETHNIC GROUPS

The Bemba, whose traditional homeland is in northern Zambia around Kasama and Lake Bangwelu, are the largest ethnic group in Zambia, forming about 20% of the population. Many also live in the Copperbelt, having migrated for work, and Bemba is now the dominant language there.

All together, speakers of Tonga as a first language make up about 15% of Zambia's population. Once primarily hunters, most Tonga are now farmers and cattle herders, while those who live along the rivers catch fish. The traditional homelands of the Tonga are the Zambezi Valley and much of the higher country to the north, thus dividing them into two groups: Valley Tonga and Plateau Tonga. The former's territory once spread into Zimbabwe, but largely disappeared when Lake Kariba was formed.

People speaking Nyanja as their first language make up about 15% of the population (the term Nyanja is used more to describe a language than a particular people); the Chewa people make up about a third of the Nyanja-speakers in Zambia. The Ngoni, descendants of Zulus who migrated here in the early 19th century, make up about 6% and live in southeast Zambia around the town of Chipata. They still maintain some Zulu traditions but have adopted Nyanja as their language. In the southeast, the Nsenga people, who also speak Nyanja, inhabit the lands around the town of Petauke, along the lower Luangwa River and along the Great East Road, making up about 5% of the population.

The Lozi have their own distinct nation called Barotseland, a significant part of Zambia's Western Province and the vast Zambezi flood plain, and with about 650,000 people, they make up roughly 6% of the population. The annual inundations provide good soil for crops and good grass for cows, so naturally the Lozi are farmers and herders, although when the flood plain is covered in water, they often have to move to villages on higher ground.

Relative newcomers to the country include South African businesspeople and Zimbabwean farmers who lost their land under Robert Mugabe's rule. There are also many Europeans and North Americans; some (such as mining consultants) have been living in Zambia for decades, while others (such as aid workers) stay for only a few years before moving on.

Environment

The Land

Landlocked Zambia is one of Africa's most eccentric legacies of colonialism. Shaped like a mangled butterfly, its borders don't correspond to any tribal or linguistic area. And Zambia is huge. At some 752,000 sq km, it's about the size of France, England and the Republic of Ireland combined.

Zambia is chock full of rivers. The Luangwa, the Kafue and the mighty Zambezi dominate western, southern and eastern Zambia, flowing through a beautiful mix of flood plains, forests and farmland. In the north, the main rivers are the Chambeshi and the Luapula; both sources of the Congo River. Northern Zambia has many smaller rivers, too, and the broken landscape helps create a stunning scenery of lakes, rapids and waterfalls.

Of course, Zambia's most famous waterfall is Victoria Falls, where the Zambezi River plunges over a mile-wide cliff before thundering down the long, zigzagging Batoka Gorge. The Zambezi flows into Lake Kariba, created by a dam but still one of the largest lakes in Africa. In northern Zambia is the even larger Lake Tanganyika – it's 675km

ZAMBIAN MUSIC

All of Zambia's ethnic groups have their own musical traditions. The Lozi are famous for the large drums played during the remarkable Kuomboka ceremony, while the Bemba are also renowned drummers. Other traditional musical instruments used by most groups include large wooden xylophones, often with gourds underneath the blocks for resonance, and tiny thumb pianos with keys made from flattened metal.

Contemporary Zambian musicians who have achieved some international fame include Larry Maluma, who blends traditional Zambian beats with reggae, and had just released his ninth album *Tusekelele* (Let's Celebrate) at the time of writing. Younger Zambians prefer reggae – both the old-school Jamaican style and the softer version popular in Southern Africa – and contemporary Zambian r'n'b and hip-hop. K'Millian is a hugely popular Zambian r'n'b artist. Also well loved is JK, who plays a mixture of hip-hop, reggae and traditional Zambian beats. Zambians love Congolese *soukous* ('rhumba' in Zambia), which is always blasted at deafening levels at local bars and nightclubs.

FOOTBALL NATION

Kennedy Mweene, the goalkeeper and captain of the Zambian national football team (who are known as Chipolopolo or 'the copper bullets'), endeared himself to Zambians during the sudden-death shootout for the 2012 Africa Cup of Nations in Libreville, Gabon. After blocking Cote d'Ivoire star Didier Drogba's shot, Mweene mimicked the hand-in-face move meant to suggest, 'I'm so fast, you can't see me', of American wrestler John Cena (both Cena and World Wrestling Entertainment, or WWE, are extremely popular in Zambia). Zambia took the Cup, a massive high for a nation that had suffered the greatest tragedy when, almost 20 years earlier, the entire national team was killed in a plane crash en route to Senegal for a World Cup qualifier.

As a somewhat deflating counterpoint to the euphoria and pride of the African Cup win in Gabon, Nkoloma Stadium in Lusaka fell into disrepair and a section of the stands even collapsed in 2012. This prompted the national team to move to the Levy Mwanawasa Stadium in Ndola until a new one is built. Keep your eyes open for enormous roadside billboard ads with Herve Renard, the French coach of the national team, in his now trademark white collared shirt open to the chest.

The quality of the country's domestic league is undermined by players lured abroad with more lucrative salaries. Some of the best Zambian footballers are recruited by TP Mazembe in the Democratic Republic of the Congo (DRC), which is widely considered the Real Madrid of Africa. However, two of the country's four most competitive teams are associated with the military – the Red Arrows of the air force and the army's Green Buffaloes. The other two are Zanarco (Lusaka) and the Warriors (Kitwe).

long, the second deepest in the world, and holds one-sixth of the earth's fresh water.

In the south and east, Zambia is cut by deep valleys, some of of which are branches of the Great Rift Valley. The Zambezi Valley is the largest, and defines the county's southern border, while the 700km-long Luangwa Valley is lined by the steep and spectacular Muchinga Escarpment.

Even the flats of Zambia can be stunning: the endless grassy Busanga Plains in Kafue National Park attract fantastic wildlife, while the Liuwa Plain – part of the even larger Upper Zambezi flood plain that makes up much of western Zambia – is home to Africa's second-largest wildebeest migration.

Some of Zambia's other geographical highlights include the breathtaking high, rolling grasslands of the Nyika Plateau, the seasonally flooded wetlands of the Kafue Flats, the teak forests of the Upper Zambezi, and the Kariba and Mpata Gorges on the Lower Zambezi.

One of the more ubiquitous features of the landscape are the sculpture-like termite mounds, some several metres high, that appear closely grouped together like a crowded cemetery. These methane-producing structures, built from a mix of termite excrement and soil, do soak up rainwater, and of course the termites themselves break down dead wood.

Wildlife

Because of Zambia's diverse landscape, plentiful water supplies, and position between Eastern, Southern and Central Africa, the diversity of animal species is huge. The rivers, of course, support large populations of hippos (at around 40,000, the Zambezi River has Africa's highest population) and crocs, and the associated grasslands provide plenty of fodder for herds of zebras, impalas and pukus (an antelope common in Zambia, but not elsewhere). Although the tiger fish of the Zambezi are related to the South American piranha, there's no record of a human being attacked (however, they are attracted to blood in the water).

Huge herds of rare black lechwe live near Lake Bangweulu, and endemic Kafue lechwe settle in the area around the Kafue River. Kasanka National Park is one of the best places on the continent to see the rare, water-loving antelopes called sitatungas. South Luangwa and Lower Zambezi National Parks are good places to see tall and stunningly graceful giraffes, and Zambia has its own subspecies – Thornicroft's giraffe. South Luangwa has its very own subspecies of wildebeest, too – the light-coloured Cookson's wildebeest – but the best place to see these creatures is the Liuwa Plain, a remote grassland area in western Zambia where

THE ZAMBEZI: RIVER OF AFRICA

The Zambezi is the fourth-longest river in Africa, after the Nile, the Congo and the Niger, and it has a long and varied course through Zambia. It rises in the far northwestern corner of the country and flows through a short section of Angola before re-entering Zambia and creating the huge flood plains around Mongu. Further downstream, the river becomes the border between Zambia and Namibia, and then between Zambia and Zimbabwe, before plummeting over the world-famous Victoria Falls and forcing its way down the Batoka Gorge to Lake Kariba.

Beyond Kariba Dam, the major Kafue River adds its waters to the flow, and the Zambezi runs between Zimbabwe's Mana Pools and Zambia's Lower Zambezi National Park. It is joined by another large tributary, the Luangwa River, before entering Mozambique and another dam-created lake – Lago de Cahora Bassa. Downstream from here the giant river crosses the last few hundred kilometres of coastal plain, finally flowing into the Indian Ocean, north of Beira.

Most of the river is wide, deep and slow-moving – ideal for canoes and even large boats. But these lazy sections are interrupted by the odd waterfall, where the river crosses bands of harder rock. These mere specks on the map were enough to prevent navigation between the interior and the coast, as the explorer David Livingstone discovered in the 19th century. Later, the colonial powers in Zambia were also unable to develop the Zambezi for serious transportation.

From time to time, boosters – often politicians and businessmen in Zimbabwe – have proposed the creation of a seaway linking the landlocked countries of southern Africa with the Indian Ocean along the Zambezi. Little progress has been made beyond the financing of feasibility studies – needless to say, the political, economic and environmental obstacles are immense.

thousands converge every year for Africa's second-largest wildebeest migration.

These animals naturally attract predators, so most parks contain lions, leopards, hyenas (which you'll probably see) and cheetahs (which you probably won't). Wild dogs were once very rare but are now encountered more frequently. Elephants, another big drawcard, are also found in huge herds in South Luangwa, Lower Zambezi and some other national parks. Zambia's herds of black rhino were killed by poachers in the 1970s and '80s, but reintroduction programs have seen rhino transported to North Luangwa National Park.

Bird lovers will love Zambia, where about 750 species have been recorded. Twitchers used to the 'traditional' Southern African species listed in the *Roberts* and *Newman's* field guides will spend a lot of time identifying unusual species - especially in the north and west. Most notable are the endangered shoebill storks (found in the Bangweulu Wetlands); fish eagles (Zambia's national bird); and the endemic Chaplin's barbets (found mostly around Monze).

One time when you might groan at biological diversity: there are 37 different species of tsetse flies in Kafue National Park. Chewing garlic cloves is said to help keep them away.

Plants

About 65% of Zambia, mainly plateau areas and escarpments, is covered in *miombo* woodland, which consists mainly of broadleaved deciduous trees, particularly various species of *Brachystegia* (another name for this type of vegetation is Brachystegia woodland). Some areas are thickly wooded, others are more open, but the trees never form a continuous canopy, allowing grass and other plants to grow between them.

In the drier, hotter valleys and best-known national parks like South Luangwa and Lower Zambezi, much of the vegetation is mopane woodland. Dominant trees are the species *Colophospermum mopane*, usually around 10m high. The baobab tree also grows here. Many legends and stories are associated with the striking and simultaneously grand and grotesque tree. One has it that the gods, upset over the boababs haughty disdain for inferior-looking flora, thrust them back into the ground, roots upward, to teach them a lesson in humility. You'll see this landscape in Zambia's best-known national parks, Lower Zambezi and South Luangwa.

With its many rivers and lakes, Zambia has some of the most extensive wetlands in Southern Africa. These include the Bangweulu Wetlands, along the southern and eastern shores of Lake Bangweulu; and the vast plains of the Kafue Flats downstream from Kafue National Park, which is dotted with seasonally flooded marshes, lagoons and oxbow lakes.

Most grassland in Zambia is low, flat and flooded for part of the year, with hardly a tree in sight. The largest flood-plain area is west of the Upper Zambezi – including Liuwa Plain National Park – where thousands of square kilometres are inundated every year. Another is the Busanga Plains in Kafue National Park.

Along many of Zambia's rivers are riverine forests. Tourists will see a lot of this type of landscape as national park camps are often built on riverbanks, under the shade of huge trees such as ebony, winter-thorn and the unmistakable 'sausage tree' (*Kigelia africana*).

Evergreen forest, the 'jungle' of Tarzan films, is found only in isolated pockets in northwest Zambia – a remnant of the larger forests over the border in Angola and the Democratic Republic of the Congo.

National Parks

Zambia boasts 20 national parks and reserves (and 34 Game Management Areas or GMAs), and some 30% of the land is protected, but after decades of poaching, clearing and general bad management, many are just lines on the map that no longer protect (or even contain) much wildlife. However, some national parks accommodate extremely healthy stocks of wildlife and are among the best in Southern Africa. Privately funded conservation organisations have done much to rehabilitate the condition of some of these.

Admission fees to the parks vary. Each ticket is valid for 24 hours from the time you enter the park, but if you're staying inside the park at official accommodation, this admission fee is valid for seven days.

Environmental Issues & Conservation

Although the population is growing rapidly it is still relatively sparse, so Zambia doesn't suffer some of the environmental problems, or at least to the same extent, as its neighbours. That being said, the country faces the daunting challenge of deforestation and consequent soil erosion and loss of productivity. Poachers set fires to ambush animals, land is regularly burned and cleared for agricultural purposes and local people chop down wood for charcoal (much of which ends up for sale in Tanzania). Despite the government's ban on the export of raw timber to other Southern African Development Community (SADC) countries, illegal logging and timber smuggling continues, now primarily to meet the demand for wood from China.

HUNTING

Hunting has greatly damaged Zambia's wildlife. The 1970s were a devastating time, when other countries' civil wars were funded with ivory coming out of the parks. In 1960 North Luangwa had 70,000 elephants; this figure dropped to an estimated 5000 by 1986. Under pressure from international organisations, however, the Zambian government introduced serious anti-poaching and development measures. Despite successes in some parks, poaching and poor management remain major problems. Jeffrey Goldberg's April 5, 2010 *New Yorker* article, 'Cry of the Kalahari' is a fascinating exploration of Mark and Delia Owens' controversial conservation work in North Luangwa National Park; *In the Eye of the Elephant* is the Owens' own account of their Zambian experiences.

In the past, people moved into some protected areas, chopped down trees, grew crops or hunted the animals. They were poor, and good land and food were scarce. Animals were a source of protein in areas where tsetse flies mean raising livestock isn't an option. ('No tsetse, no game', a commonly heard saying, refers to the fact that without the painfully annoying flies, human settlements and their accompanying livestock would devastate wildlife habitats.) Even outside the parks, on areas of land shared by people and animals, there was conflict. The same is still true today. To a poor rural subsistence farmer, wildlife is nothing but a problem: lions will kill cattle, and an elephant takes an hour to polish off a field of crops that took all year to grow. 'Chilli fences' are one method used to prevent elephants from raiding farms; pepper spray is manufactured from the four-times-a-year chilli harvest.

With this inevitable tension in mind, all of the national parks are surrounded by a ring of Game Management Areas (GMAs), a good portion of which are earmarked as hunting concessions. However, in a move surprising and encouraging to conservationists, in early 2013 Zambia announced a ban on the hunting of lions, leopards and other endangered big cats (19 hunting concessions were suspended and the director-general of ZAWA was fired because of allegations of corruption at the same time). At the time of research, though, the ban is only in effect for a year, until new baselines of big cat population figures can be established; it's also still legal on private 'game ranches' with official permits. Newly installed tourism minister Sylvia Masebo explained that photographic tourism is more economically important than hunting.

Whatever the future policies are in terms of big cats, hunting in the GMAs will continue. To many, this might seem like a compromise of conservationist ideals, but it's argued that if there was no hunting there would be indiscriminate and unregulated slaughter.

Much of the revenue from licensing fees goes to headmen or chiefs in the surrounding villages as well as ZAWA. To the frustration of conservationists, some headmen and chiefs still regard themselves as above the law, including a chief in South Luangwa who has been found unashamedly with several kills. Whether ZAWA spends the money wisely or even legitimately is also an issue of concern; however, without the proceeds ZAWA would certainly be unable to operate and would lose any leverage it has to convince communities not to hunt, themselves. Technically, the Zambian state owns all of the wildlife, while the land belongs to the traditional chiefs.

BUSH MEAT

Arguably, the biggest problem is indiscriminate snaring for commercial bush meat. If caught poaching for meat the punishment is mitigated and considered a lighter offense than for ivory (this includes if someone is caught with a dead elephant with the tusks still on). If the poacher is caught with an animal with the skin still on the animal then the punishment is a minimum five years in prison (since it's not considered a bush meat kill but rather a 'trophy'). Sold 'underground' in the back of shops or door to door to trusted customers, it's the middle and upper class, mostly in Lusaka, who are driving the bush-meat market. After all, widely available buffalo, warthog and antelope is on average 50% more expen-

ZAMBIA'S MOST IMPORTANT NATIONAL PARKS

PARK	SIZE	FEATURES	ACTIVITIES	BEST TIME TO VISIT
Bangweulu Wetlands	9800 sq km	floodplain; black lechwes, shoebills, waterbirds	walking, canoe trips, birdwatching	Dec-Mar
Kafue National Park	22,400 sq km	*miombo* woodland, open grasslands, Kafue River; red lechwes, leopards, cheetahs, lions	game drives, birdwatching, fishing	May-Oct
Kasanka National Park	390 sq km	woodlands, plains, rivers, swamps; sitatungas, wattled cranes, hippos, blue monkeys, bats (migration Oct-Dec)	boat trips, walking, game drives	Jul-Nov
Liuwa Plain National Park	3,662 sq km	vast grasslands, islands of palm trees, wildebeest migration (Nov), zebra, wild dogs, hyena	walking safaris, birdwatching	Jun-Dec
Lower Zambezi National Park	4092 sq km	Zambezi River, sandy flats, mopane woodland; crocs, hippos, elephants, buffaloes, lions	canoeing, boating, birdwatching, game drives	Jun-Sep
North Luangwa National Park	9050 sq km	Luangwa River, *miombo* woodland, plains; buffaloes, elephants, hippos, Thornicroft's giraffes, leopards, lions	walking safaris	May-Oct
South Luangwa National Park	9050 sq km	mopane & *miombo* woodland, grasslands; Thornicroft's giraffes, Cookson's wildebeest, lions, leopards, elephants, pukus	day & night game drives, walking safaris	Apr-Oct

FIND OUT ABOUT CONSERVATION IN ZAMBIA

South Luangwa Conservation Society (SLCS) and Conservation Lower Zambezi (CLZ) are the two most prominent homegrown organisations dedicated to conservation in their respective parks. To learn more about other groups doing conservation work in Zambia, or to help, try contacting the following organisations, some of whom accept volunteers:

Bird Watch Zambia (www.wattledcrane.com) Previously known as the Zambia Ornithological Society, it is dedicated to researching and monitoring the health of Zambia's birdlife.

Chipembele Wildlife Education Trust (www.chipembele.org) Focuses on educating local schoolchildren about conservation; and is also involved in anti-poaching and rehabilitation of orphaned animals.

Game Rangers International With support from the David Shepherd Wildllife Foundation, they run an elephant orphanage project in Zambia, dedicated to the rescue, rehabilitation and release of injured and orphaned elephants.

Kasanka Trust (www.kasanka.com) A private non-profit that manages the conservation of the flora and fauna of Kasanka National Park and the Bangwelu Wetlands.

Wildlife & Environmental Conservation Society of Zambia (www.conservation zambia.org) Runs environmental education programs, for children and adults, and is involved in various conservation projects.

Zambia Carnivore Program (www.zambiacarnivores.org) Works to preserve Zambia's large carnivores through research, conservation and education.

sive than beef. And there are only around a dozen private farms in Zambia where game is raised to be slaughtered for the commercial market, unlike South Africa where it's a huge industry.

CONSERVATION

As might be expected, there's considerable tension between environmental preservation and conservation and Zambia's underground wealth. A proposal for a mining concession within the Lower Zambezi National Park's boundaries was rejected in September 2012, to the surprise of some conservationists, who worry that it's only a matter of time before the profits to be wrung from the region's mineral resources (primarily coal and copper in the eastern part of the park) will be too seductive to deny. There are also oil and uranium blocks in South and North Luangwa and exploration and more informal prospecting happening in the northeastern section of Kafue.

One of the most important developments regarding conservation in recent years is the Kavango Zambezi Transfrontier Park (KAZA), a multinational effort to link the historic and instinctual migratory patterns of elephants and other wildlife between Zambia, Botswana, Namibia and Angola.

TOURISM & THE ENVIRONMENT

The detrimental impact of tourism is also a problem and most obvious along the Zambezi River (particularly near Victoria Falls). As in the national parks, locals are attracted by work opportunities and in the poor suburbs and townships around Livingstone the population has increased massively. There are frequent water shortages, leading to health problems, and sewage systems can't cope with the increased usage so waste ends up in the river. The increase in river activities such as white-water rafting, canoeing and booze cruises is damaging natural vegetation and disturbing wildlife.

SURVIVAL GUIDE

Directory A–Z

Accommodation

Accommodation prices in this book are listed for the high season (eg April/May to October/November), based on 'international rates.' Often lodges offer resident rates that can be half as much. Some lodges/camps close during the wet season (November to April); if they're open, discounts of up to 50% are common.

BOOK YOUR STAY ONLINE

For more accommodation reviews by Lonely Planet authors, check out http://hotels.lonelyplanet.com.

You'll find independent reviews, as well as recommendations on the best places to stay. Best of all, you can book online.

The accommodation in the national parks is even more skewed towards the very top end, that is on average around ZMW2000 per person; although there is some variety in terms of cost just outside park boundaries. These privately operated lodges and 'camps' (a confusing term often used to describe expensive lodges) in the parks offer the same sort of luxury and exclusivity as other lodges and camps in Southern and East Africa. Rates usually include meals, drinks, park fees and activities, such as wildlife drives, but not transfers by road, air and/or boat. A real treat of travel here are the open-air toilets and showers; most bush camps and many lodges have them.

Most cities and larger towns have campsites where you can pitch your tent, but most are way out in the suburbs (wood and charcoal usually for sale). Camping is also possible at privately run campsites just outside national park boundaries. You won't have to pay park admission fees until you actually visit the park. Some lodges around national parks have multiple types of accommodation, everything from safari tents to chalets as well as campsites – this can be a great deal as you have access to the lodge's facilities while paying a pittance for accommodation (in these cases we've placed them in the budget category in terms of its room rates).

The better budget hotels charge by the room, so two, three or even four people travelling together can get some real (if crowded) bargains. Single travellers are often charged a 'supplement'; negotiation is usually possible.

Activities

Companies in Livingstone (and Victoria Falls town in Zimbabwe) offer a bewildering array of activities, such as white-water rafting in the gorge below the falls or river boarding and canoeing on the quieter waters above the falls. Those with plenty of nerve and money can try bungee jumping or abseiling, or take a ride in a microlight or helicopter. The less adventurous may want to try hiking and horse riding.

Canoeing, either for a few hours or a few days, is a great way to explore the Zambezi River and can be arranged at lodges in the Lower Zambezi Valley and Siavonga. Fishing along the Zambezi, and at several lakes in northern Zambia, is also popular; the tiger fish provide a tough contest for anglers. Fishing and boating are also possible on Lakes Kariba, Bangweulu and Tanganyika.

Most national parks, such as Kafue, Kasanka, Lower Zambezi and South Luangwa, have activities for visitors, with wildlife drives and walks the main focus, and the main draw for visitors to Zambia. Morning drives and walks depart around 6am; night drives typically last from 4pm to 8pm.

'Fly camping,' basically trips that involve walking or boating during the day and informal bush camping at night, is becoming more popular, especially in South Luangwa, Kafue and Liuwa National Parks.

Business Hours

» **Government offices** From 8am or 9am to 4pm or 5pm Monday to Friday, with an hour for lunch somewhere between noon and 2pm.

» **Shops** Keep the same hours as government offices but are also open Saturday.

» **Supermarkets** Normally open from 8am to 8pm Monday to Friday, 8am to 6pm Saturday and 9am to 1pm Sunday; some are open 8am to 10pm daily at the big shopping centres in Lusaka.

» **Banks** Operate weekdays from 8am to 3.30pm (or 5pm), and from 8am to 11am (or noon) on Saturday.

» **Post offices** From 8am or 9am to 4pm or 4.30pm weekdays.

» **Restaurants** Normally open for lunch

SLEEPING PRICE RANGES

The following price ranges refer to accommodation rates in high season.

$ less than ZMW250

$$ ZMW250 to ZMW500

$$$ more than ZMW500

between 11.30am and 2.30pm and dinner between 6pm and 10.30pm.

» **Bar-restaurants** Can only sell alcohol until 11pm, but often stay open later on Friday and Saturday nights in Lusaka.

Climate

Late May to early October is considered prime wildlife viewing time, but October can be brutally hot. June to August is generally dry as well. December to April is the rainy season, and the landscape is vibrant; many lodges are closed during this time. If you're heading for Victoria Falls, or looking for white-water rafting, August to December, when the Zambezi's flow is reduced, is best.

Customs Regulations

There are no restrictions on the amount of foreign currency tourists can bring in or take out of Zambia. Import or export of Zambian kwacha, however, is technically forbidden; but if you take a small amount, it's unlikely to be a problem. Tourists can bring through customs 200 cigarettes or 50 cigars, and 1L of spirits or 2L of lighter alcoholic beverages.

Electricity

Electricity supply is 220V to 240V/50Hz and plugs are of the British three-prong variety.

Embassies & Consulates

Most embassies or high commissions are located in Lusaka. The British high commission looks after the interests of Aussies and Kiwis as the nearest diplomatic missions for Australia and New Zealand are in Harare (Zimbabwe). Most consulates are open from 8.30am to 5pm Monday to Thursday and from 8.30am to 12.30pm Friday; visas are usually only dealt with in the mornings.

Botswanan High Commission (Map p38; ☎0211-250555; 5201 Pandit Nehru Rd, Lusaka)

Canadian High Commission (Map p38; ☎0211-250833; 5119 United Nations Ave, Lusaka)

Democratic Republic of Congo Embassy (DRC Embassy; Map p38; ☎0211-235679; 1124 Parirenyetwa Rd, Lusaka)

Dutch Embassy (Map p38; ☎0211-253819; 5208 United Nations Ave, Lusaka)

French Embassy (Map p38; ☎0211-251322; 74 Independence Ave, Cathedral Hill)

German Embassy (Map p38; ☎0211-250644; 5209 United Nations Ave)

Irish Embassy (☎0211-291298; 6663 Katima Mulilo Rd)

Kenyan High Commission (Map p38; ☎0211-250722; 5207 United Nations Ave)

Malawian High Comission (☎0211-265768; 31 Bishops Rd, Kabulonga)

Mozambican Embassy (Map p38; ☎0211-220333; 9592 Kacha Rd, off Paseli Rd, Northmead)

Namibian High Comission (☎0211-260407; 30B Mutende Rd, Woodlands)

South African High Comission (☎0211-260999; 26D Cheetah Rd, Kabulonga)

Swedish Embassy (Map p38; ☎0211-251711; Haile Selassie Ave, Lusaka)

Tanzanian High Commission (Map p38; ☎0211-253323; 5200 United Nations Ave, Lusaka)

UK High Commission (Map p38; ☎423200; http://ukinzambia.fco.gov.uk/en; 5210 Independence Ave)

US Embassy (Map p38; ☎0211-357000; www.zambia.usembassy.gov; Kabulonga Rd, Ibex Hill)

Zimbabwean High Commission (Map p38; ☎0211-254006; 11058 Haile Selassie Ave, Lusaka)

Festivals & Events

Information about these and other festivals are on the official Zambian tourism (www.zambiatourism.com) website.

» **Kusefya Pangwena** This festival is one to look out for. Kusefya Pangwena is practised by the Bemba people of northern Zambia. This program of music, drama and dance, which is held near Kasama over four days in August, commemorates the victory of the Bemba over the marauding Ngoni in the 1830s.

» **N'cwala** A Ngoni festival held near Chipata in eastern Zambia on 24 February. There's food, dance and music to celebrate the end of the rainy season and pray for a successful harvest.

» **Kuomboka Ceremony** This ceremony is one of Southern Africa's last great festivals (p80).

Food

The staple diet for Zambians is *nshima*, a thick, doughy maize porridge that's bland but filling. It's eaten with your hands and accompanied by beans or vegetables and a hot relish, and sometimes meat or fish.

Although food isn't generally a highlight of travel in Zambia, lodges and camps in and

EATING PRICE RANGES

The following price ranges refer to a standard main course. Remember that this is a guide only and prices will be considerably more in many lodges and camps in national parks.

$ less than ZMW30

$$ ZMW30 to ZMW70

$$$ more than ZMW70

around the national parks usually offer the highest standards of culinary options. The opportunity to taste local game is perhaps the standout; kudu is very good.

The local beer is Mosi. You may also come across the discarded plastic sachets of *tujilijili* (a strong home brewed alcohol). The manufacturing and importation of *tujilijili* was declared illegal in 2012. Nevertheless, a thriving business in Malawi supplies Zambian drinkers.

Gay & Lesbian Travellers

Male homosexual activity is illegal in Zambia. Lesbian activity is not illegal but that's only due to it not being recognised. In traditional African society, same-sex relationships are a cultural taboo, so most Zambians are very conservative in their attitudes towards gays and lesbians, and homosexuality is rarely discussed sensibly in public. In Zambia, public displays of affection, while possibly not being illegal, are insensitive to local attitudes and are very much frowned upon, whatever your orientation.

Internet Access

Zamnet is the country's largest internet service provider. Internet centres are in Lusaka, Livingstone, and ones in the bigger towns such as Mongu and Ndola are spreading. Access at internet centres is cheap, costing about ZMW0.12 to ZMW0.20 per minute. The speed and reliability of connections vary.

Wireless is becoming more common, particularly as many accommodation places outside of the national parks are set up for business folk and conferences. Travelling with a laptop that has wireless connectivity can be useful, even in remote towns. In Lusaka, look for the 'I Spot' zones, which can be found at accommodation and eating places; the quality of these connections will vary.

Keep in mind that when we've listed wi-fi under specific Sleeping reviews, it can either mean it's free or guests pay a fee; it's also likely to only be available in a small area around the lobby and usually not in rooms.

Maps

The following are available at bookshops in Lusaka.

» The German *Zambia Road Map* by Ilona Hupe Verlag is currently the best available map for touring around Zambia – it shows petrol stations and important wildlife areas.

» Globetrotter's *Zambia and Victoria Falls* map is also easy to find; it includes regional and national park insets.

» *Street Guide Lusaka and Livingstone* has blow-ups of the two cities in book form.

» Self-drivers should check out **Tracks4Africa** (www.tracks4africa.com), a highly detailed downloadable GPS system.

Money

Legislation was passed in 2012 that revalued Zambia's currency; it has also prohibited any other currency from being accepted as a form of payment. As of 1 January 2013 three zeros were removed from every bank note denomination and the unit of currency changed from ZK to ZMW; eg ZK90,000 is now ZMW90. Every bank and ATM changed over to the new system on the first of January.

While tourist-oriented places might still quote prices in US dollars on websites and in promotional materials, you must by law pay in Zambian kwacha (except for international airfares, some organised tours and visas). This includes national parks, domestic flights, restaurants, etc.

CASH & ATMS

In the cities and larger towns, you can easily change cash (no commission; photo ID required) at branches of Barclays Bank, FNB, Standard Chartered Bank and Zanaco. We've received reports that many banks, including at least one at the airport, won't accept US dollars issued before 2000. You can obtain cash (kwacha) at ATMs at Barclays Bank, Stanbic and Standard Chartered banks in the cities and larger towns.

CREDIT CARDS

Some shops, restaurants and better hotels/lodges accept major credit cards. Visa is the most readily recognised, Mastercard less so and Amex even lesser. A surcharge of 4% to 7% may be added to your bill if you pay with a credit card.

It's also worth noting that payment by credit card requires a PIN to authorise the transaction; many North American tourists might not know theirs.

MONEYCHANGERS

The best currencies to take to Zambia (in order of preference) are US dollars, UK pounds, South African rands and Euros; the currencies of most neighbouring countries are worthless in Zambia, except at the relevant borders. The exception is Botswanan pula, which can also be exchanged in Lusaka.

Foreign-exchange offices – almost always called bureau de change – are easy to find in all cities and larger towns. Rates aren't significantly better than banks.

There is no black market. You might get a few kwacha more by changing money on the street, but it's illegal and there is a chance that you'll be ripped off, robbed or set up for some sort of scam. Moneychangers at the borders are more or less legitimate, but may take (slight) advantage of your ignorance about the current exchange rates. If you can't change cash at a bank or bureau de change, try a hotel or a shop.

TIPPING

While most restaurants add a 10% service charge, rarely does it actually get into the pockets of waiters; therefore, you may choose to tip the waiter directly. The top-end lodges and camps often provide separate envelopes for staff and guides if guests should wish to tip.

Public Holidays

During public holidays, most businesses and government offices are closed.

New Year's Day 1 January

Youth Day 2nd Monday in March

Easter March/April

Labour/Workers' Day 1 May

Africa (Freedom) Day 25 May

Heroes' Day 1st Monday in July

Unity Day 1st Tuesday in July

Farmers' Day 1st Monday in August

Independence Day 24 October

Christmas Day 25 December

Boxing Day 26 December

Safe Travel

Zambia is generally very safe, but in the cities and tourist areas there is always a chance of being targeted by muggers or con artists. As always, you can reduce the risk considerably by being sensible. In Zambia, thieves are known as *kabwalalas*.

For as long as the seemingly endless civil strife continues in the Democratic Republic of the Congo (Zaïre), avoid any areas along the Zambia–Congo border, especially around Lake Mweru. Foreign embassies in Zambia warn of landmines (left over from the Rhodesian civil war) in the Sinazongwe area on the shores of Lake Kariba. Avoid trekking off the beaten track in this area.

PRACTICALITIES

Newspapers *Daily Times* (www.times.co.zm) and *Daily Mail* (www.daily-mail.co.zm) are dull, government-controlled rags. The columnists at the independent *Post* (www.post-zambia.com) continuously needle the government. Published in the UK but printed in South Africa, the *Weekly Telegraph*, the *Guardian Weekly* and the *Economist* are available in Lusaka and Livingstone.

Radio Both of the Zambian National Broadcasting Corporation (ZNBC) radio stations can be heard nationwide; they play Western and African music, as well as news and chat shows in English. Radio Phoenix (89.5FM) has a call-in show called 'Let the People Talk' on Tuesdays and Fridays from 9am to 11am. MUVI TV is independently owned while ZNBC also runs the solitary government-controlled TV station, but anyone who can afford it will subscribe to South African satellite TV. BBC World Service can be heard in Lusaka (88.2FM) and Kitwe (89.1FM); Radio France Internationale (RFI) can also be heard in Lusaka.

Television Uses the PAL system.

Measures The metric system is used in Zambia.

The possession, use and trade of recreational drugs is illegal in Zambia and penalties are harsh.

Shopping

For intrepid shoppers, Zambia offers a wide range of curios and souvenirs, with different parts of the country producing distinctive localised crafts. For example, the Lozi people of western Zambia are famed for their basketry, while the Leya of Livingstone make excellent wooden carvings. The best places to buy your souvenirs are roadside stalls or curio stalls in markets. Prices here will not be fixed, and you have to bargain.

The wooden carvings are mostly representational animals and figures, or ornaments such as bowls, stools and chess-sets; quality varies immensely. As well as the conventional souvenirs, some craft-workers produce abstract or contemporary carvings; the smooth and rounded Zimbabwe-style soapstone figures are especially good.

You can buy traditional items such as gourd containers decorated with beads and cowrie shells, which originate from the Western Province. In sharp contrast are the model bikes, buses and aeroplanes made from wire – called 'jouets' in the Copperbelt (a francophone Congolese import). Simple models made by children are cheap and fun, but you can also find very intricate works, complete with opening doors and moving engine parts.

If purchasing something made from banana leaf, grass or wood such as basketry, it's best to ensure that there are no wood boring beetles living inside. One sign of infestation is if dust falls out after tapping on it several times. Freezing the item overnight should kill any bugs.

At the other end of the price market, collectors of modern art can find pieces by some of Zambia's best-known artists in galleries in Lusaka.

In shops and markets all over Zambia you can buy *chitenjes* (sheets of brightly coloured cloth that local women use as wraps, cloaks, scarves and baby carriers). They make nice souvenirs and are useful items for female travellers, especially if heading for conservative rural areas.

Telephone

Every landline in Zambia uses the area code system; you only have to dial it if you are calling outside of your area code. Remember to drop the zero if you are dialling from outside Zambia.

Almost all telecommunication services are provided by the government monopoly, Zamtel. Public phones operated by Zamtel use tokens, which are available from post offices (ZMW0.50) or local boys (ZMW1) hanging around phone booths. These tokens last three minutes but are only good for calls within Zambia. Phone booths operated by Zamtel use phone cards (ZMW5, ZMW10, ZMW20 or ZMW50) available from post offices and grocery shops. These phone cards can be used for international calls, but it's often easier to find a 'phone shop' or 'fax bureau,' from where all international calls cost about ZMW12 per minute.

International services are generally good, but reverse-charge (collect) and toll-free calls are not possible. The international access code for dialling outside of Zambia is 00, followed by the relevant country code. If you're calling Zambia from another country, the country code is 260, but drop the initial zero of the area code.

MOBILE PHONES

MTN and Airtel offer mobile (cell) phone networks. It's almost impossible to rent mobile phones in Zambia, but if you own a GSM phone, you can buy a SIM card for only around ZMW3 without a problem; this is easy to do at Lusaka Airport. You can then purchase credit in whatever denominations you need from the same company as your SIM; scratch cards range from ZMW1 to ZMW100. In Lusaka the best place to buy a cheap mobile phone is around Kalima Towers (cnr Chachacha Rd & Katunjila Rd); a basic model will cost from ZMW80 to ZMW100.

Numbers starting with 09 plus another two numbers, eg 0977, are mobile phone numbers. Mobile phone reception is getting better all the time; generally, it's very good in urban areas and surprisingly good in some rural parts of the country and patchy or non-existent in others.

Time

Zambia is two hours ahead of Greenwich Mean Time (GMT/UTC). There is no daylight saving.

Tourist Information

The regional tourist office in Livingstone is worth visiting for specific inquiries, but the main office in Lusaka is of little use.

Zambia National Tourist Board (ZNTB; www.zambiatourism.com) The official website provides links to dozens of lodges, hotels and tour agencies, but you're unlikely to recieve a reply to an email query.

Travellers with Disabilities

Although wildlife safaris are ideal for those in wheelchairs or on crutches, you'll need to be intrepid in Zambia, as there are very few facilities for the disabled – even though there are more disabled people per head of population here than in the West. It has to be said that most travellers with disabilities find travel in Zambia much easier with the assistance of a companion.

Part of the whole safari ethos in Zambia is being adaptable and flexible, so most camps and lodges in national parks have no problem catering for travellers with disabilities, provided they have some notice. Safari lodges are single storey, and getting around is fairly easy, although gaps in slatted wooden decking can easily trap a wheel or walking stick. Another great advantage at upmarket lodges is the roomy outdoor bathrooms.

In cities and towns, midrange and upmarket hotels have lifts, ramps and private bathrooms attached to the room. A few of the smart hotels in Lusaka and Livingstone have rooms with specific disabled facilities. Getting around urban areas is much harder for people with wheelchairs or walking difficulties. Footpaths (where they exist at all) are often in bad condition with cracks or damaged sections, and crossing the road can be hard because curbs don't have ramps and traffic rarely stops for pedestrians anyway.

Visas

Tourist visas are available at major borders, airports and ports, but note that you should have a Zambian visa *before* arrival if travelling by train or boat from Tanzania.

All foreign visitors – other than Southern African Development Community (SADC) passport holders who are issued visas free of charge – pay US$50 for single entry (up to one month) and US$80 for double entry (up to three months; which is good if you plan on venturing into one of the bordering countries). Applications for multiple-entry visas (US$80) must be made in advance at a Zambian embassy or high commission. If staying less than 24 hours, for example if you are visiting Livingstone from Zimbabwe, you pay only US$20.

Payment can be made in US dollars, and sometimes UK pounds. Other currencies such as euros, South African rand, Botswanan pula or Namibian dollars may be accepted at borders, but don't count on it.

Business visas can be obtained from Zambian diplomatic missions abroad, and application forms can be downloaded at www.zambiaimmigration.gov.zm.

VISAS FOR ONWARD TRAVEL

Most visas these days are available at border crossings. However, your chances of obtaining a visa for the Democratic Republic of the Congo (Zaïre) or Angola are extremely remote at borders or in Lusaka, so get it before you arrive in Zambia.

Botswana Visas on arrival valid for 30 days (and possibly up to 90 days if requested) free to passport holders from most Commonwealth countries, all EU countries, the US and countries in the Southern African Customs Union (SACU).

Malawi Most nationalities do not require a visa and are granted 30 days upon arrival. Citizens of some countires, Austria for one, must apply in advance for a single-entry visa, which costs US$150.

Mozambique Single-entry visas (US$68) are available from most land and air entry points.

Namibia Most nationalities do not require a visa and are granted 90 days upon arrival. Others need to prearrange a visa in advance.

Tanzania Visa US$50. Bring two passport photos.

Zimbabwe Visas are single/double entry US$30/45 for most nationalities, but British & Irish pay a bit extra US$55/75 (single/double). Meanwhile, Canadians pay US$75 for single visa, with no option for double entry.

VISA EXTENSIONS

» Extensions for all types of tourist visas are possible at any Department of Immigration office in any main town in Zambia. You're likely to be most successful in **Lusaka** (Cairo Rd, Memaco House) and **Livingstone** (Mosi-oa-Tunya Rd). The immigration office on Cairo Rd in Lusaka is an efficient operation.

» There's generally no queue and no fee for an additional 30 days. It's possible to seek an extension twice for a total of 90 days a year. Be aware of the expiration date of the visa; if it's a Saturday or Sunday it's best to go in on a weekday beforehand.

» If for some reason you overstay your visa, humility and politeness go a long way in dealing with Zambian authorities.

Volunteering

For information on conservation projects, see p113.

Habitat for Humanity (www.habitatzam.org.zm) Helping to build houses for the nation's poor; over 1600 houses have been built since 1984.

World Vision (www.worldvision.org) One of the bigger NGOs in Zambia with a presence for almost 30 years in many community areas including nutrition, education, healthcare, agriculture and immunisation.

Women Travellers

Women travellers in Zambia will generally not encounter gender-related problems any more than they might in other parts of the world. In fact, women travellers say that compared with North Africa, South America and many Western countries, Zambia is relatively safe and unthreatening; friendliness and generosity are encountered far more often than hostility.

Due to Zambia having a small population of people of European origin, women travellers can meet and communicate with local men – of any race – usually without being misconstrued. That's not to say that sexual harassment never happens, but local white women have done much to refute the image that females of European descent are willing to hop into bed with the first taker.

Be aware, though, that when it comes to evening entertainment, Zambia is a conservative, male-dominated society. Even in bars where women are 'allowed,' cultural conventions often dictate that you don't go in without a male companion.

Local Zambian women (like most Zambian men) are also generally friendly and approachable, once initial surprise at being greeted or addressed by a foreigner is overcome. Nevertheless, because of prevailing attitudes, it can be hard to specifically meet and talk with local women in Zambia.

Getting There & Away

ENTERING ZAMBIA

Visas are generally issued upon arrival.

A yellow fever certificate is not required before entering Zambia, but it *is* often requested by Zambian immigration officials if you have come from a country with yellow fever. A yellow fever certificate is required if you're travelling from Zambia to South Africa (although not required if you are simply in transit for another international flight). It's worth checking on this since negotiations with South Africa to drop this requirement were ongoing in late 2012. It's also worth noting that the Centers for Disease Control in the US do not recommend the vaccination for travellers to Zambia.

Air

Zambia's main international airport is in Lusaka. Some international airlines also fly to the airport at Livingstone (for Victoria Falls), Mfuwe (for South Luangwa National Park) and Ndola.

The country is increasingly well connected with direct flights to destinations outside Africa. British Airways has thrice-weekly flights from London, KLM/Air France from Amsterdam and Emirates from Dubai.

For North Americans who don't want to fly to London or Amsterdam first, **South African Airways** (www.flysaa.com) has daily direct flights from New York City to Johannesburg. From here there are regular flights to Lusaka, Ndola and Livingstone.

Zambia is also well connected with Southern Africa. **Zambezi Airlines** (☎0211-250342; www.flyzambezi.com) flies to regional destinations such as Johannesburg in South Africa

DEPARTURE TAX

The departure tax for all international flights is ZMW156. This tax is *often* included in the price of your airline ticket, but if not it must be paid at the airport (in Zambian kwacha only).

(from Lusaka and Ndola) and to Dar es Salaam in Tanzania.

Air Malawi (Map p38; ☎0211-228120; www.flyairmalawi.com; COMESA Centre, Zone B, Ground Floor, Ben Bella Road) connects Lusaka with Lilongwe and Blantyre three times a week, and with Blantyre twice a week; while **Air Zimbabwe** (www.airzimbabwe.com) flies to Harare.

It's also easy to find a flight between Nairobi (Kenya); alternatively, it's a short hop between Dar es Salaam and Lusaka. Coming from Cairo (Egypt) or Ethiopia, most flights to Southern Africa go via Nairobi.

There is also an increasing number of flights to Livingstone for Victoria Falls; South African Airways, British Airways and Kulula fly there from Johannesburg.

AIRLINES

Air Botswana (Map p38; ☎0211-255024; www.airbotswana.co.bw; Intercontinental Hotel) Flights four days a week between Lusaka and Gaborone; two are direct and two are through Kasane.

Air Malawi (Map p38; ☎0211-228120; www.flyairmalawi.com; COMESA Centre, Zone B, Ground Floor, Ben Bella Road)

Air Namibia (Map p38; ☎0211-258370; www.airnamibia.co.na; Manda Hill Shopping Centre) Direct flights between Lusaka, Livingstone and Windhoek.

Air Zimbabwe (www.airzimbabwe.com)

British Airways (www.britishairways.com)

Emirates (Map p36; www.emirates.com; Acacia Park, Arcades Shopping Centre, Great East Road, Lusaka)

Ethiopian Airlines (ET; ☎0211-236403, 0211-236402; www.flyethiopian.com) Daily flights between Addis Ababa and Lusaka.

Kenya Airways (☎0211-228886; www.kenya-airways.com; 3rd fl, Maanu Centre, Chikwa Rd) Daily flights between Lusaka and Nairobi (Kenya), Dar es Salaam (Tanzania) and Lilongwe (Malawi.).

KLM/Air France (www.klm.com)

Kulula (www.kulula.com) South African airline offering direct flights between Livingstone and Johannesburg, Cape Town and Durban.

Precision Air (Map p38; www.precisionairtz.com; Intercontinental Hotel) Wednesday, Friday and Sunday departures to Dar es Salaam (Tanzania; two hours).

South African Airlink (☎0211-254350; www.saairlink.co.za) Daily flights between Lusaka, Livingstone and Ndola and Johannesburg (South Africa).

South African Airways (www.flysaa.com; Southern Sun Ridgeway)

Zambezi Airlines (☎0211-250342; www.flyzambezi.com) Connects Lusaka to Ndola, Kitwe, Solwezi and Chipata as well as Dar es Salaam (Tanzania), Harare (Zimbabwe) and Johannesburg (South Africa). Also direct flights between Livingstone and Cape Town (South Africa); Ndola and Lubumbashi (DRC).

Land

BORDER CROSSINGS

Zambia shares borders with eight countries, so there's a huge number of crossing points. Most are open daily from 6am to 6pm; the border closes at 8pm at Victoria Falls and at 7pm at Chirundu. Before you leave the Zambian side ensure that you have enough currency of whatever country you're travelling to or South African rand to pay for your visa (if you require one).

If you are crossing borders in your own vehicle, you need a free Temporary Export Permit (TEP), which is obtained at the border – make sure to retain a copy of this form after it's stamped. Before crossing be sure to inform your rental car company in order to guarantee you have all the required documents in order. You'll likely need to purchase insurance, sometimes called COMESA. It can be bought either at the Zambian border crossings or just after you've gone through formalities on the other country's side (for Zimbabwe it'll cost around ZMW150). For Zimbabwe you also need an Interpol Certificate (good for three months), which can be obtained from the police in Zambia, and a typed 'Permission to Drive' document, which basically states that the vehicle's owner knows you're driving their car.

You also need to request a Temporary Import Permit (TIP), and pay for it. Retain the document and payment receipt for when re-entering Zambia.

Heading back into Zambia you'll might get hassled from Zambians trying to sell you insurance – you don't need this if you're in a Zambian-registered vehicle.

Note also that Zambia charges a carbon tax for non-Zambian registered vehicles; it's usually about ZMW150 to ZMW200 per vehicle.

CLIMATE CHANGE & TRAVEL

Every form of transport that relies on carbon-based fuel generates CO_2, the main cause of human-induced climate change. Modern travel is dependent on aeroplanes, which might use less fuel per kilometre per person than most cars but travel much greater distances. The altitude at which aircraft emit gases (including CO_2) and particles also contributes to their climate change impact. Many websites offer 'carbon calculators' that allow people to estimate the carbon emissions generated by their journey and, for those who wish to do so, to offset the impact of the greenhouse gases emitted with contributions to portfolios of climate-friendly initiatives throughout the world. Lonely Planet offsets the carbon footprint of all staff and author travel.

Botswana

Zambia and Botswana share what is probably the world's shortest international boundary: 750m across the Zambezi River at Kazungula. The pontoon ferry (ZMW40 for foot passengers, ZMW30/40 for an ordinary/large Zambian-registered vehicle) across the Zambezi is 65km west of Livingstone and 11km south of the main road between Livingstone and Sesheke. There are one or two buses (ZMW20, 35 minutes) here daily from Livingstone, departing from Nakatindi Rd in the morning.

US dollars and other currencies are not accepted at the Botswanan border crossing.

A quicker and more comfortable (but more expensive) way to reach Botswana from Zambia is to cross from Livingstone to Victoria Falls (in Zimbabwe), from where shuttle buses head to Kasane.

Buses to Gaborone, via Kasane and Francistown, leave several days a week from Lusaka.

Democratic Republic of the Congo (DRC, Zaïre)

This border is not for the faint hearted. DRC visas are only available to Zambian residents and this rule is strictly enforced unless you can get a letter of invitation from the Congolese government. The most convenient border to use connects Chingola in the Copperbelt with Lubumbashi in Katanga Province, via the border towns of Chililabombwe (Zambia) and Kasumbalesa (DRC). Charter taxis cost about ZMW100 from Chingola to the border. Crossing into the DRC can take a lot of time or money, so it is wise to hook up with some mining consultants or UN workers rather than venturing alone. Avoid local touts who probably want to scam you, but it is hard to avoid the official scams if the immigration officials take an interest in you. From the border to Lubumbashi a taxi is about US$50, but travelling in the other direction, the Lubumbashi taxi drivers will usually ask for US$75 as a 'security' bonus for venturing out of the city.

Malawi

Most foreigners use the border at Mchinji, 30km southeast of Chipata, because it's along the road between Lusaka and Lilongwe. One figure to keep in mind – it's only 287km from Mfuwe to Lilongwe. Note that visas into Malawi are free for most nationalities.

Further north is another border crossing at Nakonde. Going either way on public transport is extremely difficult; you really need your own wheels.

Mozambique

The main border is between Mlolo (Zambia) and fairly remote Cassacatiza (Mozambique), but most travellers choose to reach Mozambique through Malawi. There is no public transport between the two countries.

Namibia

The only border is at Sesheke (Zambia), on the northern and southern bank of the Zambezi, while the Namibian border is at Wenela near Katima Mulilo. There are bus services to Sesheke from Lusaka and Livingstone respectively; it's 200km west of the latter.

From the Namibian side, it's a 5km walk to Katima Mulilo, from where minibuses depart for other parts of Namibia.

Alternatively, cross from Livingstone to Victoria Falls (in Zimbabwe) and travel onwards from there.

South Africa

There is no border between Zambia and South Africa, but several buses travel daily between Johannesburg and Lusaka via Harare and Masvingo in Zimbabwe. Make sure you have a Zimbabwean visa (if you need one before arrival) and a yellow fever certificate for entering South Africa (and, possibly, Zimbabwe).

Tanzania

The main border by road, and the only crossing by train, is between Nakonde (Zambia) and Tunduma (Tanzania). Bus services run from Lusaka to Nakonde (ZMW140, 15 hours, 3pm) and on to Mbeya. Alternatively, walk across the border from Nakonde, and take a minibus from Tunduma to Mbeya in Tanzania.

Zimbabwe

There are three easy crossings: at Chirundu, along the road between Lusaka and Harare; between Siavonga (Zambia) and Kariba (Zimbabwe), about 50km upstream from Chirundu; and the easiest and most common of all, between Livingstone (Zambia) and Victoria Falls town (Zimbabwe). Plenty of buses travel every day between Lusaka and Harare, via Chirundu. If traveling from Siavonga, take a minibus or charter a car to the border, and walk (or take a shared taxi) across the Kariba Dam to Kariba, from where buses leave daily to Harare.

Getting Around

Air

The main domestic airports are at Lusaka, Livingstone, Ndola, Kitwe, Mfuwe, Kasama and Kasaba Bay. Dozens of minor airstrips, most notably those in the Lower Zambezi National Park (Proflight flies here regularly) and North Luangwa National Park, cater for chartered planes.

The departure tax for domestic flights is ZMW58. As of recently, Proflight tickets include this tax in the price, but for other flights it must be paid at the airport in Zambian kwacha. An additional 'infrastructure' tax applied to every ticket was passed and then subsequently cancelled in October 2012 – it may be reinstated in the future.

AIRLINES

Proflight (www.proflight-zambia.com) is the only domestic airline offering regularly scheduled flights connecting Lusaka to Chipata, Livingstone (for Victoria Falls), Lower Zambezi (Jeki and Royal airstrips), Mfuwe (for South Luangwa National Park), Ndola (also flies direct from here to Kasama) and Solwezi. The fare class with the most flexibility (in case of change of travel plans) is the most expensive. A one-way ticket from Lusaka to Mfuwe (one hour 20 minutes) ranges from ZMW810 to ZMW1500; to Jeki, from ZMW470 to ZMW1000; to Livingstone, from ZMW750 to ZMW1400. Visa,

TRAIN TO TANZANIA

Although travelling by bus to the Tanzanian border is quicker, the train is a better alternative.

The Tazara railway company usually runs two international trains per week in each direction between Kapiri Mposhi (207km north of Lusaka) and Dar es Salaam (Tanzania). The 'express train' leaves Kapiri Mposhi at approximately 3pm on Tuesdays and Fridays. The journey time is, well, anywhere between two to five days. The fares on the express train are ZMW238/200 in 1st/2nd class (both are sleeping compartments). A discount of 50% is possible with a student card.

Tickets are available on the spot at the New Kapiri Mposhi (Tazara) train station in Kapiri Mposhi and up to three days in advance from **Tazara House** (Map p38; ☎0211-222280; Independence Ave, Lusaka). If there are no more seats left at the Lusaka office, don't despair because we've heard from travellers who easily bought tickets at Kapiri Mposhi, and upgraded from one class to another while on board.

It's prudent to get a Tanzanian visa in Lusaka (or elsewhere) before you board the train; at least, contact the Tanzanian high commission in Lusaka about getting a Tanzanian visa on the train or at the border. You can change money on the train but take care because these guys are sharks.

Mastercard, Amex and Paypal are accepted for online payments.

On the Livingstone and Ndola routes, which use larger planes, passengers can check one or two bags totalling 23kg; on all other flights the limit is only 15kg (additional fees applied to excess weight). Carry-on baggage on all flights is limited to 5kg. Keep these weights in mind when transferring from another flight.

There are plenty of charter-flight companies (Proflight also does charters) catering primarily for guests staying at upmarket lodges/camps in national parks. Flights only leave with a minimum number of prebooked passengers and fares are always high, but it's sometimes worth looking around for a last-minute, stand-by flight. Two of the companies worth considering are the following:

Pro Charter (☎0974 250110; www.avocet-charters.com)

Royal Air Charters (☎0971 251493; www.royalaircharters.com)

Bicycle

If you plan on cycling around Zambia, do realise that Zambian drivers tend not to give you any room, even if there is no vehicle in the oncoming lane. Save being hit by a car, it is safe to cycle Zambia. Mountain biking is rapidly becoming popular in and around Lusaka.

Bus & Minibus

Distances are long, buses are often slow and many roads are badly potholed, so travelling around Zambia by bus and minibus can exhaust even the hardiest of travellers.

All main routes are served by ordinary public buses, which either run on a fill-up-and-go basis or have fixed departures (these are called 'time buses'). 'Express buses' are faster – often terrifyingly so – and stop less, but cost about 15% more. In addition, several private companies run comfortable European-style express buses along the major routes, eg between Lusaka and Livingstone, Lusaka and Chipata, and Lusaka and the Copperbelt region. These fares cost about 25% more than the ordinary bus fares and are well worth the extra kwacha. Tickets for these buses can often be bought the day before. There are also express buses zipping around the country.

A few general tips to keep in mind. Even on buses with air-conditioning – and it very often doesn't work – try to sit on the side of the bus opposite to the sun. Also, avoid seats near the speakers, which can be turned up to unbearably high volume.

Many routes are also served by minibuses, which only leave when full – so full that you might lose all feeling in one butt cheek. Fares can be more or less the same as ordinary buses. In remote areas the only public transport is often a truck or pick-up.

Car & Motorcycle

BRINGING YOUR OWN VEHICLE

If you're driving into Zambia in a rented or privately owned car or motorcycle, you will need a carnet; if you don't have one, a free Customs Importation Permit will be issued to you at major borders instead. You'll also be charged a carbon tax if it's a non-Zambian registered vehicle, which just means a bit more paperwork and ZMW150 to ZMW200 at the border, depending on the size of your car.

Compulsory third-party insurance for Zambia is available at major borders (or the nearest large towns). It is strongly advised to carry insurance from your own country on top of your Zambian policy.

While it is certainly possible to get around Zambia by car or motorbike, many sealed roads are in bad condition and the dirt roads can range from shocking to impassable, particularly after the rains. If you haven't driven in Africa before, this is not the best place to start. We strongly recommend that you hire a 4WD if driving anywhere outside Lusaka, and certainly if you're heading to any of the national parks or other wilderness areas. Wearing a seat belt in the front seat is compulsory.

Self-drivers should seriously consider purchasing the in-car GPS navigation system **Tracks4Africa** (www.tracks4africa.co.za), which even shows petrol stations.

DRIVING LICENCE

Foreign licences are fine as long as they are in English, and it doesn't hurt to carry an international driver's licence (also in English).

FUEL & SPARE PARTS

Diesel costs around ZMW8 per litre and petrol ZMW8.15. Shortages do occur from time to time. When petrol stations are out of gas it's not infrequently the case that station attendants are in cahoots with black market dealers selling the petrol nearby at inflated prices. Distances between towns with filling stations are great and fuel is not always available, so fill the tank at every opportunity.

It is advisable to carry at least one spare wheel, as well as a filled jerry can. If you need spare parts, the easiest (and cheapest) vehicle parts to find are those of Toyota and Nissan.

HIRE

Cars can be hired from international and Zambian-owned companies in Lusaka, Livingstone, Kitwe and Ndola, but renting is very expensive. **Avis** (Map p38; ☎Lusaka 0211-251652, airport 0211-271303; www.avis.com; Southern Sun Ridgeway, cnr Church Rd & Independence Ave) and **Europcar/Voyagers** (☎0212-620314; www.europcarzambia.com) are at Lusaka airport.

Europcar/Voyagers will charge you from ZMW365 per day for the smallest vehicle, plus ZMW2 per kilometre and this doesn't even include 16% VAT, petrol or insurance. Other companies, such as **Hemingways** (☎320996; www.hemingwayszambia.com; Mosi-oa-Tunya Rd), **4x4 Hire Africa** (☎in South Africa 721-791 3904; www.4x4hire.co.za) and **Limo Car Hire** (☎0211-278628; www.limohire-zambia.com) rent out Toyota Hiluxes and old-school Land Rover vehicles respectively, unequipped or fully decked out with everything you would need for a trip to the bush (including rooftop tents!), with prices for an unequipped vehicle starting at about ZMW680 per day. The best thing about these companies is that vehicles come with unlimited kilometres and you can take them across borders.

Most companies insist that drivers are at least 23 years old and have held a licence for at least five years.

ROAD CONDITIONS

» Many main stretches of sealed road are OK, but beware of the occasional pothole.
» Sections of main highway can be in a pretty bad way and rapidly deteriorating with gaping potholes, ridges, dips and very narrow sections that drop steeply off the side into loose gravel. Be wary and alert at all times, and seek out information about road conditions.
» Gravel roads vary a lot from pretty good to pretty terrible.
» Road conditions are probably at their worst soon after the end of the wet season (April, May, June) when many dirt and gravel roads have been washed away or seriously damaged – this is especially the case in and around national parks.

ROAD RULES

» Speed limits in and around cities are enforced, but on the open road buses and Land Cruisers fly at speeds of 140kph to 160kph.
» If you break down, you must place an orange triangle about 6m in front of and behind the vehicle.
» At police checkposts (which are very common) smile, say good morning/ afternoon, be very polite and take off your sunglasses. A little respect makes a huge difference to the way you'll be treated. Mostly you'll be met with a smile, perhaps asked curiously where you're from, and waved through without a problem.

Hitching

As in any other part of the world, hitching is never entirely safe. Despite this general warning, hitching is a common way to get around Zambia. Some drivers, particularly expats, may offer you free lifts, but you should expect to pay for rides with local drivers (normally about the same as the bus fare, depending on the comfort of the vehicle). In such cases, agree on a price beforehand.

Taxis

Often the most convenient and comfortable way of getting around, especially in the cities. They have no meters, so rates are negotiable.

 Tours

Tours and safaris around Zambia invariably focus on the national parks. Since many of these parks are hard to visit without a vehicle, joining a tour might be your only option anyway. Budget-priced operators run scheduled trips, or arrange things on the spot (with enough passengers), and can often be booked through a backpackers – try Lusaka Backpackers in Lusaka or Jollyboys Backpackers in Livingstone. Upmarket companies prefer to take bookings in advance, directly or through an agent in Zambia, South Africa or your home country.

Most Zambian tour operators are based in Lusaka and Livingstone. Several companies in Lilongwe, Malawi, may also offer tours to South Luangwa National Park. There are travel agents in Lusaka who can often organise tours and budget tours of South Luangwa.

Barefoot Safaris (☎0211-707 346; www.barefoot-safaris.com) Small group safaris, self-drive, trekking and sailing; covers Zambia, Malawi and surrounding countries.

Kiboko Safaris (☎in Mfuwe 0216-246111; www.kiboko-safaris.com) Excellent budget camping and lodge safaris in Malawi and South Luangwa, Zambia. Also luxury safaris in Malawi.

Robin Pope Safaris (www.robinpopesafaris.net) One of the most-respected operators in Zambia offering innovative and intrepid tours to destinations such as Kafue and Liuwa Plain, including mobile walking safaris.

Remote Africa Safaris (www.remoteafrica.com) Excellent small operator running safaris in the Luangwa Valley.

Wilderness Safaris (www.wilderness-safaris.com) Offers a range of tours in all Southern African countries including Zambia and Malawi. In addition to the standard luxury lodge-based tours in remote areas, it offers fly-in safaris and activity-based trips.

Land & Lake Safaris (www.landlake.net) Based in Lilongwe, Malawi, this operator has combined Malawi/Zambia safaris, as well as trips around South and North Luangwa and Victoria Falls. Good budget options available.

Train

The Tazara trains between Kapiri Mposhi and Dar es Salaam in Tanzania can also be used for travelling to/from northern Zambia. While the Lusaka–Kitwe service does stop at Kapiri Mposhi, the Lusaka–Kitwe and Tazara trains are not timed to connect with each other, and the domestic and international train terminals are 2km apart.

Zambia's only other railway services are the 'ordinary trains' between Lusaka and Kitwe, via Kapiri Mposhi and Ndola, and the 'express trains' running between Lusaka and Livingstone.

Domestic trains are unreliable and slow, so buses are always better. Conditions on domestic trains generally range from slightly dilapidated to ready-for-scrap. Most compartments have no lights or locks, so take a torch and something to secure the door at night.

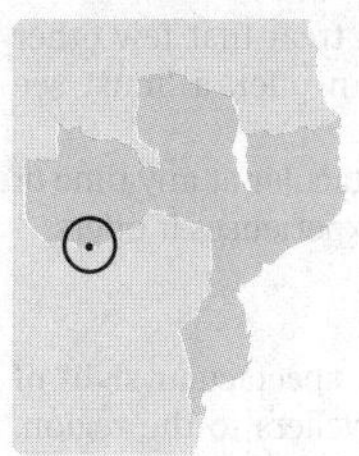

Victoria Falls

Includes »

Best Places to Eat

» Cafe Zambezi (p136)

» In Da Belly (p140)

» Olga's Italian Corner (p136)

» Mama Africa (p141)

Best Places to Stay

» Victoria Falls Hotel (p138)

» Elephant Camp (p140)

» Jollyboys Backpackers (p133)

» Stanley Safari Lodge (p135)

Why Go?

Taking its place alongside the Pyramids and the Serengeti, Victoria Falls (*Mosi-oa-Tunya* – the 'smoke that thunders') is one of Africa's original blockbusters. And although Zimbabwe and Zambia share it, Victoria Falls is a place all of its own.

As a magnet for tourists of all descriptions – backpackers, tour groups, thrill seekers, families, honeymooners – Vic Falls is one of the earth's great spectacles. View it directly as a raging mile-long curtain of water, in all its glory, from a helicopter ride or peek precariously over its edge from Devil's Pools; the sheer power and force of the falls is something that simply does not disappoint.

Whether you're here purely to take in the sight of a natural wonder of the world, or for a serious hit of adrenaline via rafting or bungee jumping into the Zambezi, Victoria Falls is a place where you're sure to tick off numerous items from that bucket list.

When to Go

There are two main reasons to go to Victoria Falls – to view the falls and to experience the outdoor activities – and each has its season.

July to December is the season for white-water rafting, especially August for hardcore rapids.

From February to June don't forget your raincoat as you'll experience the falls at their full force.

From July to September You'll get the best views of the falls, combined with lovely weather and all activities to keep you busy.

Seventh Natural Wonder of the World

Victoria Falls is the largest, most beautiful and most majestic waterfall on the planet, and is the Seventh Natural Wonder of the World as well as being a UNESCO World Heritage Site. A trip to Southern Africa would not be complete without visiting this unforgettable place.

One million litres of water fall – per second – down a 108m drop along a 1.7km wide strip in the Zambezi Gorge; an awesome sight. Victoria Falls can be seen, heard, tasted and touched: it is a treat that few other places in the world can offer, a 'must see before you die' spot.

Victoria Falls is spectacular at any time of year, yet varies in the experiences it offers.

Activities

While of course it's the spectacular sight of Vic Falls that lures travellers to the region, the astonishing amount of activities to do here is what makes them hang around. White-water rafting, bungee jumping, taking a chopper ride over the falls, walking with rhinos: Vic Falls is well and truly estab-

Victoria Falls

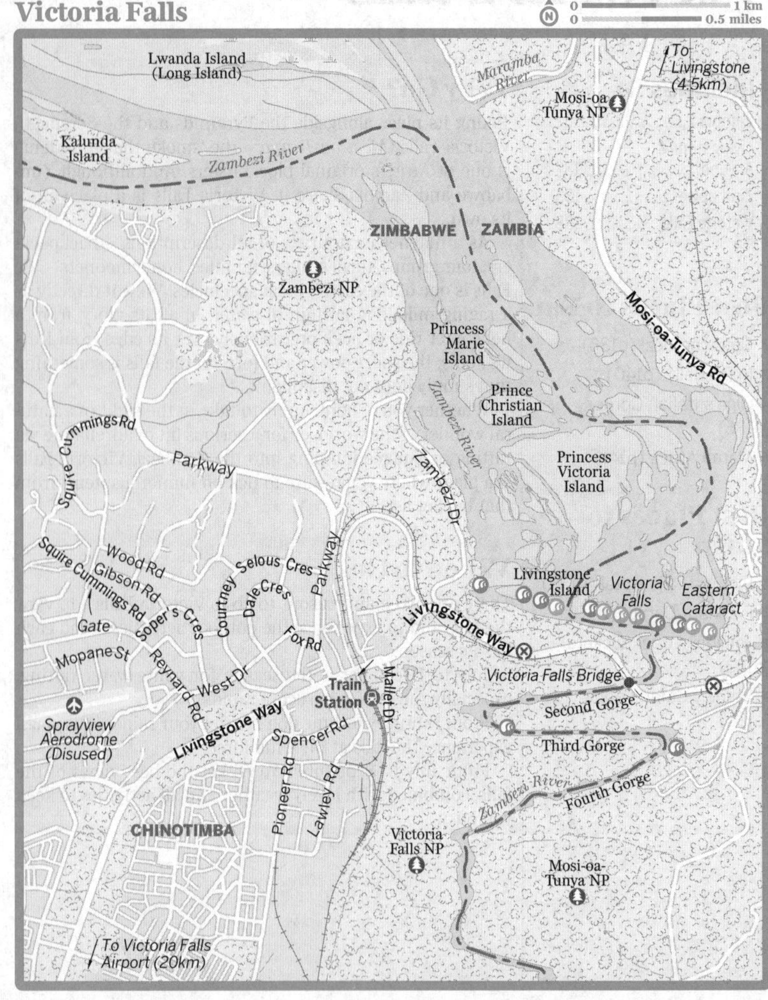

THE FALLS VIEWING SEASON

Though spectacular at any time of year, the falls has a wet and dry season and each brings a distinct experience.

When the river is higher and the falls fuller it's the Wet, and when the river is lower and the falls aren't smothered in spray it's the Dry. Broadly speaking, you can expect the following conditions during the year:

January to April The beginning of the rainy season sees the falls begin their transitional period from low to high water, which should give you decent views, combined with experiencing its famous spray.

May to June Don't forget your raincoat, as you're gonna get drenched! While the falls will be hard to see through the mist, it'll give you a true sense of its power as 500 million litres of water plummets over the edge. The mist during this time can be seen from 50kms away. If you want views, don't despair, this is the best time for aerial views with a chopper flight taking you up and over this incredible sight.

July to October The most popular time to visit, as the mist dissipates to unveil the best views and photography options from directly across the falls, while the volume maintains its rage to give you an idea of its sheer force.

November to January The least popular time to visit, as temperatures rise and the falls are at their lowest flow. But they're still impressive nevertheless, as the curtain of water divides into sections. The advantage of this time of year is you're able to swim right up to the edge of Devil's Pool on the Zambian side.

lished as one of the world's premier adventure destinations.

To get the best value out of your time here, look into packages which combine various adrenaline leaps, slides and swings for around US$125. Confirm any extra costs such as park or visa fees at the time of booking.

Costs are fairly standard across the board and activities can be organised through accommodation providers and tour operators.

Abseiling

Strap on a helmet, grab a rope and spend the day rappelling down the 54m sheer-drop cliff face for US$40.

Birdwatching

Twitchers will want to bring binoculars to check out 470 species of birds that inhabit the region, including Schalow's turaco, the African finfoot and half-collared kingfisher. Spot them on foot in the parks or on a canoe trip along the Zambezi.

Bungee Jumping & Swings

The third-highest bungee in the world (111m), this famous jump is from atop the iconic Victoria Falls bridge. It's a long way down, but man, it's a lot of fun. It costs US$125 per person.

Otherwise there's the bridge swing where you jump feet first, and free fall for four seconds; you'll end up swinging the right way up, not upside down. There are two main spots, one right off the Victoria Falls Bridge, and the other a bit further along the Batoka Gorge. Costs for single/tandem are US$125/195.

Combine bungee with a bridge swing and bridge slide, and it'll cost US$160.

Canoeing & Kayaking

On the Zambian side, take on the Zambezi's raging rapids in an inflatable kayak on a full-day trip (US$155), or learn to eskimo roll by signing up for half-/one-/three-day courses for US$82/145/412.

Otherwise there are peaceful canoe trips along the Upper Zambezi River on two-person inflatable canoes for US$125 or even more relaxed three-hour guided sunset trips for US$60 including wine and beer. Overnight jaunts cost US$200, with longer trips available.

Cultural Activities

Spend an evening by a campfire drumming under the Southern African sky, which includes a traditional meal, for US$25 for the hour. You can arrange to watch and participate in traditional dance for US$40.

Fishing

Grab a rod and cruise out to the Zambezi for the opportunity to reel in a mighty tiger fish, for around US$125 for a half day, and

ZIM OR ZAM?

Victoria Falls straddles the border between Zimbabwe and Zambia, and is easily accessible from both countries. However, the big question for most travellers is: do I visit the falls from the town of Victoria Falls, Zimbabwe, or from Livingstone, Zambia? The answer is simple: visit the falls from both sides and, if possible, stay in both towns.

From the Zimbabwean side you're further from the falls, though the overall views are better. From the Zambian side, for daring souls you can literally stand on top of the falls from Devil's Pool, though from here your perspective is narrowed.

The town of Victoria Falls was built for tourists, so it's easily walkable and located right next to the entrance to the Falls. It has a natural African bush beauty.

Livingstone is an attractive town with a relaxed ambience and a proud, historic air. Since the town of Victoria Falls was the main tourist centre for so many years, Livingstone feels more authentic, perhaps because locals earn their livelihood through means other than tourism. Livingstone is bustling with travellers year round, though the town is fairly spread out, and is located 11km from the falls.

US$255 for a full day, which includes beer, fuel and transfers. Get in touch with **Angle Zambia** (☎327489; www.zambezifishing.com) for more info.

Horse Riding

Indulge in a bit of wildlife spotting from horseback along the Zambezi. Rides for 2½ hours cost around $US90, and full-day trips for experienced riders are US$145.

Jet Boats

Power straight into whirlpools! This hair-raising trip costs US$97, and is combined with a cable-car ride down into the Batoka Gorge.

Quad biking

Discover the spectacular landscape around Livingstone, Zambia and the Batoka Gorge, spotting wildlife as you go on all-terrain quad bikes. Trips vary from ecotrail riding at Batoka Land to longer-range cultural trips in the African bush. Trips are 1 hour (US$80) or 2½ hours (US$150).

Rafting

This is one of the best white-water rafting destinations in the world, both for experienced rafters and newbies. Rafting can be done on either side of the Zambezi, in Zim or Zam, and fills up between mid-February and July, high-water season. In the river below Vic Falls you'll find Grade 5 rapids – very long with huge drops and big kicks, and not for the faint-hearted. In high-water season, day trips move downstream from rapids 11 to 24, covering a distance of around 18km.

Low-water (open) season is between July and mid-February and is considered the best time for rafting. Day trips run between rapids 1 and 19, covering a distance of around 25km. The river will usually close for its 'off season' around April/May, depending on the rain pattern for the year.

Half-/full-day trips cost about US$120/130. Overnight and multiday jaunts can also be arranged.

Other options include **riverboarding**, which is basically lying on a boogie board and careering down the rapids for US$135/150 for a half/full day. The best time of year for riverboarding is February to June. A rafting/riverboarding combo is available, US$165.

River Cruises

River cruises along the Zambezi range from civilised jaunts on the grand *African Queen* to all-you-can-drink sunset booze cruises. Prices range from US$30 to US$60. Great for spotting wildlife, though some tourists get just as much enjoyment out of the bottomless drinks. Highly recommended.

Scenic Flights

Just when you thought the falls couldn't get any more spectacular, discover the 'flight of angels' helicopter ride that flies you right by the drama for the undisputed best views available. Rides aren't cheap, but it's worth it. **Zambezi Helicopter Company** (www.shearwatervictoriafalls.com/helicopters; flights 13/25 mins US$130/250, plus US$10 park entry fee) in Zimbabwe and **United Air Charter** (☎213

323095; www.uaczam.com; Baobab Ridge, Livingstone) in Zambia both offer flights.

Another option is motorised hang-gliders, which also offer fabulous aerial views, and the pilot will take pictures for you with a camera fixed to the wing. It costs US$140 for 15 minutes over the falls.

Steam-train Journeys

To take in the romance of yesteryear, book yourself a ride on a historical steam train. On the Zimbabwe side there is the 1953 class 14A Garratt steam train through **Victoria Falls Steam Train Co** (☎13 42912; www.steamtraincompany.com; incl drinks US$40, incl dinner from US$75), that will take you over the iconic bridge at sunset or through the Zambezi National Park with either a full dinner or gourmet canapes and unlimited drinks. Even if you're not booked on a trip it's worth getting along to the station to watch the incredible drama of its departure. There are also daily vintage tram trips (one way/return US$15/30) that head over the bridge and which also have a drinks and canapes option (US$40).

In Zambia the **Royal Livingstone Express** (☎213 323232; www.royal-livingstone-express.com; Mosi-oa-Tunya Rd, Livingstone; incl dinner & drinks US$170; ⊙Wed & Sat) takes you on a 3½-hour ride including five-course dinner and drinks on a 1922 10th-class steam engine that will chug you through Mosi-oa-Tunya National Park on plush leather couches.

Wildlife Safaris

There are plenty of options for wildlife watching in the area, both in the nearby national parks and private game reserves, or further afield. Both guided walks and jeep safaris are available in the parks on both sides of the border. At **Mosi-oa-Tunya Game Park** (wildlife sanctuary admission US$10; ⊙wildlife sanctuary 6am-6pm) in Zambia, there's a chance to see white rhinos, while the Zambezi National Park in Zimbabwe has a small population of lions. Walks cost around US$70, and drives US$50 to US$90. There are also dusk, dawn or night wildlife drives (US$50 to US$90). River safaris (US$30) along the Zambezi River are another popular way to see various wildlife including elephants, hippos and plenty of birdlife.

Another convenient option, only 15km from Victoria Falls town, is the **Victoria Falls Private Game Reserve** (☎44471; www.shearwatervictoriafalls.com/safaris), a 4000-hectare private reserve run by Shearwaters. Here you can track the Big Five on a game drive (US$90), where apparently you stand a 97% (to be precise) chance of encountering a black rhino.

You can travel further afield, with operators arranging day trips to Chobe National Park in Botswana for US$170 (excluding visas). It's only a one-hour drive from Victoria Falls, and includes a breakfast boat cruise, a game drive in Chobe National Park, lunch and transfer back to Victoria Falls by 5pm. Wildlife viewing is excellent: lions, elephants, wild dogs, cheetahs, buffaloes and plenty of antelopes.

Hwange National Park (admission per day US$15; ⊙about 6am-6pm) in Zimbabwe is the other option, with one of the largest number of elephants in the world. A day trip will cost around US$250.

Zipline & Slides

Glide at 106km/h along a zipline (single/tandem US$66/105), or soar like a superhero from one country to another (from Zim to Zam) on the 'bridge slide' as you whiz over Batoka Gorge (single/tandem US$35/50). Other similar options are flying-fox rides (US$40).

Information

Tourist Information

Hands down the best independent advice is from Backpackers Bazaar (p142) in the town of Victoria Falls, run by the passionate owner, Joy, who is a wealth of all info and advice for Vic Falls and beyond. In Livingstone, the folks at Jollyboys Backpackers (p133) are also extremely knowledgeable on all the latest happenings. Both are good places to book activities and onward travel.

Travel & Adventure Companies

With activities and prices standardised across the board, all bookings can conveniently be arranged through backpacker accommodation and big hotels.

You can also go directly to the tour operators. The main ones in Zimbabwe are **Wild Horizons** (☎0712-213721, 13 42013; www.wildhorizons.co.za; 310 Parkway Dr) and **Shearwater** (☎13 44471; www.shearwatervictoriafalls.com; Parkway Dr). In Zambia try **Safari Par Excellence** (☎213 320606; www.safpar.net) and **Livingstone's Adventure** (☎213 323587; www.livingstonesadventure.com) both in Livingstone. All cover activities on either side.

VISAS

You will need a visa to cross sides between Zim and Zam. These are available at the border crossings, open from around 7am to 10pm. Note that you can't get multi-entry visas at these crossing; in most cases you need to apply at the embassy in your home country before travelling.

Crossing into Zambia, a day visit costs US$20 for 24 hours, a single-entry visa costs US$50 and double entry is US$80.

Crossing into Zimbabwe, a single-entry visa costs US$30 for most nationalities (US$55 for British/Irish, US$75 for Canadian). Double entry is US$45 for most nationalities (US$75 for British/Irish, and unavailable for Canadians).

ZAMBIA

☎260

As Zambia continues to ride the wave of tourism generated by the falls, it manages to keep itself grounded, offering a wonderfully low-key destination that has been recognised as such; it's co-host of the 2013 United Nations World Tourism Assembly. The waterfront straddling the falls continues its rapid development and is fast becoming one of the most exclusive destinations in Southern Africa.

Livingstone & Around

☎0213

Set 11km away from Victoria Falls, the relaxed town of Livingstone has taken on the role of a backpacking mecca. It attracts travellers not only to experience the falls, but to tackle the thrilling adventure scene. The town is not much to look at, but it is a safe, lively place with some fantastic restaurants. Those looking for a more scenic and luxurious experience can treat themselves to the natural setting along the Zambezi River at any number of plush lodges with river and wildlife views.

The town centres itself around one main road, Mosi-oa-Tunya Rd, 11km from the entrance to the falls. Several establishments are set right on the Zambezi River, but most of the action is set a bit back from the waterfront.

Sights & Activities

TOP CHOICE Victoria Falls World Heritage National Monument Site WATERFALL

(admission ZMW103.5; ⏲6am-6pm) This is what you're here for, the mighty Victoria Falls. It's a part of the Mosi-oa-Tunya National Park, 11km outside town before the Zambia border crossing; a path here leads to the visitor information centre, which has modest displays on local fauna, geology and culture.

From the centre, a network of paths leads through thick vegetation to various viewpoints. You can walk upstream along a path free of fences – and warning notices (so take care!) – to watch the Zambezi waters glide smoothly through rocks and little islands towards the lip of the falls.

For close-up views of the **Eastern Cataract**, nothing beats the hair-raising (and hair-wetting) walk across the footbridge, through swirling clouds of mist, to a sheer buttress called the **Knife Edge**. If the water is low, or the wind is favourable, you'll be treated to a magnificent view of the falls as well as the yawning abyss below. Otherwise, your vision (and your clothes) will be drenched by spray. Then you can walk down a steep track to the banks of the great Zambezi to see the huge whirlpool called the **Boiling Pot**. Watch out for cheeky baboons.

The park is open again in the evenings during (and just before and after) a full moon in order to see the amazing lunar rainbow. The tickets cost an extra ZMW51 – hours of operation vary, so inquire through your accommodation.

TOP CHOICE Livingstone Island VIEWPOINT

One of the most thrilling experiences not only at the falls, but in Africa, is the hair-raising journey to Livingstone Island. Here you will bathe in **Devil's Pool** – nature's ultimate infinity pool, set directly on the edge of the raging drama of Victoria Falls. You can leap into the pool and then poke your head over the edge to get an extraordinary view of the 100m drop.

Livingstone Island is in the middle of the Zambezi River, located at the top of the falls, and here you'll see a plaque marking the spot where David Livingstone first sighted the falls. The island is accessed via boat, and prices include either breakfast (ZMW333), lunch (ZMW615) or high tea (ZMW486). When the water is low, you're able to access it via walking or swimming across, but a guide is compulsory. Note that access to the island is closed from around March to May when the water levels are too high.

Mosi-oa-Tunya Game Park WILDLIFE RESERVE
(admission US$10; ⏲6am-6pm) The other part of the Mosi-oa-Tunya National Park is upriver from the falls, and only 3km southwest of Livingstone. The tiny wildlife sanctuary has a surprising range of animals including rhinos, zebras, giraffes, buffaloes, elephants and antelopes. It's most famous for tracking white rhinos on foot. Walks cost ZMW435 per person, for groups of up to eight.

Livingstone Museum MUSEUM
(Mosi-oa-Tunya Rd; admission ZMW25; ⏲9am-4.30pm) The excellent Livingstone Museum is divided into five sections covering archaeology, history, ethnography, natural history and art, and is highlighted by Tonga ritual artefacts, a life-sized model African village, a collection of David Livingstone memorabilia and historic maps dating back to 1690.

Sleeping

TOWN CENTRE

TOP CHOICE **Jollyboys Backpackers** BACKPACKERS $
(☎324229; www.backpackzambia.com; 34 Kanyanta Rd; campsite/dm/r ZMW40/50/205; @ 📶 🏊) The British and Canadian owners of Jollyboys know exactly what backpackers want, and it is wildly popular for a good reason. They have kept the needs of independent travellers at the forefront, from the sunken lounge and excellent coffee to the sparkling pool, cheap restaurant-bar and clean bright rooms. Things can get a bit hectic in the evenings, so they've

LIVINGSTONE – THE MAN, THE MYTH, THE LEGEND

David Livingstone is one of a few European explorers who is still revered by modern-day Africans. His legendary exploits on the continent border the realm of fiction, though his life's mission to end the slave trade was very real (and ultimately very successful).

Born into rural poverty in the south of Scotland on 19 March 1813, Livingstone worked in London for several years before being ordained as a missionary in 1840. The following year he arrived in Bechuanaland (now Botswana) and began travelling inland, looking for converts and seeking to end the slave trade.

As early as 1842 Livingstone had already become the first European to penetrate the northern reaches of the Kalahari. For the next several years he explored the African interior with the purpose of opening up trade routes and establishing missions. In 1854 Livingstone discovered a route to the Atlantic coast, and arrived in present-day Luanda. However, his most famous discovery occurred in 1855 when he first set eyes on Victoria Falls during his epic boat journey down the Zambezi River. Livingstone returned to Britain a national hero, and recounted his travels in the 1857 publication *Missionary Travels and Researches in South Africa*.

In 1858 Livingstone returned to Africa as the head of the 'Zambezi Expedition', a government-funded venture that aimed to identify natural resource reserves in the region. Unfortunately, the expedition ended when a previously unexplored section of the Zambezi turned out to be unnavigable.

In 1869 Livingstone reached Lake Tanganyika despite failing health, though several of his followers abandoned the expedition en route. These desertions were headline news in Britain, sparking rumours regarding Livingstone's health and sanity. In response to the growing mystery surrounding Livingstone's whereabouts, the *New York Herald* arranged a publicity stunt by sending journalist Henry Morton Stanley to find Livingstone.

After arriving in Zanzibar and setting out with nearly 200 porters, Stanley finally found Livingstone on 10 November 1871 in Ujiji near Lake Tanganyika and famously greeted him with the line 'Dr Livingstone, I presume?'.

Although Stanley urged him to leave the continent, Livingstone was determined to find the source of the Nile, and penetrated deeper into the continent than any European prior. On 1 May 1873 Livingstone died from malaria and dysentery near Lake Bangweula in present-day Zambia. His body was carried for thousands of kilometres by his attendants, and now lies in the ground at Westminster Abbey in London.

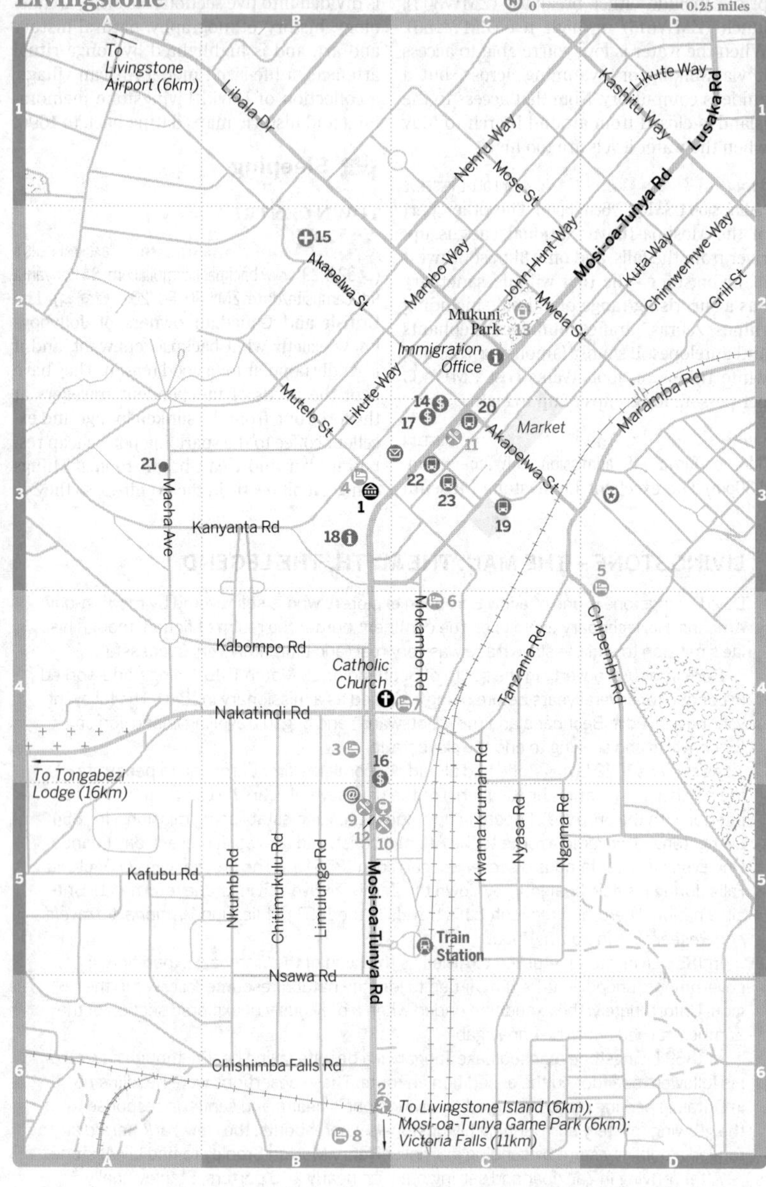

opened up the quieter **Jollyboys Camp** (Chipembi Rd) guesthouse nearby, in Chipembi Rd, to suit couples and families.

Fawlty Towers BACKPACKERS, LODGE **$$**
(☎323432; www.adventure-africa.com; 216 Mosi-oa-Tunya Rd; campsite/dm/tr ZMW40/76/215, d with/without bathroom ZMW307/205;) Once a backpacker institution, things have been spruced up here into a guesthouse full of upmarket touches: free internet and wi-fi, shady lawns, a great pool and some of the nicest and most spacious dorms we've seen. No Basil or Manuel in sight.

Livingstone

Sights
1 Livingstone Museum B3

Activities, Courses & Tours
2 Royal Livingstone Express B6

Sleeping
3 Fawlty Towers B4
4 Jollyboys Backpackers B3
5 Jollyboys Camp D3
6 Livingstone Backpackers C4
7 Olga's Guesthouse C4
8 ZigZag B6

Eating
9 Cafe Zambezi B5
Olga's Italian Corner .... (see 7)
10 Spot B5
11 Wonderbake C3
ZigZag .... (see 8)

Drinking
12 Fez Bar B5

Shopping
13 Mukuni Crafts C2

Information
14 Barclays Bank C3
15 Livingstone General Hospital B2
16 Stanbic B4
17 Standard Chartered Bank C3
18 Tourist Centre B3

Transport
19 Combi (Minibus) Stop C3
20 CR Holdings (CR Carriers) C3
21 Hemingways A3
22 Mazhandu Family Bus Services C3
23 Shalom Bus C3

ZigZag GUESTHOUSE $$
(☎322814; www.zigzagzambia.com; off Mosi-oa-Tunya Rd; s/d ZMW280/410; P❄@📶≋) Don't be deceived by the motel-meets-caravan-park exterior; the rooms here are more boutique B&B with loving touches throughout. Run by a friendly Scottish and Namibian couple, the lovely swimming pool, great restaurant and playground for kids give it a classic holiday feel.

Olga's Guesthouse GUESTHOUSE $$
(☎324160; www.olgasproject.com; cnr Mosi-oa-Tunya & Nakatindi Rds; s/d/f ZMW256/358/460; ❄📶) If you need a lie down after gorging at Olga's Italian Corner restaurant, Olga's has it covered. Clean, spacious rooms with cool tiled floors, teak furniture and slick bathrooms are just a few feet away. Profits go towards helping an organisation supporting local youth.

Livingstone Backpackers BACKPACKERS $
(☎324730; www.livingstonebackpackers.com; 559 Mokambo Rd; campsite/dm ZMW40/50; 📶≋) Resembling the *Big Brother* household, this place can be a bit 'party central', particularly when the Gen Y volunteer brigade is on holiday. You'll find them lounging by the pool or in the sandy outdoor cabana, swinging in hammocks or tackling the rock-climbing wall! There is also a hot tub, open-air kitchen and living room.

ZAMBEZI RIVERFRONT

Most prices include meals and transfers from Livingstone and reservations are recommended.

TOP CHOICE **Stanley Safari Lodge** LODGE $$$
(☎in South Africa 27-72-170 8879; www.stanleysafaris.com; per person with full board and activities from ZMW2,203; @📶≋) Intimate and indulgent, Stanley is a 10km drive from the falls in a peaceful spot surrounded by mopane forest. Rooms are as plush as can be expected at these prices; the standouts are the open-air suites where you can soak up nature from your own private plunge pool. When you tire of that, curl up by the fire in the open-air lounge. Rates are all-inclusive.

David Livingstone LODGE $$$
(☎324601; www.thedavidlivingstone.com; River Side Dr, Mosi-oa-Tunya National Park; s/d incl breakfast & activities ZMW1,745/2,675; 📶≋) The newest addition to Livingstone's luxury hotels: all rooms have river views, Rhodesian teak furniture, concertina doors, four-poster beds and stand-alone bathtubs looking out to the water. It's set within the national park, hippos honk around at night, and the decking and bar around the riverfront infinity pool is a wonderful spot for a sundowner. It's located halfway between Livingstone and the falls.

Jungle Junction Bovu Island LODGE, CAMPGROUND $
(☎0978-725282, 323708; www.junglejunction.info; campsite per person ZMW50, hut per person ZMW128–179;) Hippos, hammocks and harmony. On a lush island in the middle of the Zambezi River, around 50km from Livingstone, Jungle Junction attracts travellers who just want to lounge beneath palm trees, or engage in some fishing (ZMW77 including equipment and guide). Meals are available (ZMW36 to ZMW60).

Zambezi Waterfront LODGE $$$
(☎320606; www.safpar.net/waterfront.html; campsite per person ZMW50, s/d tent ZMW155/200, s/d incl breakfast from ZMW640/920;) Another waterfront lodge, things feel more rustic here with a wilderness charm, as crocs inhabit a small creek on the property. Accommodation ranges from luxury tents and riverside chalets to executive rooms or family suites. The riverside open-air beer garden is unsurprisingly popular at sunset. It's located 4km south of Livingstone, and a handy free shuttle service takes you to the falls and town.

Zambezi Sun RESORT $
(☎321122; www.suninternational.com; s/d incl breakfast from ZMW2,355/2,510, f ZMW2,550;) Only a 10-minute walk from the falls, this sprawling resort provides a great base for exploring the area. The North African kasbah-inspired rooms are vibrant while plenty of pools and a playground are perfect for families. It's within the perimeter of the national park, so expect to see grazing zebras but keep your distance. Rates include falls entry.

Tongabezi Lodge LODGE $$$
(☎323235; www.tongabezi.com; cottage/house per person ZMW2,200/2,710;) Here you'll find sumptuous spacious cottages and open-faced 'treehouses' and private dining decks. Guests are invited to spend an evening on nearby Sindabezi Island (per person per night US$350), selected by the *Sunday Times* as the best remote place to stay in the world.

Eating & Drinking

Livingstone is home to a number of high-quality restaurants, including a batch of excellent newcomers. Enjoy a sundowner at any of the the Zambezi riverfront resorts that allow nonguests to pop in for a drink and a stellar sunset.

TOP CHOICE **Cafe Zambezi** AFRICAN $$
(☎0978-978578; 217 Mosi-oa-Tunya Rd; mains ZMW30-48; ⏰9am-midnight;) Bursting with local flavour; vibrant decor flows from the indoor dining room to the outdoor courtyard, sunny by day and candlelit by night. The broad menu covers local *braai* (barbecue) favourites of goat meat and mopane caterpillars or an international twist of roasted veg with feta, served with *sadza* (maize porridge). Authentic wood-fired pizzas are a winner or sink your teeth into crocodile or eggplant-and-haloumi burgers.

TOP CHOICE **Olga's Italian Corner** ITALIAN $$
(www.olgasproject.con; cnr Mosi-oa-Tunya & Nakatindi Rds; pizza & pasta from ZMW40; ⏰7am-10pm;) Olga's does authentic wood-fired thin-crust pizzas, as well as delicious homemade pasta classics all served under a large thatched roof. Great options for vegetarians, include the lasagna with its crispy blackened edge served in the dish. All profits go to a community centre to help disadvantaged youth.

ZigZag CAFE $$
(off Mosi-oa-Tunya Rd; mains from ZMW25; ⏰7am-9pm;) Another string to Livingstone's bow of culinary choices, ZigZag has a drool-inducing menu of homemade muffins (such as cranberry and white chocolate), smoothies using fresh fruit from the garden, and a changing small menu of comfort food.

Spot CAFE $
(Mosi-oa-Tunya Rd; mains from ZMW40; ⏰10am-10pm) Promising 'forkin good food', this attractive little outdoor eatery with picnic tables delivers with its mix of local and international dishes, including a mean chicken schnitzel.

Wonderbake CAFE, BAKERY $
(Mosi-oa-Tunga Rd; ⏰8am-9pm;) There's nothing fancy about this bakery cafeteria, but it has a good local flavour, sells cheap pies and has free wi-fi.

Fez Bar BAR
(Mosi-oa-Tunya Rd) This open-air bar set under a garage tin roof is a popular place to kick on to with its drinking games, pool tables and menu of soft-shell tacos.

Shopping

Mukuni Crafts CRAFTS
(Mosi-oa-Tunya Rd) The craft stalls in the southern corner of Mukuni Park are a pleasant, and hassle-free place to browse for souvenirs.

Information

Dangers & Annoyances

Don't walk from town to the falls as there have been a number of muggings along this stretch of road – even tourists on bicycles have been attacked. It's a long and not terribly interesting walk anyway, and simply not worth the risk. Take a minivan for under ZMW5 or a blue taxi for ZMW40.

Emergency

Police (☎320116; Maramba Rd)

Internet Access

Computer Centre (216 Mosi-oa-Tunya Rd; internet per hr US$2; ⌚8am-8pm) Also offers international phone calls and faxes. All the hostels now have wi-fi or at least internet access.

Medical Services

Livingstone General Hospital (☎321475; Akapelwa St)

Money

Barclays Bank (cnr Mosi-oa-Tunya Rd & Akapelwa St) and **Standard Charted Bank** (Mosi-oa-Tunya Rd) both accept Visa cards, while **Stanbic** (Mosi-oa-Tunya Rd) accepts MasterCard.

Post

Post Office (Mosi-oa-Tunya Rd) Has a *poste restante* and fax service.

Tourist Information

Tourist Centre (☎321404; www.zambiatourism.com; Mosi-oa-Tunya Rd; ⌚8am-5pm Mon-Fri) Mildly useful and can help with booking tours and accommodation, but Jollyboys and Fawlty Towers have all the information you need.

Getting There & Away

Air

South African Airways (☎0212-612207; www.flysaa.com) and **British Airways** (www.britishairways.com) have daily flights to and from Johannesburg. **1Time** (☎322744; www.1time.aero) flies three times a week. The cheapest economy fare starts at around US$400 return. **Proflight Zambia** (☎0211-845944; www.proflight-zambia.com) flies daily from Livingstone to Lusaka.

Bus & Combi (Minibus)

The Zambian side of the falls is 11km south of Livingstone and along the main road to the border with Zimbabwe. Plenty of minibuses and shared taxis ply the route from the minibus terminal along Senanga Rd in Livingstone. As muggings have been reported, it is best to take a taxi.

TO LUSAKA

CR Holdings (☎0977-861063; cnr Mosi-oa-Tunya Rd & Akapelwa St) Runs four services a day to Lusaka (ZMW80, seven hours).

Mazhandu Family Bus (☎0975-805064) Seven daily buses to Lusaka (ZMW80 to ZMW115) from 6am till 10.30pm.

Shalom Bus (☎0977-747013; Mutelo St) Eight buses a day travelling to Lusaka (ZMW75), six hours), from 5.30am till 10pm, as well as to many other parts of Zambia

TO NAMIBIA

For travelling to Namibia, and crossing the Zambia–Namibia border at Katima Mulilo, see p122.

TO BOTSWANA

Buses to Shesheke (ZMW60, two hours) depart with Mazhandu Family Bus at 5am and 2pm. Otherwise there are buses to Sesheke (ZMW50) departing when full from Mingongo bus station next to the Catholic church at Dambwa village, 3km west of the town centre. To get to Mongu from Livingstone, it's best to head to Sesheke or Lusaka, and then transfer to a Mongu bus.

Combis (minibuses) to the Botswana border at Kazungula depart when they are full from Mingongo bus station and cost ZMW30. Shared taxis can be taken from the taxi rank by Shoprite and cost ZMW40.

For information about travelling to Botswana, and crossing the Zambia–Botswana border at Kazungula, see p122.

Car & Motorcycle

If you're driving a rented car or motorcycle, be sure to carefully check all info regarding insurance, and that you have all the necessary papers for checks and border crossings such as 'owners' and 'permission to drive' documents, insurance papers and a copy of carbon tax receipt. Expect to pay around $US55 in various fees when crossing the border into Zimbabwe.

Train

While the bus is a much quicker way to get around, the *Zambezi Express* is more for lovers of slow travel or trains. It leaves Livingstone for Lusaka (economy/1st class/sleeper ZMW30/45/45, 15 hours), via Choma, on Tuesday and Friday at 8pm. Reservations are available at the **train station** (☎320001), which is signed off Mosi-oa-Tunya Rd.

Getting Around

To/From the Airport

Livingstone Airport is located 6km northwest of town, and is easily accessible by taxi (ZMW50 each way).

Combis & Taxis

Combis run regularly along Mosi-oa-Tunya Rd to Victoria Falls and the Zambian border, 11km south of Livingstone (ZMW5, 15 minutes). Blue taxis cost ZMW40 to ZMW50 from the border to Livingstone. Coming from the border, combis are parked just over from the waiting taxis, and depart when full.

Car Hire

Hemingways (☎320996; www.hemingwayszambia.com; Mosi-oa-Tunya Rd) in Livingstone has new Toyota Hi-Lux 4WDs for around US$210 per day. Prices include cooking and camping equipment. Drivers must be over 25.

ZIMBABWE

☎263

There may still be a long way to go, but finally things seem to be looking up for Zimbabwe. All the bad news that has kept it in the glare of the spotlight – rampant land reform, hyper inflation and food shortages – fortunately now seem to be a thing of the past. In reality, safety has never been a concern for travellers here and, even during the worst of it, tourists were never targets for political violence. Word of this seems to have spread, as tourists stream back to the Zim side of the falls.

Victoria Falls

☎013

Having temporarily lost its mantle to Livingstone as the falls' premier tourist town, the town of Victoria Falls has reclaimed what's historically theirs as tourists return across the border in numbers.

Unlike Livingstone, the town was built for tourism. It is right upon the falls with neat, walkable streets (though not at dark, because of the wild animals) lined with hotels, bars and some of the best crafts you'll find in Southern Africa. While for a few years it felt like a resort in off-season, there's no mistake about it now – it's officially reopened for business.

Sights & Activities

TOP CHOICE **Victoria Falls National Park** WATERFALL

(admission US$30; ⏲6am-6pm) Located just before the border crossing and about 1km from the town centre, here on the Zim side of the falls you're in for a real treat. The walk is along the top of the gorge on a path, with various viewing points opening up to the extraordinary front-on panoramas of these world-famous falls. One of the most dramatic spots is the westernmost point known as **Cataract View**. Another track leads to the aptly named **Danger Point**, where a sheer, unfenced 100m drop-off will rattle your nerves. From there, you can follow a side track for a view of the **Victoria Falls Bridge**.

Hire a raincoat and umbrella just inside the gates if you go in April, or you may as well walk in your swimsuit – you will get soaked! The park is open again in the evenings during (and just before and after) a full moon, in order to see the amazing lunar rainbow (tickets cost an extra US$10).

Zambezi National Park WILDLIFE RESERVE

(admission US$15; ⏲6am-6.30pm) Consisting of 40km of Zambezi River frontage and a spread of wildlife-rich mopane forest and savannah, this national park is best known for its herds of sable antelopes, but it is also home to giraffes, elephants and an occasional lion. The entrance to the park is only 5km northwest of the Victoria Falls town centre, and is easily accessible by private vehicle. Tour operators on both sides of the border offer wildlife drives, guided hikes and fishing expeditions.

FREE **Jafuta Heritage Centre** CULTURAL CENTRE

(www.elephantswalk.com/heritage; Elephant's Walk Shopping Village, off Adam Stander Dr; ⏲8am-6pm) This worthwhile collection details the cultural heritage of local ethnic groups, from Shona, Ndebele, Tonga and Lozi people.

Sleeping

TOP CHOICE **Victoria Falls Hotel** LUXURY HOTEL $$$

(☎44751; www.victoria-falls-hotels.net; 2 Mallet Dr; s/d incl breakfast from US$312/336; ❄📶🏊) Built in 1904, this historic hotel (the oldest in Zimbabwe) oozes elegance and sophistication, and occupies an impossibly scenic location. Looking across manicured lawns (with roaming warthogs) to the gorge and bridge, you can't see the falls as such but you do see the spray from some rooms. High tea here at Stanley's Terrace is an institution.

Shoestrings Backpackers BACKPACKERS $

(☎40167; 12 West Dr; campsite per person US$6, dm/d US$9/35; @📶🏊) A perennial favourite

Victoria Falls

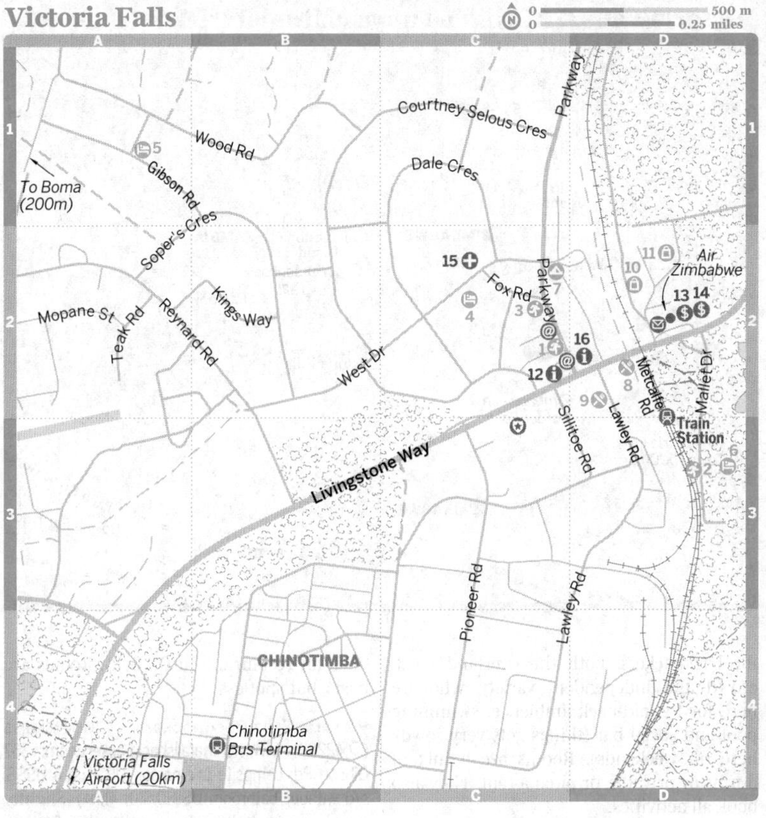

Victoria Falls

Sights
Jafuta Heritage Centre .... (see 11)

Activities, Courses & Tours
1 Shearwater Victoria Falls C2
2 Victoria Falls Steam Train Co. D3
3 Wild Horizons C2

Sleeping
4 Shoestrings Backpackers C2
5 Victoria Falls Backpackers A1
6 Victoria Falls Hotel D3
7 Victoria Falls Restcamp & Lodges C2

Eating
Africa Cafe .... (see 11)
In Da Belly Restaurant .... (see 7)
8 Lola's Tapas & Bar D2
9 Mama Africa D2

Drinking
Shoestrings Backpackers .... (see 4)
Stanley's Terrace .... (see 6)

Shopping
10 Curio Shops D2
11 Elephant's Walk Shopping & Artist Village D2
Jairos Jiri Crafts .... (see 11)
Matsimela .... (see 11)
Ndau Collection .... (see 11)
Prime Art Gallery .... (see 11)

Information
12 Backpackers Bazaar C2
13 Barclays Bank D2
14 Standard Chartered Bank D2
15 Victoria Falls Surgery C2
16 Zimbabwe Tourism Authority D2

Victoria Falls & Mosi-oa-Tunya National Parks

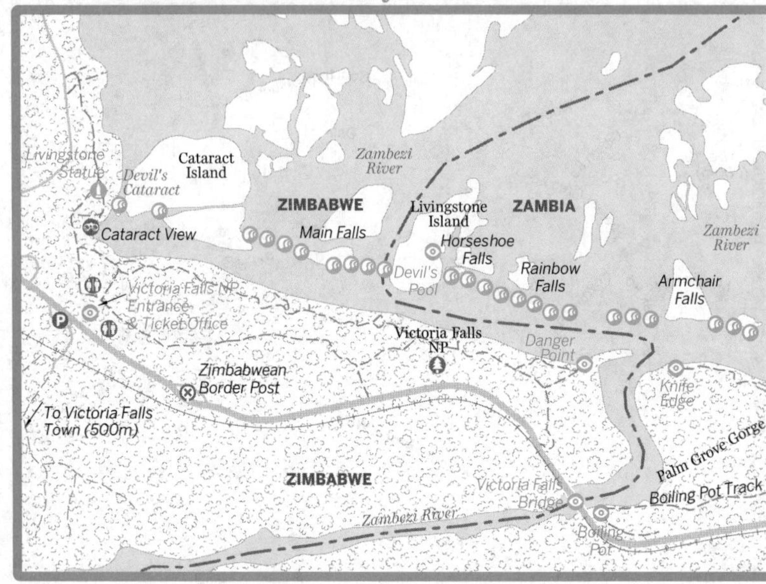

for backpackers, both the overland truck crowd and independent variety, who are here for its laid-back ambience, swimming pool and social bar (things gets very rowdy here on weekends). Rooms are a mix of dorms or privates, or pitch a tent. They also book all activities.

Elephant Camp LUXURY LODGE **$$$**
(www.theelephantcamp.com; s/d full board US$350/700; @📶🏊) One of the best spots to splash out; the luxurious 'tents' have a classic lodge feel and are set on a private game reserve looking out to the mopane woodland savannah. Each room has its own outdoor private plunge pool and balcony decking to spot grazing animals or the spray of the falls. You might get to meet Sylvester, the resident cheetah.

Victoria Falls Restcamp & Lodges CAMPSITE, LODGE **$**
(☎40509; www.vicfallsrestcamp.com; cnr Parkway & West Dr; campsite/dm/fitted dome tents US$10/11/20, s/d chalets without bathroom US$25/34, cottages US$67; 📶🏊) A great alternative for budget travellers wanting to avoid the party atmosphere of other backpackers. Rooms are basic no-frills lodge-style and tented camps. There's a lovely pool and fantastic open-air restaurant, In Da Belly. Rooms are basic, but spotless.

Victoria Falls Backpackers BACKPACKERS **$**
(☎42209; www.victoriafallsbackpackers.com; 357 Gibson Rd; campsite per person US$4, dm US$8, s/d without bathroom US$10/20; @🏊) Slightly rough around the edges, and a bit further away from the centre of town, it nevertheless remains a very good choice for budget travellers wanting a more laid-back environment.

Bengula Cottages GUESTHOUSE **$$**
(☎45945, 0778-173286; www.bengulacottages.com/; 645 Mahogany Rd; s/d/f low season US$60/100/120, high season $US100/160/220; 🏊) In the leafy suburbs, these attractive units are a solid midrange choice set around a shady pool with paper lanterns strung up and a relaxed atmosphere. The communal kitchen comes well equipped.

✗ Eating

In Da Belly Restaurant AFRICAN, INTERNATIONAL **$**
(☎332077; Victoria Falls Restcamp & Lodges; meals US$5-15; ⏰7am-9.30pm) Under a large thatched hut, looking out to a sparkling pool, this relaxed open-air eatery has a menu of warthog schnitzel, crocodile curry and impala burgers, as well as one of the

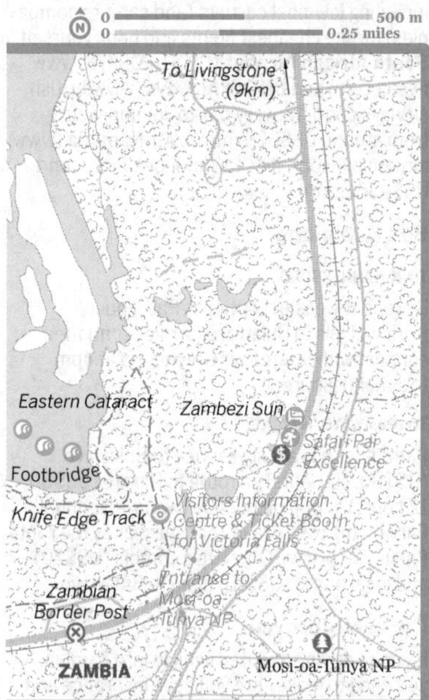

best breakfast menus in town. The name is a play on Ndebele, one of the two major population tribes in Zimbabwe.

Africa Cafe CAFE $
(www.elephantswalk.com/africa_cafe.htm; Elephant's Walk Shopping & Art Village; 8am-5pm;) This appealing outdoor cafe at the Elephant's Walk Shopping & Artist Village, with smiley staff, is a great place to refuel with quality coffee, delicious breakfast, burgers and vegetarian food.

Lola's Tapas & Bar SPANISH $$
(42994; 8B Landela Complex; tapas US$2-9; 8am-10pm;) Tapas such as *patatas bravas* and *calamares a la Romana* served by a welcoming couple from Barcelona. Dine outdoors or in the more intimate indoor area. Jugs of sangria available (US$15).

Mama Africa AFRICAN $$
(41725; www.mamaafricaeatinghouse.com; meals US$5-8; 10am-10pm) This long-time tourist haunt behind the Landela Centre specialises in local dishes, steaks and game meats. Also has regular live music and traditional dance performances.

Boma AFRICAN $$
(43211; www.thebomarestaurant.com; Squire Cummings Rd, Victoria Falls Safari Lodge; buffet US$40; dinner 7pm) While it may be a bit of a tourist trap, Boma manages to be more genuine than tacky. Enjoy a taste of Africa at this buffet restaurant set under a massive thatched roof. Dine on smoked guinea-fowl starter, impala-knuckle terrine or spit-roast warthog. There's also traditional dancing, interactive drumming and fortune telling by a witch doctor.

Drinking

TOP CHOICE **Stanley's Terrace** RESTAURANT
(Mallet Dr, Victoria Falls Hotel; high tea for 2 people US$30; high tea 3-6pm;) The Terrace at the stately Victoria Falls Hotel just brims with English colonial ambience. High tea is served with a postcard-perfect backdrop of the gardens and Vic Falls Bridge, with polished silverware, decadent cakes and three-tiered trays of finger sandwiches (cucumber? why yes, of course). Jugs of Pimms are perfect on a summer day at US$22. The only thing missing is the croquet.

Shoestrings Backpackers BAR
(12 West Dr) It's fairly laid back during the week, while weekends often feel like a house party as the dance floor gets a lot of action.

Shopping

A good selection of craft shops are located along Adam Stander Dr, with a quality items such as Shona sculpture and pieces made from recycled materials.

TOP CHOICE **Elephant's Walk Shopping & Artist Village** SHOPPING CENTRE
(0772-254552; www.elephantswalk.com; Adam Stander Dr) A must for those in the market for quality Zimbabwean and African craft, this shopping village is home to boutique stores and galleries owned by a collective that aims to promote and set up local artists.

Prime Art Gallery ART
(342783; www.primeart-gallery.com; Elephant's Walk Shopping & Arts Village) Sells original pieces by Dominic Benhura, Zimbabwe's most prominent current-day Shona sculptor whose worked has been exhibited around the world.

Matsimela BEAUTY
(www.matsimela.co.za; Elephant's Walk Shopping & Arts Village; 8am-5pm) South African bodycare brand Matsimela has set up store here with an enticing aroma of natural scented soaps and body scrubs such as rose and

lychee and baobab-seed oil. Also has a branch at Doon Estate in Harare.

Jairos Jiri Crafts CRAFTS
(Victoria Falls Curio Village; ⏲8am-5pm Mon-Fri, 8.30am-4.30pm Sat, 8.30am-1pm Sun) Good range of Shona arts and crafts, with proceeds assisting disadvantaged locals.

Ndau Collection JEWELLERY
(☎386221; www.ndaujewelry.com) Watch local artisans hand-make individually pieced silver bracelets, rings and necklaces at this store-workshop. They also sell exquisite antique African trade beads to be incorporated into custom-made jewellery.

Information

Dangers & Annoyances

Mugging is not such a problem anymore, but at dawn and dusk wild animals such as elephants and warthogs do roam the streets away from the town centre, so take taxis at these times. Although it's perfectly safe to walk to and from the falls, it's advisable to stick to the more touristed areas.

Emergency

Medical Air Rescue Service (MARS; ☎44764)

Police (☎44206; Livingstone Way)

Victoria Falls Surgery (☎43356; West Dr)

Internet Access

Econet (Park Way; per 30min/1hr US$1/2; ⏲8am-5pm Mon-Fri, to 1pm Sat & Sun)

Telco (☎43441; Phumula Centre; per hr US$1; ⏲8am-6pm)

Money

Barclays Bank (off Livingstone Way)

Standard Chartered Bank (off Livingstone Way)

Post

Post Office (off Livingstone Way)

Tourist Information

Backpackers Bazaar (☎013-45828; www.backpackersbazaarvicfalls.com; off Parkway; ⏲8am-5pm Mon-Fri, 9am-4pm Sat & Sun) Definitive place for all tourist info and bookings.

Zimbabwe Tourism Authority (☎44202; zta@vicfalls.ztazim.co.zw; 258 Adam Stander Dr; ⏲8am-5pm Mon-Fri, 8am-1pm Sat) A few brochures, but not very useful.

Getting There & Away

Air

Check out www.flightsite.co.za or www.travelstart.co.za, where you can search all the airlines including low-cost carriers (and car-hire companies) for the cheapest flights and book yourself. **South African Airways** (☎011-808678; www.flysaa.com) and **British Airways** (www.britishairways.com) fly every day to Johannesburg from around US$320 return. **Air Namibia** (www.airnamibia.com) flies to Windhoek for around US$530 return.

Bus & Minibus

TO JOHANNESBURG

By road the easiest option is Pathfinder from VicFalls to Bulawayo (arrives 1pm) then connect with Intercaper Greyhound at 4pm to Johannesburg.

TO BULAWAYO/HWANGE

Pathfinder has a daily service to Bulawayo (US$30, six hours) en route to Harare (US$60, 12 hours), stopping outside Hwange National Park on the way. Bravo Tours also plies the route for similar prices. Otherwise combis (US$20) and local buses (US$15) head to Bulawayo.

Car & Motorcycle

If you're driving a rented vehicle into Zambia, you need to make sure you have insurance and carbon tax papers, as well original owner documents. When you enter Zambia you are issued with a Temporary Import Permit, valid for while you are in the country. This must be returned to immigration for them to acquit the vehicle.

Train

A popular way of getting to/from Vic Falls is by the overnight Mosi-oa-Tunya train that leaves Victoria Falls daily at 7pm for Bulawayo, Zimbabwe (economy/2nd/1st class US$8/10/12, 12 hours). First class is the only way to go. Make reservations at the **ticket office** (☎44392; ⏲7am-10am & 2.30-6.45pm Mon-Fri, 9-10am & 4.30-6.45pm Sat & Sun) inside the train station.

Getting Around

To/From the Airport

Victoria Falls Airport is located 20km southeast of town, and is easily accessible by taxi (US$30 each way). Another option is to book a transfer with one of the companies through your hostel or travel agent in Vic Falls. Transfers are US$15 per person one way.

Car & Motorcycle

At the time of research, petrol was readily available in petrol stations. Avis and Europcar both have offices at the Vic Falls airport.

Taxis

A taxi around town costs about US$10, slightly more after dark.

Mozambique

OLIVER STREWE / GETTY IMAGES ©

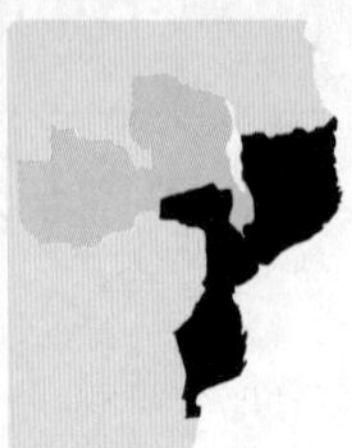

Mozambique

POP 23.5 MILLION

Includes »

Best of Nature

- Gorongosa National Park (p194)
- Chimanimani Mountains (p200)
- Quirimbas Archipelago (p240)
- Lake Niassa (p229)

Best of Culture

- Mozambique Island (p218)
- Ibo Island (p240)
- Maputo (p145)
- Inhambane (p173)

Why Go?

Mozambique beckons with its coastline and swaying palms, its traditions, its cultures, its vibe and – most of all – its adventure opportunities. This enigmatic southeast African country is well off most travellers' maps, but it has much to offer those who venture here: long, dune-fringed beaches, turquoise waters abounding in shoals of colourful fish, well-preserved corals, remote archipelagos in the north, pounding surf in the south and graceful dhows with billowing sails. Add to this colonial-style architecture, pulsating nightlife, an endlessly fascinating cultural mix and vast tracks of bush populated with elephants, lions and birds galore. Discovering these attractions is not always easy, but it is unfailingly rewarding. Bring along some patience, a tolerance for long bus rides and a sense of adventure, and jump in for the journey of a lifetime.

When to Go

Maputo

May–Oct/Nov Cooler, dry weather makes this the ideal time to visit.

Dec–Mar Rainy season can bring washed-out roads and occasional flooding in the south and centre.

Holidays In South African school holidays (Christmas, Easter, August) southern resorts fill up.

MAPUTO

☎ 21 / POP 1.59 MILLION

With its Mediterranean-style architecture, waterside setting and wide avenues lined with jacaranda and flame trees, Maputo is easily one of Africa's most attractive capitals. It's also the most developed place in Mozambique by far, with a wide selection of hotels and restaurants, well-stocked supermarkets, shady sidewalk cafes and a lively cultural scene.

The heart of the city is the bustling, low-lying baixa, spreading out northwards and eastwards from the port. Here, Portuguese-era buildings with their graceful balconies and wrought-iron balustrades jostle for space with ungainly Marxist-style apartment blocks. *Galabiyya*-garbed men gather in doorways for a chat, Indian traders carry on brisk business in the narrow side streets and women wrapped in colourful *capulanas* (sarongs) sell everything from seafood to spices at the massive Municipal Market.

A few kilometres away, along the seaside Avenida Marginal, life moves at a more leisurely pace. Fishermen stand along the roadside with the day's catch, hoping to lure customers from the constant parade of passing vehicles; banana vendors loll on their carts in the shade, with Radio Moçambique piping out eternally upbeat rhythms in the background; and local football teams vie for victory in impromptu matches in the sand.

Maputo is pricier than elsewhere in the country, especially for imported goods brought in on the toll road linking Johannesburg and the South African economy with Maputo's port and the sea. Yet there's enough selection to make it a good destination no matter what your budget. Getting to know the city is a highlight of visiting Mozambique and essential to understanding the country. Don't miss spending time here before heading north.

History

Long before Europeans discovered Maputo's charms, the local Ronga people were living here, fishing, whale hunting, farming and trading. In 1545 Portuguese navigator Lourenço Marques happened upon Delagoa Bay (now Maputo Bay), in his journey up the southern African coastline. His reports attracted other traders, who established temporary settlements offshore on Inhaca and Xefina Grande islands as bases for ivory trading forays to the mainland. Yet the Portuguese attention to the area was fleeting. They soon turned their sights northwards, all but abandoning their activities in the south.

Lourenço Marques – as the area later became known – took on a new importance in the mid-19th century, with the discovery of diamonds and gold in the nearby Transvaal Republic. Around 1898 it replaced Mozambique Island as the capital of Portuguese East Africa. A new rail link with the Transvaal, built in in 1894, and the expansion of the port fuelled the city's growth. In the 1950s and 1960s 'LM' became a favoured playground for Portuguese holiday makers and apartheid-era South Africans, who came over the border in droves seeking prawns, prostitutes and beaches. With Mozambican independence in 1975, the city's original residents reasserted themselves and in 1976 President Samora Machel changed the name to Maputo, honouring an early chief who had resisted Portuguese colonisation.

MOZAMBIQUE FAST FACTS

- **Area** 800,000 sq km
- **Capital** Maputo
- **Famous for** Beaches, islands, prawns
- **Languages** Portuguese plus Changana, Nyanja, Makhuwa and other African languages
- **Money** New Mozambican Metical (Mtc)

Orientation

Maputo sits on a low escarpment overlooking Maputo Bay, with the long avenues of its upper-lying residential sections spilling down into the baixa.

Some budget accommodation and many businesses, plus the train station, banks and the post office, are in the baixa, on or near Avenida 25 de Setembro, while embassies and most better hotels are in the city's upper section, especially in and around the Sommerschield diplomatic and residential quarter. Maputo's tallest building and a good landmark is known as '*trinta e trés andares*' or **33 Storey Building** (Mcel; Map p150; cnr Avenida 25 de Setembro & Rua da Imprensa), in the baixa. At the northernmost end of the Marginal and about 7km from the centre is Bairro Triunfo and the Costa do Sol area, with a small beach and several places to stay and eat.

Mozambique Highlights

1. Discover enchanting **Mozambique Island** (p218), with its time-warp atmosphere and cobbled streets
2. Get to know **Maputo** (p145), Mozambique's waterside capital, with lively sidewalk cafes and many museums
3. Explore the **Quirimbas Archipelago** (p239), including magical Ibo with its fort and crumbling mansions
4. Relax along the ruggedly beautiful shoreline of **Lake Niassa** (p229)
5. Watch wildlife and enjoy fine birding at **Gorongosa National Park** (p194)
6. Hike in the lush **Chimanimani Mountains** (p200)

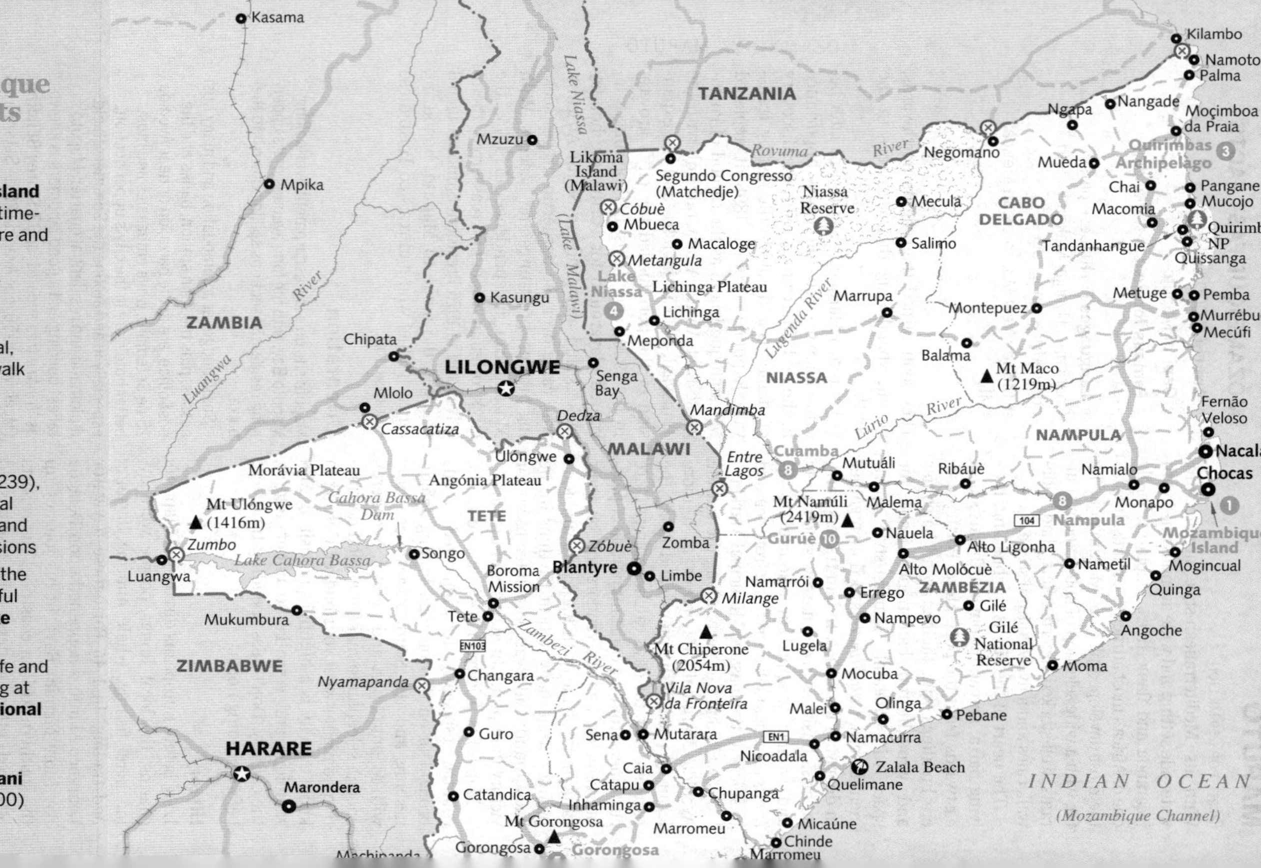

7 Wander historic **Inhambane** (p173) town's quiet streets before relaxing on nearby beaches

8 Travel by **train** (p227) between Cuamba and Nampula, and catch passing glimpses into rural life

9 Snorkel around the islands of the **Bazaruto Archipelago** (p186)

10 Walk amid tea plantations and jacaranda-lined lanes around **Gurúè** (p210)

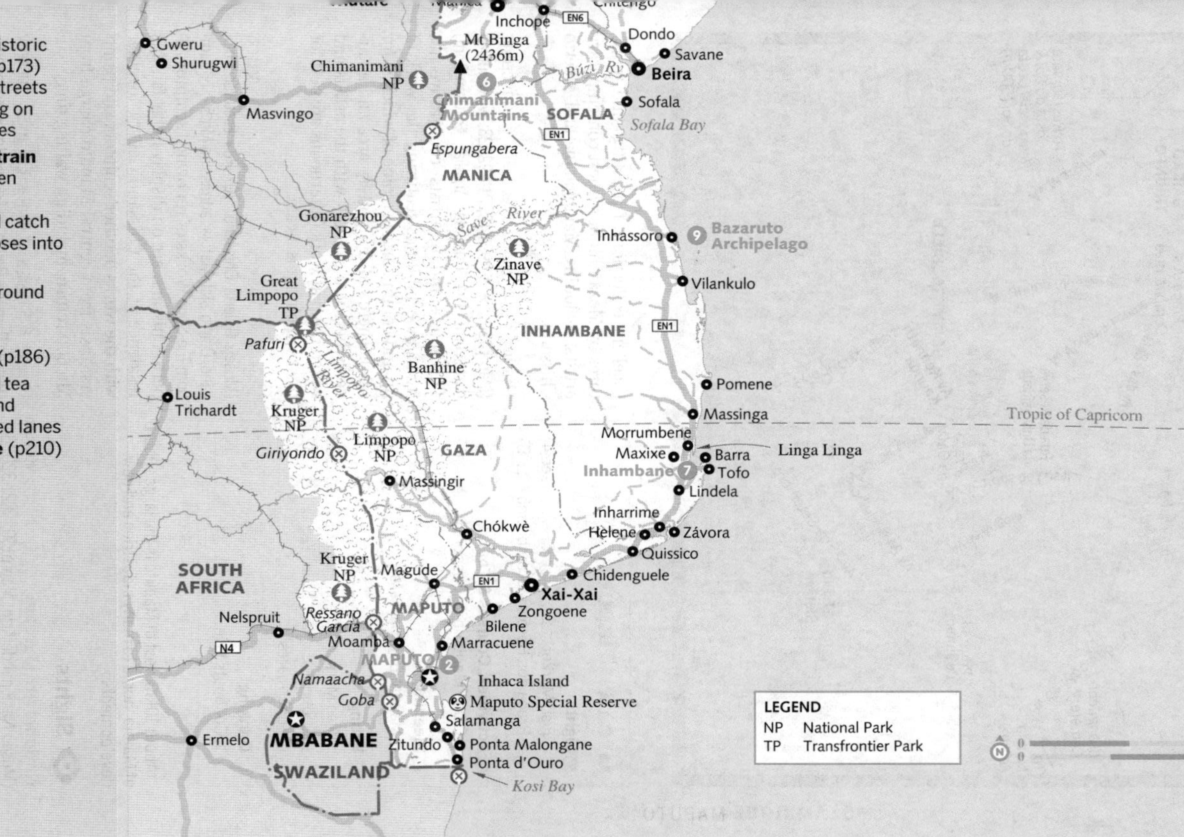

Greater Maputo

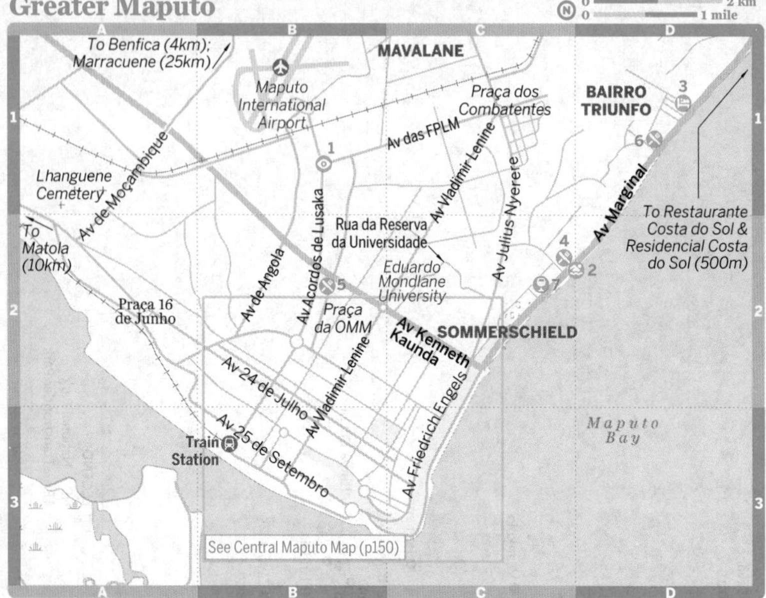

Greater Maputo

Sights

Fish Market .... (see 4)
1 Praça dos Heróis Moçambicanos B1

Activities, Courses & Tours

2 Clube Marítimo de Desportos D2

Sleeping

3 Maputo Backpackers D1

Eating

4 Fish Market C2
5 Shoprite...B2
6 Supermares D1

Drinking

7 Coconuts Live C2

About 10km west of Maputo is the large suburb of Matola, home to many industries and new developments.

Sights

National Art Museum MUSEUM

(Museu Nacional de Arte; Map p150; ☎21-320264; artemus@tvcabo.co.mz; 1233 Avenida Ho Chi Minh; admission Mtc20, Sun free; ⏲11am-6pm Tue-Fri, 2-6pm Sat & Sun) Half a block west of Avenida Karl Marx, the National Art Museum has an excellent collection of paintings and sculptures by Mozambique's finest contemporary artists, including Malangatana and Alberto Chissano.

Núcleo de Arte ARTS CENTRE

(Map p150; ☎21-499840, 21-492523; www.nucleodarte.com; 194 Rua da Argélia; ⏲10am-8pm) This long-standing artists' cooperative has frequent exhibitions featuring the work of up-and-coming artists (some of which is for sale). There's also a pottery area and a garden where you can talk with the artists and watch them at work (afternoons are best for this). Adjoining is a cafe.

Chissano Gallery GALLERY

(Museu Galeria Chissano; 307 Rua Escultor Chissano, Bairro Sial, Matola; admission Mtc50; ⏲9am-5pm Tue-Sun) Works of renowned sculptor Alberto Chissano are on display in his family's residence at the Chissano Gallery, together with the works of other sculptors and painters. Taxis from central Maputo charge from Mtc600 return, including waiting time.

House & Studio of Malangatana MUSEUM

(Rua de Camões, Bairro do Aeroporto; ⏲by appointment only) It is occasionally possible to visit the house and studio of Malangatana, Mozambique's most renowned painter. It's filled with dozens of his own paintings as well as sculptures by Alberto Chissano. Bookings are best arranged through Kulungwana Espaço Artístico (p149), at the train station. The house is located several kilometres outside the city centre; ask for directions when arranging the visit.

Train Station HISTORIC BUILDING

(Caminho dos Ferros de Moçambique, CFM; Map p150; Praça dos Trabalhadores) Maputo's landmark train station is one of the city's most imposing buildings. The dome was designed by an associate of Alexandre Gustav Eiffel (of Eiffel Tower fame), although Eiffel himself never set foot in Mozambique. Also impressive are the wrought-iron lattice work, pillars and verandas gracing the pistachio-green exterior. Inside (to the left, at the end of the platform, at 'Sala de Espera'), is the **Kulungwana Espaço Artístico** (Map p150; ☎21-333048; www.kulungwana.org.mz; ⏰10am-5pm Tue-Fri, to 3pm Sat & Sun), with a small exhibition of works by local and visiting artists, and sculptures and paintings for sale. A museum focusing on the history of Mozambique's railways is due to open at the far end of the platforms.

Natural History Museum MUSEUM

(Museu de História Natural; Map p150; ☎21-490879; Praça Travessa de Zambezi; admission Mtc50, Sun free; ⏰9am-3.30pm Tue-Fri, 10am-5pm Sat & Sun) The Natural History Museum, near Hotel Cardoso, is worth a stop simply to see its stately Manueline architecture and its garden with a mural by Malangatana. Inside are some taxidermy specimens accompanied by interactive computer terminals, a small ethnography exhibit and a fascinating display of what is probably the region's only collection of elephant foetuses.

National Money Museum MUSEUM

(Museu Nacional da Moeda; Map p150; Praça 25 de Junho; admission Mtc20; ⏰11am-5pm Tue-Fri, 9am-3.30pm Sat, 2-5pm Sun) Housed in a restored yellow building on the corner of Rua Consiglieri Pedroso, the National Money Museum dates from 1860. Inside are exhibits of local currency, ranging from early barter tokens to modern-day bills.

Geology Museum MUSEUM

(Museu da Geologia; Map p150; ☎21-313508; cnr Avenidas 24 de Julho & Mártires de Machava; admission Mtc50; ⏰9am-5pm Tue-Fri, 9am-2pm Sat, 2-5pm Sun) The Geology Museum has mineral exhibits and a geological relief map of the country.

FREE **Fort** FORTRESS

(Fortaleza; Map p150; Praça 25 de Junho; ⏰9am-5pm) The old fort was built by the Portuguese in the mid-19th century near the site of an earlier fort. Inside is a garden and a small museum with remnants from the era of early Portuguese forays to the area. The sealed, carved wooden coffin of Ngungunhane – final ruler of the famed kingdom of Gaza – is on display in one of the side rooms.

Fish Market MARKET

(Mercado de Peixe; Map p148; ⏰from about 8am) The lively Fish Market, just off Avenida Marginal, sells a good sample of what inhabits the nearby waters; choose what you'd like and get it grilled at one of the small restaurants nearby. Afternoons are best.

Municipal Market MARKET

(Mercado Municipal; Map p150; Avenida 25 de Setembro; ⏰from about 8am) With its long rows of vendors, tables piled high with produce, fresh fish and colourful spices, and stalls overflowing with everything from brooms to plastic buckets, the Municipal Market is Maputo's main market and well worth a stroll through. Get there early, when everything is still fresh, and before the crowds.

Praça da Independência PLAZA

(Map p150) This wide plaza is rimmed on one side by the white, spired **Cathedral of Nossa Senhora da Conceição** (Map p150) and on the other by the hulking, neoclassical **City Hall** (Conselho Municipal; Map p150). Just off the square is the **Iron House** (Casa de Ferro; Map p150), which was designed by Eiffel in the late-19th century as the governor's residence, though its metal-plated exterior proved unsuitable for tropical conditions.

Praça dos Heróis Moçambicanos PLAZA

(Map p148) The large Praça dos Heróis Moçambicanos, along Avenida Acordos de Lusaka near the airport, is notable for its 95m-long mural commemorating the revolution. The star-shaped white marble structure in its centre holds the remains of Mozambique's great revolutionary and post-independence heroes, including Eduardo Mondlane and Samora Machel, as well as those of national poet José Craveirinha. Photography is prohibited. The public is only permitted to visit (including walking across the praça) on 3 February.

Central Maputo

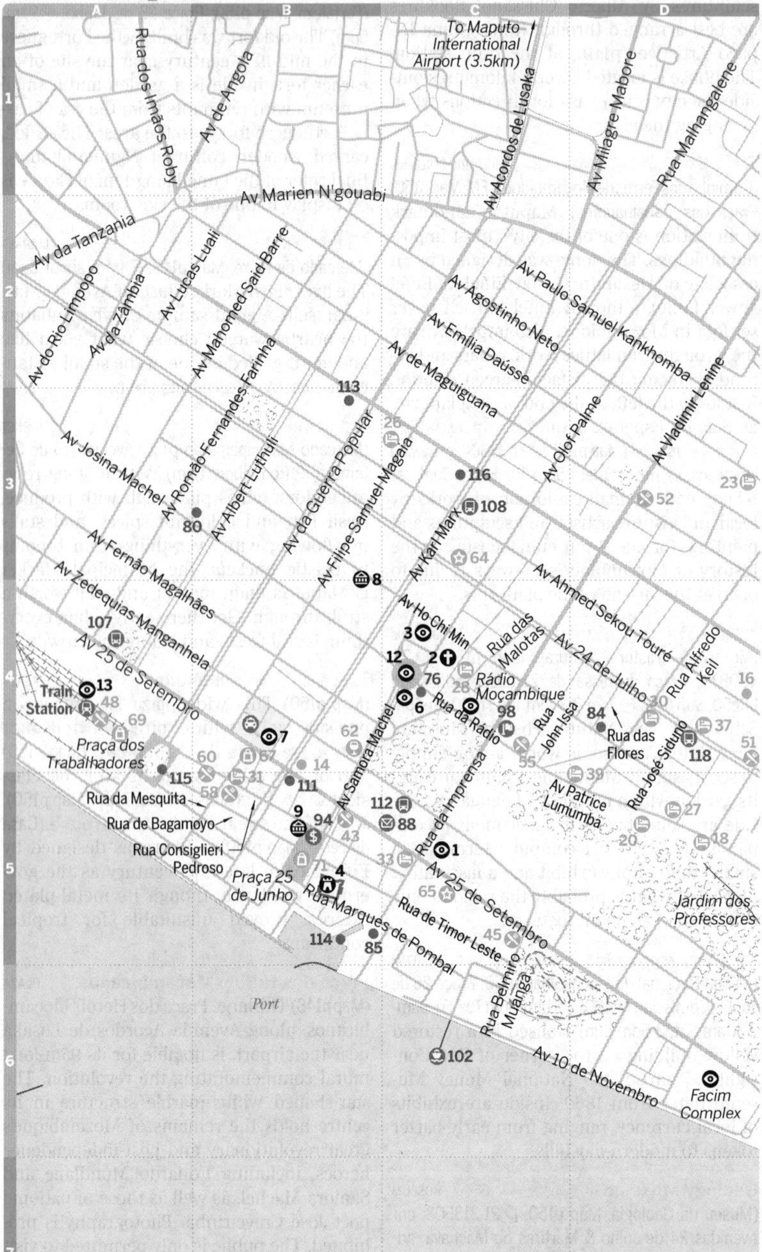
A
B
C
D
1
2
3
4
5
6
7
To Maputo International Airport (3.5km)
Rua dos Irmãos Roby
Av de Angola
Av Acordos de Lusaka
Av Milagre Mabore
Rua Malhangalene
Av Marien N'gouabi
Av da Tanzania
Av do Rio Limpopo
Av da Zâmbia
Av Lucas Luali
Av Mahomed Said Barre
Av Romão Fernandes Farinha
Av Paulo Samuel Kankhomba
Av Agostinho Neto
Av Emília Daússe
Av de Maguiguana
Av Olof Palme
Av Vladimir Lenine
Av Josina Machel
Av Albert Luthuli
Av da Guerra Popular
Av Filipe Samuel Magaia
Av Karl Marx
Av Fernão Magalhães
Av Zedequias Manganhela
Av 25 de Setembro
Av Ahmed Sekou Touré
Av Ho Chi Min
Rua das Malotas
Av 24 de Julho
Rua Alfredo Keil
Rádio Moçambique
Rua da Rádio
Rua John Issa
Rua das Flores
Rua José Sidumo
Av Samora Machel
Rua da Imprensa
Av Patrice Lumumba
Train Station
Praça dos Trabalhadores
Rua da Mesquita
Rua de Bagamoyo
Rua Consiglieri Pedroso
Praça 25 de Junho
Rua Marques de Pombal
Rua de Timor Leste
Rua Belmiro Muânga
Jardim dos Professores
Av 10 de Novembro
Facim Complex
Port
113
26
116
108
23
52
64
80
8
107
3
2
12
76
6
28
98
84
30
16
37
118
51
13
48
69
7
62
67
60
14
31
115
58
111
55
39
27
20
18
112
88
9
94
43
33
1
71
4
65
45
114
85
102

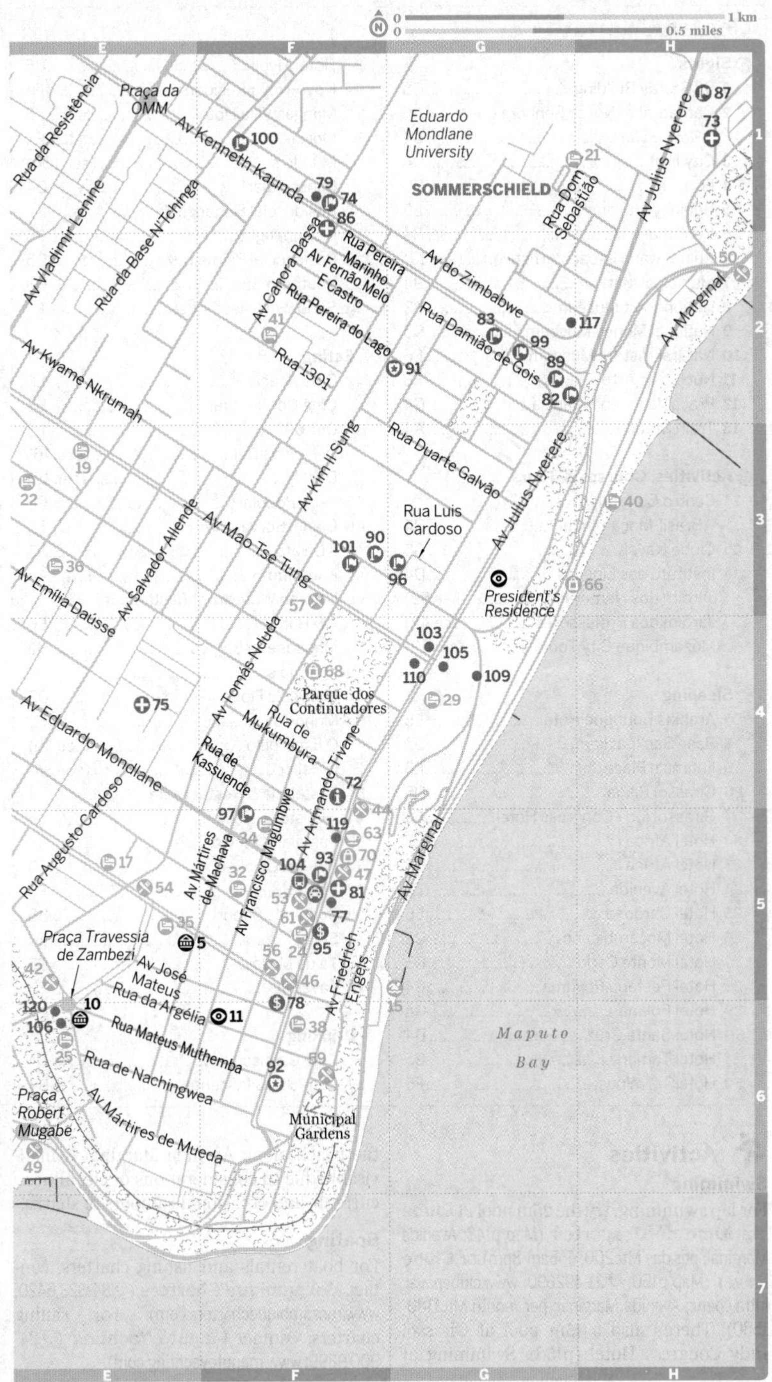
0 1 km
0 0.5 miles
Praça da OMM
Rua da Resistência
Av Kenneth Kaunda
Eduardo Mondlane University
SOMMERSCHIELD
Rua Dom Sebastião
Av Julius Nyerere
Av Vladimir Lenine
Rua da Base N'Tchinga
Av Cahora Bassa
Rua Pereira Marinho
Av Fernão Melo E Castro
Rua Pereira do Lago
Av do Zimbabwe
Rua Damião de Gois
Av Marginal
Av Kwame Nkrumah
Rua 1301
Av Kim Il Sung
Rua Duarte Galvão
Rua Luis Cardoso
Av Salvador Allende
Av Mao Tse Tung
President's Residence
Av Emilia Daússe
Av Tomás Nduda
Parque dos Continuadores
Rua de Mukumbura
Av Eduardo Mondlane
Rua de Kassuende
Av Armando Tivane
Rua Augusto Cardoso
Av Mártires de Machava
Av Francisco Magumbwe
Praça Travessia de Zambezi
Av José Mateus
Rua da Argélia
Av Friedrich Engels
Rua Mateus Muthemba
Rua de Nachingwea
Praça Robert Mugabe
Av Mártires de Mueda
Municipal Gardens
Maputo Bay

Central Maputo

Sights

- 1 33 Storey Building C5
- 2 Cathedral of Nossa Senhora da Conceição C4
- 3 City Hall C4
- 4 Fort B5
- 5 Geology Museum E5
- 6 Iron House C4
- Kulungwana Espaço Artístico .... (see 13)
- 7 Municipal Market B4
- 8 National Art Museum B3
- 9 National Money Museum B5
- 10 Natural History Museum E6
- 11 Núcleo de Arte F6
- 12 Praça da Independência C4
- 13 Train Station A4

Activities, Courses & Tours

- 14 Centro Cultural Brasil-Moçambique B4
- 15 Clube Naval G5
- 16 Instituto das Línguas D4
- Jardim dos Namorados .... (see 59)
- Jardim dos Professores .... (see 42)
- Mozambique City Tours .... (see 13)

Sleeping

- 17 Arabias Boutique Hotel E5
- 18 Base Backpackers D5
- 19 Fatima's Place E3
- 20 Girassol Bahia D5
- 21 Girassol Indy Congress Hotel G1
- 22 Hotel África I E3
- 23 Hotel África II D3
- 24 Hotel Avenida F5
- 25 Hotel Cardoso E6
- 26 Hotel Moçambicano C3
- 27 Hotel Monte Carlo D5
- 28 Hotel Pestana Rovuma C4
- 29 Hotel Polana G4
- 30 Hotel Santa Cruz D4
- 31 Hotel Tamariz B5
- 32 Hotel Terminus F5
- 33 Hotel Tivoli C5
- 34 Hoyo-Hoyo Residencial F5
- 35 Mangas Villa Hotel E5
- 36 Mozaika E3
- Mundo's .... (see 104)
- 37 Pensão Martins D4
- 38 Residencial Duqueza de Connaught F6
- 39 Residencial Palmeiras D5
- 40 Southern Sun H3
- 41 Sundown Guesthouse F2

Eating

- 42 Café Acacia E5
- 43 Café Continental B5
- 44 Deli 698 .... F5
- Deli-cious Deli .... (see 46)
- Dock's .... (see 15)
- 45 Feira Popular C5
- 46 Gianni Sorvetaria F5
- 47 Il Gelato F5
- 48 Kampfumo A4
- 49 Maputo Waterfront Restaurant & Bar E6
- 50 Marisqueira Sagres H2
- 51 Mimmo's D4
- 52 Mimmo's Flor d'Avenida D3
- 53 Mundo's F5
- O Escorpião .... (see 45)
- O Petisco .... (see 34)
- 54 Pastelaria & Restaurante Cristál E5
- 55 Pastelaria Bico d'Ouro C4
- 56 Piri-Piri Chicken F5
- 57 Pizza House F3
- 58 Sonho de Sabores B5
- 59 Surf F6
- 60 Tá de Mesa B5
- 61 Taverna F5

Drinking

- Café Camissa .... (see 11)
- 62 Café-Bar Gil Vicente B4

Activities

Swimming

For lap swimming, try the 25m pool at **Clube Marítimo de Desportos** (Map p148; Avenida Marginal; per day Mtc200; ⏲5am-8pm) or **Clube Naval** (Map p150; ☎21-492690; www.clubenaval.intra.co.mz; Avenida Marginal; per month Mtc1180-1580). There's also a 15m pool at Girassol Indy Congress Hotel (p156). Swimming at the beach along Avenida Marginal is inadvisable due to considerations of cleanliness, currents and occasional rumours of sharks.

Boating

For boat rentals and fishing charters, contact **Mozambique Charters** (☎84-323 6420; www.mozambiquecharters.com). For sailing charters, contact **Maputo Yachting** (☎84-900 9899; www.maputoyachting.com).

Dock's .... (see 15)
Hotel Terminus Pool Bar .... (see 32)
Kampfumo .... (see 13)
63 La Dolce Vita Café-Bar F5

Entertainment
64 National Company of Song & Dance C3
65 Teatro Avenida C5

Shopping
66 Artedif G3
67 Casa Elefante B4
68 Feira de Artesanato, Flôres e Gastronomia de Maputo F4
69 Himbe A4
70 Mabuku F5
71 Saturday Morning Craft Market B5

Information
72 4° Cartário Notarial F4
73 AMI Specialist Hospital H1
Cafetíssimo .... (see 46)
74 Canadian High Commission F1
75 Central Hospital E4
Centro Cultural Brasil-Moçambique .... (see 14)
76 Centro Cultural Franco-Moçambicano C4
77 Centro Cultural Português F5
78 Cotacambios F6
79 Dana Agency F1
Dana Tours .... (see 79)
80 Dinageca B3
81 Farmácia Dia e Noite F5
82 French Embassy G2
83 German Embassy G2
84 Immigration Department D4
85 Inahina B5
86 Instituto do Coração F1
87 Irish Embassy H1
88 Main Post Office C5
89 Malawi High Commission G2
90 Netherlands Embassy F3
Pizza House Internet Café .... (see 57)
91 Police Station G2
92 Police Station F6
Portuguese Embassy .... (see 77)
93 South African High Commission F5
94 Standard Bank B5
95 Standard Bank Branch F5
96 Swaziland High Commission G3
97 Tanzania High Commission F5
98 UK High Commission C4
99 US Embassy G2
100 Zambian High Commission F1
101 Zimbabwe High Commission F3

Transport
102 Catembe Ferry Pier C6
103 Chapas to Costa do Sol G4
104 Cheetah Express F5
105 Europcar G4
106 Expresso Rent-A-Car E6
107 Fábrica de Cerveja Laurentina A4
108 Greyhound C3
109 Kenya Airways G4
110 LAM Sales Office G4
111 LAM Sales Office B5
112 Luciano Luxury Coach C5
Maning Nice .... (see 112)
Museu .... (see 10)
113 Ponto Final B3
114 Porto da Pesca B5
115 Praça dos Trabalhadores Transport Stand A4
116 Ronil C3
117 South African Airways G2
TAP Air Portugal .... (see 28)
TCO .... (see 112)
118 Translux D4
119 Tuk-Tuk Stand F5
120 Tuk-Tuk Stand E6

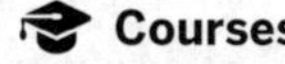

Courses

The main African languages spoken in Maputo are Shangana and the closely related Ronga. There's no formal instruction, but tutors can be easily arranged; ask around for reliable teachers at language schools, at your embassy or at local businesses and offices.

Centro Cultural Brasil-Moçambique LANGUAGE COURSE
(Map p150; ☎21-306774, 21-306840; ceb.eventos@tvcabo.co.mz; cnr Avenidas Karl Marx & 25 de Setembro) Offers Portuguese language classes and cultural events.

Instituto das Línguas LANGUAGE COURSE
(Map p150; ☎21-305473, 21-325684; marketing.il@tvcabo.co.mz; 1260 Avenida Ahmed Sekou Touré)

MAPUTO FOR CHILDREN

There's a large lawn, a playground, arcade games and several eateries at **Jardim dos Namorados** (Map p150; Avenida Friedrich Engels). Just next door are the municipal gardens, overlooking the bay. There's also a small playground attached to Mundo's restaurant (p158) and another, larger outdoor playground at the lovely **Jardim dos Professores** (Map p150; Avenida Patrice Lumumba) near Hotel Cardoso.

The swimming pool at Girassol Indy Congress Hotel (p156) has an attached play area and large surrounding gardens.

Instituto das Línguas offers Portuguese language classes.

Tours

Mozambique City Tours GUIDED TOUR
(Map p150; ☎21-333531; www.mozambiquecitytours.com; per adult/child/family Mtc855/685/995) Mozambique City Tours, with a kiosk at the train station entrance, has a hop-on-hop-off 'train' that runs in a two-hour loop to all the city's main sites, with 10 scheduled stops, and four circuits daily.

Bairro Mafalala Walking Tour CULTURAL TOUR
(☎82-418 0314; www.iverca.org; per person for 3 hr tour Mtc1000-1500) A walking tour through Mafalala bairro focusing on the area's rich historical and cultural roots, and including a stop at a local *curandeiro* (traditional healer) and a dance performance. The per person price varies depending on group size.

Jane Flood Walking Tours CULTURAL TOUR
(jane.flood@gmail.com) Specialist walking tours focusing on Maputo's architecture and art.

Festivals & Events

There's almost always an art or music festival happening in Maputo. For upcoming events check with Centro Cultural Franco-Moçambicano (p159), Kulungwana Espaço Artístico (p149) and the Living in Maputo pages on **Club of Mozambique** (www.clubofmozambique.com).

Sleeping

If you want to be in the thick of things, choose somewhere in or near the baixa or in the central area just above the baixa. For sea breezes and more tranquillity, head to the upper part of town, in and around Sommerschield and the Polana neighbourhood, or to Avenida Marginal and Costa do Sol.

BAIXA

Residencial Palmeiras BOUTIQUE HOTEL $$
(Map p150; ☎82-306 9200, 21-300199; www.palmeiras-guesthouse.com; 948 Avenida Patrice Lumumba; s/d Mtc2500/3100;) This popular place has bright decor, comfortable, good-value rooms (all but one with private bathroom, and all with TV) and a tiny garden. It's near the British High Commission, and about 10 minutes on foot from the Luciano, Maning Nice and TCO bus company offices.

Base Backpackers BACKPACKERS $
(Map p150; ☎82-452 6860, 21-302723; thebasebp@tvcabo.co.mz; 545 Avenida Patrice Lumumba; dm/d Mtc350/900; @) Small, but popular and often full, with a convenient, quiet location on the edge of the baixa. It has a kitchen, backyard bar, terrace and *braai* (barbecue) area with views to the port in the distance. Via public transport from Junta, take a 'Museu' *chapa* to the final Museu stop, from where it's a short walk.

Hotel Pestana Rovuma HOTEL $$$
(Map p150; ☎21-305000; www.pestana.com; 114 Rua da Sé; s/d from Mtc5580/6192; @) Centrally located just off Praça da Independência and opposite the cathedral, the 200-room Pestana Rovuma has well-appointed rooms, a small gym, a business centre and a selection of shops and boutiques downstairs. It's run by the Pestana Group, and offers package excursions from Johannesburg that include its sister hotels on Inhaca Island and in the Bazaruto Archipelago.

Hotel Tivoli HOTEL $$$
(Map p150; ☎82-319 3130, 21-307600; www.tdhotels.com; 1321 Avenida 25 de Setembro; s/d from US$170/202;) Completely renovated, this hotel in the baixa offers small, slick, modern rooms and a gym.

Hotel Santa Cruz HOTEL $$
(Map p150; ☎21-303006, 21-303004; www.teledata.mz/hotelsantacruz; 1417 Avenida 24 de Julho; s/d with shared bathroom Mtc1000/1600, d/ste Mtc1850/2220;) This long-standing place offers basic, decent rooms in a nondescript high-rise near the corner of Avenida Amilcar Cabral. It's not optimal for solo women travellers.

Hotel Tamariz HOTEL **$$**
(Map p150; ☎21-428608; Rua Consiglieri Pedroso; r Mtc1500; ❄) This is one of the cheapest, most reliable bets on a busy, noisy street in the heart of the baixa. Rooms are basic but acceptable, with TV and hot water. There's no food, but several restaurants are nearby. It's not optimal for solo women travellers.

Girassol Bahia HOTEL **$$$**
(Map p150; ☎21-360350, 21-360360; www.girassolhoteis.co.mz; 737 Avenida Patrice Lumumba; s/d Mtc6450/7300; ❄@📶🏊) The Girassol Bahia offers reliable rooms and service, and stunning views over the bay from the dining room, although all this comes at a steep price for what is on offer.

Hotel Moçambicano HOTEL **$$**
(Map p150; ☎82-305 2890, 21-310600; info@hotelmocambicano.com; 961 Avenida Filipe Samuel Magaia; s/tw/d Mtc3000/3350/3650; ❄🏊) This large, long-standing hotel, in a busy location convenient to the Ponto Final transport stand and the baixa, offers decent value for money.

AVENIDA MARGINAL & COSTA DO SOL

Southern Sun HOTEL **$$$**
(Map p150; ☎21-495050; www.southernsun.com; Avenida Marginal; s/d from US$270/300; ❄@📶🏊) Attractively set directly on the water (although there's no beach swimming), with comfortable rooms, attentive service, a small gym and a waterside restaurant.

Maputo Backpackers BACKPACKERS **$**
(Map p148; ☎82-467 2230, 21-451213; maputobp@gmail.com; 95 Quarta Avenida, Bairro Triunfo; dm Mtc600, r with/without bathroom Mtc1500/1000) A small, quiet place well away from the centre and near Costa do Sol, with a handful of rooms (including eight- and 10-bed dorms) with fans but no nets. Cooking is permitted if the house isn't too crowded. *Chapas* to/from town (Mtc7.50) stop nearby. Taxis charge Mtc300.

Residencial Costa do Sol MOTEL **$$**
(☎21-450115; rcs@teledata.mz; Avenida Marginal; s/d Mtc1400/2400) Above Restaurante Costa do Sol, this place has faded but tolerable rooms with fan, noise from downstairs and the beach across the road.

SOMMERSCHIELD & POLANA

Hotel Polana HOTEL **$$$**
(Map p150; ☎21-491001; www.serenahotels.com; 1380 Avenida Julius Nyerere; s/d from US$295/330; ❄@📶🏊) In a prime location on the clifftop with uninterrupted views over the sea, the Polana is Maputo's classiest hotel. Rooms are in the elegant main building or in the 'Polana Mar' section closer to the water. There's a large pool set amid lush gardens, a business centre, and a restaurant with daily breakfast and weekend dinner buffets.

Hotel Cardoso HOTEL **$$$**
(Map p150; ☎21-491071; www.hotelcardoso.co.mz; 707 Avenida Mártires de Mueda; s/d from US$240/260; ❄@📶🏊) Opposite the Natural History Museum, and on the clifftop overlooking the bay, this 130-room hotel is a Maputo classic, with good service, well-appointed rooms, a business centre and a bar with views over the water and port area.

Hotel Monte Carlo HOTEL **$$**
(Map p150; ☎82-312 8160, 21-304048; www.montecarlo.co.mz; 620 Avenida Patrice Lumumba; r Mtc2800-4000; ❄@📶🏊) A convenient central location, efficient staff, tidy rooms (some of the higher-priced ones are quite spacious) and a restaurant make this business hotel overall good value.

Hoyo-Hoyo Residencial HOTEL **$$**
(Map p150; ☎82-300 9950, 21-490701; www.hoyohoyo.odline.com; 837 Avenida Francisco Magumbwe; s/d Mtc2000/2400; ❄📶) This solid, no-frills hotel lacks pizzazz, but its 36 small rooms are comfortable, serviceable and fairly priced, and the ambience is familial. The location, just back from Avenida Julius Nyerere, is convenient, and there's a good restaurant.

Residencial Duqueza de Connaught BOUTIQUE HOTEL **$$$**
(Map p150; ☎21-492190; duqueza@tdm.co.mz; 290 Avenida Julius Nyerere; s/d Mtc3500/4500; ❄@) This lovely, quiet eight-room boutique hotel is in a restored home with polished wood, linen bedding and spotless rooms. Meals can be arranged with advance order.

Mozaika BOUTIQUE HOTEL **$$$**
(Map p150; ☎21-303965, 21-303939; www.mozaika.co.mz; 769 Avenida Agostinho Neto; s/d from Mtc3125/4610, apt Mtc7900; ❄@📶🏊) This boutique hotel, in a convenient central location one block west of the Central Hospital, is justifiably popular, with eight small rooms, each decorated with its own theme and set around a small garden courtyard with a tiny pool. There's also a self-catering apartment and a bar, although no restaurant.

Pensão Martins PENSION $$
(Map p150; ☎21-301429; pensaomartins@gmail.com; 1098 Avenida 24 de Julho; s/d/tr/ste Mtc2000/2500/3000/3500;) This peach-coloured establishment has a sleepy reception area and bland but mostly spacious rooms in a convenient central location. The suites are in a separate building behind.

Hotel Terminus HOTEL $$$
(Map p150; ☎21-491333; www.terminus.co.mz; cnr Avenidas Francisco Magumbwe & Ahmed Sekou Touré; s/d from Mtc3250/4300;) This three-star establishment in the upper part of town has small but well-appointed rooms with TV, plus good service and facilities, a business centre, a small garden, a tiny pool and a restaurant. It's popular with business travellers and often fully booked.

Fatima's Place BACKPACKERS $
(Map p150; ☎82-185 1577; www.mozambiquebackpackers.com; 1317 Avenida Mao Tse Tung; dm Mtc500, s/d without bathroom Mtc1000/1500, s/d Mtc1250/1800;) In the upper part of town, the long-standing Fatima's has an outdoor kitchen-bar, a small courtyard garden and a mix of rooms. The same management operates a hostel in Tofo (p177), and there's a daily shuttle between the two.

Sundown Guesthouse HOTEL $$
(Map p150; ☎21-497543; www.hotelmaputo.com; 107 Rua 1301; s/d from US$108/128;) This popular place offers good-value, well-appointed rooms in a small apartment block on a quiet street in the Sommerschield residential area. Meals are available on order and full breakfast is included in the price.

Girassol Indy Congress Hotel HOTEL $$$
(Map p150; ☎21-498765; www.girassolhoteis.co.mz; 99 Rua Dom Sebastião; s/d/chalet from Mtc6500/7050/12,500;) This place, in a quiet corner of Sommerschield, has well-appointed rooms as well as apartments ('chalets') set in expansive, manicured, enclosed gardens. There's a pool with an adjoining children's play area, plus a gym and a restaurant.

Hotel Avenida HOTEL $$$
(Map p150; ☎21-484400; www.tdhotels.com; 627 Avenida Julius Nyerere; s/d US$360/400;) A high-rise in a busy location in the upper part of town with efficient service, a business centre and sleek rooms with all the amenities, plus a restaurant. Room prices include use of the health club and sauna.

Mundo's GUESTHOUSE $$
(Map p150; ☎84-468 6367, 21-494080; www.mundosmaputo.com; cnr Avenidas Julius Nyerere & Eduardo Mondlane; s/d Mtc1500/2520;) Four large rooftop rooms all with TV and glimpses of the sea. Breakfast is not included in the rates.

Mangas Villa Hotel HOTEL $$$
(Villa das Mangas; Map p150; ☎21-497078; www.hipchichotels.com; 401 Avenida 24 de Julho; s/d from Mtc3630/3990;) The pluses at this tidy, whitewashed establishment are its aesthetics and its convenient central location. Rooms – most clustered around the pool in a tiny garden area – are small, with TV and mosquitoes. There's an adjoining restaurant-bar as well.

Arabias Boutique Hotel HOTEL $$$
(Map p150; ☎21-328945; www.hipchichotels.com; 698 Avenida 24 de Julho; s/d Mtc3630/3990;) The rooms at Arabias have bright red doors with *faux* Arab decor. Some rooms have interior windows only. There's a restaurant.

Hotel África I HOTEL $$
(Map p150; ☎21-312438, 84-306 0620, 21-312437; hotelafrica.reservas@gmail.com; 789 Avenida Paulo Samuel Kankhomba; s/d/ste Mtc2500/3500/4000;) Rather plain but clean and fair-value rooms in an unexciting but reasonably convenient location.

Hotel África II HOTEL $$$
(Map p150; ☎84-333 0001, 21-319191; res@hotelafrica.co.mz; 1103 Avenida Agostinho Neto; s/d Mtc3800/4500;) Clean, decent-value rooms in a centrally located highrise. There is also a restaurant.

Eating

BAIXA

Café Continental CAFE $
(Map p150; cnr Avenidas 25 de Setembro & Samora Machel; light meals Mtc150-200; ⊙6am-10pm) This classic place in the baixa is a Maputo landmark, with a good selection of well-prepared pastries, plus light meals, a large seating area and lots of ambience.

Pastelaria Bico d'Ouro CAFE $
(Map p150; cnr Avenida Patrice Lumumba & Rua John Issa; meals from Mtc130) A working-person's cafe, with sandwiches, soups and inexpensive but filling set menus.

Kampfumo PUB $$
(Map p150; ☎82-986 0137; meals Mtc350-400; ⊙12.30-3pm, 6pm-10.30pm Mon-Fri) At the train

SELF-CATERING

Deli-cious Deli (Map p150; Ground Floor, Polana Shopping Centre, cnr Avenidas Julius Nyerere & 24 de Julho) Fresh breads, cheeses and sliced meats.

Deli 698 (Map p150; 698 Avenida Julius Nyerere) Gourmet items and fresh bread.

Shoprite (Map p148; Avenida Acordos de Lusaka; ⏲9am-8pm Mon-Sat, to 1pm Sun) Just outside the city centre and en route to the airport, with ATMs in the same shopping complex.

Supermares (Map p148; Avenida Marginal, Costa do Sol; ⏲9am-7pm Mon-Sat, to 1pm Sun) A large mall with ATMs and many shops, including a Shoprite.

station, this former jazz cafe has a set daily menu for lunch, and a selection of well-prepared grilled meat and seafood in the evenings.

Tá de Mesa EUROPEAN $

(Map p150; Rua Consiglieri Pedroso; meals from Mtc150; ⏲lunch Mon-Sat) This place with counter seating is popular with locals and good for a quick, inexpensive bite.

Sonho de Sabores EUROPEAN $$

(Map p150; ☎82-307 6378; 103 Rua Consiglieri Pedroso; meals Mtc300-400; ⏲lunch & dinner Mon-Sat) Opposite Hotel Tamariz this place offers crowded seating in a tiny dining area, inexpensive grilled chicken, a large menu of local dishes and seafood and meat grills.

AVENIDA MARGINAL & COSTA DO SOL

Marisqueira Sagres SEAFOOD $$$

(Map p150; ☎21-495201; 4272 Avenida Marginal; seafood meals from Mtc400, pool per adult/child Mtc180/100; ⏲lunch & dinner Wed-Mon) This waterside place is popular for dinners and Sunday lunch, with a large menu of well-prepared seafood platters, plus meat grills and continental fare, and a small pool.

Dock's SEAFOOD $$

(Map p150; ☎82-325 5120, 21-493204; Avenida Marginal; meals Mtc350-500; ⏲9am-2am) At Clube Naval, Dock's has a daily seafood special, seafood grills and burgers, breezy waterside seating and a late-night bar. The Mtc20 Clube Naval compound entry is deducted from your meal bill.

Restaurante Costa do Sol SEAFOOD $$

(☎21-450115, 21-450038; Avenida Marginal; meals Mtc350-500; ⏲noon-11pm) A Maputo classic, this beachside place draws the crowds on weekend afternoons. There's seating on the large sea-facing porch or indoors, and an array of seafood dishes and grills, with prawns the speciality. It's about 5km from the centre at the northern end of Avenida Marginal.

Fish Market SEAFOOD $$

(Mercado da Peixe; Map p148; off Avenida Marginal) En route to Costa do Sol (the turnoff is opposite Clube Marítimo), you buy your fish fresh here, then choose a restaurant stall in the enclosed adjoining area to cook it. Cooking prices average about Mtc120 per kilo, and all the stalls also offer rice, chips or other accompaniments on order. Waits can be long on weekends, but there are shaded tables where you can sit. The best time to visit is late afternoon.

Feira Popular INTERNATIONAL $$

(Map p150; cnr Avenida 25 de Setembro & Rua Belmiro Muanga; admission Mtc20; ⏲lunch & dinner) This is a Maputo institution, where you can mix and mingle with the crowds as you wander amid dozens of small bars and restaurants set inside a large, walled compound. **O Escorpião** (Map p150; ☎21-302180; meals Mtc250-450; ⏲lunch & dinner Tue-Sun), with hearty Portuguese fare, is one of the most popular. Taxis wait outside until the early hours.

Maputo Waterfront Restaurant & Bar SEAFOOD $$$

(Map p150; ☎21-304014; www.maputowaterfront.net; Praça Robert Mugabe; meals from Mtc400; ⏲closed Sun dinner) This place has well-prepared seafood dishes (meat dishes as well), indoor and outdoor seating, views over the water and live music Wednesday, Friday and Saturday evenings.

SOMMERSCHIELD & POLANA

Pastelaria & Restaurante Cristál CAFE, EUROPEAN $$

(Map p150; ☎84-302 3560, 82-281 5180; restaurantecristal@hotmail.com; 554 Avenida 24 de Julho; meals from Mtc300; ⏲6.30am-11pm) This long-standing place has delicious pastries and breads, light meals, indoor and street-side seating and a popular, reasonably-priced restaurant serving well-prepared local and continental dishes.

O Petisco GOAN $
(Map p150; ☎82-300 9950, 21-490701; www.hoyohoyo.odline.com; 837 Avenida Francisco Magumbwe; meals from Mtc150; ⏲dinner Mon-Fri) The in-house restaurant at Hoyo-Hoyo Residencial serves tasty Goan and local fare at very reasonable prices.

Pizza House CAFE $
(Map p150; ☎21-485257; 601/607 Avenida Mao Tse Tung; pizzas & light meals Mtc170-270; ⏲6.30am-10.30pm) Popular with locals and expats, this place has outdoor seating, plus reasonably priced pastries, sandwiches, burgers, grilled chicken and other meals. There's also a small convenience store, and upstairs is an internet cafe.

Surf CAFE $
(Map p150; Jardim dos Namorados, Avenida Friedrich Engels; snacks & light meals from Mtc150; 👪) Surf is a large, amenable place with indoor and garden seating, views from the escarpment over the bay, a children's play area and fast service. It's very popular on weekends, and with families.

Café Acacia CAFE $$
(Map p150; Jardim dos Professores, Avenida Patrice Lumumba; light meals from Mtc250; ⏲7am-9pm; 👪) A tranquil garden setting with a children's play area and bay views, plus tasty pastries and coffees.

Mimmo's PIZZERIA $
(Map p150; ☎21-309491; cnr Avenidas 24 de Julho & Salvador Allende; meals Mtc200-350) At this bustling street-side pizzeria the menu also includes pastas, and seafood and meat grills. Its sister restaurant, **Mimmo's Flor d'Avenida** (Map p150; cnr Avenidas Vladimir Lenin & de Maguiguana), has air-con. At both, check your bill and your change carefully.

Piri-Piri Chicken FAST FOOD $$
(Map p150; Avenida 24 de Julho; meals from Mtc200; ⏲11am-midnight) A Maputo classic, with grilled chicken – with or without *piri-piri* (spicy chilli sauce) – plus spicy shrimp curry, cold beers and a good local vibe. It also does takeaway.

Taverna EUROPEAN $$$
(Map p150; ☎84-444 5551, 84-444 5550; www.restaurantetaverna.co.mz; 995 Avenida Julius Nyerere; meals Mtc300-500; ⏲noon-3pm & 6-10pm Mon-Fri, noon-3.30pm Sun) Delicious Portuguese cuisine with *fado* music in the background and a large wine selection; it's just up from Avenida Eduardo Mondlane.

Gianni Sorvetaria ICE CREAM $
(Map p150; Ground Floor, Polana Shopping Centre, cnr Avenidas Julius Nyerere & 24 de Julho; ice cream from Mtc70) Delicious Italian gelato, plus sandwiches and light meals.

Il Gelato ICE CREAM $
(Map p150; Avenida Julius Nyerere; ice cream from Mtc70, light meals Mtc120-250; ⏲6.30am-11pm) Excellent Italian gelato, plus light meals and indoor and street side seating. It's next to Mabuko bookstore.

Mundo's BURGERS, PUB $$
(Map p150; ☎21-494080; www.mundosmaputo.com; cnr Avenidas Julius Nyerere & Eduardo Mondlane; meals Mtc350-500; ⏲8am-midnight; 📶👪) Pizzas, burritos, burgers, and other hearty fare are all served up in large portions on wooden tables set around a street-side veranda and cooled by a misting system in the summer months. There's also all-day breakfast and a small play area for children.

Drinking

Maputo's thriving nightlife scene includes a large and frequently changing selection of cafes, pubs, bars and clubs. Thursday through to Saturday are the main nights, with things only getting going after 11pm. Cover charges at most places range from Mtc50 to Mtc250.

Dock's BAR, RESTAURANT
(Map p150; ☎21-493204; Avenida Marginal; ⏲9am-2am) The late-night waterside bar here is especially popular on Thursday ('prawns & jazz', advance reservations required), Friday (happy hour from 11pm) evenings, and when the weather is warm.

Café Camissa CAFE
(Map p150; 194 Rua da Argélia; admission Mtc100; ⏲10am-8pm) At Núcleo d'Arte with live music on Friday and Sunday evenings.

Hotel Terminus Pool Bar BAR
(Map p150; ☎21-491333; cnr Avenidas Francisco Magumbwe & Ahmed Sekou Touré) Good for a quiet drink, or if you want to stay local.

Kampfumo PUB
(Map p150; ⏲8am-11pm Thu-Sat) This former jazz cafe at the train station has a dusty, old-world ambience and a mix of live music (Saturdays) and CDs.

Café-Bar Gil Vicente BAR
(Map p150; 43 Avenida Samora Machel) A popular place with a constantly changing array of groups.

La Dolce Vita Café-Bar
CAFE

(Map p150; 822 Julius Nyerere; ⏲10am-late Tue-Sun) This sleek tapas and late-night place near Xenon cinema has live music on Thursday evening. By day, try the juices and smoothies.

Coconuts Live
LOUNGE, DISCOTHEQUE

(Map p148; Complexo Mini-Golfe, Avenida Marginal; disco Mtc250, lounge free; ⏲disco Fri & Sat, lounge Wed-Sun) A weekend disco catering to a young, informal crowd, plus a popular chill-out lounge.

☆ Entertainment

Check with the Centro Cultural Franco-Moçambicano (p159) and the www.clubofmozambique.com listings for upcoming music and dance performances.

National Company of Song & Dance
TRADITIONAL DANCE

(Companhia Nacional de Canto e Dança; Map p150; cncd@tvcabo.co.mz; Cine Teatro África, 2182 Avenida 24 de Julho) The National Company of Song & Dance, Mozambique's renowned national dance company, has occasional performances in Maputo that are well worth attending.

Teatro Avenida
THEATRE

(Map p150; ☎21-326501; teatroavenida@tvcabo.co.mz; 1179 Avenida 25 de Setembro) Teatro Avenida is home to one of Maputo's best-known theatre groups, Mutumbela Gogo. Plays are in Portuguese.

Shopping

Artedif
ARTS & CRAFTS

(Map p150; ☎21-495510; Avenida Marginal; ⏲9am-3.30pm) This cooperative for disabled people is about 400m south of Southern Sun hotel. Crafts sold here are slightly more expensive than those at the street markets, but tend to be of higher quality. Prices are fixed.

Saturday Morning Craft Market
ARTS & CRAFTS

(Map p150; Praça 25 do Junho; ⏲about 8am-1pm Sat) Woodcarvings, batiks and many other items.

Feira de Artesanato, Flôres e Gastronomia de Maputo
ARTS & CRAFTS

(Map p150; Avenida Mártires da Machava, Parque dos Continuadores; ⏲9am-5pm) Batiks, woodcarvings and more.

Himbe
ARTS & CRAFTS

(Map p150; Train Station, Praça dos Trabalhadores) A small selection of lovely crafts made by local women.

Casa Elefante
TEXTILES

(Map p150; Avenida 25 de Setembro; ⏲closed Sun) A good place to buy *capulanas* (sarongs). It's opposite the Municipal Market. There are many tailors nearby.

Mabuku
BOOKS

(Map p150; Avenida Julius Nyerere) Diagonally opposite the South African High Commission, with a small selection of English-language books and magazines.

ℹ Information

Cultural Centres

Centro Cultural Brasil-Moçambique (Map p150; ☎21-306840; ceb.eventos@tvcabo.co.mz; cnr Avenidas Karl Marx & 25 de Setembro) Exhibitions by Lusophone artists and Portuguese language courses.

Centro Cultural Franco-Moçambicano (Map p150; ☎21-314590; www.ccfmoz.com; Praça da Independência) An excellent place, with art exhibitions, music and dance performances, films, theatre and more.

Centro Cultural Português (Instituto Camões; Map p150; ☎21-493892; ccp-maputo@instituto-camoes.pt; 720 Avenida Julius Nyerere) Art and photography exhibits; opposite the South African High Commission.

Dangers & Annoyances

Although most tourists visit Maputo without mishap, be vigilant when out and about both during the day and at night, and take sensible precautions. In particular, avoid carrying a bag, wearing expensive jewellery or otherwise giving a potential thief reason to think that you might have something of value. Don't put yourself in isolating situations, and at night, always take a taxi. Areas to avoid during the day include the isolated stretches of the Marginal between Praça Robert Mugabe and the Southern Sun hotel, and the access roads leading down to the Marginal from Avenida Friedrich Engels. Also avoid the area below the escarpment just south of Avenida Patrice Lumumba.

Restricted areas that are off-limits to pedestrians (no photos) include the eastern footpath on Avenida Julius Nyerere, in front of the president's residence, and the Ponta Vermelha zone in the city's southeastern corner.

Emergency

Official emergency numbers rarely work. It's better to seek help from your hotel or embassy.

If you are the victim of a crime and need to get a police report for your insurance company, these can be obtained with time and patience at the police station nearest the site of the crime. Useful stations addresses include: **Avenida Kim Il Sung** (Map p150; ☎21-322002, 21-325031), 1½ blocks south of Avenida Kenneth Kaunda, and on **Avenida Julius Nyerere** (Map p150), three blocks south of Avenida 24 de Julho. Some insurance companies will accept a report from your embassy instead.

Central Hospital (Map p150; ☎21-325000, 21-307136; Avenida Salvador Allende, between Avenidas Eduardo Mondlane & Augustinho Neto)

Immigration

Immigration Department (Departmento Nacional de Migração; Map p150; Avenida Ho Chi Minh; ⏲7.30am-2pm to receive requests) Just up from Rua das Flores. Allow five to seven days for processing visa extensions.

Internet Access

Cafetíssimo (Map p150; Polana Shopping Centre, 3rd Fl, cnr Avenidas Julius Nyerere & 24 de Julho; ⏲8.30am-9pm Mon-Sat; ☏) Wi-fi free with food/drink purchase. Surfing only, no chatting.

Pizza House Internet Café (Map p150; Avenida Mao Tse Tung; per hr Mtc60; ⏲8am-10pm; @☏) Upstairs at Pizza House.

Medical Services

AMI Specialist Hospital (Maputo Trauma Centre; Map p150; ☎82-302 0999, 82-000 2999, 82-000 1999; 2986 Avenida Julius Nyerere; ⏲24hr) Western standards and facilities; meticais, dollars or Visa card accepted.

Farmácia Dia e Noite (Map p150; ☎84-505 8238, 82-832 3250; 764 Avenida Julius Nyerere; ⏲24hr) Opposite the South African High Commission.

Instituto do Coração (Map p150; ☎82-305 3097, 82-327 4800, 21-416347; 1111 Avenida Kenneth Kaunda; ⏲24hr) Western standards and facilities for all ailments (not just cardiac issues); meticais, dollars or Visa card accepted.

Money

There are 24-hour ATMs all over town, including at the airport and at both Shoprites. Only Millennium BIM ATMs accept MasterCard; the rest accept Visa only. BIC machines dispense up to Mtc5000 per transaction, Millennium BIM ATMs up to Mtc3000 per transaction.

Cotacambios City (Map p150; Gr Fl, Polana Shopping Centre, cnr Avenida Julius Nyerere & Mao Tse Tung; ⏲9am-9pm Mon-Sat, 10am-8pm Sun); Airport (Main terminal; ⏲open for international arrivals and departures) All change cash only. Cotacambios' airport branch also does reverse exchanges.

Notary

4° Cartário Notarial (Map p150; Avenida Armando Tivane; ⏲7.30am to 3pm Mon-Fri) Notarises documents such as passport copies.

Post

Main Post Office (CTT; Map p150; Avenida 25 de Setembro; ⏲8am-6pm Mon-Sat, 9am-noon Sun) Talk-and-pay service available 8am to 5pm weekdays (Mtc1 per impulse).

Travel Agencies

Dana Agency (Map p150; ☎21-484300; travel@dana.co.mz; Gr Fl, 1170 Avenida Kenneth Kaunda) Domestic and international flight bookings.

Dana Tours (Map p150; ☎21-495514; info@dana
tours.net; 1st Fl, 1170 Avenida Kenneth Kaunda) Specialises in travel to the coast, and can also sort you out for destinations throughout Mozambique plus Swaziland and South Africa. Midrange and up.

Mozaic Travel (☎21-451376; www.mozaictravel.com; 240 Rua de Massala, Bairro Triunfo) Excursions, including to Limpopo National Park and Bazaruto Archipelago.

ℹ Getting There & Away

Air

Kenya Airways (Map p150; ☎21-495483; www.kenya-airways.com; 33/659 Avenida Barnabé Thawé, Maputo) Shares an office with Air Mauritius.

LAM Central Reservations (☎84-147, 82-147; www.lam.co.mz) Sales Office (Map p150; ☎21-468800; cnr Avenidas 25 de Setembro & Karl Marx); Sales Office (Map p150; ☎21-490590; cnr Avenidas Julius Nyerere & Mao Tse Tung)

South African Airways (Map p150; ☎84-389 9287, 21-488970/3; www.flysaa.com; Avenida do Zimbabwe, Sommerschield) Located near the South African High Commissioner's residence.

TAP Air Portugal (Map p150; ☎21-303928, 21-303927; www.flytap.com; 114 Rua da Sé) At Hotel Pestana Rovuma.

Bus

FOR UP-COUNTRY TRAVEL

Maputo's main long-distance bus depot for up-country arrivals and departures is **'Junta'** (Avenida de Moçambique), about 7km (Mtc300 in a taxi) from the city centre. Most departures are very early, between 2.30am and 5.30am.

Some buses coming into Maputo continue into the city to **Ponto Final** (Map p150; cnr Avenidas Eduardo Mondlane & Guerra Popular), from where it's about Mtc150 in a taxi to central hotels.

Time your travels to avoid arriving at night.

TCO (Map p150; ☎82-891 3020, 82-956 0600; Avenida Zedequias Manganhela) and **Maning Nice** (Map p150; ☎82-706 2820; Avenida Zedequias Manganhela; ⏲8am-5pm) have their ticket offices and arrival/departure point in the baixa, which is much more convenient than Junta.

To **Xai-Xai** (Mtc280, four hours), **Maxixe** (Mtc475, 6½ hours), **Massinga** (Mtc550, eight hours), **Pambara Junction** (for Vilankulo, Mtc700, nine hours) and **Beira** (Mtc1780, 16 hours), TCO has an air-con bus with bathroom departing two to three times weekly at 5am from its office behind the main post office. Departure days vary; confirm when booking and expect last-minute changes.

Other transport terminals include **Benfica** (Avenida de Moçambique) for *chapas* to Marracuene and **Fábrica de Cerveja Laurentina** ('Ferroviario'; Map p150; cnr Avenidas 25 de Setembro & Albert Luthuli) for *chapas* to Swaziland, South Africa, Namaacha, Boane and Goba.

INHAMBANE Private, reasonably priced minivan transport for individuals or groups to Inhambane (about Mtc700) and Massinga can be arranged through Residencial Palmeiras (p154).

TOFO Fatima's Place (p156) has a daily shuttle between Maputo and Tofo (Mtc700).

NAMPULA To Nampula (Mtc2500), Maning Nice goes twice weekly, departing Maputo at 3.30am and arriving around 10am the next morning in Nampula, with an overnight stop in Nicoadala. From Nampula, Maning Nice has a connection on to Pemba, departing Nampula around noon and arriving in Pemba around 7pm.

TO JOHANNESBURG

Departure and ticketing points for express buses to Johannesburg include:

Greyhound (Map p150; ☎21-355700, 21-302771; www.greyhound.co.za; 1242 Avenida Karl Marx) At Cotur Travel & Tours, on the corner with Avenida Eduardo Mondlane.

Luciano Luxury Coach (Map p150; ☎82-769 9830, 84-860 2100, 21-752711; 273 Avenida Zedequias Manganhela; ⊗8am-5pm for ticketing) Behind the main post office.

Translux (Map p150; ☎21-303829, 21-303825; www.translux.co.za; 1249 Avenida 24 de Julho) At Simara Travel & Tours.

TO NELSPRUIT

Cheetah Express (Map p150; ☎21-486 3222, 82-425 0850, 84-444 3024; cheetahexpress@tdm.co.mz) Next to Mundo's restaurant.

Train

Slow trains (third class only) connect Maputo with several destinations. Rehabilitation plans are underway; get an update on routes, fares and journey times at the information window, to the left in the main train station entrance, or – with luck – at www.cfmnet.co.mz.

CHICUALACUALA (on the Zimbabwe border) Departing at 1pm on Wednesday from Maputo and at 1pm on Thursday from Chicualacuala (1st/3rd class Mtc500/182, 20 hours).

RESSANO-GARCIA (South African border) Departing Maputo at 7.45am, and Ressano Garcia at 12.10pm (Mtc15, four hours).

Getting Around

To/From the Airport

Maputo International Airport is 6km northwest of the city centre (Mtc400 to Mtc500 in a taxi).

Bus & Chapa

Buses have name boards with their destination. City rides cost about Mtc5.

Chapas go everywhere, with the average price for town trips from Mtc5. Most are marked with route start and end points, but also listen for the destination called out by the conductor. To get to Junta, look for a *chapa* going to 'Jardim'; coming from Junta into town, look for a *chapa* heading to 'Museu'.

» **Museu** (Map p150; Natural History Museum) *Chapas* to the airport and Junta (Mtc5 from Museu to Junta). *Chapas* marked 'Museu-Benfica' go along Avenida Eduardo Mondlane.

» **Ponto Final** (p160) Terminus for some upcountry buses, and for *chapas* running along Avenida Eduardo Mondlane. Also *chapas* to Costa do Sol.

» **Praça dos Trabalhadores** (Map p150) *Chapas* to Costa do Sol.

» **Corner of Avenidas Mao Tse Tung and Julius Nyerere** (Map p150) *Chapas* to Costa do Sol.

» **Ronil** (Map p150; cnr Avenidas Eduardo Mondlane & Karl Marx) *Chapas* to Junta, Benfica and Matola.

Car

Park in guarded lots when possible, or tip the young boys on the street to watch your vehicle.

Avis (☎21-465498, 82-328 4560, 21-465497; maputo.airport@avis.co.za; Airport) Offices also in Beira, Nampula and Tete.

Europcar (Map p150; ☎21-497338, 82-300 2410; www.europcar.co.mz; 1418 Avenida Julius Nyerere) Next to Hotel Polana and at the airport. Offices also in Beira, Nampula and Tete.

Expresso Rent-A-Car (Map p150; ☎21-493619; timisay@tropical.co.mz) At Hotel Cardoso; 2WD vehicles only; unlimited kilometre packages available.

Premium Rent-a-Car (☎82-527 6355, 82-762 9600, 21-466034; www.carpremium.co.mz; Airport) Offices also in Nampula, Beira, Tete and Pemba.

Sixt (☎82-300 5180, 21-465250; www.sixt.com; Airport) Offices also in Beira, Tete, Nampula and Pemba.

Taxi & Tuk-Tuk

» Taxi ranks include the **Hotel Polana taxi rank** (☎21-493255) and those in front of most other top-end hotels. Taxis also park at the **Municipal Market** and on **Avenida Julius Nyerere** in front of Mundo's restaurant. Town trips start at Mtc100. From central Maputo to Costa do Sol costs Mtc300. From Junta to anywhere in the city centre costs Mtc350 to Mtc400.

» Tuk-tuks are less expensive than taxis (town trips from Mtc50). Look for them **opposite Hotel Cardoso** (Map p150), and on **Avenida Julius Nyerere** (Map p150), just up from the South African High Commission.

AROUND MAPUTO

Catembe

Catembe, a bucolic town on the south side of Maputo Bay, offers a taste of upcountry for those who won't have a chance to leave the capital properly. Head here for a day or overnight, munch on prawns, enjoy the views of Maputo's skyline from across the bay and get into local rhythms.

Sleeping & Eating

Catembe Gallery Hotel HOTEL $$
(Marisol; ☎84-228 3623, 21-380050; www.galleryhotel.co.mz; budget/luxury d Mtc2520/4620, 6-/10-person apartment Mtc14,560/21,000; ❄☎≋) This popular spot has a tranquil waterside setting, a good restaurant, a small gallery displaying the work of local artists and an array of rooms and apartments. It's 4km north of the ferry dock. Pickups from the dock cost Mtc45 per person (advance booking only), and boat transfers from Maputo cost Mtc150 per person, minimum four people.

Esplanada-Bar Retiro de Katembe PENSION $$
(☎82-619 5273, 82-462 1140; d/tr/q Mtc2500/3000/3500; meals from Mtc250; ❄) About 400m down to the right on the beach when leaving the ferry pier, with overpriced, poorly ventilated houses in its back garden, and a good waterfront restaurant that is a popular lunch stop. Room prices exclude breakfast.

Getting There & Away

Two vehicle ferries run daily from the Maputo dock near the Ministry of Finances (per person/vehicle Mtc5/270, 20 minutes). Departures from Maputo are at 5am, 6am, 7am, 8.30am and thereafter every few hours or so until 10pm. From Catembe, the first departure is at 5.30am; evening departures are at 5pm, 6pm, 7.30pm, 9.30pm, 10.45pm and 11.30pm (final boat sometimes leaves early). Small passenger-only boats (Mtc5) run throughout the day between 7am and 7pm, although they are often unsafe, especially in bad weather.

Inhaca Island

Just 7000 years ago – almost like yesterday in geological terms – Inhaca (Ilha de Inhaca) was part of the mainland. Today, this wayward chunk of Mozambican coastline lies about 40km offshore from Maputo, and is an enjoyable weekend getaway. It's also an important marine research centre, known in particular for its offshore coral reefs. The reefs are among the most southerly in the world, and since 1976, parts of the island and surrounding waters have been designated a reserve (per person per visit US$10) to protect them and local marine life. About 3km northwest of Inhaca is tiny, uninhabited **Portuguese Island** (Ilha dos Portuguêses), a beautiful white patch of sand surrounded by clear waters. It was formerly a leper colony and is now part of the Inhaca marine reserve system.

Just south of Inhaca, across a narrow channel at the tip of Machangula Peninsula, is **Cape Santa Maria**, with quiet beaches and crystal-clear waters ideal for snorkelling. The area, which is also known for its pelicans and flamingos, is usually visited by boat from Inhaca or direct from Maputo, although there's also an overland route through the Maputo Special Reserve and a self-catering camp.

The majority of Inhaca's residents belong to a subgroup of the Tembe-Tsonga and speak a dialect of Ronga distinct from (but mutually intelligible with) that found on the mainland.

Sights & Activities

The best **beaches** are on the island's northeastern edge past the lighthouse, and on Portuguese Island. The closest good beach to the ferry pier is about 2km south, along the bay. On Inhaca's southwestern edge is a marine biology research station and a small **museum** (21-760009; admission Mtc75; 8.30-11.30am & 2-3.30pm Mon-Fri, from 9.30am Sat, Sun & holidays) with specimens of local fauna. Transport can be arranged through Pestana Inhaca Lodge (p163) or Restaurante Lucas (p163). Otherwise, it's a 50-minute walk to the marine research station, and double that to the lighthouse.

Birdwatching opportunities abound, with about 300 bird species recorded on Inhaca. This is a remarkable figure considering that the island measures only about 72 sq km in area. Among others, watch for great-winged and white-chinned petrels, mangrove kingfishers, crab plovers and greater frigate birds.

The **woodcarvers** based at Pestana Inhaca Lodge work with light-coloured wood, which is then painted, or darkened with a mixture of finely powdered charcoal and water, followed by a layer of shoe polish.

Sleeping & Eating

Marine Biology Research Station GUESTHOUSE $
(21-760013, 21-760009; fax 21-492176; r per person Mtc600) Just in from the water on the island's southwestern edge, these no-frills rooms have shared facilities and cold-water showers. It's primarily for students and researchers but is open to the public on a space-available basis. There is a kitchen, and a cook can be arranged, but you will need to bring your own food. Book rooms at least five days in advance.

Pestana Inhaca Lodge HOTEL $$$
(21-760003; www.pestana.com; s/d/f with half board from US$174/259/259;) Set in expansive, shaded gardens just north of the ferry pier on the island's western side, this four-star establishment is Inhaca's main hotel. Rooms are bright and cheery, with mosquito nets, fan and air-con. The family rooms (most are wheelchair-friendly) have a double bed, a sofa bed that can take two children, and a small verandah. Once you move past the hustle at the pier, it makes for a relaxing retreat (go midweek or in the off-season when it's quieter). There's a saltwater swimming pool, a restaurant with a lunchtime buffet, an in-house dive operator and package deals from Johannesburg (also in combination with its sister hotels in Maputo and on the Bazaruto Archipelago). Note that there's a two-night minimum stay during peak periods.

Restaurante Lucas SEAFOOD $$
(21-760007; meals Mtc250-450; from 7am) This long-standing local-style restaurant is the main place to eat. It's pricey, but the seafood grills are delicious, and the ambience is laid back. Order in advance if you're in a rush or if you fancy a particular dish. It's next to Pestana Inhaca Lodge.

Getting There & Away

Air

CFA Charters (www.cfa.co.za) does occasional charters to Inhaca from Mtc8000 per person return.

Boat

The **Vodacom ferry** (84-220 1610; www.inhaca.co.mz; 10.30am-5pm Mon, Wed, Thur & Fri) departs from Maputo's Porto da Pesca (off Rua Marques de Pombal) at 8am on Saturday and Sunday (Mtc1700 return, two hours). Departures from Inhaca are at 3pm.

There is also a boat departing from the Catembe ferry pier at 7am on Tuesday, Thursday, Saturday and Sunday (Mtc550 one-way, 1½ to two hours). Departures from Inhaca are at 2pm.

Maputo Yachting (84-900 9899; www.maputoyachting.com) does sailing charters to Inhaca and nearby Cape Santa Maria. For speedboat charters, contact **Mozambique Charters** (84-323 6420; www.mozambiquecharters.com). The ride takes about one hour, and can be rough during the windy months of August and September. All boats drop you at the beach in front of Pestana Inhaca Lodge, and usually stop at Portuguese Island en route. Transport to Portuguese Island is also easy to arrange with local fishermen on the beach in front of Pestana

Inhaca Lodge, and at low tide it's sometimes possible to walk from Inhaca. Dana Tours (p160) also organises Inhaca excursions.

Getting Around

Car hire with a driver can be arranged at Restaurante Lucas (p163) or Pestana Inhaca Lodge (p163) from about US$80 per day.

Marracuene & Macaneta Beach

Macaneta is the closest open-ocean beach to Maputo, with stiff sea breezes and long stretches of dune-fringed coast. It's on a narrow peninsula divided from the mainland by the Nkomati River, and is reached via Marracuene, 35km north of Maputo along the N1. Marracuene was a getaway for wealthy Maputo residents during colonial days and saw some heavy fighting in the 1980s during the war. Today, it's a small riverside town with a sleepy, faded charm, its main street lined with bougainvilleas and old Portuguese villas in various states of repair.

Sleeping & Eating

Jay's Beach Lodge LODGE $

(☎84-863 0714; www.jaysbeachlodge.co.za; per vehicle for day visitors Mtc200, campsite per person Mtc275, 2-/4-/6-/8-person chalet Mtc1400/2800/4200/5600) This good place is just behind the dunes on a long, beautiful beach, with a restaurant, shade and *braai* (barbecue) facilities available for day visitors, and camping and chalets for overnight. Pick-ups from Marracuene can be arranged for those without 4WD. The day visitor fee is waived if you eat at the restaurant.

GWAZA MUTHINI

Each year in February, Marracuene fills up with visitors commemorating those who died resisting colonial rule in the 1895 Battle of Marracuene, known locally as Gwaza Muthini. At the heart of the festivities is the killing of a hippo from the Nkomati River and the *kuphalha* ceremony (invocation of the ancestors), although the hippo hasn't been very forthcoming in recent times and a goat is usually roasted instead. Gwaza Muthini also marks the beginning of the season for *ukanhi* – a traditional brew made from *canhu*, the fruit of the *canhoeiro* tree found throughout Maputo and Gaza provinces, and considered sacred in much of the region.

Getting There & Away

Take any northbound *chapa* from Benfica (Mtc60, one hour) to Marracuene, from where it's a 10-minute walk through town to the **Nkomati River ferry** (return per person/vehicle Mtc4/180, five minutes; ⏲6am to 6pm). On the other side, follow the rutted road for about 5km to a junction of sorts, from where you'll find most of the Macaneta places about 5km to 8km further, and signposted. There's no public transport; hitching is slow except at weekends. For drivers, a 4WD is essential, except to get to Macaneta Lodge.

North of Marracuene

About 20km north of Marracuene and signposted just off the N1 are several useful places for breaking up your travel if you're doing a self-drive visit from South Africa, including **Blue Anchor Inn** (☎82-325 3050, 21-900559; www.blueanchorinn.com; adult/child Mtc1106/553), which has pleasant rooms and cottages in large grounds, and a restaurant. Breakfast costs extra.

SOUTHERN MOZAMBIQUE

For more than 500 years, visitors have been marvelling at the beauty of the southern Mozambican coastline. For the early Portuguese explorers, its white sands and sheltered bays served as a gateway to the fabled goldfields of the interior, and as convenient staging points on the long sea journey to the Orient. In more recent times, a steady stream of holiday-makers have been lured by promises of plates heaped with giant prawns and grilled *lagosta* (crayfish); languid days cooled by gentle Indian Ocean breezes; sultry nights enlivened by pulsating *marrabenta* rhythms; and the best diving and game fishing to be found in the region.

Mozambique's southern coast is the most developed part of the country for tourism. And its popularity is well justified. From Ponta d'Ouro, with pounding surf and windswept dunes, to the serene lagoons and shallow coastal lakes between Bilene and Závora, and the legendary beaches of Tofo and Barra, it boasts some of the most beautiful stretches of sand on the continent. In addition to the beaches, southern Mozambique has a wealth of cultural highlights, if you have the time to see them. These include the famed *timbila* (marimba) orchestras of the Chopi people and a rich body of traditional lore, much of which focuses on the old kingdom of Gaza.

Tourism infrastructure is fast expanding and caters to all budgets. Transport links, especially with nearby South Africa, are good, with sealed major roads and a reliable bus network. If you want an easy introduction to Mozambique or a beach holiday, the south is a good place to start.

Ponta d'Ouro & Ponta Malongane

☎21

The sleepy colonial-era town of Ponta d'Ouro has boomed in popularity in recent years and is the first Mozambique stop on many southern Africa overland itineraries. Its best asset is its excellent beach – long, wide and surf-pounded. Offshore waters host abundant sea life, including dolphins and whale sharks and – from July to October – whales. Thanks to Ponta d'Ouro's proximity to South Africa, it fills up completely on holiday weekends.

About 5km north is the quieter and even more beautiful Ponta Malongane, with a seemingly endless stretch of windswept coastline fringed by high, vegetated dunes and patches of coastal forest.

Activities

Diving

The Tandje Beach Resort (p166) compound is the base for **Scuba Adventures** (☎21-900430; www.africasafaris.co.za) and the **Whaler** (☎84-604 4369; www.thewhaler.co.za) dive operators. Both offer simple tented and/or reed or wooden hut accommodation sharing ablutions with the camping ground, catered or self-catering options, diving courses and equipment rental. Both also offer low-season and midweek discounts.

Devocean Diving DIVING
(www.devoceandiving.com) In the town centre next to the police station.

Ponta Malongane DIVING
(www.malongane.co.za) At Ponta Malongane.

Simply Scuba DIVING
(www.simplyscuba.co.za) At Motel do Mar (p165).

Dolphin Tours

Dolphins frequent the waters off Ponta d'Ouro, and catching a glimpse of these beautiful creatures can be a wonderful experience. However, they're wild, which means sightings can't be guaranteed; let them come to you, if they wish, and don't go off in wild pursuit or try to touch them. Prices are about Mtc1100 per person for a two-hour excursion, generally also involving snorkelling near Ponta Malongane and sailing down towards the lighthouse. Dolphins can be spotted year round (although there are no refunds if you don't spot any). Whale sharks are best seen between July and November. Between June and August it's chilly in the boats, so bring a windbreaker. If conditions are stormy or too windy, the boats don't go out. From October/November to February the sea tends to be calmest.

Dolphin Encountours BOAT TOUR
(☎84-330 3859; www.dolphin-encountours.co.za) Based at Dolphin House in the town centre.

Somente Aqua Dolphin Centre BOAT TOUR
(☎84-242 9864; www.somenteaqua.com) Just before Tandje Beach Resort. Also has self-catering accommodation.

Sleeping

PONTA D'OURO

Motel do Mar Beach Resort HOTEL $$
(☎21-650000; www.pontadoouro.co.za; 4-person chalets without/with sea view US$85/105; ❄) In a fine seaside location (though not all rooms manage to have full sea views), this motel is a throwback to colonial days. It has a restaurant that does seafood grills, a 1960s ambience and blocks of faded but nevertheless quite pleasant two-storey self-catering chalets.

Kaya Kweru BUNGALOW $$
(☎82-527 6378, 21-758403; www.kaya-kweru.com; dm with bathroom US$18; 2-/4-person cottage from US$102/163; ❄@≋) About 200m north of the town centre past the Catholic church, this efficient place has rows of closely spaced stone-and-thatch cottages with bathrooms, all set in a rather featureless compound redeemed by its location just in from the beach and its good facilities. There's also a restaurant, an open-air bar facing the sea, a grill area, a full range of activities (including a dive operator), and transfers to/from South Africa and Maputo. The dorm rooms have air-con and private bathroom.

Café PENSION $
(84-827 5275, 21-650048; pontacafe@yahoo.com; r per person Mtc875;) Café has small rooms in reed chalets closely spaced around a tiny garden behind the restaurant. All have nets, fans and shared bathrooms with hot water. It's perched on a hilltop in the town centre about 200m in from the beach; look for the bright orange building. If you're after some quiet, midweek is best; on weekends the bar has music until dawn.

Tandje Beach Resort CAMPGROUND $
('Campismo' 21-900430; campsite per person/vehicle Mtc520/15; 2-/4-/6-person bungalow from Mtc1880/4600/9400) In addition to the facilities of the Scuba Adventures (p165) and the Whaler (p165) dive camps located on its grounds, both of which have budget accommodation, Tandje has a shaded, seaside camping area with shared ablutions and basic bungalows, including a few beach-facing ones. All the bungalows have a small gas stove, but only the six-person bungalow has hot water and fridge. It's at the southern end of town. Contact them through Scuba Adventures.

Devocean Diving CAMPGROUND $
(84-206 1120; www.devoceandiving.com; r or tent per person from US$23) About 400m from the sea along the main road into town and next to the police station, this is basically a dive camp but with more pampering. Accommodation is in a few rooms in the main house or in canvas tents set around a small garden, and there's a restaurant.

Coco Rico BUNGALOW $$
(84-875 8029; www.cocorico.co.za; 8-person chalet US$340;) About 200m north of the town centre past the Catholic church, Coco Rico has large, well-equipped, eight-person wooden self-catering chalets just back from the beach.

Praia de Ouro Sul TENTED CAMP $$$
(in South Africa 012-348 2690; www.pontadoouro.co.za; d/q tent from US$164/194;) Well-appointed safari-style tents set on a forested hillside, and there's a restaurant. It's about 5km south of Ponta d'Ouro town, and is signposted from town.

PONTA MALONGANE

Ponta Malongane, without a town, is quieter and more spread out than Ponta d'Ouro, and has an excellent beach. You'll need your own transport here.

Ponta Malongane CAMPGROUND $
(in South Africa 013-741 1975; www.malongane.co.za; campsite per adult/child US$21/13, dive-camp tents US$30-60, log hut d US$74, 4-person self-catering chalets from US$161) This long-running, laid-back place is based in the sprawling and shaded Parque de Malongane. It has many accommodation options, including camping, four-person *rondavels* (round, traditional-style huts) and chalets, and small, rustic twin-bedded log huts. There's also a restaurant and a large self-catering area. You should ask about dive-accommodation deals. Breakfast costs extra.

Tartaruga Marítima Luxury Camp TENTED CAMP $$
(84-373 0067; www.tartaruga.co.za; s/d US$104/160;) About 2km north of Parque de Malongane, and well-signposted, is Tartaruga. This lovely and tranquil retreat has spacious, comfortable safari-style tents tucked away in the coastal forest behind the dunes and is just a few minutes' walk from a wonderful stretch of beach. There's no restaurant but there is a raised lounge-bar and self-catering *braai* area with views over the open ocean. Ask about midweek discounts.

Eating

Most eating options are located in Ponta d'Ouro.

Bula-Bula CONTINENTAL $$
(meals Mtc200-450; lunch & dinner Thur-Tues) The popular Bula-Bula has a large selection of well-prepared continental and Mozambican cuisine, including pastas, salads and seafood grills.

A Florestinha do Índico CONTINENTAL $
(meals from Mtc200; lunch & dinner) Next to Motel do Mar, with seating under thatched umbrellas scattered around a shady lawn and a selection of samosas and other snacks, plus standard fare.

Fishmonga SEAFOOD $$
(21-650026; meals from Mtc250; breakfast, lunch & dinner;) A popular rooftop gathering spot in front of Café, on the hilltop in the town centre, serves filling breakfasts, seafood platters and other hearty fare.

Café CAFE $$
(21-650048; pontacafe@yahoo.com; meals from Mtc250; lunch & dinner Wed-Mon;) The orange Café, perched on the hilltop in the

town centre with views to the sea, has tasty pancakes, prawns and other fare, plus a bar with a daily happy hour and live music most weekends.

Information

Ponta d'Ouro has a constantly changing array of shops in the town centre. Within a short time of arriving, you'll find surf board rental, fishing tackle shops, a pharmacy and more. The best place for self-catering supplies is the market (try the small shops on the back side). To the right of the market is a bakery. There's a BIC ATM just below Café (Visa card only). South African rands are accepted everywhere; meticals and US dollars can also be used.

Getting There & Away

Ponta d'Ouro

CAR Ponta d'Ouro is 120km south of Maputo. The road is potholed but in decent shape for the first 60km, but it's slow going through soft, deep sand thereafter. Allow about three hours in a private vehicle (4WD only).

CHAPAS Direct *chapas* depart Maputo's Catembe ferry pier by about 6am or earlier on Tuesday and Friday (Mtc175, five hours). Departures from Ponta d'Ouro are on Wednesday and Saturday from in front of the market. Otherwise, take the ferry to Catembe, where there are several direct *chapas* daily. From Ponta d'Ouro back to Catembe, there is a *chapa* most weekdays departing at 4am. Arrange with the driver the evening before to pick you up at your hotel.

SHUTTLE Kaya Kweru (p165) has a twice weekly shuttle from Maputo (Mtc4000 per person return).

FROM SOUTH AFRICA Kosi Bay border crossing is 11km south of Ponta d'Ouro along a sandy track (4WD), and most *chapas* from Catembe pass here first, before stopping at Ponta d'Ouro (Mtc50 from the border to Ponta d'Ouro). Coming from South Africa, there's a guarded lot just over the border where you can leave your vehicle in the shade for R30 per day. All the hotels do pick-ups from the border from about US$10 to US$15 per person (minimum two people). Allow about five hours for the drive to/from Durban (South Africa).

Ponta Malongane

There's no public transport to Ponta Malongane, though *chapas* between Maputo and Ponta d'Ouro stop at the signposted turn-off, about 5km before Ponta Malongane. To get between Ponta d'Ouro and Ponta Malongane, you can walk along the beach at low tide (7km) or go via the road.

Maputo Special Reserve

En route to Ponta d'Ouro and just two hours from the capital is the 90-sq-km **Maputo Special Reserve** (adult/child/vehicle Mtc200/100/200), which runs along a spectacularly beautiful and completely isolated stretch of coastline. It was gazetted in 1969 to protect the local elephant population (about 350 in the late 1970s), plus several turtle species. Until recently it was known as the Maputo Elephant Reserve. The elephants, who suffered from the effects of the war and poaching, are estimated to number only about 180 today – most quite skittish and seldom seen, but planned restocking should improve chances of sightings. There are also small populations of antelope, hippo and smaller animals. The main attractions are the pristine wilderness feel – it offers a true bush adventure close to the capital – and the birding. Over 300 different types of birds have been identified, including fish eagles and many wetland species. The coastline here is also an important nesting area for loggerhead and leatherback turtles; peak breeding season is November to January.

The heart of the reserve is **Ponta Milibangalala**, about 35km from the main gate along the sea. While there are few spots that can rival the beauty of the coastline here, the bush road in from the gate is also interesting, as it passes through the reserve's rich diversity of habitats, including woodlands, grasslands and dry forest.

Although rehabilitation is scheduled – in conjunction with the planned extension of the reserve, and its ultimate merger with South Africa's Tembe Elephant Park – there are currently no facilities, apart from a basic beachside **camping ground** (campsite adult/child Mtc200/100) at Ponta Milibangalala. You'll need to be completely self-sufficient, including food and water (water suitable for washing is sometimes available at the main entrance). There's also an area at the main entrance next to the reserve office where you can pitch a tent, although almost everyone goes further in to camp along the beach. A lodge is scheduled to open in the park within the next several years; check www.anvilbay.com for updates.

Outside the reserve, about 8km south of Salamanga town and signposted along the road to Ponta d'Ouro, is the community run **Tsakane ka Madjadjane** (☎82-215 1360; campsite per person w/ own tent Mtc150/250, dm

Mtc300, s/d Mtc500/750). It offers very basic accommodation and the chance to arrange cultural activities, including learning about honey harvesting and mat weaving. Advance bookings are recommended.

Continuing north within the reserve, past its northern boundary and on to the tip of the Machangula Peninsula, brings you to **Ponta Torres Nhonguane Lodge** (☎84-318 2443; www.nhonguanelodge.co.za; 4-person tent Mtc4000, self-catering houses per person from about Mtc2000) on Cape Santa Maria, with large safari-style tents and well-equipped self-catering chalets. Bring all food and drink. A 4WD is essential and you'll need to pay vehicle and entry fees for the reserve.

Getting There & Away

Dana Tours (p160) operates day and overnight trips to the reserve. Otherwise, you'll need your own transport (4WD). The main entrance, known as *campeamento principal*, is about 65km from Catembe along the Ponta d'Ouro road. From here, it's 3km to the park gate, and then about 35km further through the reserve along a rough road to the coast and the camping ground. There's a second entrance further along the Ponta d'Ouro road, marked with a barely legible signpost, from where it's about 22km into the reserve.

Namaacha

Cool Namaacha lies on the border with Swaziland, about 70km west of Maputo. Its streets are lined with lavender jacaranda and bright-orange flame trees, and thanks to its favourable climate, it is the source of many of the flowers for sale on Maputo's street corners. The ornate colonial-era church is the main building of interest.

Located on the main road in the town centre, **Hotel Libombos** (☎21-960102; d/ste Mtc3000/3500; ❄) has comfortable rooms, some with views over the hills, plus a restaurant and a casino.

Chapas run throughout the day to/from Maputo (Mtc70, 1½ hours), departing Namaacha from the border, and stopping in front of the market on the main road.

Bilene

☎282

This small resort town sits on the large Uembje Lagoon, which is separated from the open sea by a narrow, sandy spit. Thanks to its sheltered waters and its position as the first resort area north of Maputo, it's a popular destination with vacationing South African families, and on holiday weekends you'll be tripping over motorboats, windsurfing boards and quad bikes. If you're based in Maputo with a car at your disposal, it makes an enjoyable getaway, but if you're touring and want some sand, head further north to the beaches around Inhambane or south to Ponta d'Ouro.

Unlike most of Mozambique's other coastal lakes and lagoons, Uembje gets influxes of fresh water via a narrow channel to the sea, so conditions vary with the seasons. In general the winter months are best, with breezes and waves.

In the 19th century the area around Bilene served as capital for the Gaza chief, Soshangane. During colonial days Bilene was known as São Martinho, and the saint's feast on 4 November is still celebrated, often with processions, singing and dancing in the upper part of town away from the beach.

Sleeping & Eating

Complexo Palmeiras CAMPGROUND $
(☎82-304 3720, 282-59019; http://complexopalmeiras.blogspot.com; campsite US$6, plus per person US$5, 4-person chalets US$97) At the northern edge of town on the beach, it has camping, no-frills chalets with fridge, *braai* facilities and a restaurant. Bring your own towels, linens, pans and cutlery. It's about 500m past the market and transport stand: follow the main road into town to the final T-junction, then go left for 1km.

Praia do Sol RESORT $$
(☎82-319 3040; www.pdsol.co.za; s/d US$67/133, chalets per person US$67; ✖) About 4km south of town along the beach, this place has a collection of spacious two- and four-person A-frame chalets overlooking the lagoon, plus some double rooms. There are also larger four- and five-person self-catering chalets (per chalet US$218/266) and a restaurant-bar, as well as diving, canoeing, snorkelling and quad-bikes, plus boat trips across the lagoon to the ocean. Turn right onto the beachfront road and continue for about 3km, staying right at the fork. Prices for the rooms and non-self-catering chalets include breakfast.

Complexo Aquárius LODGE $$
(☎82-301 9000, 282-59000; www.aquariusbilene.co.mz; r Mtc2500; ❄) Just to the right (south) of the main T-junction on a nice, semi-shaded

section of beach, with red-roofed stone chalets and a restaurant featuring seafood grills and Portuguese cuisine.

Café O Bilas CAFE **$**
(pizzas from Mtc120) This longstanding place next to the petrol station is good for pizzas and snacks.

Tchin-Tchin AFRICAN **$**
(Beachfront road; meals from Mtc150) Inexpensive grilled chicken and chips.

Getting There & Away

Bilene is 140km north of Maputo and 35km off the main road. A direct bus departs Maputo's Praça dos Combatentes ('Xikelene') at about 7am (Mtc130, five hours). Otherwise, go to Junta and have any northbound transport drop you at the Macia junction, from where pick-ups run throughout the day to/from Bilene (Mtc25, 30 minutes).

Leaving Bilene, direct departures are daily at 6am (and sometimes again at 1pm) from the town centre near the market.

If you're driving, the road to Bilene is tarmac throughout. With a 4WD (or by chartering a boat – possible at most hotels), it's possible to reach the other side of the lagoon and beach on the open sea. Boats can also be arranged with local fishermen from about Mtc250 return.

Limpopo National Park

Together with South Africa's Kruger National Park and Zimbabwe's Gonarezhou National Park, **Limpopo National Park** (Parque Nacional do Limpopo; ☎21-713000; www.limpopopn.gov.mz; adult/child/vehicle Mtc200/100/200, payable in meticais or South African rand) forms part of the Great Limpopo Transfrontier Park. Gonarezhou connections are still in the future, but Kruger and Limpopo are now linked via two fully functioning border crossings.

Wildlife on the Mozambique side can't compare with that in South Africa's Kruger, and sightings are still very hit and miss; it's quite possible to spend time in the park without seeing large animals, yet Limpopo's bush ambience is alluring, and the park area also offers the chance for cultural and adventure tourism. There are people living within the park boundaries so it's likely that you'll see some of these communities on the park's eastern fringes.

Most visitors use Limpopo as a transit corridor between Kruger and the coast. There's also the five-day Shingwedzi 4WD Trail, starting at Kruger's Punda Maria camp and continuing south through Limpopo park to the Lebombo/Ressano Garcia border crossing (book through www.dolimpopo.com or www.sanparks.org).

Additional offerings include a four-day hiking trail from Massingir Dam west along the Machampane River, and a three-day canoe expedition along the Elefantes (Olifants) River from its confluence with the Shingwedzi River to its confluence with the Limpopo River. Both can be booked through Machampane Wilderness Camp (p169).

Sleeping & Eating

Campismo Aguia Pesqueira CAMPGROUND **$**
(campsite per person Mtc210, 2-person chalet Mtc1500) This good park-run camping ground is along the edge of the escarpment overlooking Massingir Dam, about 50km from Giriyondo border crossing. All campsites have views over the dam, plus *braai* facilities. There's a communal kitchen and ablutions, plus several rustic self-catering chalets, also with views.

Machampane Wilderness Camp TENTED CAMP **$$$**
(www.dolimpopo.com; s/d tent with full board US$363/558) The upmarket Machampane has five spacious, well-appointed safari tents in a tranquil setting directly overlooking a section of the Machampane River, where you're likely to see (or at least hear) hippos plus a variety of smaller wildlife and many birds. Activities are the highlight here and include guided walks, a multi-night hiking trail and a four-day canoe expedition along the Elefantes River. Machampane Camp is about 20km from Giriyondo border crossing, and pick-ups can be arranged from Massingir village or from Kruger park's Letaba camp (where you can leave your car).

Covane Fishing & Safari Lodge LODGE **$$**
(☎in South Africa 011-023 9901; www.covanelodge.com; campsite per person US$12, tw in traditional house US$60) This place – jointly run by Barra Resorts and the local community – is about 13km outside Limpopo's Massingir gate on a rise overlooking the dam. It was in the process of being upgraded as this book was researched, and price changes are likely. Currently on offer are camping and accommodation in local-style bungalows or twin-bedded chalets, plus the chance to rent houseboats. Boat excursions,

THE GAZA KINGDOM

Gaza province is now famous for its beaches and coastal lakes, but as recently as the mid-19th century it was renowned as the seat of the kingdom of Gaza, one of the most influential in Mozambican history. At the height of its power around the 1850s, it stretched from south of the Limpopo River northward to the Zambezi and westward into present-day Zimbabwe, Swaziland and South Africa.

One of Gaza's most famous chiefs was Soshangane, who ruled most of southern Mozambique from his base at Chaimite. Soshangane died in 1858 and was succeeded by his son, Umzila, who in turn was succeeded by his son, Ngungunhane. Ngungunhane's first priority was to defend the Gaza kingdom from ever-increasing European encroachment. While outwardly acknowledging Portuguese sovereignty, he allowed raiding parties to attack Portuguese settlements and struck numerous deals with the British, playing off the two colonial powers against each other.

By the mid-1890s, the tides began to turn. In 1895 Ngungunhane was captured by the Portuguese, and spent the remainder of his life in exile in the Azores. He died in 1906, and the mighty Gaza kingdom came to an end.

fishing trips, village walks and visits to the park can be arranged. Breakfast costs US$5 extra and local-style lunch and dinner are available. Advance bookings are recommended.

Getting There & Away

The main park entrance on the Mozambique side is **Massingir Gate** (6am-6pm), about 5km from Massingir town (which has an ATM). It's reached via a signposted turn-off from the N1 at Macia junction that continues through Chokwé town (where there's also an ATM) on to Massingir. While daily *chapas* go between Maputo's Junta and Massingir (Mtc180), there is currently no possibility for onward transport within the park, so Limpopo remains primarily a self-drive destination.

To enter Limpopo from South Africa's Kruger park, you'll also need to pay Kruger park entry fees, and Kruger's gate quota system applies (see www.sanparks.org for information).

If you transit between the Pafuri border crossing, at Limpopo's northern tip, and Vilankulo, it's worth detouring about 30km before reaching Mapinhane to visit the overgrown ruins of **Manyikeni** (signposted to the north of the Mapinhane road). Manyikeni was once the seat of a major trading centre and chieftaincy which was occupied between the 13th and 17th centuries, and which had links to Great Zimbabwe. At the moment the site is neglected, although it has been proposed for inclusion as a Unesco World Heritage site.

The closest tanking up stations on the Mozambique side are in Xai-Xai, Chókwè and Massingir. Travelling via Mapai, there is no fuel until Mapinhane.

Xai-Xai

282

Xai-Xai (pronounced 'shy-shy', and known during colonial times as João Belo) is a long town, stretching for several kilometres along the N1. It's of little interest to travellers, but the nearby **Xai-Xai Beach** (Praia do Xai-Xai), about 10km from the town centre, has invigorating sea breezes, and is an agreeable overnight stop if you're driving to/from points further north.

The capital of Gaza province, Xai-Xai was developed in the early 20th century as a satellite port to Maputo, although its economic significance never approached that of the national capital. Running just south of Xai-Xai is the 'great, grey-green greasy' Limpopo River of Rudyard Kipling fame. It's Mozambique's second largest waterway, with a catchment area of more than 390,000 sq km, and drains parts of Botswana, South Africa and Zimbabwe as it makes its way to the sea. Despite its size, water levels vary dramatically throughout the year, leaving some sections as just small streams during the dry winter months. The wetlands around the Limpopo's lower reaches are rewarding birdwatching areas, and are most accessible near Zongoene.

Sleeping

Complexo Halley HOTEL $$
(282-35003; complexohalley1@yahoo.com.br; Xai-Xai Beach; d Mtc2250-2750;) This longstanding beachfront hotel is the first place you reach coming down the beach access

road from town, and is an amenable, recommended choice. It has stiff sea breezes, a seaside esplanade, a good restaurant and pleasant, homy rooms (ask for one that's sea-facing). All rooms have hot-water bathroom and some have air-con and TV. On Friday evening there's a disco at the hotel; on Saturday it's across the road at the beachside esplanade.

Kaya Ka Hina PENSION $
(☎282-22391; N1; s/d without bathroom Mtc750/850, tw/d with bathroom from Mtc1200/1500; ❄) The centrally located Kaya Ka Hina is convenient if you're trying to catch an early bus or if you don't want to drive down to the beach. It has no-frills, clean rooms upstairs and an inexpensive restaurant below. It's on the busy main road about 100m north of the *praça* transport stand. The hotel entrance is around to the side of the restaurant.

Eating

Pastelaria Chave CAFE $
(EN1; meals from Mtc150) Inexpensive local dishes and snacks.

Pastelaria Mukokwene CAFE $
(snacks & light meals from Mtc50) Pastries, breads and light meals. It's one block east of the main street, directly east of (and one block behind) Pastelaria Chave, as the crow flies.

KFC FAST FOOD $
(just off EN1) For those missing American-style fried chicken.

Information

There are ATMs at **Millennium BIM** (N1, near Kaya Ka Hina), **Standard Bank** (one block behind Kaya Ka Hina) and **Barclays** (N1, opposite the church). For internet access try **Telecomunicações de Moçambique** (per min Mtc1; ⏲7.30am-7pm), diagonally opposite Standard Bank and just behind the central market.

Getting There & Away

The main '*praça*' transport stand is near the old Pôr do Sol complex on the main road at the southern end of town. Buses to Maputo depart daily at about 6am (Mtc280, four hours). It's marginally faster to take one of the north–south through buses, although getting a seat can be a challenge. Wait by the Pôr do Sol complex or, better, take a *chapa* to the *pontinha* (bridge control post), where all traffic needs to stop.

To Xai-Xai Beach (Mtc5), *chapas* depart from the *praça* transport stand, or catch them anywhere along the main road. They run at least to the roundabout, about 700m uphill from the beach, and sometimes further.

Around Xai-Xai

The lagoon-studded coast north and south of Xai-Xai has a string of attractive beaches – all quiet, except during South African school holidays. The area is particularly suited to travellers with their own vehicle, as many of the lodges are located well off the N1, although some offer transfers.

The beach is particularly lovely at **Chidenguele**, about 70km north of Xai-Xai and just 5km off the N1 down an easy access road. The coast here is fringed by high, vegetated dunes stretching into the horizon in each direction. There's also an old **lighthouse**, reached via an unsignposted sandy track off the Chidenguele access road, and climbable when the keeper is around. Chidenguele village is notable for its large **cathedral** (visible from the N1), its bakery and its small market. About 12km north along the beach is **King's Pool** – a sheltered tidal pool that is ideal for snorkelling, and for fishing from the outer reef.

Paraíso de Chidenguele (☎84-390 9999; www.chidbeachresort.com; 'overnight' r per person US$36, 2-/4-/6-person chalets US$85/121/204; 👪) is a lovely place with accommodation in simple, twin-bed 'overnight' rooms, or in spacious, well-equipped self-catering cottages – some with stunning views over the sea, others nestled in the coastal forest. There's a restaurant-bar and a large, sparkling clean swimming pool. It's ideal for families. It also rents snorkelling equipment for trips to King's Pool.

Well south of here – south of Xai-Xai and about 7km north of Bilene – is another lovely stretch of beach, and the pleasant **Zongoene Lodge** (☎282-42003, in South Africa 015-295 9038; www.zongoene.com; campsite per person US$16, d US$156, 4-person self-catering house from US$235; ✉). It's just south of the mouth of the Limpopo River with spacious 'pool chalets', or more rustic self-catering houses set back from the beach. There's also camping, a restaurant and an array of activities including fishing and sunset cruises on the Limpopo River. The turn-off is about 15km south of Xai-Xai at Chicumbane, from where it's about 35km further down a sandy track that can be negotiated by 2WD during the dry months.

Quissico

About 130km northeast of Xai-Xai on the N1 is Quissico, capital of Zavala district. It is noteworthy for being one of the main meal and bathroom stops on long-haul bus routes along the N1. If the bus stops for long enough, look down the escarpment eastward to a chain of shimmering, pale blue lagoons in the distance. Quissico's other claim to fame is that it is the centre of the famed Chopi *timbila* (marimba) **orchestras**, and the site of an annual *timbila* **festival** (last weekend in August).

Lagoa Eco Village (☎84-577 2946; info@lagoaecovillage.com; campsite per person Mtc300, dm/d MTc400/1750, 5-/8-person self-catering chalet Mtc4300/5940), on the edge of the lagoon about 7km from Quissico town down a rough track, has a lagoon-side setting, swimming and kite surfing (with your own equipment), and various types of rustic, thatched accommodation and camping. There's a *braai* area, a communal kitchen and a small bar, but no restaurant, so bring your own food and drink (Quissico town has basics and an ATM), or book meals with them in advance. Via public transport, take a *chapa* from the main Quissico junction heading to Macomane. Get off at the T-junction, from where it is about 1km further on foot to the right. Driving, the turnoff is signposted opposite the hospital.

Závora Beach

About 55km north of Quissico and roughly 80km south of Inhambane is Závora Beach, with a lighthouse that is possible to climb if you can find someone around to open it. It's also home to the rustic, slightly frayed but fairly priced and backpacker-friendly **Závora Lodge** (☎84-288 8584; www.zavoralodge.com; 4-person bungalow US$97, 4-/8-/10-person sea-view house US$146/291/364; ❄@). There's a large array of accommodation, including camping sites (per person US$12 to US$14) both behind and on the visibly eroding dunes, self-catering chalets (some in a compound behind the dunes and better ones on top of the dune with views and breezes), rooms (US$85 to US$109) and a backpackers' dorm (US$13). There's also a restaurant overlooking the sea. The bungalows, houses and sea-view rooms come with bedding and towels; for the other options, you'll need to bring your own. Závora Lodge's main attraction is its good in-house **dive operator** (http://mozdivers.com) who will guide you to see the area's many underwater attractions (manta rays, sharks, a nearby shipwreck) at reasonable prices.

CHOPI TIMBILA ORCHESTRAS

The intricate rhythms and pulsating beat of Chopi *timbila* music are among southern Africa's most impressive musical traditions. The music is played on *timbila* (singular: *mbila*) – a type of marimba or xylophone made of long rows of wooden slats carved from the slow-growing *mwenje* (sneezewood) tree. In age-old rites of passage, young Chopi boys would go into the bush to plant *mwenje* saplings, which would then be harvested for *timbila* construction years later when their grandsons came of age.

At the heart of *timbila* music is the *m'saho* (performance), which involves an orchestra (*mgodo*) of up to 20 or more instruments of varying sizes and ranges of pitch, singers and dancers, rattle or shaker players and a single composition with movements similar to those of a Western-style classical symphony. Rhythms are complex, often demanding that the players master different beats simultaneously with each hand, and the lyrics are full of humour and sarcasm, dealing with social issues and community events.

Following a decline during the immediate post-independence and war years, *timbila* music is now experiencing a renaissance, due in part to the efforts of Venáncio Mbande, a master composer, player and *timbila* craftsman par excellence. Like many other Chopi, Mbande left Mozambique at a young age to seek work in the South African mines but kept the art of *timbila* alive and ultimately formed his own orchestra. In the mid-1990s Mbande returned to his home near Quissico, where he began teaching *timbila* music and craftsmanship. His orchestra, Timbila ta Venáncio, has received international acclaim. Numerous other orchestras have since been formed around Zavala district and Quissico is a centre for training young players. For information on the annual festival in Quissico, try contacting **Amigos de Zavala** (www.amizava.org).

Getting There & Away

Závora is 17km from the N1 (usually negotiable with 2WD); the turn-off is signposted 11km north of Inharrime town. Free pick-ups to/from Inharrime can be arranged with Závora Lodge. Otherwise, there's a daily *chapa* (Mtc30, 45 minutes), departing Inharrime at about noon and Závora (just up from Závora Lodge) at about 7am. Transfers can also be arranged from Inhambane and Tofo.

Lindela

This junction village is where the road to Inhambane splits off the N1. **Quinta de Santo António** (84-490 5105, 82-489 2420, 293-56030; www.stayonthebeach.co.za; N1; campsite per person Mtc200, d from Mtc1200, 4-/6-person chalet Mtc12500/3500;) has rooms (some with air-con), well-equipped self-catering chalets with fans, nets and microwaves, a shop selling a few basics, a resident parrot, meals with advance notice, and among the cleanest bathrooms along this stretch of the coastal road.

Inhambane

293

With its serene waterside setting, tree-lined avenues, faded colonial-style architecture and mixture of Arabic, Indian and African influences, Inhambane is one of Mozambique's most charming towns and well worth a visit. It has a history that reaches back at least 10 centuries, making it one of the oldest settlements along the coast. Today Inhambane is the capital of Inhambane province, although it's completely lacking in any sort of bustle or pretence. It is also the gateway to a fine collection of beaches, including Tofo and Barra.

History

As early as the 11th century, Inhambane served as a port of call for Arabic traders sailing along the East African coast. Textiles were an important commodity, and by the time the Portuguese arrived in the early-16th century, the area boasted a well-established cotton-spinning industry. In 1560 Inhambane was chosen as the site of the first Jesuit mission to the region. Development was also helped along by Inhambane's favourable location on a sheltered bay, and before long it had moved into the limelight as a bustling ivory trading port. By the early-18th century, the Portuguese had established themselves here, together with traders from India. This mixture of Indian, Christian and Muslim influences continued to characterise Inhambane's development in later years, and is still notable today.

In the coming decades, the focus of trade shifted from cloth and ivory to slaves. By the mid-18th century, an estimated 1500 slaves were passing through Inhambane's port each year, and this human trafficking had become the town's economic mainstay.

In 1834 Inhambane was ravaged by the army of the Gaza chief, Soshangane. However, it soon recovered to again become one of the largest towns in the country. The abolition of the slave trade in the late-19th century dealt Inhambane's economy a sharp blow. The situation worsened in the early-20th century as economic focus in the region shifted southward to Lourenço Marques (now Maputo). Many businesses moved south or closed, and Inhambane began a gradual decline from which it still has not recovered.

LAND OF THE GOOD PEOPLE

Upon his arrival in Inhambane, 15th-century Portuguese explorer Vasco da Gama was reportedly so charmed by the locals that he gave the area the name Terra da Boa Gente (land of the good people).

Sights & Activities

Strolling around Inhambane's quiet traffic-free streets comes as a surprise treat if you've been frequenting some of Mozambique's other urban areas. The **Cathedral of Nossa Senhora de Conceição**, dating from the late 18th century, is one of the main landmarks. It rises up behind the newer **cathedral**, just north of the jetty. North of here, reached by following the waterfront road, is the small **old mosque** (1840). The **new mosque** is several blocks further east. Don't miss strolling along the **waterfront** at sunset, and watching the sun sink into the flamingo-frequented Inhambane Bay.

Inhambane's colourful **market** is at its best in the early morning. Also recommended is the tiny **museum** (Avenida da Vigilância; admission free, donations welcome; 9am-5pm Tue-Fri, 2-5pm Sat & Sun) near the new mosque. Its displays include collections of traditional musical instruments, clothing and household items from the surrounding area, with some captions in English.

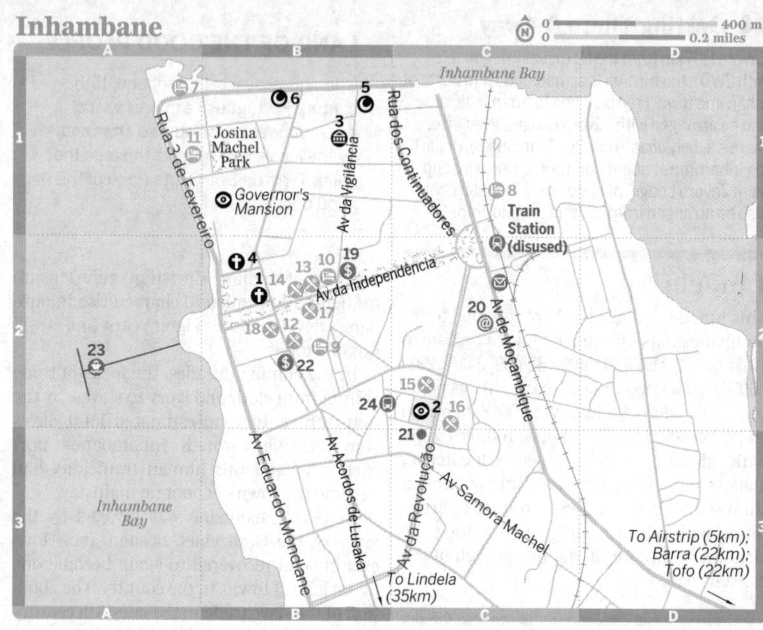

Inhambane

Sights

- 1 Cathedral of Nossa Senhora de Conceição B2
- 2 Market C2
- 3 Museum B1
- 4 New Cathedral B2
- 5 New Mosque B1
- 6 Old Mosque B1

Sleeping

- 7 Casa do Capitão A1
- 8 Escola Superior de Hotelaria e Turismo C1
- 9 Hotel Africa Tropical B2
- 10 Hotel Inhambane B2
- 11 Pensão Pachiça A1

Eating

- 12 Á Maçaroca B2
- 13 Café d'Hotel B2
- Clube do Comodore ..... (see 7)
- 14 Famous Fried Chicken B2
- 15 Padaria de Inhambane C2
- 16 Supermarket C2
- 17 TakeAway Sazaria B2
- 18 Verdinho's B2

Information

- 19 Barclays Bank B2
- 20 Centro Provincial de Recursos Digitais de Inhambane C2
- 21 Litanga Travel & Services C3
- 22 Millennium BIM B2

Transport

- 23 Boats & Dhows to Maxixe A2
- 24 Bus Station B2

Sleeping

Casa do Capitão HOTEL **$$$**
(☎293-21409, 293-21408; www.hotelcasadocapitao.com; s/d from Mtc4800/6750; ❄📶) This beautiful new hotel is in a fantastic location overlooking Inhambane Bay on two sides. Views are wonderful and rooms are beautifully appointed. It's a nice treat if you're in Inhambane on a honeymoon or if you just want pampering. There's also a good restaurant (p175). Significant low season and weekend discounts are available.

Hotel Inhambane HOTEL $$
(☎84-389 3837, 293-21225; www.hotelinhambane.co.mz; Avenida da Independência; d/tr/ste Mtc2200/3200/5900; ❄) Central Hotel Inhambane has simple, clean, mostly spacious rooms with minifridge, TV and hot water.

Pensão Pachiça BACKPACKERS $
(☎84-389 5217, 84-412 5297, 293-20565; www.barralighthouse.com; Rua 3 de Fevereiro; dm/s/d/f Mtc400/900/1500/2200, meals Mtc300-400) This backpackers on the waterfront has clean rooms and dorm beds (the family room has its own bathroom), a restaurant-bar serving pizzas and local cuisine, and a rooftop terrace overlooking the bay. From the ferry, take a left coming off the jetty and continue about 300m. The same management runs campgrounds at Tofinho and Barra lighthouse.

Hotel Africa Tropical PENSION $
(Sensasol; ☎82-777 4871; s/d/tr Mtc500/1200/1700; ❄) The Tropical has a row of tidy rooms facing a small garden. Some have double bed, others have a double plus a single bed. All have fan, net and hot water, and most also have TV and minifridge. Breakfast costs extra, and there's a small restaurant. It's well-located just off Avenida da Independência.

Escola Superior de Hotelaria e Turismo HOSTEL $
(☎293-20755, 293-20781; www.eshti.uem.mz; Avenida de Moçambique; tw/q Mtc1125/2250) By the train station at the eastern edge of town, this place has functional attached twins (no nets), with each two-room (four-bed) unit sharing a bathroom. Unless they are full, you can often negotiate to only be charged per occupied bed, rather than for the entire room. From the ferry jetty, continue straight through town to the end of the main road.

Eating

TakeAway Sazaria CAFE $
(Avenida da Independência; meals from Mtc80; ⊙8am-5pm Mon-Fri) At Fatima's Paradise, with tasty, inexpensive soups, pregos and sandwiches to eat there or take away.

Café d'Hotel AFRICAN $
(Avenida da Independência; meals Mtc150-200) Inexpensive, tasty daily menus and local dishes. It's just down from Hotel Inhambane.

Verdinho's CONTINENTAL $$
(☎82-389 9038; Avenida Acordos de Lusaka; salads from Mtc185, meals from Mtc280; ⊙8am-10pm Mon-Sat; 📶) Features a large menu including meze, gourmet salads and burgers, pizzas and continental dishes, and seating indoors or at shaded tables outside on the patio, where you can watch the passing scene.

TANGERINAS DE INHAMBANE

Mention Inhambane province to a Mozambican, and chances are they will say something about *tangerinas de Inhambane*. In season, you'll see bushel baskets of tangerines lining the roadsides, piled to overflowing. The fruit has even made it into local pop culture through the poem, *As saborosas tanjarinas d'Inhambane*, written by renowned Mozambican poet José Craveirinha.

Clube do Comodore CONTINENTAL $$
(Rua 3 de Fevereiro; meals from Mtc300) At Casa do Capitão, with well-prepared seafood and meat grills and wonderful views over the bay.

Padaria de Inhambane BAKERY $
(Avenida da Revolução) For hot, fresh rolls. It's next to the market, and close enough to dash over to from the bus stand.

Á Maçaroca EUROPEAN $$
(☎293-20489; Avenida Acordos de Lusaka; meals from Mtc300-450; ⊙7am-11pm Mon-Sat) One block south of Avenida da Independência, this Swiss-Mozambican place has a selection of grilled fish, meat, curries and other dishes.

Famous Fried Chicken FAST FOOD $
(Avenida da Independência; fried chicken from Mtc140) American-style fried chicken and clean bathrooms.

Supermarket SUPERMARKET $
(Avenida da Revolução) Diagonally opposite the market and reasonably well-stocked.

Information

Immigration (for visa extensions) is in Maxixe.

Barclays Bank (Avenida da Independência) With an ATM.

Centro Provincial de Recursos Digitais de Inhambane (Avenida da Revolução; per min Mtc1; ⊙8am-8pm Mon-Fri, 9am-4pm Sat) Internet access.

Millennium BIM (Avenida Acordos de Lusaka) With an ATM.

Litanga Travel & Services (☎293-21024; litanga servicos@gmail.com; Avenida da Revolução) Near the entrance to the central market. Walking tours, *dhow* trips and LAM bookings.

Getting There & Away

Air

LAM (www.lam.com.mz; airport) has several flights weekly connecting Inhambane with Maputo, Vilankulo and Johannesburg.

Boat

Small motorised passenger boats operate from sunrise to sundown between Inhambane and Maxixe (Mtc10, 25 minutes). The pier on the Maxixe side is just across the N1 from the main bus stand. Sailing *dhows* do the trip more slowly for Mtc5, and one of Inhambane's great morning sights is sitting on the jetty and watching them load up. It's also possible to charter a motorboat (about Mtc200, 10 minutes).

Bus & Chapas

The **bus station** is behind the market. *Chapas* to Tofo run throughout the day (Mtc15, one hour). There is a daily direct bus to Maputo, departing at 5.30am (Mtc500, seven hours, 450km). Fatima's Nest (p177) in Tofo also has a daily shuttle to Maputo (Mtc700) that stops by Inhambane. For other southbound buses, and for all northbound transport, you'll need to head to Maxixe.

Coming from Maputo, a direct bus departs Junta between 5am and 6am, or take any northbound bus to Maxixe.

There's at least one daily *chapa* to Maxixe (Mtc40 to Mtc50) via the shortcut road; the turnoff from the N1 is at Agostinho Neto area, 20km south of Maxixe.

Tofo

☎293

Thanks to its sheltered azure waters, white sands, easy access and fine diving, the beach at Tofo has long been legendary on the southern Africa holiday circuit. The beach runs in a long arc, at the centre of which is a small town with a perpetual party atmosphere. Many people come to Tofo expecting to spend a few days, and instead stay several weeks or more. For something quieter, head around the point to Barra, or further north or south.

Activities

Diving

Tofo is Mozambique's unofficial diving capital. The following operators also organise whale shark snorkelling safaris:

Diversity Scuba DIVING
(☎293-29002; www.diversityscuba.com; town centre)

Liquid Adventures DIVING
(☎84-060 9218; www.divingtofo.com) Behind Tofo OnLine in the town centre.

Peri-Peri Divers DIVING
(www.peri-peridivers.com) At Albatroz Lodge.

Surfing

Waterworks Surf & Coffee Shop (Town Centre), next to Diversity Scuba, rents kayaks and surfboards.

Horse Riding

For horse riding on the beach (catering to riders of all levels), contact Cavalheiros do Tofo in person (it's set back from the beach just before reaching Bamboozi Beach Lodge) or go through www.tofotravel.com.

Quad Biking

Quad-biking excursions to Barra Point and beyond can be arranged with **Tofo Quad Bike Adventures** (☎84-817 7597) at Casa Anlija, just up from Fatima's.

Sleeping

For rentals of self-catering cottages in Tofo and Tofinho, contact **Tofo Beach Cottages** (www.tofo.co.za). See also www.tofotravel.com.

Note that some of the lower-lying camping areas behind the dunes can get extremely wet and flooded during the rainy season.

Casa do Mar B&B $$
(☎in South Africa 82-455 7481; www.casa-do-mar.co.za; s/d from Mtc1600/2700; ❄🏊) This beautiful B&B-style place has bright, spotless and impeccably decorated rooms in a large private home, some with sea views, and a chef who prepares delicious gourmet meals. Breakfast costs extra (Mtc250 per person).

Casa Azul GUESTHOUSE $$
(☎82-821 5921; www.casa-azul-tofo.com; s US$72-108, d US$80-150) Casa Azul, a lovely converted white with blue trim, colonial-era house on the beach at the southeastern end of Tofo, is bright and cheery, and has pleasant rooms named for different colours. There are semi-open-air bathrooms, each one different, and a 'treehouse' room with its own veranda, plus a small garden in front, and meals.

Albatroz Lodge LODGE $$$
(☎293-29005; www.albatrozlodge.com; 4-/6-/8-person chalets Mtc3800/4600/5850) Large, rustic thatched self-catering cottages in a

quiet setting on the bluff overlooking the beach. There's a restaurant and an on-site dive operator (p176). Some cottages are well ventilated, while others have an exterior window and a semi-interior one covered with thatching that can block air flow.

Aquático Ocean Annex PENSION **$$**
(☎82-857 2850; www.aquaticolodge.com; tr Mtc1700; ❄) This place has four attached, spacious self-catering rooms in a good location directly on the beach. Each has one double and one twin bed, fan, nets, a refrigerator and a mini-cooker. There are no meals, but there's a restaurant next door.

Nordin's Lodge BUNGALOW **$**
(☎82-312 4770, 293-29009; binos50@hotmail.com; 2-/4-person chalets Mtc1500/3000) The unassuming Nordin's is at the northern edge of town in a good, shaded location directly on the beach. It has four rustic, rather faded but decent-value thatched chalets that come with hot water, fridge and self-catering facilities. There are no meals.

Fatima's Nest BACKPACKERS **$**
(☎82-185 1575; www.mozambiquebackpackers.com; campsite per person Mtc250, dm Mtc400, s/d/tr/q Mtc1000/1600/2300/3000, s/d bungalow Mtc700/1300) The long-standing Fatima's, ever popular and now considerably expanded, has camping, dorm beds and a mix of very basic bungalows and rooms, all on low dunes overlooking the beach behind and just north of Nordin's Lodge. There's also a kitchen, a bar, pool table, and evening beach bonfires.

Bamboozi Beach Lodge BACKPACKERS **$**
(☎293-29040; www.barraresorts.com; campsite per person US$16; dm US$17, d hut US$36, d bungalow/sea-view chalet US$102/136) Popular Bamboozi has dorm beds and extremely basic reed huts – some with floor mattresses and others with beds, and all with just a bottom sheet and net – set down low behind the dunes and sharing rather scruffy ablutions. There are also five stilted reed A-frame 'chalets' with bathrooms, and a better sea-view chalet up on the dune with views. It's 3km north of town along a sandy road. The views from the dune-top bar-restaurant are magnificent, but prices are high for what is on offer. Wednesday and Friday are party nights.

Mango Beach BUNGALOW **$**
(☎82-943 4660; www.mangobeach.co.za; d Mtc865-2000, 4-/6-person chalets Mtc2125/4375) About 4km north of town along the road paralleling the beach, and signposted from the entrance to Tofo, is Mango Beach. It has a dune-top bar/eating area with impressive views over the beach (which is rocky just in front, so you'll need to head south for swimming). Behind the dunes is a cluster of basic bungalows with shared bathrooms. Bring your own towels and linens. Nicer are the houses (also with shared bathroom), and the chalets, which come with their own kitchenette and bathroom. There's no electricity for the entire compound from sunset to dawn, and it gets very dark.

CFM Lodge PENSION **$$**
(☎293-29020; r Mtc1800; ❄) CFM Lodge is smack in the centre of things, opposite the market and about 100m back from the beach behind Hotel Tofo Mar. Its row of attached rooms come with nets and hot water. Check that your air-con is working first, as the rooms aren't well-ventilated otherwise. There's no food, although a restaurant is planned.

Hotel Tofo Mar HOTEL **$$$**
(www.hoteltofomar.com) Situated in a prime location directly on the beach in the town centre, Hotel Tofo Mar is the only 'proper' hotel (ie non bungalow-style place) in Tofo. It was being completely renovated at the time of writing, but should reopen imminently. Check with them for an update.

Eating & Drinking

Casa de Comer FUSION **$$**
(☎293-29004; meals from Mtc300-450; ⏲9am-10pm Wed-Mon; ✎) Tasty Mozambique-French fusion cuisine, including vegetarian dishes, and some local artwork on display in the small adjoining garden. It's in the town centre.

Tofo Tofo AFRICAN **$**
(meals from Mtc150) Inexpensive snacks and local food, and a small grocery store.

Blend CAFE **$**
(At Liquid Adventure; snacks from Mtc70) This sandwich and smoothie shop also has good breakfasts, burgers and more.

Dino's Beach Bar CAFE **$$**
(www.dinosbeachbar.com; meals from Mtc200; ⏲10am-late Thu-Tue) One of Tofo's main hangouts, Dino's is located on the beach just past Fatima's Nest, with good vibes, good music and tasty food (pizzas, seafood, toasted sandwiches, desserts and more).

Chili's Deli DELI $

(Inhambane road; snacks from Mtc50) Hidden away behind the petrol station several kilometres before Tofo (on the right when coming from Inhambane) is this little place with fresh cheese, freshly made tortilla chips and homemade fudge. It's a worthwhile stop for those with their own transport.

Restaurante Concha CONTINENTAL $$

(meals Mtc250-400) Opposite the market in the town centre, with local flavour and Western prices. There's a wide selection of Mozambican and continental standards, and a bar.

Information

The closest ATMs are in Inhambane and Barra.

Tofo On-Line town (per min Mtc3; ⌚9am-6pm Wed-Mon); beach (per min Mtc3; ⌚10am-6pm Thu-Tue) has internet access. The town branch also has pre-paid wireless access.

Getting There & Away

Chapas run throughout the day along the 22km sealed road between Tofo and Inhambane, departing Tofo from about 5am (Mtc10-15 for a large bus, one hour). To Maputo's Junta, there's usually one direct bus daily, departing Tofo by about 4.30am (Mtc500, 7½ hours). Fatima's Nest (p177) also has a daily shuttle to Maputo (Mtc700). Otherwise, you'll need to go via Inhambane or Maxixe. If you do this and want to catch an early north/southbound bus, it's possible in theory to sleep in Tofo, but for a more sure connection, stay in Inhambane the night before.

If you leave early from Maputo, it's possible to get to Inhambane in time to continue straight on to Tofo that day, with time to spare.

Tofinho

Just around the point (to the south) and easily accessed from Tofo (by walking or catching a lift) is Tofinho. It's set on a green hillside looking out over turquoise waters, and is Mozambique's unofficial surfing capital. Board rental should be arranged in Tofo (p176).

Sleeping & Eating

For eating, Turtle Cove (p178) is the place to go, with its eclectic mix of dishes, sometimes featuring sushi, and a laid-back ambience. Bar closing time is 11.30pm. Everywhere else in Tofinho is self-catering.

Turtle Cove Surf & Yoga Lounge BUNGALOW $

(☎82-719 4848; www.turtlecovetofo.com; campsite per person US$8.50, dm US$12-18, d chalet US$48-60; ❄) This is the spot to go if you're interested in surfing or chilling, with Moorish-style stone houses with bathrooms, a few very basic grass huts, camping, a yoga centre and a restaurant. Breakfast is extra. There's a 20% discount for longer stays.

Casa de John GUESTHOUSE $$

(Casa Amarela; ☎082-451 7498; www.casajohn.co.za; 2-/3-bedroom house US$164/242) Just back from the cliff near the monument, this place has lovely, well-appointed two- and three-bedroom self-catering houses in a breezy setting on the cliff overlooking the sea.

Tofinho Back Door Campsite CAMPGROUND $

(☎84-389 5217; www.barralighthouse.com; campsite per adult/child US$12/6, 6-person house US$146) Has campsites overlooking the sea (all with *barracas*, power point and water) and simple reed *casitas* (bungalows) with hammocks, mosquito nets and shared hot-water ablutions.

Barra

☎293

Barra sits at the tip of the Barra Peninsula, where the waters of Inhambane Bay mix with those of the Indian Ocean. On the bay side are stands of mangrove and wetland areas that are good for birding. It's all beautiful, but unlike Tofo, there's no town, and everything's spread out. Many self-drivers prefer Barra's quieter scene and its range of midrange accommodation options, but Tofo is a better bet if you're backpacking or relying on public transport. There's an ATM at Barra Lodge. For diving and instruction, contact **Barra Dive** (www.barradiveresorts.com; Barra Lodge).

Sleeping & Eating

Barra Lodge LODGE $$$

(☎293-20561; www.barraresorts.com; 6-person self-catering cottages US$173, s/d beach chalet US$216/400; ❄📶🏊) One of Barra's largest, longest-running and most outfitted places, with a range of accommodation – from small twin-bed reed *casitas* with bathroom (s/d with half board US$126/230), to larger, well-equipped self-catering cottages – plus a beachside bar-restaurant, a full range of activities, and excursions to its sister lodge at Pomene, further up the coast.

Flamingo Bay Water Lodge LODGE $$$
(293-56007, 293-56005; www.barraresorts.com; s/d with half board US$177/327;) Well-appointed wood-and-thatch stilt houses lined up in a row directly over the bay. There's also a good restaurant known for its 'double meat pizzas'. No children under 12 years of age permitted. It's under the same management as the nearby Barra Lodge, and transfers to/from the Barra Lodge beach are provided.

Areia Branca Lodge LODGE $$
(www.areiabranca.co.za; campsite per person U$15, 6-bed bungalow US$127) A collection of rustic self-catering reed chalets on the beach almost at the northwesternmost edge of the Barra Peninsula; just continue along the increasingly sandy track past Flamingo Bay Water Lodge.

Barra Lighthouse CAMPGROUND $
(Farol de Barra; 84-389 5217, 84-573 4525; www.barralighthouse.com; campsite per person US$12) This place has rustic camping next to the lighthouse at Barra point, with hot and cold ablutions, plug points, good security and views. Boats can be launched; quad bikes aren't permitted. Take the signposted sandy right off the Barra road (4WD only), when coming from Bar Babalaza.

Bar Babalaza PUB $
(meals from Mtc250) Apart from the lodge restaurants, the main eating option is Bar Babalaza, about 6km from Barra at Josina Machel junction where the roads to Tofo and Barra diverge. It's a local institution, with meals and drinks, air for your tyres and local information. In Barra itself, there are no shops or nonhotel restaurants but fish is available from local fishers.

Getting There & Away

AIR Barra Lodge (p178) and Flamingo Bay (p179) offer fly-in packages from Johannesburg. There are connections by air to/from Inhambane (from where all the Barra lodges do transfers).

BUS Daily *chapas* go between Inhambane and Conguiana village along the Barra road. From here, you'll need to sort out a pick-up or walk (about 4km to Barra Lodge).

CAR & MOTORCYCLE The turn-off for Barra is about 15km from Inhambane en route to Tofo; go left at the Bar Babalaza junction. You can easily make it in a 2WD most of the way, but you'll need a 4WD to reach Barra lighthouse and the self-catering anglers' places at the point. Hitching is easy in high season from Bar Babalaza.

Maxixe

293

Maxixe (pronounced ma-sheesh) is about 450km northeast of Maputo on the N1 and is convenient as a stopping point for traffic up and down the coast. It's also the place to get off the bus and onto the boat if you're heading to Inhambane, across the bay.

Sleeping & Eating

Maxixe Camping CAMPGROUND $
(293-30351; N1; campsite per person Mtc130) Maxixe Camping, just south of the jetty, has an enclosed and scruffy but serviceable camping ground overlooking the bay with reasonable ablutions. You can leave your vehicle here while visiting Inhambane (Mtc75 per vehicle per day).

Stop Residencial MOTEL $$
(82-125 2010, 293-30025; stopmaxixe96@hotmail.com; d/tw/ste Mtc1500/1500/1800;) Tidy, functional rooms with hot-water bathrooms. Most of the rooms are just up the road next to Barclays Bank. For bookings, directions and check-in, go to Restaurante Stop next to the ferry.

Restaurante Stop CONTINENTAL $$
(293-30025; N1; meals from Mtc225; 6am-10pm) Stop, on the north side of the jetty, has prompt service, clean toilets, tasty meals and a swimming pool (per person Mtc100).

Information

Inhambane Province's **Department of Immigration** (Migração; 7.30am-3.30pm) for visa extensions, is in Maxixe, one block back from the main road. Turn at Barclay's Bank, then take the first left; Immigration is just up on the left. No visa extensions are done in Inhambane town.

There are ATMs at Millennium BIM, just in from the main road near Pousada de Maxixe, and at Barclays Bank, about 600m further north and just off the N1.

Getting There & Away

Buses to Maputo (Mtc475, 6½ hours, 450km) depart from the bus stand by the Tribunal (court) from 6am. There are no buses to Beira originating in Maxixe; you'll need to try to get space on one of those coming from Maputo that stop at Maxixe's main bus stand (Mtc1000 from Maxixe to Beira). Thirty-seater buses to Vilankulo originating in Maputo depart Maxixe from about 10am from the main bus stand. Otherwise, *chapas* to Vilankulo (Mtc180, 3½ hours) depart throughout the day from Praça 25 de Setembro (Praça de Vilankulo), a couple of blocks north of the bus stand in front of the Conselho Municipal.

If you're driving to Inhambane, take the short-cut road signposted to the east about 20km south of Maxixe in the Agostinho Neto area.

Massinga

The bustling district capital of Massinga is a convenient stocking up point, with numerous shops, a petrol station and garage.

There are several ATMs, including **Millennium BIM** (one block west of the N1) and **BCI** (N1), at the southern end of town.

For accommodation, try **Dalilo's Hotel** (☎293-71043; N1; tw with/without bathroom from Mtc800/550; ❄) at the northern end of town, with meals at **Dalilo's Restaurant** (N1; meals from Mtc180), just south of Dalilo's Hotel.

Getting There & Away

Most north–south buses stop at Massinga. The first departure to Maputo (Mtc550, eight hours) is by about 6am. Going north, buses from Maputo begin to arrive in Massinga by about 11am, en route to Vilankulo.

Morrungulo

About 8km north of Massinga is the signposted turn-off for Morrungulo Beach (Praia de Morrungulo), a stunning stretch of coastline. **Ponta Morrungulo** (☎293-70101; www.pontamorrungulo.co.za; campsite adult/child Mtc400/200, 4-person seafront/garden chalet Mtc4500-5000) has a mix of rustic, thatched beachfront and garden self-catering chalets and campsites, all on a large, manicured bougainvillea- and palm-studded lawn running directly onto the beach with magnificent views of Morrungulo Bay from the top of the escarpment. There's also a restaurant (closed Monday). The setting is outstanding, although the antiquated colonial-era ambiance may be a turnoff for some.

About 1.5km north of here is the unassuming **Sylvia Shoal** (☎in South Africa 083-270 7582; www.mozambique1.com; campsite per person US$13, barracas US$22, 2-/4-person chalet US$82/107), with shaded campsites, a handful of self-catering chalets set behind low dunes and a restaurant (open during low season with advance bookings only).

> **TROPIC OF CAPRICORN**
>
> There are no signs marking the spot, but you cross the Tropic of Capricorn (the southernmost latitude – 22.5° – at which the sun is directly overhead) about 15km south of Massinga town on the border between Massinga and Morrumbene districts.

Getting There & Away

Morrungulo is 13km from the main road down a good dirt track that is negotiable with a 2WD. Sporadic *chapas* (Mtc30) run from the Massinga transport stand (on the N1) to Morrungulo village, close to Ponta Morrungulo, and within about 3km walk of Sylvia Shoal.

Pomene

Pomene, the site of a colonial-era beach resort, is known for its fishing and birding, and its striking estuarine setting. The area is part of the **Pomene Reserve** (per adult/child above 12/vehicle Mtc200/50/200), which was gazetted in 1972 with 20,000 hectares to protect the mangrove ecosystems, dune forests and marine life of the area, including dugongs and turtles. The reserve has been long neglected, although now it is receiving renewed attention. The beach here – one of our favourites – is beautiful, especially up near the point by the lighthouse and the now derelict Pomene Hotel.

Pomene Lodge LODGE **$$**
(☎82-369 8580, in South Africa 011-023 9901; www.barraresorts.com; campsite per person US$18, 4-/6-person self-catering bungalow US$177/219, s/d water chalet US$145/245; ❄) Pomene Lodge, in a fine setting on a spit of land between the estuary and the sea, has no-frills self-catering reed bungalows just back from the beach, plus a row of newer, spacious and very lovely 'water chalets' directly over the estuary – a great splurge. There's also camping (hot and cold water), and a restaurant/bar. Diving, quad-bike rental and estuary boat trips can be arranged, as can transfers to/from Barra Lodge.

Pomene View LODGE **$$**
(☎84-465 4572; www.pomeneview.co.za; 5-/6-person chalets US$152/182; ❄) Pomene View, on a rise amid the mangroves and coastal vegetation on the mainland side of the estu-

ary, is small and tranquil, with its own special appeal and wide views. Accommodation is in self-catering brick-and-thatch chalets, and there's a bar and restaurant. Take the signposted turn-off north of Massinga, and then follow the Pomene View signs. Transfers across the estuary to the beach are easily arranged, as are mangrove excursions and fishing charters.

Getting There & Away

Pomene is on the coast about halfway between Inhambane and Vilankulo off the N1. The turn-off is about 11km north of Massinga (which is the best place to stock up) and is signposted immediately after the Morrungulo turn-off. From the turn-off, which is also the end of the tarmac, it's about 58km (1½ to two hours) further along an unpaved road to Pomene Lodge, and about 54km to Pomene View (branch left at the small signpost). In the dry season, it's possible to reach Pomene View in a 2WD with clearance. For Pomene Lodge, you'll need 4WD. There's an airstrip for charter flights from Inhambane and Vilankulo.

Via public transport, there are one or two *chapas* weekly from Massinga to Pomene village (Mtc120), which is a few kilometres before Pomene Lodge. Most locals prefer to take a *chapa* from Massinga to Mashungo village (Mtc100, daily) on the north shore, and then a boat across the estuary to Pomene Lodge and village. However, the chapa *departs* Massinga about 3pm, reaching Mashungo about 8pm or 9pm. There is nowhere in Mashungo village to sleep, although you could try your luck asking locally for permission to camp.

Vilankulo

☎293

Vilankulo is the finishing (or starting) point of Mozambique's southern tourism circuit, and an institution on the southern Africa backpacking and overlanding scenes. It's also the gateway for visiting the nearby Bazaruto Archipelago, separated from the mainland by a narrow channel of turquoise sea. During South African holidays, Vilankulo is overrun with pick-ups and 4WDs, but otherwise it's a quiet, slow-paced town with some lovely nearby beaches.

Sights

At the northern end of town on the beach is the white and pink **Dona Ana Hotel**, built by tycoon-entrepreneur Joachim Alves and about to reopen after renovations. Just inland are the Millennium BIM building (p185), which used to be Alves' residence, and the colourful **Mukoke market** (Bairro Mukoke).

The **fish-market beach**, below Varanda, is a hive of activity in the early mornings and late afternoons when the fishers return with their catch.

Activities

Diving

Diving is very good, although the main sites are well offshore (about a 45-minute boat ride), around the Bazaruto Archipelago.

Dive Bazaruto DIVING
(www.divebazaruto.com) At Archipelago Resort (p184) in Chibuene.

Big Blue DIVING
(www.bigbluevilankulo.com) About 2km north of the Dona Ana Hotel, next to Aguia Negra.

Odyssea Dive DIVING
(www.odysseadive.com) About 500m south of the Old Market, next to Baobab Beach Backpackers.

Dhow Safaris

For day or overnight dhow safaris around the Bazaruto Archipelago, there are several outfits, including the recommended **Sailaway** (☎82-387 6350, 293-82385; www.sailaway.co.za), on the road paralleling the beach road, about 400m south of the Dona Ana Hotel. Prices average from US$120 per person per day for overnight safaris and from US$70 to US$80 for a day snorkelling excursion to Magaruque, including park fees, lunch, snorkelling equipment, protective footwear (important, as the rock ledge can be sharp) and lunch. Day trips to Bazaruto, with its beautiful sand dunes, are difficult from Vilankulo (given the comparatively long travel distance) and are best arranged with Marimba Secret Gardens (p184) (Mtc1700 to

CHIEF VILANKULO

Like many towns in Mozambique, Vilankulo takes its name from an early local chief *(régulo)*, Gamala Vilankulo Mukoke. The name was rendered as 'Vilanculos' during colonial times, but was then changed back to Vilankulo after independence. Bairro Mukoke (Mucoque), west of Millennium BIM, is named after Gamala Vilankulo's son, who lived there.

Mtc2300 per person including park fees, snorkelling equipment and lunch). There is officially no camping on the islands in the park; most operators camp along the mainland coast.

There are also many independent dhow operators in Vilankulo. If you go with a freelancer, remember that while some are reliable, others may quote tempting prices, and then ask you to 'renegotiate' things once you're well away from shore. Check with the tourist information office or with your hotel for recommendations and don't pay until you're safely back on land. For nonmotorised dhows, allow plenty of extra time to account for wind and water conditions; it can take two to three hours (sometimes longer) under sail from Vilankulo to Magaruque, and much longer to the other islands.

Horse Riding

Mozambique Horse Safari (www.mozambiquehorsesafari.com), based in Chibuene, offers rides on the beach, including a fishing village tour, for riders of all levels.

Kite Surfing

Try **Kite Surfing Vilankulo** (www.kitesurfingvilankulo.com) at Casa Rex and **Kite Surfing Centre** (www.kitesurfingcentre.com), north of town, next to Casbah Beach Bar and just up from Samara.

Vilankulo

Sights
1 Fish Market ... B4

Activities, Courses & Tours
Kite Surfing Vilankulo ... (see 3)
2 Sailaway ... B2

Sleeping
3 Casa Rex ... A1
Complexo Âncora ... (see 14)
4 Complexo Turístico Josef e Tina ... B3
5 Hotel Central ... B2
6 Luxus ... B2
7 Palmeiras Lodge ... B2
8 Pescador ... A1
9 Smugglers ... B2
10 Varanda ... B4
11 Zombie Cucumber Backpackers ... B3

Eating
12 Café Moçambicano ... B3
13 Café Zambeziana ... B4
14 Complexo Âncora ... B1
Kilimanjaro Café ... (see 6)
15 Samara ... A1
16 Taurus Supermarket ... B2

Shopping
17 Mukoke Market ... A1

Information
18 Barclays Bank ... B3
19 BCI ... B3
20 Conservatoria dos Regístos e Notariado de Vilankulos ... B3
21 iCloud Internet Café ... B2
22 Millennium BIM ... B2
23 Tourist Information Office ... B4

Transport
24 Buses to Maputo ... B4
25 New Market Transport Stand ... B2

Sleeping

VILANKULO

Complexo Turístico Josef e Tina BUNGALOW $
(☎82-789 7879; www.joseftina.com; campsite per person Mtc200, chalet r Mtc800, r Mtc1200, guesthouse Mtc3900) Just back from the sea this tidy, peaceful, locally run place has camping in the enclosed garden, reed chalets sharing bathrooms, and simple rooms in a small self-catering house. All rooms have nets, there's a small self-catering kitchen area and meals are available on order.

Vilanculos Beach Lodge LODGE $$$
(☎293-82388; www.vilanculos.co.za; s/d US$207/354;) This place, about 3km north of the Dona Ana hotel along the water, has large, manicured grounds sloping down to the beach, a garden swing, a large infinity pool and spacious, well-appointed rooms.

Aguia Negra LODGE $$$
(☎293-82387; www.amazingmozambique.com; d US$206, 4-person chalet from US$73 per person;) Aguia Negra has breezy, rustic, thatched A-frame chalets, each with an open loft area set around a large, grassy compound overlooking the sea. There are also double rooms with air-con, TV and minifridge, and there's a restaurant and a dive operator next door (p181). It's about 2km north of the Dona Ana Hotel.

Casa Rex BOUTIQUE HOTEL $$$
(☎293-82048; www.casa-rex.com; s/d from US$140/220, f US$360;) This lovely, midsized boutique hotel is the place to go if you're after an upmarket getaway. It sits in peaceful, manicured grounds about 500m north of the Dona Ana Hotel, and has a range of rooms and suites, all with sea views. Meals are homemade and excellent, and the hotel is known for its personalised style.

Vila la Mar LODGE $$$
(☎293-82302; vilalamar@yahoo.com; 6-/10-person houses US$265/290;) Spacious and well-equipped self-catering chalets, some overlooking the water, in manicured grounds. It's about 2km north of the Dona Ana Hotel, and just up from Aguia Negra.

Pescador BOUTIQUE HOTEL $$$
(☎293-82312; www.amazingmozambique.com; d US$150;) This boutique place is just up from and diagonally opposite Casa Rex and lacks a beachfront, although the rooms have views of the sea. It has six well-appointed rooms, classical music piping through the lobby and a poolside restaurant.

Palmeiras Lodge LODGE $$$
(☎84-380 2842, 293-82050; www.palmeiras-lodge.net; s/d from Mtc2700/4320) Just in from the beachfront road, this place is light, bright, airy and clean, with well-appointed, white-washed stone-and-thatch cottages set in lush, green grounds. There's a restaurant.

Smugglers LODGE $$
(☎84-071 0792, 293-82253; www.smugglers.co.za; d with/without bathroom Mtc2900/1800, 6-person cottage Mtc4500;) Just southwest of the Dona Ana Hotel on the inland side of the road, this place has seen better days, although it remains an amenable choice. Rooms are set around large, lush gardens with two small pools (not operational at the time of our visit). Most of the rooms have twin beds with shared hot-water bathrooms, fans and nets. There are also larger rooms with bathrooms, a two-room family cottage and a scruffy restaurant. Breakfast costs extra.

Baobab Beach Backpackers BACKPACKERS $
(☎82-731 5420; www.baobabbeach.net; campsite per person Mtc200, dm Mtc270, d bungalow with/without bathroom Mtc1400/680) With its waterside setting, chilled vibe and straightforward bungalows, Baobab Beach is a favourite with the party set. It's about 500m south of the Old Market. Walking from town is fine by day; at night, always take a taxi.

Zombie Cucumber Backpackers BACKPACKERS $
(☎82-804 9410, 84-686 9870; www.zombiecucumber.com; dm Mtc350, chalet d Mtc1500;) Chilled vibe, hammocks, a bar, circular dorm, small chalets and meals on order. Very relaxing. It's just back from the beach road.

Muha Backpackers BACKPACKERS $
(☎84-577 8394; s/d with fan Mtc400/800;) This locally-run place has eight simple but tidy rooms (a mix of twins and doubles) with fans and nets, a small restaurant and a rooftop terrace. It's about 350m south of the Old Market area, and shortly before Baobab Beach Backpackers. Next door is an internet cafe (p185).

Complexo Âncora PENSION $$$
(☎82-389 9999, 293-82444; www.ancorasuites.com; s/d Mtc3000/4155;) A block of spacious, darkish rooms, all with one double bed and one couch bed plus cable TV and mini-

fridge, and all overlooking a small garden, the beach and the harbour. Next door is a restaurant.

Varanda PENSION $$
(☎84-746 0707, 293-82412; varanda.barko@yahoo.com; d with/without sea view Mtc4000/2500) This long-standing place overlooking the beach has pleasant, spotless rooms. From the compound, it's an easy walk down the dune to the fish market on the beach. At night, always use a taxi for heading out. Breakfast costs extra. At the time of research, the restaurant was only open to hotel guests or with advance order.

Luxus MOTEL $$
(☎82-851 1301, 84-030 3151; r Mtc2500, apt Mtc3500; ❄) This place has rather soulless, albeit spacious, rooms (no nets), most with the main window opening on to a hallway. There's also a two-room apartment with cooking facilities (although no pans). It's located in a small shopping mall at the end of the main street and just opposite Taurus Supermarket.

Hotel Central HOTEL $$
(☎293-82024; d/tw/ste/f Mtc2000/2500/2600/3600; ❄) The former Pensão Central is being upgraded and is worth a look if you have an early bus, as it's directly opposite the new market bus station. Once renovations are completed, prices are likely to change.

SOUTH OF VILANKULO

For visitors with their own vehicle or backpackers willing to put up with erratic public transport, there are several good spots on quiet Chibuene beach, about 7km south of Vilankulo town.

Archipelago Resort RESORT $$$
(☎84-775 8433, 293-84022; www.archipelago-resort.com; 6-person garden/sea view bungalow US$200/213; ❄) This wonderful resort has 18 spacious, well-appointed Indonesian-style self-catering bungalows set in expansive green grounds overlooking the sea. All have large verandas, two bedrooms and two bathrooms downstairs, and a two-bed loft. There's also a restaurant, an on-site PADI dive operator (p181) and horse riding nearby.

Casa Guci LODGE $$
(☎84-237 8702; www.casaguci.com; per person with/without breakfast from US$88/77; ❄) This small place is about 7km south of town just back from the water. It has modern, well-equipped two- and four-person self-catering chalets set around large grounds and a good restaurant (p185). Each chalet has its own little patio, garden and fully equipped kitchen. Note that self-catering rates are also available.

Blue Water Beach Resort BUNGALOW $
(☎in South Africa 011-781 1661; sales@anthology.co.za; campsite Mtc350, d bungalow Mtc700) Rustic, faded bungalows and camping in neglected but attractive grounds overlooking the water.

NORTH OF VILANKULO

Marimba Secret Gardens BUNGALOW $
(☎84-048 9098, 82-005 3015; www.marimba.ch; dm/d/tw without bathroom from Mtc500/1400/1500; @) We've had good reports about this place, on the beach about 25km north of Vilankulo along a bush track. Accommodation is in stilted rooms and dorms sharing clean ablutions, and there's a restaurant (where you'll have to eat, as there's nothing else around), gardens and evening bonfires. It's a good bet if you're looking for a quiet spot to relax away from Vilankulo's bustle and seeking a chance to get acquainted with local life. It's also a good base for excursions to Bazaruto Island as sailing times are shorter than from Vilankulo. Bush walks are possible and kite surfing is planned. Transfers to/from Vilankulo are free for stays of three or more nights (otherwise Mtc200 per person one-way).

Eating

VILANKULO

Café Zambeziana CAFE $
(light meals from Mtc120) Immediately to your right when exiting the old market, this local place has tasty but inexpensive grilled chicken and barbecue sandwiches.

Café Moçambicano CAFE $
(Avenida Eduardo Mondlane; pastries from Mtc15) Pastries, bread, yoghurt, juice and a bakery next door. It's opposite Barclays Bank.

Kilimanjaro Café CAFE $$
(breakfast Mtc140-280, sandwiches and light meals Mtc200-300; ⏰7.30am-6pm Mon-Sat; 📶) Salads, sandwiches, pizza, pasta and a changing daily menu plus smoothies and gourmet coffees. It's in the Lexus shopping mall opposite Taurus supermarket.

Complexo Âncora SEAFOOD, PIZZERIA $$
(☎293-82444; pizzas & meals Mtc200-350; ⏰7am-10pm Wed-Mon) This waterside place near

the port has pizzas and continental dishes. Portions are large and there's an eating area overlooking the water. Everything is halal (no alcohol) and there's a takeaway service.

Samara SEAFOOD $$
(☎82-380 6865; samara@tdm.co.mz; meals from Mtc250; ⊙lunch & dinner in season) Just back from the beach, Samara features Portuguese-style cuisine and is known for its prawns and other seafood, as well as for long meal waits. Management also rents out some rooms (single/double Mtc2880/3200) in stone-and-thatched chalets in the gardens behind the restaurant. Follow the main road to where the tarmac ends, take the small, signposted right-hand fork and continue down about 200m further.

Taurus Supermarket SUPERMARKET $
(Avenida Eduardo Mondlane; ⊙closed Sun) Well-stocked for self-catering. It's near the end of the tarmac road, diagonally opposite Millennium BIM.

CHIBUENE

Casa Guci EUROPEAN, PIZZERIA $$
(☎84-237 8702; www.casaguci.com; meals from Mtc350) The restaurant at this lodge (p184) is known for its delicious pizzas and relaxing garden setting. It's 7km south of town; you'll need either your own vehicle or a taxi to get here.

Information

Money

Barclays Bank (Avenida Eduardo Mondlane) ATM. Near the town entrance, diagonally opposite Café Moçambicano.

BCI (Avenida Eduardo Mondlane) ATM. Near the town entrance, just down from Barclays.

Millennium BIM (☎Bank; Avenida Eduardo Mondlane, Bairro Mukoke) ATM (Visa & MasterCard).

Internet

Babylon Internet Café (per hr Mtc100; ⊙9am-noon & 2-7pm) Next to Muha Backpackers. Also rents mountain bikes and snorkelling gear.

iCloud Internet Café (Avenida Eduardo Mondlane; per min Mtc3; ⊙9am-noon & 2pm-7pm Mon-Fri, 9am-noon Sat) At Lexus Shopping Centre.

Notary

Conservatoria dos Regístos e Notariado de Vilankulos (Avenida Eduardo Mondlane; ⊙8am-3.30pm Mon-Fri) Near Barclays; for getting your documents notarised.

Tourist Information

Tourist Information Office (www.vilankulo.com; Rua da OMM; ⊙8am-3.30pm Mon-Fri, 9am-1pm Sat) A helpful stop with town maps, general info and sometimes internet access. It's in the town centre.

Getting There & Away

Air

Offices for all airlines are at the airport, which also has an ATM. The airport turnoff is along the road running to Pambara junction, 1.5km from the main roundabout at the entrance to town. From the turnoff, it is 2km further.

LAM (www.lam.com.mz) has five times weekly flights to/from Maputo (from about US$200 one way) **Federal Air** (www.fedair.com) has daily flights between Johannesburg and Vilankulo, sometimes via Nelspruit.

Bus

Vilankulo is 20km east of the N1, down a tarmac access road, with the turn-off at Pambara junction. *Chapas* run between the two throughout the day (Mtc15). Except for large buses to Maputo and *chapas* to Chibuene, all transport departs from the transport stand at the **new market** ('Mercado Novo') on Avenida Eduardo Mondlane.

TO MAPUTO To Maputo (Mtc750, nine to 10 hours), there are usually two buses daily, departing by 4.30am, and sometimes as early as 2am; book your ticket with the drivers the afternoon before and verify the time. Departures are from in front of the small red shop one block up from the old market, opposite the tribunal and to the west of the main road. Coming from Maputo, departures from Junta are between 2.30am and 3.30am. More comfortable TCO buses running between Maputo and Beira stop only at Pambara junction, and need to be booked in advance.

TO BEIRA To Beira (Mtc550, 10 hours) buses depart Vilankulo at 4.30am at least every second day; book the afternoon before.

TO CHIMOIO

There's no direct bus to Chimoio. You'll need to take a Beira bus as far as Inchope junction (Mtc550 from Vilankulo), and then get a minibus from there.

TO MAXIXE To Maxixe (for Inhambane and Tofo), several minibuses depart each morning (Mtc180, three to four hours). Allow six to seven hours for the entire journey from Vilankulo to Tofo.

TO INHASSORO To Inhassoro (Mtc75, 1½ hours), minibuses depart from just east of the market.

Getting Around

Vilankulo is very spread out. For a taxi, try contacting **Sr Eusébio** (☎82-681 3383), or arrange through your hotel. Occasional *chapas* run along the main road, but not out to the beach places on the northeastern edge of town, and not to the airport. *Chapas* to Chibuene (Mtc15, 30 minutes) depart from next to Afro Bar just down (west) from the old market. They can take a long time to fill; for Mtc100, drivers are usually willing to leave when you are ready. The *chapa* terminus in Chibuene is at the T-junction near Casa Guci. Go left from here for Casa Guci and Blue Waters. For Archipelago Resort, ask the driver to drop you at the turnoff shortly before the T-junction.

At night, always take a taxi in the area near Baobab Beach Backpackers, to/from the Maputo bus terminus and near the old market and anywhere near the beachfront.

Bazaruto Archipelago

The Bazaruto Archipelago has clear, turquoise waters filled with colourful fish, and offers opportunities for diving, snorkelling and birding. It makes a fine upmarket holiday destination if you're looking for the quintessential Indian Ocean getaway.

The archipelago consists of five main islands: Bazaruto, Benguera (also spelled Benguerra, and formerly known as Santo António), Magaruque (Santa Isabel), Santa Carolina (Paradise Island or Ilha do Paraíso) and tiny Bangué. Until about 10,000 years ago – relatively recent in geological terms – the larger islands were connected to the mainland at the tip of São Sebastião peninsula. The small population of Nile crocodiles that laze in the sun in remote corners of both Bazaruto and Benguera islands is evidence of this earlier link.

Since 1971 much of the archipelago has been protected as **Bazaruto National Park** (Parque Nacional de Bazaruto; adult/child Mtc200/100). In late 2002 the park boundaries were extended southward to encompass all of the islands, bringing the area under protection to about 1400 sq km. Thanks to this protected status, and to the archipelago's relative isolation from the ravages of war on the mainland, nature bursts forth here in full force. You'll see dozens of bird species, including fish eagles and pink flamingos. There are also red duikers, bushbucks and, especially on Benguera, Nile crocodiles. Dolphins swim through the clear waters, along with 2000 types of fish, plus loggerhead, leatherback and green turtles.

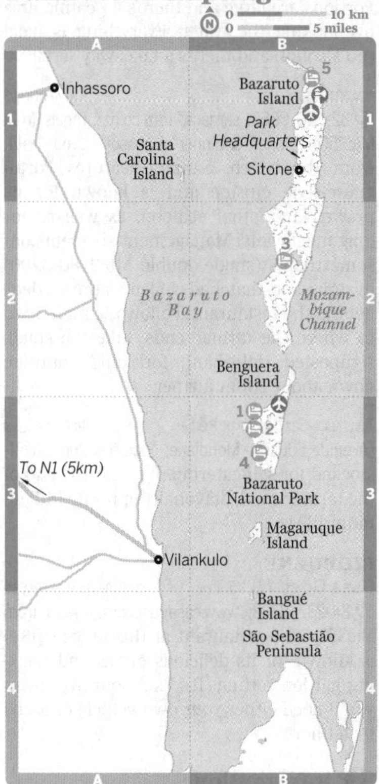

Bazaruto Archipelago

Sleeping

1 Azura at Gabriel's B3
2 Benguerra Lodge B3
3 Indigo Bay Island Resort & Spa B2
4 Marlin Lodge B3
5 Pestana Bazaruto Lodge B1

Most intriguing are the elusive dugongs, who spend their days foraging among seagrass meadows around the archipelago. As a backdrop to all this are excellently preserved coral formations, with up to 100 species of hard coral and over two dozen soft coral species identified so far.

Living amid all the natural beauty are about 3500 Mozambicans who call the archipelago home.

Just south of the Bazaruto Archipelago is the São Sebastião Peninsula, which is dotted with small lakes, lagoons and stands of mangrove, and edged by the same turquoise waters that lap the islands of the archipelago. It's known especially for its flamingos and other water birds. Day excursions (via speedboat charter) are best arranged from Vilankulo.

History

Although many of the island residents are relatively recent arrivals who sought haven during the war years, the archipelago's history reaches well back. The islands (previously known as the Hucicas or Vacicas) were long famed for their pearls and ambergris. By at least the 15th century, they were the site of a thriving maritime community sustained by the coastal dhow trade. The earliest Portuguese trading settlements dated from the mid-16th century, while the first permanent Portuguese settlement was established on Santa Carolina in the mid-19th century. Today, all of the islands except Bangué are inhabited.

Activities

Diving

Dives, equipment rental and certification courses can be organised at any of the lodges, or in Vilankulo (p181).

Game Fishing

Game fishing (tag-and-release) can be arranged at all of the lodges.

Sailing

Sailing trips around the archipelago can be arranged with island hotels, and with the Vilankulo-based dhow safari operators (p181). Magaruque – the closest island to Vilankulo and the main destination for day sailing/snorkelling safaris from the mainland – has a rock shelf with lots of fish, although only isolated coral patches, on its western side. Surf shoes or other protective footwear are essential, as there are many sharp edges; most operators provide these.

Sleeping & Eating

BAZARUTO ISLAND

Pestana Bazaruto Lodge LODGE $$$
(84-308 3120, 21-305000; www.pestana.com; s/d with full board from US$359/446;) This unpretentious four-star getaway is at the northwestern end of Bazaruto island overlooking a small, tranquil bay. Accommodation is in two dozen A-frame chalets amid lush gardens beneath the sand dunes. There is also a honeymoon suite and some family-style chalets. There's a two night minimum stay.

Indigo Bay Island Resort & Spa RESORT $$$
(21-301618; www.indigobayresort.com; r per person with full board from US$545;) Indigo Bay is the largest and most outfitted lodge in the archipelago. It offers a mix of villas and beachfront chalets, and a range of activities. While it lacks the laid-back island touch of many of the other places, for some visitors this will be compensated for by the high level of comfort and amenities.

BENGUERA ISLAND

Benguerra Lodge LODGE $$$
(in South Africa 011-452 0641; www.benguerra.co.za; r per person with full board from US$575;) Generally considered to be one of the most intimate of the island lodges, with well-spaced and spacious luxury chalets and villas near the beach. It's at the centre of the island's western coastline, and offers the usual activities.

Marlin Lodge LODGE $$$
(in South Africa 012-940 4212; www.marlinlodge.co.za; per person with full board US$395-580) Marlin Lodge has 17 sea-view chalets and a full range of activities. Unlike most of the other island lodges, they don't charge a single supplement.

Azura at Gabriel's RESORT $$$
(in South Africa 0767-050599; www.azura-retreats.com; r per person with full board US$575-875;) A lovely setting, full facilities and accommodation in villas of varying degrees of luxury.

MAGARUQUE ISLAND

The original hotel on Magaruque was founded by tycoon-entrepreneur Joaquim Alves in colonial days and was long a favoured haunt of the rich and famous. Completely refurbished (and in part newly built) accommodation is underway, but was not yet open at the time of research. For now, the small island is ideal if you fancy relaxing on a patch of tropical sand. It can be circled in a

CHEAP ACCOMMMODATION?

There is no budget accommodation on the islands. The best options if you have limited funds are arranging an island dhow cruise from Vilankulo, or visiting in the off-season, when some of the lodges offer special deals.

few hours, but bring plenty of shade or sunscreen. There's also fine snorkelling in the crystal clear shallows just off the beach on the island's southwestern corner.

SANTA CAROLINA ISLAND

The prettiest of the islands, with stands of palm and other vegetation, Santa Carolina was formerly the site of another Joaquim Alves property. Today the old hotel is closed and crumbling, although a renovation is planned, but in the meantime you can visit the island as a day excursion. It's an easy walk around its perimeter, but snorkelling here – among the best in the archipelago – is the highlight, and it is possible just offshore.

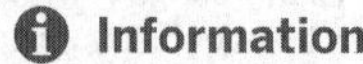

Information

Entry fees are normally collected by the island hotels, and in advance by most Vilankulo-based dhow safari operators. Park headquarters are located at Sitone, on the western side of Bazaruto Island. While fees for diving, walking and other activities within the archipelago have been approved in principle, they are not currently being enforced.

Getting There & Away

Air

Federal Air (www.fedair.com) flies between Johannesburg, Nelspruit and Vilankulo, from where you can arrange island helicopter or boat transfers with the lodges. **CFA Charters** (293-82055; www.cfa.co.za; Vilankulo Airport) has flights connecting Bazaruto Island with Vilankulos (about US$200 one way).

Boat

All the top-end lodges arrange speedboat transfers for their guests. Most day visitors reach the islands by dhow from Vilankulo, where there are a number of sailing safari operators (p181).

Inhassoro

Sleepy Inhassoro – the last of the 'main' coastal towns before the N1 turns inland – is a popular destination for South African anglers. Its sunbaked, white-sand shoreline is uncluttered and inviting, although there's no surf or breeze, except during storms when the wind stirs up the waves a bit. Boat transfers to Bazaruto and Santa Carolina islands, both visible off-shore, can be arranged at any of the hotels, often on-the-spot, but it's best to give advance notice. Expect to pay about Mtc10,000/12,000 for a seven-person boat transfer to Santa Carolina/Bazaruto. BCI and Millennium BIM have ATMs.

Sleeping & Eating

Complexo Turístico Seta BUNGALOW **$$**
(293-91001, 82-302 0990, 293-91000; www.inhassorosetahotel.co.cc; campsite per person Mtc300, tw chalet Mtc2500, 6-person self-catering chalet Mtc6000; ❄) Complexo Turístico Seta, a long-standing place at the end of the main road leading into town from the N1, has large, quiet grounds, a restaurant-bar overlooking the sea, campsites (towards the back of the property), and accommodation in small sea-facing chalets (several sizes available). There are also basic self-catering cottages in an unappealing setting behind the parking-lot reception area.

Getting There & Away

Inhassoro is 15km east of the main road. *Chapas* run daily to/from Vilankulo (Mtc70, 45 minutes). To Beira, go to Vulanjane (the junction with the N1, Mtc10 in a *chapa*) and wait for passing northbound buses from there; ask staff at your hotel to help with the timing. Driving northwards, there's a bridge across the Save River.

CENTRAL MOZAMBIQUE

In the annals of ancient Africa, central Mozambique – Sofala, Manica, Tete and Zambézia provinces – had a much higher profile than it does today. It was here, at the old port of Sofala, that 15th-century traders from as far away as India and Indonesia gathered in search of vast caches of gold. And it was here that some of the region's most powerful kingdoms arose, including the Karanga (Shona) confederations along the Zimbabwe border and the legendary kingdom of Monomotapa southwest of Tete. It was also in central Mozambique, along the Zambezi River, that early explorers and traders first penetrated the vast Mozambican hinterlands. During the 17th and 18th centuries, they set up a series of *feiras* (trading fairs) that reached as far inland as Zumbo on the Zambian border.

Today, the tides have turned and central Mozambique seldom gets more than passing mention in the tourist brochures. Yet while it lacks the accessible beaches of the south, the region has many attractions. In addition to wildlife watching at Gorongosa National Park, there's hiking amid the misty mountain landscapes of the Chimanimani range and in the tea country around Gurúè; fishing and relaxing around Lake Cahora Bassa; and birdwatching.

Central Mozambique is also an important transit zone, flanked by the Beira corridor (connecting landlocked Zimbabwe with Beira and the sea) and the Tete corridor, which links Zimbabwe and Malawi. As such, it makes a convenient route for travellers combining Mozambique with neighbouring countries.

Beira

☎ 23, POP 546,000

Beira, capital of Sofala province, is Mozambique's second-largest city. It's also the country's busiest port, and as famed for its seafood as for its tawdry nightlife. Yet, despite a somewhat tarnished image, Beira is a reasonably pleasant place with a compact central area, an addictive harbour-town energy, attractive colonial-era architecture and a short, breezy stretch of coastline.

Beira has a reputation as one of the easiest places in the country to catch malaria, so cover up well in the evenings, and travel with a net.

History

Settlement of the area around Beira dates to at least the 9th century AD, when small fishing and trading settlements dotted the nearby coastline. The most important of these was the fabled Sofala (p193). Following Sofala's decline, trade continued well into the 19th century, although on a smaller scale.

In 1884 a Portuguese landholder and imperialist named Joaquim Carlos Paiva de Andrada established a base at the mouth of the Púngoè River (at the site of present-day Beira) as a supply point for his expeditions into the interior. He also wanted to promote development of the Mozambique Company – one of the many charter companies set up by the Portuguese in their attempts to solidify their control over the Mozambican hinterlands. Paiva de Andrada was not the only one enamoured of Beira's charms. The British also found the area enticing as an export channel from their landlocked inland territories to the sea. Over the next decade, it became a focus of dispute between the two colonial powers before ultimately going to Portugal in 1891.

Andrada, who meanwhile had made Beira the headquarters for his Mozambique Company, began to develop its harbour facilities. At the same time, a railway line to the interior was completed and Beira soon became a major port and export channel for Southern Rhodesia (Zimbabwe).

From the mid-20th century, Rhodesia's links with South Africa increased, cutting into Beira's transport monopoly. By this time, however, Beira's significance as a port was established and it continued to be one of Mozambique's hubs.

During the war years, Renamo leader Afonso Dhlakama had his headquarters at Maríngué, northwest of Beira near Gorongosa, and both Beira and Sofala province continue to be Renamo strongholds.

Orientation

The heart of the city is the area around the squares of Praça do Município and Praça do Metical. Near here, you'll find shops, banks, telecom and internet facilities, plus an array of street-side cafes. North of the two squares is the old commercial area of the baixa, with the port and some impressive colonial-style architecture, while about 1km east is Praça do Maquinino, the main bus and transport hub. From Praça do Município, tree-lined streets lead south and east through the shady and charming Ponta Gêa residential area to Avenida das FPLM. This then runs for several kilometres along the ocean, past the hospital to Makuti, another residential area fringing Beira's small stretch of beach. At the end is the old red-and-white Makuti **lighthouse**, dating to 1904.

Sights & Activities

Beira's spired **cathedral** (Avenida Eduardo Mondlane), southeast of the centre, was built in the early-20th century with stones taken from the ruins of San Caetano fort in Sofala. Also worth a look are the surrounding **Ponta Gêa** area, with some charming old houses; **Praça do Metical**; and the area around the port, where the streets are lined with faded colonial-era buildings. One to watch for is the restored **Casa Infante de Sagres** (Port), now the offices of Manica Shipping Company.

Makuti Beach (Praia de Makuti; Avenida das FPLM) is one of the better places in town to relax, though it can't compare with the coastline further south or north. The water is moderately clean, currents strong (ask locally where swimming is possible) and the breezes good. There's a **swimming pool** (Avenida das FPLM; admission Mtc300) at Clube Náutico.

The **Central Market** (Mercado Central; Rua Correia de Brito) in the town centre is the best place to buy fruit and vegetables. **Praia Nova Market**, west of Praça do Município, has piles of fresh seafood and much more.

Beira

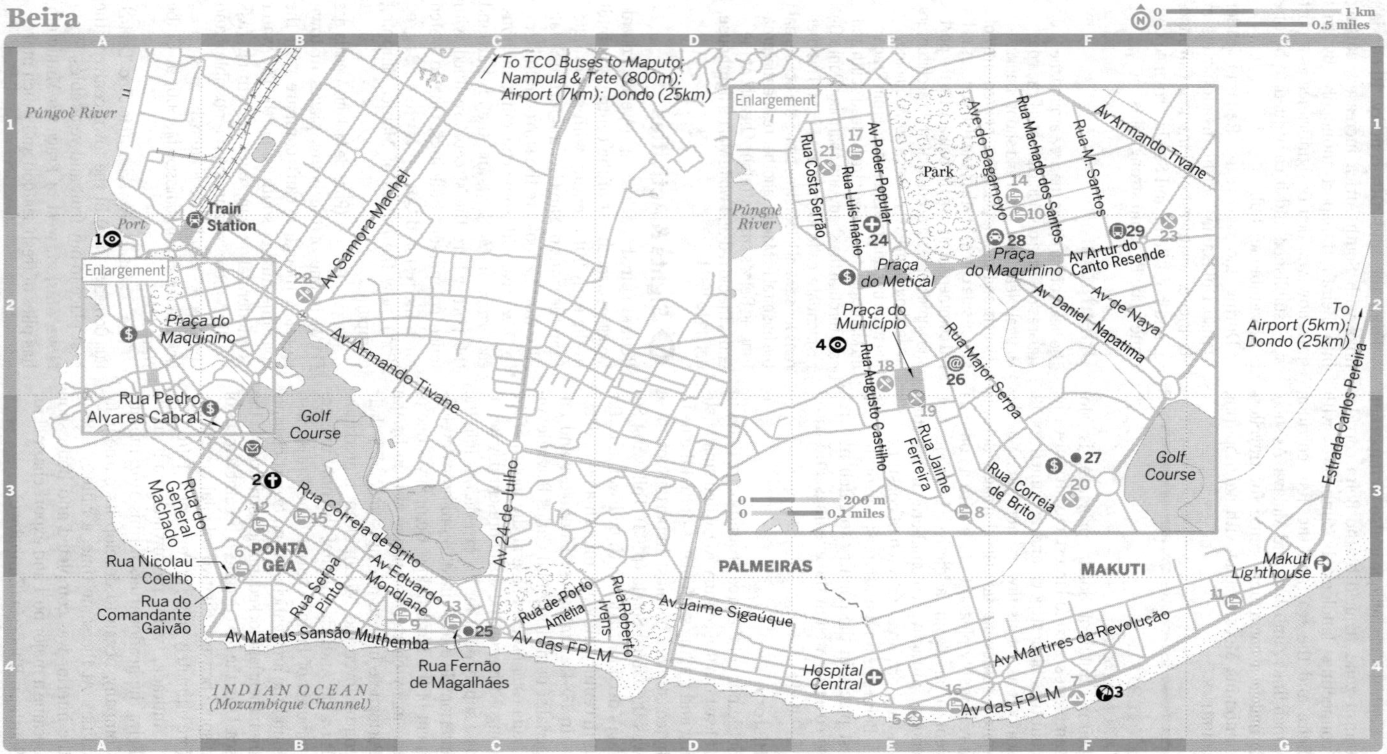

0 1 km
0 0.5 miles

Púngoè River
Port
1
Train Station
Enlargement
Praça do Maquinino
Rua Pedro Alvares Cabral
22
Av Samora Machel
Av Armando Tivane
To TCO Buses to Maputo; Nampula & Tete (800m); Airport (7km); Dondo (25km)
Golf Course
2
Rua do General Machado
12
15
Rua Correia de Brito
6
PONTA GÊA
Rua Nicolau Coelho
Rua do Comandante Gaivão
Rua Serpa Pinto
Av Eduardo Mondlane
9
13
25
Av Mateus Sansão Muthemba
Rua Fernão de Magalhães
Av 24 de Julho
Rua de Porto Amélia
RuaRoberto Ivens
Av das FPLM
Av Jaime Sigaúque
PALMEIRAS
INDIAN OCEAN
(Mozambique Channel)
Hospital Central
5
16
Av das FPLM
Av Mártires da Revolução
7
3
MAKUTI
11
Makuti Lighthouse
Estrada Carlos Pereira
To Airport (5km); Dondo (25km)

Enlargement
Púngoè River
Rua Costa Serrão
21
17
Rua Luís Inácio
Av Poder Popular
24
Park
Praça do Metical
Ave do Bagamoyo
14
10
28
Praça do Maquinino
Rua Machado dos Santos
Rua M. Santos
29
23
Av Armando Tivane
Av Artur do Canto Resende
Av de Naya
Av Daniel Napatima
Praça do Município
4
18
Rua Augusto Castilho
19
Rua Jaime Ferreira
26
Rua Major Serpa
8
Rua Correia de Brito
27
20
Golf Course
0 200 m
0 0.1 miles

Beira

Sights
1 Casa Infante de Sagres A2
2 Cathedral B3
3 Makuti Beach F4
4 Praia Nova Market E2

Activities, Courses & Tours
5 Clube Náutico Swimming Pool E4

Sleeping
6 Beira Guest House B3
7 Biques F4
8 Hotel Infante E3
9 Hotel Miramar C4
10 Hotel Tivoli F1
11 Jardim das Velas G4
12 Pensão Moderna B3
13 Pousada Tropical C4
14 Residencial BeiraSol F1
15 Royal Guest House B3
16 Sun, Sand & Beach Guesthouse E4
17 VIP Inn Beira E1

Eating
Biques .... (see 7)
18 Café Riviera E2
19 Central Market E3
Clube Náutico .... (see 5)
20 Restaurante Kanimambo F3
21 Restaurante Pic-Nic E1
22 Shoprite B2
23 Take-Away 2 + 1 .... F2

Information
24 Clínica Avicena E2
25 Palácio do Governador C4
Shoprite .... (see 22)
26 Teledata E2

Transport
27 LAM F3
28 Main Taxi Stand F2
29 Main Transport Stand F2

Sleeping

Rio Savane CAMPGROUND $
(82-596 2560, 23-323555; campsite per person Mtc300) This rustic place, 40km north of town in a serene setting on the Savane River, is separated from the sea by a narrow peninsula and makes a fine getaway. It has camping, *barracas* (thatched shelters, Mtc400 plus Mtc200 per person) with mattresses and bedding, a couple of self-catering chalets (d/q Mtc1500/3000), and meals. The surrounding wetlands are ideal for birding. Follow the Dondo road past the airport to the right-hand turn-off for Savane. Continue 35km to the estuary, where there's secure parking and a small boat (until 5pm) to take you to the camp.

Jardim das Velas HOTEL $$
(23-312209; jardimdasvelas@gmail.com; 282 Avenida das FPLM, Makuti Beach; d/f Mtc3325/3850;) This quiet place near the lighthouse has spotless, well-equipped rooms with views to the sea upstairs, and a couple of four-person family rooms with bunk beds downstairs. All rooms have mosquito nets. There's no breakfast and no meals, but there is a small garden with *braai* facilities, and filtered water. The beach is just across the street. It's very popular and often full; advance bookings recommended.

Beira Guest House GUESTHOUSE $$
(82-315 0460; woodgateangola@yahoo.co.uk; Rua Nicolau Coelho; r Mtc3500;) Beira Guest House has clean, comfortable and well-appointed rooms in Ponta Gêa, just off Rua do Comandante Gaivão. Breakfast is included; there are no other meals.

Royal Guest House GUESTHOUSE $$
(23-324030; 1311 Avenida Eduardo Mondlane; r Mtc3500;) This cosy residential-style B&B in the shady Ponta Gêa area has pleasant, well-appointed rooms with minifridge, TV and laundry service. Breakfast is included; no other meals are available. It's diagonally opposite the cathedral.

Pousada Tropical GUESTHOUSE $$$
(23-327202; Rua Fernão de Magalhæs; r Mtc3500-4000;) Spacious, well-appointed rooms in a restored private villa with polished wood floors and lots of windows. It's just off Avenida Eduardo Mondlane, on the side street immediately next to the **governor's residence** *(palácio do governador)*. If they are full, the same management runs the similarly-priced guesthouse nearby.

Sun, Sand & Beach Guesthouse GUESTHOUSE $$
(84-565 7114, 23-311036; www.ssbguest.com; 2196 Avenida das FPLM; d from Mtc3000;)

MOZAMBIQUE BEIRA

This small, well-located and colourful guesthouse, just back from the beach and up from Clube Náutico, has a handful of comfortable, mostly spacious rooms, some with sea views.

VIP Inn Beira HOTEL $$$
(☎82-305 4753, 23-340100; www.viphotels.com; 172 Rua Luís Inácio; s/d from MTc4100/4400; ❄📶) Modern, comfortable rooms in the heart of the baixa, one and a half blocks north of Praça do Metical.

Residencial BeiraSol GUESTHOUSE $$
(☎82-492 4848, 23-236420; 168 Rua da Madeira; r Mtc1700-2500; ❄) Opposite Hotel Tivoli, this place has modern rooms, although most have only interior windows; ask for a room to the front for more views. Despite this drawback, it is a clean, secure option in the baixa. There is no breakfast.

Hotel Tivoli HOTEL $$$
(☎23-320300; bookings.tivolibeira@tdhotels.com; cnr Avenida de Bagamoyo & Rua da Madeira; s/d US$190/228; P❄@📶) Small and tidy albeit rather faded rooms with TV and amenities in a high-rise in the baixa. Downstairs is a sleek restaurant/bar. Buffet breakfast is included in the price.

Biques CAMPGROUND $
(☎84-5977130, 23-313051; www.biques.com; Makuti Beach; campsite per person Mtc100; P) Set on a breezy rise overlooking Makuti beach at the end of Avenida das FPLM, this long-standing camping ground remains popular, as does the bar-restaurant. It's the only camping in town, and a good spot for watching the sunset. Take any *chapa* towards Makuti and ask them to drop you at the turnoff, from where it's about 400m further on foot.

Hotel Miramar HOTEL $
(☎23-322283; http://miramar.no.sapo.pt/; Rua Vilas Boas Truão; s/d Mtc800/1600; ❄) The Miramar has reasonably priced, no-frills rooms – some with private bathroom, most with TV – near the water (no beach), but inconvenient for the rest of town.

Pensão Moderna PENSION $
(☎23-329901; Rua Alferes da Silva; d/tr Mtc1755/2750) One of the better budget bets, with adequate rooms, most with fan and shared bathroom. It's two blocks south of the cathedral.

Hotel Infante HOTEL $$
(☎23-326603; Rua Jaime Ferreira; non-renovated d Mtc1750, renovated s/d Mtc2500/3000; ❄) In a high-rise building in a congested section of town a few blocks from LAM, Infante has small, clean rooms (some with fan and shared bathroom, others with air-con and private bathroom) and a restaurant.

Eating

Beira's restaurants and cafes are full of faded charm, and the dining scene is where you can experience this port city at its best.

Café Riviera CAFE $
(Praça do Município; light meals from Mtc150; ⏲7.30am-9pm) This classic, pink Old World streetside cafe is a good spot to sit with a cup of coffee and *bolo de mandioca* (almond cake) and watch the passing scene. There are soft, plump sofas inside and tables outdoors overlooking the plaza.

Clube Náutico SEAFOOD $$
(☎23-311720; Avenida das FPLM; meals from Mtc200, plus per person entry Mtc20; ⏲lunch & dinner) This colonial-era swimming and social club is a popular waterside hangout, with average food and slow service redeemed by the relaxing beachside setting.

Restaurante Kanimambo CHINESE $
(☎23-323132; Rua Pero de Alenquer; meals from Mtc200; ⏲lunch & dinner Sun-Fri) Down a small side street opposite LAM, with tasty Chinese food and a friendly proprietor.

Biques SEAFOOD $$
(☎84-597 7130, 23-313051; www.biques.com; Makuti Beach; meals Mtc250-350) This restaurant-bar has long been popular with South African and Zimbabwean overlanders. Apart from the satellite TV, the main features are good seafood and meat grills, the beachside ambience and sunset views.

Restaurante Pic-Nic CONTINENTAL $$
(☎23-326518; Rua Costa Serrão; meals Mtc180-320; ⏲lunch & dinner) For years this place it was reputed to be one of the city's best restaurants and while its reputation is somewhat outsized for what you get, portions are large and service reasonable. Dining is in a windowless, red-draped interior, with black-suited waiters at your beck and call.

Take-Away 2 + 1 AFRICAN $
(Avenida Artur do Canto Resende; meals from Mtc100) A small restaurant serving a selection of inexpensive local fare, just northeast of Praça do Município.

Shoprite SUPERMARKET $
(cnr Avenidas Armando Tivane & Samora Machel) For self-catering.

Information

EMERGENCY **Clínica Avicena** (☎23-327990; Avenida Poder Popular; ⊙24hr) Just north of Praça do Metical.

INTERNET ACCESS **Teledata** (Rua Companhia de Moçambique; per hr Mtc60; ⊙8am-6pm) Internet connection; diagonally opposite the telecom office.

MONEY There are many ATMs, including at the airport; at **Shoprite** (Avenida Samora Machel); at **BCI** (Rua Major Serpa), opposite LAM; and at **Standard Bank** (Praça do Metical)

Getting There & Away

Air

There are flights on **LAM** (☎23-324142, 23-303112, 23-306000, 23-324141; 85 Rua Major Serpa) twice weekly to/from Johannesburg, daily to/from Maputo, and several times weekly to/from Tete, Nampula, Pemba and Lichinga. **SAAirlink** (☎23-301570, 23-301569; www.flyairlink.com; Airport) flies several times weekly between Beira and Johannesburg.

Bus & Chapa

Beira's main transport hub is in the Praça do Maquinino area, bounded by Avenida Daniel Napatima and Avenida Samora Machel. There's no real order to things; ask locals where to go for buses to your destination.

» **TCO** (☎82-304 8163; tcobeira@tdm.co.mz; 28 Rua dos Irmãos Roby) departs several times weekly at 4am to **Maputo** (Mtc1780, 15 to 16 hours) and **Nampula** (Mtc1900, 16 to 17 hours), and three times weekly to **Tete** (Mtc890, seven hours). All departures are from the TCO office in Bairro dos Pioneiros, 1km north of the centre, and just off Avenida Samora Machel. For intermediate stops between Beira and Maputo (including Pambara junction for Vilankulo, and Maxixe for Inhambane), you'll still be charged the full Maputo fare. For **Quelimane** (Mtc650, 10 hours) direct buses leave daily by 5.30am. Alternatively, TCO en route to Nampula stops at Nicoadala, from where you can get a *chapa* the remaining 40km.

» To **Vilankulo** (Mtc550, seven to eight hours, daily), there's a direct bus departing by about 4.30am.

» To **Chimoio** (Mtc200, three hours), minibuses go throughout the day from the main transport stand.

» Another option for any northbound or southbound transport is to go to Inchope, a scruffy junction 130km west of Beira (Mtc130, three hours), where the EN6 joins the N1, and try your luck with passing buses there, although they are often full and waits are long.

Getting Around

The airport is 7km northwest of town (Mtc200 to Mtc250 in a taxi).

CHAPAS *Chapas* to Makuti (Mtc5) depart from the main transport stand.

CAR HIRE For vehicle rentals head to **Sixt** (☎23-302 651, 23-302 650, 82-300 5190; www.sixt.com) or **Europcar** (☎23-303 090), both at the airport.

TAXI The **main taxi stand** is at the western edge of Praça do Maquinino. Taxis don't cruise for business, and companies come and go, so ask your hotel for the updated numbers.

SOFALA

About 40km south of Beira and just south of the Búzi River is the site of the ancient gold-trading port of **Sofala**, dating from at least the 9th century AD. Sofala's importance lay in its role as the major link between the gold trade of the interior and the powerful sultanate at Kilwa in present-day Tanzania. By the 15th century it had become one of East Africa's most influential centres, with ties as far away as Madagascar, India and Indonesia. San Caetano, the first Portuguese fort in Mozambique, was built at Sofala in 1505 with stones shipped from Portugal. However, soon after the Portuguese arrived, trade routes shifted northwards, Mozambique Island eclipsed Sofala as the main coastal base and Sofala and its fort rapidly sunk into oblivion. Today nothing remains of Sofala's former glory and the ruins of the fort have been overtaken by the sea. The area is, however, beautiful and inviting for exploration by anyone wanting to get off the beaten track.

To get here from Beira by public transport, take any bus heading along the N6 towards Chimoio and get off at Tica, from where there is sporadic public transport south to Búzi, where there are several *pensões*. If you are approaching by road from the N1, the turn-off is at Chiboma; ask locally about conditions from Chiboma to the coast. Alternatively, there's a daily ferry from Beira, which stops at various points along the coast, including Búzi and the small, modern-day port of Nova Sofala.

Around Beira

GORONGOSA NATIONAL PARK

About 170km northwest of Beira is **Gorongosa National Park** (Parque Nacional de Gorongosa; ☎82-308 2252; www.gorongosa.net; adult/child/vehicle per day US$20/10/45; ⏰6am-6pm Apr-Dec), which was gazetted in 1960 and soon made headlines as one of southern Africa's premier wildlife parks. It was renowned for its large prides of lions, as well as for its elephants, hippos, buffaloes and rhinos. During the 1980s and early 1990s, hungry soldiers and poachers brought an end to this abundance. Because Renamo headquarters was nearby, the surrounding area was heavily mined and the park's infrastructure was destroyed. Rehabilitation work began in 1995, and in 1998 Gorongosa reopened to visitors. In recent years, the park has received a major boost thanks to assistance from the US-based Carr Foundation, which has joined with the Government of Mozambique to fund Gorongosa's long-term restoration and ecotourism development.

Animal numbers still pale in comparison with those of earlier times, and can't compare with those in other southern African safari destinations. However, wildlife is making a definite comeback and the park is highly recommended on any Mozambique itinerary. It's likely that you will see impalas, waterbucks, sable antelopes, warthogs, hippos, crocodiles and perhaps even elephants and lions.

A wildlife sanctuary has been created in the park, where restocking of zebras, buffaloes, wildebeests and other animals has begun. Another major attraction is the birdlife, with over 300 species, including many endemics and near-endemics and an abundance of water birds in the wetland areas to the east around the Urema River.

Just as much of a highlight as the wildlife is Gorongosa's unique and beautiful mixture of ecological zones, with jade-green floodplains, savannah, woodlands, forests of fever trees, stands of palm and hanging vines. Within its 5370 sq km it encompasses the southernmost part of the Great Rift system, the hulking Gorongosa massif, expanses of coastal plain and the Zambezi valley, and is considered to be the most biologically diverse of all Mozambique's conservation areas. The park's rehabilitation also involves a strong community development element, and the chance to see some of this work is another draw.

Sleeping & Eating

Girassol Gorongosa Lodge LODGE $$
(☎82-308 2252; www.gorongosa.net; campsite per person Mtc320, s/d tent Mtc1480/2100, s/d garden room Mtc2600/3500, s/d/f bungalow from Mtc3500/4400/7200; ❄🏊) Located at Chitengo park headquarters, with comfortable, recently renovated *rondavels* scattered around an expansive, grassy compound, a handful of rooms and a camping ground with ablution blocks and hot water. There's also a restaurant and a swimming pool.

Explore Gorongosa TENTED CAMP $$$
(www.exploregorongosa.com; s/d with full board US$728/970; ⏰Apr-Nov) Explore Gorongosa runs walking safaris and canoe trips from its base in a semi-permanent tented camp in one of the most scenic sections of the park. Its tents are spacious and comfortable, and for multinight bush walks, it operates a series of fly camps. Everything is custom-tailored and it's an excellent bet for experiencing the bush. Rates include accommodation, meals, beverages and safari activities. Children below 10 years of age by advance arrangement only.

Gorongosa Adventures Campsite CAMPGROUND $
(☎82-957 1436; http://gorongosa-adventures.blogspot.com) About 9km outside the main gate, and 500m off the park access road, is this unsignposted, unnamed campsite with lovely camping. It has twin-bed permanent tents under bamboo roofs; clean, hot showers; well-equipped cooking facilities and a small shop selling basic supplies. Staff can also help you organise walks and excursions in the area, including birdwatching trips to Mt Gorongosa (US$24 to US$64 per person, depending on group size), as well as transport to the park gate (where you can hire a park vehicle for a safari). Accommodation prices were still being sorted out as this book was researched, so you'll need to contact the campsite, but everything was very reasonable and good value, and considerably less expensive than the park accommodation. Meals can be arranged in advance for about Mtc300 per person.

Pensão Azul PENSION $
(r with/without bathroom Mtc1000/500, with aircon Mtc1200) If you're coming from the north and get stuck in Vila Gorongosa, this place (white with yellow trim) has no-frills rooms and inexpensive meals. It's just east of the main road, opposite the main junction.

Information

Park headquarters (☎82-302 0604, 23-535010; contact@gorongosa.net) are in Chitengo, about 15km east of the entry gate, from where rough tracks branch out to other park areas. Vehicle rental, guides for wildlife drives, and excursions to a nearby village can be arranged at park headquarters. Multinight bush walks and (in the wetter months) canoe trips can be arranged through Explore Gorongosa (p194).

Getting There & Away

AIR **CFA Charters** (☎21-466 881, 293-82055; www.cfa.co.za) flies on request between Vilankulo and Gorongosa National Park.

ROAD The park turn-off is at Inchope, about 130km west of Beira, from where it's 43km north along good tarmac to Nota village and then 17km east along an all-weather gravel road to the park gate. You can easily reach the park entrance with a 2WD, but for exploring, you'll need a 4WD. *Chapas* heading north from Inchope to Gorongosa town (Vila Gorongosa), about 25km beyond the park turn-off, will drop you at the turn-off, from where you can arrange a pick-up with staff (advance booking essential). Pick-ups are also possible from Beira, Chimoio and Inchope; see www.gorongosa.net for prices.

MT GORONGOSA

Outside the park boundaries to the northwest is **Mt Gorongosa** (1862m), Mozambique's fourth-highest mountain. Steeped in local lore, it's known for its rich plant and birdlife and its abundance of lovely waterfalls. The mountain's slopes are the only place in southern Africa to see the green-headed oriole, and one of just a handful of places where you can see the dappled mountain robin and Swynnerton's forest robin.

Mt Gorongosa is considered sacred, but it's possible to climb to its upper slopes with a local guide. A base camp for hikers and birdwatchers has been set up near the beautiful **Morumbodzi Falls**, which are on the mountain's western side at about 950m. From the camp, there are paths to the falls (about one hour's easy walk away), **birding walks** and overnight climbs to the **summit** (about six hours one way). Hikes to the falls can be organised through park headquarters (contact@gorongosa.net) from about US$70 per person including transport. Gorongosa Adventures Campsite (p194), outside the park gate, can also help with hikes to the falls, as well as to the summit, as can the small community-based group, **Mangwana** (www.ecomangwana.com).

According to tradition, no red can be worn when climbing the mountain and the climb must be undertaken barefoot, though this latter requirement seems to be conveniently waived these days. This is just as well: the mountain receives about 2000mm of rain a year, and the wet, humid conditions, combined with the steepness of the path on the upper reaches, make the going slippery approaching the summit. Good shoes and a reasonable degree of fitness are essential.

To get to the Morumbodzi base camp area, follow the N6 from Beira to the turn-off at Inchope. Continue north along the tarmac road, passing the turn-off for Gorongosa park and continuing another 25km or so further to Gorongosa town. About 10km beyond Gorongosa town, turn off the main highway to the right, and continue 10km along an unpaved track to the base camp. Transport from the park can be organised through park staff.

Chimoio

☎251

Chimoio is the capital of Manica province and Mozambique's fifth-largest town. While its tourist attractions are modest, it's a pleasant place with an agreeable climate and worth a stop if you're in the area. It's also the jumping-off point for exploring the Chimanimani Mountains to the southwest.

Sights & Activities

About 5km northeast of town is **Cabeça do Velho**, a large rock that resembles the face of an old man at rest. To get here, take Rua do Bárue past Magarafa market and continue along the dirt road; you'll see the rock ahead of you in the distance. Once at the base, you can climb up in about 10 minutes to enjoy some views. As with all mountains and high places in Mozambique, there are legends and traditions associated with this one and locals may still offer a prayer to the spirits once at the top.

Sleeping

Pink Papaya BACKPACKERS $
(☎82-555 7310; http://pinkpapaya.atspace.com; cnr Ruas Pigivide & 3 de Fevereiro; dm Mtc400, s/d/q Mtc800/1000/2000; P) Pink Papaya is the best budget option in town, with helpful management, a convenient central location, clean dorm beds and doubles, a well-equipped kitchen and *braai* area, and breakfast available on request. Note that there is no camping. The owner can also

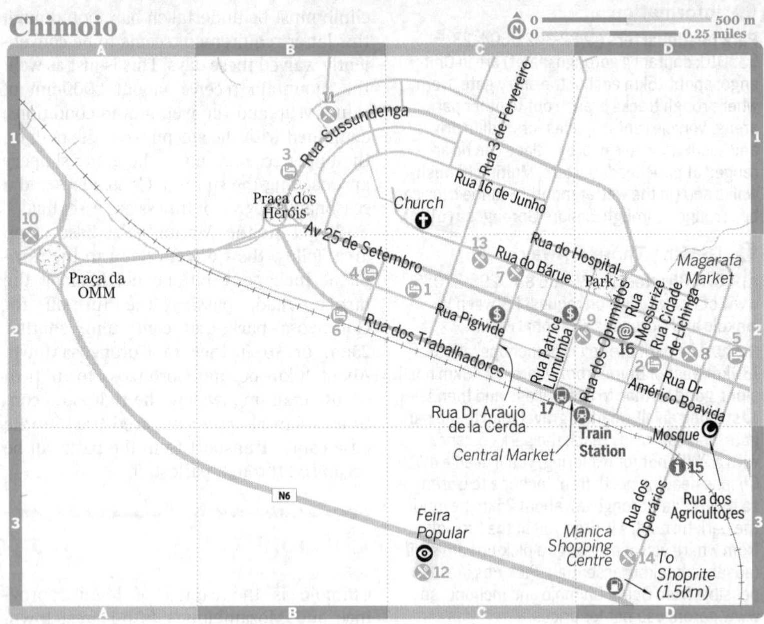

Chimoio

Sleeping

1 Complexo Hoteleiro Vila Pery............C2
2 Hotel Inter...............................D2
3 Hotel-Residencial Castelo Branco.........B1
4 Pink Papaya...............................B2
5 Residencial Dabhad........................D2
6 Residencial Safari........................B2

Eating

7 Café Atlântida............................C2
8 Café-Bar Xeirinho.........................D2
9 Karachi...................................D2
10 La Plaza.................................A2
11 Pizzeria Vapor...........................B1
12 Restaurante Maúa.........................C3
13 Restaurante-Bar Jumbo....................C2
14 Shawarma Castle..........................D3

Information

Chimoio Forex.........................(see 14)
15 Provincial Tourism Directorate...........D3
16 Teledata.................................D2

Transport

17 Main Bus Station.........................C2

help with information on excursions to the Chimanimani Mountains, Gorongosa National Park and Penha Longa. It's about 10 minutes on foot from the bus stand. With the bus stand to your right and train station to your left, walk straight and take the fourth right into Rua 3 de Fevereiro. Go one block to Rua Pigivide. On request, staff will accompany you to the bus stop for early morning departures.

Hotel-Residencial Castelo Branco HOTEL $$$

(☎82-522 5960, 251-23934; Rua Sussundenga; s/d Mtc3800/4200; P❄📶) Catering to business travellers, this place has modern, comfortable twin- and double-bed rooms – all with minifridge and satellite TV – around a small garden, and offers a breakfast buffet. There's also a restaurant, and apartments are available for long-term rentals. It's signposted just off Praça dos Heróis and is often full.

Residencial Dabhad PENSION $$

(☎82-385 5480, 251-23264; http://dabhad.com; cnr Ruas do Bárue & dos Agricultores; r Mtc1500; P❄) This friendly, no-frills place has a mix of twin- and double-bed rooms with air-con, TV and hot water. Continental breakfast is included, but there are no other meals.

Hotel Inter HOTEL $$$
(☎84-242 0000, 251-24200; www.interhotels.co.mz; Avenida 25 de Setembro, near Rua Cidade de Lichinga; r/ste from Mtc4000/5200; ❄☎✉) This multistorey place in the town centre compensates for its lack of ambience with comfortable, modern rooms and good facilities. There's also a restaurant.

Residencial Safari PENSION $
(☎251-22894; Rua dos Trabalhadores; s/tw with shared bathroom Mtc1000/1500, d Mtc1200; ❄) This place, targeted at local business clientele, is worth checking out if you're on a budget. Rooms have TV and hot water, and there's internet connection if you have your own laptop. Breakfast is included, otherwise there are no meals.

Quinta Sol CAMPGROUND $
(☎251-23759; info@mozecotours.com; per tent Mtc400) This campsite on the eastern edge of town, about 2km south of Shoprite in the Manjoro area, has camping, hot water for ablutions and cooking facilities. At the time of research it was due to open soon.

Hotel Milpark HOTEL $$
(☎82-763 2312; milparkhotel@hotmail.com; tw & d from Mtc2500-4000; ✉) About 7km outside town along the Beira road, with straightforward rooms around expansive grounds, a restaurant and a pool.

Complexo Hoteleiro Vila Pery HOTEL $$
(☎82-501 4520; vilapery@tdm.co.mz; Rua Pigivide; d/tw Mtc2600/2800) Bright paintings give a bit of ambience to this otherwise rather soulless hotel. Rooms (located around a central cement courtyard) are clean and fine.

Eating

Café Atlântida AFRICAN $
(cnr Ruas do Bárue & Dr Araújo de la Cerda; meals from Mtc130) Inexpensive local meals in a rather cavernous interior.

La Plaza CONTINENTAL $
(☎82-601 4980, 251-23716; Praça da OMM; meals from Mtc150; ⏱lunch & dinner Mon-Sat) The recently renovated La Plaza has good, reasonably priced pizzas, plus Portuguese cuisine and seafood.

Restaurante-Bar Jumbo CONTINENTAL $
(Rua do Bárue; meals about Mtc200) The basic but reliable Jumbo has grilled chicken and continental dishes. Seating is downstairs in the bar or in a cosy wood-panelled room upstairs.

Café-Bar Xeirinho EUROPEAN $$
(☎82-384 7950; Avenida 25 de Setembro; meals about Mtc250; ⏱lunch & dinner Wed-Mon) This Portuguese-run place has an amenable ambience, a pool table and a tasty menu ranging from coffees and milkshakes to continental dishes. It's just before Rua Cidade de Lichinga.

Shawarma Castle FELAFEL $
(☎84-282 0285; Manica Shopping Centre, Rua dos Operários, N6; ⏱lunch & dinner) Reasonably priced, good Lebanese food. When heading out of town towards Shoprite, cross the railroad tracks. Manica Shopping Centre is at the next intersection to your right, by the petrol station.

Karachi INDIAN $
(☎82-628 6629; Cnr Avenida 25 de Setembro & Rua Patrice Lumumba; meals from Mtc120; ⏱until 8.30pm daily) This unassuming spot near the Central Market is popular for its inexpensive Indian food and snacks. It's upstairs (go up and to your left) at the Liga Muçulmana/\Desportivo complex. It also has takeaway.

Restaurante Maúa AFRICAN $
(off N6; meals from Mtc200; ⏱lunch & dinner Tue-Sun) This is one of the most popular of the several restaurants at the Feira Popular, featuring grills and well-prepared Mozambican cuisine. It's at the southern end of town just off the N6, and is mainly an option for those with their own transport, as taxis are difficult to find in the evenings.

Pizzeria Vapor PIZZERIA $
(Rua do Mercado; pizza from Mtc180) Just down from Castelo Branco, Pizzeria Vapor has delicious pizzas. Go left when exiting Castelo Branco, past the market area; take the first left, and Pizzeria Vapor will be on your right-hand side.

Shoprite SUPERMARKET $
(N6) For self-catering; 2km east of Chimoio town centre.

Information

Internet

Internet Café (cnr Ruas do Bárue & Dr Araújo de la Cerda; per min Mtc1; @) Above Café Atlântida.

Teledata (cnr Avenida 25 de Setembro & Rua Mossurize; per min Mtc1; ⏱8.30am-6pm Mon-Fri, 9am-noon Sat; ☎) Slow, but has wi-fi.

Money

Barclays Bank (Rua Dr Araújo de la Cerda) Has an ATM.

Chimoio Forex (N6) At Manica Shopping Centre, just beyond the railway tracks and next to the petrol station; changes cash.

Standard Bank (cnr Avenida 25 de Setembro & Rua Patrice Lumumba) ATM.

Tourist Information

Mozambique Ecotours (www.mozecotours.com), reachable through the **Eco-Micaia office** (☎251-23759; www.micaia.org; just off Rua Josina Machel, behind the Chimoio International School), is the best source of information on hiking in the Chimanimani Mountains. To get here, follow Avenida Liberdade north past the church. After crossing Rua Sussundenga, continue for three more blocks to Rua Josina Machel, where you take a left. Continue along Rua Josina Machel until the paved road turns right, and Eco-Micaia is immediately on your right.

 Getting There & Around

Air

There are three flights weekly on **LAM** (☎82-392 6000, 251-24715; tandamoia@tandamoia.co.mz; Shoprite Complex, N6) to Maputo. The airfield is 10km from town, and signposted about 5km west of Chimoio along the Manica road.

Bus & Chapa

All transport leaves from the main bus station, near the train station.

TETE & MAPUTO Buses depart daily at 4am to Tete (Mtc400, seven hours) and between 2.30am and 4am to Maputo (Mtc1200, 14 hours).

VILANKULO There's no direct bus; take the Maputo bus and get dropped at Pambara junction. While the price should be pro-rated, it's difficult from Chimoio to get the drivers to come down from the full Mtc1200.

BEIRA & MANICA To Beira (Mtc200, three hours) and Manica (Mtc25, one hour) chapas run throughout the day.

QUELIMANE & NAMPULA To Quelimane (Mtc550, eight hours) and Nampula (Mtc1200, 15 hours), there are departures three times weekly on Maning Nice.

Taxi

Chimoio has a few taxis; find them in front of the park on Avenida 25 de Setembro or by the market.

Around Chimoio

About halfway between Chimoio and Manica is **Chicamba Real Dam** (Barragem de Chicamba Real), set among low hills, and popular with bass anglers. **Casa Msika** (☎251-66044; www.casamsika.com; campsite per person Mtc125, d Mtc1060, 3-/4-person chalets Mtc1670/1940; 🍽) has lakeside camping with a good setting (but dirty ablutions facilities), simple rooms and chalets overlooking the lake, and a restaurant. Advance bookings are essential on weekends and holidays. From Chimoio, head west for about 45km to the signposted turn-off, from where Casa Msika is about 4km further. There's no public transport, but transfers from Chimoio can be arranged.

Manica

Tiny Manica, 70km west of Chimoio, is situated in what was once the heart of the kingdom of Manica and an important gold-trading area.

Millennium BIM (N6) and **Barclays** (N6) both have ATMs.

 Sights

Near the town entrance, in a red-roofed colonial-era house, is a **Geology Museum** (Museu de Geologia; ☎251-24433; admission free; ⏲8am-3.30pm).

EXPLORING MANICA PROVINCE

Although the Chimanimani National Reserve (p200) is the undisputed highlight, Manica province has many other attractions including stunning terrain, a wealth of historical sites and rock-art sites. Catandica town, en route to Tete, offers access to the beautiful Serra Choa plateau for self-drivers, while tiny Nhacolo, which has basic accommodation on the Zambezi River, offers an interesting self-drive loop going via Sena, Caia and the N1 south to Gorongosa park or north into Zambézia province. Work is well underway to open up tourism throughout the province, with an emphasis on ecotourism and community engagement, although as yet there is little organised. Contact **Mozambique Ecotours** (www.mozecotours.com) for information on the latest developments and for help with suggested routes and itineraries, as well as for information on combining exploration of Manica with visits to off-the-beaten track coastal destinations in Sofala province.

About 5km from town are the impressive **Chinamapere rock paintings**. To get here, go west from Manica about 3km, and then south for about 1km along a dirt road, following signs for *'pinturas rupestres'*. The site of the paintings is considered sacred by local residents, and before your visit an elderly lady will conduct a brief prayer ceremony. According to tradition, no pregnant or menstruating women can visit the site.

Northwest of town, off the Penha Longa road and signposted from Manica, are the ruins of **Macequece Fort** (Fortaleza de Macequece), the location of an old gold-trading fair and site of an 1891 battle between Portuguese colonial forces and Cecil Rhode's British South Africa Company. You'll need a 4WD to get here.

Sleeping & Eating

Pensão Flamingo PENSION $
(☎251-62385; EN6; r Mtc1100) On the main road a few blocks west of Millennium BIM, this spiffy place has simple rooms with bathroom and fan, plus a garden and a restaurant.

Manica Lodge LODGE $$
(☎82-872 6668, 251-62452; d in small/large rondavel Mtc1117/1755) At the western end of town, about 400m off the main road (watch for the signposted turn-off just after the immigration office), this amenable establishment has stone *rondavels* scattered around tranquil, manicured gardens. The larger ones are reasonably spacious, with TV and private bathrooms. Out the back are several less appealing *rondavels* that are tiny, and do not have TV. There's also a restaurant and a three-room self-catering house.

Getting There & Away

All transport departs from the market, diagonally opposite Millennium BIM. *Chapas* run frequently to/from Chimoio (Mtc65, one hour) and to the Zimbabwe border (Mtc25, 30 minutes).

Penha Longa

The mountainous Penha Longa area straddles the border with Zimbabwe, beginning about 20km north of Manica. It's cool and scenic and offers many walks, all of which can be easily undertaken from Casa Gaswa or Quinta da Fronteira. The area is also home to the Shona people and you'll see their traditional painted dwelling compounds dotting the hillsides. Although there is plenty of local cross-border activity, the only official border crossing is between Machipanda and Mutare (Zimbabwe) on the main road.

THE MUTASA

Since long before colonial boundaries were drawn, the people of Penha Longa have been loyal to the *mutasa*, the dynastic title of the ruler of the kingdom of Manica, who controls the area from present-day Mutare (Zimbabwe). Despite a divisive 1891 Anglo-Portuguese treaty that put western Penha Longa under British control, and the eastern part under Portuguese control, cross-border ties remain strong.

It's possible to arrange to sleep in the compound of a local family at **Casa Gaswa** (☎82-380 2330, 82-659 0358; giftmashiri@yahoo.com.br; 2-person rondavel Mtc500), a simple but nice *rondavel* in Penha Longa's Mutombombwe area. Local-style meals can be arranged, but it's a good idea to bring some food and drink with you from Manica. If Casa Gaswa is occupied, you can also pitch a tent on the grounds (campsite per person Mtc150).

Next door and under the same management is **Casa Mutombombwe** (☎82-380 2330, 82-659 0358; giftmashiri@yahoo.com.br; 4-person house Mtc1500), a simple but well-equipped self-catering house with electricity that sleeps up to four people. Hiking guides can be arranged at both places.

There's also camping and a few basic rooms in darkish thatch-and-brick cottages at **Quinta da Fronteira** (Penha Longa Inn; ☎84-839 5311; penhalongainn@gmail.com; campsite per person Mtc250, s/d Mtc600/1350), an old mansion about 3km from Casa Gaswa with a stream nearby and a once-lovely botanical garden. Bring all your own food and drink. Pink Papaya (p195) in Chimoio can help with arrangements for all of these places.

Getting There & Away

CHAPAS *Chapas* run several times daily between Manica and Penha Longa (Mtc25, one hour). From the chapa terminus in Penha Longa, it's a 20-minute walk to Mutombomwe and Casa Gaswa, and from there, about 3km further to Quinta da Fronteira. Ask locals to point out the way.

CAR Driving, turn north at the Millennium BIM intersection in the centre of Manica town towards the market. Continue past the market, staying left at the first fork. Penha Longa village

A LEGEND OF PENHA LONGA

During the late-19th century, Penha Longa lay in the centre of a disputed area. To the west were the lands of the kingdom of Manica. To the southeast was the territory of the powerful Gaza chief Ngungunhane.

These two kingdoms had long been enemies, and Ngungunhane's troops staged frequent raids into Manica. To protect themselves from the invaders, the people of Penha Longa would send heralds up the mountain to Mudododo village (on what is now the Zimbabwe border), from where they had wide views down over the valleys. When these heralds saw Ngungunhane's forces coming, they would notify the villagers, who would set out roots from a certain plant for the invaders and then flee the village. Although this type of root closely resembled yam, a local staple, it was actually poisonous. The invaders were not able to tell the difference and would eat it and then fall ill. In this way, the residents of Penha Longa were able to protect themselves and resist the Gaza invaders.

is reached after about 19km. Mutombomwe bairro (neighbourhood), Casa Gaswa and Casa Motombombwe are about 2km further. The road is unpaved, but in reasonable condition during the dry season.

Chimanimani Mountains

Silhouetted against the horizon on the Zimbabwe border southwest of Chimoio are the Chimanimani Mountains, with Mt Binga (2436m), Mozambique's highest peak, rising up on their eastern edge. The mountains are beautiful and exceptionally biodiverse, with vegetation ranging from lowland tropical forests and *miombo* woodland to evergreen forests and afro-alpine grasslands on the highest reaches. Much of the range is encompassed by the **Chimanimani National Reserve** (Reserva Nacional de Chimanimani; www.actf.gov.mz; adult/child/vehicle Mtc200/50/200), which is part of the larger Chimanimani Transfrontier Conservation Area (ACTF), together with Chimanimani National Park in Zimbabwe.

Chimanimani is notable for its abundance of rare plants, with at least 90 species whose range is restricted to the Chimanimani area alone. Many are prized by traditional healers for their medicinal value. There is also a multitude of birds, including the rare southern banded snake eagle, Chirinda apalis and the barred cuckoo. Rounding out the picture are bushbuck, eland, sable, duiker, klipspringer and countless smaller animals.

Like the Penha Longa area to the north, the Chimanimani Mountains have a long history and rich traditional life. Rock art estimated to be 2000 years old, but possibly as much as 10,000 years old, has been found at several locations. Many of the rivers and pools in this area are considered sacred by local communities, as are some of the forest areas in the foothills of the mountains, and some of the peaks themselves.

 Activities

It's possible to hike throughout the mountains, with plenty of suitable camping sites on the high plateaus close to mountain streams. Mt Binga can be climbed in two days, with one night spent on the mountain, but the highlands offer endless options for hikes of anything from a day to a week or more.

There are many possible routes. For climbing Mt Binga, a good starting point is Chikukwa, where guides and porters can be arranged. Allow two to three days for the climb, including travel time to/from Chimoio.

Another possible destination in the area is the lovely Moribane Forest, which features beautiful low- to mid-altitude tropical rainforest in the Chimanimani National Reserve buffer zone, and can be accessed from the Sussungenga–Dombe road.

For those with a 4WD, Mt Tsetserra is another possible route. From its base you can climb up a rough 4WD track through some beautiful, bird-filled montane rainforest to the top of the Tsetserra plateau (three to four hours return), or do various day or overnight walks. At the summit are the ruins of an old mansion (a hotel is planned), and camping.

Once up in the mountains you have to be entirely self-sufficient. Be prepared for sudden changes in weather, especially for mist, rain and cold, and keep in mind that the routes are physically demanding. Hikes begin at about 700m in altitude, the highlands are at around 1800m and the highest peaks well above 2000m.

Sleeping

There are twin-bed tents (d Mtc1250) with bucket baths and a basic self-catering kitchen at the main entrance to Chimanimani National Reserve, and rudimentary huts (per person Mtc200) at Chikukwa. However, carrying a tent is recommended (camping costs Mtc100 per person). If you plan on using the reserve tents or huts, check first at the **Provincial Tourism Directorate** (Direcção Provincial de Turismo; INSS Bldg, Rua dos Operários) in Chimoio to confirm availability.

Ndzou Camp CAMPGROUND $
(www.mozecotours.com; campsite per tent Mtc400, 3-person tent Mtc1300, d rondavel Mtc2150, 6-person self-catering house Mtc3200) Ndzou Camp, a joint venture between **Eco-Micaia** (www.micaia.org) and the local community, is a wonderful, well-run place in the middle of Moribane Forest Reserve with camping, *rondavels* and a small family lodge. Staying here is a real highlight of exploring the Chimanimani area. Also on offer at Ndzou are guided forest walks, eco-learning activities and the chance to track the local population of forest elephants. The camp can be reached via public transport. Pick-ups from Chimoio airfield can also be arranged.

Information

The best contact for getting started exploring the mountains and the Chimanimani region in general is the highly recommended **Mozambique Ecotours** (www.mozecotours.com).

The main reserve entrance (*'portão'*), where you pay your entry fees, is at the Mussapa Pequeno River, about 70km southwest of Chimoio off the road to Rotanda. For all hikes, you'll need to have a guide. These can be arranged at various points, including at the Mussapa Pequeno reserve entrance, at Chikukwa camp (about 26km southwest of the reserve entrance) and at Mahate (southeast of the reserve entrance). Guide fees are Mtc450 per day both for shorter hikes, and for Mt Binga climbs.

In addition to food supplies (nothing is available in the reserve), bring along a sturdy water bottle for refilling at streams, and some water purifying tablets. Chimoio is the best place for stocking up for hikes, and an array of basics is also available in Sussundenga. Waterproofing your gear is essential, as is bringing along a bag to pack out your rubbish. As always, stick to beaten paths to avoid potential dangers from old landmines, especially in the forest areas.

Getting There & Away

The best access to the Chimanimani area on the Mozambique side is from Chimoio via Sussundenga and Rotanda. If you're driving, you'll need a 4WD to reach the sites in this area.

MAIN RESERVE ENTRANCE To reach the main reserve entrance on the Mussapa Pequeno River via public transport, take a *chapa* from Chimoio to Sussundenga. Once in Sussundenga, you'll need to wait for another vehicle going towards Rotanda. After passing Muoha, watch for the signposted Chimanimani turn-off. Ask the bus driver to drop you at the 'container', from where you'll have to walk 4km along a track through lovely *miombo* woodland to the entrance. From there, it's 26km further to Chikukwa Camp.

NDZOU CAMP & MORIBANE CAMP For Ndzou Camp, and for the very basic Moribane camp (shortly before Ndzou along the Sussundenga–Dombe road), there's usually at least one direct *chapa* daily from Chimoio to Dombe, leaving Chimoio by 8am or earlier, which can drop you. It's often just as fast to take a *chapa* to Sussundenga, from where you can catch onward transport to Dombe and the camps. It's approximately 60km from Chimoio to Sussundenga, and about 40km from Sussundenga to Ndzou.

MT TSETSERRA For Mt Tsetserra, take the signposted turn-off for Chicamba Real Dam for about 15km southward to the dam administration buildings. From here, continue southwest as the road winds scenically for about 60km up to the Tsetserra plateau. You will need a 4WD.

Tete

☎ 252, POP 50,000

Dry, dusty Tete doesn't have much in the way of tourist attractions and its reputation as one of the hottest places in Mozambique often discourages visitors. Yet the arid, brown landscape, dotted with baobab trees and cut by the wide swathe of the Zambezi River, gives it a unique charm and an atmosphere quite unlike that of Mozambique's other provincial capitals.

History

Tete was an important Swahili Arab trading outpost well before the arrival of the Portuguese and today remains a major transport junction. It grew to significance during the 16th and 17th centuries when it served as a departure point for trade caravans to the goldfields further inland. At the end of the 17th century, it was all but abandoned when the Portuguese lost their foothold in the hinterlands. In the 18th century, it again began

TETE PROVINCE

Tete province is an anomaly within Mozambique, lying inland and almost divided from the rest of the country by Malawi. While the south is hot and arid, northern Tete, much of which is at altitude, enjoys a cooler climate with beautiful hill panoramas. Tete province is also interesting as one of the few areas in Mozambique (in addition to Cabo Delgado) where you can see masked dancing, although it can be difficult to find. Try asking at Tete's Casa de Cultura (Av Eduardo Mondlane) at the northwestern edge of town.

to prosper with the opening of the gold fair at Zumbo to the west and the expansion of goldmining north of the Zambezi. It became a regional administrative centre in 1767, and a hospital and a house for the governor were built. More recently, Tete received a boost with the building of the dam at Cahora Bassa, which opened in 1974. Today, with a population of roughly 50,000, it is one of the major towns in the Mozambican interior.

The main languages are Nyungwe, around Tete city; Chewa, near the Malawi border; and Ngoni.

Sights & Activities

Tete's main sights are the impressive 538m-long **suspension bridge** that spans the Zambezi River and the remains of an old Portuguese **fort** on the river near the bridge.

About 25km northwest of Tete, overlooking the river, is the **Missão de Boroma** (Boroma Mission). Founded in 1885 by Jesuit missionaries, it was known for its *colégio* (school), its carpentry-training centre and its attractive church. After being abandoned for many years, activities have recommenced on a small scale.

Northeast of Tete near the Malawi border is the district of **Angónia**, which is set on a plateau between 1000m and 1500m in altitude, and has a wonderfully cool and refreshing climate, especially if you've just come from Tete. It's also a scenic area and good for walks, although there are no tourist facilities. Ulóngwe, its pleasant capital, is just 20km west of the border and is closely tied into the Malawian economy; kwacha are accepted here as well as meticais.

Sleeping

Finding any accommodation in Tete can be difficult, as many hotels are booked long-term by mining and other businesses and finding good budget accommodation is close to impossible. There are currently no camping grounds. Several new upmarket hotels are currently under construction, meaning that rooms may become easier to find, although still pricey.

Prédios Univendas GUESTHOUSE $$
(252-23199, 252-22670, 252-23198; Avenida Julius Nyerere; s/d with shared bathroom Mtc1300/1550, s/d from Mtc1550/1750;) Straightforward, clean rooms in Tete town centre. The entrance to the rooms (most with fan, air-con and TV) is just around the corner from the Univendas shop on Avenida da Independência.

Motel Tete MOTEL $$
(82 588 2040, 252-22345; N103; r Mtc3500;) On the river, about 25 minutes on foot from Tete town centre along the main road to Changara, this unassuming place is a Tete institution. Rooms are simple but pleasant, the older ones are low-ceilinged, and all are spacious with TV. There's also a riverside restaurant (no alcohol).

Park Inn Tete HOTEL $$$
(84-337 2009, 252-27900; www.parkinn.com/hotel-tete; Zambia Rd; s/d weekdays from Mtc8400/9000, weekends from Mtc6000/7000;) This new place is a welcome addition to Tete's hotel scene, with modern, wheelchair-friendly rooms and a quiet location outside the city centre on the other side of the bridge. It's 3km from the town centre, just off the N103, along the road to Moatize and the airport.

Hotel Zambeze HOTEL $$$
(252-24000, 252-23101; Avenida Eduardo Mondlane; s/d Mtc4500/5500;) This large, multistorey place in the centre of town has straightforward, rather overpriced rooms with TV and minifridge, but it's often the only place with availability. There's also a restaurant and snack bar. It's next to Standard Bank.

Villa Habsburg GUESTHOUSE $$
(84-724 6435, 252-20323; www.villahabsburg.com; r US$120-150) This lovely B&B is in a renovated mansion on the north bank of the river about 1km downriver from the bridge. It has four well-appointed rooms, tranquil grounds and river views.

Hotel Nhungué HOTEL $$$

(☎252-24071, 84-749 3547, 252-24069; www.teteadventures.com/hotelnhungue; Rua Agostinho Neto; s/d Mtc3600/3950; ❄📶) Just back from the river, and just off the N103, Hotel Nhungué has unexciting but spacious rooms around a courtyard. All come with satellite TV, and there's a restaurant. Ask about weekend discounts.

Hotel Sundowner HOTEL $

(☎82-306 1589; N103; r Mtc1000; ❄) Just back from the river and just up from Motel Tete, with OK rooms (inspect a few, as they're not the cleanest) and meals.

Paraíso Misterioso HOTEL $$

(☎82-431 9560; Avenida Liberdade; r Mtc2500; ❄) In an amenable location overlooking the river and just below the bridge, with decent value rooms and a nice restaurant.

Eating & Drinking

Good spots to enjoy a cool drink while watching the sun set over the Zambezi include the outdoor patio at Motel Tete (p202) and the garden at Paraíso Misterioso (p203).

Le Petit Café CAFE $

(cnr Avenidas Julius Nyerere & Liberdade; snacks & light meals from Mtc150; ⏱7.30am-8pm Mon-Sat) In Centro Comercial Fatima, with light meals, pastries, snacks and juices.

Paraíso Misterioso CONTINENTAL $

(Avenida Liberdade; meals from Mtc170; ⏱lunch & dinner) On the riverbank just below the bridge and just up from Hotel Sundowner, with a small garden, river views and good meals. They also have rooms.

Pino's Restaurant PIZZERIA $$

(cnr Avenidas Julius Nyerere & Liberdade; pizzas & meals from Mtc220; ⏱dinner) Just down from Le Petit Café at Clube de Chingale, with pizzas and Italian dishes.

Information

Immigration Office (Rua Macombre) A few blocks up from Hotel Zambeze.

Barclays (Avenida Eduardo Mondlane) ATM; diagonally opposite Hotel Zambeze.

Millennium BIM (Avenida Julius Nyerere) ATM; around the corner from Hotel Zambeze.

Standard Bank (cnr Avenidas Julius Nyerere & Eduardo Mondlane) ATM; next to Hotel Zambeze.

Getting There & Away

Air

LAM (☎252-22056; Avenida 24 de Julho) flies several times weekly to/from Maputo, Beira, Lichinga, Nampula, Quelimane and Chimoio. The airport is 6km from town on the Moatize road (from Mtc100 in a taxi); take any *chapa* heading to Moatize.

Bus & Chapa

A new bridge across the Zambezi is under construction about 6km downriver from the existing bridge (which is currently operating one lane only, and is frequently backed up).

BEIRA To/from Beira, the best option is **TCO** (☎252-22191; cnr Avenidas Julius Nyerere & Liberdade), departing Tete Tuesday, Thursday and Saturday at 5am (Mtc890, seven to eight hours) from the TCO ticketing office opposite the gas station by Clube de Chingale. Departures from Beira are Monday, Wednesday and Friday at 6am. Travellers to Chimoio will be charged the full Beira fare.

CHIMOIO To/from Chimoio (Mtc400, six to seven hours), transport leaves from opposite Prédio Emose on Avenida da Independência, just down from Smart Naira hotel and near Univendas. The first departures in each direction are between 4.30am and 5am, which means that if you're travelling from Chimoio to Blantyre (Malawi) via Tete, you'll be able to make the journey in one long day without overnighting in Tete, after walking across the bridge to catch transport to Zóbuè.

SONGA To Songo (for Cahora Bassa Dam), several pick-ups daily depart from the old *correios* (post office) building in the lower part of town near the cathedral (Mtc150).

MOATIZE For Moatize (Mtc10), *chapas* depart throughout the day from the Moatize bus stand on Rua do Qua.

BOROMA To Boroma, there are occasional direct *chapas* leaving from Mercado da OUA on Avenida 25 de Junho. It's possible to hitch, although the going is slow. The best place to wait is at the Boroma road junction, about 1.5km west of Mercado da OUA.

ULÓNGWE To Ulóngwe, there is at least one direct *chapa* departing daily from Mercado da OUA. Otherwise, take any car heading to Zóbuè, get out at the Angónia junction about 15km before Zóbuè and get onward transport from there.

MALAWI For Malawi, *chapas* run to Zóbuè (Mtc150, 1½ to two hours, 115km northeast of Tete) from the far (Moatize) side of the bridge (to your left, just after crossing the bridge). After crossing the border and passing through 'no man's land', you'll need to switch to Malawi transport on the other side.

HARARE (ZIMBABWE) For Harare, take a *chapa* to Changara (Mtc100, 1½ hours) from Mercado 1 de Maio, and get transport from there.

ZAMBIA For Zambia, take a Moatize *chapa* over the bridge past the SOS compound to the petrol station, where you'll find *chapas* to Matema, and from there, infrequent transport to Cassacatiza on the border.

Getting Around

Sixt Car Rental (☎82-302 1344, 252-20261; www.sixt.com) and **Europcar** (☎252-20171; www.europcar.com) are at the airport.

Taxis are at the airport, and near the intersection of Avenidas Julius Nyerere and Avenida Liberdade.

Cahora Bassa Dam & Songo

About 150km northwest of Tete, near the town of Songo, is massive Cahora Bassa, the fifth-largest dam in the world. It was completed in 1974, and is set at the head of a magnificent gorge in the mountains. It makes a good day or overnight trip from Tete. It's also a wonderful destination for anglers, and is renowned for its tiger fish.

History

Cahora Bassa Dam had its beginnings during the colonial era, when it was proposed as a means of flood control and for water storage to irrigate plantations downstream. The scheme was later enlarged to include a hydroelectric power station, with South Africa agreeing to buy most of the energy. Construction of the dam was highly politicised, with the Portuguese government intending it as a statement of its permanent presence in the region. Plans were made to place up to one million settlers, white and African, on the new farmland that the dam waters would irrigate. This was vigorously opposed by Frelimo (Mozambique Liberation Front). Party leadership viewed Cahora Bassa as a perpetuation of white minority rule in Southern Africa, and made blocking the dam's construction a major objective in the late 1960s. Opposition was organised on an international scale, as sympathetic groups in Western countries worked to discourage private investment.

Ultimately the contracts were signed and, despite repeated Frelimo attacks during construction, the massive undertaking was completed in 1974. To move all the equipment needed for the dam, existing roads and railways had to be modified, and a suspension bridge was built across the Zambezi at Tete. While resettlement of people living in the area was not as great a problem as it was with the construction of the nearby Kariba Dam on the Zambia–Zimbabwe border, more than 24,000 new homes had to be built.

Three decades after its construction, Cahora Bassa has not come close to fulfilling early expectations. One major reason was the destruction of power lines by Renamo rebels in the 1980s. Even after repairs were completed, power supplies remained grounded by contractual and pricing disputes between Mozambique, South Africa and Portugal. Silt is another impediment. Most of it is brought in via the Luangwa River, where overgrazing and poor farming practices lead to soil erosion and turn the waters muddy brown. In 2007 Portugal turned majority control of the dam over to Mozambique, opening the door for the dam to begin to reach its potential.

LAKE CAHORA BASSA

Lake Cahora Bassa, created by the dam, stretches for 270km westwards to the confluence of the Zambezi and Luangwa rivers on the Zambian border, and has the potential to generate more than 3500 megawatts of energy – enough to illuminate the entire region. En route, it partially covers the thundering Cahora Bassa rapids, which blocked David Livingstone's Zambezi River expedition in the late 1850s when he attempted to find a direct route into the interior.

Sleeping & Eating

Centro Social do HCB BUNGALOW $$
(☎252-82666; r Mtc2500;) This pleasant place in the town centre has clean, comfortable twin-bed rooms set in large, manicured grounds. All rooms have fridge, window screens and private bathrooms with hot water. Breakfast costs extra. Also here is **Restaurante O Teles** (☎252-82454; meals from Mtc200).

Ugezi Tiger Lodge LODGE $$
(☎84-599 8410; www.ugezitigerlodge.co.za; campsite per person Mtc350, s/d Mtc1500/2280;) Anglers, or anyone wanting an escape to nature, will love this rustic fishing camp

ZAMBEZI RIVER

The mighty Zambezi tumbles into Mozambique at Zumbo in western Tete province and flows about 1000km through the country before spilling into the sea near Chinde, south of Quelimane.

Up to 8km wide at points, it has long served as a highway between the coast and the interior. One of the notables it has carried is David Livingstone, who took a paddle steamer upriver from the Zambezi delta to Tete before his progress was thwarted by the Cahora Bassa rapids. Earlier, Arab traders made their way upriver at least as far as Sena and Tete, and the Portuguese built settlements near the river delta in the hope of gaining access to western goldfields.

Apart from the bridge at Caia, the only links over the Mozambican portion of the river are the suspension bridge at Tete and the Dona Ana rail bridge between Mutarara and Sena.

perched on a hill overlooking Lake Cahora Bassa. There's a choice of camping; basic, somewhat faded chalets on the densely vegetated hillside; or two eight- to 12-person self-catering houses. It's all very no-frills but the morning scenery on the lake at the base of the property (there's no beachfront) is beautiful. The restaurant serves delicious grilled fish, and boats are available for fishing charters and for lake tours up towards the dam. It's about 14km from Songo town and 6km beyond the dam.

Information

The dam, including the impressive underground turbine rooms, can be visited with advance arrangement only. Contact the offices of **Hidroeléctrica de Cahora Bassa** (HCB; ☎252-82221, 252-82224, 252-82157) in Tete, or in Songo town (look for the HCB office in the *substação* or substation) and ask for Relações Públicas (Public Relations), which will help you organise things. There's no charge for a visit, and permits are no longer necessary to enter Songo. However, you'll need to get a letter of approval from HCB; allow at least 24 hours.

Getting There & Away

Chapas run several times daily between Tete and Songo (Mtc150, three to four hours), departing Tete from the old *correios* building. Once in Songo, it's another 7km down to the dam, which you'll have to either walk or hitch. Ugezi Tiger Lodge does pick-ups from Tete.

Zumbo

Remote Zumbo's history dates back to at least 1715, when the Portuguese established a gold-trading fair at the eastern edge of the Luangwa River at its confluence with the Zambezi. The settlement grew rapidly and by the mid-18th century was one of the most prosperous European cities in Southern Africa, with numerous Portuguese trading houses. This boom was short-lived, and by 1765, Zumbo's wealth began to decline. The difficult overland journey along the Zambezi from Tete, shifting trade patterns, the town's fragile economic foundation and drought were all factors. By the mid-19th century, Zumbo had been all but abandoned and today it is little more than an oversized village.

About 15km downstream of Zumbo is Chawalo Camp (www.cmsafaris.com), a rustic fishing lodge that needs to be booked as part of a multinight package based out of Luwangwa (Zambia).

The easiest access to Zumbo from Tete is via Zimbabwe or Zambia. On the Mozambican side, you can reliably get as far as Fingoé (north of the lake, and at the midway point between Songo and Zumbo) via public transport. From Fingoé to Zumbo, there's no public transport, but the road is passable with a 4WD. There is also a cargo barge known as the *Kuza*, which sails roughly every two weeks between Zumbo and Songo, taking anywhere from four to eight days for the journey.

Sena & Mutarara

About 250km downstream from Tete along the Zambezi are the twin villages of Sena and Mutarara, known for the 3.6km Dona Ana railway bridge (built in 1934) which spans the river here (no vehicles). There are a few basic *pensões* in both towns. The river here is known for its hippos, which you can sometimes see if you happen to be flying over in a charter flight, or by asking at your *pensão* for help organising a boat.

From Mutarara, you can continue north on an unpaved road and a generally hassle-free border crossing into Malawi, or eastwards over the Shire River (bridged by a small, hand-cranked ferry) and then on to Morrumbala (where there's a *pensão*) and the main road to Quelimane.

Caia

About 60km further downstream from Sena and Mutarara is Caia, the main north–south crossing point. There's no decent accommodation in Caia itself, but in Catapu, 32km south of Caia along the main road, is the very good **M'phingwe Camp** (☎82-301 6436; www.dalmann.com; s/tw without bathroom Mtc600/850, s/d with bathroom from Mtc850/1150, 4-person cottage from Mtc1550), with six rustic but spotless double cabins sharing facilities, plus one with its own bathroom. There is no camping. Breakfast can be arranged with advance notice and there's a restaurant with tasty meals and cold drinks. The surrounding forest is a fine birding area. The turn-off is signposted on the N1, from where M'phingwe is about 1.5km further.

About 7km north of Caia, signposted 1km north of the bridge and 800m off the N6, is **Cuácua Lodge** (☎84-839 2350, 82-312 0528; cuacualodge@gmail.com; campsite per person Mtc300; s/d/tr without bathroom Mtc1000/1250/1500; s/tw Mtc1950/2400; ❄🍴), with well-appointed stone-and-thatch cottages, budget rooms sharing bathroom and a restaurant with lovely views over the river. Birdwatching, river trips, forest walks and other excursions can be arranged.

Chapas go daily between Caia and Sena. Tolls at the Armando Emílio Guebuza bridge over the Zambezi River at Caia are Mtc80/100 for small/large vehicles.

Marromeu

Marromeu is an old sugar-growing centre beside the Zambezi River, dating back to the late-19th century when the Portuguese Sugar Society of East Africa built a plantation and sugar factory here. After years of neglect, the factory has been rehabilitated under Mauritian ownership, and is now Mozambique's largest sugar processing mill.

About 45km upriver from Marromeu, and easily accessed with 4WD from Caia, is **Chupanga Mission**, where Mary Moffat, wife of the missionary and explorer David Livingstone, is buried. She died here on 17 April 1862.

South of Marromeu begin the extensive wetlands of the Zambezi River delta, home to a wealth of water birds, including wattled crane, flamingo and pelican. On the coast is the **Marromeu Special Reserve** (Reserva Especial de Marromeu), which was formerly known for its vast herds of buffalo – put by some estimates at about 55,000 in the 1970s. Today only a fraction of that number remain, although plans are underway for restocking. The reserve is also home to populations of waterbuck, sable antelope, zebra and elephant, as well as rich levels of birdlife, with the highest density of waterbirds in Mozambique. In 2004, it was proclaimed as a 'wetland of international importance' under the Ramsar convention.

In Marromeu town, basic accommodation is available. It's better, however, to base yourself at Catapu and explore from there. *Chapas* go daily to Marromeu from both Inhamitanga and Caia.

Quelimane

☎24

Bustling Quelimane is the capital of Mozambique's densely populated Zambézia province and heartland of the Chuabo people. While lacking the architectural charm of some other Mozambican towns – with the exception of the **abandoned Portuguese cathedral** near the waterfront, and the nearby **mosque** – its compact size and energetic atmosphere make it an agreeable place to break your travels.

Well outside town are several beaches that can't rival the coastal stretches further north or south, but make fine getaways if you're based in Quelimane longer term. The riverfront is at its best at sunset.

History

Quelimane stands on the site of an old Arab trading settlement dating to at least the 15th century and built on the banks of the Bons Sinais River in the days when this was still linked to the Zambezi River. Until the 19th century, when the river channel became clogged with silt, Quelimane served as the main entry port to the interior. It was also an important export point for agricultural products, and a major slave-trading centre. Today few traces of this long history are evident and, apart from the cathedral, almost no old buildings remain.

Quelimane

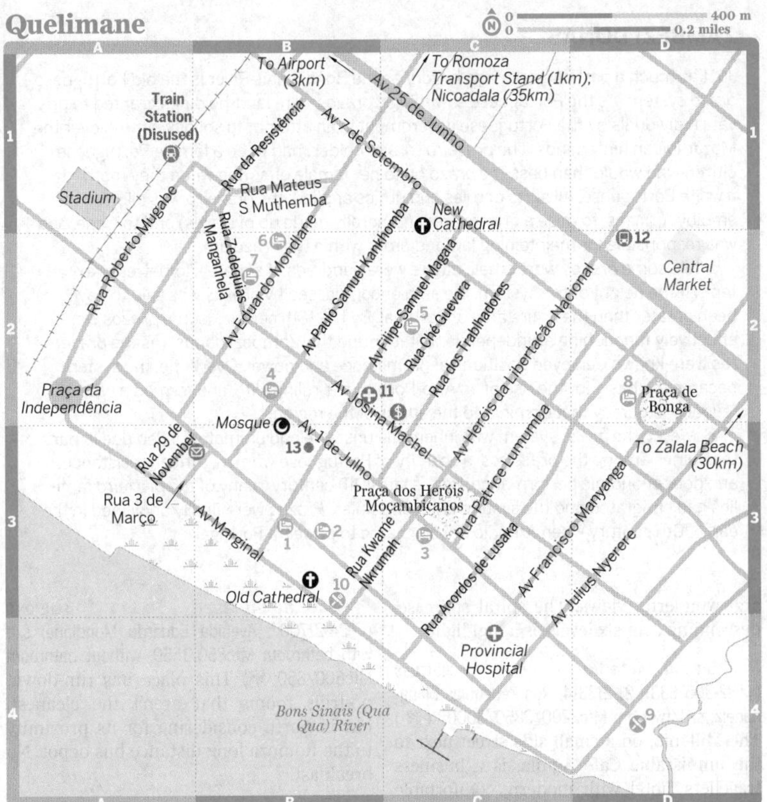

Sleeping

Hotel Flamingo HOTEL $$

(☎82-552 7810, 24-215602; www.hotelflamingo quelimane.com; cnr Avenidas Kwame Nkrumah & 1 de Julho; s Mtc2000-3200, d Mtc2500-3800; ❄📶🏊) This popular midrange hotel opposite Praça dos Heróis has bland but good-value rooms, efficient staff, a small pool, tiny gym and a restaurant. It's often fully booked.

Hotel Chuabo HOTEL $$$

(☎24-213182, 24-213181; hotelchuabo@teledata.mz; Avenida Samora Machel; s/d Mtc3175/3900; ❄) The Chuabo is a Quelimane institution, one of the few hotels anywhere in the country that managed to stay running throughout the war years. The spacious, faded rooms come with TV, fridge and air-con, and many have views over the river. The usually empty rooftop restaurant has surprisingly decent meals, waiters in starched shirts,

Quelimane

Sleeping

1 Hotel 1 de Julho B3
2 Hotel Chuabo B3
3 Hotel Flamingo C3
4 Hotel Rosy B2
5 Pensão Ideal C2
6 Pensão Quelimane B2
7 Residencial Millénio B2
8 Villa Nagardas D2

Eating

9 Centro Turístico Gany Marina D4
10 Estilo China B3

Information

11 Farmácia Calêndula B2

Transport

12 Chapas to Zalala Beach D2
13 LAM B3

ZAMBEZI DONAS

Just as much a part of Quelimane history as the Bons Sinais River is the old Portuguese *prazo* system. As the Portuguese saw things, *prazos* were land-holdings granted to private individuals by the Portuguese government in an attempt to solidify control over the Mozambican hinterlands. The *prazeiro* (*prazo* holder) had to be a female Portuguese citizen who would then pass the *prazo* on to her female offspring when they married a white Portuguese. All sorts of rules and duties applied: the *prazeiro* was allowed to employ Africans, to raise a private army (generally made up of slaves) and to trade, and was responsible for maintaining law and order within the *prazo* area.

While some *prazos* were small, others were hundreds of square kilometres in extent. At the height of the system, the area encompassed by *prazos* was said to have been greater than the entire area of Portugal. By the 18th century, some *prazos* were effectively functioning as independent states, and the 'Zambezi *donas*' (as the *prazeiros* were known), enjoyed positions of prominence and power. Over time, the system became the basis for the rise of an Afro-Portuguese ruling elite, and formed a type of feudal aristocracy that dominated the affairs of the region.

However, the *prazo* system was inherently unstable and ultimately failed due in part to rivalries among the *prazeiros*, a scarcity of Portuguese women, African resistance, and poor economic performance. By the late-19th century, many of the *prazeiro* families had emigrated and the system lay in shambles. *Prazos* were finally abolished in the early 20th century when António Salazar came to power in Portugal.

and wonderful views. The spiral staircase, descending over six levels, is a highlight.

Residencial Millénio HOTEL **$$**
(☎82-305 6331, 21-213314; Rua Zedequias Manghanela; s/d/tw from Mtc2200/2850/3000; P Wi-Fi) The Millénio, on a small side street next to the unmissable Café Águila, is a business travellers' hotel with modern, comfortable rooms in tiny grounds, and a restaurant.

Villa Nagardas BOUTIQUE HOTEL **$$**
(☎24-212046; 79 Praça de Bonga; s/d Mtc3400/3700; air-con) The small Villa Nagardas has African decor, pleasant, cosy rooms and a restaurant. It's near the municipal library.

Hotel 1 de Julho HOTEL **$**
(☎24-213067; cnr Avenidas Samora Machel & Filipe Samuel Magaia; tw with shared bathroom Mtc1000, with bathroom & air-con Mtc1500; air-con) Near the old cathedral, this faded budget choice has reasonable rooms with fan, sink and bucket showers, a central location near the river and inexpensive meals. Breakfast costs extra.

Pensão Ideal PENSION **$**
(☎24-212731; Avenida Filipe Samuel Magaia; r with bathroom Mtc800-1500, without bathroom Mtc550-650; air-con) This long-standing place is well-located near the cathedral, with reasonable rooms, some with fan, some with air-con, and all with continental breakfast.

Pensão Quelimane PENSION **$**
(☎24-217007; Avenida Eduardo Mondlane; s/d with bathroom Mtc850/1550, without bathroom Mtc600/850; air-con) This place has run-down, no-frills rooms that aren't the cleanest, but is worth considering for its proximity to the Romoza long distance bus depot. No breakfast.

Hotel Rosy PENSION **$**
(☎24-214969; cnr Avenidas 1 de Julho & Paulo Samuel Kankhomba; s/d/tw Mtc1050/1200/1250; air-con) In a noisy, busy location near the central mosque, the Rosy has faded, overpriced rooms that are worth considering only if other budget options are full. Rooms on the ground floor have air-con, while those upstairs are marginally nicer, but with fan only. There's no food.

Eating

Estilo China CHINESE **$**
(Bar Refeba, cnr Avenida Marginal & Rua Kwame Nkrumah; meals Mtc190-350) In an ideal location just back from the river, Estilo China has Chinese food plus seafood and meat grills, and terrace seating with amenable views.

Centro Turístico Gany Marina SEAFOOD **$$**
(Náutica; Avenida Marginal; meals Mtc300-550) The sometimes on, sometimes off Gany has a modest selection of overpriced seafood

meals, seating in a cavernous interior and something of a faded pub ambience. It's at the easternmost end of Avenida Marginal, near where it turns in to Avenida Maputo, and past the port.

Information

Farmácia Calêndula (24-213393; Avenida Josina Machel; 8am-6pm Mon-Sat, 9am-1pm Sun) For medical assistance.

Millennium BIM (Avenida Josina Machel) ATM

Getting There & Away

Air

LAM (84-307 0737, 24-212801; Avenida 1 de Julho) flies several times weekly to/from Maputo, Beira, Nampula and Tete. The airport is about 3km northwest of town at the end of Avenida 25 de Junho (Mtc150 to Mtc200 in a taxi).

Bus & Chapa

The transport stand (known locally as 'Romoza') is at the northern end of Avenida Eduardo Mondlane. *Chapas* run frequently to/from **Nicoadala** (Mtc30, 45 minutes) at the junction with the main road.

NAMPULA To Nampula, a **Grupo Mecula** (Mtc480, 10 hours) bus departs daily at 4.30am. Several vehicles also run daily to **Mocuba** (Mtc200, two to three hours), from where you can get onward transport to Nampula via Alto Molócuè, or to the Malawi border at Milange (Melosa). Another option is to take a *chapa* to Nicoadala, and from there, catch the Beira–Nampula **TCO** (82-304 8163, 23-354822; tcobeira@tdm.co.mz) bus; advance bookings are essential.

GURÚÈ To Gurúè (Mtc300, six to seven hours), there's a bus daily at 4.30am; buy your ticket the day before. Even with a ticket, it's best to show up early at the bus stand to be sure of a seat.

BEIRA To Beira (Mtc650, 10 hours), there's a daily bus leaving by 5am. Alternatively, TCO passes Nicoadala from about 1pm, but advance booking is necessary.

CHIMOIO To Chimoio (Mtc550, eight hours), Maning Nice departs daily at 3am from their office on Avenida Eduardo Mondlane, about 1km past the Romoza transport stand and on the opposite side of the road.

ZALALA *Chapas* to Zalala (Mtc25, one hour) depart Quelimane from next to the central market, at the corner of Avenida Heróis da Libertação Nacional & Avenida 25 de Junho.

Pebane

About 280km northeast of Quelimane is Pebane, a fishing port and popular holiday destination during colonial times, and today a faded, quiet town near a long beach.

The South African–run **Pebane Fishing Charters** (82-950 2605, 84-766 0037, in South Africa 034-414 1058; www.pebane.com; per person full board Mtc2870;) has seven well-maintained, beach-facing stone-and-thatch cottages with hot water, and a restaurant.

Pebane is reached in slow stages by public transport, or with a 4WD. The best route from Quelimane is via Malei (95km north of Quelimane on the Nampula road), from where it's about 200km further on a dirt road via Olinga and Mucubela. A good option from Pebane northwards is along a

WORTH A TRIP

ZALALA BEACH

The closest beach to Quelimane is Zalala Beach, about 30km northeast of town. Long and wide, with a row of fringing palms and a large village nearby, it's an ideal day excursion for getting a taste of local Zambézian life. The drive out from Quelimane is bumpy and scenic, through extensive coconut plantations formerly owned by Companhia da Zambézia.

Residencial Sonho do Mar (r Mtc750), at the main junction just a few minutes walk from the *chapa* terminus, is the best budget option, with small, clean rooms and meals on order.

The still-getting-started **Zalala Beach Lodge** (84-390 1630, 24-217055; www.zalalabeach.com; s/d from Mtc3750/5625;), about 100m back from a lovely stretch of beach, is 12km north of Zalala and accessed via a signposted, sandy track (4WD only). It is out of the way and a bit misplaced in the middle of nowhere, but rooms are very comfortable and well-appointed and meals are tasty. As there's nothing else around, half- or full board packages are recommended.

Chapas to Zalala (Mtc25, one hour) depart Quelimane from next to the central market.

bush track (4WD) via the Gilé National Reserve to Gilé village and on to Alto Ligonha, from where it is straightforward to continue on to Nampula.

Gilé National Reserve

Prior to the war, the 2100-sq-km Gilé National Reserve (Reserva Nacional de Gilé) was home to elephants, buffaloes and other wildlife. It's now being rehabilitated with French development assistance. According to recent surveys, there are still small populations of buffaloes, elephants, sable antelopes, leopards and other mammals.

The best road access is via Pebane or Alto Molócuè. Camping is possible near Mulela (Mualama) on the reserve's southwestern corner and in Musseia, and there is camping and basic tented accommodation inside the reserve at **Camp Lice** (campsite per person Mtc300, d tent Mtc1500) on the Lice River.

Mocuba

The large, lively town of Mocuba is the junction for travel between Quelimane and Nampula or Malawi. About 40km north, near Munhamade in Lugela district, are some **hot springs**. Also in Lugela district are the large **Mt Mulide caves** (cavernas do Monte Mulide), used during the war as a place of refuge by local populations. Both spots are considered sacred, and there are no facilities at either.

Pensão Cruzeiro (☎24-810184; Avenida Eduardo Mondlane; tw/d Mtc1000/1200; P), on the main street, has decent rooms and meals. **Padaria e Pastelaria Zambeze** (Avenida Eduardo Mondlane; snacks from Mtc50), about 400m further north along the main road and near Millennium BIM, has samosas, burgers, yoghurt and other light meals.

Transport to Quelimane (Mtc120, two to three hours) leaves from the market throughout the day. For Nampula (Mtc350), the best bet is to try to get a seat on the Mecula bus from Quelimane, which passes Mocuba from about 7am. There are several vehicles daily in the morning between Mocuba and Milange (Mtc200, four hours) departing from Mocuba's market, though you'll maximise your chances of a lift by walking west past the airstrip to the Milange road junction. Mocuba to Gurúè costs Mtc200.

Milange

Milange is a busy town with more than its share of hustlers, about 3km from the border (Melosa) with southeastern Malawi. Millennium BIM has an ATM.

Pensão Reis (r Mtc1100), with hot running water, and **Pensão Lili** (r Mtc750) are both centrally located and have been recommended as safe, although it's better to push on if possible and stay in either Mocuba or over the border in Mulanje (Malawi).

The road between Milange and Mocuba is fairly well travelled, and finding a lift usually isn't a problem. To Gurúè, there is sporadic public transport along a road to Molumbo, and from there to Lioma, from where you can get a *chapa* to Gurúè.

Gurúè & Mt Namúli

Gurúè sits picturesquely amid lush vegetation and tea plantations in one of the coolest, highest and rainiest parts of the country. Tea has long been one of the most important crops in Mozambique, and there are extensive holdings dating from colonial days here. The surrounding area offers fine walking and if you don't mind foregoing certain comforts, it would be easy to spend a week or more here hiking in the hills.

Sights & Activities

A good way to start is with a walk through the jacarandas on the northern edge of town. To get here, find the small church in the centre of Gurúè and head north along the road running in front of it. Continue for five to 10 minutes, following the edge of the hill and staying on the uphill side at the forks.

Cascata WATERFALLS

A popular destination for longer hikes is the *cascata* (waterfall) in the hills north of town. To get here, head first to the UP4 tea factory (also known as Chá Sambique), which you can see in the distance to the north; ask locals to point out the way and allow about 45 minutes on foot. From UP4, it's another 1½ hours on foot through overgrown tea plantations and forest to the falls, which will be to your right. En route are several detours offering beautiful views back down towards Gurúè. Swimming is possible in the pools above the falls. There are said to be some wild horses from colonial days in the surrounding hills, as well as herds of cattle.

As the falls are situated in the middle of tea plantations, you'll need permission to visit. This is free and can be obtained from the Gulamo company at their UP6 warehouse, a complex of white buildings several kilometres out of town off the Quelimane road; ask for Senhor Rafiq. At UP6 you may also be able to arrange to tour one of the tea factories, which still have much of their original equipment, including an old steam engine.

Mt Namúli MOUNTAIN

Rising up from the hills about 15km northeast of Gurúè are the mist-shrouded slopes of Mt Namúli (2419m), from which flow the Licungo (Lugela) and Malema Rivers. If you find yourself in the area with time to spare, it makes a scenic but challenging climb for which you'll need a good level of fitness and lack of a fear of heights (as there are several near-vertical spots where you'll need to clamber on all fours). The mountain is considered sacred by the local Makua people, so while climbing is permitted, you'll need to observe the local traditions, although this has taken on a very commercial aspect these days. Guides (essential, as the route isn't straightforward and it's easy to get lost) can be arranged in Gurúè through Pensão Gurúè (p212), but allow several extra days to sort out the logistics. The going rate for a guide is from about Mtc300. If you try to organise things on your own, it is helpful to get a letter of introduction from the **Conselho Municipal** (Avenida da República; ⏲7am-3pm), in the upper part of town, to bring to the chief.

Before setting out, buy some *farinha de mapira* (sorghum flour) at the market in Gurúè (it shouldn't cost more than Mtc50), to be used to appease both the spirits and the local *régulo* (chief, who is currently a queen). Also set aside an additional Mtc300 to Mtc500 per person for further appeasement of the queen, and pack along some water purification tablets for yourself.

The climb begins about 6km outside Gurúè near UP5, an old tea factory. To reach here, head south out of Gurúè along the Quelimane road. Go left after about 2km and continue several kilometres further to UP5. With a vehicle, you can drive to the factory and park there. With a 4WD it's also possible to drive further up the mountain's slopes to Mugunha Sede, about 40km from Gurúè by road and the last village below the summit. There's no public transport.

Shortly before reaching UP5 you'll see a narrow but obvious track branching left. Follow this as it winds through unrehabilitated tea plantations and stands of bamboo and forest, until it ends in a high, almost alpine, valley about 800m below the summit of Mt Namúli. The views en route are superb. On the edge of this valley is Mugunha Sede, where you should seek out the queen, request permission to climb further and ask for a local guide for the remainder of the way. If you don't speak Portuguese, bring someone along with you who knows either Portuguese or the local language, Makua. If you've come this far with a 4WD, you'll need to arrange to leave it here. The sorghum flour that you bought in Gurúè should be presented as a gift to the queen, who may save some to make traditional beer and scatter the remainder on the ground to appease the ancestors. The queen will then assign someone to accompany you to the top of the mountain, where another short ceremony may be performed for the ancestors.

About two-thirds of the way from the village is a spring where you can refill your water bottle, although it's considered a sacred spot and it may take some convincing to persuade your guide to show you where it is. Just after the spring, the climb steepens, with some crumbling rock and places where you'll need to use your hands to clamber up. Once near the summit, the path evens out and then gradually ascends for another 1.5km to the mountain's highest point. The top of Namúli is often shrouded in clouds, so you may have better views during the climb than from the summit itself.

THE MAKUA

Although widely scattered today throughout large areas of central and northern Mozambique, most Makua people consider Mt Namúli as a common home. According to tradition, the Makua ancestors – all once living in the area around the mountain – split into several groups. Some followed the Malema River from its source on the mountain northwards into Nampula province, while others made their way southward along the Licungo River (which also has its source on Namúli) into present-day Zambézia, thus resulting in the distinct Makua groupings of modern times.

It's theoretically possible to do the climb in a long day from Gurúè if you get an early start and drive as far as Mugunha Sede (three to four hours), from where it's about five hours on foot to the summit. However, in practice this often doesn't work out, as you need to allow time to track down and talk with the queen; it's better to plan on at least an overnight.

To do the entire climb on foot from Gurúè, allow three days, walking the first day as far as Mugunha Sede (about seven to eight hours from Gurúè), where the *régulo* will show you a spot to camp or arrange basic accommodation in a local house. The second day, head up to the summit and back, sleeping again in Mugunha Sede and returning the next day to Gurúè. With an early start and good fitness levels, it's possible to combine the second and third stages into one long day. If you have an extra day available, there's a longer detour route possible via the UP4 warehouse and a beautiful waterfall. Camping on the summit isn't permitted (and isn't a good idea anyway because of rapidly and often dramatically changing weather conditions). At any time of year, be prepared for rain and cold during the climb. Also, if it's raining, the guide will definitely want an extra incentive to continue up to the summit.

Sleeping & Eating

For meals, other than what you can arrange at the hotels, try **Restaurante Zamzam** (Ave Eduardo Mondlane; light meals Mtc100-150), on the roundabout, just up from Pensão Gurúè.

Catholic Mission GUESTHOUSE $
(Centro Polivalente Leão Dehon; ☎24-910096; cpldgurue@gmail.com; dm Mtc300, tw without bathroom Mtc600, d with bathroom from Mtc1000) Located on the edge of town in Bairro Artes e Ofício, this tranquil place has clean, good-value rooms, tasty meals with advance notice and hot-water bathrooms. The gates close at 9pm.

Pensão Gurúè PENSION $
(☎82-576 0040, 24-910050; Avenida Eduardo Mondlane; d Mtc1200, s/tw without bathroom Mtc800) On the main street in the lower part of town and diagonally opposite Pousada Monte Verde (p212), this guesthouse has had a face lift and offers clean, cheery rooms and a restaurant next door. It's also possible to arrange to pitch a tent in the small gardens behind.

Pousada Monte Verde PENSION $
(☎84-588 4311; s/d Mtc550/650) This place on the main roundabout near Millennium BIM, and a short walk uphill from the market area/transport stand has simple rooms with bathrooms.

Information

Millennium BIM (Avenida Eduardo Mondlane) ATM; in the lower part of town.

BIC (Avenida Samora Machel) ATM; in the upper part of town.

Getting There & Away

Transport in Gurúè departs from near the market at the lower end of town.

NAMPULA From Nampula, take any bus to Alto Molócuè (Mtc200), where you can then get a waiting *chapa* on to Gurúè (Mtc200). Going in the other direction, you'll need to depart Gurúè by 5am at the latest for Nampevo junction to get a connection on to Nampula.

QUELIMANE For connections to/from Quelimane, there's a daily direct *chapa* departing at 4.30am (Mtc300, six hours); buy tickets the day before. Otherwise there are several vehicles daily to Mocuba (Mtc200, 3½ to four hours), from where you can continue to Quelimane.

VIA MUTUALI It's also possible to take the train from either Nampula or Cuamba to Mutuali, where you'll find a waiting open-backed pick-up truck on to Gurúè (Mtc150, four to five hours). This works best coming from Cuamba; coming from Nampula, most of the journey to Gurúè will be at night. There's also usually one vehicle daily between Cuamba and Gurúè (Mtc200 to Mtc250, five hours). To Milange, it's fastest to go via Mocuba.

Alto Molócuè

This agreeable town is a refuelling point between Mocuba and Nampula. **Pensão Famba Uone** (d Mtc700), just up from the market, has extremely basic doubles and meals with advance notice. Several vehicles daily go to/from Nampula (Mtc200, 3½ hours) and Mocuba (four hours). There's also at least one vehicle daily to Gurúè via Nauela (50km from Alto Molócue to Nauela, 56km from Nauela to Gurúè) along a wonderfully scenic route.

NORTHERN MOZAMBIQUE

If southern Mozambique's lures are the accessible beaches and relaxing resorts, in the north it's the paradisiacal coastal panoramas, the sense of space and the sheer adventure of travel. This is one of Africa's last frontiers, wild, beautiful and untamed. Inland are vast expanses of bush where enough lions and elephants still roam to be the stuff of local lore and wreak havoc on villages. Along the coast is an almost endless succession of unspoiled beaches and islands, including Mozambique Island – one of southern Africa's most alluring destinations.

In many respects, the north (the provinces of Nampula, Niassa and Cabo Delgado) might as well be a separate country. It's divided from the rest of Mozambique by several major rivers and hundreds of kilometres of road. And, although home to one-third of Mozambique's population, it accounts for only one-fifth of the gross national product, has the lowest adult literacy rates and often seems to drop out of sight for the southern-oriented government.

Culturally, northern Mozambique is intriguing as the home of many matrilineal tribes, in contrast with the strictly patrilineal south. Islamic influences are also stronger here, with centuries-old ties to the ancient Swahili trading networks. The north is also the birthplace of Mozambique's independence struggle. It was here, in the bush, that the Frelimo cadres did their training, and it was here – in the unlikely village of Chai – that the first shots of war were fired.

In the main destinations – Nampula, Mozambique Island, Pemba, the Quirimbas Archipelago and Lichinga – there is enough infrastructure to travel as comfortably as you like. Elsewhere, most journeys are rough and rugged.

Nampula

☎26

Nampula, Mozambique's third-largest city, is a crowded city with a hard edge. As the jumping-off point for visiting Mozambique Island, it's also an inevitable stop for many travellers. While there are few tourist attractions, Nampula's negatives are redeemed somewhat by its good facilities, broad avenues and its main plaza, graced by an imposing white cathedral and rimmed by flame trees.

Another plus is the lush surrounding countryside dotted with enormous inselbergs – large masses of smooth volcanic granite, which intruded into the earth's crust aeons ago and were then exposed over the millennia by the erosion of the softer surrounding rock. Some soar close to 1000m into the air. For any technical climbing, you'll need to get permission from the local district administrator.

History

It's only recently that Nampula has come into its own, having spent much of the 19th century languishing in the shadow of nearby Mozambique Island. The construction of a rail link from the coast in the 1930s and the expansion of nearby Nacala's port in the late 1940s boosted Nampula's growth as a rail junction and administrative centre. Today, it's the capital of Nampula province (Mozambique's second most populous province after Zambézia) and the commercial centre of the north.

Sights & Activities

Nampula doesn't have as much to offer architecturally as Maputo and Beira, but there are a few intriguing buildings. The main one is the imposing **Cathedral of Nossa Senhora de Fátima**, in a large plaza flanked at one end by the **governor's house**.

National Ethnography Museum MUSEUM
(Museu Nacional de Etnografia; Avenida Eduardo Mondlane; admission Mtc100; ⏲9am-5pm Tue-Fri, 2-5pm Sat & Sun) The National Ethnography Museum is worth a visit, with a collection documenting various aspects of local life and culture, and explanations in English and Portuguese.

Complexo Bamboo Swimming Pool SWIMMING
(Ribáué Rd; adult/child Mtc200/100) A good spot to cool off.

Sleeping

Ruby Nampula BACKPACKERS $
(☎82-717 9923; claudilhas@hotmail.com; Rua Daniel Napatima; dm/d Mtc700/1600; wi-fi) This backpackers in a converted private house is highly recommended, especially for travellers using Nampula as a jumping off point for Mozambique Island. It has spotless, good value rooms and dormitories – Nampula's best value in the budget category – plus hot water, a self-catering kitchen and a small bar selling snacks and cakes. The staff is very helpful with onward travel information. It's a block from the Museum, next to the well-signposted offices of World Vision.

Nampula

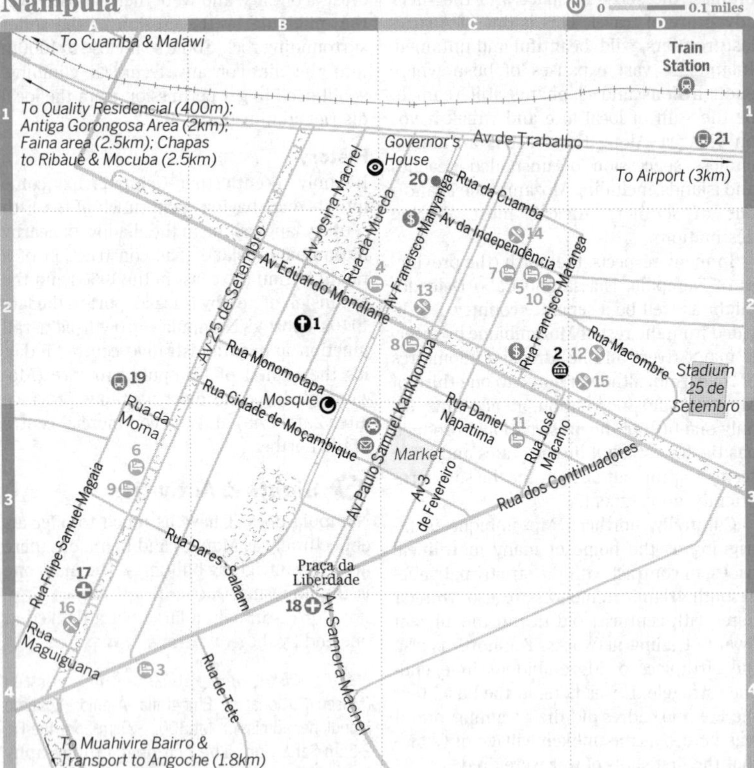

Nampula

Sights
1 Cathedral of Nossa Senhora de Fátima B2
2 National Ethnography Museum C2

Sleeping
3 Hotel Brasília A4
4 Hotel Girassol B2
5 Hotel Lúrio C2
6 Hotel Milénio A3
7 Pensão África C2
8 Residencial A Marisqueira C2
9 Residencial da Universidade Pedagógica A3
10 Residencial Expresso C2
11 Ruby Nampula C3

Eating
A Marisqueira .... (see 8)
Café Atlântico .... (see 4)
12 Copacabana D2
13 Frango King C2
14 Restaurante Dona Amélia C2
15 Sporting Clube de Nampula D2
16 Supermarket A4
Supermercado Ideal .... (see 4)

Information
Centro Comercial de Nampula .... (see 4)
17 Farmácia 25 de Setembro A3
18 Provincial Hospital B4
Teledata .... (see 4)

Transport
19 Grupo Mecula A2
20 LAM C1
Maning Nice .... (see 21)
Nagi Trans .... (see 21)
21 Padaria Nampula Transport Stand D1
TCO .... (see 14)

Complexo Bamboo CHALETS **$$**
(☎26-216595, 26-217838; bamboo@teledata.mz; Ribáué Rd; s/d/tw/ste Mtc1950/2450/2450/2950; P❄≋♿) Pleasant, well-maintained rooms (the twins are nicer than the doubles) in expansive grounds with a children's playground make this a good choice for families. All rooms have TV and minifridge and there's a popular restaurant. It's about 5km out of town; follow Avenida do Trabalho west from the train station, then right onto the Ribáuè Rd; Bamboo is 1.5km down on the left.

Residencial Expresso HOTEL **$$**
(☎26-218809, 26-218808; 574 Avenida da Independência; tw from Mtc2200-2500; P❄) A dozen large, spotless, modern twin-bed rooms with fridge and TV. Breakfast is included and meals can be arranged.

Hotel Milénio HOTEL **$$**
(☎26-218989, 26-218877; hotelmilenio@tdm.co.mz; 842 Avenida 25 de Setembro; tw/d/ste Mtc3200/3200/4500; ❄@) Large, modern rooms convenient to the Mecula bus garage, and a pricey restaurant downstairs. Wi-fi is in the lobby only.

Residencial da Universidade Pedagógica HOSTEL **$**
(☎82-833 7434; 840 Avenida 25 de Setembro; s/d/tw Mtc1400/2000/2400) This university accommodation is in a quiet area next to Hotel Milénio, with simple, secure, good-value rooms and breakfast. It's also convenient to the Mecula bus depot.

Hotel Brasília HOTEL **$**
(☎26-212127; 26 Rua dos Continuadores; s/d/tw Mtc800/900/1100; ❄) Hotel Brasília is currently rented out long term, but is worth checking as its clean rooms are among the better-value choices in the budget category. All come with bathroom, and there's a small restaurant. It's a 20-minute hike from the bus and train depots.

Pensão África HOTEL **$**
(Pensão Nampula; ☎84-925 0798, 82-259 6886; Avenida 3 de Fevereiro; s/tw/d Mtc1000/1250/1500) Basic but acceptable budget rooms in a busy central location. There's no food.

Hotel Girassol HOTEL **$$**
(☎26-216000; www.girassolhoteis.co.mz; 326 Avenida Eduardo Mondlane; s/d from Mtc2800/3250; P❄) Upstairs in the Centro Comercial de Nampula high-rise, this four-star place has modern rooms with TV and minifridge, although the price difference with the other options in this category isn't justified. Ask for a room with views over the cathedral and town.

Complexo Montes Nairucco CAMPGROUND **$**
(☎26-215297, 26-240081; idalecio@teledata.mz; Ribáuè Rd; campsite per person Mtc150, s/d Mtc1395/1775, day visit per person Mtc50) This Portuguese-run working farm is nestled under the towering Monte Nairucco about 16km west of town, and is dotted with mango and orange groves. It makes a peaceful weekend retreat or day trip (open 6am to 10pm), with a reservoir where you can swim, a restaurant and a bar and a *braai* area. The camping ground overlooks the reservoir and gets high marks from overlanders. Taxis from town charge about Mtc400. If you're driving, follow the Ribáuè Rd for about 15km to the signpost, from where it's 1km further down a small lane.

Hotel Lúrio HOTEL **$$**
(☎82-827 8587, 26-218631; hotelurio@gmail.com; Avenida da Independência; s/d/ste Mtc2600/2700/3400) Recently renovated, this centrally-located hotel offers bland rooms and a restaurant. It's diagonally opposite petrol station Fabião.

Quality Residencial HOTEL **$$**
(☎26-217872, 26-216871; www.residencialquality.com; 953 Avenida do Trabalho; s/d/ste from Mtc2200/2500/2950; ❄) This new, good-value place is about 1km out of town along the Quelimane road, with modern rooms and a restaurant downstairs. It's a good option for self-drivers wanting to head south out of town early.

Residencial A Marisqueira HOTEL **$**
(☎26-213611; cnr Avenidas Paulo Samuel Kankhomba & Eduardo Mondlane; s/d/tw Mtc1350/1500/1750; ❄) On a busy corner, with no-frills rooms (ask for one of the 'newer' ones), all with TV, plus a convenient (albeit noisy) central location. There's no hot water, and the hallways and common areas seem to be permanently under construction.

Eating

Self-caterers can try the **Supermarket** (Avenida 25 de Setembro; ⏲9am-8pm Mon-Sat, to 3pm Sun) at the lower end of Avenida 25 de Setembro near the junction with Rua dos Continuadores or **Supermercado Ideal** (326 Avenida Eduardo Mondlane), in the Hotel Girassol building.

Restaurante Dona Amélia AFRICAN **$$**
(Casa Fabião, Avenida da Independência; daily menu Mtc300-400; ⌚lunch & dinner) This small place is hidden away almost in the Galp Fabião petrol station, and next to the TCO booking office. Just ask the gas station attendants to point you to the right doorway. Inside, Dona Amélia prepares soup and one or two different lunch and dinner specials each day. The food is good and reasonably priced, and the ambience authentic, with a TV in the background and locals coming and going.

Copacabana CONTINENTAL **$$**
(Rua Macombre; meals Mtc200-350; ⌚7am-9pm Mon-Fri, until 11pm Sat & Sun) This popular place behind the museum has outdoor seating under a large thatched roof, tasty pizzas, and seafood and meat grills.

Complexo Bamboo CONTINENTAL **$$**
(☎26-216595; www.teledata.mz/bamboo; Ribáué Rd; meals from Mtc200) The outdoor restaurant at this hotel serves tasty versions of all the usual dishes in pleasant, leafy surroundings.

Sporting Clube de Nampula CONTINENTAL **$$**
(Avenida Eduardo Mondlane; meals from Mtc200; ⌚8am-10pm) Next to the National Ethnography Museum, this long-standing watering hole features the usual chicken and fish grills, plus *feijoada* (a bean and sausage dish). There's inside and outdoor seating.

Café Atlântico CAFE **$**
(Centro Comercial de Nampula, Avenida Eduardo Mondlane; snacks & meals from Mtc150; ⌚6am-9pm) Burgers, pizzas and other light meals.

Frango King FAST FOOD **$**
(Avenida Eduardo Mondlane; half/whole chicken Mtc125/200; ⌚7.30am-4am) Grilled chicken to go, at almost any hour.

A Marisqueira CONTINENTAL **$**
(☎26-213611; cnr Avenidas Paulo Kankhomba & Eduardo Mondlane; meals from Mtc170) Reasonably priced plates of the day.

Shopping

Sunday Morning Craft Market ARTS & CRAFTS
(Stadium; ⌚dawn-dusk) The best place for crafts. It's held in the large stadium downhill from Copacabana restaurant. Go early, before things get hot and crowded.

Information

Internet Access

There's wi-fi access in the lobby of Hotel Milénio (p215).

Teledata (Centro Comercial de Nampula, Avenida Eduardo Mondlane; per hr Mtc1; ⌚8am-noon & 2-8pm Mon-Fri, 9am-5pm Sat) Internet access.

Medical Services

Consultório Médico Boa Saude (☎84-460 5170, 84-601 5600; Rua dos Viveiros, Bairro Muahivire) One of the better bets if you're ill. Just off Avenida das FPLM.

Farmácia 25 de Setembro (Avenida 25 de Setembro; ⌚8am-6pm Mon-Sat, 9am-1pm Sun) Just down from Hotel Milénio.

Provincial Hospital (Praça da Liberdade) Malaria testing.

Money

Centro Comercial de Nampula (Avenida Eduardo Mondlane) ATM inside; same location as Hotel Girassol.

Millennium BIM (cnr Avenidas da Independência & Francisco Manyanga) ATM.

Standard Bank (Avenida Eduardo Mondlane) ATM; just up from the museum.

Getting There & Away

Air

There are flights on **LAM** (☎26-212801, 26-213322; Avenida Francisco Manyanga; ⌚7.30am-12.30pm & 2.30-5.30pm Mon-Fri) to Maputo daily, and Beira, Lichinga, Quelimane, Tete and Pemba several times weekly.

The airport is about 4km northeast of town (Mtc150 in a taxi).

Bus & Chapa

The main bus companies currently serving Nampula are:

Grupo Mecula (☎26-213772; grupomecula@teledata.mz; Rua da Moma) Departures and ticketing from the Grupo Mecula garage, just off Avenida 25 de Setembro and one block south of Rua Cidade de Moçambique in the area known as 'Roman'. All departures at 5am. Ticketing office opens at 3pm.

Maning Nice (☎82-706 2820; Avenida do Trabalho) Departures and ticketing from Padaria Nampula transport stand, in the same place as *tanzaniano chapas* to Mozambique Island. All departures between 3am and 5am.

TCO (☎84-601 6861, 82-509 2180) Ticketing office adjoins Galp petrol station ('Casa Fabião') on Avenida da Independência, just east of Avenida Paulo Samuel Kankhomba. Departures are from 'Antiga Gorongosa', about 2km from the train station along Avenida do Trabalho, between the Sasol and GALP petrol stations, on your left as you're heading to Quelimane. Schedules vary on a weekly basis.

Nagi Trans (☎86-318 4004, 84-265 7082, 84-955 1669; Avenida do Trabalho) Ticketing and departures from Nagi Investimentos, next to the Millennium BIM branch in the Antiga Gorongosa area.

PEMBA To Pemba (Mtc350, seven to eight hours): Grupo Mecula (daily); Maning Nice (three times weekly, with one bus at 4.30am and one at noon, which awaits the Maning Nice bus arriving from Maputo); Nagi Trans (daily at noon)

QUELIMANE To Quelimane (Mtc480, 11 hours): Grupo Mecula (daily); Maning Nice (daily); Nagi Trans (daily)

MOÇIMBOA DA PRAIA, MUEDA & MONTEPUEZ Maning Nice services Moçimboa da Praia (Mtc500, 13 hours, daily), Mueda (Mtc500, daily) and Montepuez (Mtc300, nine hours, daily).

MOZAMBIQUE ISLAND To Mozambique Island (Mtc140, three to four hours) *chapas* depart between 5am and 11am from the Padaria Nampula transport stand along Avenida do Trabalho east of the train station. Look for one that's going direct; many go only to Monapo, where you'll need to stand on the roadside and wait for another vehicle. The best connections are found on one of the *tanzaniano chapas*, which depart Nampula between about 7am and 10am, depending on how early they arrive from Mozambique Island, and which continue more or less nonstop to the island. The Padaria Nampula transport stand is also the place to find *chapas* to Mossuril, Namapa, and other points north and east.

ANGOCHE *Chapas* go to Angoche (Mtc150, three hours) daily, departing from 4.30am from Muahvire bairro, along the extension of Avenida das FPLM. Go over the small bridge and continue all the way up the hill to the start of the Angoche road.

BEIRA TCO and Maning Nice both service Beira (Mtc1900, 16 hours) twice weekly.

MOCUBA *Chapas* to Mocuba (Mtc350) leave from the 'Faina' area, about 2.5km west of the train station along Avenida do Trabalho near the Ribáuè road junction, but it's faster to take the Mecula bus to Quelimane and have them drop you off.

CUAMBA It's possible in theory to get transport from the Faina area, although most people go via Gurúè or by train.

CHIMOIO Maning Nice services Chimoio (Mtc1200) three times weekly.

MAPUTO TCO, Maning Nice and Nagi Trans all run to Maputo (Mtc2500, 30 hours) twice weekly

VILANKULO There are no direct buses to Vilankulo. The best connection is Nampula to Chimoio on Maning Nice, and then continuing from Chimoio to Vilankulo.

Train

A six-times-weekly passenger train connects Nampula and Cuamba.

 Getting Around

The main **taxi rank** (Avenida Paulo Samuel Kankhomba) is near the market. For car hire, **Sixt** (☎82-300 5170, 26-216312; www.sixt.com), **Europcar** (☎84-322 3473; www.europcar.com) **Safari Rent-a-Car** (☎84-333 3555, 26-12255; safari@tdm.co.mz) and **Premium Rent-a-Car** (☎26-217864; www.carpremium.co.mz) are all at the airport.

Angoche

Angoche, an old Muslim trading centre dating from at least the 15th century, was one of the earliest settlements in Mozambique. While little evidence of its long history remains, the area, and especially the nearby islands, are caught in an intriguing time warp, and you can still hear Arabic spoken in many areas.

History

Angoche (formerly António Ennes) initially gained prominence as a gold and ivory trading post. By the late-16th century, the town had been eclipsed by Quelimane as an entry port to the interior. However, it continued to play a role in coastal trade and was an important economic and political centre, with close ties to Mozambique Island. In the 19th century, Angoche became the focus of the clandestine slave trade, which continued until the 1860s, when the town was attacked by the Portuguese. While effective Portuguese administration was not established until several decades later, the attack marked the beginning of Angoche's downfall and the town never regained its former status.

Sights & Activities

There's a small but lively afternoon **fish market** near the Catholic church. Go left and down towards the water after passing the church.

About 7km north of town is the long, wide and stunning **Praia Nova** (New Beach), with perhaps the whitest sand that you'll see anywhere. It has no shade or facilities. The start of the road to reach Praia Nova is a few blocks past the far (northern) end of the park (past O Pescador restaurant), from where it's 7.5km further; you'll need to walk or hitch. About 45km further on is the village of **Quinga**, near another beautiful stretch of sand for which you'll need your own 4WD transport.

Dhows or motorised boats to the nearby islands can be arranged at the *capitania* (maritime office), at the base of the main road near Praça dos Heróis. Dhows also leave frequently from the fish market.

Stretching well south of Angoche towards Moma and on to Pebane are the archipelagos of the **Primeiras and Segundas Islands**, slated to be Mozambique's newest protected area. Several of the islands are favoured as nesting areas by local green turtles and many are encircled by coral reefs. Dugongs are also frequent visitors. There are no tourist facilities yet, although several projects are underway.

Sleeping & Eating

Hesada Apartments APARTMENTS $
(☎82-666 8880, 84-666 8880, 26-720327/8; www.hesadapartments.webs.com; d/apt Mtc1000/2500; ❄) This is Angoche's best accommodation, with several rooms in the city centre, plus two self-catering, two-room apartments in a quiet area on the outskirts of town. All have bathrooms and 24-hour water supply (a rarity in Angoche). The owner also has a 4WD vehicle available for rent.

Pensão Mafamete HOTEL $
(s/d/tw Mtc350/450/500) This very basic place is the best of the local *pensões* (inexpensive hotels), with a few basic rooms in a multistorey building. All have fan, but no nets (although the windows are screened), and all share bathrooms without water. There's no food. When entering town, turn off the main road to the left at the first round marker in front of the Governo building. Go three blocks down; Mafamete is on your left, on the final block before reaching a small park.

Restaurante O Pescador SEAFOOD $
(☎84-470 8481; meals from Mtc200; ⊙lunch & dinner Mon-Sat) O Pescador has good, well-prepared meals, a cool interior with checked tablecloths, and shaded parking. On Sunday, it's sometimes possible to arrange meals in advance with the proprietress. It's around the corner from Pensão Mafamete on the park; look for the blue-and-white parking awning.

Information

Millennium BIM (Avenida Liberdade) Has an ATM.

Getting There & Away

Chapas go daily to/from Nampula (Mtc150, four hours), departing from the transport stand at the top entrance to town, about 1km from the central area. The first departure is at 2.30am (4.30am from Nampula to Angoche). All go via Nametil. Going via Corrane (Nampula–Corrane–Liupo–Angoche) is possible with your own high-clearance 4WD, but not recommended, as the stretch from Corrane to Liupo is in poor condition.

With your own transport (4WD), or with time and persistence on public transport, it's possible to travel between Angoche and Monapo (near Mozambique Island) via the sizeable settlement of Liupo on a good dirt road.

Mozambique Island (Ilha de Moçambique)

Crescent-shaped Mozambique Island (Ilha de Moçambique) measures only 3km in length and barely 500m in width at its widest section. Yet it has played a larger-than-life role in East African coastal life over the centuries, and today is one of the region's most fascinating destinations – part slowly reawakening ghost town, part lively fishing community. It's also a picturesque and exceptionally pleasant place to wander around.

Mozambique Island's fusion of cultures is best seen in Stone Town, as the quiet, cobwebbed northern half of the island is known. Here, you'll find the majority of historic buildings, most constructed between the early-16th and late-19th centuries when the Portuguese occupied the island and most original residents were banished to the mainland. Graceful praças rimmed by once-grand churches, colonnaded archways and stately colonial-era buildings line the quiet, cobbled streets. Makuti Town – the island's younger, more colourful southern half – reflects Mozambique Island's other face. It dates from the late-19th century, and is where most islanders now live, with its thatched-roof huts, narrow alleyways echoing with the sounds of children playing and chickens squawking, and fishermen sitting on the sand repairing their long, brightly coloured nets. The waterfront in between, along the island's eastern edge, is known as the *contracosta*.

History

For most of its history Mozambique Island has served as a meeting point of cultures and a hub of Indian Ocean trade. As early as the 15th century it was an important boat-building centre, and its history as a trading settlement – with ties to Madagascar, Persia, Arabia and elsewhere – dates back well before that. Vasco da Gama landed here in 1498, and in 1507 a permanent Portuguese settlement was established on the island. Unlike Sofala to the south, where the Portuguese also established a foothold at about the same time, Mozambique Island prospered as both a trading station and naval base, with connections to places as far away as Macau and Goa. In the late-16th century, the massive Fort of São Sebastião was constructed. The island soon became capital of Portuguese East Africa, a status that it held until the end of the 19th century when the government was transferred to Lourenço Marques (Maputo). As focus shifted southward, Mozambique Island's star began to fade. The construction of a rail terminus at nearby Nacala in 1947 and the development of the Nacala port during the 1950s sealed the island's fate and sent it into an economic decline from which it never recovered.

Apart from its early strategic and economic importance, Mozambique Island also developed as a missionary centre. Beginning in the 17th century, numerous orders established churches here and Christians intermixed with the island's traditional Muslim population and Hindu community. Various small waves of immigration over the years – from places as diverse as East Africa, Goa and Macau – contributed to the ethnic and cultural mix, and the resulting melange is one of the island's most intriguing aspects. Over the last century, as the Portuguese presence on the island has faded, Muslim influence has reasserted itself and, together with local Makua culture, is now dominant.

Since 1991, this cultural melting pot has been a Unesco World Heritage site and, while there are still many crumbling ruins, there's fresh paint and restoration work aplenty.

Sights

While wandering through Stone Town, watch for the restored, ochre-toned **BIM** (Avenida Amilcar Cabral) and the ornate **colonial administration offices** overlooking the gardens east of the hospital. A few blocks north of the market is the recently restored **Hindu temple** and, on the island's western edge, a fairly modern **mosque** painted an unmissable shade of green.

Palace & Chapel of São Paulo MUSEUM

(Palácio de São Paulo; ☎26-610081; adult/child Mtc100/50; ⊙8am-4.30pm) This imposing edifice – the former governor's residence and now a museum – dates from 1610 and is the island's historical showpiece. The interior, which is currently under renovation and closed to the public, gives a remarkable glimpse into what upper-class life must have been like during the island's 18th-century heyday. In addition to knick-knacks from Portugal, Arabia, India and China, there are many pieces of original furniture, including an important collection of heavily ornamented Indo-Portuguese pieces. In the chapel (currently open), don't miss the altar and the pulpit, the latter of which was made in the 17th century by Chinese artists in Goa. On the ground floor is the small but fascinating **Maritime Museum** (Museu da Marinha), with gold coins, ship compasses, Chinese porcelain and other items recovered from local shipwrecks. Behind the palace are the **Church of the Misericórdia** (still in use) and the **Museum of Sacred Art** (Museu de Arte Sacra), containing religious ornaments, paintings and carvings. The museum is housed in the former hospital of the Holy House of Mercy, a religious guild that assisted the poor and sick in several Portuguese colonies from the early 1500s onwards. The ticket price includes entry to all three museums and an English-speaking guide.

Fort of São Sebastião FORTRESS

(per adult/child Mtc100/50; ⊙8am-4.30pm) The island's northern end is dominated by the massive Fort of São Sebastião, which is the oldest complete fort still standing in sub-Saharan Africa. Construction began in 1558, and about 50 years later the final stones were laid. Just beyond the fort, at the island's tip and accessed via the fort entrance, is the tiny **Chapel of Nossa Senhora de Baluarte**. Built in 1522, it's considered to be the oldest European building in the southern hemisphere and one of the best examples of Manueline vaulted architecture in Mozambique. At the southern end of the island, overlooking Makuti Town and the fishing port, is the large (and no longer used) **Church of Santo António**. Nearby is a **cemetery** with Christian, Muslim and Hindu graves.

Activities

Mozambique Island is not a beach destination and strong tidal flows make it dangerous to swim around the island's northern and southern ends. The cleanest of the island's patches of sand is Nancaramo Beach, next to the fort. For beautiful, clean sand, head across Mossuril Bay to Chocas and Cabaceira Pequena, or to the beach on Goa Island. There are swimming pools at O Escondidinho (p221) (Mtc150 per person for non-guests) and Villa Sands (p221) (free if you have a meal at the restaurant).

Sleeping

Casa Branca GUESTHOUSE $

(☎82-454 3290, 26-610076; http://ilhamocambique.com.sapo.pt; Rua dos Combatentes; r with shared bathroom Mtc1100, with minifridge & bathroom Mtc1600) On the island's eastern side near the **Camões statue**, Casa Branca has three simple but spotless rooms with views of the turquoise sea just a few metres away, and a shared kitchen. One room has its own bathroom, and the other two share. Rates include breakfast. Adjoining is a seaside garden/sitting area.

Mooxeleliya GUESTHOUSE $

(☎82-454 3290, 26-610076; http://ilhamocambique.com.sapo.pt; d without/with air-con Mtc1000/1500, f Mtc2000) Mooxeleliya (the Makua name translates roughly as, 'Did you rest well?') has five simple but spacious high-ceilinged rooms upstairs and two darker, three- to four-person family-style rooms downstairs. All rooms have their own bathroom, breakfast is included and there's a small cooking area with refrigerator and a communal TV/sitting area. It's just down from the Church of the Misericórdia.

Patio dos Quintalinhos GUESTHOUSE $

(Casa de Gabriele; ☎82-419 7610, 26-610090; www.patiodosquintalinhos.com; Rua do Celeiro; &s/d with shared bathroom US$26/30, d/q from US$42/64, ste US$64; P@🛜≋) Opposite the green mosque, with a handful of comfortable, creatively designed rooms around a small courtyard, including one with a loft, and a suite with its own skylight and private rooftop balcony with views to the water. All have bathroom, except for two small rooms to the back. There's also a rooftop terrace, pool and secure parking; breakfast is included. Staff can help with bicycle rental and excursions.

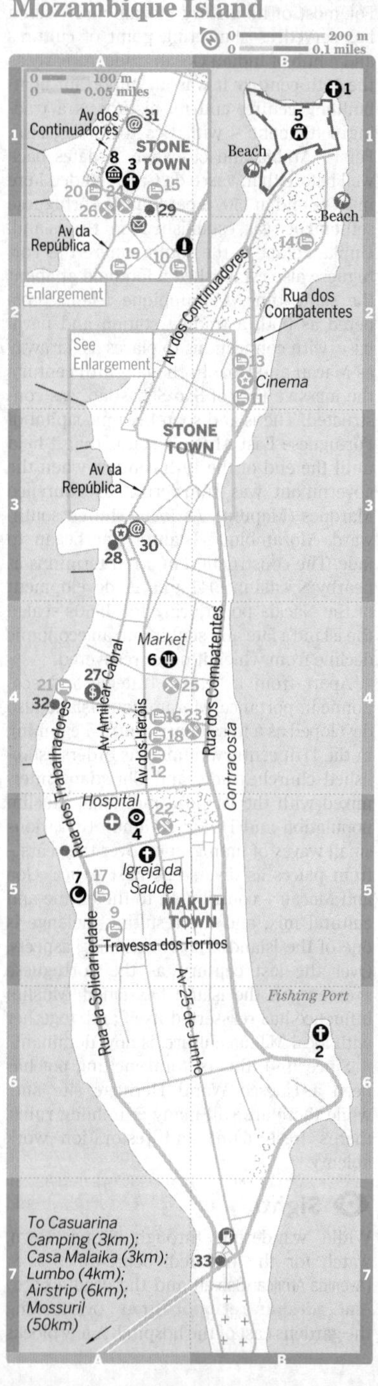

Mozambique Island

Sights
BIM Bank (see 27)
1 Chapel of Nossa Senhora de Baluarte B1
2 Church of Santo António B6
3 Church of the Misericórdia A1
4 Colonial Administration Offices A5
5 Fort of São Sebastião B1
6 Hindu Temple A4
Maritime Museum (see 8)
7 Mosque A5
Museum of Sacred Art (see 3)
8 Palace & Chapel of São Paulo A1
Pool (see 16)

Activities, Courses & Tours
Pool (see 21)

Sleeping
9 Amakuthini (Casa de Luís) A5
10 Casa Branca A2
11 Casa das Ondas B2
12 Casa de Dona Shamu A4
13 Casa de Yasmin B2
14 Hotel Omuhi'piti B2
15 Mooxeleliya A1
16 O Escondidinho A4
17 Patio dos Quintalinhos A5
Pensão Watólofu (see 23)
18 Residencial Amy A4
19 Ruby Backpacker A2
20 Terraço das Quitandas A1
21 Villa Sands A4

Eating
22 Bar Flôr de Rosa A5
23 Bar-Restaurante Watólofu B4
24 Café-Bar Âncora d'Ouro A1
O Escondidinho (see 16)
25 O Paladar A4
26 Relíquias A1

Information
27 BIM A4
28 Capitania (Port Captain's Office) A3
29 Immigration Office A1
30 Mcel A3
31 Telecomunicações de Moçambique A1

Transport
32 Dhows to Cabaceira Grande A4
33 Transport Stand B7

Ruby Backpacker BACKPACKERS $
(☎84-398 5862; ruby@themozambiqueisland.com; Travessa da Sé; dm Mtc500, tw/d Mtc1100/1100; @) Great value for money, this place, in a renovated 400-year-old house, has dorm beds upstairs and downstairs, twin and double rooms, a self-catering kitchen, hot showers, a bar, a fantastic rooftop terrace, bicycle rental, laundry service, a traveller's notice board and lots of information about onward travel. From the 'arcade' street, take the first left after passing the Missanga craft shop (to your right), then take the next left.

O Escondidinho HOTEL $$
(☎26-610078; www.escondidinho.net; Avenida dos Heróis; s Mtc1400-2700, d Mtc1600-2900, extra bed Mtc650;) This atmospheric place has spacious, high-ceilinged rooms, all with nets, ceiling fans and mosquito netting in the windows, plus a garden courtyard, and a good restaurant. A few rooms have private bathroom. It's near the public gardens.

Hotel Omuhi'piti HOTEL $$
(☎26-610101; s/d from Mtc3000/3400;) In a good setting at the island's northern tip, this once pleasant hotel, now run by CFM, has begun to fade and is no longer good value for money. However, the setting is quiet and lovely, and most rooms have large windows and sea views. Breakfast is included, and there's a restaurant.

Villa Sands BOUTIQUE HOTEL $$
(☎82-744 7178; www.villasands.com; d Mtc3200-3700, ste Mtc4500;) This sleek, boutique hotel overlooks the water on the northwestern side of the island. Most ground floor rooms have only a skylight, although they are light and airy, with ceiling fans. The upstairs suite has wide views. The upstairs rooms also have their own pool, and there's a restaurant (meals from Mtc400) and a rooftop terrace.

Terraço das Quitandas B&B $$$
(☎84-6131243, 26-610115; www.terracodasquitandas.com; Avenida da República; s US$125-175, d US$200-250) This B&B is in a restored colonial-era house on the water next to Relíquias restaurant. It has six well-appointed rooms, each with authentic but rather heavy period decor and all but two with

A WATERLESS ISLAND

Interestingly, there are no wells on Mozambique Island; it was settled despite the lack of water sources because of its favourable location and natural harbour. To compensate, most houses in the early days had cisterns, as did the Fort of São Sebastião, which had three. Now, water is piped in from the mainland.

private bathroom. While atmospheric and comfortable, service can be rather sporadic.

Casa de Yasmin GUESTHOUSE $
(☎82-676 8850, 26-610073; Rua dos Combatentes; r Mtc750-1500, ste Mtc2000; ❄) Near the cinema at the island's northern end, with a handful of clean rooms – some with bathroom and some with air-con – in an annex next to the family house. The larger double suite has air-con and a glimpse of the sea. There's no food.

Casa das Ondas GUESTHOUSE $
(☎82-438 6400, 82-569 2888; r with/without bathroom Mtc1200/1000) Three basic, somewhat rundown rooms (one with private bathroom), a sitting area and a kitchen. It's just to the left of the cinema and unmarked; look for the arched windows.

Casuarina Camping CAMPGROUND $
(☎84-616 8764; casuarina.camping@gmail.com; campsite per person Mtc200, d with/without bathroom from Mtc1000/800; 📶) On the mainland opposite Mozambique Island, and just a two-minute walk from the bridge (to your right, coming from the island), Casuarina has a well-maintained camping ground on a small, clean beach, plus simple bungalow-style rooms, ablution blocks with bucket-style showers and a restaurant with pizza oven, local dishes, seafood and ice cream.

Pensão-Bar-Restaurante Watólofu GUESTHOUSE $
(☎82-629 2505; off Rua dos Combatentes; r Mtc1000) The rooms at Watólofu, inside an unmarked walled compound, are simple and small, but good for the price. All have fan, double bed and private bathroom, and there's a restaurant.

Local Homes with Rooms

The cheapest options are in local homes, most with small, basic rooms in the family quarters.

Amakuthini GUESTHOUSE $
(Casa de Luís; ☎82-540 7622, 82-436 7570; dm Mtc350, s/d with shared bathroom Mtc600/800) Very basic and rough around the edges, but welcoming and the only accommodation in the midst of crowded Makuti Town. It has an eight-bed dorm and several small, dark rooms with fan in a tiny garden behind the family house. All accommodation has nets, and the room price includes breakfast. There are also basic cooking facilities, laundry service and a refrigerator. Meals can be arranged with advance notice. Take the first left after passing the green mosque (to your right), make your way down the narrow, rocky path to the first corner and turn right.

Residencial Amy GUESTHOUSE $
(Avenida dos Heróis; d Mtc500-700, tr Mtc800) Near the park, with several basic, dark rooms (most lacking exterior windows) in the main house and a common area with TV. There's no food.

Casa de Dona Chamo GUESTHOUSE $
(☎84-747 1200, 82-130 3346; Avenida dos Heróis; d without bathroom Mtc600-700, d/tr with bathroom and air-con Mtc1200/1500) This place near the park has basic, darkish rooms, a common area and a friendly proprietress. There's no food.

Casa Malaika HUT $
(☎84-426 5893; fotografiasinfronteras@gmail.com; campsite per person Mtc100, dm/r Mtc200/500) On the mainland, just to the left of the bridge when coming from the island, this place was just getting started when we passed through. It offers a chance to stay in a very basic traditional style house and become acquainted with the local community. Volunteering can also be arranged, as can local style meals.

Eating

For self-caterers, there are several well-stocked shops just inside the market entrance. For great ambience, ask around for the 'barraca restaurants' near the hospital, especially Barraca Sara.

O Paladar AFRICAN $
(meals Mtc250; ⏲lunch & dinner Thu-Tue) At the eastern corner of the old market, O Paladar is the place to go for local cuisine. Stop by in the morning and place your order with Dona Maria for lunchtime or evening meals.

Relíquias FUSION $$

(☎82-5252318; Avenida da República; meals Mtc260-600; ⏰10am-10pm Tue-Sun) This pleasant, popular spot has well-prepared seafood and meat dishes, plus delicious prawn curry, *matapa* (cooked cassava leaves with peanut sauce) and coconut rice. It's near the museum, and has seating indoors or outside overlooking the water.

Café-Bar Âncora d'Ouro CAFE $$

(☎26-610006; meals about Mtc350; ⏰8am-11pm Thurs-Tues) Muffins, pizzas, sandwiches, soups, homemade ice cream, waffles and other goodies, plus more substantial fare, prompt service and airy seating. It's opposite the Church of the Misericórdia.

Bar Flôr de Rosa ITALIAN $$

(☎82-745 7380; meals Mtc300-350; ⏰5pm-midnight Mon-Sat) This small, chic Italian-run place has coffees and espressos, a selection of pastas, soups and sandwiches, and a rooftop terrace for sundowners, plus live music on Friday and Saturday in season. It's near the hospital.

O Escondidinho EUROPEAN $$

(☎26-610078; meals about Mtc500) The restaurant at this hotel has a changing daily menu featuring well-prepared shrimp, crayfish and other seafood dishes with French overtones and tables near the small garden.

Bar-Restaurante Watólofu SEAFOOD $

(off Rua dos Combatentes; meals Mtc160-280; ⏰lunch & dinner) This quiet establishment is tucked into an unsignposted walled compound behind O Escondidinho. It serves tasty grilled chicken, squid, shrimp and other local dishes.

Information

BIM (Avenida Amilcar Cabral) Has an ATM (Visa and MasterCard), and changes cash (US dollars, euro and rand).

Immigration Office Diagonally opposite Mooxeleliya, but visa extensions are handled only in Nampula.

Mcel (per min Mtc1; ⏰9.30am-6pm Mon-Fri) Internet access; just down from the police station.

Telecomunicações de Moçambique (per min Mtc1; ⏰8am-8pm Mon-Fri, 8am-1pm Sat) Internet access; near the Palace and Chapel of São Paulo.

Getting There & Away

Air

There's an airstrip at Lumbo on the mainland for charter flights.

Bus & Chapa

Mozambique Island is joined by a 3.5km bridge (built in 1967) to the mainland. Most *chapas* stop about 1km before the bridge in Lumbo, where you'll need to get into a smaller pick-up to cross over Mossuril Bay, due to vehicle weight restrictions on the bridge.

Leaving Mozambique Island, all transport departs from the bridge.

NAMPULA The only direct cars to Nampula (Mtc140, three hours) are the *tanzaniano* minibuses, with one or two departing daily between 3am and 5am. The best thing to do is to ask at your hotel for help to get a message to the driver to collect you at your hotel pre-dawn. For all later departures, you will need to change vehicles at Monapo and sometimes also at Namialo. Chartering a vehicle from Nampula to Mozambique Island costs from about Mtc3000 one way.

PEMBA For travel direct to Pemba, take the 4am *tanzaniano* to the main junction in Namialo (Mtc100, one hour). Large buses from Nampula

MUSIRO

All along the northern coast, and especially on Mozambique Island, you'll frequently see women with their faces painted white. The paste is known as *musiro* (also *n'siro* or *msiro*), and is used as a facial mask to beautify the skin, and sometimes as a sunscreen by women working in the fields or as a medicinal treatment (though the medicinal paste usually has a yellowish tinge). *Musiro* was also traditionally applied in ways that conveyed messages (for example, whether the wearer was married, or whether her husband was away), although most of the meanings have since been lost.

Musiro is made by grinding a branch of the *Olax dissitiflora* tree (known locally as *ximbuti* or *msiro*) against a stone with a bit of water. Local women usually leave the mask on for the day, and sometimes overnight. If you go walking in villages early in the morning and see women with white paste on their hands, chances are that they are in the midst of preparing *musiro*.

start passing the Namialo junction from about 6am and usually have space (about Mtc300, six hours from Namialo to Pemba). If you miss these, there are always smaller vehicles going north, and by 2pm or earlier you should be in Pemba.

QUELIMANE For travel south to Quelimane, you'll need to overnight in Nampula.

LUMBO *Chapas* to Lumbo cost Mtc10 (Mtc5 just to cross the bridge). If you're driving, wide vehicles won't pass over the bridge, and maximum weight is 1.5 tonnes. There's a Mtc10 toll per vehicle payable on arrival on the island.

Around Mozambique Island

GOA ISLAND

This tiny island (known locally as Watólofu) is about 5km east of Mozambique Island. It has a lighthouse that was built during the 1870s, and is today run by a lighthouse keeper and his family who have lived on Goa for more than 20 years. The lighthouse is now solar powered and according to the keeper the batteries give out about 1am. You can climb to the top for views. Below is a lovely beach.

The island's name comes from its position on the sea route from Goa, India, which was the base for Portuguese Mozambican government between 1509 and 1662.

Boat charter from Mozambique Island costs from Mtc1000 for four passengers; check with your hotel for a reliable captain. If you arrange a visit on your own, get permission first at the *capitania* on Mozambique Island; it's free and can be arranged on the spot. Be prepared for choppy seas, and tidal limits on the length of time you can spend on the island. Allow about 40 minutes one way with favourable winds and currents; in unfavourable conditions, allow at least double this.

SENA ISLAND

About 2km south of Goa Island is Sena Island (also known as the Island of Cobras). It takes its name from its location along the old sea route aiming towards the trading centre of Sena, on the Zambezi River. It's rocky, accessed with difficulty and seldom visited, although it has a lovely lagoon. Permission from the *capitania* on Mozambique Island is necessary to visit. Boat charter costs from Mtc1000 for four passengers; check with your hotel for a reliable captain.

Around Mozambique Island

SÃO LOURENÇO ISLAND

Just off the southern tip of Mozambique Island is this tiny island, which is completely covered by an eponymous fort dating from 1695. You can walk across the channel at low tide (watch that you don't get stuck out there), but will need to clamber up over the walls, as the ladder into the fort is missing.

LUMBO

Sleepy Lumbo, on the mainland opposite Mozambique Island, was formerly the terminus of a railway line from the interior. Today it is of interest for its Commonwealth war cemetery, a once grand but now abandoned hotel, a few old Portuguese houses, and salt flats.

CHOCAS, CABACEIRA PEQUENA & CABACEIRA GRANDE

North of Mozambique Island and across Mossuril Bay is the old Portuguese holiday town of Chocas. The town itself is of minimal interest, but just south along a sandy track roughly paralleling the beach is **Cabaceira Pequena**, with a long, beautiful white-sand beach and views across the bay to Mozambique Island. Just inland are the ruins of an old Swahili-style mosque and the remains of a cistern used as a watering spot by Portuguese sailors. **Carrusca Mar & Sol** (☎26-213302, 82-516 0173; 4-/7-person bungalows Mtc1750/3500) is a wonderful spot on weekdays (unpleasantly crowded on weekends), with a handful of rustic but spacious, nicely outfitted bungalows with hammocks and terraces, all set on a rise between the mangroves and one of the best stretches of beach. There's also a restaurant featuring seafood, pasta and pizza (meals from about Mtc300), a small children's playground and sunset views of Mozambique Island. It's about 2km south of Chocas town, en route to Cabaceira Pequena. Advance bookings are essential on weekends and holidays.

About 2km further up the beach is **Coral Lodge 15.41** (82-902 3612; www.corallodge1541.com; s/d US$595/900;), an upmarket spot with 10 luxury villas that makes a lovely base for visiting Mozambique Island. There is snorkelling in the lagoon just in front.

Further along (northwest) from Cabaceira Pequena is **Cabaceira Grande**, with a small treasure-trove of ruins, including a well-preserved church (Nossa Senhora dos Remédios) dating from the late 16th-century and the ruins of the mid-19th-century governor-general's palace. You can carefully climb up the latter for superb views.

MOSSURIL

Apart from Chocas, the closest major village in the area is Mossuril, which you'll pass en route when travelling to Chocas by road, and which hosts a lively Saturday market.

Pensão-Restaurant Sunset Boulevard (82-401 5416; www.hotelsunsetboulevard.com; dm/d US$8/20) is in the São João area of Mossuril, about 800m from the Mossuril Governo building, and a good half-hour walk from the main Mossuril village transport junction. It is a restored residence with simple but surprisingly nice rooms (given its unlikely location on the road to nowhere) and meals, and lots of information on and help with organising exploration of the surrounding area. It's part of the **Téran Foundation** (www.teranfoundation.org) effort to provide local tourism training, and is a potential chill-out spot if you're interested in seeing Mozambique well away from any sort of established route. Volunteering opportunities are also available. Nearby is a small patch of beach.

Getting There & Away

Boat

There's at least one dhow daily connecting Mozambique Island with Cabaceira Grande and Mossuril, departing the island between about noon and 1pm from the beach down from BIM bank next to Villa Sands, and departing Mossuril about 6am (Mtc25). For Sunset Boulevard, ask to be dropped off at 'São João', from where the *pensão* is just a five to 10 minute walk up from the beach. From Mossuril village, it's about 1½ hours on foot to Cabaceira Grande. If you want to return the same day, you'll need to charter a boat (about Mtc1500 for a motorised dhow). Hotels on Mozambique Island can also organise Chocas/Cabaceira excursions. For all travel to/from the Cabaceiras, be prepared for lots of wading and walking.

Bus

There's one daily direct *chapa* between Nampula and Chocas, departing Nampula between 10am and noon, and departing Chocas about 4am (Mtc150, five hours). Otherwise, take any transport between Nampula or Monapo and Mozambique Island to the signposted Mossuril turn-off, 25km southeast of Monapo (Mtc100 from Nampula to the Mossuril turn-off). Sporadic *chapas* go from here to Mossuril (20km), and on to Chocas (12km further, Mtc50), with no vehicles after about 3pm. From Chocas, it's a 30-minute walk at low tide to Cabaceira Pequena, and from one hour to 1½ hours to Cabaceira Grande.

Nacala

26

Nacala town is set on an impressive natural harbour and its port, developed in the mid-20th century, is northern Mozambique's busiest. The town itself has nothing of interest for travellers (apart from several ATMs), but there's fine diving in the bay and attractive nearby beaches, including **Fernão Veloso** about 12km to the north.

Sleeping & Eating

Libélula LODGE $$
(82-306 6473, 82-304 2909; www.divelibelula.com; Fernão Veloso; campsite per person US$10, dm US$15, d US$60-70, 2- to 4-person chalets US$60-75;) Most travellers head to Libélula, about 10km outside town in Fernão Veloso in a fine setting on an escarpment overlooking the beach and the aqua waters of Nacala Bay. On offer are rustic reed-and-thatch chalets, dorm beds, camping, a good waterside restaurant, snorkelling and diving. Pick-ups can be arranged from Nacala town or Nampula.

Nuarro Lodge LODGE $$$
(82-305 3028; www.nuarro.com; per person with full board and activities US$295) This laudable eco venture is a lovely place with 12 rustic but comfortable and spacious chalets. All are constructed out of traditional materials and use solar power, are beautifully decorated, and each is set on its own along a low vegetated dune overlooking the sea.

Various activities are available including sea kayaking, diving (excellent – the only lodge in Mozambique where you can do wall dives from the shore), snorkelling and visits to the nearby village. It's about 90km north of Nacala in Memba on the Baixa do Pindo peninsula; transfers can be arranged from Nacala, Nampula and Pemba. Ask also about special deals, especially during the low season.

Hotel Maiaia HOTEL $$
(☎82-601 5440, 26-526842; Rua Principal; s/d Mtc3040/3400; ❄) This centrally located three-star establishment caters to business travellers, with simple rooms with TV (some also have a tiny balcony) and a restaurant. It's on the main street diagonally opposite the central market.

ℹ Getting There & Away

Grupo Mecula buses to Pemba (Mtc350, seven hours) depart Nacala daily at 5am from the Mecula garage. Head down Rua Principal to the large roundabout, then follow the street going left and uphill next to Mozstar. Mecula is about 400m up on the left, behind an unmarked wall.

There are *chapas* each morning to Nampula (Mtc160), Namialo (Mtc80) and Monapo (Mtc75, one hour), departing from the big tree next to Telecomunicações de Moçambique. Once in Monapo (ask your hotel for help in timing the connection), there's onward transport to Mozambique Island and Namialo (the junction town for Pemba).

ℹ Getting Around

To get to Fernão Veloso, follow the left fork where the road splits after after entering Nacala, and continue for 2km to the unmarked airport and military base turn-off to the right. Go right here. After about 9km watch for the signposted Libélula left-hand turn-off opposite the base, from where it's another 1.5km.

Chapas run frequently from the port area past Hotel Maiaia and on to Nacala Alta (Mtc5) – the best place to catch these is from the blue container opposite Hotel Maiaia – and then from Nacala-Alta to Fernão Veloso (Mtc10).

Cuamba

☎271

This lively rail and road junction was formerly known as Novo Freixo. With its dusty streets, flowering trees and large university student population, it is the economic centre of Niassa province and a convenient stop-off if you're travelling to/from Malawi. The surrounding area is known for its garnet gemstones and for its scenic panoramas, especially to the east around Mt Mitucué (Serra Mitucué).

Sleeping & Eating

Quinta Timbwa CHALETS $
(☎82-300 0752, 82-692 0250; quintatimbwa@yahoo.com.br; tw with shared bathroom Mtc750, d from Mtc1000, rondavel with/without air-con Mtc2000/1500; ❄👪) This place is set on a large estate about 2.5km from town, and signposted. It's tranquil and good value, with spotless, pleasant rooms (some in attached rows, some in small *rondavels*) surrounded by expansive grounds and a small lake. It's ideal for families, or for anyone coming with their own transport. There's also a restaurant.

Hotel Vision 2000 HOTEL $
(☎271-62632; cnr Avenidas Eduardo Mondlane & 25 de Junho; r Mtc1400; ❄) Vision 2000, at the main intersection, is not the newest of hotels, as its name gives away, and it's rather down at the heel these days, although the shower-bidet combo in a few of the rooms might be an attraction for some. The attached restaurant has a small selection of meals, and visits to the nearby garnet mines (about 5km from town) can be arranged.

Pensão São Miguel PENSION $
(☎271-62701; r with shared bathroom Mtc500, r with fan/air-con Mtc800/1000; ❄) This long-standing, local-style guesthouse has small, clean rooms crowded behind the restaurant-bar area. Each room has one small double bed. While it's not the most luxurious of establishments, it's the best value-for-price option in the town centre, and located an easy 10-minute walk from the train station and bus stand. Breakfast is included in the deal.

Supermercado Pera-Doce SUPERMARKET $
(Town Centre) Just down from Pensão Namaacha, this supermarket has a good selection of basics and is convenient for stocking up before the train ride to Nampula.

ℹ Information

Millennium BIM (Avenida Eduardo Mondlane) ATM; near the post office.

Telecomunicações de Moçambique (Avenida Eduardo Mondlane; per min Mtc1; ⏲8am-noon & 2-6pm Mon-Sat) Internet access; a few doors up from Millennium BIM.

Getting There & Away

Bus & Chapa

Most transport leaves from Maçaniqueira market, at the southern edge of town and just south of the railway tracks. *Chapas* also come to meet arriving trains. The best times to find transport are between 5am and 6am, and again in the afternoon at the station, when the train from Nampula arrives.

GURÚÈ & NAMPULA To Gurúè, the best routing is via train to Mutuali, from where you can find waiting pick-ups on to Gurúè. This generally works best going from Cuamba to Gurúè; going in the other direction entails long waits and travel at night. There's also a direct pick-up most days to Gurúè (Mtc200 to Mtc250), departing Cuamba by about 6am. Once in Gurúè, you can connect to Mocuba (Mtc200 Gurúè to Mocuba) and Nampula (Mtc350 Mocuba to Nampula) the same day. At the time of research, there were only sporadic direct vehicles from Cuamba to Nampula. You'll need to take the train, or go via Gurúè (Mtc400 Gurúè to Nampula direct).

LICHINGA To Lichinga (Mtc500, seven hours), there are several trucks daily via Mandimba, with the first departure at about 4am.

MALAWI To Malawi, there is at least one pick-up daily from Cuamba to Entre Lagos (Mtc170, 1½ hours). Once at Entre Lagos, you'll need to walk across the border, where there's a weekly train on the Malawi side to Liwonde.

Train

A train connects Cuamba with Nampula (Mtc350/140 for 2nd/3rd class, 10 to 12 hours), departing in each direction at 5am Tuesday to Sunday. Second class only runs in each direction on alternate days (currently from Cuamba on Wednesday, Friday and Sunday and from Nampula on Tuesday, Thursday and Saturday). It's well worth planning your travels to coincide with a day when 2nd class is running, as third class is crowded and uncomfortable. Second-class tickets can be purchased between 2pm and 5pm on the day before travel (but not earlier). Third class tickets are always available, up until the time of departure.

It's a great ride, with the train stopping at many villages along the way and offering a fine taste of rural Mozambican life. Vendors sell food at every stop, but it's worth supplementing this by bringing some snacks along, and you should bring enough bottled water for the trip as well.

To transport your vehicle on the train (about US$100), you'll need to load it the night before and arrange a guard. During the journey you can ride with the car.

Mandimba

Mandimba is a small, bustling border town and transport junction. If you get stuck here, **Bar-Restaurante Ngame** (Senhor Liton's; d Mtc500), near the transport stop, has basic rooms looking out on a small courtyard, and does meals with advance notice.

About 1km along the road to Cuamba, on the opposite side, is **Bar-Restaurante Massinga** (d Mtc1200; ❄), which has double 'chalet' *rondavels* with air-con in a separate, pale pink, compound 500m beyond the restaurant along the main road.

Vehicles go daily to Lichinga (Mtc250) and Cuamba (Mtc250). Expect to pay Mtc30/50/100 for a bicycle/motorbike/taxi lift to cover the approximately 4km from Mandimba to the border, and Mtc50 for a moto-taxi across the 1500m of no-man's land to the Malawi border crossing (although frequently the moto-taxi drivers will stop in the middle and demand that the price be 're-negotiated').

Lichinga

☎271 / ELEV 1300M

Niassa's capital is pretty, low-key Lichinga (formerly Vila Cabral), which sits at about 1300m altitude, with an invigorating, cool climate and quiet, jacaranda-lined streets. It's worth a day or two in its own right and is also the best jumping-off point for exploring the Lake Niassa. The surrounding area – home mainly to Yao people, as well as smaller numbers of Nyanja and Makua people – is dotted with pine groves and ringed by distant hills.

Orientation

Lichinga is set out in a series of concentric circles, with a large plaza at the centre and the main transport stand at its southeastern edge near the market. It's easy to cover on foot – nothing is more than about a 10-minute walk.

The section of road running past the governor's mansion on the northwestern edge of town is closed to vehicle traffic and the area immediately in front of the mansion is also closed to pedestrians.

Sleeping

The owner of O Chambo (p228) rents rooms (singles/doubles Mtc1250/1500) in her house; it's on the Cuamba road just after Socin supermarket.

Lichinga

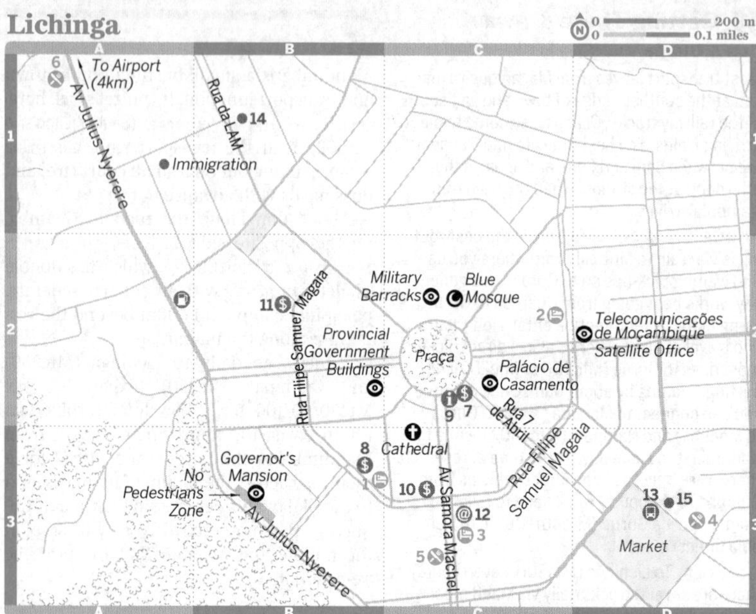

Lichinga

Sleeping

- 1 Hotel Girassol Lichinga B3
- 2 Ponto Final C2
- 3 Residencial 2+1 .... C3

Eating

- 4 O Chambo D3
- 5 Padaria Mária C3
- 6 Supermercado Socin A1

Information

- 7 Barclays C2
- 8 BCI B3
- 9 Lúrio Empreendimentos C2
- 10 Millennium BIM C3
- 11 Standard Bank B2
- 12 Sycamore Services C3

Transport

- 13 Bus Stand D3
- 14 LAM B1
- 15 Transport to Tanzania D3

Ponto Final HOTEL $

(☎82-304 3632, 271-20912; Rua Filipe Samuel Magaia; s with shared bathroom Mtc800, d Mtc1200) At the northeastern edge of town, this long-standing place has clean, low-ceilinged rooms, a big bright zebra painting in the courtyard as well as a popular restaurant-bar. Turn down the road at the small green-and-white Telecomunicações de Moçambique satellite office.

Residencial 2+1 HOTEL $$

(☎82-381 1070; angelina.rosario.guita@gmail.com; Avenida Samora Machel; s/d Mtc1500/1800) Clean, efficient and central, within easy walking distance of the bus stand. Attached is a reasonably priced restaurant.

Hotel Girassol Lichinga HOTEL $$$

(☎271-21280; www.girassolhoteis.co.mz; Rua Filipe Samuel Magaia; s/d Mtc3750/4200; ❄@🏊) Hovering between three and four stars, this is Lichinga's most upmarket option and one of the few places in the province catering to business travellers. It has satellite TV, huge rooms (most with large windows), a restaurant and tennis court. Book in advance for a discount; walk-in rates are higher.

Eating

In addition to the hotel restaurants, there are several other good options.

O Chambo AFRICAN $

(☎84-319 8800, 271-21354; meals from Mtc150) A cosy place in the Feira Exposição Niassa

(FEN) compound next to the market, with soups and local meals. The owner also rents out rooms.

Padaria Mária CAFE $
(Avenida Samora Machel; snacks & light meals from Mtc100) Opposite Residencial 2+1, with a good selection of pastries, plus light meals and yoghurt.

Supermercado Socin SUPERMARKET $
(Cuamba road; ⌚9am-1pm & 3-7pm Mon-Fri, 9am-noon Sat) For self-catering.

Information

Internet Access

Sycamore Services (Avenida Samora Machel; per min Mtc1; ⌚10am-6pm Mon-Fri, to noon Sat)

Money

Barclays (Main Roundabout) ATM.

BCI (Rua Filipe Samuel Magaia) ATM; in the Hotel Girassol complex, next to the hotel entrance.

Millennium BIM (cnr Avenida Samora Machel & Rua Filipe Samuel Magaia) ATM.

Standard Bank (Rua Filipe Samuel Magaia) ATM.

Travel Agencies

Lúrio Empreendimentos (☎84-308 4080, 82-492 3780, 271-21705; lempreendimentos@teledata.mz; Main Roundabout; ⌚8am-noon & 2-5.30pm Mon-Fri, 9am-noon Sat), next to Barclays, is efficient, reliable and recommended. It's the best bet for car rentals, LAM bookings and for help organising travels anywhere in Niassa. This includes drop-offs and pick-ups in Cóbuè (for Nkwichi Lodge) and transport to/from and within the Niassa Reserve.

Getting There & Away

Air

LAM (☎271-20847, 271-20434; Rua da LAM), just off the airport road, operates several flights weekly to/from Maputo, going via Tete (weekly) or Nampula (three times weekly) and sometimes Beira. Flights out of Lichinga tend to be heavily booked, so reconfirm your reservation and show up early at the airport.

Bus & Truck

All transport departs from beside the market, with vehicles to most destinations leaving by around 6am.

CUAMBA VIA MANDIMBA To Cuamba (Mtc500, seven hours) trucks go daily via Mandimba (Mtc250), with the first vehicle departing between 3am and 4am.

METANGULA To Metangula (Mtc150, 2½ hours) several vehicles go daily.

SEGUNDO CONGRESSO/MATCHEDJE & ROVUMA RIVER To Segundo Congresso/Matchedje and the Rovuma River (Mtc500, six hours), at least one pick-up truck goes daily, leaving anywhere between 7am and noon from the dusty street just before the transport stand; look for the blue *barracas* near Safi Comercial and inquire there. Once over the bridge, you can get transport to Songea for about US$7. In both directions, you'll need to have your visa in advance if using this crossing.

MARRUPA To Marrupa (Mtc500, three hours), there's a daily vehicle. However, there is no public transport from Marrupa onwards, either to Niassa Reserve or to Montepuez.

Getting Around

Lúrio Empreendimentos has a variety of 4WD vehicles for rent, with or without driver, at very fair rates. A taxi usually waits near Hotel Girassol Lichinga. Otherwise, Lúrio Empreendimentos can help with booking taxis.

Lake Niassa" (Lake Malawi)

The Mozambican side of Lake Niassa (Lago Niassa) is beautiful and, in contrast to the Malawian side, almost completely undeveloped. It sees a small but steady stream of adventure travellers and is an excellent destination for anyone wanting to get off the beaten track.

The main area for exploring is the coast between Metangula and Cóbuè, with a succession of narrow beaches – some sandy, others gravel – backed by mountains and steep hills rising up directly from the

FIM DO MUNDO

Fim do mundo (the end of the world) is how many Mozambicans describe Niassa – the least populated of Mozambique's provinces – and as far as the rest of the country is concerned, it might as well be. The area is generally overlooked by the government and other locals and ignored by tourists. Yet if you're after adventure and time in the bush, it's an ideal destination. Apart from Niassa's scenic rugged terrain, the main attractions are the Lake Niassa coastline and the wild Niassa Reserve (p231).

lakeshore. Most local residents are Nyanja ('People of the Lake'), and their distinctively painted square, thatched dwellings dot the countryside. Fishing is the main source of livelihood, though it's mostly small scale. The only commercial fishing operation on the Mozambican side of the lake is at Metangula.

Allow plenty of time for getting around and be prepared to rough it. When venturing onto the lake, keep in mind that squalls can arise suddenly, often with strong winds.

METANGULA

Bustling Metangula is the capital of lake district, the largest Mozambican town along the lakeshore, and the site of a small naval base. The town is divided into two areas: the staid administrative quarters perched on a small escarpment with wide views over the lake, and the lower lying residential areas along the lake shore. Metangula itself has little for visitors, however, about 8km north of town is the tiny village of **Chuwanga**, which is on an attractive beach, and is a popular weekend getaway from Lichinga.

About 5km northeast of Chuwanga is **Messumba**, site of a well-known Anglican mission that traces its history back to the arrival of the first missionaries in the area in 1882. Until being forced to close during the war, Messumba served as headquarters for Anglican missionary activity in northern Mozambique. It was renowned for its hospital and for the Colégio de São Felipe, where numerous notables studied, including several members of Frelimo's elite. Most of the mission buildings are now in disrepair, although you can still visit the church and walk around the grounds.

Sleeping & Eating

Mbuna Bay CHALETS $$$
(☎82-536 7781; www.mbunabay.ch; s/d with full board in bush bungalow US$140/220, in beach chalet US$180/280) About 15km south of Metangula, the eco-friendly Mbuna Bay has four wooden beachfront cottages, four brick cottages set back in the bush, and one wattle-and-daub cottage. All have creatively designed bathrooms (some open-air), and all are comfortable in a rustic way. Snorkelling, dhow sails, kayaking and yoga can all be arranged, as can transfers from Lichinga.

Chuwanga Beach Hotel BUNGALOWS $
(Complexo Cetuka, Catawala's; Chuwanga Beach; ⏲campsite per person Mtc150, d Mtc500) This long-standing popular place is about 8km from Metangula on Chuwanga beach. It offers camping and basic reed bungalows on the sand, with shared rather scruffy ablutions facilities (bucket baths). Meals and drinks are available and there's a grill for cooking your own food.

Casa de Hospedes Bela Vista PENSION $
(r with shared bathroom Mtc150) Bleak but reliable rooms sharing grubby ablutions. There's no running water. It's down from the main junction and Bar Triângulo, and next to Immigration.

Getting There & Away

CHAPAS

Daily *chapas* connect Metangula and **Lichinga** (Mtc150, 2½ to three hours), most departing Lichinga early. There's also one *chapa* daily between Metangula and **Cóbuè** (Mtc170, four hours). Departures in Metangula are from the fork in the road just up from the market at Bar Triângulo; look for the yellow Mcel wall. The final 20km or so of the tarmac road from Lichinga to Metangula are very scenic as they wind down to the lakeshore.

There are occasional *chapas* between Metangula and Chuwanga, and hitching is easy on the weekend. Otherwise, get a Cóbuè *chapa* to drop you at the Chuwanga turn-off, though it's probably just as fast to walk from Metangula. To get to Messumba, you'll need your own 4WD.

FERRY

The Ilala ferry is currently out of service; when running, it connects Metangula and **Malawi**. At the time of research, a new ferry was supposed to start 'soon' serving ports on the Mozambican side of the lake, including Metangula and Cóbuè.

LAKE NIASSA FAST FACTS

» At more than 550km long, up to 75km wide, and 700m deep in parts, Lake Niassa (Lake Malawi) is the third-largest lake on the African continent after Lake Victoria and Lake Tanganyika.

» About 25% of the lake's area is in Mozambique.

» Within its deep blue waters are over 500 species of fish, including over 350 that are unique to the lake. Lake Niassa is also home to about one-third of the earth's known cichlid (freshwater fish) species, including the brightly coloured mbuna.

Check with local lodges if it has begun service. Departures in Metangula are from the small dhow port just down from Bar Triângulo and below the Catholic church.

CÓBUÈ

Tiny Cóbuè is the gateway into Mozambique if you're travelling from Malawi via Likoma Island, about 10km offshore. The island is surrounded by Mozambican waters, but belongs to Malawi.

In addition to its immigration post, Cóbuè's attractions include a lakeside setting dotted with mango trees, the remains of a school once used as a wartime base by Frelimo, and the ruins of an old church, with goats lying around in the shade. Cóbuè is also the jumping-off point to reach Nkwichi Lodge.

Sleeping & Eating

Khango Beach BUNGALOW $
(☎99-962 0916, from Mozambique 00-265-856 7885, in Malawi 88-856 7885; r with shared bathroom per person Mtc250; P) This rustic place, run by the affable, English-speaking Julius, has simple reed bungalows directly on the sand. All have nets and clean shared ablutions facilities. Tasty, filling meals can be arranged with advance notice.

Rest House Mira Lago PENSION $
(Pensão Layla; r with shared bathroom Mtc250; P) Directly in the village centre, this place has solar-powered lighting and a row of no-frills, clean rooms. Each has a small double bed. Meals can sometimes be organised with advance notice.

Getting There & Away

AIR

There's an airstrip in Cóbuè for charter flights. More common is to charter a flight from Lilongwe (Malawi) to Likoma Island (about US$300 per person one way, book through Nkwichi Lodge (p232)) and then arrange a boat transfer from there with the lodge.

BOAT

The *Ilala* ferry was out of service at the time of research. Meanwhile, fishing boats ply daily in the mornings between Cóbuè and Likoma Island (about US$7 one-way). Mozambique visas are issued in Cóbuè. If you're travelling to/from Malawi, you'll need to go to Immigration (on the hill near the large antenna) to get your passport stamped.

Ferry service is supposed to restart imminently at ports on the Mozambican side of the lake, including Cóbuè, so check with the lodges for an update.

BUS & CAR

A daily *chapa* runs between Metangula and Cóbuè, departing Metangula about 7am and Cóbuè about 8am (Mtc150, four to five hours).

The road between Cóbuè and Metangula (75km) is unpaved but in good condition, and there's secure parking at Khango Beach and Rest House Mira Lago in Cóbuè. Walking between Cóbuè and Metangula takes about two days, going along the river via the villages of Ngoo and Chia.

Niassa Reserve

About 160km northeast of Lichinga on the Tanzanian border is the **Niassa Reserve** (Reserva do Niassa; www.niassareserve.org; adult/child/vehicle per day Mtc200/50/200), a vast tract of wilderness with the largest wildlife populations in Mozambique, although the animals are often difficult (or impossible) to spot. Wildlife includes elephants (estimated to number about 16,000), sable antelopes (14,000), lions (800), buffaloes and zebras. There are also duikers, elands, leopards, wildebeests, hippos and a population of the endangered African wild dog, as well as over 400 different types of birds.

The reserve is also notable for its ruggedly beautiful scenery – dense bush and woodlands laced with rivers and dotted with massive inselbergs. It's twice the size of South Africa's Kruger National Park, and was established in the early 1960s to protect local elephant and black rhino populations. However, because of inaccessibility, scarce finances and the onset of war it was never developed. Although wildlife populations here suffered during the 1980s from poaching and the effects of armed conflict, losses were far less than those in other protected areas further south. In more recent times significant progress has been made in curbing poaching and there has been a trend of increasing animal numbers. Ongoing poaching and hunting in reserve areas has contributed to great skittishness on the part of wildlife; go to Niassa primarily for adventure, rather than for wildlife watching.

In the late 1990s Niassa Reserve was given new life when a group of private investors, working in partnership with the Mozambican government, was granted a 10-year renewable lease on the area. The reserve's size was increased to about 42,000

WORTH A TRIP

NKWICHI LODGE

Apart from its convenient location as part of a larger southern Africa circuit linking Mozambique and Malawi, the main reason to come to Cóbuè is to get to the highly recommended **Nkwichi Lodge** (www.mandawilderness.org; s/d with full board in chalet US$395/640, in private house US$450/700). It's one of the most appealing and genuinely community-integrated lodges we've seen in the region, and worth the splurge. It offers the chance to explore an area of southern Africa that is about as remote as it gets, while enjoying all the comforts, and contributing to benefit the local community and environment. The lodge is linked with the Manda Wilderness Community Conservation Area, a privately initiated conservation area along the lakeshore that also promotes community development and responsible tourism. The surrounding bush is full of birds, with ospreys, palm nut vultures, Pell's fishing owls and fish eagles all regularly seen.

Accommodation is in six spacious hand-crafted bungalows, with private outdoor baths and showers built into the bush, and several looking out onto their own white-sand coves. There are also two private houses, each with lake views, private chef, and lots of space and privacy; they're ideal for groups. The lake at Nkwichi is crystal clear and safe for swimming and there's a dhow for sails and sunset cruises. You can also arrange canoeing and multinight wilderness walking safaris, or visits to the lodge's demonstration farm. Boat transfers from Cóbuè and Likoma Island can be arranged.

sq km, and the boundaries now stretch from the Rovuma River in the north to the Lugenda River in the south and east.

An estimated 35,000 people live within the reserve's boundaries, which also encompass a 20,000 sq km buffer zone. You'll undoubtedly come in to contact with locals setting their fish traps, walking, or paddling in dugout canoes (for which a few words of Swahili or Yao will stand you in better stead than Portuguese).

Sleeping & Eating

At the time of writing, there was no official public camping ground, although there is a rudimentary area near Mbatamila headquarters where you can pitch a tent, and another camping area at Kiboko, on the Lugenda River by the park gate. Bring all food, drinking water and supplies with you.

Lugenda Bush Camp TENTED CAMP **$$$**
(☎21-301618; www.lugenda.com; per person with full board from US$500; ⏲Jun-Nov) This lovely place on the Lugenda River near the eastern edge of the park caters primarily to fly-in guests, and offers a unique safari experience that's likely to appeal to well-heeled safari connoisseurs seeking an 'unpackaged' adventure experience with all the amenities. There's a set of maintained roads around the camp to facilitate wildlife tracking.

Information

Reserve headquarters are about 40km southwest of Mecula at Mbatamila.

Wildlife in Niassa Reserve is spread relatively thinly over a vast area, with dense foliage and only a skeleton network of bush tracks. As a result, most tourism to date has been exclusively for the well-heeled, with the most feasible way to visit by charter plane from Pemba. With the gradual upgrading of road connections linking Cabo Delgado and Niassa provinces, this is beginning to change, although the reserve's main market is likely to remain top end for the foreseeable future.

For self-drivers it is possible in theory to do drive-in visits. However, given the lack of a developed network of tracks, this is only recommended for the adventure and the wilderness, rather than for the safari or 'Big Five' aspects. Note that Niassa's tsetse flies are very aggressive and very numerous. Any activity in a vehicle will need to be done with windows up.

At the time of research, fees were not being collected at the reserve entrance, but rather are payable in advance – in person or via cheque – through the Maputo office of the **Sociedade para a Gestão e Desinvolvimento da Reserva do Niassa** (SGN; ☎21-329807; sgdrn.map@tvcabo.co.mz; 1031 Avenida Mao Tse Tung), the entity charged with managing the reserve. The receipt should then be presented when you reach the reserve. That said, the entire reserve infrastructure is still in very early stages, and we haven't heard of anyone being turned away at the gate for lack of a receipt.

Getting There & Around

Air

There are about 11 airstrips that can accommodate charter flights, including one at Mecula. The reserve sits roughly midway between Lake Niassa to the west and the Indian Ocean to the east, both about an hour's flight away via small plane. **CFA Charters** (☎82-575 2125; www.cfa.co.za) flies three times weekly between Lugenda Camp and Pemba (US$538/889 one-way/return). Book directly, or through Kaskazini in Pemba.

Car

By road it's possible to reach Mbatamila in the dry season via Montepuez, Balama and Marrupa. The Balama–Marrupa section is in poor condition, although currently being rehabilitated. Allow a full day from Pemba, with bush camping the only accommodation en route. Approaching the reserve from Lichinga, there is good tarmac as far as Marrupa, where there is petrol. At Marrupa, there is camping and basic accommodation with bucket baths at **Quinta Manlia** (campsite per person Mtc100, r Mtc600), about 3km out along the Pemba route. From Marrupa, the remaining 100km stretch up to the Lugenda River and on into the reserve is dirt but in reasonable shape. The unpaved road from Cuamba to Marrupa is another doable option, especially during the dry season. Petrol is generally also available on the roadside in Mecula, although this should not be relied upon, and on the whole, driving itineraries in the reserve will be limited by how much extra fuel you can carry.

Once across the Lugenda, you'll need to sign in at the reserve before continuing on towards Mecula and Mbatamila park headquarters – about 45km from the gate, and set in the shadow of the 1441m-high Mt Mecula – where you can arrange a guide.

Montepuez

☎272

Montepuez, a busy district capital, previously rivalled Pemba as the largest town in Cabo Delgado. Today it's known for its marble quarries and as the start of the wild 'road' west across Niassa province towards Lichinga. It would also be the overland gateway to the Niassa Reserve, were it not for a challenging 100-or-so kilometre stretch of road to the west from Balama to Marrupa that is currently just a bush track, although it's in the process of being rehabilitated. Allow one full day for this section.

The main road in Montepuez is Avenida Eduardo Mondlane; most places are either on or just off it.

Sleeping & Eating

For meals, there's a **refrigerator** (from 7am Mon-Sat) next to the bakery (which is on a side street one block before the bus stand) with juice, yoghurt and (sometimes) apples. Also try the small **café** (light meals from Mtc100) behind the park with the aeroplane.

Vivenda Angelina GUESTHOUSE $
(Avenida Julius Nyerere; r Mtc600) Vivenda Angelina has clean, quiet rooms in a private house sharing a bathroom, and (often) running water. There's no food and no signpost. Coming from the main road, turn right at the Plexus signboard at the western end of town, go two short blocks, and then turn left onto Avenida Julius Nyerere. It's the second house on the left.

Residencial do Geptex PENSION $
(☎272-51114; Avenida Julius Nyerere; d without/with bathroom Mtc400/500) Has very basic rooms with double beds, bucket baths, fan and no nets. It's at the western end of town, two blocks north of the main road.

Getting There & Away

The transport stand is about two blocks south of Avenida Eduardo Mondlane; turn down the street with Millennium BIM. Several *chapas* daily go between Pemba and Montepuez (Mtc170, three hours). Heading west, there's regular transport to Balama (Mtc160), but from there to Marrupa (for Niassa Reserve) there is no option other than hitching a lift with a tractor or a truck. If you're driving, the Balama–Marrupa stretch is only feasible in the dry season.

Pemba

☎272

Pemba sprawls across a peninsula jutting into the enormous and magnificent Pemba Bay, one of the world's largest natural harbours. It was established in 1904, as administrative headquarters for the Niassa Company, and for much of its early life was known as Porto Amelia. Today it's the capital of Cabo Delgado province, the main town in Mozambique's far north, and gateway to the Quirimbas Archipelago and an endless string of white-sand beaches. Although lacking the charm to be a destination in itself, the town makes for a relaxing and enjoyable stop, with almost perpetual sunshine and blue skies, a long beach nearby and a lazy, languid ambience.

Pemba's baixa area is home to the low-lying port and old town, with a row of small shops and traders lining the main street. Steeply uphill from here, the busier and less atmospheric town centre is the place to get things done, with banks and offices, a few restaurants and hotels, and the main bus stand. About 5km east of the town centre is Wimbi (also spelled Wimbe) Beach, the main hub of tourist activity and the favoured destination of most visitors.

Sights

Almost everyone heads straight for **Wimbi Beach**, where you can swim and enjoy the sea breezes.

On Pemba's outskirts are several colourful and vibrant *bairros* (neighbourhoods). The most intriguing is **Paquitequete**, which is on the southwestern edge of the peninsula and is Pemba's oldest settlement. In contrast with the other *bairros*, which are newer and more heterogeneous, the population here is almost exclusively Muslim, and predominantly Mwani and Makua. The atmosphere is at its best in the late afternoon just before sunset. At Paquitequete's northern edge is a small **fish market**. The nearby beach buzzes with activity in the early morning as *makuti* (dried palm fronds used for constructing roofs), bamboo and other building materials are unloaded and readied for market.

Up on the hill behind the governor's mansion is a large **cemetery**, with fragrant frangipani trees shading the Christian and Muslim graves. Close to the sea is a section containing Commonwealth war graves.

Beginning about 10km south of town is a string of tranquil, attractive beaches, including **Murrébuè**, ideal for kite surfing.

Activities

Swimming

Swimming Pool SWIMMING
(per adult/child Mtc200/100; 10am-6pm) Clube Naval has a small swimming pool.

Diving

There's rewarding diving around Pemba. Pemba Beach Hotel (p235) has resident dive instructors available for its guests.

CI Divers DIVING
(272-20102; www.cidivers.co.za; Complexo Náutilus, Avenida Marginal, Wimbi Beach) The main operator, offering PADI open-water certification, equipment rental and boat charters.

Dhow Safaris & Sailing

For pricey day trips around Pemba Bay or upmarket multinight dhow safaris to the Quirimbas Archipelago, contact **Pemba Sailing Safaris** (82-408 6694; www.pembasailingsafaris.com) or Kaskazini (p238).

Sleeping

Book Pemba accommodation in advance if travelling during the December/January and South African Easter school holidays.

TOWN CENTRE

Central Pemba has slim accommodation offerings. For most travellers it's only worth considering staying in town if you can't find anything at Wimbi Beach or if you have an early morning bus.

Hotel Cabo Delgado HOTEL $
(272-21552; cnr Avenidas 25 de Setembro & Eduardo Mondlane; s/d/tw/ste Mtc700/1000/1100/1500) This ageing hotel on the main street is well past its prime, although the central location (diagonally opposite Mcel) is convenient. The faded rooms come with bathroom (though not always with water) and fan (though not always with electricity). There's no food.

OUTSIDE THE TOWN CENTRE

Pemba Dive & Bushcamp CAMPGROUND, BUNGALOWS $
(Nacole Jardim; 82-661 1530; www.pembadivecamp.com; campsite per person US$10, dm US$20, d/q chalet US$100/160;) Ideal for families and overlanders, with Pemba's best camping, plus dorm beds, rustic chalets, a beachside bar and *braai* area, and botanical walking tours on request. It's about 10 minutes from town (Mtc400 in a taxi), behind the airport in an excellent setting on the bay, and about 3km off the main road down an unpaved track.

WIMBI BEACH

Residencial Reggio Emilia GUESTHOUSE $$
(82-888 0800, 272-21297; www.wix.com/akeelz/Residencial-Reggio-Emilia; 8696 Avenida Marginal; r Mtc3000, 4-person self-catering chalet Mtc7000;) This tranquil spot along the extension of the Wimbi Beach road has clean, spacious rooms – all with hot water, air-con, satellite TV, minifridge and quality mattresses – and a few self-catering chalets in quiet grounds. All are nicely decorated with locally-sourced materials such as Palma mats, and all have mosquito screens on the

windows. Breakfast costs extra, and a restaurant will be opening imminently.

Pemba Beach Hotel HOTEL **$$$**
(272-21770; www.pembabeachresort.com; 5470 Avenida Marginal; s/d from Mtc7076/8613, 4-6 person self-catering apartment Mtc13,833;) This five-star establishment has expansive grounds overlooking the water, well-equipped rooms, a restaurant (closed at the time of research) and a yacht for charters around the Quirimbas Archipelago. Package deals from Johannesburg are available that also include sister lodges in the Quirimbas and Bazaruto archipelagos.

Kauri Resort HOTEL **$$**
(82-151 4222, 272-20936; www.kauriresort.com; r Mtc3000-4000;) A newish place along the extension of Wimbi beach, with small, clean, modern rooms and a restaurant (closed Monday).

Pieter's Place GUESTHOUSE **$$**
(82-682 2700, 272-20102; cidivers@teledata.mz; Avenida Marginal; s/d from US$45/60) Along the extension of the Wimbi beach road with a few small, airy rooms in the shaded grounds of a private residence. Breakfast costs extra. There's also an open-air restaurant (closed Monday), and a huge baobab tree in the courtyard, with a treehouse sitting area built into its upper branches.

Wimbi Sun Residencial GUESTHOUSE **$$**
(82-318 1300, 272-21946; wimbisun@yahoo.com; 7472 Avenida Marginal; r/ste Mtc1600/1900;) Clean, modern rooms (the best are the spacious 'suites'), none with nets and all with bathrooms and TV. It's at the start of the Wimbi Beach strip, diagonally opposite Complexo Náutilus on the inland side of the road. Breakfast costs Mtc150 extra.

Simples Aldeia Lda APARTMENT **$$**
(SAL; 272-20134; Avenida Marginal; s/d from Mtc2000/2500, 2-room cottage s/tw Mtc3500/4250;) This self-catering place, about 2km from the roundabout on the beach side of the road, has simple, faded rooms in three small cottages, all with twin beds, TV, screens, fridge and hotplate.

Pemba Magic Lodge CAMPGROUND **$**
('Russell's Place'; 82-527 7048, 82-686 2730; pembamagic@gmail.com; campsite per person US$10, dm US$20, d, tr & q chalets US$65, self-catering family bungalow US$100;) About 3.5km beyond Complexo Náutilus along the beach road extension, this place has campsites with ablutions facilities (although no cooking facilities) just next to the very busy restaurant, plus a handful of simple chalets with fan and bathroom. There's also a bar-restaurant with a large menu including pizzas. Full breakfast costs Mtc300. The beach is just a few minutes' walk away (high-tide swimming only). Security here is on-again/off-again.

CRAFT SHOPPING

Even if you don't think you want to buy crafts, it's worth stopping in at the excellent **Artes Maconde** (artesmaconde@yahoo.com), with branches at **Pemba Beach Hotel** and next to CI Divers at **Complexo Náutilus**. It sells a wide range of quality carvings, crafts and textiles sourced from throughout Mozambique, as well as from elsewhere in the region. It's one of the best craft shops in the country, as far as quality of the artistry and uniqueness of the art are concerned, and craftsmen come from outlying villages throughout Cabo Delgado and as far away as the DR Congo (Zaïre) to deliver their wares. It does international air and sea shipping, and also takes orders.

Eating

TOWN CENTRE & BAIXA

For self-catering try **Osman's** (Avenida 25 de Setembro; 8.30am-6pm Mon-Fri, 9am-4pm Sat), about 1.5km east of the main junction, or the pricey but well-stocked **Procongel** (Petromoc road; 9am-1pm & 2-5pm Mon-Fri, 9am-1pm Sat) attached to Wilson's Wharf restaurant in the baixa, with produce, imported cheeses and gourmet items.

Pastelaria Flor d'Avenida CAFE **$**
(272-20514; Avenida Eduardo Mondlane; meals from Mtc180-220; 7am-9pm Mon-Sat) A long-standing, informal eatery with outdoor tables on a small, street-side plaza offering a selection of standards and pastries.

Restaurante-Bar Samar SEAFOOD **$**
(272-20415; Avenida 25 de Setembro; meals Mtc180-220; 9am-10pm Sun-Fri) Tucked away in the car park of the Igreja Reino de Deus, this place features hearty Portuguese cuisine served on a shaded porch.

Pemba

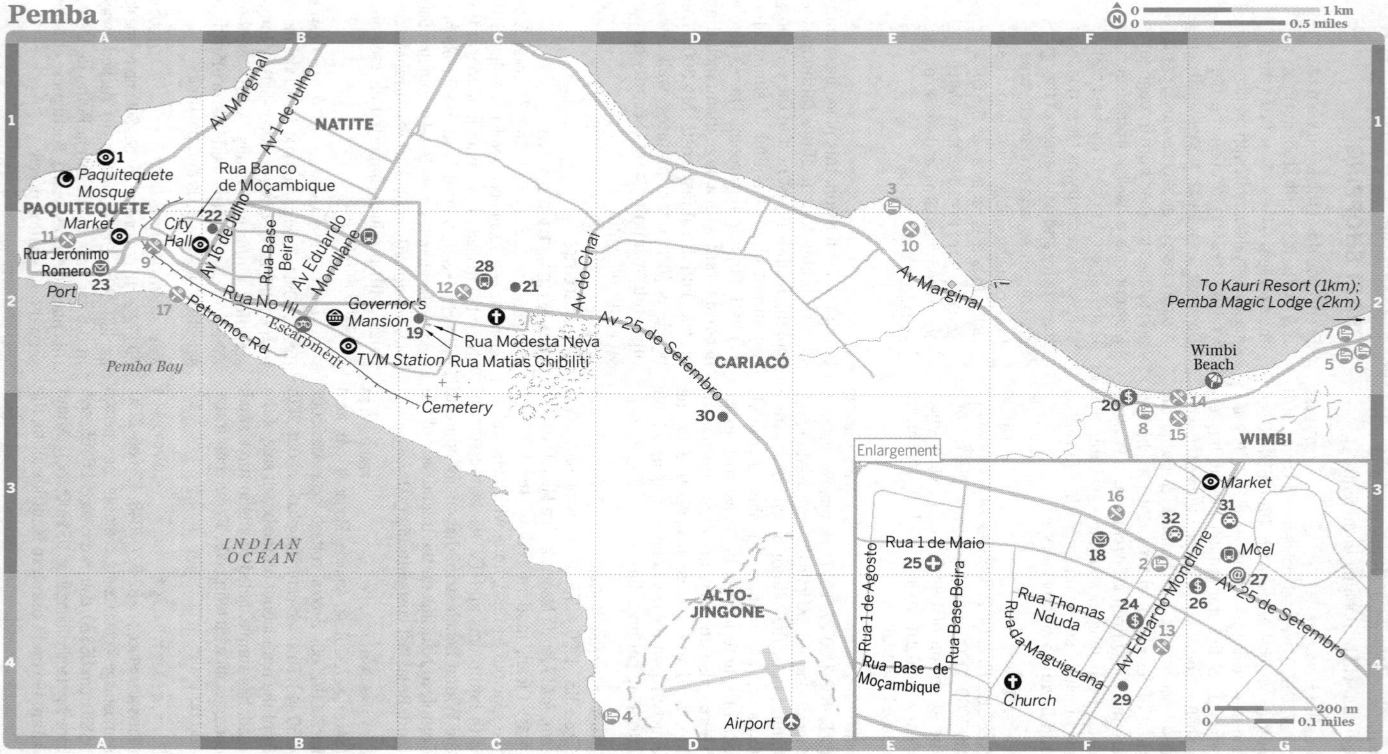

0 1 km
0 0.5 miles
NATITE
PAQUITEQUETE
1
Paquitequete Mosque
Market
11
Rua Jerónimo Romero
23
Port
9
City Hall
22
Rua Banco de Moçambique
Av Marginal
Av 1 de Julho
Av 16 de Julho
Rua Base Beira
Av Eduardo Mondlane
Rua No III
17
Petromoc Rd
Escarpment
Pemba Bay
Governor's Mansion
19
TVM Station
Rua Modesta Neva
Rua Matias Chibiliti
Cemetery
12
28
21
Av do Chai
Av 25 de Setembro
CARIACÓ
30
3
10
Av Marginal
To Kauri Resort (1km); Pemba Magic Lodge (2km)
7
5
6
Wimbi Beach
20
8
14
15
WIMBI
INDIAN OCEAN
ALTO-JINGONE
4
Airport
Enlargement
Market
16
32
31
18
Mcel
2
27
26
24
Av 25 de Setembro
Av Eduardo Mondlane
13
Rua 1 de Maio
25
Rua 1 de Agosto
Rua Base Beira
Rua Thomas Nduda
Rua da Maguiguana
Rua Base de Moçambique
Church
29
0 200 m
0 0.1 miles

Pemba

Sights

	CI Divers	(see 20)
1	Fish Market	A1

Sleeping

2	Hotel Cabo Delgado	F3
3	Pemba Beach Hotel	E1
4	Pemba Dive & Bush Camp	D4
5	Pieter's Place	G2
6	Residencial Reggio Emilia	G2
7	Simples Aldeia Lda	G2
8	Wimbi Sun Residencial	F3

Eating

9	556	A2
10	Clube Naval	E2
11	Locanda Italiana	A2
12	Osman's	C2
13	Pastelaria Flor d'Avenida	F4
14	Pemba Dolphin	F3
	Procongel	(see 17)
15	Restaurante Rema	F3
16	Restaurante-Bar Samar	F3
17	Wilson's Wharf	A2

Shopping

	Artes Maconde	(see 3)
	Artes Maconde Branch	(see 20)

Information

18	Branch Post Office	F3
19	Clínica de Cabo Delgado	C2
	Complexo Náutilus & ATM	(see 20)
20	Complexo Náutilus ATM	F3
21	Farmácia São Carlos Lwanga	C2
22	Immigration Office	B2
	Kaskazini	(see 3)
23	Main Post Office	A2
24	Millennium BIM & ATM	F4
25	Provincial Hospital	E3
26	Standard Bank & ATM	G4
27	Sycamore Services	G4

Transport

28	Grupo Mecula Buses	C2
29	LAM	F4
30	Main Transport Stand/Rodoviario	D3
	Safi Rentals	(see 20)
31	Taxi Rank	G3
32	Taxi Rank	F3

Locanda Italiana ITALIAN $$
(☎82-688 9050, 272-20672; locandaitaliana@tdm.co.mz; 487 Rua Jerónimo Romero; meals Mtc280-350) Tasty pizza and pastas in the quiet courtyard of a restored building in the baixa. The pizza oven is fired up during evenings only, from 6pm.

Wilson's Wharf SEAFOOD, BURGERS $$
(☎84-303 8197, 84-742 2909; Petromoc road; breakfast Mtc200-250, meals Mtc250-750; ⏰8am-late Mon-Sat;) Burgers, seafood and meat grills, hearty breakfasts and views over the port. Rooms are planned.

556 STEAKHOUSE $$
(☎272-21487; Rua No III; meals Mtc180-400; ⏰10am-10pm Mon-Sat) On the hill overlooking the port and the bay, with South African meats, plus chicken grills, pizzas, hamburgers, grilled prawns, squid, pub food and ice cream.

WIMBI BEACH

Restaurante Rema AFRICAN $
(Avenida Marginal; meals from Mtc170) A good spot for local meals and local vibes. It's just opposite Pemba Dolphin.

Clube Naval SEAFOOD, CONTINENTAL $$
(☎82-304 4887, 272-21770; Avenida Marginal; meals from Mtc250; ⏰10am-11pm) This waterside restaurant-bar has a beachside setting and a large menu featuring salads, seafood, chicken, ribs, pizzas and desserts. There's a volleyball area on the sand, a swimming pool and a small children's playground.

Kauri INTERNATIONAL $$
(Avenida Marginal; meals Mtc300-700; ⏰lunch & dinner Tue-Sun) The restaurant at Kauri Resort is reasonably fast, with a beachside setting, tasty seafood and meat grills, and Chinese and Indian dishes.

Pemba Dolphin SEAFOOD $$
(☎272-20937; Avenida Marginal; pizza Mtc150-250, seafood grills Mtc250-550; ⏰from 7am) Directly on the beach, with music and a beach-bar ambience, plus seafood grills and pizzas.

Information

Immigration

Immigration Office (Rua 16 de Junho; ⏰7.30-11am & 2-4pm Mon-Fri) Just off Rua Base de Moçambique.

Internet Access

Sycamore Services (☎272-21999; 1282 Avenida 25 de Setembro; per hr Mtc100; ⏰7.30am-8pm Mon-Sat, 8am-noon Sun) Internet connection; it's just after Mcel.

Medical Services

Clínica de Cabo Delgado (☎272-21462; Rua Modesta Neva 10) For basic medical treatment, although quality is erratic.

Farmácia São Carlos Lwanga (⏰7am-6.30pm Mon-Fri, 8am-5pm Sat) One block back from Avenida 25 de Setembro, on the same street as the Mecula bus office.

Provincial Hospital (cnr Ruas Base Beira & 1 de Maio) Malaria tests and basic medical treatment.

Money

Barclay's (Avenida Eduardo Mondlane) ATM.

Millennium BIM (Avenida Eduardo Mondlane) ATM; there's also a Millennium BIM ATM in front of Complexo Náutilus at Wimbi Beach.

Standard Bank (Avenida Eduardo Mondlane) With ATM.

Tourist Information

Kaskazini (☎82-309 6990, 272-20371; www.kaskazini.com; Pemba Beach Hotel, Avenida Marginal, Wimbi Beach; ⏰8am-3pm Mon-Fri, 8.30am-noon Sat) Efficient, knowledgeable and a good first stop. It gives free information on Pemba and elsewhere in northern Mozambique, helps with accommodation and flight bookings, and can organise everything from dhow safaris to sunset cruises.

ℹ Getting There & Away

Air

LAM (☎272-21251; Avenida Eduardo Mondlane; ⏰7am-4.30pm Mon-Fri, 9.30-11.30am Sat) flies daily to/from Maputo (via Nampula and/or Beira), and twice weekly to/from Dar es Salaam (Tanzania). **SAAirlink** (☎272-21700; www.flyairlink.com; Airport) flies twice weekly between Johannesburg and Pemba.

CFA (☎82-575 2125; www.cfa.co.za) flies five times weekly to the Quirimbas Archipelago and three times weekly to Niassa Reserve. Book directly, or through Kaskazini (p238).

Expect to pay from Mtc350 to Mtc500 for a taxi from the airport to town.

Bus & Chapa

Grupo Mecula (☎272-20821; grupomecula@teledata.mz; Rua Josina Machel) has daily buses to **Nampula** (Mtc350, seven hours), **Moçimboa da Praia** (Mtc270, seven hours) and **Mueda** (Mtc280, nine hours), with the same bus going first to Moçimboa da Praia and then on to Mueda. There's also a daily bus to **Nacala** (Mtc350, seven hours); otherwise take the Nampula bus to Namialo junction and wait there for onward transport. All of Mecula's Pemba departures are at 4.45am from the Grupo Mecula office, just off the main road and about 1.5km from the centre on a small side street behind Osman's supermarket.

For **Mozambique Island** the best bet is to continue to Nampula, and then get onward transport from there the next day. You can also try your luck getting out at Namialo junction and looking for onward transport from there, but the timing often doesn't work out, and Namialo is unappealing as an overnight spot.

For other destinations, head to the **main transport stand** ('Rodoviario') about 2km from the centre (Mtc100 in a taxi) along the extension of Avenida 25 de Setembro, where there are vehicles in all directions, including **Macomia** (Mtc170, two hours) and **Montepuez** (Mtc170, three hours). Maning Nice and Nagi Trans buses also depart from here to Nampula daily.

ℹ Getting Around

Bus & Taxi

There are taxi ranks on Avenida Eduardo Mondlane **just down from Mcel** and at the **same junction** along Avenida 25 de Setembro, or call ☎84-600 0008. Town to Wimbi Beach costs Mtc150 to Mtc200. There's also a public bus that runs between 6am and 7pm from town to Wimbi Beach and beyond (Mtc10), and the occasional *chapa* from the **Mcel corner** to Complexo Nautilus roundabout (Mtc7.50).

Rental Car

Safi Rentals (☎82-380 8630; www.pembarentacar.com) comes highly recommended, offering reliable car rentals at very reasonable prices. Rates include unlimited kilometres, and open the door to many attractions in the north that would be otherwise inaccessible for budget and midrange travellers. They are based at Complexo Náutilus. It's also possible to arrange car rentals through Kaskazini (p238).

Around Pemba

Within about a 2½- to three-hour drive from Pemba are a couple of camps and lodges that offer visitors a chance to experience a part of Cabo Delgado's wild, untamed bush and possibly see an elephant or two.

On the northern side of Pemba Bay, **Londo Lodge** (www.londolodge.com; per person full board from US$500; ✉) has beach-facing villas overlooking the bay, a restaurant and a range of water sports. Short bushwalks can also be arranged, and sunset dhow cruises are included in the price.

CABO DELGADO

Although remote geographically and otherwise from Maputo, Cabo Delgado province has played a disproportionately important role in recent Mozambican history. It's known in particular as the birthplace of the independence struggle, which began here, supported from bases in nearby Tanzania. Cabo Delgado is also where some of the most protracted fighting took place during the 1980s. At the height of the war, it could take up to a month to travel – convoy-style and moving only at night – between Pemba and Moçimboa da Praia, which makes the seven-hour bus ride today seem like a stroll in the park. A legacy of the war years is that most district capitals in the north have airstrips, including some large enough to accommodate jets.

As in neighbouring Niassa province, large tracts of Cabo Delgado are wild and trackless, and local lore is full of tales about the dangers of lions and the like.

Major ethnic groups include the Makonde, the Makua and, along the coast, the Mwani.

Taratibu (per person full board from US$60) is a rustic bush camp set in a wilderness tract within Quirimbas National Park boundaries, about 160km northwest of Pemba in Ancuabe district. There are a handful of pleasant double bungalows, and the chance for bush walks and vehicle safaris. Advance bookings are essential, and should be made through Kaskazini (p238) in Pemba.

MURRÉBUÈ

About 12km south of Pemba is Murrébuè, a lovely, long and undeveloped stretch of white sand fringed by turquoise waters that is famed for its optimal kite-surfing conditions.

Sleeping & Eating

Ulala BUNGALOWS $$
(☎82-710 9117, 82-741 5104; www.ulala-lodge.com; s/d in bungalow Mtc2400/2800, in stilt bungalow Mtc3600/4000) This new place has a lovely beachside setting, a large dining/relaxing area, and accommodation in two spacious, breezy stilt houses just back from the beach, or two other non-stilted family bungalows somewhat further back. All have hot water, nets and the whole setting is lovely. Airport transfers are free for stays of two or more nights.

Il Pirata BUNGALOWS $$
(☎82-380 5790; www.murrebue.com; d with full board US$135-180) At the northern end of the beach, and about 3km north of Ulala, is this hub of activity. It has three lovely bungalows and delicious Italian meals. Airport transfers can be arranged.

Upeponi GUESTHOUSE $
(☎82-669 8540, 82-397 2659; r with/without air-con Mtc1500/750) This relaxed, locally-run place is a popular weekend destination for day visitors offering a pleasant stretch of beach and a restaurant (weekends only) for lunch and dinner.

nZuwa BUNGALOWS $$
(☎82-730 6365, 82-589 4692; www.nzuwa.com; campsite US$15, dm US$10-15, r US$60-80, f bungalow from US$120;) At the far northern end of the beach, just before Il Pirata, nZuwa was just about to get started when we passed through, with various accommodation options, meals and day volunteer opportunities.

Getting There & Away

To reach Murrébuè, head out of Pemba along the main road for about 5km; turn left at the signposted Mecufi district road and wind your way along the sandy road downhill. At the T-junction at the bottom, after the police station, Ulala and Upeponi are signposted to the right. Il Pirata and nZuwa are to the left.

Quirimbas Archipelago

The Quirimbas Archipelago consists of about two dozen islands and islets strewn along the 400km stretch of coastline between Pemba and the Rovuma River. Some are waterless and uninhabited, while others have histories as long as the archipelago itself.

Throughout, the archipelago's natural beauty is astounding, with searingly white patches of soft sand surrounded by brilliant turquoise and azure waters alternating with greener, vegetated islands and extensive stands of mangroves. Dense mangrove forests also link some of the islands with each other and with the coast, with only skilled dhow captains able to navigate among the intricate channels that were cut during colonial times.

Today, many of the southern islands, including Ibo, Quirimba and Matemo, are part of the **Quirimbas National Park** (Parque Nacional das Quirimbas; adult/child Mtc200/100), which also includes large inland areas on the fringing coastline. The one-time entry fee is collected by hotels within the park area. There are also various other park fees, including Mtc100 per person per day for camping, but their enforcement status is still in flux.

In addition to its pristine natural beauty, the archipelago is known for diving – which is considered to be especially good around Quilaluia, Vamizi and Rongui – and for birding.

History

Ibo and Quirimba, the two main islands in the archipelago, were already important Muslim trading posts when the Portuguese arrived in the 15th century. The islands were renowned in particular for their production of silks, cottons and maluane cloth; on some old maps, they are shown as the Maluane Islands. Ivory, ambergris and turtle shell were also important items in local commerce, and trade extended south as far as Sofala, Zambézia and north to Malindi, off the Kenyan coast.

By the early-17th century the Portuguese had established a mission on Quirimba and a fortified settlement on Ibo. They also built cisterns to store rainwater, which encouraged the development of agriculture, and the islands began to supply food to Mozambique Island. Beginning in the mid-18th century, the archipelago, particularly Ibo Island, served as a base for the clandestine slave trade, attracting boats from as far away as Zanzibar and Kilwa in present-day Tanzania. In the late-19th century, as the slave trade came to an end and colonial attention shifted to the mainland, trade in the archipelago began to decline. Today Quirimba, with its coconut and sisal plantations, is probably the most economically active of the islands, though all are quiet – largely ignored until recently and caught in a fascinating time warp.

Getting There & Away

Air

CFA Charters (☎82-575 2125; www.cfa.co.za) flies five times weekly between Ibo and Pemba (US$310 return, 25 minutes), with stops on request at Matemo, Medjumbe and several other islands. Book directly or through Kaskazini (p238) in Pemba.

Boat

To reach the islands under your own steam, you'll need to go first to Quissanga, on the coast north of Pemba. A direct *chapa* departs Pemba from the fish market behind the mosque in Paquitequete bairro (Mtc200, five to six hours) at about 4.30am daily. Once in Quissanga, most vehicles continue on to Tandanhangue village (Mtc200 from Pemba), 5km further, which is the departure point for dhows to Ibo (Mtc50). In a private car, the trip to Quissanga and Tandanhangue takes about 3½ hours. For drivers (4WD), there's secure parking at Gringo's (James') Place next to the Tandanhangue dhow port for Mtc100 per day.

Dhows leave Tandanhangue only at high tide (with a window of about two hours on either side of the high-tide point), and non-motorised boats take from one to six hours to Ibo (about 45 minutes with motor). There's no accommodation in Tandanhangue. Chartering a motorised boat for yourself to Ibo will cost about Mtc1500 one way. Kaskazini (p238) in Pemba offers road transfers between Pemba and Tandanhangue followed by a motorboat transfer to Ibo for US$270 one-way for up to four people.

Dhows to Quirimba Island depart from Quissanga. Alternatively, you can inquire with Pensão Quirimba about space on their boat.

For overnight sailing charters from Pemba direct to the islands, contact Kaskazini.

IBO ISLAND

Ibo, the best-known of the Quirimbas islands, is an enchanting place. Its quiet streets are lined with dilapidated villas and crumbling, moss-covered buildings, and echo with the silent, hollow footsteps of bygone centuries. Architecturally it is more open than Mozambique Island, although its ambience is more insulated and its pace more subdued. The best time to visit is during a clear, moonlit night, when the old colonial houses take on a haunting, almost surreal aspect.

Ibo was fortified as early as 1609 and by the late-18th century had become the most important town in Mozambique outside of Mozambique Island. During this era the island was a major export point in the slave trade, with demand spurred by French sugar plantation owners on Mauritius and elsewhere. In the late-19th century, it served briefly as headquarters for the Niassa Company. However, in 1904, the headquarters were relocated to Pemba (then Porto Amelia) to take advantage of Pemba's better sea access routes and harbour, and Ibo faded into oblivion.

At the island's northern end is the star-shaped **Fort of São João** (per person Mtc50; 7am-4pm), which was built in 1791 and designed to accommodate up to 300 people. In the days when Ibo was linked into the slave trade, the fort's dark, cramped lower chambers were used as slave holding points. Today it's known for the **silver artisans** who have set up shop near the entrance. Much of the silver used is made from melted-down coins and is often of inferior quality, but the distinctive and refined Swahili artisanship is among the best in the region. Inside is also the small but fascinating **Maritime Museum** (Museu Marítimo), focusing on local Mwani culture. Explanations are in Portuguese, with an English translation available.

There are two other forts on the island, neither well preserved. The **Fort of São José** to the southwest dates from 1760, but ceased to have any military use once the larger fort of São João was built. The **Fort of Santo António** near the market was built around 1830. Other places of interest include a large church near the fort of São José, and the island's three cemeteries, including an old Hindu crematorium along the road running northwest from the port.

Traditional religious practices are alive and well on Ibo and if you spend some time on the island, you'll undoubtedly come into contact with them. One of the best times to see dancing is in late June, when the feast of São João (24 June) is celebrated with numerous festivities.

Ibo doesn't have many beaches, but as compensation there are magical sunset views over the mud flats just north of the tiny port. With some time, you can also take day excursions to a nearby sandbank, or to a lovely patch of beach on the other side of the island.

For a walking tour and explanations of Ibo's history, ask your hotel to put you in contact with Rual, who is taking over from **Senhor João Baptista**, Ibo's venerable official historian. Another contact for walking tours around town is the enterprising and reliable **Hamisi** (82 039 2069).

There are no ATMs or banks on Ibo, and most places on the island do not accept credit cards.

Sleeping & Eating

It's possible to arrange homestays with local families. Contact **Ibraimo Assane** (82-551 1919; r Mtc250-400). You'll get a taste for local life and get to sample local meals. Be prepared for extremely basic conditions.

Miti Miwiri GUESTHOUSE **$$**
(82-543 8564, 26-960530; www.mitimiwiri.com; d/tr/f US$65/75/80, 3-course dinner about Mtc500; @) A lovely, atmospheric place in a restored house with a handful of spacious, good-value rooms with bathroom and fan, including one family room with two double beds. There's a large, walled garden with three swings, a bar and sheesha lounge, and a restaurant with excellent meals, including vegetarian selections. Staff can also help with tourist information and excursions, flight bookings to/from Pemba and international telephone calls. It's in the heart of the town, and about 10 minutes on foot from the dhow port – ask any of the children who come to meet the boat to show you the way. Continental/full breakfast costs Mtc150/250 extra.

Tikidiri HOSTEL **$**
(82-590 3944; Airfield road; campsite per person Mtc100, s/d Mtc150/300) This community-run place, about 2km from the dhow port opposite the old Catholic cemetery along the path leading to the airfield, has basic but clean stone-and-thatch bungalows with nets, bucket baths and clean drop toilets. There's no electricity and no breakfast, but good local meals can be arranged (from Mtc100), as can guides for exploring the island and elsewhere in the archipelago.

Casa de Lucy GUESTHOUSE **$**
(82-815 2892; d Mtc800) Just up from the dhow port and before Ibo Island Lodge, with two nice rooms (one overlooking the water), and some more under construction. Meals can be arranged.

Panela Africana Guesthouse & Restaurant GUESTHOUSE **$**
(African Pot; 82-535 3113; sstephanec@hotmail.com; d US$30-40, meals Mtc250-350, set menu Mtc500; restaurant noon-3pm & 6pm until late) About 75m past and diagonally opposite Santo António fort in Bairro Rituto, with three rooms attached to the family house and a gourmet restaurant, featuring Mozambican-French fusion cuisine. During the dry season, Stephane, the owner, can

also arrange dhow safaris to the other islands on his sleeper dhow, *Maisha*.

Ibo Island Lodge LODGE $$$
(www.iboisland.co.za; s/d with full board US$460/720;) This nine-room luxury boutique hotel – the most upmarket accommodation on Ibo – is housed in two restored mansions in a prime setting overlooking the water near the dhow port. Relax on the sea-facing verandas, enjoy a sundowner overlooking the water, or luxuriate in the comforts of the rooms.

Pensão Café do Ibo PENSION $
(Ibo Coffee Guesthouse; 82-551 7501, 82-658 7111; Airfield rd; r Mtc1200-1500) This private home has clean, quiet, slightly cramped rooms in a small house opposite a coffee plantation. It's about a 10-minute walk from the dhow port, following the road towards the airfield, with the water to your right.

Cinco Portas GUESTHOUSE $$
(www.cincoportas.net; s US$50-80, d US$65-100, 4-person house US$180-250;) This comfortable place is in a restored mansion with a lovely garden. It's about a five minute walk from the dhow port, one street back from the water.

Karibuni HOSTEL $
(Campsite do Janine; 82-703 2200; campsite per person Mtc120, r Mtc400-800) This place is next to Ibo Island Lodge and just up from the dhow port. It has some very basic rooms and space in a small garden to pitch your tent. Meals can be prepared, but you'll need to bring your own food.

QUIRIMBA ISLAND

Quirimba, just south of Ibo, is the most economically active island of the archipelago, with large coconut plantations, a sizeable sisal factory and an airstrip. While it is more bustling than Ibo, it is less interesting from an architectural and historical perspective and not nearly as scenic as the little patches of paradise further north, although it has some lovely stretches of sand. It is possible to walk between Quirimba and Ibo at low tide, but it's a long route through dense mangrove swamps and you'll need a guide.

Historically, Quirimba was an important Muslim trading centre well before the arrival of the Portuguese. In 1522 it was raided by the Portuguese and the town was destroyed, although it was later rebuilt. In the 16th century Quirimba served as a centre for missionary work.

Quirimbas Pensão (82-308 3930, 82-576 7264; quirimba.island@gmail.com; r US$50, meals US$20), on the grounds of an old coconut estate, has four clean rooms and meals. Advance bookings are essential.

QUILALUIA

Until recently, tiny Quilaluia was inhabited only by seasonal fishing communities. Now it's a protected marine sanctuary and home to **Quilálea** (www.azura-retreats.com/quilalea; r per person with full board US$665-795), a luxurious private resort with nine sea-facing villas. The surrounding waters offer prime diving and snorkelling immediately offshore.

MEDJUMBE & MATEMO

Idyllic Medjumbe is a narrow sliver of island draped with white coral sand and home to **Medjumbe Island Resort** (www.medjumbe.com; per person with full board from US$530;). Accommodation is in 13 thatched wooden chalets set directly on the sand. Diving and fishing are available just offshore.

Unlike Medjumbe, which is unpopulated except for the resort, the much larger island of Matemo, north of Ibo, has been inhabited for generations and was an important centre for cloth manufacture into the 17th century. Today villages dot much of the north and interior of the island. The upmarket **Matemo Island Resort** (www.matemoresort.com; per person with full board from US$440;) has two dozen chalets, all with sliding glass doors opening onto the beach, indoor and outdoor showers and Moorish overtones in the common areas. It's also possible to arrange camping on Matemo at Sr Dade's campsite near Matemo Island Resort; the best contact for this is Miti Miwiri (p241) on Ibo.

Both Medjumbe Island Resort and Matemo Island Resort are run by Rani Africa, which also runs the Pemba Beach Hotel (p235) in Pemba and Lugenda Bush Camp (p232) in the Niassa Reserve; island/mainland packages are available.

VAMIZI, RONGUI & MACALÓÈ

These three islands are part of a privately funded, community based conservation project. For now, only Vamizi has accommodation, with lodges on Rongui and Macalóè and an inland luxury bush lodge planned.

Historically, the most important of the three islands was Vamizi, a narrow, paradisal crescent about midway between Moçimboa da Praia and Palma at the northernmost end of the archipelago. It was long

MAPIKO DANCING

If you hear drumming in the late afternoons while travelling around Cabo Delgado, it's likely *mapiko*, the famed masked dancing of the Makonde.

The dancer (always a man) wears a special wooden *lipiko* (mask; plural: *mapiko*), decorated with exaggerated features, hair (often real) and facial etchings. After being carved, the masks are kept in the bush in a special place known as the *mpolo*, where only men are permitted to enter. Traditionally, they cannot be viewed by women or by uncircumcised boys unless they are being worn by a dancer.

Before *mapiko* begins, the dancer's body is completely covered with large pieces of cloth wrapped around the legs, arms and body so that nothing can be seen other than the fingers and toes. All evidence that there is a person inside is supposed to remain hidden. The idea is that the dancer represents the spirit of a dead person who has come to do harm to the women and children, from which only the men of the village can protect them. While boys learn the secret of the dance during their initiation rites, women are never supposed to discover it and remain in fear of the *mapiko*. (*Mapiko* supposedly grew out of male attempts to limit the power of women in matrilineal Makonde society.)

Once the dancer is ready, distinctive rhythms are beaten on special *mapiko* drums. The dance is usually performed on weekend afternoons, and must be finished by sunset. The best places to see *mapiko* dancing are in and around Mueda and in Macomia.

a Portuguese and Arabic trading post and there are ruins of an old Portuguese fort at its western end, plus a large village and several stunning beaches to the north and east. All three islands are important seasonal fishing bases.

Vamizi Island Lodge (www.vamizi.com; per person with full board & activities US$1250) is a 24-bed luxury getaway on a long arc of spectacular white sand draped along Vamizi's northern edge, and one of the most beautiful places to relax along the northern Mozambican coast. The 13 spacious beach chalets have large, open sitting areas and private verandas, plus all the comforts you could want, presented in a tasteful and low-key way. There's diving and snorkelling offshore. Deep-sea fishing, walks – including to some hawksbill and green turtle nesting areas – and birding excursions can be arranged.

Macomia

The small district capital of Macomia is the turn-off point for the beach at Pangane and the end of the good tarmac if you're heading north.

Pensão-Residencial Caminho do Norte (r Mtc400), on the main road just north of the junction, has no-frills rooms. **Bar Chung** (at the junction) has a few very basic rooms in the family compound to rent (rates are cheap and negotiable), and can help with meals.

Several vehicles daily go to Mucojo (Mtc70) along a rough road, sometimes continuing on to Pangane. Hitching is possible but very slow. If you're stranded, a good place to ask for a lift is at Bar Chung, at Macomia's main intersection.

To continue southward to Pemba (Mtc170, two hours), buses from Moçimboa da Praia and Mueda pass Macomia from about 9am. Going northwards, you'll often need to wait until around 9am or 10am for a vehicle to pass through.

Chai

It was in the large village of Chai that Frelimo's military campaign against colonial rule began in 1964. There's a small monument near the main road and every year on 25 September (Revolution Day), national attention turns here as the independence struggle is remembered with visits by high-ranking officials and re-enactments of historical events.

Chai is about 40km north of Macomia along the main road between Pemba and Moçimboa da Praia. Take any vehicle heading to/from Pemba and ask to be dropped off, but do it early enough in the day so that you have a chance of onward transport, as there's no accommodation.

Pangane

☎26

Pangane is a large village on a long, lovely palm-fringed beach about 10km north of Mucojo, and 50km off the main north–south road. Many seasonal fishermen come up from Nacala and other places in the south, so the sand near the point isn't always the cleanest, but the setting is beautiful, just on the edge of paradise. Offshore is Macalóè Island, and beyond that the St Lazarus Bank, known for its diving.

Sleeping & Eating

Guludo LODGE $$$

(☎26-960569; www.guludo.com; r per person with full board from US$345) This upmarket fair-traded camp makes a fine base if you want to get a taste of northern Mozambique's coastal paradise while learning about and supporting local community development initiatives. Accommodation is in safari-style tents or more upmarket 'adobe bandas'. There's also a family banda. Island excursions, diving and elephant tracking can be arranged, as can visits to see the village school and other community initiatives. It's about 15km south of Mucojo junction; transfers can be arranged from Pemba and Macomia.

Savana Beach Lodge LODGE $$$

(Messano Flower Lodge; ☎26-960558; www.savanabeachmozambico.com; campsite US$30, s/d US$150/250;) This lodge, run by the Italian Ora hotel chain, is between Pangane and Mucojo, and is currently the only accommodation near Pangane. It consists of several nicely appointed bungalows (more planned), without water at our visit (although this should be fixed imminently) in a beautiful location directly on the beach, and a camping area.

Getting There & Away

Pangane is 50km off the main north–south road (the turn-off is at Macomia), and about 9km north of Mucojo, a tiny junction village on the coast. There is at least one daily *chapa* between Macomia (where fuel is usually available) and Pangane (Mtc80), departing Pangane at about 5am. Departures from Macomia are at about 9am; the *chapa* waits until the Pemba–Moçimboa da Praia and Moçimboa da Praia–Pemba through buses arrive. There are also several *chapas* daily from Macomia to Mucojo (Mtc70), from where you can usually find a pick-up on to Pangane. Dhows to the Quirimbas islands can be arranged at the lodges or with local fishermen. There are also dhows from Ibo or the other islands to Pangane.

There's an airstrip at Mucojo for charter planes.

Mueda

Mueda, the main town on the Makonde Plateau and the centre of Mozambique's Makonde people, is rather lacking in charm. However this is compensated for by a wonderfully cool climate, a rustic, highland feel and an attractive setting, with views down from the escarpment along the southern and western edges of town. The surrounding area holds the potential for some good hiking, but it was heavily mined during the war and is not yet completely de-mined, so stick to well-trodden paths. The plateau itself lies at about 800m altitude, with water available only on its slopes and at its base.

The closest ATM is in Moçimboa da Praia.

Sights & Activities

Mueda was originally built as an army barracks during the colonial era. In 1960 it was the site of the infamous massacre of Mueda. There's a statue commemorating Mueda's role in Mozambican independence and a mass grave for the 'martyrs of Mueda' at the western end of town. Maria José Chipande – wife of Alberto Chipande, a well-known Makonde guerrilla commander during the independence struggle, one of the founding members of Frelimo and a former minister of defence – is also buried here. Just behind this monument is a ravine (known locally as *xiudi)* over which countless Mozambicans were hurled to their deaths.

The outlying villages are good places to see Makonde woodcarvings.

Sleeping & Eating

Pensão Mtima PENSION $

(☎86-314 5303; Rua 1 de Maio; r with/without bathroom Mtc800/500) On the main road, with basic, clean rooms with bucket baths and meals on order.

Getting There & Away

Grupo Mecula has a daily bus between Pemba and Mueda via Moçimboa da Praia (Mtc280, nine hours), departing at 5am. Several vehicles go each morning between Mueda and Moçimboa da Praia (Mtc150, two hours). There's also one vehicle daily to the Negomano border (Mtc500),

THE MAKONDE

The Mueda Plateau around Mueda is home to the Makonde people, who are renowned throughout Africa for their amazing woodcarvings. Like many tribes in the north, the Makonde are matrilineal. Children and inheritances normally belong to the woman and it's common for a husband to move to the village of his wife after marriage, setting up house near his mother-in-law. Settlements are widely scattered – possibly a remnant of the days when the Makonde sought to evade slave raids – and there is no tradition of a unified political system. Each village is governed by a hereditary chief and a council of elders.

Due to their isolated location, the Makonde remained largely insulated from colonial and postcolonial influences. Even today, many Makonde still adhere to traditional religions, with the complex spirit world given its fullest expression in their carvings.

Traditionally the Makonde practised body scarring and, while it's seldom done today, you may see older people with markings on their faces and bodies. It's also fairly common to see elderly Makonde women wearing a wooden plug in their upper lip, or to see this depicted in Makonde artwork.

departing between about 8am and 9am. All transport leaves from the main road opposite the market. After about 10am, it's difficult to find vehicles to any destination.

If you're driving there are two roads connecting Mueda with the main north–south road. Most traffic uses the good road via Diaca (50km). The alternate route via Muidumbe (about 30km south of Diaca) is scenic, winding through hills and forests, but rougher. Near Muidumbe is **Nangololo**, a mission station and an important base during the independence struggle, with an old airstrip large enough to take jets.

Moçimboa da Praia

272

This bustling outpost is the last major town before the Rovuma River and the Tanzanian border. Most local residents are Mwani ('People of the Sea') – a Swahili, and hence Muslim, people known for their textiles and silver craftsmanship, as well as for their rich song and dance traditions. Moçimboa da Praia does a brisk trade with Tanzania, both legal and illegal, and from here northwards, a few words of Swahili will often get you further than Portuguese.

The town itself is long, stretched over several kilometres between the main road and the sea. In the upper-lying section is a small market, several *pensões*, a petrol station and the transport stand. About 2km east, near the water, are a few more places to stay, plus police and immigration, a lively fish market and the colourful dhow port.

Together with nearby Palma, Moçimboa da Praia has become a hub for the current influx of oil money in northern Mozambique, so expect changes here.

Sights & Activities

Watching all the activity at the fish market, especially early morning or late afternoon, is fascinating. It's also possible to arrange a dhow to visit some of the outlying islands, or to visit the attractive swimming beach near Ncamangano; ask at the petrol station near the immigration office.

Sleeping & Eating

Pensão Leeta, at the town entrance opposite the transport stand, is currently rented out in its entirety, but you may still be able to pitch a tent in its grounds.

Hotel Chez Natalie CHALET **$$**
(82-439 6080, 272-81092; natalie.bockel@gmail.com; campsite per person Mtc300, d without bathroom Mtc800, 4-person chalets without/with internet & hot water Mtc2000/2200; @) The best bet in town if you have your own transport, with large grounds overlooking the estuary, camping, a handful of spacious family-style four-person chalets with running water and mosquito nets, and a grill. Very tranquil. Breakfast and other meals are available with advance arrangement only. It's 2.5km from the town centre; watch for the barely signposted left-hand turn-off from Avenida Samora Machel onto Avenida Eduardo Mondlane just after passing Clubé de Moçimboa. Continue along Avenida Eduardo Mondlane past the small Praça do Paz on your left for 400m. Turn left next to a large tree onto a small dirt path, and continue

about 1km past a row of local-style houses to Chez Natalie. With advance notice, *mapiko* dancing can be arranged.

Complexo de Contentores de Ilha Vumba BUNGALOW **$$**
(☎82-311 4750; r small/large Mtc1420/2500; ❄) This place, a temporary housing complex for oil and tourism project workers, has clean, air-conditioned rooms in trailers. It also has Moçimboa's best **restaurant** (meals from Mtc180). It's along the road paralleling the beach.

Pensão-Residencial Magid PENSION **$**
(☎272-81099; Avenida Samora Machel; r Mtc500) A short walk downhill from the transport stand and convenient to the Grupo Mecula bus 'garage', with basic rooms sharing facilities.

Restaurante Estrelha AFRICAN **$**
(Avenida Samora Machel; meals from Mtc150) Restaurante Estrelha is opposite the police station and on the right, just before the park. There's outdoor seating and, with luck, a choice of grilled chicken or fish.

Information

If you're travelling by dhow and enter or leave Mozambique here, have your passport stamped at the immigration office just back from the beach in the lower part of town. An immigration officer meets arriving international flights.

Barclays, Millennium BIM and BCI all have ATMs. Barclays changes US dollars cash. **Telecomunicações de Moçambique** (Avenida 7 de Março; per min Mtc1) has internet access.

Getting There & Away

Air

CFA Charters (☎82-575 2125; www.cfa.co.za) flies three times weekly between Moçimboa da Praia, Pemba and several of the Quirimbas islands, including Ibo, Matemo and Medjumbe, in coordination with Coastal Aviation flights from Dar es Salaam (Tanzania).

Bus & Pick-Up

The transport stand is near the market at the entrance to town, close to the large tree. Several pick-ups go daily to/from the Rovuma ('Namoto') via Palma (Mtc250, two hours). The road to Palma is being paved, and is in good shape. To Pemba, the Mecula bus departs daily at 5am (Mtc270, seven hours). Maning Nice departs daily by 3am. Several pickups also do the journey, departing by 7am from the main road in front of the market. Maning Nice goes daily between Moçimboa da Praia and Nampula (Mtc500, 13 hours), and several vehicles go daily to/from Mueda (Mtc150, two hours).

Palma

The large fishing village of Palma lies nestled among the coconut groves about 45km south of the Tanzania border. It's a centre for basketry and mat weaving (though most of this is done in the outlying villages) and for boat making, and it is fascinating to watch craftspeople using centuries-old techniques. The area is also a melting pot of languages, with Makwe, Makonde, Mwani, Swahili and Portuguese all spoken.

Palma has an upper, administrative section of town with immigration, the post office, a guesthouse and a small market, and a lower section, about 2km downhill along the water, with the main market and many local houses. There's nowhere to change money, although changing meticais and Tanzanian shillings at the markets is no problem.

Sights & Activities

About 15km offshore across Túnguè Bay is idyllic **Tecomaji Island**. Just south of Tecomaji is Rongui Island, followed by Vamizi Island. All are privately owned. Beaches in town are not clean enough for swimming.

About 20km north of Palma is tiny Kiwiya junction, where a sandy track branches about 17km seawards to **Cabo Delgado** (the point of land from which Cabo Delgado province takes its name) and a lighthouse.

Sleeping & Eating

Pensão Managanha PENSION **$**
(r Mtc500) This place in the upper part of town has simple, clean rooms and a loud disco on weekends.

Getting There & Away

All transport leaves from the Boa Viagem roundabout at the town entrance. Some drivers continue down to the main market.

Chapas from Moçimboa da Praia en route to the Rovuma River pass Palma from about 6am (Mtc100 from Palma to the border). Transport from the Rovuma south to Moçimboa da Praia passes through Palma from about 10am, and there's at least one vehicle from Palma to Moçimboa da Praia each morning (Mtc150, one hour) along a good, graded road that will soon be paved.

UNDERSTAND MOZAMBIQUE

Mozambique Today

Since the signing of peace accords in 1992, and the first multiparty elections in 1994, Mozambique has been remarkably successful in moving beyond its history of war and transforming military conflict into political competition. In December 2004, Armando Guebuza, an insider in the ruling Frelimo political party, was elected to succeed long-serving former president Joaquim Chissano (also Frelimo), who had earlier announced his intent to step down. An easy re-election for Guebuza followed in 2009. The next national elections are scheduled for 2014.

Thanks to these relatively smooth political transitions, Mozambique has won acclaim and donor funding over the past decade as a successful example of postwar reconciliation and democracy-building in Africa. The country is also set to benefit economically from major coal and natural gas finds in the north. However, challenges continue, including widespread corruption, rising organised crime and opposition party Renamo's ongoing struggles to prove itself as a viable political party. Yet, despite these shadows, the long-term outlook is positive. Throughout its long history, Mozambique has shown a remarkable ability to rebound in the face of adversity, and most observers still count the country among the continent's bright spots.

History

From Bantu-speaking farmers and fishers to Arabic traders, Goan merchants and adventuring Europeans, Mozambique has long been a crossroads of cultures.

In the Beginning

The first Mozambicans were small, scattered clans of nomads, possibly distant cousins of the San, who were likely trekking through the bush as early as 10,000 years ago. They left few traces and little is known about this era.

About 3000 years ago, Bantu-speaking peoples from the Niger Delta in West Africa began moving through the Congo basin. Over a period of centuries they journeyed into East and southern Africa, reaching present-day Mozambique sometime around the 1st century AD, where they made their living farming, fishing and raising livestock.

Early Kingdoms

Most of these early Mozambicans set themselves up in small chiefdoms, some of which gradually coalesced into larger states or kingdoms. These included the Karanga (Shona) in central Mozambique; the renowned kingdom of Monomotapa, south and west of present-day Tete; and the Maravi (also known as the Malâwi), who exercised dominion over a large area extending from the Zambezi River into what is now southern Malawi and Zambia.

Southern Mozambique, which was settled by the Nguni and various other groups, remained decentralised until the 19th century when consolidation under the powerful kingdom of Gaza gave it at least nominal political cohesion.

Arrival of the Arabs

From around the 8th century AD sailors from Arabia began to arrive along the East African coast. Trade flourished and intermarriage with the indigenous Bantu-speakers gave birth to the Swahili language and culture. By the 9th century several settlements had been established, including Kilwa island, in present-day Tanzania, which soon became the hub of Arab trade networks throughout southeastern Africa. Another was Sofala, near present-day Beira, which by the 15th century was the main link connecting Kilwa with the old Shona kingdoms and the inland goldfields. Other early coastal ports and settlements included those at Mozambique Island, Angoche, Quelimane and Ibo Island, all ruled by local sultans.

Portuguese Adventurers

In 1498 Vasco da Gama landed at Mozambique Island en route to India. Within a decade after da Gama's arrival, the Portuguese had established themselves on the island and gained control of many other Swahili–Arab trading posts – lured in part by their need for supply points on the sea route to the east and in part by their desire to control the gold trade with the interior.

Over the next 200 years the Portuguese set up trading enclaves and forts along the coast, making Mozambique Island the capital of what they called Portuguese East Africa. By the mid-16th century, ivory had replaced gold as the main trading commodity and by the late 18th century, slaves had been added to the list, with close to one million Africans sold into slavery through Mozambique's ports.

Portugal's Power Struggle

In the 17th century the Portuguese attempted to strengthen their control by setting up *prazos* (vast agricultural estates) on land granted by the Portuguese crown or by wresting control of it from local chiefs. This, however, did little more than consolidate power in the hands of individual *prazeiros* (holders of the land grants).

The next major effort by the Portuguese to consolidate their control came in the late 19th century with the establishment of charter companies, operated by private firms who were supposed to develop the land and natural resources within their boundaries. In reality these charter companies operated as independent fiefdoms, and did little to consolidate Portuguese control. Most were also economic failures, and they soon became notorious for labour abuses and for the cruel and appalling conditions under which the local populations within their boundaries were forced to live.

With the onset of the 'Scramble for Africa' in the 1880s, when various European powers competed to assert control over parts of the continent, Portugal was forced to strengthen its claims in the region. In 1891 a British–Portuguese treaty was signed formalising Portuguese control in the area.

The Early 20th Century

One of the most significant events in early-20th-century Mozambique was the large-scale labour migration from the southern provinces to South Africa and Rhodesia (present-day Zimbabwe). This exodus was spurred by expansion of the Witwatersrand goldmines and by passage of a new labour law in 1899. The new law divided the Mozambican population into non-indigenous (*não indígenas* or *assimilados*), who had full Portuguese citizenship rights, and indigenous *(indígenas)*, who were subject to the provisions of colonial law and forced to work, to pay a poll tax and to adhere to passed laws.

Another major development was the growing economic importance of the southern part of the country. As ties with South Africa strengthened, Lourenço Marques (now Maputo) took on increasing importance as a major port and export channel and in the late 19th century the Portuguese transferred the capital here from Mozambique Island.

In the late 1920s António Salazar came to power in Portugal. He sealed off the colonies from non-Portuguese investment, abolished the remaining *prazos* and consolidated Portuguese control over Mozambique. Overall, conditions for Mozambicans worsened considerably.

Mueda Massacre

Discontent with the situation grew and a nationalist consciousness gradually developed. In June 1960, at Mueda in northern Mozambique, an official meeting was held by villagers protesting peacefully about taxes. Portuguese troops opened fire on the crowd, killing many demonstrators. Resentment at the 'massacre of Mueda' helped politicise the local Makonde people and became one of the sparks kindling the independence struggle. External support came from several sources, including Julius Nyerere's government in neighbouring Tanganyika (now Tanzania). In 1962, following a meeting of various political organisations working in exile for Mozambican independence, the Frente pela Libertação de Moçambique (Mozambique Liberation Front; Frelimo) was formed in Dar es Salaam, Tanzania, led by Eduardo Chivambo Mondlane.

The Independence Struggle

Frelimo was plagued by internal divisions from the outset. However, under the leadership of the charismatic Mondlane and operating from bases in Tanzania, it succeeded in giving the liberation movement a structure and in defining a program of political and military action to support its aim of complete independence for Mozambique. On 25 September 1964 Mondlane proclaimed the beginning of the armed struggle for national independence.

In 1969, Mondlane was assassinated by a letter bomb at his office in Dar es Salaam. He was succeeded as president by Frelimo's military commander, Samora Moises Machel. Under Machel, Frelimo sought to extend its area of operations to the south. The Portuguese meanwhile attempted to eliminate rural support for Frelimo by implementing a scorched earth campaign and by resettling people in a series of *aldeamentos* (fortified village complexes).

However, struggles within Portugal's colonial empire and increasing international criticism sapped the government's resources. In 1974, at a ceremony in Lusaka (Zambia), Portugal agreed to hand over power to Frelimo and a transitional government was established. On 25 June 1975 the independent People's Republic of Mozambique was proclaimed with Samora Machel as president and Joaquim Chissano, a founding member of Frelimo's intellectual elite, as prime minister.

Early Years of Independence

The Portuguese pulled out virtually overnight, leaving the country in a state of chaos with few skilled professionals and virtually no infrastructure. Frelimo, which found itself suddenly faced with the task of running the country, threw itself headlong into a policy of radical social change.

Frelimo's socialist program proved unrealistic, and by 1983 the country was almost bankrupt. Onto this scene came the Resistência Nacional de Moçambique (Mozambique National Resistance; Renamo), a ragtag group that had been established in the mid-1970s by Rhodesia (now Zimbabwe) as part of its destabilisation policy, and later kept alive with backing from the South African military and certain sectors in the West.

Ravages of War

Renamo, which had been created by external forces rather than by internal political motives, had no ideology of its own beyond the wholesale destruction of social and communications infrastructure in Mozambique, and destabilisation of the government. Many commentators point out that the war which went on to ravage the country for the next 17 years was thus not a 'civil' war, but one between Mozambique's Frelimo government and Renamo's external backers. Recruitment was sometimes voluntary but frequently by force. Roads, bridges, railways, schools and clinics were destroyed. Atrocities were committed on a horrific scale.

The drought and famine of 1983 crippled the country. Faced with this dire situation, Frelimo opened Mozambique to the West in return for Western aid.

In 1984 South Africa and Mozambique signed the Nkomati Accord, under which South Africa undertook to withdraw its support of Renamo, and Mozambique agreed to expel the African National Congress (ANC) and open the country to South African investment. While Mozambique abided by the agreement, South Africa exploited the situation to the full and Renamo's activity did not diminish.

Samora Machel died in a plane crash in 1986 under questionable circumstances, and was succeeded by the more moderate Joaquim Chissano. The war between the Frelimo government and the Renamo rebels continued, but by the late 1980s political change was sweeping through the region. The collapse of the USSR altered the political balance, and the new president of South Africa, FW de Klerk, made it more difficult for right-wing factions to supply Renamo.

Peace

By the early 1990s, Frelimo had disavowed its Marxist ideology. A ceasefire was arranged, followed by a formal peace agreement in October 1992 and a successful UN-monitored disarmament and demobilisation campaign.

Mozambique Way of Life

You don't need to travel for long in Mozambique before hearing the word *paciência* (patience). It's the great Mozambican virtue and most Mozambicans have it in abundance, with each other and with outsiders. You'll be expected to display some in return, especially in dealings with officialdom; impatience is always counterproductive.

Mozambique is also characterised by its cultural diversity. Each of its 10 provinces has its own unique history, culture and tradition. There has long been an undercurrent of north–south difference, with geographically remote northerners often feeling neglected by powerhouse Maputo, where proximity to South Africa and good road links have pushed economic development along at a rapid pace. Yet this tension has remained low-level. Religious frictions are also minimal, with Christians and Muslims living side by side in a relatively easy coexistence.

Population

There are 16 main ethnic groups, including the Makua (Cabo Delgado, Niassa, Nampula and parts of Zambézia), Makonde (Cabo Delgado), Sena (Sofala, Manica and Tete), and the Ronga and Shangaan (Gaza and Maputo). Smaller groups include the Lomwe and Chuabo (both Zambézia), Yao and Nyanja (Niassa), Mwani (Cabo Delgado), Nyungwe (Tete) and Tswa and Chopi (Inhambane).

TRADITIONAL RELIGIONS & TRADITIONAL HEALERS

Traditional religions based on animist beliefs are widespread in Mozambique. The spirits of the ancestors are often regarded to have significant powers over the destiny of living people. In connection with these beliefs, there are many sacred sites, such as forests, rivers, lakes and mountains, that play important roles in the lives of local communities.

Closely intertwined with traditional religions is the practice of traditional medicine, which is found throughout the country, sometimes in combination with Western medical treatment. *Curandeiros* (traditional healers) are respected and highly sought-after. They are also often relatively well paid, frequently in kind rather than in cash. In some rural areas far from health clinics or a hospital, the *curandeiro* may be the only provider of medical assistance. In addition to *curandeiros,* you may encounter *profetas* (spirit mediums or diviners) and *feticeiros* (witch doctors).

Most markets have a traditional-remedies section selling bird claws, dried leaves and plants, and the like. Diviners often carry a small sack of bones (generally matching male and female parts of the same species) which facilitate communication with the ancestors.

About 1% of Mozambique's population is of Portuguese extraction, most of whom are at least second generation and consider themselves Mozambicans first.

Mozambique's Cuisine

Mozambique's cuisine blends African, Indian and Portuguese influences, and is especially noted for its seafood as well as its use of coconut milk and *piri-piri* (chilli pepper).

Where to Eat

Roadside or market *barracas* (food stalls) serve plates of local food such as *xima* (a maize- or casava-based staple) and sauce for about US$6 or less.

Most towns have a cafe, *pastelaria* or *salão de chá* serving coffee, pastries and inexpensive snacks and light meals such as omelettes, *pregos* (thin steak sandwiches) or burgers.

Restaurant prices and menu offerings are remarkably uniform throughout the country, ranging from about Mtc250 to Mtc400 for meals such as grilled fish or chicken served with rice or potatoes. Most restaurants also offer hearty Portuguese-style soups.

Markets in all larger towns sell an abundance of fresh tropical fruits along with a reasonably good selection of vegetables. High-quality meats from nearby South Africa are sold in delis and supermarkets.

Staples & Specialities

STAPLES

» **Xima or upshwa** A maize- or cassava-based staple (called *xima* or *upshwa*) or rice, served with a sauce of beans, vegetables or fish.

» **Frango grelhado** (grilled chicken) Cheap and easy to find; usually served with chips or rice.

SPECIALITIES

» *matapa* (cassava leaves cooked in a peanut sauce, often with prawns or other additions) in the south

» *galinha á Zambeziana* (chicken with a sauce of lime juice, garlic, pepper and *piri-piri*) in Quelimane and Zambézia provinces

» *caril* (curry) dishes

» *chamusas* (samosas; triangular wedges of fried pastry, filled with meat or vegetables) and *rissois de camarão* (similar to *chamusas* but semicircular, and with a shrimp filling)

» grilled prawns, lobster and crayfish, *lulas* (calamari) and other seafood

» fresh bread rolls

» *peixe grelhada* (grilled fish), which are delicious and served with rice or chips

» *prego* (thin steak sandwich)

DRINKS

» *Água mineral* (bottled water) is widely available

» *Refrescos* or 'sodas' (soft drinks) are widely available

» Beer Manica, Laurentina, Dois M (2M), plus South African and Namibian beers; sold by the *garafa* (bottle) or *lata* (can).

» Wine (*vinho*) Portuguese and south African wines are widely available

» Juice (*sumo*) Nonsweetened fruit juices from South Africa are widely available

The Arts

Dance

On Mozambique Island and along the northern coast, watch for *tufo* (a dance of Arabic origin). It is generally performed by women, wearing matching *capulanas* (sarongs) and scarves, and accompanied by drums (some more like tambourines) known as *taware*.

In the south, one of the best-known dances, particularly in Maputo, is *makwaela*, characterised by a cappella singing accompanied by foot percussion.

A good place to get information on traditional dance performances are the *casas de cultura* (cultural centres), found in every provincial capital.

Literature

During the colonial era, local literature generally focused on nationalist themes. Two of the most famous poets of this period were Rui de Noronha and Noémia de Sousa.

In the late 1940s José Craveirinha (1922–2003) began to write poetry focusing on the social reality of the Mozambican people and calling for resistance and rebellion, which eventually led to his arrest. Today, he is honoured as Mozambique's greatest poet, and his work, including 'Poem of the Future Citizen,' is recognised worldwide.

As the armed independence struggle gained strength, Frelimo freedom fighters began to write poems reflecting their life in the forest, their marches and the ambushes. One of the finest of these guerrilla poets was Marcelino dos Santos.

With Mozambican independence in 1975, writers and poets felt able to produce literature without interference. This new-found freedom was soon shattered by Frelimo's war against the Renamo rebels, but new writers emerged, including the internationally acclaimed Mia Couto, whose works include *Voices Made Night* and *The Last Flight of the Flamingo*. Contemporary female writers include Lilia Momple (*The Eyes of the Green Cobra*) and Paulina Chiziane (*Niketche – A Story of Polygamy*).

Music

The *timbila* orchestras of the Chopi people in southern Mozambique (see p172) are one of the country's best-known musical traditions.

Modern music flourishes in the cities and the live music scene in Maputo is excellent. *Marrabenta* is considered Mozambique's national music. It developed in the 1950s in the suburbs of Maputo (then Lourenço Marques) and has a light, upbeat style and distinctive beat inspired by the traditional rural *majika* rhythms of Gaza and Maputo provinces. It is often accompanied by a dance of the same name.

Sculpture & Painting

Mozambique is known for its woodcarvings, particularly for the sandalwood carvings found in the south and the ebony carvings of the Makonde.

The country's most famous painter is Malangatana Valente Ngwenya – universally known as Malangatana – whose style is characterised by dramatic figures and flamboyant yet restrained use of colour, and by its highly symbolic social and political commentary. Other internationally acclaimed artists include Bertina Lopes and Roberto Chichorro.

Mozambique's Natural Environment

Mozambique has extensive coastal lowlands forming a broad plain 100km to 200km wide in the south and leaving it vulnerable to seasonal flooding. In the north, this plain narrows and the terrain rises to mountains and plateaus on the borders with Zimbabwe, Zambia and Malawi. In central Mozambique, the predominant geographical feature is the Zambezi River valley and its wide delta plains. In many areas of the north, particularly in Nampula and Niassa provinces, towering granite outcrops or inselbergs dominate the landscape.

Wildlife

ANIMALS

While more than 200 types of mammals wander the interior, challenging access, dense vegetation and skittishness on the part of the animals can make spotting difficult, and Mozambique shouldn't be viewed as a 'Big Five' destination. Work is proceeding in reviving several parks and reserves, especially Gorongosa National Park, which offers Mozambique's most accessible wildlife watching.

BIRDS

Of the approximately 900 bird species that have been identified in the southern Africa region, close to 600 have been recorded in Mozambique. Among these are numerous aquatic species found primarily in the southern wetlands. On Inhaca Island alone, 300 bird species have been recorded. Rare and unique species (most of which are found in isolated montane habitats such as the Chimanimani Mountains, Mt Gorongosa and Mt Namúli) include the dappled mountain robin, the chirinda apalis, Swynnerton's forest robin, the olive-headed weaver and the green-headed oriole.

MARINE LIFE

Coastal waters host populations of dolphins, including spinner, bottlenose, humpback and striped dolphins, plus loggerhead, leatherback, green, hawksbill and olive ridley marine turtles. The coast also serves as a winter breeding ground for the humpback whale, which is found primarily between Ponta d'Ouro and Inhambane. Between July and October, it's also common to see whales in the north, offshore from Pemba.

Dugongs have been sighted around Inhambane Bay, Angoche, Mozambique Island, Nacala and the Quirimbas and Bazaruto Archipelagos.

Plants

Almost 6000 plant species have been recorded, including an estimated 250 that are thought to be found nowhere else in the world. The Maputaland Centre of Plant Diversity, straddling the border with South Africa south of Maputo, is one of the most important areas of the country in terms of plant diversity and has been classified as a site of global botanical significance. The Chimanimani Mountains are also notable for their plant diversity, with at least 45 endemic species. Other important highland areas include Mt Namúli, the Gorongosa Massif, Mt Chiperone (western Zambézia province) and Mt Mabu.

National Parks & Reserves

Mozambique has six national parks: Gorongosa, Zinave, Banhine and Limpopo in the interior; Bazaruto National Park offshore; and Quirimbas National Park, encompassing both coastal and inland areas in Cabo Delgado province. Zinave and Banhine have no tourist infrastructure.

Wildlife reserves include Niassa, Marromeu, Pomene, Maputo and Gilé. The Chimanimani National Reserve has a network of rustic camps for hikers.

Environmental Issues

From rampaging elephants that destroy farmers' crops to massive flooding and the plundering of natural resources by unscrupulous timber harvesters and commercial fishing operators, Mozambique's challenges in preserving its ecosystems read like a high-adventure novel. Fortunately these natural resources have come increasingly into the international spotlight, and great strides have been made in protecting the country's wealth.

Highlights include the creation of Quirimbas National Park, the extension of Bazaruto National Park, and ongoing efforts to declare a new protected marine area around the Primeiras and Segundas Islands.

SURVIVAL GUIDE

Directory A–Z

Accommodation

» Accommodation along the coast, especially in the south, fills during Christmas and New Year's, Easter and

MOZAMBIQUE'S COASTAL LAKES

Mozambique is one of two countries in East Africa with major coastal barrier lakes or lagoons (the other being Madagascar). The lakes are separated from the sea by well-developed longshore dune systems, and most are no more than 5m deep. They include Uembje Lagoon at Bilene, Lake Inhampavala north of Xai-Xai, Lake Quissico, just east of Quissico town, and Lake Poelela, about 30km north of Quissico and traversed by the N1.

With the exception of Uembje, none of the lakes have links with the sea and their brackish waters are rich with marine and birdlife. These include numerous freshwater fish species, and white storks, little egrets and pink flamingos. At Lake Quissico alone, between 50 and 60 bird species have been recorded.

SACRED FORESTS

An example of the contributions made by local traditions to biodiversity conservation is seen in the foothills of the Chimanimani Mountains. Communities here recognise various types of sacred areas. One is the *dzimbahwe* (chief's compound), where each chiefdom has its own spot, generally in a densely forested area, and access is strictly limited. Another is the *gwasha*, a forest area used by chiefs, elders and spirit mediums for rainmaking and other ceremonies. Both the *dzimbahwe* and the *gwasha* are treated with great respect and no development, wood cutting or harvesting are permitted. Hunting is under the control of the chiefs, as is the gathering of medicinal and other plants.

other South African school holidays (all of which are considered 'high season'); book accommodation in advance.

» Always ask about low season (ie, during the February to April rainy months) and children's discounts.

» When quoting prices, many establishments distinguish between a *duplo* (room with two twin beds) and a *casal* (double bed).

» Rates are often quoted in US dollars or South African rand. Payment can almost always be made in meticais, dollars or rand.

» In this chapter, the following price ranges refer to a double room in high sesason:

$ Less than Mtc1250

$$ Mtc1250 to Mtc3750

$$$ More than Mtc3750

BACKPACKERS LODGES

Backpacker lodges ('backpackers') offer dorm beds (average cost Mtc400), private rooms, cooking facilities and, sometimes, campsites. They're always worth seeking out and are usually the best-value budget accommodation.

CAMPING

» There are many camping grounds. Carry a tent to save money, and for travel in rural areas. Per person prices: Mtc150 to Mtc250 per night.

» Officially, camping is permitted only in designated areas. Where there is no established campsite, ask the local *régulo* (chief) for permission to camp; you'll invariably be welcomed, and should reciprocate with a modest token of thanks (eg what you would pay at an official camping ground or a bit less).

HOTELS & PENSÕES

» The cheapest hotels *(pensão,* singular, or *pensões,* plural) may have a bucket bath, probably won't have air-conditioning and may or may not have electricity.

» At the midrange level, expect private bathroom, hot running water, electricity, air-conditioning (sometimes) and a restaurant on the premises. Top-end hotels come with all the amenities, at a price.

SELF-CATERING & RENTALS

Many coastal places offer self-catering options, with a kitchenette or *braai* (barbecue) area, kitchen utensils and sometimes plug points. Some supply bed linens, mosquito nets and towels; for others you'll need to bring these yourself. Some also have a restaurant.

Activities

BIRDWATCHING

Prime birding areas include the following:

» Bazaruto Archipelago

» Gorongosa National Park and Mt Gorongosa

» Chimanimani Mountains

» Mt Namúli

» Maputo Special Reserve

» Area around Catapu, near Caia.

Useful websites with bird lists and announcements of regional birding activities include the following:

Avian Demography Unit (http://web.uct.ac.za/depts/stats/adu/p_mozat.htm)

Indicator Birding (www.birding.co.za)

BOOK YOUR STAY ONLINE

For more accommodation reviews by Lonely Planet authors, check out http://hotels.lonelyplanet.com.

You'll find independent reviews, as well as recommendations on the best places to stay. Best of all, you can book online.

PRACTICALITIES

- **Currency** New Mozambican Metical (Mtc)
- **Newspapers** *Notícias* and *Diário de Moçambique* (dailies); *Savanna* (weekly). Mozambique News Agency (AIM; www.poptel.org.uk/mozambique-news) website for English-language news
- **TV** TVM (www.tvm.co.mz; state run), RTK (commercial), RTPI (Portuguese TV)
- **Weights & measures** Metric system

Southern African Birding (www.sabirding.co.za)

African Bird Club (www.africanbirdclub.org)

DIVING & SNORKELLING

Attractions include the chance to sight dolphins, whale sharks, manta rays and dugongs; opportunities to discover new sites; the natural beauty of the Mozambican coast; seasonal humpback whale sighting; excellent fish diversity; and a generally untouched array of hard and soft corals, especially in the north. You'll also have most spots almost to yourself.

Equipment, instruction and certification are available in Ponta d'Ouro, Závora, Tofo, Vilankulo, the Bazaruto Archipelago, Nacala, Pemba and the Quirimbas Archipelago. Prices are comparable to elsewhere in East Africa, although somewhat higher than in South Africa.

HIKING

Mountain climbs include Mt Gorongosa and Mt Namúli. For hiking, head to the Chimanimani Mountains, which is where you'll find Mt Binga, Mozambique's highest peak. The hills around Gurúè offer good walking.

SURFING & KITE SURFING

The best waves are at Ponta d'Ouro in the far south of the country and at Tofinho. Boards can be rented at both places.

Kite surfing has a small but growing following in Mozambique, especially in the north near Pemba, and around Vilankulo. A good initial contact is **Pirate Kites** (www.murrebue.com).

WILDLIFE WATCHING

The main wildlife-watching destination is Gorongosa National Park. Other possibilities include Niassa Reserve, Maputo Special Reserve and Limpopo National Park. Apart from Gorongosa, the chances of spotting significant wildlife are small, and Mozambique shouldn't be considered a 'Big Five' destination.

Business Hours

Banks 8am to 3pm Monday to Friday

Foreign exchange bureaus (*casas de câmbio*) 8.30am to 5pm Monday to Friday, 8.30am to noon Saturday

Government offices 7.30am to 3.30pm Monday to Friday

Eating Breakfast 6am to 11am, lunch noon to 3pm, dinner 6pm to 10.30pm

Drinking 5pm to late

Shopping 8am to noon and 2pm to 6pm Monday to Friday, 8am to 1pm Saturday

Children

- The main considerations for travel here will likely be the scarcity of decent medical facilities, the length and discomfort involved in many road journeys, the challenge of maintaining a balanced diet outside the major towns, and the difficulty of finding clean bathrooms outside of midrange and top-end hotels.
- The beaches are ideal for visiting with young children. Many resorts have swimming pools and most offer kids' discounts.
- In beach areas, be aware of the risk of hookworm infestation in populated areas, as well as the risk of bilharzia in lakes. Other things to watch out for include sea urchins at the beach (beach shoes are a good idea for children and adults) and thorns in the bush.
- Bring mosquito nets from home for your children and ensure that they sleep under them. Also bring mosquito repellent from home, and check with your doctor regarding the use of malaria prophylactics. Long-sleeved shirts and trousers are the best protection at dawn and dusk.

PRACTICALITIES

Cots & spare beds Easily arranged; average cost Mtc500

Child seats for hired cars Occasionally available; confirm in advance

High chairs Occasionally available

Formula, disposable nappies & wet wipes Available in pharmacies, large supermarkets and markets in larger towns

Child care Easy to arrange informally through your hotel

Customs Regulations

» It's illegal to export any endangered species or their products, including anything made from ivory or tortoiseshell.

» Reasonable' quantities of souvenirs for personal (rather than commercial) purposes can be exported without declaration.

Electricity

Electricity is 220V to 240V AC, 50Hz, usually accessed with South African–style three-round-pin plugs or two-round-pin plugs.

Embassies & Consulates

All of the following embassies are located in Maputo. The closest Australian representation is in South Africa.

Canadian High Commission (Map p150; ☎21-492623; www.canadainternational.gc.ca/mozambique; 1138 Avenida Kenneth Kaunda) **Dutch Embassy** (Map p150; ☎21-484200; http://mozambique.nlembassy.org; 324 Avenida Kwame Nkrumah)

French Embassy (Map p150; ☎21-484600; www.ambafrance-mz.org; 2361 Avenida Julius Nyerere)

German Embassy (Map p150; ☎21-482700; www.maputo.diplo.de; 506 Rua Damião de Gois)

Irish Embassy (Map p150; ☎21-491440; maputoembassy@dfa.ie; 3332 Avenida Julius Nyerere)

Malawian High Commission (Map p150; ☎21-492676; 75 Avenida Kenneth Kaundam)

Portuguese Embassy (Map p150; ☎21-490316; www.embpormaputo.org.mz; 720 Avenida Julius Nyerere)

South African High Commission (Map p150; ☎21-243000; www.dfa.gov.za/foreign/sa_abroad/sam.htm; 41 Avenida Eduardo Mondlane)

Swazi High Commission (Map p150; ☎21-491601; swazimoz@teledata.mz; 1271 Rua Luís Pasteur) Located behind the Netherlands Embassy.

Tanzanian High Commission (Map p150; ☎21-490110/3, 21-491051; ujamaa@zebra.uem.mz; 852 Avenida Mártires de Machava) Near the corner of Avenida Eduardo Mondlane.

UK High Commission (Map p150; ☎82-313 8580; http://ukinmozambique.fco.gov.uk; 310 Avenida Vladimir Lenine)

US Embassy (Map p150; ☎21-492797; http://maputo.usembassy.gov; 193 Avenida Kenneth Kaunda)

Zambian High Commission (Map p150; ☎21-492452; 1286 Avenida Kenneth Kaunda)

Zimbabwean High Commission (Map p150; ☎21-486499, 21-490404; 1657 Avenida Mártires de Machava)

Food

In this chapter, the following price ranges refer to a standard main course.

$ Less than Mtc250

$$ Mtc250 to Mtc500

$$$ More than Mtc500

Legal Matters

» The use or possession of recreational drugs is illegal in Mozambique. If you're offered anything, it is often a set-up, usually involving police, and if you're caught, penalties are very stiff. At the least, expect to pay a large bribe to avoid arrest or imprisonment (which is a very real risk).

» If you're arrested for more 'legitimate' reasons, you have the right to talk with someone from your embassy, as well as a lawyer, though don't expect this to help you out of your situation with any rapidity.

» Driving on the beach, driving without a seatbelt (for all passengers), exceeding speed limits, driving while using your mobile phone, turning without using your indicator lights, and driving without carrying two red hazard triangles and a reflective vest in the boot are all illegal, and can often attract police attention and demands for a bribe or *multa* (fine).

Maps

Excellent Coopération Française maps cover Maputo, Beira, Quelimane, Nampula and Pemba; check at the local municipal council. Also useful are Reise Know-How's *Mosambik & Malawi* and Globetrotter's *Mozambique* map.

Tracks for Africa (www.tracks4africa.co.za) Downloadable GPS maps for self-drivers in the bush.

Instituto Nacional de Hidrografia e Navegação (Inahina; ☎21-429108, 21-429240;

DOCUMENTS

All foreigners are required to carry a copy of their passport when out and about.

Rather than carrying the original, carry a notarised copy of the name and visa pages, plus notarised copies of your drivers license and other essential documents. If you're stopped on the street or at a checkpoint and asked for any of these, always hand over the notarised copy, rather than parting with the original, and always insist on going to the nearest police station *(esquadrão).* The more you can do to minimise the impression that you're a newly arrived tourist, the lower your chances of getting stopped for a document check.

Notary facilities are available in Maputo and provincial capitals; see the town listings, or ask at your hotel for a recommendation. Some Mozambique embassies will also provide this service before you travel.

Rua Marques de Pombal, Maputo) Coastal and maritime maps *(cartas náuticas)* and tide tables (*tabelas de marés*); at the *capitania*, behind the white Safmar building near the port.

Direcção Nacional de Geografia e Cadastro (Dinageca; ☎21-302555; 537 Avenida Josina Machel, Maputo) Detailed topographical maps.

Money

» Mozambique's currency is the metical (plural *meticais,* pronounced 'meticaish') nova família, abbreviated in this chapter as Mtc. Note denominations include Mtc20, Mtc50, Mtc100, Mtc200, Mtc500 and Mtc1000, and coins include Mtc1, Mtc2, Mtc5 and Mtc10.

» One metical is equivalent to 100 centavos (Ct), and there are also coins of Ct1, Ct5, Ct10, Ct20 and Ct50, plus a few old metical coins (not acceptable as tender) floating around.

» Visa card withdrawal from ATMs is the best way of accessing money.

» Carry a standby mixture of US dollars (or South African rand, especially in the south) and meticais (including a good supply of small denomination notes, as nobody ever has change) for times when an ATM is nonexistent or not working.

ATMS

» All larger and many smaller towns have ATMs for accessing cash meticais. Most of them (including Barclays, BCI and Standard Bank) accept Visa card only; Millennium BIM machines also accept Mastercard.

» Many machines have a limit of Mtc3000 (US$120) per transaction. BCI's limit is Mtc5000 (US$200) and some Standard Bank machines dispense up to Mtc10,000 (US$400) per transaction.

CASH

» US dollars are easily exchanged everywhere; together with South African rand (which are especially useful in southern Mozambique), they are the best currency to carry.

» Only new-design US dollar bills will be accepted. Euros are easy to change in major cities, but elsewhere you're likely to get a poor exchange rate.

» Most banks don't charge commission for changing cash, and together with foreign exchange bureaus, these are the best places to change money. BCI branches are generally good. Many Millennium BIM branches will let you change cash only if you have an account.

» *Casas de câmbio* (foreign exchange bureaus) usually give a rate equivalent to or slightly higher than the banks, and are open longer hours.

» Changing money on the street isn't safe anywhere and is illegal; asking shopkeepers is a better bet.

CREDIT CARDS

» Credit cards are accepted at most (but not all) top-end hotels, many midrange places, especially in the south, and at some car-hire agencies, but otherwise are of limited use in Mozambique.

» Visa is by far the most useful, and is also the main (often only) card for accessing money from ATMs.

TIPPING & BARGAINING

In low-budget bars and restaurants tipping is generally not expected, other than perhaps rounding up the bill. At upmarket and tourist establishments, tipping is customary (from 10% to 20%, assuming service has been good). Tips are also warranted, and always appreciated, if someone has gone out of their way to do something for you.

TRAVELLERS CHEQUES

Travellers cheques can only be exchanged with difficulty (try BCI) and with a high commission plus original purchase receipts. Nowhere accepts travellers cheques as direct payment.

Public Holidays

New Year's Day 1 January

Mozambican Heroes' Day 3 February

Women's Day 7 April

International Workers' Day 1 May

Independence Day 25 June

Lusaka Agreement/Victory Day 7 September

Revolution Day 25 September

Peace & Reconciliation Day 4 October

Christmas/Family Day 25 December

For South African school holiday dates see the calendar link at www.saschools.co.za.

Safe Travel

Mozambique is a relatively safe place and most travellers shouldn't have any difficulties. That said, there are a few areas where caution is warranted.

CRIME

» Petty theft and robbery are the main risks: watch your pockets or bag in markets; don't leave personal belongings unguarded on the beach or elsewhere; and minimise (or eliminate) trappings such as jewellery, watches, headsets and external money pouches.

» If you leave your vehicle unguarded, don't be surprised if windscreen wipers and other accessories are gone when you return. Don't leave anything inside a parked vehicle.

» When at stoplights or slowed in traffic, keep your windows up and doors locked, and don't leave anything on the seat next to you where it could be snatched.

» In Maputo and southern Mozambique (due to the proximity of South African organised-crime rings) carjackings and more violent robberies do occur, although most incidents can be avoided by taking the usual precautions: avoid driving at night; keep the passenger windows up and the doors locked if you are in a vehicle (including taxis) at any time during the day or night; don't wander around isolated or dark streets; avoid walking alone or in a group at dusk or at night, particularly in isolated areas or on isolated stretches of beach; and avoid isolating situations in general. At all times of day, try to stick to busier areas of town, especially if you are alone, and don't walk alone along the beach away from hotel areas. If you're driving and your car is hijacked, hand over the keys immediately.

» When riding on chapas or buses, keep your valuables well inside your clothes to avoid falling victim to unscrupulous entrepreneurs who take advantage of overcrowded conditions to pick their fellow passengers' pockets.

» All this said, don't let these warnings deter you, simply be a savvy traveller. The vast majority of visitors travel through this beautiful country without incident.

HASSLES & BRIBES

More likely than violent crime are simple hassles with underpaid authorities in search of a bribe. The worst offenders here are regular (ie, gray uniformed non-traffic) police. If you get stopped you should not have any problem as long as your papers are in order. Being friendly, respectful and patient helps (you won't get anywhere otherwise), as does trying to give the impression that you know what you're doing and aren't new in the country. Sometimes the opposite tack is also helpful – feigning complete ignorance if you're told that you've violated some regulation, and apologising profusely. It's also worth remembering that only traffic police are authorised to stop you for traffic infractions. If stopped, keep in mind that you can request to wait until a traffic police arrives. Often this will diffuse the bribe attempt.

» If you are asked to pay a *multa* (fine) for a trumped-up charge, playing the game a bit (asking to speak to the supervisor or *chefe,* and requesting a receipt) helps to counteract some of the more blatant attempts, as does insisting on going to the nearest *esquadrão* (police station); you should always do these things anyway.

LANDMINES

Thanks to a massive demining effort, many of the unexploded landmines littering Mozambique (a legacy of the country's long war) have been eliminated; however, mines are still a risk in a few areas. To be on the safe side, stick to well-used paths, including on roadsides in rural areas, and don't free camp or go wandering off into the bush without first seeking local advice.

Areas that should always be avoided include the bases of bridges, old schools or abandoned buildings, and water tanks or other structures.

Telephone

Mobile phone numbers are seven digits, preceded by 82 for Mcel, 84 for Vodafone and 86 for Movitel.

Do not use an initial zero; seven-digit mobile numbers listed with zero at the outset are in South Africa, and must be preceded by the South Africa country code (27) when dialling.

All companies have outlets in major towns where you can buy Sim-card starter packs (Mtc50), fill out the necessary registration form, and buy top-up cards.

TELEPHONE CODES

Country code 258

International dialling code 00

Land-line area codes Included with all numbers in this chapter; must be used whenever dialling long-distance. As with mobile numbers, there is no initial zero.

Time

Mozambique time is GMT/UTC plus two hours. There is no daylight savings.

Visas

» Visas are required by all visitors except citizens of South Africa, Swaziland, Zambia, Tanzania, Botswana, Malawi, Mauritius and Zimbabwe.

» Single-entry visas (only) are available at most land and air entry points (but not anywhere along the Tanzania border) for Mtc2085 (or the US dollar equivalent) for one month.

» To avoid long visa lines at busy borders, or for a multiple-entry visa, arrange your visa in advance. If you're arriving in Maputo via bus from Johannesburg (South Africa) it's recommended (though not essential) to get your visa in advance.

» Fees vary according to where you buy your visa and how quickly you need it. The maximum initial length of stay available is three months. Same-day visa service is available at several places including Johannesburg and Nelspruit (South Africa), but at a price.

» No matter where you get your visa, your passport must be valid for at least six months from the dates of intended travel, and have at least three blank pages.

» For citizens of countries not requiring visas, visits are limited to 30 days from the date of entry, after which you'll need to exit Mozambique and re-enter.

» The length of each stay for multiple-entry visas is determined when the visa is issued, and varies from embassy to embassy; only single-entry and transit visas are available at Mozambique's borders.

VISA EXTENSIONS

» Visas can be extended at the *migração* (immigration office) in all provincial capitals provided you haven't exceeded the three-month maximum stay, at a cost of Mtc2085 for one month.

» Processing takes from two days (with payment of an approximately Mtc200 supplemental express fee) to one week.

» Don't wait until the visa has expired, as extensions are not granted automatically; hefty fines are levied for overstays.

Getting There & Away

Entering the Country

A valid passport and visa are required to enter, and a yellow fever vaccination certificate if coming from an infected area.

Air

AIRPORTS

Maputo International (MPM) Mozambique's modern main airport

Vilankulo (VNX) Regional flights

Beira (BEW) Regional flights

Nampula (APL) Regional flights

Moçimboa da Praia (MZB) Regional flights

Pemba (POL) Regional flights

AIRLINES

Coastal Aviation (safari@coastal.co.tz) Dar es Salaam (Tanzania) to Moçimboa da

Praia, with connections to Pemba and the Quirimbas Archipelago.

Federal Air (www.fedair.com) Johannesburg (South Africa) to Vilankulo via Kruger Mpumalanga International Airport.

Kenya Airways (www.kenya-airways.com) Nairobi to Maputo.

Linhas Aéreas de Moçambique (LAM; www.lam.co.mz) Domestic routes plus flights between Johannesburg, Maputo, Vilankulo and Beira; Dar es Salaam, Pemba and Nampula; Lisbon (Portugal) and Maputo.

SAAirlink (www.flyairlink.com) Johannesburg to Beira, Nampula and Pemba; Durban to Maputo.

South African Airways (www.flysaa.com) Johannesburg to Maputo.

TAP Air Portugal (www.flytap.com) Lisbon to Maputo.

Land

MALAWI

Border Crossings

Cóbuè On Lake Niassa

Dedza 85km southwest of Lilongwe

Entre Lagos Southwest of Cuamba

Mandimba Northwest of Cuamba

Melosa (Milange) 120km southeast of Blantyre

Metangula On Lake Niassa

Vila Nova da Fronteira At Malawi's southern tip

Zóbuè On the Tete Corridor route linking Blantyre (Malawi) and Harare (Zimbabwe); this is the busiest crossing

To/From Blantyre

Via Zóbuè: vehicles go daily from Blantyre to the border via Mwanza. Once in Mozambique (the border posts are separated by about 5km of no man's land), *chapas* go daily to Tete (Mtc150, 1½ hours Zóbuè to Tete).

Via Vila Nova da Fronteira: daily minibuses go from Blantyre to Nsanje and onto the border. Once across, there are *chapas* to Mutarara, and from there to Sena and onto Caia on the main north–south road.

Via Melosa (about 2km from Milange town, and convenient for Quelimane and Gurúè): buses go from Blantyre via Mulanje to the border. Once across, several vehicles go daily to Mocuba, from where there is frequent transport south to Quelimane and north to Nampevo junction (for Gurúè) and Nampula.

Entre Lagos (for Cuamba and northern Mozambique): possible with your own 4WD (allow about 1½ hours to cover the 80km from Entre Lagos to Cuamba), or by *chapa* (about 2½ hours between the border and Cuamba). On the Malawi side, minibuses go from the border to Liwonde. Another option: the weekly Malawi train between the border and Liwonde (currently Thursday morning from Liwonde to Nayuchi on the border, and from Nayuchi back to Liwonde that same afternoon). There is basic accommodation at Entre Lagos if you get stuck.

Via Mandimba: Malawian transport goes frequently to Mangochi, where you can get minibuses to Namwera, and onto the border at Chiponde. Once in Mozambique (moto-taxis bridge the approximately 1.5km of no man's land for Mtc50, and then vehicles take you to Mandimba town), several vehicles daily go from Mandimba to both Cuamba (three hours) and Lichinga.

To/From Lilongwe

The **Dedza** border is linked with the N103 to/from Tete by a scenic tarmac road. From Tete, there's at least one *chapa* daily to Vila Ulongwé and on to Dedza. Otherwise, go in stages from Tete via Moatize and the junction about 15km southwest of Zóbuè. Once across, it's easy to find transport for the final 85km to Lilongwe.

SOUTH AFRICA

Border Crossings

Giriyondo (8am–4pm October–March, to 3pm April–September) 75km west of Massingir town, 95km from Kruger's Phalaborwa Gate

Kosi Bay–Ponta d'Ouro (8am–4pm) 11km south of Ponta d'Ouro

Lebombo–Ressano Garcia (6am–10pm) Northwest of Maputo; very busy

Pafuri (6am–5.30pm) 11km east of Pafuri Camp in Kruger National Park

CLIMATE CHANGE & TRAVEL

Every form of transport that relies on carbon-based fuel generates CO_2, the main cause of human-induced climate change. Modern travel is dependent on aeroplanes, which might use less fuel per kilometre per person than most cars but travel much greater distances. The altitude at which aircraft emit gases (including CO_2) and particles also contributes to their climate change impact. Many websites offer 'carbon calculators' that allow people to estimate the carbon emissions generated by their journey and, for those who wish to do so, to offset the impact of the greenhouse gases emitted with contributions to portfolios of climate-friendly initiatives throughout the world. Lonely Planet offsets the carbon footprint of all staff and author travel.

To/From Nelspruit & Johannesburg

Large 'luxury' buses do the route daily (US$40 to US$50 one way, nine to 10 hours). All lines also service Pretoria. It's best to organise your Mozambique visa in advance, although most of the companies will take you without a visa. The risk: if lines at the border are long, the bus may not wait, in which case you'll need to take a *chapa* the remaining 85km to Maputo.

Cheetah Express (84-444 3024, 21-486 3222; Av Eduardo Mondlane) Daily between Maputo and Nelspruit (Mtc1100 one way), departing Maputo at 7am from Avenida Eduardo Mondlane next to Mundo's, and departing Nelspruit at about 4pm from Mediclinic, Crossings and Riverside Mall.

Greyhound (in South Africa 083-915 9000; www.greyhound.co.za) Daily from Johannesburg's Park Station complex at 8am and 10pm, and from Maputo at 7am and 7pm.

Luciano Luxury Coach (84-860 2100, in South Africa 83-993 4897) Daily except Sunday from Johannesburg (Hotel Oribi, 24 Bezuidenhout Ave, Troyville) at 5pm; from Maputo daily except Saturday at 9pm.

Translux (in South Africa 011-774 3333; www.translux.co.za) Daily from Johannesburg at 8.45am; from Maputo at 7.45am.

To/From Kruger National Park

Neither the Pafuri nor the Giriyondo crossing is accessible via public transport. Visas are available on both sides of both borders. Officially, you're required to have a 4WD to cross both borders, and a 4WD is essential for the Pafuri border, which crosses the Limpopo River near Mapai (for which there is a makeshift ferry during the rains). Allow two days between Pafuri and Vilankulo. **Nhanfule Campsite** (per person US$6) at Limpopo National Park's Mapai entry gate has hot-water showers.

Note that if you are entering/leaving South Africa via Giriyondo, you will be required to show proof of payment of one night's lodging within the Great Limpopo Transfrontier Park (ie, either in Limpopo National Park or South Africa's Kruger park) to fulfil SANParks' requirement for one compulsory overnight within the transfrontier park for all visitors.

To/From Durban

Luciano Luxury Coach (84-860 2100, in South Africa 83-993 4897) goes between Maputo and Durban via Namaacha and Big Bend in Swaziland (Mtc1110, nine hours) departing Maputo at 6.30am Tuesday and Friday and Durban (Pavillion Hotel, North Beach) at 6.30am Wednesday and Sunday.

To/From Ponta d'Ouro

For travel via the Kosi Bay border post, see our Ponta D'ouro coverage (p167).

SWAZILAND

Border Crossings

Goba–Mhlumeni (7am–8pm) Southwest of Maputo

Lomahasha–Namaacha (7am–8pm) In Swaziland's extreme northeastern corner

To/From Manzini

While there are at least one or two direct *chapas* daily between Maputo and Manzini (about Mtc350), it's faster and cheaper to take a *chapa* between Maputo and Namaacha (Mtc70, 1½ hours), walk across the border, and then get Swaziland transport on the other side (about US$6 and three hours from the border to Manzini).

For self-drivers, the Namaacha border is notoriously slow on holiday weekends; the quiet border at Goba (Goba Fronteira), reached via a scenic, winding road from Maputo, is a good alternative. The road from Swaziland's Mananga border, connecting north to Lebombo–Ressano Garcia, is another option.

TANZANIA

Border Crossings

For all Mozambique–Tanzania posts it is essential to arrange your Mozambique (or Tanzania) visa in advance.

Kilambo 130km north of Moçimboa da Praia, and called Namiranga or Namoto on the Mozambique side

Moçimboa da Praia (Mozambique) Immigration and customs for those arriving by plane or dhow

Mtambaswala/Negomano Unity Bridge

Mtomoni Unity Bridge 2; 120km south of Songea (Tanzania)

Palma (Mozambique) Immigration and customs for those arriving by dhow

To/From Mtwara

Vehicles go daily from 6am from Mtwara (Tanzania) to Kilambo (Tsh4000, one hour) and on to the Rovuma, which is crossed via a combination of walking and dugout canoe (Tsh5000, 10 minutes to over an hour, depending on water levels, and dangerous during heavy rains). The border is a rough one, and it's common for touts to demand up to 10 times the 'real' price for the boat crossing, and for boat captains to stop mid-river and demand higher fees than those that have already been agreed upon. Watch your belongings, especially when getting into and out of the boats, and keep up with the crowd.

Once in Mozambique, several pick-ups go daily to the Mozambique border crossing (4km further) and on to Moçimboa da Praia (Mtc250, two hours).

Depending on water levels, it is sometimes possible to arrange to take your vehicle across the Rovuma at Kilambo via dugout canoes strapped together by local entrepreneurs. This is obviously risky. And, it's potentially expensive (from US$100 to US$400 for the crossing depending on your negotiating skills).

To/From Masasi

The main vehicle crossing over the Rovuma is via the Unity Bridge at Negomano (7.30am–4pm in Mozambique, 8.30am–5pm in Tanzania), near the confluence of the Lugenda River. From Masasi, go 35km southwest along the Tunduru road to Nangomba village, from where a good 68km track leads down to Masuguru village. The bridge is 10km further at Mtambaswala. Once over, there is 160km on a bush track with fine, deep, red dust (mud during the rains, and often blocked by trucks). This track continues through low land bordering the Rovuma before climbing up to Ngapa (shown as Moçimboa do Rovuma on some maps), where there is a customs and immigration checkpoint, as well as stunning views down over the Rovuma River basin. From Ngapa to Mueda is 40km further on a reasonable dirt road (four to six hours from the bridge to Mueda, longer during the rains).

There's a daily *chapa* from Masasi to Mtambaswala (Tsh5000) each morning. On the other side, a *chapa* leaves Negomano by about 1pm for Mueda (Mtc500). Going in the other direction, if you arrive at Mtambaswala after the *chapa* for Masasi has left (it doesn't always coordinate with the vehicle arriving from Mueda), there are some basic guesthouses for sleeping.

To/From Songea

One or two vehicles daily depart from Majengo C area in Songea (Tsh10,000, three to four hours) to Mtomoni village and the Unity 2 bridge. Once across, take Mozambique transport to Lichinga (Tsh25,000, five hours). Pay in stages, rather than paying the entire Tsh35,000 Songea–Lichinga fare in Songea, as is sometimes requested.

ZAMBIA

Border Crossings

Cassacatiza (7am–5pm) 290km northwest of Tete; main crossing

Zumbo (7am–5pm) At the western end of Lake Cahora Bassa

To/From Zambia

The **Cassacatiza–Chanida** border is seldom used as most travellers combining Mozambique and Zambia go via Malawi. *Chapas* go daily from **Tete** to Matema, from where there's sporadic transport to the border. On the other side, there are daily vehicles to Katete (Zambia), and then on to Lusaka or Chipata.

The rarely used crossing at **Zumbo** is accessed with difficulty from Mozambique via Fíngoę and is of interest primarily to anglers and birdwatchers heading to the western reaches of Lake Cahora Bassa.

ZIMBABWE

Border Crossings

Espungabera In the Chimanimani Mountains

Machipanda On the Beira Corridor linking Harare with the sea

Mukumbura (7am–5pm) West of Tete

Nyamapanda On the Tete Corridor, linking Harare with Tete and Lilongwe (Malawi)

To/From Harare

From **Tete** there are frequent vehicles to Changara and onto the border at Nyamapanda, where you can get transport to Harare. Through buses between Blantyre and Harare are another option.

From **Chimoio** there is frequent transport to Manica and from there to the border, from where you'll need to take a taxi 12km to Mutare, and then get Zimbabwe transport to Harare.

The seldom-used route via the orderly little border town of **Espungabera** is slow and scenic, and an interesting dry-season alternative for those with a 4WD.

Mukumbura (4WD only) is of interest mainly to anglers heading to Cahora Bassa Dam. There is no public transport on the Mozambique side.

Lake

MALAWI

The *Ilala* ferry, which services several Mozambican ports on its way up and down Lake Niassa, was grounded for repairs at the time of research. Contact **Malawi Lake Services** (☎in Malawi 1-587221; ilala@malawi.net) for an update. Meanwhile, the journey between Cóbuè and Likoma Island (Malawi) can be done by local fishing boats (about US$7 one way), which wait each morning at both destinations for passengers.

There are immigration posts in Metangula and Cóbuè (and on Likoma Island and in Nkhata Bay, for Malawi). You can get a Mozambique visa at Cóbuè, but not at Metangula.

Getting Around

Air

AIRLINES IN MOZAMBIQUE

Linhas Aéreas de Moçambique (LAM; ☎82-147, 84-147, 21-468000; www.lam.co.mz) The national airline, with flights linking Maputo with Inhambane, Vilankulo, Beira, Chimoio, Quelimane, Tete, Nampula, Lichinga and Pemba. Always reconfirm your ticket, and check in early. Visa cards are accepted in most offices. Advance purchase tickets are significantly cheaper than last-minute fares. Sample one-way fares and flight frequencies: Maputo to Pemba (US$320, daily), Maputo to Vilankulo (US$180, daily), Maputo to Lichinga (US$225, four weekly).

CFA Charters (www.cfa.co.za) Scheduled and charter flights to the Bazaruto Archipelago, Quirimbas Archipelago and Gorongosa National Park.

Boat

On Lake Niassa there is passenger service between Metangula, Cóbuè and several other villages.

Bus

» Direct services connect all major towns at least daily, although vehicle maintenance and driving standards leave much to be desired.

» A large bus is called a *machibombo,* and sometimes also *autocarro.* The main companies include TCO, with comfortable buses and constantly changing schedules; Maning Nice; Nagi Trans; and Grupo Mecula.

» Most towns don't have central bus stations. Instead, transport usually leaves from the bus company garage, or from the start of the road towards the destination. Long-distance transport in general, and all transport in the north, leaves early – between 3am and 7am. Mozambican transport usually leaves quickly and close to the stated departure time.

» Sample journey fares and times: Maputo to Vilanculos (Mtc750); Nampula to Pemba (Mtc350, seven hours); Maputo to Beira (Mtc1780, 16 hours); Pemba to Maputo (Mtc2500, 3 days).

» There is no luggage fee for large buses. For smaller buses and *chapas,* if your bag is large enough that it needs to be stowed on the roof, you will be charged, with the amount varying depending on distance and size of the bag, and always negotiable.

» Where there's a choice, always take buses rather than *chapas.*

RESERVATIONS

Book TCO buses in advance, as its routes fill quickly. Maning Nice and Grupo Mecula should be booked the afternoon before. Otherwise, showing up on the morning of travel (about an hour prior to departure) is usually enough to ensure a place.

If you are choosy about your seat (best is in front, on the shady side), get to the departure point earlier.

The more luggage on the roof, the slower the service.

Car & Motorcycle

» A South African or international drivers licence is required to drive in Mozambique. Those staying longer than six months will need a Mozambique drivers licence.
» *Gasolina* (petrol) is scarce off main roads, especially in the north. *Gasóleo* (diesel) supplies are more reliable. On bush journeys, always carry an extra jerry can and top up whenever possible, as filling stations sometimes run out.
» Temporary import permits (US$2) and third-party insurance (US$25 for 30 days) are available at most land borders, or in the nearest large town.

HIRE

» There are rental agencies in Maputo, Vilankulo, Beira, Nampula, Tete and Pemba, most of which take credit cards. Elsewhere, you can usually arrange something with upmarket hotels.
» Rates start at about US$100 per day for 4WD, excluding fuel.
» None of the major agencies offer unlimited kilometres, although some of the smaller ones do.
» With the appropriate paperwork, rental cars from Mozambique can be taken into South Africa and Swaziland, but not into other neighbouring countries. Most South African rental agencies don't permit their vehicles to enter Mozambique.

INSURANCE

» Private vehicles entering Mozambique must purchase third-party insurance at the border.
» It's also advisable to take out insurance coverage at home or (for rental vehicles) with the rental agency to cover damage to the vehicle, yourself and your possessions.
» Car-rental agencies in Mozambique have wildly differing policies (some offer no insurance at all, those that do often have high deductibles and most won't cover off-road driving); inquire before signing any agreements.

ROAD HAZARDS

» Drunk driving is common, as are excessive speeds, and there are many road accidents. Throughout the country, travel as early in the day as possible, and avoid driving at night.
» If you are not used to driving in Africa, watch out for pedestrians, children and animals on the road or running onto the road.
» Tree branches on the road are the local version of flares or hazard lights, and mean there's a stopped vehicle, crater-sized pothole or similar calamity ahead.

ROAD RULES

» In theory, traffic in Mozambique drives on the left.
» Traffic already in a roundabout has the right of way (again, in theory).
» The driver and all passengers are required to wear a seatbelt.
» Other relevant provisions of Mozambique's traffic law include a prohibition on driving while using a mobile phone, a requirement to drive with the vehicle's insurance certificate, and a requirement to carry a reflector vest and two hazard triangles.
» Speed limits (usually 100km/h on main roads, 80km/h on approaches to towns and 60km/h or less when passing through towns) are enforced by radar.
» Fines for speeding and other traffic infringements vary, and should always be negotiated (in a polite, friendly way), keeping in mind that official speeding fines range from Mtc1000 up to Mtc24,000, depending on how much above the speed limit you are travelling and where the infringement occurs.
» Driving on the beach is illegal.

Hitching

» As anywhere in the world, hitching is never entirely safe, and we don't recommend it. This said, in parts of rural Mozambique, your only transport option will be hitching a lift. Payment is usually not expected, but clarify before getting in. A small token of thanks is always appreciated. If you do need to pay, it is usually equivalent to what you would pay on a bus or *chapa* for the same journey.

» To flag down a vehicle, hold your hand out at about waist level and wave it up and down; the Western gesture of holding out the thumb is not used.

» Hitching in pairs is safer. Women should avoid hitching alone.

» Throughout the country, the prevalence of drunk drivers makes it essential to try and assess the driver's condition before getting into a vehicle.

Local Transport

CHAPA

» The main form of local transport is the *chapa,* the name given to any public transport that runs within a town or between towns, and isn't a bus or truck. On longer routes, your only option may be a *camião* (truck). Many have open backs, and the sun and dust can be brutal unless you get a seat up front in the cab.

» *Chapas* can be hailed anywhere, and prices are fixed. Intra-city fares average Mtc5; long-haul fares are usually slightly higher than the bus fare for the same route. The most comfortable seat is in the front, next to the window, though you'll have to make arrangements early and sometimes pay more.

» *Chapa* drivers are notorious for their unsafe driving and there are many accidents. Where possible, bus is always a better option.

» Like buses, long-haul *chapas* in Mozambique tend to depart early in the day and relatively promptly, although drivers will cruise for passengers before leaving town.

TAXI

Apart from airport arrivals, taxis don't cruise for business, so you'll need to seek them out. While a few have functioning meters, you'll usually need to negotiate a price. Town trips start at Mtc100.

Tours

Dana Tours (www.danatours.net) Long-established and highly reliable, Dana Tours covers most of Mozambique, plus Mozambique–South Africa combination itineraries, focusing particularly on mid-range and upmarket.

Mozaic Travel (www.mozaictravel.com) Another long-standing and reliable operator catering to all budgets.

Train

The only passenger train regularly used by tourists is the slow line between Nampula and Cuamba. Vendors are at all stations, but bring extra food and drink. Second class is reasonably comfortable, and most cabins have windows that open. Third class is hot and crowded. Book the afternoon before travel. If you have the time, it's one of southern Africa's great journeys.

Malawi

ARIADNE VAN ZANDBERGEN / GETTY IMAGES ©

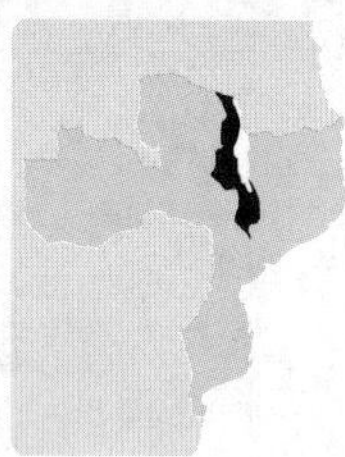

Malawi

☎ 265 / POP 16.3 MILLION

Includes »

Best Places to Eat

» Latitude 13° (p269)
» Buchanan's Grill (p273)
» Casa Mia (p329)
» Kaya Mawa (p297)

Best Places to Stay

» Huntingdon House (p339)
» Kaya Mawa (p297)
» Mumbo Island (p312)
» Mkulumadzi Lodge (p340)
» Latitude 13° (p269)

Why Go?

Often dismissed as 'Africa for beginners', Malawi has long been viewed as an interloper at the table of great safari destinations. That is, until a lion reintroduction program commenced in 2012 and travel editors started salivating.

Aside from its animals, what immediately captures you about Malawi is its geographical diversity. Slicing through the landscape in a trough formed by the Great Rift Valley is Africa's third largest lake – Lake Malawi; a shimmering mass of clear water, its depths are swarming with colourful cichlid fish. Whether it's diving, snorkelling, kayaking or chilling out on one of its desert islands, a visit to the lake is a must.

Suspended in the clouds in Malawi's deep south are the dramatic peaks of Mt Mulanje and the mysterious Zomba Plateau; both are a trekker's dream, with mist-cowled forests and exotic wildlife. Head further north and you'll witness the otherworldly beauty of Nyika Plateau, its rolling grasslands resembling the Scottish Highlands.

When to Go

Lilongwe

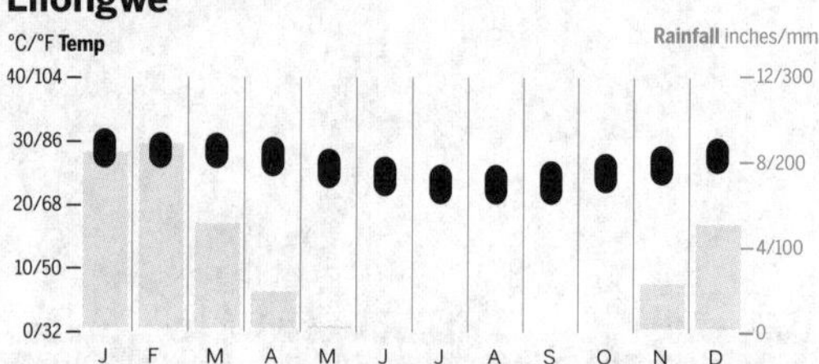

May–Jul Dry season, with cooler temperatures and lush vegetation.

Oct–Nov The end of the dry season is best for wildlife viewing, but can be uncomfortably hot.

Dec–Mar The rainy season; temperatures remain high and flash flooding can occur.

Malawi Highlights

1. Kayaking to Mumbo Island across bottle-green **Lake Malawi** (p312)
2. Heading to **Majete Wildlife Reserve** (p339) to see lions reintroduced in 2012
3. Scrambling up the twisted peaks of **Mt Mulanje** (p334) and admiring the astounding views
4. Spotting hippos and crocs on the Shire River in **Liwonde National Park** (p318) and getting up close to elephants
5. Escaping to dreamy **Kaya Mawa** (p297) boutique hotel on Likoma Island
6. Cruising past crocs on a kayak in the Bua River in **Nkhotakota Wildlife Reserve** (p302)
7. Cycling the rugged grasslands of **Nyika National Park** (p285), home to zebras and leopards

LILONGWE

☎01 / POP 781,500 / ELEV 1050M

Sprawling, chaotic and bustling with commerce, Lilongwe feels fit to burst. The nation's capital is initially a little underwhelming and it takes some time to get your bearings – you may wonder where the centre is – but once you've decided on your favorite restaurants, ferreted out the best malls and discovered those hidden leafy oases, the place really grows on you. A trip to the city market is an eye opener, with gleaming fruit and African music dancing over the animated faces of hawkers. It's also worth visiting Lilongwe Nature Sanctuary, which has recently been reinvigorated (though not after midnight, as lately hyenas have been appearing and opportunistically feasting on inebriated locals). A visit to the tobacco auction floors on the outskirts of town is a great photo opportunity, and within easy reach of the city are cool forest reserves and a famed pottery workshop at Dedza.

Lilongwe has two centres: City Centre (Capital City), home to ministries, embassies, smart hotels, airline offices and travel agents; and Old Town, with its guesthouses, backpacker hostels and campsites, bus station, main market, banks, tour companies and malls. The two centres are 3km apart and minibuses frequently run between them. The heart of Old Town is the market on Malangalanga Rd. Just south of the market is the main bus station. Just to the north of the market is Devil St, a narrow road lined with bars and cheap hotels, where you'll also find the departure points for buses headed to Zambia or Tanzania.

Sights & Activities

Main Market — MARKET

(Map p270; Malangalanga Rd, Old Town) The main market near the bus station in Old Town is a pocket of frenetic activity and worth a visit even if you don't want to buy anything. You'll find all manner of things on sale here – bicycle parts, live chickens, vegetables, dustbins, underwear… the list goes on. Be aware, however, that pickpockets operate in the crowds. What's more, some visitors with large bags have been violently robbed, so travel light here to avoid unwanted attention and don't bring any valuables, such as a camera, with you. Dozens of little stores blast out Malawian music and sell counterfeit CDs.

FREE Tobacco Auction Floors — GALLERY

(☎01-710377; admission free) For a view of Malawi's economic heart, go to the public gallery overlooking the auction floors at the vast Auction Holdings warehouse about 7km north of the city centre, east of the main road towards Kasungu and Mzuzu. This is best reached by taxi, but local minibuses serve the industrial area. The auction season is April/May to September.

Lilongwe Wildlife Centre — WILDLIFE RESERVE

(Map p270; ☎01-757120; www.lilongwewildlife.org; Kenyatta Rd; admission MK1500; ⏲8am-4pm Mon-Fri, to noon Sat) In between City Centre and Old Town and alongside the Lingadzi River are 180 hectares of wilderness area, otherwise known as the Lilongwe Nature Sanctuary. After the sanctuary fell into disrepair, a joint agreement between the Lilongwe Wildlife Trust and the Department of National Parks and Wildlife has returned some of the area to its former glory. The new Lilongwe Wildlife Centre is Malawi's only sanctuary for orphaned, injured and rescued wild animals and plays an active role in conservation. Local residents include: a one-eyed lion rescued from Romania, bush babies, python, baboons, duikers, serval, blue monkeys and a leopard. The centre is considered by the UK-based Born Free Foundation, among others, to be a safe space for injured animals and for those that have been rescued from the bushmeat and wildlife trades, poorly kept zoos and private collections. The centre's ultimate aim is to rehabilitate the animals for a life back in the wild and it has a strict no breeding, no trade and a non-essential contact policy. They also run an outreach program to schools.

You're not allowed to wander around the centre on your own, but the entry fee includes a tour of the animal enclosures. This isn't a zoo so you aren't guaranteed to see any animals, but you will get to walk through a lovely wilderness area and learn about the centre's aims and animal conservation in Malawi in general.

Parliament Building — HISTORIC BUILDING

To get up close to the country's movers and shakers, head to the Parliament Building, which moved in the mid-1990s from Zomba to the ostentatious palace of former president Banda on the outskirts of Lilongwe. At the time of writing, work was underway on a shiny new parliament building near Capital Hill, which should be completed by 2011.

Kamuzu Mausoleum TOMB

(Map p270; Presidential Way) If you're interested in seeing the final resting place of Malawi's first president, Dr Banda, head for the marble and granite Kamuzu Mausoleum in Heroes Acre. Adorned with a huge portrait of Malawi's first 'president for life' at the entrance, the mausoleum also houses a library and research centre. Construction finished in 2006 at a whopping cost of US$600,000.

Sleeping

Lilongwe has a diverse range of accommodation. Most budget digs are located in Old Town, which is convenient with its eating, drinking and transport facilities. Midrange places have restaurants for residents and rates usually include breakfast, while facilities at top-end hotels include travel and car-hire agents, business centres, swimming pools, restaurants and bars.

TOP CHOICE **Latitude 13°** BOUTIQUE HOTEL **$$$**

(☎0882-200849, 0996-403159; www.thelatitudehotels.com; 60/43 Mphonongo Rd; s/d suites in house US$170/220, garden suites US$220/270;) Lilongwe's first and only world-class boutique hotel, this gated, 9-roomed oasis sets new standards for the country's accommodation. From the moment you step into its rarefied atmosphere of shadowy chic pulsing with glowing pod lights you're transported right off the African continent!

With its walls peppered with pop art, bespoke art installations – like driftwood threaded with fairy lights – at every turn, to the sumptuous rooms with buffed cement floors, four-poster beds, black walls and plunge baths, Latitude is special. Resident chef Richard Greenhall trained under Jamie Oliver and alchemises in the kitchen to serve what may be the best food in the country.

Sunbird Capital Hotel HOTEL **$$$**

(Map p270; ☎01-773388; www.sunbirdmalawi.com; Chilembwe Rd; s/d US$175/205, deluxe US$185/215;) A cut above the competition, you can almost sense the ghosts of past presidents and foreign dignitaries who've stepped down Capital's swank corridors. Set in lush gardens, rooms here are tastefully conservative with bureaus, bouncy beds and large en suites. The main restaurant dishes up Italian and Indian cuisine and very tasty grilled food (mains MK3000).

There's also a gym, pool, hairdresser, shops and travel agents here.

> **MALAWI FAST FACTS**
>
> » **Area** 118,484 sq km
>
> » **Capital** Lilongwe
>
> » **Famous for** The lake, laid-back beach resorts and friendly locals
>
> » **Languages** English, Chichewa
>
> » **Money** Malawian kwacha (MK) and US dollars

Kumbali Country Lodge LODGE **$$$**

(☎0999-963402; www.kumbalilodge.com; Nature's Gift Ltd, Capital Hill Dairy Farm, Area 44; s/d from US$180/220;) A short drive from the city centre, in a gentle rural setting, is a choice of swanky individual thatched chalets (Madonna has stayed here on her controversial visits to Malawi) with beautiful views all the way to nearby Nkhoma Mountain.

This is a working farm so the food, including fresh vegetables from the farm gardens and delicious homemade yoghurts and cheese, is fantastic. There are also plenty of nature trails and bird-spotting opportunities here. Hyenas, wild pigs and even leopards are also occasionally spotted here.

Sunbird Lilongwe Hotel HOTEL **$$$**

(Map p274; ☎01-756333; Kamuzu Procession Rd; s/d from US$109/134;) This white, colonial-style building, with 94 rooms, is set in manicured gardens. International standard rooms are naturally present for this excellent chain, fresh and well furnished with fridges, spotless en suites and bureaus. There's a classy restaurant too, as well as a gym and pool to cool off in.

Crossroads Hotel HOTEL **$$$**

(Map p270; ☎01-750333; www.crossroadshotel.net; Mchinji Roundabout, Crossroads Complex; r MK26,000, deluxe r MK33,000;) With a distinct international feel, newish Crossroads has all the facilities you'd expect: friendly, professional staff, and 100 rooms based around a pleasant courtyard. There's a nice cafe, bar and pool and you're close to the amenities of Crossroads Mall. Rooms have cable TV and are very comfy indeed. There's also a car-hire agent: Crossroads Car Hire (p362).

Mabuya Camp CAMPING, HOSTEL **$**

(Map p270; ☎01-754978; www.mabuyacamp.com; Livingstone Rd; campsite per person US$4, dm

Lilongwe

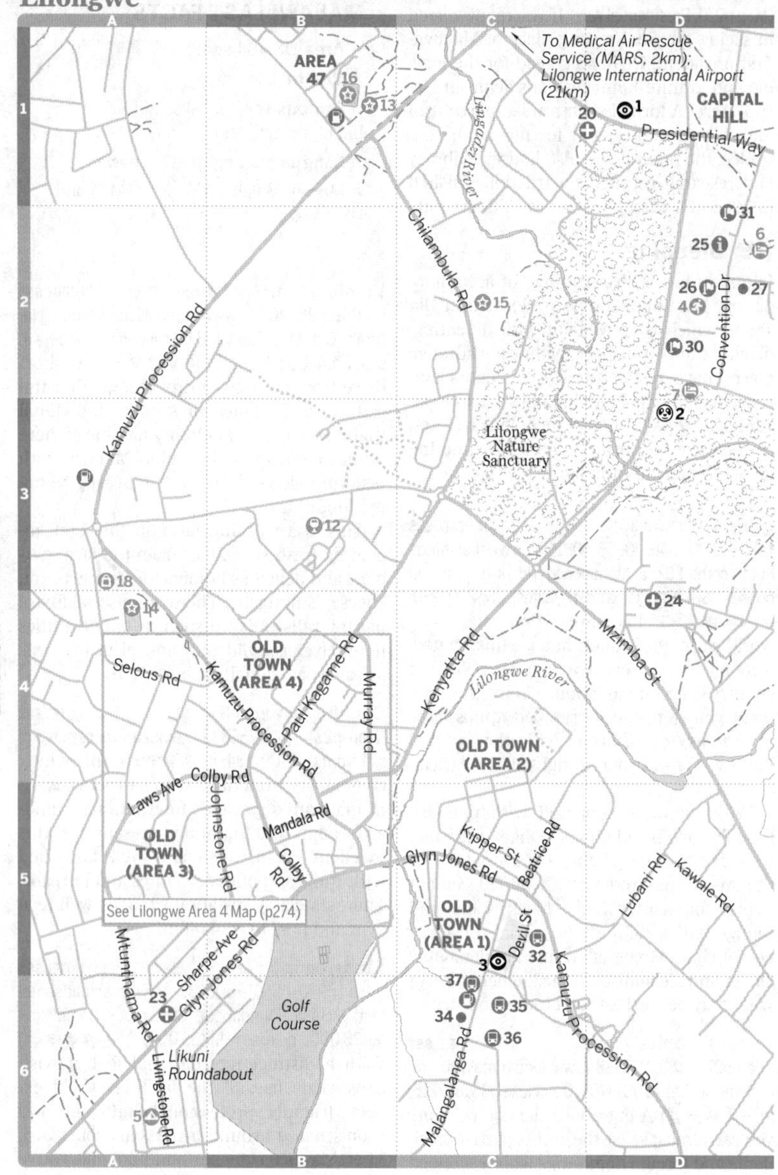

US$6, d/tw US$18/18, chalet d US$45; P@) Lilongwe's liveliest backpacker spot buzzes with a mix of solo travellers, overlanders and volunteers relaxing by the pool and in the large shady gardens. There are dorms and a double in the main house as well as chalets and camping pitches in the garden, and rooms share clean showers set in thatched *rondavels* (round, traditional-style huts).

There's also a bar with sport on TV, its menu featuring wraps, salads, breakfasts and sandwiches. If you want to self-cater,

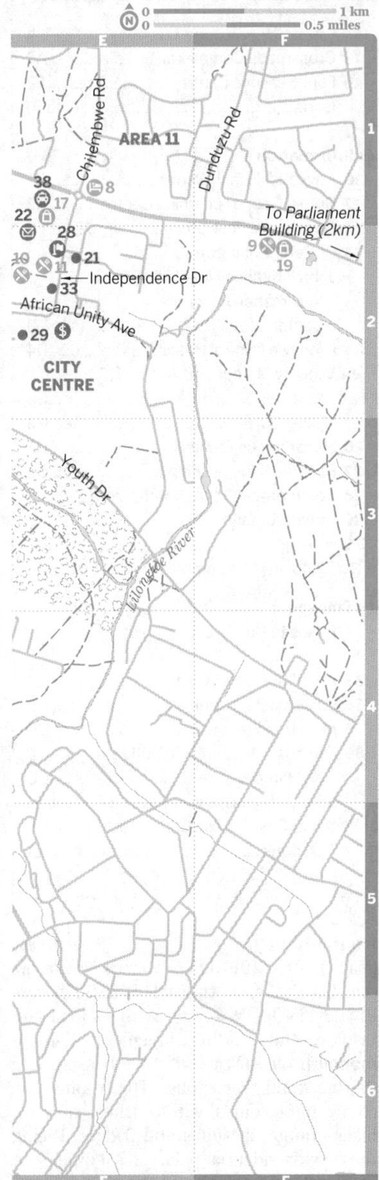

there are barbecues. Fifteen minutes' walk from the centre of Old Town.

Mufasa Lodge HOSTEL, GUESTHOUSE **$$**
(Map p274 ☎0999-071665; www.mufasamalawi.com; Kamuzu Procession Rd, Area 4; dm from US$8, s/d US$21/33; P@) Very popular with the backpacker crowd, friendly Mufasa has relocated to a leafy road. Its clean rooms vary, with cramped singles, decent dorms and spacious doubles and twins with en suites. There's a little kitchen, storage lockers, laundry service, a tourist info point as well as an exchange library and bags of space in the garden to chill.

Continental breakfast is included and there's an all day menu and well stocked bar. You can also arrange airport drop offs and pick ups here.

Barefoot Safari Lodge GUESTHOUSE, CAMPING **$$**
(☎01-707346; www.barefoot-safaris.com; campsite per person US$10, s/d tent rental US$15/25, s/d/family chalet US$60/110/190; P@) Set in 16 acres of lush gardens, Barefoot makes for a quieter alternative. There are five nicely finished chalets with private verandahs, and five walk-in tents, plus loads of space for pitching tents. The ablutions block is spotless and clean linen can also be provided.

Better still is the tempting 'Nightjar' restaurant/bar with its well-stocked fridge. There's even an on-site mechanic for your wheels. The lodge is 10km out of town on the road towards Mchinji.

Kiboko Town Hotel GUESTHOUSE **$$$**
(Map p274; ☎01-751226; www.kiboko-safaris.com; Mandala Rd; s/d incl breakfast from US$59/69, s/d deluxe incl breakfast US$69/79; @) This fresh upstairs guesthouse on Mandala Rd is splat in the centre of Old Town. Staff are friendly and rooms are equally pleasant, with four-posters, ochre walls, fresh linen, mozzie nets, en suites and cable TV.

There's also a great adjoining cafe in their courtyard – as well as a kids playground – serving up big breakfasts, pancakes, burgers and decent coffee. Come evening the bar is a real traveller/expat magnet.

Sanctuary Lodge LODGE **$$$**
(Map p270; ☎01-775202, 01-775201, 01-775200; www.thesanctuarylodge.net; campsite per adult/child US$9/6, s/d incl breakfast from US$135/160; P@) From the outside, these chalets – just outside Lilongwe Nature Sanctuary – look less than impressive but within they're well appointed with boutique flair, featuring tiled floors, step-in showers, wicker chairs and African chic decor. Add to this the peaceful setting in quiet leafy gardens and you have a winner.

Lilongwe

Sights
1 Kamuzu Mausoleum ... D1
2 Lilongwe Wildlife Centre ... D3
3 Main Market ... C5

Activities, Courses & Tours
4 Wilderness Safaris ... D2

Sleeping
Crossroads Hotel ... (see 18)
5 Mabuya Camp ... A6
6 Pacific Hotel ... D2
7 Sanctuary Lodge ... D2
8 Sunbird Capital Hotel ... E1

Eating
Ama Khofi ... (see 19)
9 Buchanan's Grill ... F2
10 Food Stalls ... E2
Food Zone Supermarket ... (see 18)
11 Metro Supermarket ... E2
Sanctuary Restaurant ... (see 7)

Drinking
Chameleon Bar ... (see 9)
12 Harry's Bar ... B3

Entertainment
13 Chez Ntemba ... B1
14 CIVO Stadium ... A4
15 Shack ... C2
16 Silver Stadium ... B1

Shopping
17 City Centre Shopping Centre ... E1
18 Crossroads Complex ... A3
19 Four Seasons Centre ... F2
Ishq ... (see 9)

Information
20 Adventist Health Centre ... D1
21 British Council Learning Centre ... E2
22 City Centre Post Office ... E2
23 Dr Peter Kalungwe ... A6
John F Kennedy Memorial Information Resource Center ... (see 17)
24 Lilongwe Central Hospital ... D4
25 Ministry of Tourism, Wildlife & Culture ... D2
Money Bureau ... (see 18)
26 Mozambique Embassy ... D2
27 Reserve Bank Building ... D2
28 South African High Commission ... E2
29 Standard Bank ... E2
30 USA ... D2
31 Zambian High Commission ... D2

Transport
32 Buses to Dar Es Salaam & Lusaka ... C5
33 KLM & Kenya Airways ... E2
34 Local Minibus Rank ... C6
35 Main Bus Station ... C6
36 Minibuses to Zomba, Blantyre and Limbe ... C6
South African Airways ... (see 8)
37 Super Sink Buses ... C6
38 Taxi Rank ... E1

There's also a campsite with plenty of *braai* (barbecue) sites and hot showers. The lodge's restaurant is equally charming. Keep your ears open to hear the Nature Sanctuary's one-eyed lion at night. It's a good idea to ask a guard to accompany you from the restaurant to your chalet if it's late, as there have been reported muggings.

St Peter's Guesthouse GUESTHOUSE **$**
(Map p274; ☎08-317769, 01-752812; Glyn Jones Rd; r with shared bathroom MK2000; P) Anglican-owned St Peter's has four pleasant rooms next to a red-brick chapel. Very peaceful with a tranquil, leafy garden. There's also a dorm with four beds and a shared bathroom.

Pacific Hotel HOTEL **$$$**
(Map p270; ☎01-776133; www.pacifichotelmw.com; City Centre; s/d standard US$85/105, deluxe US$113/135; P) With its gym and tasty restaurant, this three-floor, 47-room monolith off Africa Unity Ave boasts more marble than Persepolis. The rooms are comfy and colourful with couches, cable TV, black-granite en suites and fridges. Facing the new presidential palace, it's a quiet spot with welcoming staff and the air-con is super efficient!

Korea Garden Lodge HOTEL **$$$**
(Map p274; ☎01-759700, 01-757854, 01-753467; www.kglodge.net; Tsiranana Rd; s/d from US$45/57, s/d executive with air-con from US$57/66;) Something of an oasis, this sprawling

hotel has plenty of rooms of varying standards – the more you pay, the lighter and larger they get (some with fridges). On-site there's a very tempting pool flanked by a lovely restaurant serving Korean food, all of it teeming with plants.

Lilongwe Golf Club CAMPING $
(Map p274; ☎01-753598/118; campsite per person MK1800; P📶🏊) A clean, safe and comfortable (hot showers!) option for campers, just off Glyn Jones Rd. Rates include access to the members bar, restaurant and swimming pool.

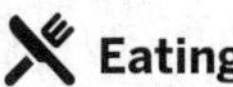

Eating

Lilongwe has a good selection of places to eat, from cafes serving cheap, local food (mostly found around Old Town) to European-style places, as well as some very good Indian restaurants.

Most midrange and top-end hotels have restaurants open to nonguests.

Buchanan's Grill STEAKHOUSE $
(Map p270; Presidential Way, Four Seasons Centre; mains MK1500-2300; ⊙lunch & dinner Mon-Sat) At this stylish and traditional steakhouse, you can sit in the old-world restaurant with a relaxing sports bar attached, or outside beside an ornamental pool overlooking manicured gardens. It's a carnivore-friendly menu with excellent renditions of rump, sirloin and fillet steak as well as salads and soups. A restful oasis.

TOP CHOICE **Don Brioni's Bistro** BISTRO $
(Mandala Rd; mains from MK2500; ⊙lunch & dinner; 📶👪) Burgers, steaks, spaghetti, t-bone, spare ribs, fish and chips or cappuccinos and cool beers – Don Brioni's deserves every inch of its regular patronage from travellers and expats for its gregarious owner and the high quality of its cuisine.

Open seven days a week, this carnivore's heaven has walls decked in reservation placards, and checked-cloth tables bathed in low-lit ambience. Take a pew in the atmospheric dining room or outside on a candlelit terrace. Recommended.

Korea Garden Restaurant KOREAN $
(3056 Tsiranana Av; mains MK3000; ⊙breakfast, lunch & dinner; P📶👪) This tin-roofed poolside affair is a sanctuary choked with plants and atmosphere. Its menu spans Korean-style grub like chicken in sesame seeds and soy sauce, to fried fish, pepper steaks and snacks like omelets and chambo.

Mamma Mia ITALIAN $
(Old Town Mall; mains from MK1400; ⊙lunch & dinner; P📶🍸👪) With its traditional Italian decor and old-world style, Mamma's has a wide-ranging menu featuring antipasti, salads, panini and homemade pasta. The pizza bases are delicious.

TOBACCO

Tobacco is Malawi's most important cash crop, accounting for more than 60% of the country's export earnings, and Lilongwe is the centre of this vital industry. Most activity takes place in the Kenengo Industrial Area on the northern side of Lilongwe, the site of several tobacco-processing factories and the huge and impressive tobacco auction rooms.

Large-scale tobacco farming started in the area around Lilongwe in the 1920s and has grown steadily in importance ever since. Two types of tobacco are produced in Malawi: 'flue', which is a standard quality leaf, and 'burley', which is of a higher quality and is in demand by cigarette manufacturers around the world.

Tobacco is grown on large plantations or by individual farmers on small farms. The leaves are harvested and dried, either naturally in the sun or in a heated drying room, and then brought to Lilongwe for sale (in southern Malawi the crops go to auction in Limbe).

In the auction rooms (called auction 'floors'), auctioneers sell tobacco on behalf of the growers. It's purchased by dealers who resell to the tobacco processors. The tobacco comes onto the floors in large bales and is displayed in long lines. Moisture content determines the value of the leaves: if the tobacco is too dry, the flavour is impaired; if it's too wet, mould will set in and the bale is worthless.

A small proportion of tobacco is made into cigarettes for the local market, but most gets processed in Malawi before being exported to be made into cigarettes abroad. Most processed tobacco goes by road to Durban, South Africa, to be shipped around the world.

Lilongwe Area 4

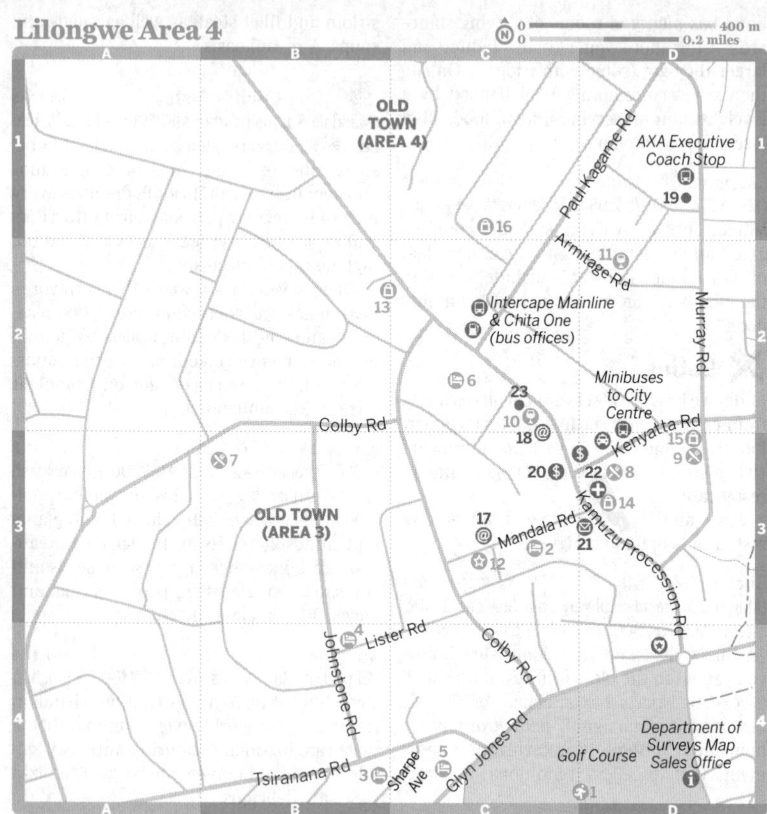

Ama Khofi

CAFE $

(Map p270; Presidential Way, Four Seasons Centre; mains MK2300; ⏲7.30am-5pm Mon-Sat, 9am-5pm Sun; P 📶 🌱 👪) Follow your nose to this delightful Parisian-style cafe with wrought-iron chairs, a bubbling fountain and pretty gardens. The menu has carrot cakes, ice cream and salads, and main courses like beef burgers and roast beef sandwiches. Great coffee too.

Sanctuary Restaurant

INTERNATIONAL $

(Map p270; www.thesanctuarylodge.net; meals from MK2000; ⏲10am-10.30pm Mon-Sat, 9am-4pm Sun; P ❄ 📶 🌱 👪) With fan-cooled dining in exposed-brick decor, Sanctuary is swimming in atmosphere. Shaded by mature fig trees singing with cicadas, this low-slung tin-roofed lodge boasts a veggie menu as well as breakfasts, meatballs, fish and steaks. At night the restaurant is romantically candlelit. On the corner of Kenyatta Dr and Youth Dr.

Monsoon

THAI $

(Pacific Parade Shopping Mall; mains from MK1750; ⏲10.30am-2pm & 6-11pm; ❄ 📶 🌱) This new Thai restaurant in the Pacific Parade Shopping Mall is a pleasant spot for Thai faves like *tom yum* soup, Thai green curry and satay.

Blue Ginger

INDIAN $

(Pacific Parade Shopping Mall; mains MK1400-3000; ⏲noon-2pm & 6-11pm Mon-Sat; P ❄ 📶 🌱 👪) Could this be the best Indian food in Lilongwe? Everything is wonderfully fresh, subtly spiced and beautifully presented in a sleek, glossy dining room that's perfect for a special night out. Try the chicken vindaloo in this Northern Indian spot off Mphonongo Rd.

Kiboko Town Hotel

INTERNATIONAL $

(Mandala Rd; dishes MK500-1300; ⏲breakfast & lunch; 📶 🌱 👪) Set in a cool courtyard with a recycled Land Rover serving as a kids playground; sit alfresco or in the cozy bar. Food

Lilongwe Area 4

is mainly omelets, sandwiches and savoury Dutch pancakes. Nice crowd.

Bohemian Cafe CAFE $
(Map p274; Laws Ave at Land & Lake Safaris; snacks from MK450; ⌚8am-4.30pm Mon-Fri, 9am-2pm Sat; P) This tempting garden cafe has plenty of shade and very tasty choc-infused coffees, as well as homemade cakes, bagels, healthy sandwiches and salads. At Land & Lake Safaris' headquarters.

Self-Catering

There are decent supermarkets all over the city, the newest and best being **Spar** (Map p274; Lilongwe City Mall, Kenyatta Rd) at Lilongwe City Mall in Old Town. Near the City Centre Shopping Centre there's a Peoples Supermarket and at the Crossroads Complex there's a Food Zone Supermarket, which has a good range of food and imported treats.

Drinking & Entertainment

Bars & Nightclubs

Chameleon Bar BAR, LIVE MUSIC
(Map p270; Presidential Way, Four Seasons Centre; ⌚11am-midnight Mon-Sat, to 10pm Sun;) Stylish, with a glass bar and purple walls, this cocktail bar sits opposite Buchanan's Grill in a leafy compound. Popular with Malawians and expats both, it puts on live music and DJ nights, poetry readings and theme parties. It also has a great cocktail menu and tables outside at which to enjoy them.

Harry's Bar BAR
(Map p270; ⌚6pm-late) Owned by Harry (a great person to get the low-down from on local bands and DJs), this is a lively wood shack dishing up a bubbling atmosphere, live jazz in the garden and revolving entertainment. A Lilongwe institution and a must for any self-respecting hedonist. It's located off Paul Kagame Rd.

Chez Ntemba NIGHTCLUB
(Map p270; Area 47; ⌚6pm-late) Live acts – with a distinctly African flavour – and disco magnetises locals and *mzungu* (white foreigners) in a fleshpot of sweaty bodies. Great fun.

Shack BAR, LIVE MUSIC
(Map p270; Chilambula Rd; ⌚6pm-late Wed & Fri) A fave with local expats; there's a pool table,

volleyball court, darts, global sports on the huge TV and live music at this simple wood shack affair. Wednesday night is disco night. They also do great barbecued food – the steaks are huge (MK2000).

Diplomat Bar BAR
(Kamuzu Procession Rd; ⊙noon-late;) Enjoying a recent refurb with a wood interior and chic red-glass chandeliers, Diplomat packs a punch despite its pint-size. A mixed crowd of expats, travellers and locals. It's right in the heart of Old Town.

Goodfellows Pub BAR
(Armitage Rd; ⊙11.30am-late Mon-Sat) With movies on the flatscreen and sport fixtures on the other screen, there's a mixed crowd of *mzungus* and locals at this rough n' ready joint. The menu is snack-focused with chicken wings, chambo and *nshima* (maize porridge).

Theatre

Umunthu Theatre THEATRE
(☎01-757979; www.umunthu.com) Off Paul Kagame Rd, Umunthu is the highlight of Lilongwe's cultural scene. It puts on regular live music, films, club nights and variety shows, showcasing the best of Malawian talent.

Sport

Football matches are played at **CIVO Stadium** (Map p270; Area 9), off Kamuzu Procession Rd, on Sunday, and at **Silver Stadium** (Map p270; Area 47). Look out for posters or ask local fans for information.

Lilongwe Golf Club GOLF
(☎01-753 598, 01-753118;) If you're the sporting type, Lilongwe Golf Club, off Glyn Jones Rd, offers daily membership for around US$10. This allows you to enter the club, and use the bar or restaurant. To use the sports facilities there's a small extra charge.

Shopping

Photography

Lee Photo Studio PHOTOGRAPHY
(Nico Shopping Centre; ⊙7.30am-5pm) Prints photos, takes passport-sized pics, sells phones, batteries and cameras.

Bookshops

Grey Matter BOOKS
(Lilongwe City Mall) Great range of thrillers, biographies, kids books and travel titles.

MARKETS

To see what Malawians buy, go to the city's main market by the bus station. It's always lively and colourful and is a great place to buy secondhand clothes, although photography is not appreciated.

There's also a craft market outside the Old Town post office, where vendors sell everything from trinket woodcarvings, basketry and jewellery to traditional Malawian chairs. If you go late in the day you're likely to get a better deal.

Bookmart BOOKS
(Kamuzu Procession Rd, Uplands House; ⊙8.30am-4.30pm Mon-Fri, to 1pm Sun) Excellent secondhand bookshop with a wide range of recent bestsellers, classics and travel books.

Central Africana BOOKS
(www.centralafricana.com; Old Town Mall; ⊙8.30am-5pm Mon-Fri, to 1pm Sat) Has a small selection of English-language novels, pictorial travel books and some very nice prints of Malawi for keepsakes.

Malls

TOP CHOICE **Four Seasons Centre** SHOPPING
(Map p270; Presidential Way;) An oasis of fine dining and upscale shopping, featuring clothing and design boutiques, a couple of bars, restaurants and a tempting cafe, Four Seasons is a restful one-stop shop.

Lilongwe City Mall MALL
(Kenyatta Rd) The newest and best mall in the city for fast food joints, supermarkets and dead central location in Old Town.

City Centre Shopping Centre MALL
(Map p270) A collection of buildings off Independence Dr containing shops, travel agents, restaurants, a bank and a post office.

Crossroads Complex MALL
(Map p270; Kamuzu Procession Rd) This houses banks, a swanky hotel, minigolf, Crossroads Car Hire, a variety of upmarket shops, supermarkets and services, and a branch of the South African Steers.

Old Town Mall MALL
(off Chilambula Rd) Off Paul Kagame Rd, this small mall has a couple of bookshops and craft stores as well as the Mamma Mia restaurant. Chic and quiet.

Arts & Crafts

African Habitat HANDICRAFTS
(Old Town Mall; ⌚8.30am-5pm Mon-Fri, to 1pm Sat) Excellent for sculpture, woodcarvings, sarongs, cards and jewellery, as well as T-shirts and bags.

Ishq HANDICRAFTS
(Map p270; Four Seasons Centre; ⌚9am-5.30pm Mon-Sat, 10.30am-4pm Sun) Selling a range of recycled mahogany and glass tables, stylish natural-coloured linen chemises, bespoke jewellery, hand-woven throws, bags and pashminas, Ishq is pure style. Cheap it's not.

La Galleria HANDICRAFTS
(lacaverna@malawi.net; Old Town Mall; ⌚9am-4.30pm Mon-Fri, to 1pm Sat) Pleasant boutique selling vivid African paintings, masks, bags and jewellery by local artists.

Things of Africa HANDICRAFTS
(Mandala Rd; ⌚7.30am-5pm Mon-Sat) A souvenir shop selling T-shirts, postcards, jewellery and other crafts.

Information

Dangers & Annoyances

You definitely don't want to be around Lilongwe Nature Sanctuary after dark thanks to the late-night hyena appearances, which have taken a few locals in recent years. Also, there have been isolated cases of muggings around the Sanctuary Lodge, so ask for a security guard to escort you to your cabana.

During the day it's fine to walk everywhere around Old Town and City Centre, although it's much quieter at City Centre at the weekend so you should be on your guard then. At night, Malangalanga Rd can be dangerous, and walking to Area 3 is not recommended. The bridge between Area 2 and Area 3 is still a favourite haunt for muggers. Always watch out for your things when at the city's main bus station, and if you arrive on a bus after dark take a minibus or taxi to your accommodation. As a general rule, it isn't safe to walk around anywhere in the city after dark.

Bus tickets should only be bought at the bus station; some travellers have been conned out of money by buying tickets on the street when there is no such service.

Emergency

Ambulance (☎998)
Fire (☎01-757999)
Police (☎01-753333)
Rapid Response Unit (☎01-794254)

Internet Access

Internet access is readily available in Lilongwe and there are several cheap options both in Old Town and City Centre. Skyband wi-fi hotspots are available throughout the city.

Comptech (Mandala Rd; per 10min MK75) Fast internet connection, printing and photocopying as well as Skype web telephone service. There is also a branch on Kamuzu Procession Rd (Kamuzu Procession Rd; per 10min MK75).

Libraries

The **British Council Learning Centre** (Map p270; ☎01-773244; info@britishcouncil.org.mw; ⌚noon-4pm Mon, 9am-4pm Tue-Thu, 9am-noon Fri), off Independence Dr, and the **John F Kennedy Memorial Information Resource Center** (Map p270; ☎01-772222; Old Mutual Bldg, City Centre Shopping Centre; ⌚9am-4.30pm Mon-Wed, 9am-noon Thu & Fri) allow nonmembers to read books and magazines in the library, but not to take them away. Both places also show films on some afternoons and evenings – check their noticeboards for details.

Medical Services

Adventist Health Centre (Map p270; ☎01-775680; Presidential Way) Good for consultations, plus eye and dental problems.

Dr Peter Kalungwe (Map p270; ☎0999-969548, 01-750404) Available for private consultations.

Likuni Mission Hospital (☎01-766574, 01-766602; Glyn Jones Rd) A better option than Lilongwe Central Hospital, this hospital, 7km southwest of Old Town, has public wards, private rooms and some expat European doctors on staff.

Lilongwe Central Hospital (Map p270; ☎01-753555; off Mzimba St) Basic facilities.

Lilongwe Private Clinic (☎01-774972, 01-927035; Mphonongo Rd, Area 10 Plot 10131) Ask for Dr Chirwa.

Medical Air Rescue Service Clinic (MARS; ☎01-794967, 01-795018, emergency line 01-794242; www.marsmalawi.com; Ufulu Rd, Area 43) Has an intensive care unit, a dental surgery and offers laboratory tests for malaria, bilharzia and HIV among others. MARS also has road and air ambulances with staff highly trained in emergency treatment. MARS is linked to Health International and can arrange evacuation to Harare or Jo'burg if things get serious.

Michiru Pharmacy (☎01-754294; Nico Shopping Centre; ⌚8am-5pm Mon-Fri, to 1pm Sat & Sun) Sells antibiotics and malaria pills (MK8000 for 6 tablets) as well as the usual offerings.

Pharmacare (☎01-753230; Nico Shopping Centre; ⌚8am-4pm Mon-Fri, to 1pm Sun) Also sells malaria pills.

Money

Money Bureau (⌚8am-4.30pm Mon-Fri) City Shopping Centre (☎01-772239; Centre House Arcade, City Shopping Centre); Crossroads Complex (p276); Nico Shopping Centre (☎01-750659; Kamuzu Procession Rd, Old Town) Has good rates, doesn't charge commission and does cash advances on credit cards.

National Bank of Malawi (Kamuzu Procession Rd, Old Town) You can change money here and get a cash advance on your Visa card. There's also a 24-hour ATM that accepts Visa.

Standard Bank African Unity Ave (Map p270; City Centre) Offers the same facilities as National Bank of Malawi but the ATM also accepts MasterCard and Maestro. Another branch on Kamuzu Procession Rd.

Post

City Centre Post Office (Map p270) Located next to City Centre Shopping Centre.

Old Town Post Office (Kamuzu Procession Rd)

Telephone & Fax

Internet cafes offer an international telephone service or can hook you up to Skype on their computers.

Tourist Information

Immigration Office (☎01-754297; Murray Rd)

Ministry of Tourism, Wildlife & Culture (Map p270; ☎01-755499; Tourism House; ⌚7.30am-5pm Mon-Fri, 8-10am Sat) Information and advice is minimal at this tourist office. For details on tours, flights and hotels you're better off at a travel agency.

Travel Agencies & Safari Operators

Barefoot Safaris & Adventure Tours (☎00270-78-6309734, 01-707346; www.barefoot-safaris.com) Organises horse riding, hiking, climbing, walking and 4WD safaris throughout Malawi and beyond. Based at the Barefoot Safari Lodge 10km out of Lilongwe, on the road to Mchinji.

Kiboko Safaris (☎01-751226; www.kiboko-safaris.com; Mandala Rd) Specialises in budget camping safaris throughout Malawi and Zambia. For example, a four-day southern Malawi trip costs US$450, while for South Luangwa National Park a two-day trip costs US$510.

Land & Lake Safaris (☎01-757120; www.landlake.net; 84 Laws Rd, Area 3) In a new garden location, this trusted company has tours for all budgets in both Malawi and Zambia. A four-day trip to South Luangwa National Park will cost US$590, while a five-day trip to Victoria Falls will set you back US$1115.

Robin Pope Safaris (☎01-795483; www.robinpopesafaris.net; Plot 10/144, Tsoka Road, Area 10) Robin Pope and African Parks have put Majete Wildlife Reserve back on the map with a dazzling new lodge, Mkulumadzi. They also operate in Zambia and are based in South Luangwa National Park where they have four camps.

They offer a tailor-made range of safari combos including the Victoria Falls and Lower Zambezi, Kafue and North Luangwa National Parks, Liuwa Plain in western Zambia and the best of Malawi.

Ulendo Travel Group (☎01-794555; www.ulendo.net; 441 Chilanga Drive, Area 10; 👪) Fifteen-year-old Ulendo distinguishes itself as a one-stop travel shop for accommodation, prebooking flights (it also has its own airline, Ulendo Airlink, that ferries travellers to national parks and Likoma Island), car hire and a variety of expertly tailored tours and safaris in Malawi and Zambia. The reliable, specialist staff is its biggest selling point. It's recently moved to a great location in Area 10.

Wilderness Safaris (Map p270; ☎01-771153, 01-771393; www.wilderness-safaris.com; Bisnowaty Complex, Kenyatta Dr) Specialising in safari trips to their high-luxe lodges in Liwonde and Nyika National Parks, Wilderness are the country's top safari operator. They also provide top-end safaris and lodge bookings throughout Southern Africa. Ask about their 'Children in the Wilderness' eco-education programs.

ℹ Getting There & Away

Air

If you're buying a ticket, it's worth trying an agent first as they offer a wider range of options, charge the same rates as the airlines and sometimes have special deals. Air Malawi, KLM & Kenya Airways and South African airways have offices in Lilongwe.

Air Malawi (☎01-700811; Kamazu International Airport)

KLM & Kenya Airways (Map p270; ☎01-774227; City Centre)

South African Airways (Map p270; ☎01-770307, 01-772242; Capital Hotel, City Centre)

Bus

AXA City Trouper and commuter buses leave from the main bus station where you'll find the AXA ticket office, though you can also buy tickets at Postdotnet inside the City Centre Peoples Supermarket, Nico Shopping Centre and at Crossroads Complex.

AXA executive coaches depart from outside the City Centre Peoples Supermarket before stopping at the immigration office on Murray Rd and making their way to Blantyre. An executive ticket between the two cities costs MK6000.

Destinations from the main bus station include Mzuzu (MK3500, five hours), Blantyre (MK2000, four hours), Kasungu (MK1500, two hours), Nkhata Bay (MK3500, five hours) and Dedza (MK1300, one hour).

A number of other bus companies, including Coachline and Zimatha, also leave from the main bus station at similar rates and times. Super Sink buses depart from the Engen Petrol Station at 6.30pm to Mzuzu (MK2000, six hours) and at 6.30pm to Songwe (MK5000).

Long-distance minibuses depart from behind the bus station to nearby destinations such as Zomba (MK2500, four to five hours), Dedza (MK1000, 45 minutes to one hour), the Zambian border (MK1500, two hours), Ntchisi (MK1200, 2½ hours), Mangochi (MK2500, 4½ hours), Limbe (MK1900, three to four hours), and Nkhotakota (MK1800, three hours).

Intercape Mainline (☎0999-403398; www.intercape.co.za) has modern buses and leaves from the Total petrol station in Old Town on Tuesday, Wednesday, Saturday and Sunday at 6am, arriving in Jo'burg at 6am the following day (one way MK29,500). **Chiwale Bus Co** (☎0999-034014) leaves for Jo'burg at 6am on Saturday from the same location (one way MK21,000).

Zambia–Botswana Coach (☎0999-405340) leaves Wednesday and Saturday at 6am, arriving in Lusaka (Zambia) at 5pm (MK9500). Kob's Coach leaves the same days, for the same price, also at 6.00am (get there a half hour early for a good seat). The **Taqwa bus** (☎0999-670468) departs from Devil St at 7pm on Saturday, Sunday and Tuesday for the 27-hour journey to Dar es Salaam (Tanzania), continuing on to Nairobi (Kenya).

ℹ Getting Around

To/From the Airport

Lilongwe International Airport is 21km north of the city. A taxi from the airport into town costs MK8000. Maddeningly, there is currently no airport bus.

Public Transport

The most useful local minibus service for visitors is between Old Town and City Centre. From Old Town, local minibuses (marked Area 12) leave from either the bus rank near the market or next to Shoprite. They then head north up Kenyatta Rd, via Youth and Convention Drs or via Independence Dr, to reach City Centre. From City Centre back to Old Town, the bus stop for the return journey is at the northern end of Independence Dr.

Taxi

The best places to find taxis are the main hotels. There's a rank on Presidential Way, just north of City Centre Shopping Centre. Taxis also congregate outside Shoprite in Old Town. The fare between Old Town and City Centre is about MK2500. Short journeys within City Centre or Old Town cost around MK1500. Negotiate a price with the driver first. **Charlie Kandoje** (☎0888-953373, 0999-935281) is particularly reliable, with two cabs and one 7-seater minibus. He can take you around the city for a half-day for as little as MK6500.

AROUND LILONGWE

Dzalanyama Forest Reserve

Dzalanyama is a beautiful forest reserve in a range of hills about 60km by road southwest of Lilongwe. The area is famous for birdwatching, and species found here include the olive-headed weaver and Stierling's woodpecker.

The only place to stay in the reserve is **Dzalanyama Forest Lodge** (s/d with shared bathroom US$30/50, whole house US$160), run by Land & Lake Safaris. It's simple and there's only one bathroom and toilet between eight people, but the romantic atmosphere makes up for it. The lodge overlooks a stream and trees brimming with birds and butterflies; at night it's lit up by tons of candles and lanterns. You can spend your days exploring walking trails, mountain biking, birdwatching or simply relaxing. There's no food provided, but if you bring you own provisions there's a cook to prepare meals for you should you choose.

If you don't have your own transport, Land & Lake Safaris arranges transfers to the forest for US$100 per car from Lilongwe, as there's no public transport here.

Dedza

Dedza is a small town 85km southeast of Lilongwe, just off the main road between Lilongwe and Blantyre. The town, one of the highest and coolest places in Malawi, is surrounded by forested hills and sits in the shadow of stately Dedza Mountain. The road south of Dedza skirts the border of Mozambique, revealing vast plains of rust-red earth and grass on both sides, broken by conical granite peaks and a quilt of farmland.

Sights & Activities

There are numerous walks, all with spectacular views, in the **Dedza Mountain Forest Reserve**.

On the northern outskirts of town is Dedza Pottery. Follow the road to the left from town and it's signposted 1km down a dirt road off the main street. It's a pottery workshop and boutique, selling crockery, tiles and garden ceramics that are all hand painted with colourful illustrations of Malawian life – stay for any length of time in Malawi and you're bound to come across its stuff in tourist hotels and restaurants.

Sleeping & Eating

There are a number of cheap resthouses on Dedza's main street.

Dedza Pottery Lodge LODGE **$$$**
(☎01-223069; www.nyasalodges.com; per person full board US$62) The spacious rooms here are decorated with local art and bright ceramics from the pottery. The rooms all have fridges, which are replenished with soft drinks and beers daily, as well as plenty of tea, coffee and fresh milk. They sit in a large garden and have small terraces from which to enjoy the views.

Dedza Pottery Restaurant INTERNATIONAL, MALAWIAN **$**
(meals from MK635, desserts from MK500) Mention Dedza Pottery and people in the know will wax lyrical about its cheesecake – and it is indeed a berry-and-cream-laden plate of heaven. But the restaurant doesn't just serve desserts. You can scoff hearty plates of cafe standbys like moussaka and lasagne or go for healthier options like salads (the mountain salad with ginger and green mangoes is recommended). While you eat you can take in views of the pottery garden and the hills beyond, and in the winter there's a log fire to keep you warm.

Ntchisi Forest Reserve

This small and rarely visited forest reserve is about 80km north of Lilongwe, near the large village of Ntchisi (*nch*ee-see). At the centre of the reserve is Ntchisi Mountain, covered in beautiful evergreen forest, as well as some of the last remaining indigenous rainforest in Malawi, and boasting stunning views of the surrounding area. Birdlife is incredibly varied, and on the mammal side of things you might see blue monkeys, baboons, bush pigs, bushbuck and duikers.

Activities

The folks at **Ntchisi Forest Lodge** can point you to a number of marked trails that you can walk with or without a guide. A popular route is the trail through the forest to the summit of Ntchisi Mountain. It's about 4km away, so allow about three hours for a return walk (more if you enjoy birdwatching). You can also hire mountain bikes, visit the nearby villages and meet a local healer, learn how to cook *nshima*, or even take drumming classes.

Sleeping

Ntchisi Forest Lodge LODGE **$$$**
(☎0999-741967; www.ntchisi.com; campsite per person US$8, d/tw/f per person US$95, children under 12 US$65) Originally built as a 'hill station' in 1914 for the colonial district commissioner who came here to escape the heat of his normal base in Nkhotakota, the lodge used to be run by the Department of Forestry, but has now been privatised.

There are five bedrooms, a lounge with fireplace, a large terrace, a garden with plenty of comfy chairs and chill-out spots, and a restaurant serving delicious locally sourced produce, including herbs and veggies from the garden. Electricity is provided by solar and wind power, evenings are candlelit, and it supports the local community and economy.

This is a very child-friendly place. It can provide babysitters during the day and make special kids meals, and is planning to build a special children's play area.

Getting There & Away

There is no public transport to the lodge so you'll have to have your own wheels. To get here from Lilongwe, aim north on the M1 and turn right (east) at Mponela on the T350. You will reach a crossroads after about 35km; turn right here towards the village of Dowa, then after another 10km, turn left (north) at a junction to Ntchisi village. About 12km north of this junction (you'll pass through the village of Chindembwe first), a dirt road turns right (east) to the forest reserve; there is a signpost to Ntchisi Forest Lodge.

NORTHERN MALAWI

Remote northern Malawi is where ravishing highlands meet hippo-filled swamps, vast mountains loom large over empty beaches, and colonial relics litter pristine islands and hilltop villages. It is Malawi's most sparsely populated region and the first taste many travellers get of this tiny country after making the journey down from East Africa.

Hugging the border with Zambia is Nyika National Park – an otherworldly wilderness where zebras pose on the skyline and pine forests hide leopards and hyenas. Head south a little and the sultry flat woodland and swamps of Vwaza Marsh Wildlife Reserve bring forth huge herds of elephants, antelopes and buffaloes. Sitting within easy striking distance of both of them is Livingstonia, which sucks you into a time warp with its old missionary buildings and quiet, unhurried atmosphere.

This part of Lake Malawi is lined with gleaming coves and pristine beaches straight out of a Caribbean dream. Budget travellers will do particularly well here – there's a huge choice of beachfront campsites, while those on a higher budget have the fine hotels of the Chintheche Strip.

Karonga

Dusty little Karonga is the first place you'll come across if making the journey down from Tanzania and while it won't enrapture you, it suffices for an overnight stay or to check your emails, stock up on cash and have a close encounter with a 100-million-year-old dinosaur. Karonga has the proud title of Malawi's 'fossil district', with well-preserved remains of dinosaurs and ancient humans. Its most famous discovery is the Malawisaurus (Malawi lizard) – a fossilised dino skeleton found 45km south of the town. See it at the **Culture & Museum Centre Karonga** (CMCK; ☎01-362579; www.palaeo.net/cmck; ⏰8am-5pm Mon-Sat, 2-5pm Sun). If you do decide to stay, opt for **Sumuka Inn** (☎0999-444816; standard/deluxe/executive MK8500/10,500/12,500, suites from MK15,000) or **Safari Lodge Annex** (☎01-362340; standard/executive/chalet MK4500/4800/6500).

Apart from the **Mbandé Cafe** (⏰8am-5pm Mon-Sat, 2-5pm Sun), eating options are slim, but there's a Standard Bank and National Bank of Malawi, internet at the museum and the locals are friendly.

Super Sink Buses (Map p270) leave at 8pm for Lilongwe. Alternatively, head to Mzuzu (MK1600, four hours) from where AXA City Trouper buses also leave for Lilongwe and Blantyre. Minibuses go to numerous destinations, including Songwe (MK1200, 45 minutes) and Mzuzu (MK1600, four hours). Taxis to the Tanzanian border go from the main bus station and cost MK1200.

If you've got a 4WD you can cross into northern Zambia via Chitipa in northern Malawi. It's four hours from Karonga to Chitipa on a rough dirt road (there's no public transport but you might be able to get a lift on a truck). After going through customs it is another 80km or four hours' drive to the Zambian border crossing at Nakonde.

Chitimba

Sitting on the main north–south road at the junction for the road to Livingstonia, Chitimba has a happy, almost Caribbean air to it. Brightly coloured shops and shacks hug the main drag but the real treasure lies a short walk away, fringing the glassy waters of Lake Malawi – sand, powdery fine, and lots of it. If you're making the hellish road trip down from mountainous Livingstonia, there are a couple of decent places to stay with bars to steady your nerves over a cool Carlsberg Green.

Sleeping & Eating

There are two places close to the junction with the main road. They can safely store your gear and arrange a guide if you want to walk up to Livingstonia – a much more pleasant option.

Chitimba Campsite CAMPING, GUESTHOUSES $
(☎0888-387116; www.chitimba.com; Chitimba; campsite per person MK1200, dm MK2400, chalets with bathroom MK5400; @📶) This chilled out *palapa*-style complex, off the main drag, is gated, safe and very well organised. The bar and restaurant dish up excellent steaks and salads, or if you're in a rush, carb food like toasties. Better still, it looks out onto the beach (fenced off to deter hawkers) and the sapphire water of Lake Malawi 150m away.

You can play volleyball, use the wi-fi at the bar, or chat to overlanders. Stilted thatch-and-brick cabanas are nicely positioned around a manicured courtyard with clean linen, mozzie nets and simple padlocked

Northern Malawi

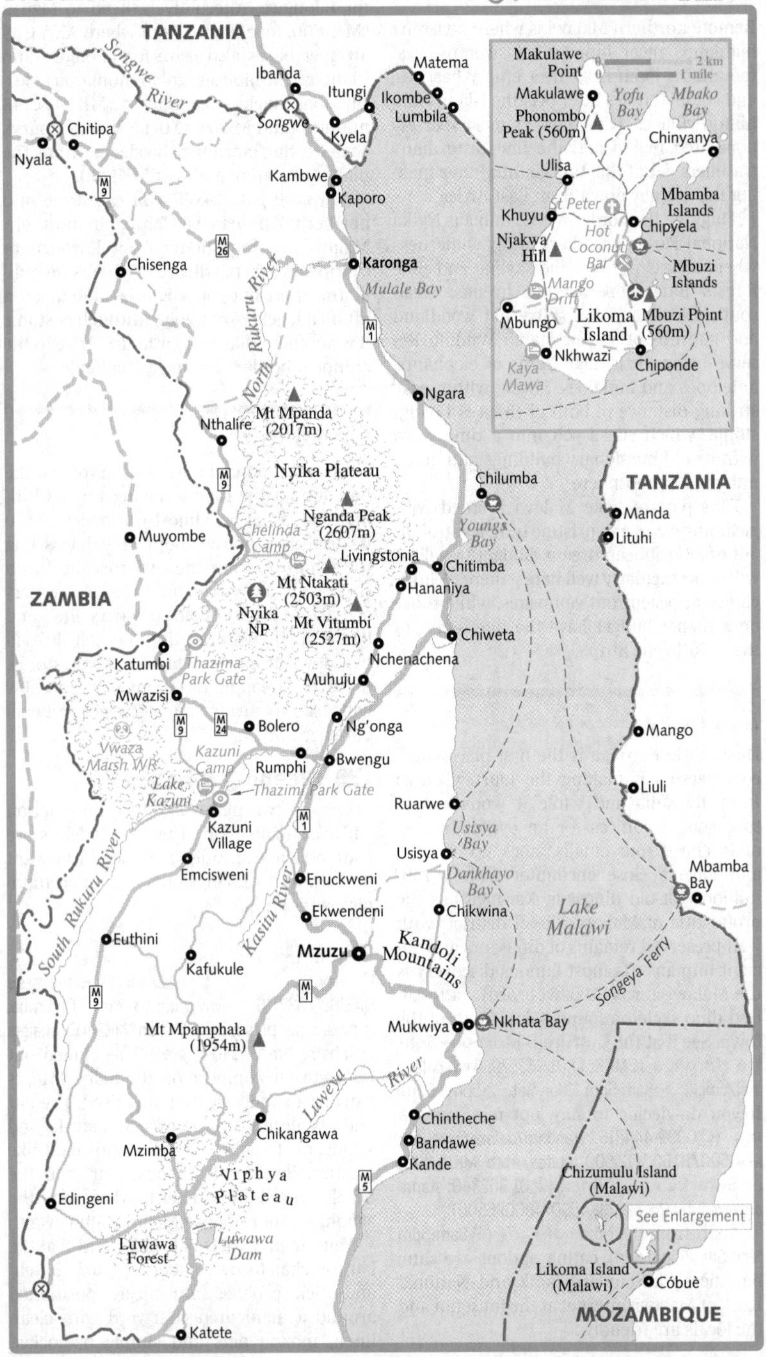

0 50 km
0 25 miles

TANZANIA
Songwe River
Ibanda
Matema
Itungi
Ikombe
Lumbila
Songwe
Kyela
Chitipa
Nyala
M9
Kambwe
Kaporo
M26
Chisenga
Karonga
Mulale Bay
North Rukuru River
M1
Ngara
Mt Mpanda (2017m)
Nthalire
Nyika Plateau
M9
Nganda Peak (2607m)
Chelinda Camp
Muyombe
Livingstonia
Mt Ntakati (2503m)
Nyika NP
Mt Vitumbi (2527m)
ZAMBIA
Chilumba
Youngs Bay
Chitimba
Hananiya
Chiweta
Nchenachena
Katumbi
Thazima Park Gate
Muhuju
Mwazisi
M9
M24
Bolero
Ng'onga
Vwaza Marsh WR
Kazuni Camp
Rumphi
Bwengu
Lake Kazuni
Thazimi Park Gate
Kazuni Village
M1
Ruarwe
Usisya Bay
Usisya
Emcisweni
Enuckweni
Dankhayo Bay
South Rukuru River
Kasitu River
Ekwendeni
Chikwina
Euthini
Kafukule
Mzuzu
Kandoli Mountains
Lake Malawi
M9
M1
Mukwiya
Nkhata Bay
Songeya Ferry
Mt Mpamphala (1954m)
Luweya River
Chintheche
Bandawe
Kande
Chikangawa
Mzimba
Viphya Plateau
M5
Edingeni
Luwawa Forest
Luwawa Dam
Katete
TANZANIA
Manda
Lituhi
Mango
Liuli
Mbamba Bay
Chizumulu Island (Malawi)
See Enlargement
Likoma Island (Malawi)
Cóbuè
MOZAMBIQUE

0 2 km
0 1 mile
Makulawe Point
Makulawe
Yofu Bay
Mbako Bay
Phonombo Peak (560m)
Chinyanya
Ulisa
St Peter
Mbamba Islands
Khuyu
Chipyela
Hot Coconut Bar
Njakwa Hill
Mbuzi Islands
Mango Drift
Mbungo
Likoma Island
Mbuzi Point (560m)
Nkhwazi
Kaya Mawa
Chiponde

MALAWI

doors. Chitimba Campsite can also arrange day trips up to Livingstonia.

Hakuna Matata CAMPING, GUESTHOUSE $
(☎0881-262337; www.hakunamatata.chitimba.com; camping/tent rental MK700/950, cabanas s/d/dm MK1300/1500/1300; @) Right beside Chitimba Campsite off the main drag, Makuna feels more like authentic backpacker turf, with an emphasis on camping (plenty of shaded pitches). There's a charming beachside bar, volleyball court, spotless toilet and shower block, and basic but clean cabanas, plus a colourful dorm. Owner Willie is a character and conducts historical day tours to Livingstonia. Check his website for details.

TOP CHOICE **Sangilo Sanctuary Lodge** LODGE $$$
(☎0888-392611, 0999-395203; www.sangilo.net; campsite per person US$5, d chalets with/without bathroom US$75/60) According to Ewan McGregor, who stayed here on his *Long Way Down* journey, Sangilo Sanctuary Lodge is 'just about the perfect retreat'. Nestled on a quiet cove, 8km north of Chitimba, this ecofriendly lodge has the most striking setting of any digs in the immediate area.

Handsome chalets perched on the cliffs boast awesome lake views. The food is a draw too; served on the outdoor restaurant deck down on the beach, they offer a couple of different choices that change daily. Call in advance to arrange pick-up from the *Ilala* ferry at Chilumba.

Getting There & Away

A minibus or *matola* (pick-up) between Chitimba and Mzuzu or Karonga is around MK1500.

Livingstonia

Built by missionaries, Livingstonia feels sanctified, special and otherworldly; its tree-lined main street is graced with old colonial-style buildings and smartly attired folk who look as if they're all en route to church. But for the stunning mountain views, there's not much to do in town but visit the Stone House. Staying at the latter or at one of the nearby permaculture farms will make for a magical, peaceful chapter in your journey.

After two failed attempts at establishing a mission at Cape Maclear and at Bandawe (too many people kept dying from malaria), the Free Church of Scotland moved its mission 900m above the lake to the village of Khondowe. Called Livingstonia after Dr David Livingstone, the mission was built under the leadership of Dr Robert Laws in 1894. The town provides a fascinating glimpse into Malawi's colonial past – most of the old stone buildings are still around today (many of them are used by the local university).

Sights & Activities

Stone House Museum MUSEUM
(admission MK250, photos MK100; ⌚7.30am-5pm) The fascinating museum in Stone House (the original home of Dr Robert Laws and now a national monument) tells the story of the European arrival in Malawi and the first missionaries. Here you can read Dr Laws' letters, peruse black-and-white photos of early missionary life in Livingstonia and browse a collection of Dr Laws' books, including the old laws of Nyasaland. Also on display is an excellent collection of original magic-lantern slides, an early anaesthesia machine, an old gramophone and the cloak that Dr Laws used when he was a moderator.

The nearby mission **church**, dating from 1894, has a beautiful stained-glass window featuring David Livingstone with his sextant, his medicine chest and his two companions, with Lake Malawi in the background. There are services here every Sunday and if you're in town you are welcome to attend.

You might also like to take a look at the **clock tower**. The nearby industrial block was built by the early missionaries as a training centre and is now a technical college. The excellent **Craft Coffee Shop** sells inexpensive carvings and crafts made by local people, as well as their excellent locally produced coffee; all proceeds go directly to the hospital and mission.

Down the road from here is the **David Gordon Memorial Hospital**, once the biggest hospital in Central Africa, and the **stone cairn** marking the place where missionary Dr Robert Laws and his African companion Uriah Chirwa camped in 1894 when they decided to build the mission here. Also nearby is **House No 1**, the original home of Dr Laws before he moved into Stone House.

About 4km from town, the impressive **Manchewe Falls** thunders 125m into the valley below. Follow a small path behind the falls and there's a cave where, as the story goes, local people hid from slave traders a hundred years ago. Allow an hour for going down and 1½ hours to get back up. Alternatively, if you're walking to/from Chitimba, you can visit on the way.

The more adventurous can also arrange abseiling trips for half a day or longer. For more details contact Mick at the Mushroom Farm.

Sleeping & Eating

Stone House GUESTHOUSE **$**
(01-368223; campsite per person MK900, r MK1500-2000;) This atmospheric granite house was built on the crest of the mountain in the early 20th century and its rooms are still redolent with history; cozy rugs, shadowy hardwood floors, and a twee lounge, which might have been transplanted from an Edinburgh tearoom (they also serve scones just to complete the conceit!).

Rooms here are comfy with thick blankets and plenty of space. The menu includes pancakes, *nshima* and homy stews. You can also use the internet for MK15 per minute or do a load of laundry for MK200. By the time you read this they may have built new cabanas in the garden.

Mushroom Farm LODGE **$$**
(0999-652485; www.themushroomfarmmalawi.com; campsite per person US$5, tent hire US$6, s/d US$16.50/23.50, cob chalet s/d US$33/41;) Perched on the edge of the Livingstonia escarpment (aka abyss!), this permaculture campsite and ecolodge run by genial Aussie, Mick, is worth the arduous journey for the warm welcome and views that will have you manually closing your jaw. Three chalets offer simple accommodation – though better still is the cob cottage with its own en suite.

There's also fire-heated communal showers and a compost loo. Wake up in the morning to mist drifting up the mountain, Miles Davis on the speakers, and Mick dishing up amazing food (think pancakes, *nasi goreng*, pasta and succulent steaks...). If you've got the energy there are plenty of adrenalin activities on offer including abseiling and rock-climbing (US$40). Mick can also pick you up from Chitimba to save you the horrible drive (US$50 each way for four persons).

TOP CHOICE **Lukwe Permaculture Camp** CAMPING, ECOLODGE **$$**
(0999-792311, 0999-434985; www.lukwe.com; campsites US$5, tent hire US$6, s/d cabins US$12/20;) Located 10km from Chitimba, above the steep zigzag hairpins, or an hour's downhill walk (about 5km) east from Livingstonia on the mountain road to Chitimba, Lukwe is special. With extraordinary, unbroken views from its funky timber verandah, watch the mountain literally drop at your feet to an infinity below.

The verandah-style cafe is pretty on the eye and serves delectably tasty grub: pancakes, organic veg, fish, sirloin steak and great breakfasts. Four super-clean chalets are set in leafy terraced gardens, and enjoy mozzie nets, balconies and – shall we call it – permaculture-chic? Tasteful Lukwe is all about being part of the environment and the community around it; helping local farmers and being completely self-sufficient. Ask its owner to give you a tour of their inspiring allotments.

Getting There & Away

From the main north–south road between Karonga and Mzuzu, the road to Livingstonia (known as the Gorode) turns off at Chitimba, forcing its way up the escarpment. This twisting, ulcerated road is a test for the most steely drivers; a white-knuckle experience of 21 switchbacks and hairpins, with a boulderous, mainly unpaved surface – at times single track – with the mountain abysmally close to you.

Don't attempt this in anything but a 4WD and *never* in rain – it's just not worth the risk, as your nerves will be frayed even in dry conditions. Better still is to ask Mick at the Mushroom Farm to come and get you from Chitimba, or walk the 2½ hour, 15km trip up the mountain, leaving your bag in the lock-up room at Chitimba Campsite. There's no bus, and you'll wait a very long time if you're hitching. Take care on this road though; isolated incidents of muggings have occurred so it's best to check the latest situation before you set off, or take a local guide from Chitimba Campsite.

The other way to reach Livingstonia, especially if you're coming from the south, is to drive up the dirt road from Rumphi, for which you'll also need a 4WD – that said, it's an easy, dusty and very pretty drive. It's also possible to get a truck up this route, which leaves at 2pm on Tuesdays and Thursdays from outside the Peoples Supermarket in Rumphi and takes about five hours.

A third option is to walk to Livingstonia from the Nyika Plateau, which can by done through Chelinda Camp or the Mushroom Farm.

Rumphi

Rumphi (*rum*-pee), west of the main road between Mzuzu and Karonga and backdropped by hills, is an authentic but forgettable little town. There's a couple of Visa-friendly ATMs, restaurants, a supermarket and a clutch of guesthouses if you get stuck here en route to Nyika National Park, Vwaza Marsh Wildlife Reserve or Livingstonia.

Sleeping & Eating

Matunkha Eco-Tourism LODGE $$$
(☎0888-202643, 0888-293424; campsite per person MK500, dm MK6500, s/d chalets MK7500/9000; @📶) This friendly lodge and orphanage is 3km out of town on the main road to Nyika National Park. You can relax in the pleasant restaurant and bar between volunteering. There are simple en suite *rondavels* (traditional-style huts) here as well as dorms and camping, and all of the profits go towards the orphanage and other community projects. Long-term teachers are welcome.

Country Resthouse GUESTHOUSE $
(☎01-372395; s/d MK2000/2500) The best option on the main road, this guesthouse has small rooms with tiled floors, pastel-coloured walls, fans and en suites. The attached Chef's Pride restaurant serves chicken and chips, meatballs and chicken curry, all accompanied by a blaring TV (mains MK700; 6am to 9pm).

Getting There & Away

Minibuses run to and from Mzuzu (MK1000, one hour). Trucks on their way to Chitipa might drop you off at the turning to Chelinda Camp. Minibuses and *matolas* to Kazuni village (from where you can get to Vwaza Marsh Wildlife Reserve) should cost around MK500. Most transport leaves from outside the Peoples Supermarket.

Nyika National Park

Accessed by a rough road, Malawi's oldest reserve is easily one of the most magical experiences in any trip to the country. Turning burnt amber in the afternoon sun, the highland grass flickers with the stripes of zebras and is punctuated by glittering boulders that look like set dressing from a *Star Trek* movie. Towering at over 2500m above sea level, 3200 sq km **Nyika National Park** (per person/car US$5/2; ⏲6am-6pm) is enigmatic; one moment its rolling grasslands remind

HOW NYIKA WAS FORMED

A small population of hunter-gatherers is believed to have inhabited Nyika (meaning 'wilderness') more than 3000 years ago, and ancient rock art has been found at Fingira Cave, at the southern end of the plateau. When the Bantu people arrived in northern Malawi, most stayed on the plains below the Nyika.

The first Europeans to see the Nyika were probably Scottish missionaries, who reached this area in 1894 after it was brought to the attention of the British government by explorer David Livingstone, although it's quite possible that it was seen by Portuguese explorers who were active in the area long before Livingstone came through. The mission station built by the Scottish missionaries, between Nyika's eastern edge and Lake Malawi, was named Livingstonia and is still a thriving centre today.

Scientists and naturalists who visited Nyika Plateau in the early 20th century recognised the biological importance of the area, and in 1933 measures were taken to protect the stands of juniper trees on the southern part of the plateau from bushfires. In 1948 this section was made into a forest reserve, and at the same time, pine plantations were established around Chelinda, near the centre of the plateau.

There were later plans to extend the plantations and develop the area as a source of wood for a proposed pulp mill on Lake Malawi, but access for logging vehicles proved difficult and the scheme was abandoned. Plantations were, however, established on the Viphya Plateau, and although plans for a Lake Malawi mill were shelved, they were still occasionally discussed, even as late as the 1990s.

In 1965 the entire upper Nyika Plateau was made a national park, and in 1976 this area was extended further to include the lower slopes of the plateau – an important water-catchment area. This most recent boundary extension included several small settlements, and the people living here were relocated to areas outside the park. When they moved they took the names of their villages with them and now, in the area bordering the park, there are several settlements that share names with valleys and other features inside the park itself.

of the Yorkshire Dales, but then an antelope leaps across your bonnet, you note the nearby mound of steaming elephant spore and you remember you're in Africa (and that Nyika is home to a very large population of leopards!).

There are plenty of zebras, bushbucks, reedbucks, roan antelopes and elephants and you may also spot elands, warthogs, klipspringers, jackals, duikers and possibly hyenas and leopards (one until recently could be seen at Chelinda Camp's lake in the morning, taking a drink; between playing voyeur outside chalet windows!). Twitchers should note that more than 400 species of bird have been recorded, including rarities such as the wattled crane and moustached green-tinkerbirds. And after the wet season, the landscape bursts into life in a blaze of wildflowers. There are around 200 species of orchid alone growing on the plateau.

Rather than just driving around in a safari vehicle, you can explore on a mountain bike, ramble through the hills on foot or simply sit down by a gin-clear stream for a spot of fishing. But who knows for how much longer you'll be able to do this on your own, for in 2013, lions (and possibly cheetahs) are due for reintroduction, which will add brilliantly to the drama.

It can get surprisingly cold on the Nyika Plateau, especially at night from June to August when frost is not uncommon. Log fires are provided in the chalets and rooms, but bring a warm sleeping bag if you're camping. During dry periods, sectors of the park are burnt to prevent larger fires later in the season. Before setting off for drives or walks, inquire at the park headquarters too find out about areas that are being burnt.

Activities

Wilderness Safaris (01-771393; www.wilderness-safaris.com) has run the concession at Nyika National Park since 2009; they run a comprehensive range of activities with excellent guides and equipment.

Wildlife Watching

Daytime wildlife drives start from Wilderness Safaris' Chelinda Lodge or Camp at 8am every morning. Thanks to their top guides your chances of seeing wildlife are extremely high (with brazen zebra being very content to pose for photos).

The most exciting wildlife drives, however, are by night. Wilderness Safaris' guides have a decent hit rate (about 40%) for scoping out leopards in the woods near the camp or out in the grasslands. The current population sits at a plump 100. Imagine nursing a Carlsberg Green as you take in the panorama of stars above the open-top Landcrusier, watching pieces of the nocturnal jigsaw slot together – the back end of one of the park's 200 elephants here, the chatter of a hyena there, an eagle owl executing a kill – unforgettable!

Wildlife viewing is good year round, although in July and August the cold weather means the animals move to lower areas. Birdwatching is particularly good between October and April when migratory birds are on the move.

Day Hiking

Although you can't enter the park on foot, hiking is allowed once you've checked into

HIKING & TREKKING ON THE NYIKA PLATEAU

There are a number of long-distance routes available on the Nyika Plateau. For advice contact the excellent Wilderness Safaris who can avail you with the *obligatory* guides and porters, who supply their own sleeping bags, tents, cooking pots and food; you must provide all the equipment and food you need.

Routes to the peaks and viewpoints on the western and northern escarpments are especially popular. The wilderness trails are not designed to help you get the best animal close-ups with your camera, but rather to show you that animals are part of a wider environment and to help you best enjoy the feeling of freedom and space that Nyika provides.

The only set route on Nyika – and by far the most popular – goes from Chelinda to Livingstonia. It's a hugely rewarding and spectacular walk, crossing east through high grassland then dropping steeply through the wooded escarpment and passing through villages and farmland to reach the old mission station at Livingstonia. This route takes three days. The third night is spent in Livingstonia and on the fourth day you can walk down to Chitimba at the lakeshore. For further information there's a chapter on Malawi in Lonely Planet's *Trekking in East Africa*.

Nyika National Park

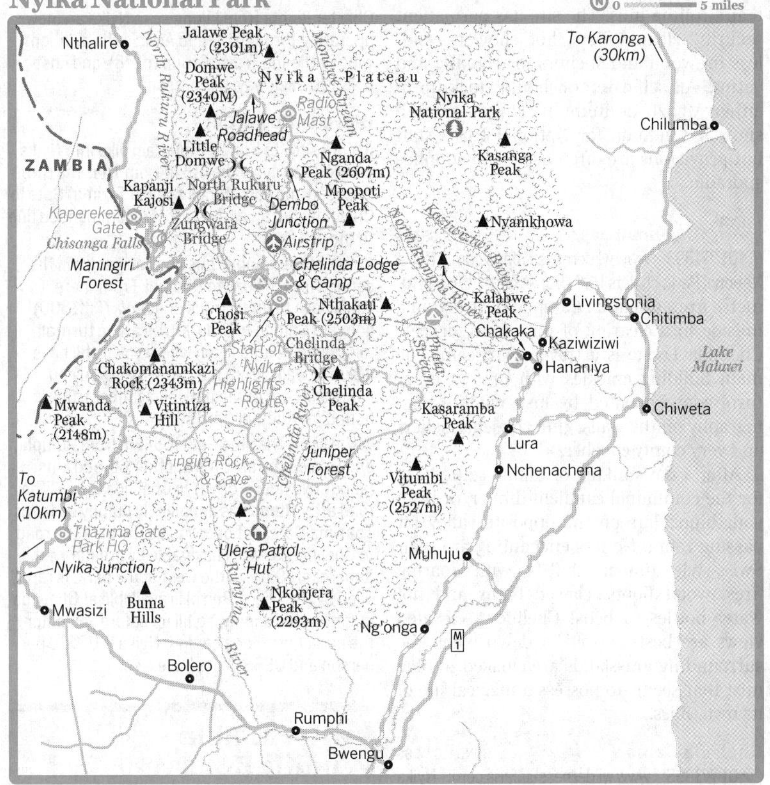

Chelinda Camp – but only with a guide, thanks to an increase in leopard and elephant populations. Wilderness Safaris organise different treks, the main highlight of which is the three-day hike to Livingstonia (guide per day US$90).

Mountain Biking

Nyika's network of dirt roads is ideal for mountain biking. You can base yourself at Chelinda and go for day rides (per day bike/guide US$40/40, kids half price) in various directions or camp out overnight (for which you'll need to hire a guide). Make sure you leave plenty of time to return before dark.

Horse Riding

Nyika's wide, open landscape lends itself perfectly to horse riding and this is by far the most enjoyable and exhilarating way to experience the plateau. You can also get much closer to animals such as zebras, elands and roans when on horseback.

Wilderness Safaris won the concession for horse riding in 2011 and by the time you read this they should *hopefully* have found a suitable partner to reinstate horseback safaris once again.

Fishing

Some anglers reckon Nyika National Park offers some of the best rainbow trout fishing in Malawi. The best time of year to fish is October and November. Fishing is allowed in the dams near Chelinda Camp (Dam One has the lion's share) and in nearby streams. Only fly fishing is permitted and there's a limit of six fish per rod per day to maintain numbers. Cost of rod per hour/day is US$4/20.

Sleeping & Eating

Camping Ground CAMPING $

(campsites per person US$15) About 2km from the main Chelinda Camp, this camp is set in a secluded site with vistas of the plateau's rolling hills. The site has permanent security, clean toilets, hot showers, endless firewood and shelters for cooking and eating. All self-caterers should stock up in either Mzuzu or Rumphi. There's a small shop at Chelinda for National Parks staff but provisions are often basic and supplies sporadic.

TOP CHOICE Chelinda Lodge LODGE **$$$**

(☎01-771393; www.wilderness-safaris.com; Nyika National Park; chalets US$450;) One kilometre from Chelinda Camp and sitting on a hillside in a clearing of pine trees, upscale Chelinda Lodge is a traveller's dream. The main building crackles with fires at every turn, complemented by lush wildlife photography on the walls, glittering chandeliers and very comfy couches.

After a day's hiking or biking settle back for the communal candlelit dinner, or train your binoculars on the opposite valley for passing zebra. No less enchanting are their Swiss-style timber chalets with roaring fires, wood floors, clawed baths and hot water bottles in beds! Chelinda's elevated views are best enjoyed at dawn when the surrounding grasslands are cloaked in blue mist that seems to possess a magical life of its own. Bliss.

Chelinda Camp BUNGALOW **$$$**

(☎01-771393; www.wilderness-safaris.com; Nyika National Park; chalets US$160;) Nestled into the lee of a valley beside a small lake, Chelinda Camp (run by Wilderness Safaris) is insanely picturesque. Its bungalows have an unfussy '70s aspect to them and are ideal for families, with decent self-catering facilities, cosy sitting rooms and stone fireplaces.

Keep your eyes peeled for leopards drinking at the lake come dawn (and ask to see their claw marks on one of the chalet walls!). Reception and a highly atmospheric restaurant are but a few yards away.

Getting There & Away

Despite most maps showing otherwise, there is no road of any sort between Chelinda and Livingstonia or any other town on the eastern side of the plateau. Getting to the park by public transport can be a bit of an ordeal, so it's much easier if you can hire wheels in Lilongwe. Wilderness Safaris can also organise transfers here from their base in Lilongwe as can Ulendo Travel Group (p278).

Air

Charter flights from Lilongwe to Nyika are now operating through Ulendo Airlink, the aviation wing of Ulendo Travel Group (p278), and cost US$500 each way, per person.

Bicycle, Bus & Car

It's possible to bring a mountain bike into Nyika and you can cycle the 60km from Thazima (pronounced and sometimes spelled Tazima) Gate to Chelinda, but an early start is recommended due to the distance.

The nearest public bus you can get is via the service from Mzuzu to Rumphi. From there, you'll have to find a truck or *matola* (MK1500) going to Chitipa to drop you off at the turn-off to Chelinda Camp, from where you'll still have 20km to walk. From the camp itself you can catch a lift out of the park on a timber truck bound for Rumphi (MK1500).

The main Thazima Gate is 54km from Rumphi; once inside the park it's another 60-odd kms (about two hours' drive) to Chelinda Camp. The road after Rumphi is appallingly bumpy as far as Thazima Gate, but once inside the park the road to Chelinda is easily navigable by ordinary car. Kaperekezi Gate, in the west of the park, is rarely used by travellers. Petrol is available at Chelinda but in limited supply, so fill up before you enter the park. Entry for a car into Nyika is US$10 per person and US$3 per vehicle.

Vwaza Marsh Wildlife Reserve

This 1000-sq-km reserve is not on the mainstream tourist track, but with its compact size and plentiful buffalo, elephant and hippo population, this is a park that shouldn't be overlooked.

The park ranges in appearance from large flat areas of mopane woodland to open swamp and wetlands. The Luwewe River runs through the reserve (draining the marshland) and joins the South Rukuru River (the reserve's southern border), which flows into Lake Kazuni. It joins the Zambian Luangwa ecosystem to the west.

A good network of driveable tracks in the reserve is easily explored in a 4WD or high-clearance vehicle; if you're in a 2WD, ask at Kazuni Camp for advice on the condition of the tracks. The best driving route is along the southern edge of the reserve, parallel to the river, heading to Zoro Pools. A better way to witness wildlife is on foot – either around Lake Kazuni or on a longer wilderness trail – but you must be accompanied by a guide.

Like many of Malawi's parks, poachers have hit Vwaza. As well as a plethora of antelope – puku, impala, roan and kudu, to name a few – there are around 2000 buffaloes and 300 elephants; it's not unusual to see herds of 30 or 40 of them. Vwaza's birdwatching is also excellent. There are some 300 species present here and this is one of the best places in Malawi to see waders, including storks and herons. There are few predators here but occasionally lions and leopards are spotted, as are wild dogs that sometimes pass through from Zambia.

In fact, just sitting around Vwaza's main camp will bring plenty of animal sightings for it looks over Lake Kazuni (which is inhabited by more than 500 hippos), and on most days you'll see crocodiles lying out in the sun, hippos popping their heads out of the water and a steady parade of animals coming down to the lake to drink.

The best time of year to visit is in the dry season; just after the rainy season, the grass is high and you might go away without seeing anything. There are whispers that the excellent Barefooot Safaris may tender to run the concession here which will be good news for travellers looking for more security and comfort. The park costs US$10 entry fee per person and US$3 per vehicle.

Sleeping

Lake Kazuni Safari Camp CAMP **$$**
(☎0884-462518; huts US$40) The camp's basic en-suite, thatch-and-brick cabanas are perfectly positioned on the lakeshore – the local residents are so plentiful, it feels as if you've just stepped into the pages of a children's picturebook.

Although the management is seriously depleted in its offerings – since the original concession manager pulled a runner – the National Parks' skeleton staff is doing its best and can cook you dinner in the camp's kitchen if you stock up on food in nearby Rumphi.

There are no vehicles at present that can take you on a wildlife-watching drive, however, friendly guide **Godwin** (☎0994-418625) is happy to accompany you in your own vehicle as long as it's a 4WD (per trip for 90 minutes US$10). Alternatively, a walking safari costs US$10 per trip. Contact Manuel the **Park Manager** (☎884-462518) to get a status report on whether the lodge is still open.

Getting There & Away

If you're travelling by public transport, first get to Rumphi (reached from Mzuzu by minibus for MK1000). From Rumphi there are plenty of *matolas* travelling to and from the Kazuni area and you should be able to get a lift to the main gate for around MK1000. Otherwise buses and minibuses to Mzimba might drop you at Kazuni village, which is about 1km from the park gate.

By car, head west from Rumphi. Turn left after 10km (Vwaza Marsh Wildlife Reserve is signposted) and continue for about 20km. Where the road swings left over a bridge, go straight on to reach the park gate and camp after 1km.

Mzuzu

Dusty, busy, sprawling Mzuzu is the largest town in northern Malawi and serves as the transport hub for the region. Travellers heading to Blantyre, Lilongwe, Nkhata Bay, Nyika or Viphya, or to and from Tanzania are likely to spend a night or two here. Mzuzu has banks, shops, a post office, supermarkets, pharmacies, petrol stations and other facilities, which are especially useful if you've come into Malawi from the north.

Sights

The **museum** (M'Mbelwa Rd; admission MK200; ⏲7.30am-noon & 1-5pm, tours at 9am, 11am, 1.30pm & 2pm) has displays on the people and the land of northern Malawi. Exhibits include traditional hunting implements, musical instruments, and a mock-up of a traditional hut. If you're planning to head up to Livingstonia there's an interesting exhibition telling the story of the missionaries' journey.

Sleeping

TOP CHOICE **Mzoozoozoo** HOSTEL **$**
(☎0888-864493; campsite MK500, r MK3800, dm MK1400; @📶) This funky backpackers haven delights with its lovely garden, quiet location (a few minutes' walk out of town off Jomo Kenyatta Rd), and colourful basic rooms. The friendly vibe, art-spattered walls and warm management, plus the terrific comfort food (steaks and chicken) may change your travel plans by a night or two.

Some nice touches include flip-flops in the showers, a huge DSTV in the communal room, a book exchange, and if ordered in advance, dinner served on the verandah.

Mzuzu

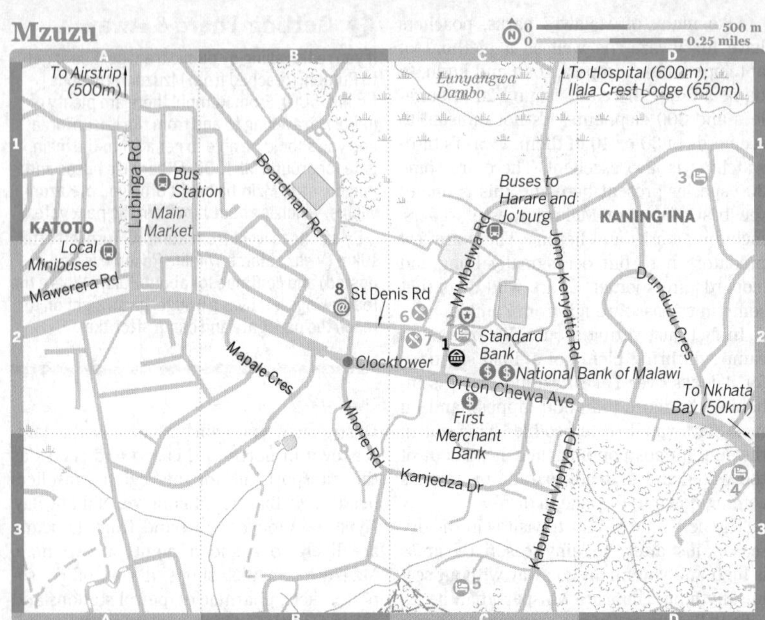

Mzuzu

Sights

1 Museum C2

Sleeping

2 Mimosa Court Hotel C2
3 Mzoozoozoo D1
4 Mzuzu Lodge D3
5 Sunbird Mzuzu Hotel C3

Eating

6 A1 Restaurant C2
7 Greenvee Restaurant C2
Sombrero Restaurant .... (see 2)

Information

8 Postdotnet B2

Sunbird Mzuzu Hotel HOTEL **$$$**
(✆01-332622; www.sunbirdmalawi.com; s/d from US$160/180; P❄@📶) Easily the plushest digs in the city, this large hotel is set in imposing grounds and has huge rooms with deep-pile carpets, DSTV, and views of the town's golf course just off Kabunduli Viphya Dr. As you'd expect from the Sunbird Group, the service is friendly and efficient and the place feels of an international standard. There's also a cosy cafe selling posh coffee with wi-fi for laptops.

Mzuzu Lodge LODGE **$$$**
(✆01-310224/226; Orton Chewa Ave; s/d standard US$50/65, executive US$65/95; P❄@📶) If you stay in this motel-style digs (it's in a nice, peaceful location east of town), go for an executive room – away from the noise of the bar and with all the hotel amenities you could want like armoires and TVs. Standard rooms, on the other hand, are dingy, overpriced and next to a noisy bar.

Mimosa Court Hotel HOTEL **$$**
(✆01-312609, 01-312833; s/d MK12,700/14,500; P) Set back from the road, behind the museum, Mimosa is clean and friendly and has a decent restaurant and pleasant bar. Rooms are large, scrupulously clean and well catered for with mozzie nets, DSTVs, en suites, bureaus and fans. It's in a convenient location in the centre of town, off M'Mbelwa Rd.

Flame Tree Campsite CAMPING **$**
(✆0999-511423; campsite per person MK700; P) Run by Maggie, the owner of Flame Tree Guesthouse, this lovely campsite, 6km south of town on the M1, sits in manicured gardens spilling over with wild fruit trees and is popular with campervans and campers. There are two shower and toilet blocks and an on-site mechanic. At the time of research there was no cafe or shop.

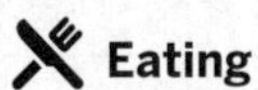

Eating

TOP CHOICE **A1 Restaurant** RESTAURANT $
(St Denis St; mains around MK1000; 11.45am-2pm & 6-10pm;) Super-fresh indigo-walled A1 has DSTV on the wall, abstract art and a menu featuring North Indian cuisine. It offers classic dishes like tikka masala and rogan josh; the chicken korma is tasty.

Greenvee Restaurant INDIAN, MALAWIAN $
(0888-899666; St Denis Rd; mains from MK800; 6am-10pm) With its red checked-cloth tables, airy interior and verandah, Greenvee is a nice spot to people-watch between tucking into *nshima*, Indian curries, steak, and chicken and chips.

Sombrero Restaurant MALAWIAN $
(01-312833; mains MK800; breakfast, lunch & dinner;) The food here has a reputation as some of the best in town and the small sunny terrace and congenial atmosphere make it a fun place for a meal. Steaks, fish and curries are on the menu. It's located at the Mimosa Court Hotel.

Information

The National Bank of Malawi, Standard Bank and First Merchant Bank, all on Orton Chewa Ave, exchange travellers cheques and money, and offer credit-card withdrawals. National and Standard Banks have ATMs that accept foreign cards. If you're heading to Nkhata Bay, there are now a couple of ATMs but just in case stock up on cash here.

Internet access is available at **Postdotnet** (per 30 min MK300; 8am-5pm Mon-Fri, to 12.30pm Sat) on Boardman Rd.

Getting There & Away

AXA City Trouper buses go to Lilongwe at 7am and 5pm (MK3500, five hours) and local buses leave at 7.30am and 6pm (MK2200, six to seven hours). AXA buses also go to Karonga, leaving at 6.30am and 10am (MK1500, four hours) and local buses leave to Karonga at 6.30am (MK700, five hours) via Rumphi (MK1000) and Chitimba (MK540).

Minibuses go to Nkhata Bay (MK850, one to two hours), Karonga (MK2000, three to four hours), Chitimba (MK1700, two hours), Rumphi (MK1000, one hour) and the Tanzanian border (MK2500, four hours).

National Bus Company has daily departures to Lilongwe (MK2250), Blantyre (MK3000) and Salima (MK3000).

The Taqwa Bus, originating in Lilongwe, travels between Mzuzu and Nairobi (Kenya) daily (MK24,000), calling at Songwe for the border (MK5000), Mbeya (Tanzania; MK7000) and Dar es Salaam (Tanzania; MK13,000). You should report to the station at 11.30pm for a midnight departure. The bus crosses the border at first light, goes through Mbeya in the morning, gets to Dar es Salaam at around 10pm and leaves for Nairobi the next morning.

KM Bus Services (0888-639363) leaves from the forecourt of Mbacheda Guest House at 7pm on Fridays, going to Harare (Zimbabwe; MK17,000) and Jo'burg (South Africa; MK23,000).

Nkhata Bay

There's something distinctly Caribbean about this place; with banana-coloured fishing boats buzzing across the green bay, vivid market stalls hawking barbecued fish, and music filling the air. For backpackers there's a clutch of perfectly positioned guesthouses perched on cliffs tumbling down to the lake, plus a few upscale family options. Be careful not to entirely give yourself over to lotus eating though, for there are loads of activities to enjoy before you hammock flop; be it snorkelling, diving, fish-eagle feeding, kayaking or forest walks.

Strung along the coast from the town centre, most lodges are secreted in small bays. All are reached via a road that climbs up and down a hill to the next bay. Be careful of walking between town and your lodge at night; the road is unlit and muggings are not infrequent (though thanks to a heightened police presence they are getting less). Walk in numbers or take a guard from your lodge with you.

Activities

Swimming

On the southern side of Nkhata Bay, **Chikale Beach** is a popular spot for swimming and lazing on the sand, especially at weekends. Snorkelling equipment is free for guests at most of the lodges.

Kayaking

Monkey Business (0999-437247; blondieleap@hotmail.com), based at Butterfly Space, and **Chimango Tours** (0999-268595), based at Mayoka Village, can organise paddling excursions personally tailored to your needs – anything from half a day to a few days down the coast. A full day usually costs US$40.

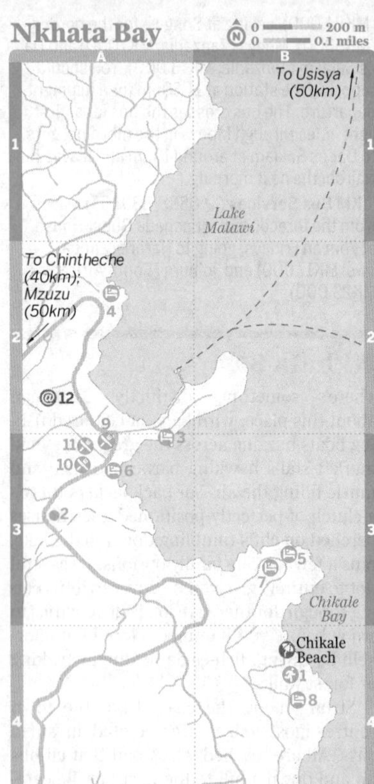

Nkhata Bay

Activities, Courses & Tours

Chimango Tours .... (see 7)
1 Monkey Business B4
2 Nkhata Bay Safari A3

Sleeping

3 Aqua Africa A3
4 Big Blue Star A2
5 Butterfly Space B3
6 Ilala Bay Lodge A3
7 Mayoka Village B3
8 Njaya Lodge B4

Eating

9 Hot Spot A3
10 Kaya Papaya A3
Mayoka Village .... (see 7)
11 Take Away Palace A3

Information

Aqua Africa .... (see 3)
12 L-Net Internet Cafe A2

Typical itineraries include idyllic spots along the northern lakeshore such as Usisya and Ruarwe.

Diving

Aqua Africa DIVING

(☎0999-921418, 01-852284; www.aquaafrica.co.uk) The bay's only dive operator, this dependable western-run outfit sits up the hill two minutes' walk from the harbour. Casual dives for certified divers cost US$50, and full PADI four-day beginner courses cost US$375 (including all materials). Colourful chiclid fish, the kind you've probably seen in a dentist's aquarium, swim throughout the lake, but more spectacular are the schools of dolphinfish who are drawn to your torch on night dives.

Aqua Africa also offers windsurfing rentals (per half day US$20) and snorkelling gear (per half day US$15). There's also a very tasty cafe bar where you can snack on wraps and posh coffee as you learn your theory.

Fish-Eagle Feeding & Snorkelling

Both Monkey Business and Chimango Tours offer enjoyable trips out on the lake to feed fish eagles. Typically this takes a half day and costs US$15. The excellent Kumbu who runs Monkey Business can also take you cliff jumping with an enjoyable barbecue and snorkel combined for US$15.

Tours

Nkhata Bay Safari TOUR

(☎0999-265064; daviemzungu@yahoo.co.uk; ⊙office 7am-5pm) Run by Dave, this tour company offers combined five-day trips to Vwaza, Nyika and Livingstonia for US$500, as well as tailored trips further afield. He can also arrange bus bookings for Tanzania, cabins for the *Ilala* ferry, flights and lodges. Sunset cruises cost US$20.

Sleeping

Nkhata Bay has several places to stay, all strung out in a line along the road into town and along the lakeshore. Beds at most places have mosquito nets. To get from town to the lodges at Chikale Beach, stay on the road, cross the bridge and then head up the big hill. It's about one to two kilometres, depending on the lodge.

TOP CHOICE Butterfly Space GUESTHOUSE $

(☎0999-265065; www.butterfly-space.com; campsite per person MK750, dm MK1500, chalet with/without bathroom MK4000/2500; P@🛜) Run by Alice and Khumbu, inspiring, colourful and socially committed Butterfly, next to Mayoka Village, is a rare backpackers oasis. There's a palapa-style lounge or spacious beachfront bar to chill in, a private beach, internet cafe, media centre, self-catering block and a restaurant serving authentic Tongan cuisine, as well as pancakes, steak and chips, or muffins.

It gets better too: Butterfly Space is passionately involved in youth programs, so you can volunteer on-site in the youth centre helping with computer, painting or English lessons. There's also a craft shop. Rooms in the A-frame cabanas are basic but very clean.

Aqua Africa LODGE $$

(☎0999-921418, 01-352284; www.aqua-africa.co.uk; r from US$35-80; P❄@🛜) With cozy en suite rooms with polished stone floors, private balconies, huge beds and step-in mozzie nets, this lovely accommodation is often used by resident divers. The Dive Deck Cafe, complete with wicker loungers and viewing deck, has an excellent menu ranging from full breakfasts to salads, tortilla wraps and muffins. Staff are equally friendly and helpful.

Mayoka Village LODGE $$

(☎0999-268595, 01-994025; www.mayokavillage.com; dm US$8, s/d chalet US$20/40, s/d chalet without bathroom US$15/28; P@🛜) Cleverly shaped around the rocky topography of a cliff, boutique-style Mayoka cascades down in a series of beautiful bamboo-and-stone chalets. There are myriad romantic nooks to take in the lake below, or to grab some rays on sun loungers. There's also a great waterfront bar.

All chalets are nicely finished with tasteful furniture, fans and some have wraparound verandahs. Check out what has to be the most stylish compost loo in Nkhata Bay! Lovely.

Njaya Lodge LODGE $

(☎0999-409878, 01-352342; www.njayalodge.com; camping MK800, reed/stone chalets MK2000/2000, family chalets MK4500-7000; P❄@🛜) Set in terraced gardens bursting with frangipani trees and palms, with manicured lawns tumbling down to the spearmint water, Njaya has tasteful family-sized chalets up on the hill, cosy reed huts, and striking stone cottages right by the lake. Think wicker chairs, choice linen and cool floors.

Njaya also has a restaurant whose verandah is the perfect sundowner spot; it serves great barbecued chambo and chips, bluefish and bubblefish.

Big Blue Star GUESTHOUSE $

(☎01-352316; campsite per person MK1000, dm/s/d without bathroom MK1500/1700/3750; P@🛜) With a pulsy reggae beat from its lively bar, and its hillside spot with great lake views, Big Blue Star is immediately appealing. There's a book exchange, free storage, a boho chill-out lounge with a billowing sarong ceiling, free dugout canoes for guests, overlander parking spaces and free wi-fi.

Accommodation comes in small colourful dorms (with mozzie nets) or reed huts, plus a few shaded spots for tents. The staff are friendly too.

Ilala Bay Lodge LODGE $$

(☎01-352362; s/d MK4000/5000; P@🛜) Ilala looks run down on the outside but its rooms, with cream interiors and denim-blue trim, are fresh, spacious and have large tiled bathrooms as well as TVs, mozzie nets, bureaus and fans. Not really a traveller haunt but peaceful all the same. Has its own private beach and there's a restaurant serving Malawian staples.

Eating & Drinking

TOP CHOICE Kaya Papaya THAI, MALAWIAN $

(mains from MK900; ⏲7am-late, food served to 9pm; 🛜✍) Close to the harbour, with its purple and orange livery and shadowy interior, Kaya Papaya has more than a touch of Afro-chic; it's matched by a Thai-accented menu of zesty salads, pizza and Malawian fare like butterfish with *nshima*. If you are still hungry, you should try the fruit pancake and homemade cakes.

Mayoka Village INTERNATIONAL $

(mains from MK950; ⏲7am-3pm & 6-8.30pm; P🛜✍) This guacamole-green bar is infused with African sounds and the lapping waves of the lake a few feet away. The alfresco lounge bar is a great place to enjoy organic salads, breakfasts, hamburgers, baguette sandwiches and stir-fries. The staff may even be dancing!

WHERE TO ON THE LAKE

Lake Malawi is the defining feature of this little country's landscape, enticing travellers with its glassy bottle-green waters, abundance of colourful underwater life and endless saffron beaches. It has often been described as an inland sea and, when trying to spot Mozambique's hazy silhouette on the horizon, it's easy to see why. The lake's enigmatic weather often entertains storms thick enough to rouse 5m waves and intimidating swells, shifting within an hour to reveal flawless blue skies reflected in the water's glassy veneer.

The lakeshore's environment changes starkly from dramatic escarpments in the north to flat, sandy bays in the south. It can be tough figuring out where to go, so the following should help you decide.

The North

The least-developed section of the lake is home to Chitimba Campsite, which serves as a magnet for overland trucks coming in from Tanzania.

Nkhata Bay

Lush hillside framing indented bays makes the landscape reminiscent of the Caribbean (and so is the laid-back vibe). This is above all a beach resort for backpackers, but those in search of a little more comfort will find it too, and the excellent diving, kayaking and socialising will keep them here.

Likoma & Chizumulu Islands

Sublime beaches, unparalleled diving, breathtaking walks, preserved cultures and a beautiful missionary cathedral make these islands a must-see. There's excellent accommodation, from budget beach huts to five-star luxury, and it provides a rare opportunity to immerse yourself in untainted village life.

Chintheche Strip

A secluded collection of camping grounds, lodges and resorts pepper this picturesque stretch of the lake, which is a hop, skip and jump from the wooded hills of the Viphya Plateau.

Senga Bay

The nearest beach paradise to Lilongwe offers a wide range of places to stay, excellent snorkelling and bush walking, and trips to the nearby islands to see giant monitor lizards.

Cape Maclear

Blissful beach vistas, chilled-out resorts and a friendly little village all mix quite happily in Cape Maclear. It's also the staging post for trips to the exquisitely pretty Mumbo Island.

Monkey Bay to Mangochi

A smattering of top-end hotels, midrange resorts and budget lodges, many with a few kilometres of private beach and the facilities to keep you from moving far.

Take Away Palace INDIAN $
(MK1000; ☑) Run by a local Indian family, sit in the diner-style interior or outside, feasting on a menu spanning Northern Indian cuisine to Western dishes. It also does takeaways. On the main drag by the harbour.

Hot Spot MALAWIAN $
(Main Street; mains MK800; ⏱7am-9pm; ☑) With plenty of local characters frequenting it, this simple eatery has vibrant red walls and sits on the main drag by the harbour. Authentic Malawian fare like fresh fish, beef, *nshima*, beans and rice.

The **Peoples Supermarket** on the main drag sells toiletries, biscuits and milk.

ℹ Information

There's nowhere to change money but there are two ATMs at the top of the hill (50m before you reach Big Blue Star hostel). While they accept Visa they don't accept MasterCard. Alternatively, some of the lodges accept credit cards, US currency and travellers cheques for payment. Internet access is available at **Aqua Africa** (per min MK20; ⏲10am-4pm Mon-Sat) and **L-Net Internet Cafe** (per half hour MK250; ⏲7am-5pm Mon-Fri, 8am-12.30pm Sat & Sun).

Dangers & Annoyances

Travellers have been attacked and robbed when walking outside the town centre (in particular to and from Chikale Beach at night), so take extra care when walking this route as it can be quite deserted. Most travellers will encounter a fair amount of hassle from local beach boys offering a bewildering amount of services, from beach barbecues to personalised key rings. If you're not interested, be polite but very firm and they should leave you alone.

Getting There & Away

All buses and minibuses go from the bus stand on the main road. AXA buses run to Mzuzu (MK800, two hours) and minibuses run to Nkhotakota (MK1000, five hours), Chintheche (MK600, one hour) and Mzuzu (MK700, one to two hours). To reach Lilongwe the quickest option is to go to Mzuzu and transfer bus.

Many travellers also come or go on the *Ilala* ferry which arrives at 1am on Sunday then heads for Ruarwe and Usisya at 7am. On Monday it returns at 1pm to head south that day at 8pm for Likoma and Chizumulu Islands. Various transport boats also go to the above islands; ask at the harbour office for more info.

Around Nkhata Bay

North of Nkhata Bay, the steep slopes of the Rift Valley escarpment plunge straight down to the lake and there's no room for a road alongside the shore. The isolated villages along this stretch provide a remote experience that is well worth the hike.

Fifteen kilometres north of the village of Usisya is **Zulukhuni River Lodge** (☎0995-636701, 0999-492774; campsite US$4, dm US$8, chalets US$13, stone house US$16), a gorgeous hideaway barely visible from the water. Stone-and-thatch chalets teeter over the water, backed by a wild, jungly garden, and there's an impressive bar and restaurant area nestled underneath the curve of a cliff. A troop of fish eagles, kingfishers and otters regularly entertain guests and there are plenty of walks to the nearby river and waterfall to be had.

The *Ilala* ferry stops at Ruarwe village, 20 minutes' walk south of the lodge. Alternatively, 'Jack Boat' leaves Nkhata Bay on Wednesday and Friday at 12pm for Ruarwe (eight hours; call ☎0999-071914 to book a place). Monkey Business (p291) can also charter a boat (MK3000) anytime to reach Zulukhuni Lodge – speak to Khumbu. You can book the lodge at Kaya Papaya (p293) in Nkhata Bay.

Chintheche Strip

About 40km south of Nkhata Bay, this endlesss stretch of golden sand fringed by woods and dazzling blue water, known as the 'Chintheche Strip', is a destination for weekenders from Lilongwe and self-drive travellers. Swim, horse-ride, cycle or just flop and wait for the approach of fish eagles whose crowing punctuates the still of the vast denim sky. Chintheche was also home to the original Lake of Stars festival before it moved south. Chinteche Inn is now organising a new 'Moon Rock' festival, focusing on local bands.

Most lodges are situated at least 2km east of the main road that runs between Nkhata Bay and Nkhotakota. If you're travelling by bus, the express services may not stop at every turn-off, but minibuses stop almost anywhere on request. The access roads for the majority of the lodges require 4WD or a high-clearance car, as the tracks are pretty bad.

Activities

Boat Rides

Chintheche Inn can organise speedboat trips to nearby Morning Star Island (maximum six persons, per boat US$60). You can also hire a wooden fishing boat to go snorkelling (US$80, maximum eight persons).

Birdwatching Walks & Treks

Organised by Wilderness Safaris based at Chintheche Inn, accompany Wesley the guide to see blue-spotted doves, fish eagles, malachite kingfishers, nightjars as well as purple bandit sunbirds. Walks cost US$10 per person. **Wilderness Safaris** (☎01-771393; www.wilderness-safaris.com; Kenyatta Rd, Bisnowaty Service Centre, Lilongwe) also run cultural walks to a local tree nursery and the deaf school at Bandawe Mission. Walks also encompass a trip to a fishing village and local orphanage (US$10 per person).

LIVINGSTONIA TAKE TWO

If you're visiting one of the lodges on the Chintheche Strip, you should try to visit the **Old Bandawe Mission**, a cavernous church built between 1886 and 1900, which was the short-lived location of the Livingstonia mission. Dr Robert Laws moved the mission north to Bandawe from its original site at Cape Maclear when members of his flock kept falling ill with malaria. Unfortunately, after a few years, the same thing happened at Bandawe, and Dr Laws eventually moved the mission to the cool, malaria-free hillside town of Khondowe, in 1894.

Perhaps the most interesting thing at Bandawe is the graveyard where several of the early Scottish missionaries are buried. It's some 400m from the church in a hauntingly beautiful spot – their graves silhouetted against the lake and surrounded by a series of low white walls. The church is near Makuzi Beach Lodge. Follow the signs to the lodge from the main road and the church is 2.5km down the track.

Diving

Aquanuts Dive School DIVING
(☎0991-922242; www.aquanutsdivers.com; Kande Beach Resort) Run by Justin, Aquanuts Dive School, based at Kande Beach Resort, has an on-site training pool and offers introductory four-day PADI courses (US$350), casual dives (US$40) and PADI scuba refresher courses. They also run night dives (US$50).

Horse Riding

A professionally run stable, **Kande Horse** (☎0888-500416; www.kandehorse.com; Chinteche strip) has 28 horses and organises a variety of excursions from two-hour forest rides (adult/child MK7500/4000) to swimming with the horses and riding through the forest (MK15,000). You can also stay here fullboard and ride for US$220 per day. Accommodation is in a stone farmhouse at the stables. It is 50km south of Nkhata Bay, just outside the village of Kande, and is well signposted from the road.

Sleeping

TOP CHOICE **Chintheche Inn** LODGE $$$
(☎01-771393; www.wilderness-safaris.com; campsite per person US$10, s/d US$210/320; P⊖❄@☎) Set in gardens choking on oleander, flame and mango trees, stylish Chintheche Inn has 10 tin-roofed, low slung chalets and one family cottage. While they might look ordinary on the outside, the rooms are beautifully finished within, enjoying unblemished lake views, separate lounges, step-through mozzie nets, capacious bathrooms, myriad candles and upscale African chic.

The hotel restaurant is decked in wicker chairs, a crackling stone fireplace come evening, and you can eat in or alfresco. The hotel can also organise a host of activities including cycling and walks (through owner Wilderness Safaris). There's also an immaculate shower block for campers set in its own area.

Kande Beach Resort RESORT $$
(☎01-357376; www.kandebeach.com; campsite per person US$5, dm US$10, cabins per person US$13, beach chalets US$26, chalets with bathroom US$45, family chalet US$60; P@☎) About 7km from the Makuzi turn-off (55km south of Nkhata Bay), this traveller's paen to hedonism has a lovely reed bar, bags of alfresco seating and hammocks to flop on, plus beach *palapa* shelters for added shade.

There's a volleyball court, on-site dive centre (Aquanuts), as well as very nice chalets with tree-trunk four-posters (unfortunately the latter are set away from the beach behind the overland truck camping area, so you might not have a peaceful night). There are also dorms and plenty of room to pitch a tent.

Sambani Lodge LODGE $
(☎0888-713857; campsite per person MK1500, s/d incl breakfast MK5000/7000; P) Set in peaceful, shaded gardens aglow with frangipani trees and flowers, chalets here are faded but not without charm. Rooms come with bureaus, mozzie nets and en suites, and the views from the verandah are serene. Reached by a rutted road.

Makuzi Beach Lodge LODGE $$$
(☎01-357296; www.makuzibeach.com; campsite per person US$5, r incl breakfast US$70, r superior US$85; P❄@☎) Your first glimpse of the beach Makuzi sits on is trippy; it's bookended by hill and woods, and in between are

tree-spouting granite boulders angled in powder-fine sand.

Set in paradisical gardens, Makuzi's thatch-roofed, witches' hat *rondavels* are very tempting, with boutique flourishes like four posters, tasteful linen and choice artwork. For activities there's free kayaking, snorkelling and fishing. You can find Makuzi Beach by continuing south down the main road past Chintheche.

Ngala Beach Lodge LODGE **$$$**
(☎0888-192003, 01-295359; www.ngalabeach.com; standard chalet s/d US$60/100, superior chalet US$120/200; P@🛜) This lovely traditional thatch lodge has tiled floors, high ceilings and gardens dripping in bougainvillea. A-frame chalets are romantically finished with hardwood furniture, Persian rugs and billowing white linen. One caveat – the lodge sits on a stretch of beach near a reed bank (to the left), and come dusk its waters are a hunting spot for crocs.

The restaurant serves freshly caught chambo, and has a revolving a la carte menu.

Likoma Island

Likoma and Chizumulu Islands are on the Mozambican side of Lake Malawi, but are part of Malawi. Blissful Likoma measures 17 sq km and is home to around 6000 people.

Likoma's flat and sandy south is littered with baobabs, and offers a constant panoramic view of Mozambique's wild coast only 40km away. The island's main drawcard is an abundance of pristine beaches and the activities revolving around them, but there's a healthy dose of other activities, both cultural and physical, to fill several days here.

Sights

In Chipyela, the huge Anglican **Cathedral of St Peter**, which is said to be the same size as Winchester Cathedral, should not be missed; its stained-glass windows, crumbling masonry and sheer scale are a testament to the zeal of its creators' religious conviction. Climb the tower for spectacular views. If you're lucky you might meet the charming old verger who'll happily give you a tour, and you're welcome to join in the vibrant service on Sunday morning. Nearby, the **market place** contains a few shops and stalls. The *Ilala* ferry stops at a beach about 1km to the south.

> **IMMIGRATION OFFICE: GETTING TO MOZAMBIQUE**
>
> The main Mozambique border crossing to the east (where you can also get visas on arrival) is Cóbuè, a short ride over the water from Likoma Island. Local boats will take you there for US$3 and you pay US$70 for a visa. In the market by the Cathedral in Cóbuè there's an Immigration Office to fill in your exit pass. Right beside the office are the boatmen.

Activities

Swimming is a must on Likoma and is best on the long stretches of beach in the south. The tropical fish population has been unaffected by the mainland's overfishing, and the **snorkelling** is excellent. Kaya Mawa arranges three-day open-water PADI **scuba-diving** courses (US$315) run by Josh and Kevin. The island's compact but diverse area is also perfect for **walking** or **mountain biking** – you can bring bikes across on the ferry or hire them from Mango Drift for US$10 per day.

Sleeping & Eating

TOP CHOICE **Kaya Mawa** BOUTIQUE HOTEL **$$$**
(☎0999-318359; www.kayamawa.com; per person chalets full board US$375-435; ❄@🛜) Remember Scaramanga's pad in *The Man with the Golden Gun*? Kaya Mawa, set on an amber-coloured beach lapped by turquoise water, is the ultimate location to live out your inner Bond. A place to chase away crow's feet, its cliffside chalets, cleverly moulded around the landscape, are so beautiful you'll never want to leave; think plunge baths, the gentle lap of waves and the tinkle of a waiter quietly appearing with a bottle of chilled Champagne at your verandah. Tempted? You should be, for this is one of the finest boutique experiences on the continent. The bar-cum-restaurant is somewhere between a Bedouin dream and Caribbean shack. Dinner is set by candlelight on the beach, staff are almost elfin in their diplomacy and discretion, while the food is dreamed up by a chef who trained under Jamie Oliver. Massages can be had for US$65 or reflexology for US$50 and there's a boutique selling exquisite handmade jewellery and sarongs. It's only when you leave Kaya Mawa that you truly appreciate how special it is.

LIKOMA MISSIONARIES & THE CATHEDRAL OF ST PETER

European involvement on Likoma Island began in 1882 when members of Universities Mission to Central Africa (UMCA) chose the island as a protective base from attacks from the warlike Ngoni and Yao peoples.

Between 1903 and 1905 the huge cathedral was built and dedicated to St Peter – appropriately a fisherman. Today it remains one of Malawi's most remarkable buildings. The cathedral measures over 100m long by 25m wide and has stained-glass windows and elaborate choir stalls carved from soapstone. The crucifix above the altar was carved from wood from the tree where Livingstone's heart was buried in Zambia, and the altar itself sits on what used to be the old slave market back when Likoma was a stopping-off point on the slave route from the interior to the coast.

Mango Drift HOSTEL **$$$**
(☎0999-746122; www.mangodrift.com; campsite/dm per person US$6/8, chalets US$30, d chalets US$70; @📶) The slacker, rough-and-ready sibling of Kaya Mawa perhaps, but really, this place is hardly backpacker hardship – in fact, it has to be the country's most idyllic hostel. Its lake-caressing cabanas were recently rebuilt in stone and boast some serious boutique genes like hibiscus petals scattered on snow-white linen, painted wicker sofas, and sundown verandahs.

The shared toilets and shower block are no less immaculate. Double en suite cabanas can be found up the hill and have been lavished with typical Kaya Mawa detail. There's also a boutique selling pashminas, beaded jewellery and dresses. Chill out in the bar, grab a book from the exchange, scuba dive or just flop on the golden beach shaded by mango trees. You just arrived in heaven.

Hunger Clinic MALAWIAN **$**
(mains MK750; ⏰6am-6pm; 🖉) Right by the water opposite the Immigration Office, this simple cafe serves up *nshima* with veg and great fish and chips.

ℹ Getting There & Away

Ulendo Airlink (☎01-794 555; www.ulendo.net/flyer; 441 Chilanga Drive, Area 10, Capital City, Lilongwe) provides charter flights to Likoma. The more of you there are, the cheaper it is per person. For example, a one-way flight from Lilongwe to Likoma Island ranges from US$210 to US$320 per person depending on how many of you there are.

The *Ilala* ferry – out of service for repairs at the time of research but hopefully now back on the water – stops at Likoma Island twice a week, usually for three to four hours, so even if you're heading elsewhere, you might be able to nip ashore to have a quick look at the cathedral. Check with the captain before you leave the boat. Heading south, the ferry then sails to Metangula on the Mozambican mainland. Local dhows also sail to Cóbuè for MK500 and for a little extra can pick you up or drop you off from Mango Drift on Likoma.

Chizumulu Island

Stretches of azure water and white rocky outcrops give Chizumulu Island a Mediterranean flavour, while the backdrop of dry scrub is positively antipodean.

Sometimes known as Nick's Place, **Wakwenda Retreat** (☎0999-348415; campsite/dm US$3.50/6, r from US$14), smack bang on a postcard-perfect beach, is utter chill-out material. The sizeable bar is constructed around a massive, hollow baobab tree, and there are small wooden chill-out platforms constructed on and around a cluster of boulders in the sand – perfect for sundowners. The shaded lounge area is often the focus of lazy activity such as snorkelling (free gear), card games and goat barbecues. The restaurant (meals from MK500) serves food communal style, so it's easy to get to know the other guests.

The *Ilala* ferry stops right outside Wakwenda Retreat, so even if you're not staying on the island, you can pop over for a drink. There are daily dhow ferries between Likoma and Chizumulu costing around MK500 per person. The trip can take anywhere from one to three hours depending on the weather; it's an extremely choppy ride when the wind is blowing, and potentially dangerous if a storm comes up. If you're unsure, ask at Wakwenda Retreat for advice.

CENTRAL MALAWI

This small corner of Malawi is chiefly famed for its dazzling white beaches and scattering of desert islands. Backpackers' mecca Cape Maclear, is the first to spring to mind; a sunny peninsula where travellers slip into a daze of snorkelling, sunbathing and laid-back village life. And just over the water is the idyllic Mumbo Island, home to one of Malawi's top ecolodges. Stylish resorts dot the coastline and luxury seekers will be rewarded aplenty with international-standard accommodation with top-notch service.

Just a short drive up from the lake, is the Viphya Plateau, a haunting wilderness of mountains, grasslands and mist-shrouded pines. And nearby, Nkhotakota Wildlife Reserve, Malawi's most rugged reserve, now has fine lodges, improved access, and increased wildlife stocks.

Viphya Plateau

ELEV 1200M

The Viphya Plateau forms the spine of central and northern Malawi, snaking a cool path through the flat scrubland, dusty towns and sunny beaches that reign on either side. It may be called a plateau, but there's nothing flat about this part of the country in looks or in atmosphere. Tightly knit forests give way to gentle valleys and rivers, and huge granite domes rise softly from the earth like sleeping beasts. Indigenous woodland bristles with birds and wildflowers, antelope can often be seen, and monkeys are regularly spotted darting through the trees.

The main route to Mzuzu from Lilongwe passes through the plateau and much of it is lined by pine trees, encasing the road in an eerie silence on misty days (and there are plenty). When the mist lifts you'll be rewarded with a line of sweeping grey- and purple-tinged mountains lining the western horizon in the distance. If you want to stay for a few days, there are a few peaceful forest lodges and plenty of hiking, cycling and rock climbing to be done.

Sights & Activities

Hiking is the main activity here and the nearby accommodation will be able to give you advice on where the best places are to roam, though there's a lot to be said for simply sitting back and taking in the views.

Otherwise, for activity junkies the best place to head is to Luwawa Forest Lodge where activities organised on the plateau include **rock climbing** (half day per person US$40), **mountain biking** (half day per person US$18), **fishing** (rod hire US$4) and **walking** (guides from US$10). Walking trails include the Luwawa–Chintheche Trail, a two-day hike down to the lakeshore.

Sleeping

TOP CHOICE **Luwawa Forest Lodge** LODGE **$$**
(☎01-342333, 01-991106; www.luwawaforestlodge.com; campsite per person US$7, tw/tr with shared bathroom per person US$40, chalets with half board/full board per person US$68/75, cottages per night US$160; P @) Set at 1585m, homy Luwawa sits in a clearing of pine trees, its manicured gardens spilling with colourful flowers and morning mist. The centrepiece lounge is dominated by the impressive baobab-inspired fireplace, crackling from dawn until late at night.

Outside is a verandah to take breakfast and soak up the gorgeous view of the forests and nearby lake. There are four chalets with bunk beds, bathrooms, self-catering facilities and swallow-you-up four-posters which are perfect for families (sleep up to six), as well as three new cottages, and also a well shaded camping area.

Activities on offer include mountain biking with a guide on solid Trek bikes, abseiling and rock climbing with an experienced instructor, three-day hikes to Lake Malawi, camping under the stars, and various hiking trails (there's a booklet in your room with suggested one- to five-hour hikes on well-marked trails through montane forest). The lodge's organic food should also be credited. From the ridgeback dogs that greet you on arrival to the warm service of the staff and owner George, Luwawa Forest Lodge is a rare treat.

There's no public transport to Luwawa, so you'll have to ask the bus driver to drop you at the Luwawa turn-off and either walk from the main road or call the lodge for a pick-up (US$10 per group). The lodge lies 10km east of the main M1 road between Kasungu and Mzuzu and is well signposted, but in the wet season you'll definitely need a 4WD to reach it. *Matolas* (pick-ups) regularly pass by on the M1 between 8am and 9am if you're headed back to Lilongwe.

Central Malawi

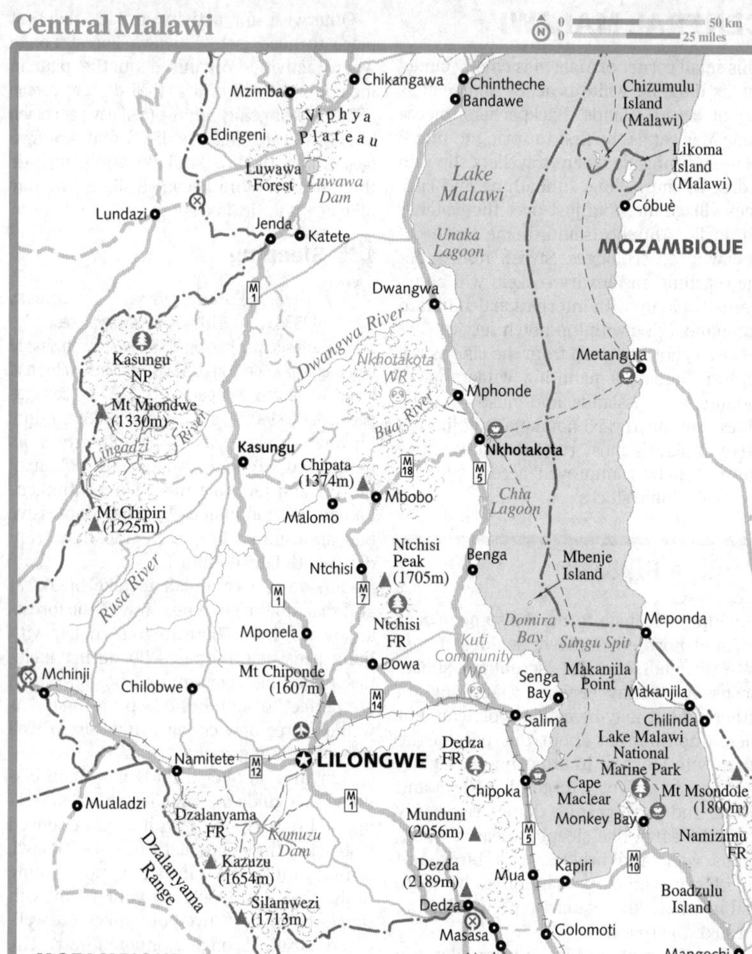

Nkhotakota

Described as one of the oldest market towns in Africa, unassuming Nkhotakota had a significant and sinister part to play in Malawi's history. In the 1800s the town was home to a huge slave market, set up by Arabic trader Jumbe Salim bin Abdullah. From here thousands of unfortunate captives were shipped annually across the lake to Tanzania, before being forced to march to the coast.

Today the town is strung out over 4km between the busy highway and the lake and makes a break in any journey along the lakeshore, but don't expect much action. In the grounds of the St Anne's Mission Hospital is a large tree called the **Livingstone Tree**, where the explorer David Livingstone camped while leading an expedition to Malawi in the 1860s. When he returned a few years later, he met with a local chief called Jumbe, and tried (unsuccessfully) to persuade him to abandon the slave trade.

Sleeping & Eating

TOP CHOICE **Stima Inn** HOTEL $$
(☎0999-260005; www.sanibeachresort.com; dm per person US$8, standard r US$40-55, superior

r US$75; P @) Within staggering distance of the *Ilala* ferry, this low-slung, cream building with art deco aspirations is quirky to say the least – somewhere between a tug boat and an inspired architectural feat. Adorned with nautical motifs, it sits in isolation looking out over sand-flats to the nearby lake.

Atmospheric, houseproud rooms with warmly coloured rugs, sequined cushions and mozzie nets, come in all shapes and sizes. The central courtyard lounge is a good place to feast on a menu of Caribbean chicken, steaks, English breakfasts and more intrepid dishes like crocodile tail in honey.

Pick & Pay Resthouse GUESTHOUSE $
(0991-356762; s/d without bathroom MK1000/1500, s/d MK2000/2500) Friendly digs with locals playing *bawo* (similar to checkers) on the front verandah. Rooms are super basic with the odd fan and prison-style toilet. The walls though don't seem to have been painted since the days of Hastings Banda! A cafe serves cheap local fare for around MK600.

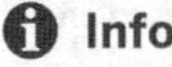

Information

There's a branch of the Commercial Bank of Malawi on the main north–south road, which offers foreign-exchange facilities. A petrol station

MINI-ITINERARIES: CENTRAL MALAWI

How Long & How to Get There

If you've got your own wheels, head to **Mangochi** from Lilongwe and spend a few days making your way up the coast, through **Cape Maclear**, **Senga Bay**, and on to **Nkhotakota**. You'll have to limit yourself on public transport – perhaps head straight for Cape Maclear for a couple of days and then bus it up to Nkhotakota via **Monkey Bay**. Then either drive yourself around **Nkhotakota Wildlife Reserve** for a day (you'll need a 4WD), bus it and get picked up by **Bua River Lodge**, or arrange a day trip to the reserve through one of the lakeshore lodges. After you've had your fill of wildlife, head north to the **Viphya Plateau**, where you can stop off for a day or two's hiking and cycling through the hills. Minibus and bus drivers will drop you off at the turn-off to one for the lodges if you don't have transport.

How Much?

In this part of the country there's something to suit every style and budget, from dirt-cheap campsites to five-star lodges.

Budget

If you're looking for beach frolics on a budget, head for backpackers' favourite, Cape Maclear, where you can camp for around US$5 or bed down in a dorm for around US$10. Bua River Lodge in Nkhotakota Wildlife Reserve has, aside from its luxury safari tents, budget accommodation from around US$17 per head, and in the Viphya Plateau the wonderful Luwawa Forest lodge also has bunks and cheap camping with million-dollar views, aside from its more upscale cabins.

Midrange

Both Senga Bay and Cape Maclear have some good options for midrange travellers and you can pick up a room for US$50 to US$60. All midrange lodges have restaurants serving a mixture of Malawian and European food.

Top End

The strip of beach between Mangochi and Monkey Bay has a couple of large resort hotels where you'll find a double room from around US$100 and up. Pumulani (p353), a super luxury lodge in Lake Malawi National Park, costs US$460 per person all-inclusive.

Tip

Don't miss a walking safari in Nkhotakota Wildlife Reserve, and if you're feeling *really* intrepid you can kayak (p353) past crocs.

CICHLID FISH

There are around 500 species of fish in Lake Malawi. Most of these are of the family *Cichlidae* – the largest family of fish in Africa – and 99% of these cichlids are endemic to the lake. Chambo, familiar to anyone who has eaten in a restaurant in Malawi, are one type of cichlid. Others include the small *utaka*, which move in big shoals and are caught by fisherfolk at night. But Lake Malawi is most famous for the small and colourful *mbuna*, of which there are many species. As well as being attractive to snorkellers and divers, *mbuna* are popular with aquariums, and for scientists they provide a fascinating insight into the process of evolution. *Mbuna* identification and classification is an ongoing process and it is thought that many species of *mbuna* remain undiscovered.

and a Peoples Supermarket are also on the main road. Buses and minibuses stop at the petrol station. Get online at the **Nkhotakota Internet Cafe** (☎01-292284; per min MK300; ⏰7.30am-4.30pm Mon-Fri, 8am-6pm Sat, 2-6pm Sun).

Getting There & Away

You can get to Nkhotakota by the *Ilala* ferry. AXA buses go to and from Lilongwe (MK2000, three hours). The bus will drop you off roughly outside Nkhotakota's Shell petrol station, which is on the highway. Minibuses also leave from here and go to Salima (MK1100, two hours) and Nkhata Bay (MK1500, four to five hours).

South of Nkhotakota

You may like to visit the **Nkhotakota Pottery** (☎0999-380105; www.dedzapottery.com; 👪), whose turn-off is signposted 15km south of Nkhotakota town, on the main road. It offers a range of pottery workshops, and courses last anything from three days to three weeks, and include accommodation, food, tuition and excursions to local attractions. Participants are housed in lovely chalets on the beach. If you don't have time for a long course, there is also a workshop where you can make your own pots or decorate some that are already made (MK560 per hour), and an Aladdin's cave of a boutique where you can purchase all manner of colourful hand-painted crockery. To get here from Nkhotakota town catch a *matola* (MK215).

Sleeping

Nkhotakota Pottery Lodge LODGE $$
(☎0844-581098, 01-751743; www.nyasalodges.com; campsite per person MK800, dm MK5000, s/d chalets MK8000/11,000; P@📶) This is the perfect place to indulge your creative side staying a skip away from a wild, sandy cove.

You don't have to be taking a pottery course to stay here but the chalets are often full of potters (and named after them too – rooms don't have numbers, but instead take their names from tales of a certain schoolboy wizard). You also have the option of dorm rooms and camping and there's an excellent restaurant that provides welcome respite from meat, *nshima* and chips. Accepts credit cards.

Fish Eagle Bay Lodge LODGE $$$
(☎0999-331134; www.fisheaglebay.com; chalets s/d US$35/52; P@📶) This ecolodge boasts six delightful whitewashed chalets (two are self-catering), with tasteful decor, as well as a decent beach bar and excellent beach where you can flop, sail, kayak or play tennis.

For those with vigilant eyes you may see sun-loving crocs lounging on the nearby rocks (though we're glad to report there has never been an altercation with one). Situated 10km south of Nkhotakota in Mblame village, Fish Eagle is a little further down the dirt track past Sani Beach Resort.

Nkhotakota Wildlife Reserve

West of the main lakeshore road lies **Nkhotakota Wildlife Reserve** (per person/car US$10/3; ⏰6am-6pm), comprising 1800 sq km of rough, inhospitable terrain – dense *miombo* woodlands, bush and evergreens – and a couple of navigable roads. Before its recent renaissance the park had been through hard times; abandoned to poachers because of a lack of funding, and plentiful human settlements encroaching along its borders.

Fast forward to 2010 and enter two very different safari lodges to redress the balance. Thanks to increased funding (in 2012 the park received an US$850,000 cash injection from the World Bank), successful wildlife conservation programs and increased road networks, the reserve is coming back into its own. There are also plans afoot to ringfence at least a third of its core area to improve the survival of wildlife.

The Bua River flows green and scaly with a very healthy population of crocs, and come evening at the lodges there's a very good chance you'll see elephants crossing the river, your cockles warmed by a fire, your liver glowing with a decent Bloody Mary in hand. There are also roan and sable antelopes here, buffaloes, baboons, waterbucks, leopards and even itinerant lions – it's just that wildlife can be difficult to spot because of the dense vegetation. Several large rivers cross the reserve, so the birdlife is also varied; there are more than 200 species including palm-nut vultures, kingfishers and ground hornbills. The Bua River is also excellent for salmon fishing.

The best way to really experience the nature is walking with a guide, or kayaking down the Bua River, your heart in your mouth as crocs upstream slip soundlessly into the murk to come and take a closer look.

Sleeping

There are currently two lodges in the park: the romantic Bua River Lodge, which sits conveniently close to the entrance of the park, and Tongole Wilderness Lodge, a further hour's drive into the heart of the reserve. The roads are currently navigable with a 2WD car, if a little steep on certain stretches.

TOP CHOICE **Tongole Wilderness Lodge** LODGE $$$ (0991-337681, 0881-433168; www.tongole.com; adult/child per night US$345/172; P @) Built

WORTH A TRIP

KUTI COMMUNITY WILDLIFE PARK

Kuti Community Wildlife Park (0993-800289; admission per person MK500, per vehicle MK500) is a beautiful wildlife reserve located 1½ hours from Lilongwe, and 30 minutes from Senga Bay.

As well as providing a marvellous place to stay and a vibrant wildlife headcount to enjoy, Kuti's key objective is protecting wildlife and conserving the environment by working together with the local communities. They're also partnered with Lilongwe Wildlife Centre (p268) and act as a release site for wild animals from the sanctuary. Formed from a former government cattle ranch, Kuti consists of 30 sq km of grasses, woodland, wetland and savannah grassland. A haven for wildlife, the park is home to kudus, duikers, bushbucks, genets, civet cats, bush pigs, giraffes, zebras, nyalas, sables, impalas, warthogs and 87 species of bird.

Over the last 10 years the park has developed a great deal, with new accommodation, roads and sponsorship of important community projects. The 11 villages around Kuti Ranch are all stakeholders in its development and 50% of the park's revenue is invested in the local community. The park has an environmental education centre that local schoolchildren can visit to learn about conservation. Malawi has the world's fifth highest rate of deforestation, and those local to the area will know that Salima District's population is growing at an astronomical rate – the population will increase an estimated 37% in the next 10 years. Kuti provides communities with alternatives to destructive practices that benefit both the people and the environment, restoring habitats and promoting sustainable livelihoods.

You can visit the wildlife park for the day or stay the night in a range of accommodation: camping at either Landirani Camp or Sanga Camp, both with ablutions and cooking facilities (US$10 per person, kids under 12 are free); A-Frame cabanas (sleeping up to four) set in a clearing with cooking area and ablutions (US$20 per person); or Bush Villas (sleep up to six) set in woodlands, with bathrooms, kitchenettes, fridges and private barbecue areas (US$100 to $120 per villa).

Wildlife walks and drives cost US$10 per person (guides are $10 for up to three hours), or hire a bike at $10 per half day and tackle the web of marked trails, wending your way to the Sunset Deck and its marvellous views.

Kuti is located about 1km from the Nkhotakota turn-off, when coming from Lilongwe. The park is signposted and about 5km down the dirt road.

with local materials and opened in late 2011, Tongole Wilderness Lodge has an ecoconscious ethos to help the local population and environment. It runs a community development project focusing on sports education and is funding the creation of a school block. The lodge sits at elevation above the Bua River, and a well-worn elephant crossing. Its thatched, near church-high lodge is a Herculean feat in itself; with a mezzanine walkway leading to an aerial viewpoint – the perfect place to balance a G&T with your binoculars.

Come late afternoon, elephants come to the water, while other regular visitors include baboons, and you may even hear the occasional lion. Activities include flyfishing and conventional fishing (when the Bua River is running strong), and kayaking upstream with a coolbox of sundowner Greens (scant reward after being scared witless by crocs watching you like periscopes!).

Crafted from local materials, huge chalets include plunge baths, marble basins, rain showers, natural ventilation and wrought-iron doors that protect though fully immerse you in the widescreen views at your door. All activities are included. The management is lovely.

Tongole is situated 160km (a three-hour drive) from Lilongwe Airport, and has just also opened its own airstrip for private charters. For more information contact **Ulendo Airlink** (☎01-794555; www.ulendo.net; 441 Chilanga Drive, Area 10).

Bua River Lodge LODGE, CAMPGROUND **$$$**
(☎0888-03981, 0990-476887; island/riverside tents US$115/95, hillside rooms US$75, basic rooms not incl dinner US$17; P@) Run by likeable Englishman (and Eric Sykes lookalike) John, this place – perched on the edge of a very beautiful boulder-strewn section of the Bua River – is an adult Neverland. By night, flickering parrafin trails deter nosy wildlife and snake their way to beautiful safari tents kitted out with alfresco rain showers, African chic decor, thick duvets and locally carved chairs.

The main prize though goes to the central lodge; crafted from eucalyptus trunks, it's a multilevel, thatched, open-sided affair. Up top, the verandah is good for spotting animals, there's a decent book exchange, and the restaurant serves up tenderised steaks, pasta dishes and cutlets marinated in red wine, by candlelight. Three-course dinner is included in the price. It's probable you'll see crocs, lots of them, on the sandbars next to the river. Better still is to take a free morning or pre-sunset safari walk, in the company of a guard, to the cascades (2km). You may also see vervet monkeys, elephants, baboons, bushbucks and khudus.

The turn-off to Bua is 10km north of Nkhotakota town, followed by a rough dirt track. You will need your own wheels to get here. You could also enter the park from the south via the very potholed Nkhotakota–Kasungu road. Axa buses headed from Mzuzu can drop you off at the park gate (ask to be dropped at the Lozi Trading centre) then call John at Bua River Lodge for a lift (MK2000 per person). From Nkotakota a lift will cost you MK4000. To walk to to Bua River Lodge it's about 10km.

Salima

The small town of Salima is spread out about 20km from the lake, where the road from Lilongwe meets the main lakeshore road. It's friendly and low-key, useful as a place to change transport, stock up on provisions and go to the bank before hitting the lakeshore places at Senga Bay. Don't bother staying overnight though.

Sleeping & Eating

Mwambiya Lodge GUESTHOUSE **$**
(☎01-262314; r MK3000; P) The rooms at this joint across the railway line from the bus station look as if they haven't been painted since *Starsky & Hutch* first aired. That said they're large, have mozzie nets and bathrooms, and there's also a restaurant (meals around MK1000) and bar.

Half London Lodge GUESTHOUSE **$**
(☎01-262885; s/d MK4000/4800; P) Kitsch rooms looking out onto a courtyard, with Liberace-style bedspreads, bathrooms and TVs are what you can expect here. All rooms have Brit-related names – check out 'Grasgow'! Staff are very sweet and the place is clean if paint thirsty. It's on the way into town opposite the BP petrol station.

Canoe Ice Cream Den MALAWIAN **$**
(mains MK900) Right beside the Petroda petrol station on the main drag, this sunny little cafe is redolent with tempting food: steak, chicken, curry, *nshima* and beef stew, and – true to its name – ice cream.

Senga Bay

Sitting at the eastern end of a broad peninsula that juts into the lake, Senga Bay by night thrums with music; by day, fishing nets dry on the beach, boats are propped up photogenically on the shore and backstreets are vivid with playing kids. The trickle of travellers who pass through may find it a little sparkless, but it's an OK place to break your journey en route to Nkhata Bay, and there are a couple of really nice hotels and some great budget digs.

Sights & Activities

Windsurf, snorkel, take a boat ride or learn to dive. You could also take a trip out to nearby **Lizard Island** to see its population of giant monitor lizards and its cormorant colony. Many lodges and local guides can arrange this and it should cost about US$60. Alternatively, from Senga Bay town, you can go hiking in the nearby **Senga Hills**; the woodland is beautiful, and the viewpoints overlooking the lake are well worth the effort. It's best to hire a local guide from your hotel to show you the way (and also because there have been isolated incidents of robbery and harassment here).

You might also aim for the **hippo pools** about half an hour's walk up the lakeshore, or reached by descending the north side of the Senga Hills. Hippo numbers have recently been depleted due to a necessary cull, as the overswollen population was damaging nearby crops. Again, a local guide is recommended. The hippos have a reputation for being timid, but aggressive when worried, so take care here.

If you're looking for souvenirs, there's a strip of **craft stalls** a few kilometres out of Senga Bay, on the Salima road.

About 10km south of Senga Bay you'll find **Stewart Grant's Tropical Fish Farm** (☎01-263165), which breeds and exports cichlids. If you're genuinely interested you can do a half-hour tour of the farm.

Sleeping

TOP CHOICE **Safari Beach Lodge** LODGE $$$
(☎0999-365494, 01-263143; www.safaribeachlodge.net; s/d US$110/140, children under 12 US$60; P❄@🛜) Safari's magical hillside gardens cascade in a riot of bougainvillea and boulders down to the beach. There are four rooms in the lodge, five stone chalets and two family-sized chalets (hut 7 is the best).

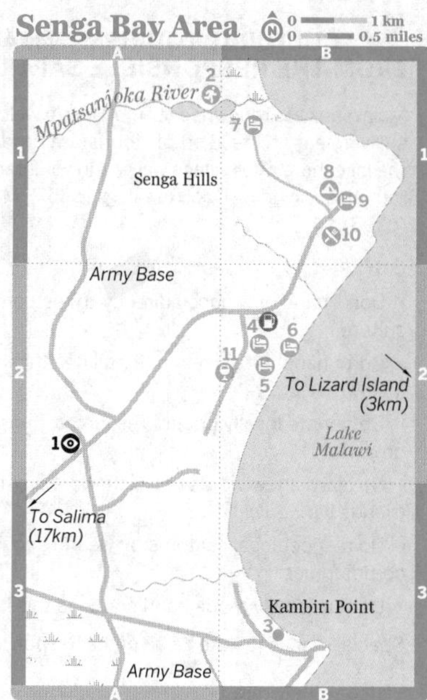

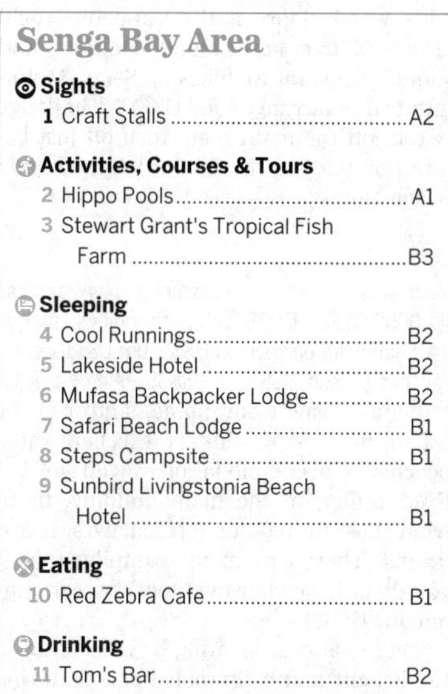
Senga Bay Area

Sights

The beach is a mere two minutes' walk through a wood singing with monkeys, but there's also a spotless kidney-shaped pool. The rooms themselves are delightful, with warm-patterned bedspreads, choice art, fridges, air-con and driftwood bureaus and

CULTURAL TOURISM IN MALAWI – A FEW GUIDELINES FROM THE RESPONSIBLE SAFARI COMPANY

Malawians are renowned for their warm welcome, and with tourism still in its infancy it's still very easy to head off the tourist trail and experience rural Africa. Many lodges along the lakeshore offer village walks and volunteering opportunities within their local communities, including Cool Runnings (p357), Mayoka Village (p293) and Butterfly Space (p293).

Guidelines for Visiting Community Projects in Malawi

» Don't hand out money directly to the community – this encourages a begging culture.

» Don't hand out sweets – dental healthcare is not accessible for most people in Malawi!

» Do donate locally bought resources, pens, papers, books etc to local schools and projects.

» Do learn a few words of Chichewa – a smile and a local greeting will make you friends very quickly!

» Do respect local customs by wearing conservative clothing when visiting local communities.

» Do buy locally made handicrafts as this helps to support the local economy.

Special thanks to Kate Webb of the Responsible Safari Company.

DSTV. The deluxe rooms are *even* nicer with wood floors and verandahs. You'll also find free kayaks and snorkels, and should you want to, hikes up Senga Mountain can be arranged for US$15. The lodge is 1km off the main road; turn off just before the gates to the Sunbird Livingstonia Beach Hotel.

TOP CHOICE Cool Runnings GUESTHOUSE, CAMPGROUND **$$**
(☎0999-915173,01-263398;coolrunnings@malawi.net; campsite per person US$5, dm US$10, caravan per person US$12, r US$35; P@≈) Like a home away from home, and run by warm host Sam, this is excellent-value beachside accommodation. Sleep in the fixed trailer, in the main building, or in what has to be one of Malawi's nicest dorms. There's room for camping too (if you don't have your own tent you can rent one for US$7).

There's also an inviting bar flickering in candlelight and a tin-roofed cafe featuring fresh fish and chicken. Boat charters can be arranged as well as car hire and if you feel like it you can get involved in one of the many social programs on offer; Cool Runnings built a school, runs a football team, set up a volunteer police force and built a library! Inspiring.

Sunbird Livingstonia Beach Hotel HOTEL **$$$**
(☎01-263444, 01-263222; www.sunbirdmalawi.com; standard s/d from US$100/130, deluxe US$145/175; P⊖❄@≈≋) Formerly the Grand Beach Hotel, this spearmint-white pile (built back in the 1920s and once a favourite haunt for fancy colonial balls) with its columned entrance and manicured lawns, takes you back to another era. The beach is immaculate and tempting for swimming with decent views of nearby Lizard Island crested in white guano.

Take dinner on the alfresco terrace, plunge in the spotless pool or head for a massage, for this is a place to do very little but unwind. Rooms vary in size but are traditional with international standard furnishings. Pure quality.

Steps Campsite CAMPGROUND **$**
(campsite per person MK1500; P@≈) Perfectly situated by the giant boulders that bookend the golden stretch of beach, this campsite is owned by the Sunbird Hotel Group and benefits from its premier-level service.

There are loads of pitches under shade, hot showers, individual power points and round-the-clock security; a beach bar that leaps from a Martini ad; a volleyball court; and a spotless ablution block. In a word – perfect!

Mufasa Backpacker Lodge LODGE $$
(☎0884-0746676; campsite US$4, dm US$8, r with/without bathroom US$38/35; P@) This faded banana-and-pastel-green beachfront digs has a sandy patio with scattered loungers, a little bar and Caribbean vibe. Fastidiously clean rooms have vividly coloured linen, African art on the walls and are tantalisingly close to the lull of the surf.

There's also an airy dorm and dining room decked out in plenty of wood and bright local fabrics. The food is excellent.

Lakeside Hotel HOTEL $$
(☎01-263500, 01-263400; standard/superior r MK10,000/13,000; P@) On the outside these peeling, white motel-style digs are unprepossessing, but step within and they become more tempting, especially the ones facing the lake. Rooms have fridges, loads of room, bathrooms, TV and fans. You'll see plenty of corporate jolly types here so it's not exactly 'backpacker' writ large.

Eating & Drinking

Red Zebra Cafe MALAWIAN $
(mains MK1000; 7am-10.30pm; P) Situated in a garden off the main road, this zesty, Caribbean-infused restaurant covers the bases with grilled chops, steak, fruit salads, ice cream and cupcakes. Eat within its colourful interior or alfresco. Things kick off on weekend evenings and live bands occasionally put in an appearance.

Tom's Bar BAR
(8am-late) Popular little spot with both locals and visitors communing for a cold beer. It closes when the last person leaves.

Information

Dangers & Annoyances

Take great care when swimming near the large rocks at the end of the beach at Steps Campsite; there's a surprisingly strong undertow. Some of the beaches here are flat and reedy – perfect conditions for bilharzia, so get advice from your hotel or lodge to see if it's safe. Finally, never swim in the lake at dusk as this is when crocs and hippos are at large; from then on and through the night.

Getting There & Away

First get to Salima. From there, local pick-ups run to Senga Bay (MK250), dropping you in the main street. If you want a lift all the way to Steps Campsite, negotiate an extra fee with the driver. If you're travelling to/from Cape Maclear, consider chartering a boat; it's not too expensive (around US$250 to US$300) if you get a group together. Ask at Cool Runnings guesthouse.

Mua

Wedged between Salima and Balaka, and sitting on a hill thick with flame trees, Mua is a rare treat; the red-brick terracotta-tiled mission seems transplanted from Tuscany, and the church itself is strangely beautiful even if you're not religious. Built at the beginning of the 20th century by Catholic White Fathers, Mua Mission houses a school, a hospital and the fascinating Kungoni Centre of Culture & Art. Established more than 30 years ago, the centre is dedicated to breeding greater understanding of Malawi's culture and history among tourists and Malawians alike.

Sights

Kafukufuku Research Centre CULTURAL BUILDING
(☎01-262706; www.kungoni.org; per day MK600) For people with a genuine interest in learning more about Malawian history and culture there's the research centre where you can delve into photographs, books and research papers. The centre also runs sporadic courses on Malawian culture, history, art and language. They include a visit to the museum, group participation, videos and free access to the library.

Kungoni Centre of Culture & Art CULTURAL BUILDING
(☎01-262706; www.kungoni.org; 7.30am-4pm Mon-Sat) The Kungoni Centre of Culture & Art, part of the Mua Mission, is made up of several different workshops and exhibitions. Set up in 1976 by a Canadian, Father Claude Boucher (who still directs the centre), it has developed into an important focal point for cultural information and training.

Chamare Museum MUSEUM
(admission MK900; 7.30am-4pm Mon-Sat) If you only visit one thing here, make it the Chamare Museum, beautifully decorated with vibrant murals depicting scenes from Malawian history. Its three rooms concentrate on the three main cultural groups of the region (Chewa, Ngoni and Yao) and their approach to traditional beliefs, with a huge collection of Gule Wamkulu masks. A guide is included in the entrance fee; the tour takes at least an hour.

Carving Workshop HANDICRAFT

You can watch the talented artists go to work on blocks of wood, carving them into exquisite sculptures. The workshop also operates as a training centre where the experienced carvers train new recruits. It also runs sporadic courses on Malawian history and culture, and there are frequent performances of dances and songs from the Chewa, Ngoni and Yao cultures.

Kungoni Art Gallery GALLERY

(admission MK1500) The Kungoni Art Gallery showcases woodcarvings and other artwork, such as painting and embroidery. Proceeds from the sale of these go to help the local community.

Sleeping & Eating

TOP CHOICE **Namalikhate Hostel** HOSTEL $$

(☎01-262706; s/d MK9750/13,000; P@ᯤ) Set in Edenic gardens crowded with flowers, this series of chalets overlooking a narrow gorge may be one of the prettiest lodges in the country. Rooms don't disappoint either with heavy drapes, downlights and step-through mozzie nets. It's impossibly romantic for couples, the restaurant (MK1400 for meals) too; with postcard views of locals fishing below in the gorge.

Getting There & Away

Mua is about 50km south of Salima on the road to Balaka. The Mua Mission is about 1km from the main road and is clearly signposted.

Monkey Bay

Hidden behind the Cape Maclear headland, sultry Monkey Bay is enchantingly slow; languid locals, a petrol station and a couple of shops are all that you'll find here. Backpacker country it is, with a couple of magic traveller joints on the beach, and conveniently it's also where the *Ilala* ferry stops at the quaint harbour. Fish, snorkel or hammock flop – whatever you do, you may need to recalibrate that calendar. There's a Peoples Supermarket near the harbour and one FMB ATM which *sometimes* works, so stock up on funds before arriving.

Sleeping

Mufasa Rustic Camp CAMPGROUND, CABANAS $

(☎0993-080057; campsite per person MK850, s/d MK5250/6750, dm MK2250; P) Something of a traveller's magnet, Mufasa has its own sheltered beach bookended by smooth boulders, and is only 400m from the main harbour. Rooms are basic bamboo affairs, but the bar is much more appealing with lounging cushions, wicker swing chairs and a very relaxed vibe.

Come dusk expect communal fires and bonhomie. The owners can arrange snorkel and boat trips for around (MK3500). There's also a rowing boat you can use (MK2500). Be careful though of swimming over to the reedy inlet next to the camp's main beach – a traveller was recently mauled by a croc here. Note: if there are reeds, mudbanks or a stream or river flowing into the lake, there may well be crocs too.

Venice Beach Backpackers HOSTEL $

(☎0844-16541; campsite per person MK800, dm MK2000, r MK4000; P@ᯤ) Cool and very rough-and-ready rooms can be found in this beachside backpacker joint about 1.5km from the main road. Hammock flop, fraternise with the locals or kayak (MK5000) or dive if you feel like it (non–PADI certified).

MALAWI'S LAKE OF STARS

Since 2004, Malawi's sandy shores have been regularly rocking to the sound of Malawi's greatest pop acts and a smattering of international DJs. Organised by a British club promoter who fell in love with Malawi while working on a gap year, the three-day Malawi Lake of Stars Festival takes place (almost) every October at different locations by the lake. The aim is to raise funds for local charities, as well as to boost the profile of Malawian music and have loads of fun. Think miniature Glastonbury with heat and flip-flops instead of mud and rubber boots. All kinds of acts have taken to the stage, from Malawian reggae superstars the Black Missionaries, to up-and-coming African hip-hop stars, to British folk musicians. The event attracted over 3000 people in 2008 and by 2011 big names such as Foals and Vampire Weekend were guests. The event was cancelled in 2012 but should be rocking again come 2013. For further info on where and when it will be when you visit, check out www.lakeofstars.org.

GULE WAMKULU

Performed at funerals, major celebrations and male initiation ceremonies, Gule Wamkulu or 'Great Dance' is the most popular dance among the Chewa. It can't be performed by just anyone; only members of a secret society, sometimes called the Nyau brotherhood, are allowed to participate. Dancers perform clad in magnificent costumes and brightly painted masks made from cloth, animal skins, wood and straw. Each dancer represents a particular character (there are more than 150 Gule Wamkulu characters) – a wild animal, perhaps, or an ancestral spirit, sometimes even a modern object such as a car or a plane. Each character has its own meaning – for example lions represent strength and power and often appear at the funeral of a chief.

Supported by an entourage of drummers and singers, the dancers achieve a state through which they can summon up the spirits of animals or dead relatives. As the drumbeats quicken, they perform dances and movement with incredible energy and precision. Some of this is pure entertainment, some of it is a means of passing on messages from ancestral spirits, and some of it aims to scare the audience – as a moral lesson or a warning. Through acting out mischievous deeds, the Gule Wamkulu characters are showing the audience, as representatives of the spirit world, how not to behave.

There are both individual and group performances and they take place during the day and at night – when the audience watches from afar. The dance is widespread in central and southern Malawi and is also performed in Zambia's Eastern Province and the Tete province of Mozambique.

You can also spear fish. Aside from this there are drumming classes, beach volleyball and a reggae-fuelled bar.

The two-storey, thatched building has a selection of dorms and doubles as well as a top-floor viewing deck with plenty of hammocks. There are also a couple of chalets next to the main building. You can buy good meals here (snacks MK400, dinner and lunch MK850).

Getting There & Away

From Lilongwe, AXA buses go to Monkey Bay, usually via Mua and the southern lakeshore (MK1800, four hours). From Lilongwe you're probably better off going by minibus to Salima (MK1500, one hour), from where you might find a minibus or *matola* going direct to Monkey Bay.

It's much easier to reach Monkey Bay from Blantyre on the ordinary bus that travels via Liwonde and Mangochi (MK2500, five to six hours). A quicker option is to go by minibus (MK2500, four to five hours), but you'll need to leave early in the morning and you might have to change at Mangochi. Many travellers also use the *Ilala* ferry to travel up and down the country to or from Monkey Bay.

From Monkey Bay, a *matola* ride to Cape Maclear should cost MK600. Although not far away, it can take forever to get there and you could have to wait hours for a *matola* departure. To Mangochi, a minibus costs around MK600 and the AXA bus MK550.

Cape Maclear

A long stretch of powder-fine sand bookended by mountains and lapped by dazzling water, Cape Maclear deserves all the hype thrown at it. By day the bay glitters a royal blue, studded by nearby islands and puttering, crayon-coloured fishing boats. On shore women wash clothes, dry fish, and nautical types spread out vermilion nets to dry. And there's bags of things to do aside from lotus eating on a hammock, be it kayaking, sailing, snorkelling, walking or diving. Come afternoon the streets ring with music from the backstreet gospel choirs... Prepare to be lulled!

There are plenty of sleeping options here to keep all sorts happy – from reed huts and tents on the beach to upmarket lodges serving fine French cuisine.

Sights

Much of the area around Cape Maclear, including several offshore islands, is part of **Lake Malawi National Park** (per person/car US$5/1) one of the few freshwater aquatic parks in Africa, and designated a Unesco World Heritage Site back in 1986. The park headquarters are just inside the gate, where you'll also find a visitor centre which doubles as a small **museum and aquarium** (7.30am-noon & 1-5pm Mon-Sat, 10am-noon & 1-4pm Sun).

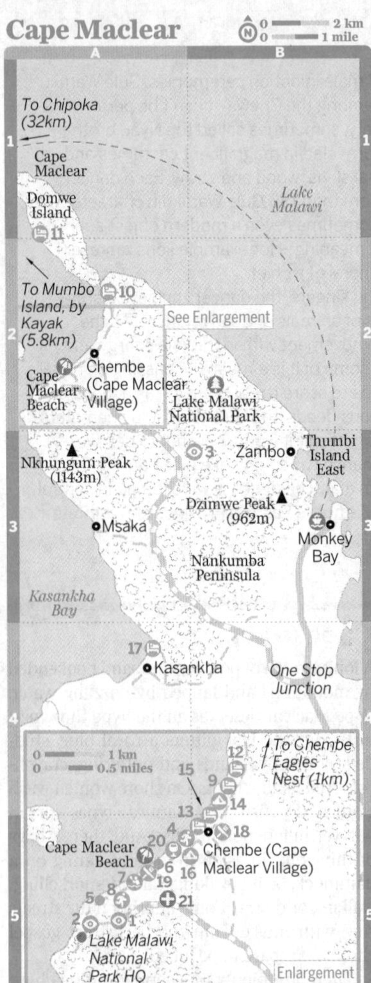

Cape Maclear

Sights

1 Missionary Graves A5
2 Museum and Aquarium A5
3 Mwala Wa Mphini B3

Activities, Courses & Tours

4 Billy Riordan Memorial Trust A5
5 Danforth Yachting A5
6 Frogman Scuba A5
7 Kayak Africa A5
8 Panda Garden A5

Sleeping

9 Cape Mac Lodge B4
10 Chembe Eagles Nest A2
Danforth Yachting .... (see 5)
11 Domwe Island Adventure Camp A1
12 Fat Monkeys B4
13 Gecko Lounge B5
14 Malambe Camp B4
15 Mgoza Lodge B5
16 Mufasa Camp A5
17 Pumulani A4

Eating

18 Boma/Hiccups Pub B5
Gecko Lounge .... (see 13)
Mgoza Restaurant .... (see 15)
19 Thomas's Grocery Restaurant and Bar A5

Drinking

20 Seattle Reggae Beach Bar A5

Information

21 Billy Riordan Clinic A5

The aquarium isn't exactly brimming over with marine life and is more like a little information centre, with explanatory panels about the lake life overshadowing the one functioning tank with its few fish and solitary turtle. The museum charts the area's history and you'll be offered a guided tour. The museum also provides a good backstory on Livingstone's first mission if you're off to visit the nearby missionary graves.

Just before the entrance gate to the national park is a sign pointing to a path, which leads towards the hills overlooking the bay. A few hundred metres up is a small group of **missionary graves**, marking the last resting place of the missionaries who attempted to establish the first Livingstonia Mission here in 1875.

Activities

The phantom 'boat tour boys' who took your money and never turned up seem to have evaporated since the establishment of the **Cape Maclear Tour Guides Association** – a membership organisation for the area's guides ensuring business is fairly distributed among them. All registered guides work to a set price list, and circulate at different resorts along the beach on a weekly basis, so it's more than likely you'll be *softly* approached by one within an hour or two of arrival.

Snorkelling

Guides registered with the Cape Maclear Tour Guides Association can organise a number of half- and full-day trips involving snorkelling. For example, trips to Thumbi Island West will cost around US$45 per person including food, snorkel hire, park fees and fish-eagle feeding.

If you prefer to go snorkelling on your own, many places rent gear (rates start at about US$10, but check the quality of your mask). Otter Point is a small rocky peninsula and nearby islet that is popular with snorkellers and even more so with fish. You may even see otters here.

Diving

For diving, go to **Frogman Scuba** (☎0999-952488, 01-599156) or Danforth Yachting. Both offer PADI four-day Open Water courses for around US$375, as well as casual dives for experienced divers.

Kayaking

If you prefer to stay on top of the water, several of the lodges rent out kayaks. For a longer expedition, **Kayak Africa** (☎0999-942661; www.kayakafrica.net) is great, as you can arrange to kayak to one of its beautiful camps on Domwe and Mumbo Islands, or even between them. The cost includes accommodation, good meals, hot showers, snorkel gear and park fees.

Boat Trips

Yet another option is sailing on a yacht with **Danforth Yachting** (☎0999-960770, 0999-960077; www.danforthyachting.com). A sunset cruise around Cape Maclear aboard the *Mufasa* costs US$50 per person (minimum six people required); a full-day island-hopping cruise costs US$900 per boat, including lunch; and an overnight cruise including all meals, as well as snorkelling and fishing equipment, also costs US$900 per boat. The owners also have exquisite accommodation.

Guides registered with the Cape Maclear Tour Guides Association can arrange a number of boat trips to Thumbi Islands and Otter Point from US$45 per person. Sunset Booze cruises are also popular and cost around US$20 per person (not including drinks).

Hiking

There's a range of hikes and walks in the hills. Entry into the national park is US$5, and the park's rate for a guide is US$15 per person for a full-day trip. There are also hippo trips (US$45 per person, minimum three people). It's better to hire a guide.

The main path starts by the missionary graves and leads up through woodland to a col below **Nkhunguni Peak**, the highest on the Nankumba peninsula, with great views over Cape Maclear, the lake and surrounding islands. It's six hours' return to the summit; plenty of water and a good sun hat are essential.

Another interesting place to visit on foot is **Mwala Wa Mphini** (Rock of the Tribal Face Scars), which is just off the main dirt road into Cape Maclear, about 5km from the park headquarters. This huge boulder is covered in lines and patterns that seem to have been gouged out by long-forgotten artists, but are simply a natural geological formation.

Volunteering

Billy Riordan Memorial Trust VOLUNTEERING
(www.billysmalawiproject.org) The inspiring Billy Riordan Memorial Trust was set up in memory of a young man, Billy Riordan, who drowned in the lake in 1999. The trust has established a clinic and provides medical care in the area. The trust always needs medical volunteers (doctors, dentists, nurses, lab technicians), and work in administration, agriculture and horticulture is also available. They prefer volunteers who can commit for a minimum of four months.

Panda Garden VOLUNTEERING
(☎0999-140905; www.heedmalawi.net; Main St, Chembe village) Help out with art classes (artists very welcome), gardening and bilharzia research on the lake, identifying host-carrying snail areas (scuba divers welcome).

Sleeping

TOP CHOICE **Mumbo Camp** CAMPGROUND $$$
(☎0027-21-783 1955, 0999-942661; per adult/child incl meals, kayak & snorkelling gear US$290/145, family tent US$725) Situated exclusively on Mumbo Island (p312), this ecoboutique campsite has seven walk-in tents on wooden platforms with bathrooms, tucked beneath trees and above rocks, with spacious decks and astounding views.

Most people choose to get to the island by kayak from the **Kayak Africa** (www.kayakafrica.net) reception in Cape Maclear – the camp

WORTH A TRIP

MUMBO ISLAND: THE ECO PEARL IN A BED OF EMERALDS

Half an hour's putter by boat from Cape Maclear lies a mystery of a desert island cloaked in thick jungle, ballasted by giant boulders and fringed by turquoise water so greeny-blue that it looks as if it's leapt from an ad campaign. Welcome to Mumbo Camp (p311), the ecoresort with a solid green soul and low-key approach to pampering. Staff are sufficiently visible but know how not to break your Robinson Crusoe fantasy by over cossetting you.

The accommodation is simple and that's half the charm; you don't feel as if you've stepped into the pages of a glamour magazine; rather it feels authentic – and yes, those are 1.5m monitor lizards swimming across the perfect little inlet, and yup, that screech is a pair of noisy resident fish eagles on the hunt for chambo. The water here is perfect for snorkelling and kayaking (all equipment included in the price), so clear in fact, you can see swarms of chiclid dancing like coloured jewels under the surface. But before you take to the lake or follow a well-marked trail through the jungle, take a moment to savour your room – a safari tent with a bedouin-style ceiling billowing with a walk-in mozzie net, brilliantly positioned for 180-degree views giving you the impression that there's no one else on the island. And that's almost the case; there are no thumping tunes here, no tinkle of glasses, just the sound of the lapping waves and your slowing pulse.

staff will bring along your stuff in a separate boat. You can catch this boat if you're feeling lazy...

It would be perfectly acceptable to just laze around on the hammocks and decks of the camps and indulge in that castaway feeling, but there are kayaks, snorkels and scuba lessons to be had should you choose. Frogman Scuba (p311) offers casual dives for US$4, or PADI four-day courses for US$375. A maximum of 14 people can stay here.

TOP CHOICE Danforth Yachting LODGE $$$
(☎0999-960770, 0999-960077; www.danforthyachting.com; full-board per person US$190; P❄@📶) Beautifully finished Danforth has stylish, mint-fresh rooms set in lush beachside gardens. There's a top-notch restaurant with a menu spanning Mediterranean fare to roast beef and Yorkshire pudd.

An active crowd stay here to take advantage of the various yachting options on offer, but should you want to flop and read there's a peaceful chill-out hut looking out over the water, and the rooms themselves are sumptuous, with nautical-blue linen contrasting white walls.

Gecko Lounge LODGE $$$
(☎0999-787322, 01-599188; www.geckolounge.net; chalet d/tr US$110/120, s/d US$80/90; P@📶) A firm family favourite and with good reason, Gecko chalets are almost *upon* the manicured beach, with kitchenettes and self-catering facilities. There are bunk beds too for large families, fridges, fans, cool tile floors and mozzie nets, as well as plenty of hammocks and swing chairs outside.

The thatch- and wicker-accented restaurant is worth a mention for its tasty pizzas and burgers, as well as being the perfect sundowner spot for a Malawi gin. There's also DSTV in the bar showing rugby and soccer matches. You can rent kayaks and snorkel gear, or hire DVD players and DVDs to watch in the comfort of your own room.

Mgoza Lodge LODGE $$
(☎0995-632105; www.mgozalodge.com; chalets US$55, dm MK1500; P@📶) Cheaper and more low-key than nearby Gecko, Mgoza has bags of charm with brick-and-thatch cottages spaced around a leafy garden. Rooms are spacious, cool and split-level with wood-panel baths, pretty curtains, huge beds, and billowing step-in mozzie nets.

There's also an inviting restaurant with an upstairs viewing deck for sundowners. And finally, the staff, run by Kay, are especially warm.

Fat Monkeys GUESTHOUSE $$$
(☎0999-948501; campsite per person US$3, vehicle US$6, dm US$10, s/d US$55/75; P@📶) Monkeys' dorms and rooms are clean and cool with fans, while pitches are shaded. Come evening the bar stacks up with a lively crowd. It also holds the traveller crown as Cape Mac's most popular midscale place to eat – probably thanks to its easy vibe, tasty salads, pizza, and excellent chambo and kampango fish.

Malambe Camp CAMPGROUND $
(☎0999-258959; malambecamp@africaonline.net; campsite per person MK600, tent hire MK950, dm MK1000, hut s/d MK2000/3000; @📶) Malambe has shaded pitches facing the beach just a few yards away, a spotless ablution block, and a cool bar piping out Boney M. In fact with its tempting loungers and many hammocks, it feels like a slice of Jamaica.

The cafe dishes up toasties, pasta and curries as well as decent breakfasts. You can also hire snorkel gear here (US$5). Choose from simple huts constructed from reed mats, permanent tents (with proper beds inside) or a large, light reed dorm.

Mufasa Camp CAMPGROUND, GUESTHOUSE $
(☎0999-374631; campsite US$4, dm US$6, s/d US$14/18; P@📶) This simple accommodation close to the beach has shared bathrooms and basic but very clean rooms huddled around a courtyard bursting with bougainvillea. It makes for a good-value, peaceful alternative to party-style guesthouses and is run by an award-winning British photographer and his lovely wife. There's also a welcoming bar.

Chembe Eagles Nest LODGE $$$
(☎0999-966507; www.chembenest.com; campsites US$10, chalets incl breakfast US$75; @📶) At the far northern end of Cape Maclear Beach, this lodge sits in an idyllic spot on a beautiful and very clean broad stretch of private beach, strewn with palm trees and shaded tables, and nestled against the side of the hills. Chalets have cool, tiled floors, granite bathrooms and thatched roofs.

The restaurant serves up Malawian dishes and there's plenty to do including catamaran hire (US$45 per full day, includes lunch) and sunset cruises (US$15 per person).

Cape Mac Lodge LODGE $$$
(☎0999-621279; rogerl@africa-online.net; s/d/tr US$105/150/155; P❄@📶) On a quiet stretch of the beach in well-tended gardens, these oxblood thatch rooms are full of African flair with mezzanines, huge bathrooms, private verandahs and a cool bar. If you're feeling active there's volleyball, sailboards and kayaks for free. Cape Mac also has a restaurant, **Froggies**, which serves excellent French cuisine and some of the best steaks in Cape Mac. There's also pool and a whirlpool.

Domwe Island Adventure Camp ECOLODGE $$$
(☎0027-21-783-1955; www.kayakafrica.co.za; standard safari tents s/d/child US$75/120/30, camp tents US$25) Based on nearby Domwe Island, this is the smaller and more rustic of Kayak Africa's two lodges, run on solar power and romantically lit by paraffin lamps. It's self-catering, with furnished safari tents, fridges, shared ecoshowers and toilets. It also has a bar and a beautiful staggered dining area, open to the elements and set among boulders. There are two full-time staff employed here. It costs US$30 each way to be dropped off/picked up at the island. Kayaks cost US$30 to hire, snorkel gear US$15.

Eating & Drinking

Popular with travellers are beach barbecues arranged by local guides. A chicken or fish barbecue accompanied by drummers costs around US$10 per person and can be arranged by your lodge, or just ask around the village.

TOP CHOICE **Mgoza Restaurant** INTERNATIONAL $
(mains MK1300; P📶) With shaded *palapa* shelters in a garden facing the lake, this

MALAWI, C'EST CHIC

Pumulani (☎01-794491; www.pumulani.com; all-inclusive rate per person US$460; P❄@📶) is a stylish lakeside lodge with nature-inspired rooms – think grass roofs and huge windows to let in the light, views of the surrounding forest and lake, and massive wooden terraces from which to gaze at the clear waters and sweep of golden sand below. The food here is equally amazing and private candlelit barbecues on the beach can be arranged. Yes, it's expensive, but a number of activities are included in the price, including snorkelling, fishing and trips on the romantic old traditional wooden dhow.

Other touches of luxury in Malawi? How about Kaya Mawa (p297), where you can step directly from the terrace of your rustic-luxury rock-hewn bungalow into the crystal waters of the lake, or Mvuu Wilderness Lodge (p319) for 'camping' with a sky-high romance quotient?

is a cool spot to chat in the friendly bar or chill outside and take dinner.

Based at Mgoza Lodge, the restaurant serves up great full English breakfasts, healthy fruit smoothies and come evening, it's flickering in candlelight as you lick your chops over fresh fish, and perhaps the best homemade hamburgers in Malawi.

Boma/Hiccups Pub INTERNATIONAL, BAR **$**
(dishes MK1500; noon-late;) A slice of sophistication, the bar is all shadow and backlit wall-mounted masks. A projector screens live sport or news while a maze of alcoves and woody corridors scattered with wicker loungers invites you to explore. This is a great place for dinner; feast on salads, Hungarian goulash, veggie lasagna, steak and chips or chambo.

Thomas's Grocery Restaurant & Bar MALAWIAN **$**
(dishes from MK1000) This simple joint run by Thomas sells biscuits and toiletries, and dishes up chicken curry, chapatis, chambo, catfish and chips. Authentic and shaded, it's a nice place to stop, the outdoor bench seating perfect for people-watching passing villagers.

Gecko Lounge INTERNATIONAL **$**
(dishes MK800-1000;) The restaurant at Gecko is a good place to drop in for a meal by the water. It is well known for its pizzas (from MK1200), which have an eclectic range of toppings, from fish to mango. You can get your pizzas to go for an extra MK100.

Seattle Reggae Beach Bar BAR
A little orange-green shack on the beach with cheap beers and spirits and (of course) a reggae soundtrack. It was closed for a face lift when we passed.

Information

Bilharzia is rife in Cape Maclear, so it may be the case you need to drop in to the **Billy Riordan Clinic** (consultations adult/child US$80/40; minor complaints 8am-noon & 2-4pm Mon-Fri, emergency 10am-noon & 3-4pm Sat & Sun), which dispenses bilharzia medicine.

Skyband has come to Cape Maclear so most of the lodges have wi-fi and many will lend you a laptop to check your emails. You can also buy Airtel phone vouchers at the more upscale lodges.

Dangers & Annoyances

Bilharzia, a water-borne parasitic infection, is rife in Cape Maclear. In order to treat it, take a course of praziquantel tablets no less than six weeks after your last swim here. Tablets are easier to find in places such as Lilongwe and Blantyre, but do buy them from a reputable source – fakes abound.

Travellers sometimes receive hassle from beach boys selling jewellery; a firm 'No' should suffice.

Getting There & Away

By public transport, first get to Monkey Bay, from where a *matola* should cost MK400. If you're driving from Mangochi, the dirt road to Cape Maclear (signposted) turns west off the main road, about 5km before Monkey Bay.

From Cape Maclear, if you're heading for Senga Bay, ask around about chartering a boat. It will cost around US$300, but it's not bad when split between four to six people and much better than the long, hard bus ride. *Matolas* leave for Monkey Bay from around 6am, on a fill-up-and-go basis, and take about an hour. From there you can get onward transport.

Monkey Bay to Mangochi

From Monkey Bay the main road runs south to Mangochi. Along this stretch of lake are several places to stay, catering for all tastes and budgets. Most are signposted off the main road.

Sleeping

TOP CHOICE **Norman Carr Cottage** BOUTIQUE HOTEL **$$$**
(0888-355357, 0999-207506; www.normancarrcottage.com; r from US$100-155;) Norman Carr Cottage balances simplicity, character and luxury with aplomb. Six suites and a family cottage have massive handmade king-sized beds, small living areas and open-air garden showers.

The beach and gardens are full of hanging chairs and sun beds and there's a beachside pool and whirlpool – a perfect setting to indulge in that Malawian gin and tonic. Food is great (the English breakfast comes particularly recommended) and rates include all activities and food so you can snorkel to your heart's content. It is about 15km south of Monkey Bay.

Sunbird Nkopola Lodge LODGE **$$$**
(01-580444; www.sunbirdmalawi.com/nkopola; s/d/family incl breakfast US$145/175/220;) Located about 18km north of Mangochi, accommodation here ranges from an excellent campsite to large rooms for families. Rooms are clean – family rooms have bunk beds for kids – and well equipped,

and most open out onto private patios with views of the beach.

The most atmospheric rooms are the originals, shaded by tamarind and strangler fig trees, set up on the hill. The campsite is separate with its own clean hot showers and toilets, as well as a smattering of chalets with a bathroom. On-site facilities include a swimming pool, volleyball court and even a bird sanctuary. Staff can organise a range of excursions around the area. There's also an ATM here.

Club Makokola RESORT **$$$**
(☎01-580244/5, 01-580469; www.clubmak.com; s/d/family incl breakfast US$120/186/351; P❄@📶🏊) With its spa, golf course, squash and tennis courts, Club Mak exudes charm from the instant you pass down its drive lined with pink and orange bougainvillea. Aside from the myriad facilities perfect for keeping the kids busy, the hotel sits on a manicured, golden stretch of sand.

Ponder the lake view from the thatched poolside restaurant, before wandering the tropical gardens scattered with well-placed *rondavels*. Decor within rooms is understated ethnic chic, and includes hand-carved tables and wooden lamps, Malawian art and painted ceramic sinks. Mak also has its own airstrip!

Mangochi

Mangochi makes a good overnight stop if you're on the way to Liwonde, and lies near the southern end of Lake Malawi, strung out between the main lakeshore road and the Shire River. It's not immediately captivating until you head to the river down the shaded boulevard, where the scene is a little more pleasing to the eye. The town was once an important slave market, and then an administrative centre in colonial days, when it was known as Fort Johnston. Facilities include several shops, supermarkets, a post office and National and Standard Banks with ATMs.

Sights

The excellent **Lake Malawi Museum** (admission MK200; ⏰7.30am-5pm Mon-Sat) houses ethnographic, environmental and historical exhibits, telling the history of the lake. There's also a replica of the foredeck and bridge of the old gunboat HMS *Guendolin*. To get here, turn right at the clock tower, by the waterfront.

On the waterfront is the **Queen Victoria Clock Tower**, built in 1901 in memory of the queen. Just behind it is the squat stone **MV Vipya Memorial**, dedicated to the 145

HMS GUENDOLIN

HMS *Guendolin* was a military boat, made in Britain and assembled in Mangochi in 1899. At 340 tonnes, it was for many years the largest boat on the lake and had a top speed of 12 knots. It also had two powerful guns on board. Such a show of strength was thought necessary by the colonial authorities in order to deter slave-traders who crossed the lake in dhows with their human cargo, but also because colonial rivals Germany and Portugal had territory facing Lake Malawi and were believed to want to increase their influence in the region.

The Germans also had a gunboat, called *Herman von Wissemann*, but despite the friction between their two governments, the captains of the two ships were apparently great friends and would often meet at various points around the lake to drink beer and shoot the breeze.

When WWI was declared in 1914, the *Guendolin* was ordered to destroy the German boat. The British captain knew where the *von Wissemann* would be, as he and the German captain had previously arranged a rendezvous.

But the German captain wasn't aware that war had erupted, and his ship was completely unprepared. The *Guendolin* steamed in close, then bombed the *von Wissemann* and rendered it unuseable. The German captain and crew were then informed of the commencement of hostilities and taken prisoner. This rather unsporting event happened to be the first British naval victory of WWI and Lake Malawi's only recorded battle at sea.

In 1940 the *Guendolin* was converted to a passenger ship, and one of the guns was set up as a memorial in Mangochi, near the clock tower. Some years later the ship was scrapped. All that remains today is the gun; the compass and the ship's bell are on display at the Lake Malawi museum.

passengers and crew who died when the *Vipya* sank on 30 July 1946. Next to that stands the **6PR Hotchkiss Gun** that stood on the *Guendolin* Patrol Gun Boat from 1889 to 1940.

Sleeping

Villa Tafika Lodge LODGE $
(☎01-593544; www.villatafika.com; standard/classic/river view MK5000/6000/14,500; P) Without doubt the best place in town, this old-fashioned custard-hued pile sits right by the clock tower overlooking the river, and has pleasant rooms with mozzie nets, bathrooms, TV and polished stone floors, and wicker chairs in shaded spots to drink up the mountain views. The restaurant also serves up fresh chambo and chips and various pizzas.

The villa was built in 1895 and was the house of EL Rhodes, the commander of the gunboat *Guendolin*. The river-view room, right at the top of the house, has an elegant balcony from where you can survey the town.

Eating & Drinking

All around the bus station are cheap cafes selling beans and *nshima* or stews for around MK600. Villa Tafika has outdoor dining where you can eat grills (MK1200) with a view of the clock tower and the mountains.

Getting There & Away

All buses between Blantyre and Monkey Bay stop in Mangochi. There are minibuses to/from Liwonde (MK780), Ulongwe, for Liwonde National Park (MK900), Blantyre (MK2500) and the Mozambican border at Chiponde (MK1100).

CHIFUNDO ARTISANS NETWORK

If you're near the large market town of **Balaka**, pay a visit to the **Chifundo Artisans Network** (☎0888-365960; ⏱8am-4pm daily, tours Mon-Fri; P) a craft studio and community initiative that employs (and trains) some 40 local people to make a range of different crafts, from Malawian dolls to colourful hand-painted textiles, to handmade recycled paper. You can visit the studio and afterwards buy some of the products at the on-site store; there's also a small cafe here. To get here stay on the road past Balaka – Chifundo is signposted behind the mission church.

SOUTHERN MALAWI

Southern Malawi is home to the country's commercial capital, and receives the highest proportion of foreign visitors who venture here to scale the country's mountains and watch wildlife in an incredibly diverse landscape.

To the east, on the border with Mozambique, and flanked by emerald-green tea plantations, is mist-shrouded Mt Mulanje, Malawi's highest peak. A short way north is the Zomba Plateau, a stunning highland area. Safari lovers can experience luxury and adventure combined, in two of the country's best parks – Liwonde, where you can get up close to elephants, hippos, rhinos and crocodiles, and Majete, the south's brightest star thanks to huge investment and the reintroduction of lions. Blantyre, the country's most dynamic city, is a pit stop for restaurants and bars.

Liwonde

Straddling the Shire River, Liwonde is one of the gateways to Liwonde National Park. The river divides the town in two; to the east you'll find the main bus stations, the market, supermarkets and the train station. West of the river are several tourist lodges. It can be a pleasant place to spend the night, or if you want to do a DIY safari on a budget – heading into the park just for a day.

Sleeping & Eating

Shire Camp GUESTHOUSE $
(☎0999-210532, 0888-909236; campsite per person MK500, chalet incl breakfast MK3500; P) Shire Camp has a colourful restaurant-bar serving chambo, chips and cool greens, and has friendly staff. Bamboo-and-brick cabanas are meticulously clean with tiled floors, fans, hot-water bathrooms and netted breeze vents.

The campsite is less appealing with hard, rocky ground and a basic ablutions block. Shire camp can take you on a river safari (US$25 per person), which lasts for 4½ hours and heads deep into Liwonde National Park. The camp is on the river's north bank. Take the dirt road on the right just before the National Bank.

Southern Malawi

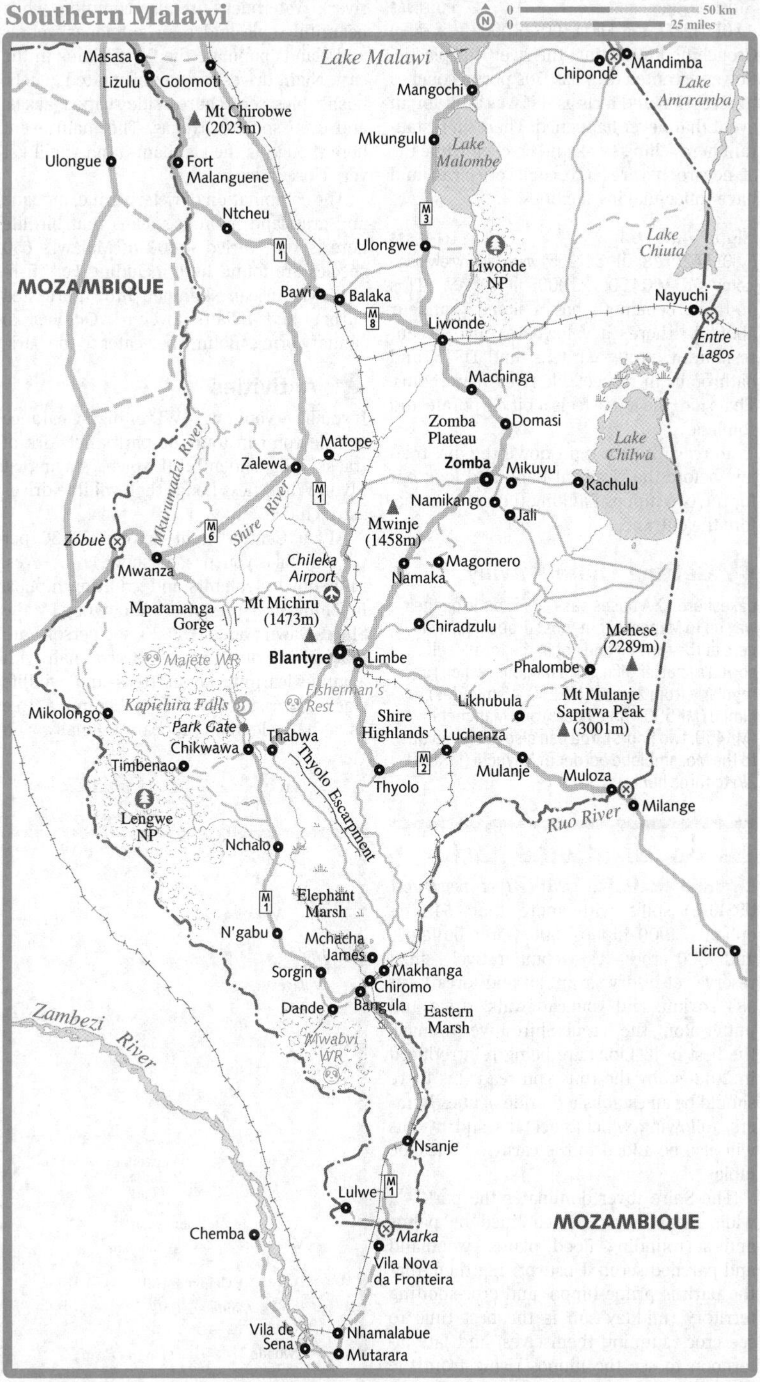

0 50 km
0 25 miles

Masasa
Lizulu
Golomoti
Lake Malawi
Chiponde
Mandimba
Lake Amaramba
Mangochi
Mt Chirobwe (2023m)
Mkungulu
Lake Malombe
Ulongue
Fort Malanguene
M3
Ntcheu
M1
Ulongwe
Liwonde NP
Lake Chiuta
MOZAMBIQUE
Bawi
Balaka
Nayuchi
M8
Liwonde
Entre Lagos
Machinga
Domasi
Zomba Plateau
Lake Chilwa
Mkurumadzi River
Matope
Zalewa
Zomba
Mikuyu
Kachulu
M1
Shire River
Namikango
Jali
Mwinje (1458m)
M6
Zóbuè
Chileka Airport
Magornero
Namaka
Mwanza
Mpatamanga Gorge
Mt Michiru (1473m)
Chiradzulu
Mchese (2289m)
Blantyre
Limbe
Phalombe
Majete WR
Fisherman's Rest
Kapichira Falls
Likhubula
Mt Mulanje
Sapitwa Peak (3001m)
Mikolongo
Park Gate
Shire Highlands
Thabwa
Chikwawa
Luchenza
M2
Timbenao
Thyolo Escarpment
Mulanje
Thyolo
Muloza
Milange
Lengwe NP
Ruo River
Nchalo
M1
Elephant Marsh
N'gabu
Mchacha James
Liciro
Makhanga
Sorgin
Chiromo
Bangula
Dande
Eastern Marsh
Zambezi River
Mwabvi WR
Nsanje
M1
Lulwe
MOZAMBIQUE
Marka
Chemba
Vila Nova da Fronteira
Vila de Sena
Nhamalabue
Mutarara

Shire Lodge HOTEL $$$
(☎01-542277; s/d MK14,500/23,000; P❄@📶) Crouching low against the river this plastic-flower-accented digs has '70s porno couches in reception and feels as if it was built for an event that never happened. There's a restaurant here selling steak and chicken while the 52 new rooms are large, cool, very clean, and have coffee-making facilities.

Hippo View Lodge LODGE $$$
(☎01-542116/8, 01- 542255; www.hippoviewlodge.com; s/d MK14,500/23,000; P❄@📶) This 95-room behemoth has a faded grandeur about it; there's a volleyball court, decent restaurant, pretty gardens, and DSTV and bathrooms in respectable river-view rooms. That said, the lodge feels a bit corporate and soulless.

To reach it turn right down the dirt road just before the National Bank and look out for the two hippos flanking the road just before the entrance.

Getting There & Away

Lakeshore AXA buses pass by Liwonde on their way up to Mangochi but most drop off passengers at the turn-off and not in the town itself, so you're better off using a minibus, which run regularly from Zomba (MK250, 45 minutes), Limbe (MK500, three hours) and Mangochi (MK450, two hours). You can also get a minibus to the Mozambique border at Nayuchi (MK850, 2½ to three hours).

Liwonde National Park

Liwonde National Park (per person/car US$10/3) spills with more than 545 elephants, 1900 hippos, 500 water buffaloes and 1800 crocs. It's a comparatively small reserve set in dry savannah and forest over 584 sq km, and you can walk, drive and putter along the serene Shire River to make the best of it. Lions are being reintroduced in 2013, so by the time you read this there should be an established pride of apex hunters; following which, cheetahs and hyenas will also be added to the carnviore's league table.

The Shire River dominates the park – a wide, meandering stretch lined by palms and surrounding flood plains, woodland and parched scrub. Unsurprising then, that the park is prime hippo- and croc-spotting territory (midday sun is the best time to see crocs sunning themselves, and late afternoon to see the hippos rising from the river). Waterbucks are also common, while beautiful sable and roan antelopes, zebras and elands populate the flood plains in the east. Night drives can reveal spotted genets, bushbabies, scrub hares, side-striped jackals and even spotted hyenas. The main event here though is the elephants, and you'll get very close indeed.

The combination of rich riverine, mopane and grassland habitats means that birdlife here is very varied – 400 of Malawi's 650 species are found here including Pel's fishing owl, African skimmer, brown-breasted barbet, and Lilian's lovebird. October to January brings Böhm's bee-eater to the park.

Activities

If you have your own 4WD or high-clearance vehicle you can tour the park's network of tracks independently. If you're staying at Mvuu Wilderness Lodge then wildlife drives are included.

Mvuu Camp's night drives (US$30 per person) take you past flashing crocs' eyes, ninja-quiet elephants and grunting hippos, finishing in a romantic sundowner by the Shire. Dawn walks (US$20 per person) are magical as you wander the savannah with a guide learning about trees and wildlife tracks (occasionally hiding behind a tree as a bull elephant appears!) Finally, you

Liwonde National Park

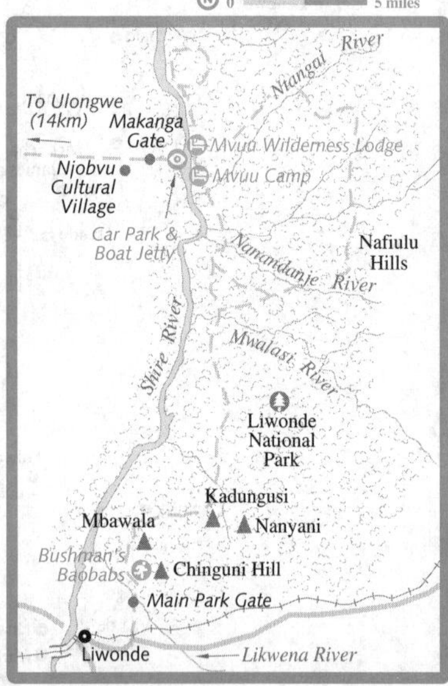

LIWONDE RHINO SANCTUARY

The **rhino sanctuary** (www.wilderness-safaris.com; admission US$3) is a fenced-off area within the park, developed for breeding rare black rhinos. It has since been expanded to protect a number of mammal species from poaching. At the time of research 10 black rhinos were living in the enclosure along with populations of Lichtenstein's hartebeest, Cape buffalo, Burchell's zebra, and eland and roan antelope. Organised in conjunction with Wilderness Safaris at Mvuu Camp, you can go on three-hour hikes with scouts (US$45, leaves at 5.30am) searching for the rhinos in the 48-sq-km reserve. Prior to your departure you'll need to learn some basic sign language back at Mvuu Camp, as speaking around the intensely shy and nervous rhinos is counter productive.

can't visit Mvuu and not take a boat safari (US$30 per person). Don't be alarmed if an aggressive male guarding a brace eyes your boat then ducks under the water to make a charge for you; the rangers at the tiller are brilliantly adept at moving away at the last minute.

Bushman's Baobabs offer wildlife drives, village walks, boat trips and kayaking excursions, all for around US$25 per person. Alternatively, Hippo View Lodge in Liwonde town operates wildlife-viewing boat trips along the Shire River.

Near the park's Makanga Gate, **Njobvu Cultural Village** (☎0888-623530, through Mvuu Camp reception 01-542135; www.njobvuvillage.com; r per person US$16, r incl full board & activities US$50; 👪) offers visitors a rare opportunity to stay in a traditional Malawian village, sleeping in traditional mud-brick huts (with or without a mattress – your choice!). During the day you are invited to take part in the villagers' daily lives, visiting traditional doctors, the village school and eating local food such as *nshima*. All proceeds go directly to the community.

Sleeping

Places to stay in Liwonde remain open all year – you can reach them by boat even if rain closes some of the park tracks. Be warned though, the rains send the elephants further inland, making them harder to spot.

TOP CHOICE Mvuu Camp LODGE **$$$**

(☎01-771153, 01-771393; www.wilderness-safaris.com; campsite per person US$15, all-inclusive chalets per person US$260; @📶) Run by the excellent Wilderness Safaris, Malawi's premier safari provider (also operating Chelinda Camp in Nyika National Park), Mvuu sits on the river in the realm of myriad hippos and crocs.

The camp comprises a main restaurant building and nearby, a scattering of chalets with cosy interiors; step-in mozzie nets, comfy beds, immaculate linen and stone-walled bathrooms. By night, walk past warthogs to your quarters, and perhaps wake (as we did) to a bull elephant grazing on fallen figs next to your window, or lumbering hippos passing your door. There's a small campsite with spotless ablution blocks and self-catering facilities. Eat at the open-plan, thatched restaurant; dinner is communal and the food is hearty. Look out for the nightly firepit and once-weekly cultural evening of traditional drumming and dancing.

Mvuu Wilderness Lodge LODGE **$$$**

(☎01-771153, 01-771393; all-inclusive chalets per person US$445; 🏊) A short distance upriver from its rugged cousin, Mvuu Camp, this intimate, upscale lodge is full of romantic atmosphere. Sumptuous safari tents have huge beds covered with billowing mosquito nets, and semi-alfresco roofs and bathrooms.

Private balconies overlook a water hole where there are plenty of birds and crocs sunning themselves on the banks. There's a small swimming pool, a restaurant serving excellent food and a raised lounge area overlooking the lagoon. Rates include park fees and all wildlife drives, boat rides and bird walks.

Bushman's Baobabs LODGE **$$$**

(☎0995-453324, 0888-838159; www.bushmansbaobabs.com; per person campsite/dm/tented chalet US$7.50/15/60, per person tent US$45; P@📶🏊) Since its reincarnation from Chinguni Hills Camp, reports are good. The campsite lies in the south of the park, there are comfortable rooms in the main house as well as a number of walk-in safari tents with bathrooms, a pool and a large viewing deck.

Expect delicious, home-cooked meals, prepared daily, and a warm host. There's also a campsite, **Nkalango Camp**, five minutes' walk away, with dorms, space for tents, *braai* (barbecue) spots, and a bar and restaurant. Bushman's offers wildlife drives, village walks, boat trips and kayaking excursions, all for around US$25 per person.

Getting There & Away

The main park gate is 6km east of Liwonde town. There's no public transport beyond here, though you might find a *matola* to take you as far as Bushman's Baobabs for around MK600. From the gate to Mvuu Camp is 28km along the park track (closed in the wet season); a 4WD vehicle is recommended for this route.

Another way in for vehicles is via the dirt road (open all year) from Ulongwe, a village between Liwonde town and Mangochi. This leads for 14km through local villages to the western boundary. A few kilometres inside the park is a car park and boat jetty, where a watchman hoists a flag to arrange a boat from Mvuu Camp to come and collect you. This service is free if you're staying at the camp.

Alternatively, if you make a booking in advance for Mvuu Camp through Wilderness Safaris in Lilongwe the camp can arrange a boat transfer from Liwonde town for US$80.

For those without wheels, the best option is to get any bus or minibus between Liwonde town and Mangochi and get off at Ulongwe (make sure you say this clearly, otherwise the driver will think you want to go to Lilongwe). In Ulongwe locals wait by the bus stop and will sometimes take you by bicycle to the park (this takes about an hour).

Zomba

With its chilly elevation, decrepit red-brick church, faded cricket club and old colonial buildings nestled in the wooded foothills, Zomba is hauntingly special; like a chapter of the British Empire hanging by a tenuous thread. Yes it has the typical chaos of a dusty market, but the higher you head up the ghostly Zomba Plateau, the more stunning and pristine the scenery becomes. The capital of Malawi from 1891 until the mid-1970s, it's home to wide, tree-lined streets, and an easy charm. East of the main road is the town's friendly commercial centre. There's a lively market, banks, bureau de change, internet cafes and a couple of decent eateries.

Sleeping

TOP CHOICE Annie's Lodge LODGE $$
(01-527002; Livingstone Rd; standard s/d MK8250/9400, superior s/d MK10,600/11,800; P❄@) Set in the foothills of the Zomba Plateau, Annie's has appealing black-and-white brick chalets with green-tin roofs, swallowed in palm trees and flowers.

Rooms are carpeted, clean and welcoming with DSTV, air-con and bathrooms. The executive rooms are housed in a new wing and sit at the top of the plot; what they lack in old-fashioned charm, they make up for in great views. There's a bar and restaurant too.

Hotel Masongola HOTEL $$
(01-524688; hotelmasongola@clcom.net; Livingstone Rd; s/d from MK10,600/15,300; P) Built in 1886, this tin-roofed, turreted old dame has bags of charm. Choose between a superior room with an aerial view or one of the brick-red chalets in gardens of roses and geraniums. Rooms are cosy, clean and have bureaus and bathrooms.

Ndindeya Motel MOTEL $
(01-525558; s/d MK2250/2700; P) Off a small turn-off, this powder-blue motel is charmless with lacklustre staff. Rooms have cold-water showers, stone floors and are equally lukewarm, but just about adequate for a cheap night. There are lovely gardens at the back of the property though, which make a nice sundowner spot, and the restaurant serves tasty portions of grilled meats.

Eating

There are plenty of cheap hole-in-the-wall places around the bus station where you can pick up plates of chicken and *nshima* or chips for around MK400.

TOP CHOICE Tasty Bites INTERNATIONAL $
(Kamuzu Hwy; dishes from MK1000; 9.30am-8pm Mon-Sat, 10.30am-8pm Sun; P❄) Set inside or outside under an awning this popular roadside expat hangout is a real sanctuary, with an Afro diner feel to its fuschia-muralled interior. Enjoy a menu spanning pizzas, burgers, various curries, chambo and chips, ice cream and brownie and various delicious cakes. The large dining room has a notice board with information about the local area and beyond.

Dominos INTERNATIONAL $
(Macleod Rd; mains MK1000; 10am-midnight; P) In a leafy part of town, Domino's is fun for lunch, dinner or sundowners, thanks to its lushly gardened outside patio and excellent wood-fired pizzas, chambo, steak and fries.

Zomba

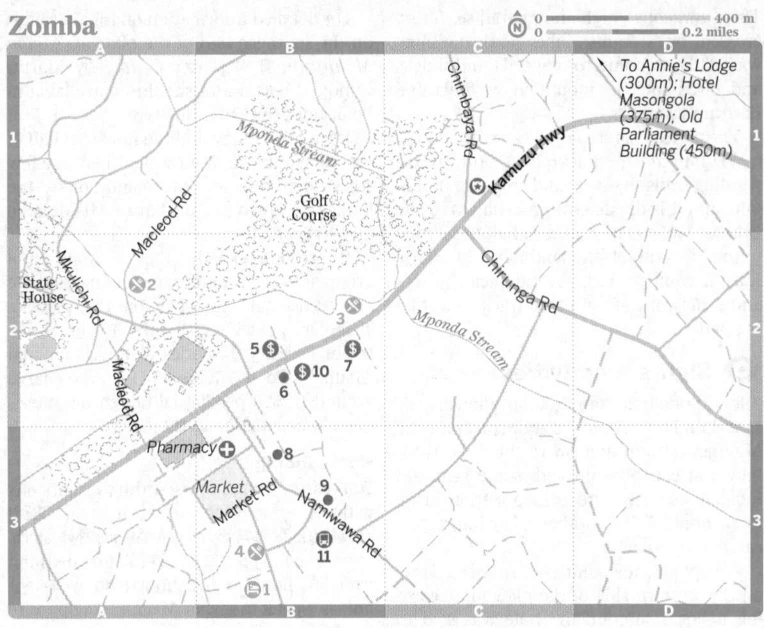

Zomba

Sleeping

1 Ndindeya Motel.....B3

Eating

2 Dominos.....A2
3 Tasty Bites.....B2
4 Uncle Dan's Café.....B3

Information

5 First Merchant Bank.....B2
6 Metro Cash & Carry.....B2
7 National Bank.....B2
8 Peoples.....B3
9 Shoprite.....B3
10 Standard Bank.....B2

Transport

11 Bus Station.....B3

Uncle Dan's Café MALAWIAN $
(☎01-527114; dishes from MK400; ⏰7.30am-6pm Mon-Fri, 7.30am-7pm Sat, 8.30am-4.30pm Sun; P✍) Rough-'n'-ready Dan's is friendly and fresh walled, with plastic tables and chairs, but genuine service. Order from a range of *nshima* and steak, chips, eggs and breakfast. Look for the sign saying 'Aaron & Lisa Pizzeria' – Uncle Dan's is inside.

Information

There are **Standard**, **National** and **First Merchant Banks** in the town with ATMs. For supplies, there's a **Shoprite**, a **Peoples** supermarket and a **Metro Cash & Carry**.

Getting There & Away

Zomba is on a main route between Lilongwe and Blantyre. The bus station is in the town centre, off Namiwawa Rd. AXA buses run to/from Lilongwe (MK2000, five to six hours), Blantyre (MK750, 1½ to two hours), Liwonde (MK650, one hour) and Nkhata Bay (MK3950) via Mangochi (MK1000) and Mzuzu (MK4000).

Minibuses go every hour or so to Limbe (MK1000, one hour) and also head to Lilongwe (MK2000, four to five hours), Liwonde (MK700, 45 minutes) and Mangochi (MK800).

Zomba Plateau

Rising nearly 1800m behind Zomba town, and carpeted in thick stands of pine, Zomba Plateau is beguilingly pretty. As you ascend the snaking road past wildflowers, stoic locals heaving huge burdens of timber, and roadside strawberry vendors, the place feels like Alpine France; then a vervet monkey jumps out, a pocket of blue mist envelops your car, and you realise you're in Africa.

This gorgeous highland paradise, criss-crossed by streams, lakes and tumbling waterfalls, is home to leopards, bushbucks and birds such as mountain wagtails and Bertram's weavers.

The plateau can be covered on foot, by car (4WD only on the backroads), and myriad winding trails that ring and cross the mountain, and it is divided into two halves by the Domasi Valley. The southern half has a road to the top, a hotel (the landmark Ku Chawe Inn), a campground, several picnic places and a network of driveable tracks and hiking paths.

Sights & Activities

A few kilometres from Ku Chawe Inn are the **Mandala Falls**. A nature trail runs past the Mulunguzi Dam and on to the falls. From here you can hike through some beautiful indigenous forest and passed a trout farm, to **Williams Falls**, another fairly impressive cascade.

A popular viewpoint is **Chingwe's Hole** on the western side of the plateau. According to local rumour, the hole was said to lead to the bottom of the Rift Valley and, in days of old, local chiefs would throw their enemies down there.

For even more impressive views, head for the eastern side of the plateau, where **Queen's View** (named after Queen Elizabeth, wife of King George VI, who visited Zomba in 1957) and **Emperor's View** (after Emperor Haile Selassie of Ethiopia, who visited in 1964) overlook Zomba town and out towards Mulanje.

Hiking

The southern half of the plateau is ideal for hiking. The network of tracks and paths can be confusing though, so for more help with orientation there's a 3D map of the plateau in the **Model Hut**.

For detailed information on hiking routes on the southern half of the plateau, *Zomba Mountain: A Walker's Guide,* by Martin Cundy, is useful and should be available in bookshops (p330) in Blantyre.

Keen hikers may find the northern half of the plateau more interesting. There are few tracks here and no pine plantations – the landscape is similar to that of Mt Mulanje and Nyika Plateau.

It's recommended either to walk in a group or to use a guide when hiking, as there are occasional muggings on the plateau. There are guides registered with the Ministry of Forestry, Fisheries & Environmental Affairs based at the Model Hut, who charge around US$20 per day, although the rate is open to negotiation as there's no set price.

Horse Riding

You can arrange horse-riding excursions with **Zomba Plateau Stables** (☎0888-714443, 0888-714445; maggieparsons@iwayafrica.com; per person per hour US$35) for anything from an hour to five hours, on well-kept horses. Speak to owner Maggie. It's opposite the Mulunguzi Dam.

Sleeping & Eating

There are no shops on the plateau so campers and self-caterers should bring everything they need up from Zomba town. Accommodation options are now down to three: camping, guesthouse or upscale hotel.

TOP CHOICE **Ku Chawe Inn** HOTEL **$$$**
(☎01-773388, 0888-965141, 01-514237; s/d US$125/160, hilltop rooms s/d US$185/210;) Set in elevated botanical gardens dripping with honeysuckle and blue gum trees, Ku Chawe boasts amazing views of the distant plain. Inside its charming red-brick exterior (built 1969) service is warm, while

THE POTATO PATH

The Potato Path is the Zomba Plateau's most popular hike; it's a direct route from Zomba town leading all the way up to the plateau. Look for the signpost at a sharp bend on the main road to the plateau, some 2km from Zomba town. The path climbs steeply through woodland to near Ku Chawe Inn.

From here, the Potato Path then goes straight across the southern half of the plateau, sometimes using the park tracks, sometimes using narrow short cuts, and leads eventually to Old Ngondola Village, from where it descends quite steeply into the Domasi Valley, well known for its fertile soil and good farming conditions. Here locals grow potatoes and take them along the Potato Path (hence the name) down to Zomba town to sell.

Allow two to three hours for the ascent, and about 1½ hours coming down.

Zomba Plateau (Southern Section)

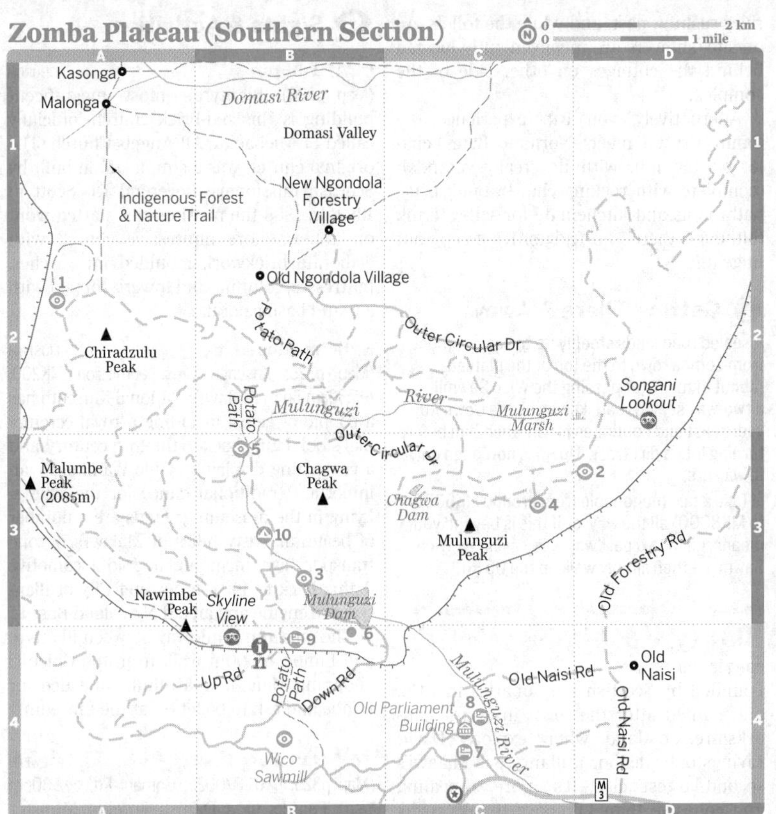

Zomba Plateau (Southern Section)

Sights
1 Chingwe's Hole A2
2 Emperor's View D3
3 Mandala Falls B3
4 Queen's View C3
5 Williams Falls B3

Activities, Courses & Tours
6 Zomba Plateau Stables B4

Sleeping
7 Annie's Lodge C4
8 Hotel Masongola C4
9 Ku Chawe Inn B4
10 Ku Chawe Trout Farm B3

Information
11 Model Hut B4

rooms are equally appealing, with outside verandahs and international-style decor and cosy stone fireplaces.

There are two restaurants and a welcoming bar, or if it's warm, eat on the patio. The menu features sirloin steaks, pork chops and king-sized prawns. There's also bags to do here, such as grabbing a mountain bike and exploring the plateau, or going for a horse ride.

Ku Chawe Trout Farm CAMPGROUND, BUNGALOWS $
(☎0888-638524, 01-525271; campsite per person MK600, chalets per person MK2000, 4-bed self-contained chalets MK7000; Ⓟ) This idyllic campsite in the lee of a valley and the middle of giant gum- and cedar-tree clearing, is perfect for camping. It's very basic, boasting only barbecue facilities and a small

river rushing past, and while the toilets are on-site, showers are inconveniently located behind the cottages on other side of the complex.

Alternatively, you can experience the Camp Crystal–meets–Norman Bates chalet on the hill, with its creaky verandah (complete with rocking chair!), bunk beds, bathrooms and kitchenette for self-catering (although there's no fridge). It's creepy but huge fun.

Getting There & Away

A sealed road leads steeply up the escarpment from Zomba town to the top of the plateau (about 4km). After passing the Wico Sawmill, a two-way sealed road, known as the Down Rd, veers east and continues for another 2km before turning into a dirt track. Up Rd is now open only to walkers.

Take a taxi (negotiable from around MK6000 to MK8000) all the way, or if this is beyond your means, get a taxi part way – say as far as Wico Sawmill – then simply walk up the Up Rd.

Blantyre & Limbe

POP 728,000

Founded by Scottish missionaries in 1876, and named after the town in South Lanarkshire, Scotland, where explorer David Livingstone was born, Blantyre is Malawi's second-largest city. It's more appealing and cohesive than Lilongwe thanks to its compact size and hilly topography, and though there's not much to do here, it makes for a good springboard for exploring remote areas such as Mulanje and the Lower Shire Valley. Attached to the city's eastern side (as of 1956) is Limbe; home to a grand old mission church, minibus station and excellent golf club. Unlike Blantyre, however, which has seen a finessing of its restaurants and hotels, Limbe has fallen into disrepair over the last couple of decades.

Blantyre serves as the country's commercial and industrial hub and has the best and most diverse choice of restaurants in the country, several happening bars, and a fascinating library and archives. Add to that tour operators, banks, internet cafes and other practicalities, and Blantyre makes a pleasant stopover. The main focus of shops, banks and shops is on Victoria Ave and adjoining Glyn Jones Rd.

Sights & Activities

CCAP Church CHURCH

(Map p326) Blantyre's most magnificent building is this red-brick church, officially called St Michael & All Angels Church. The original church was a simple affair, built by Scottish missionary Reverend DC Scott in 1882. In 1888 the missionaries started work on a new, more impressive church with elaborate brickwork moulded into arches, buttresses, columns and towers, topped with a grand basilica dome.

National Museum MUSEUM

(Map p325; Kasungu Cres; admission MK200; 7.30am-5pm) Malawi's National Museum has a couple of gems, including a royal ceremonial stool dating back to the 16th century, and a fascinating display on Gule Wamkulu – an important traditional dance for the Chewa. Lying in the museum grounds are a number of beautiful, rusty relics of Malawi's bygone transport age including an old locomotive dating back to 1904, a decrepit City of Blantyre fire engine and an old Nyasaland Bus.

The museum is midway between Blantyre and Limbe, a 500m walk from the Chichiri Shopping Mall. Take a minibus headed for Limbe and ask to be let off at the museum.

FREE **Carlsberg Brewery** BREWERY

(Map p325; 01-870022; Gomani Rd; 2.30pm Wed) Thanks to a Danish Foreign Minister who visited Malawi during the independence celebrations in 1966 and wasn't too impressed by the beers available, a Carlsberg brewery was established here; and thus began the story of the country's favourite drink, the 'Green'. Beerophiles can head to the brewery, east of the centre every Wednesday at 2.30pm, when free tours are laid on (but have to be booked in advance). You'll be told all about the brewing process after which you'll be rewarded with a free tasting.

Mandala House HISTORIC BUILDING

(Map p326; 01-871932; Mackie Rd; 8.30am-4.30pm Mon-Fri, to 1pm Sat) This is the oldest building standing in Malawi and was built back in 1882 as a home for the managers of the Mandala Trading Company. It's a quietly grand colonial house, encased in wraparound verandahs and set in lovely gardens. Inside the house is the inviting Mandala Cafe (p329), the eclectic La Galleria (p330) art gallery and the **Society of Malawi Library & Archive** (Map p326; Mandala House,

Greater Blantyre & Limbe

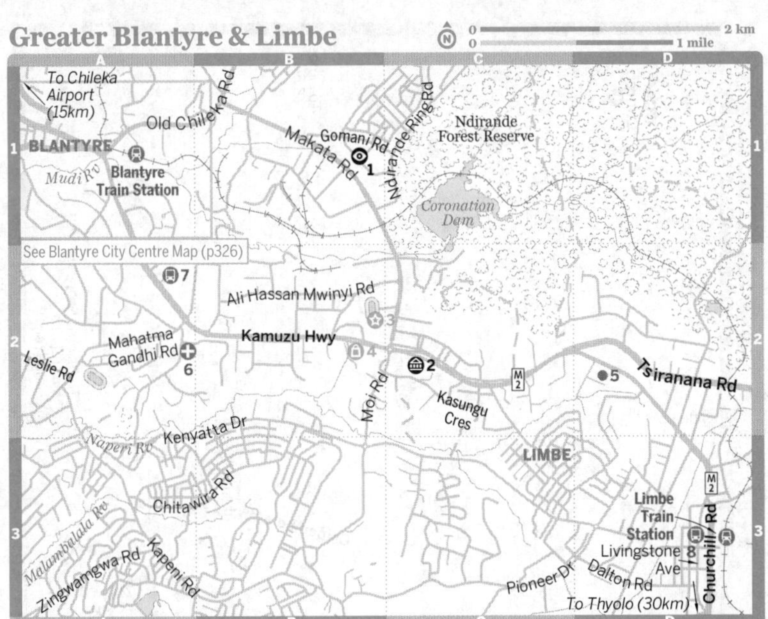

Mackie Rd; ⏰9am-noon Mon-Fri & 6-7.30pm Thu), which contains a vast number of journals, books and photographs, some dating as far back as the 19th century. You could easily while away a spare afternoon perusing old volumes on politics, history, exploration and wildlife.

Blantyre Sports Club HEALTH & FITNESS
(Map p326; ☎01-835095, 01-821172; cnr Victoria Ave & Independence Dr) Established in 1896 and whiffing of colonialism, this is a great place to work up a sweat or keep the kids amused. Take lunch in the breezy checked-cloth-tabled restaurant, enjoying a range of samosas, salads, burgers and steaks.

There are tennis and squash courts, a gym and a pool. Daily membership costs MK2000, which allows you to enter the club and use the bar and restaurant (there's a good buffet on Sunday lunchtimes). You can then pay to use the pool (MK500), play squash or tennis (MK250) or to take a round of golf (nine holes MK700). Equipment can be hired.

Greater Blantyre & Limbe

Sights
1 Carlsberg Brewery B1
2 National Museum C2

Eating
Game .... (see 4)
Jungle Pepper .... (see 4)
Shoprite .... (see 4)

Entertainment
Cine City Cinema .... (see 4)
3 Kamuzu Stadium B2

Shopping
Central Bookshop .... (see 4)
4 Chichiri Shopping Mall B2

Information
5 Mozambique Consulate D2
6 Queen Elizabeth Central Hospital A2

Transport
7 Automotive Centre A2
8 Limbe Bus Station D3

☞ Tours

Wilderness Safaris ADVENTURE TOUR
(Map p326; ☎01-820955; www.wilderness-safaris.com; Protea Hotel Royalis, 2 Hanover Ave) The country's leading light in adventure travel, Wilderness Safaris have an office at the Protea Hotel Ryalls (p328), and can organise excursions for Liwonde National Park staying

Blantyre City Centre

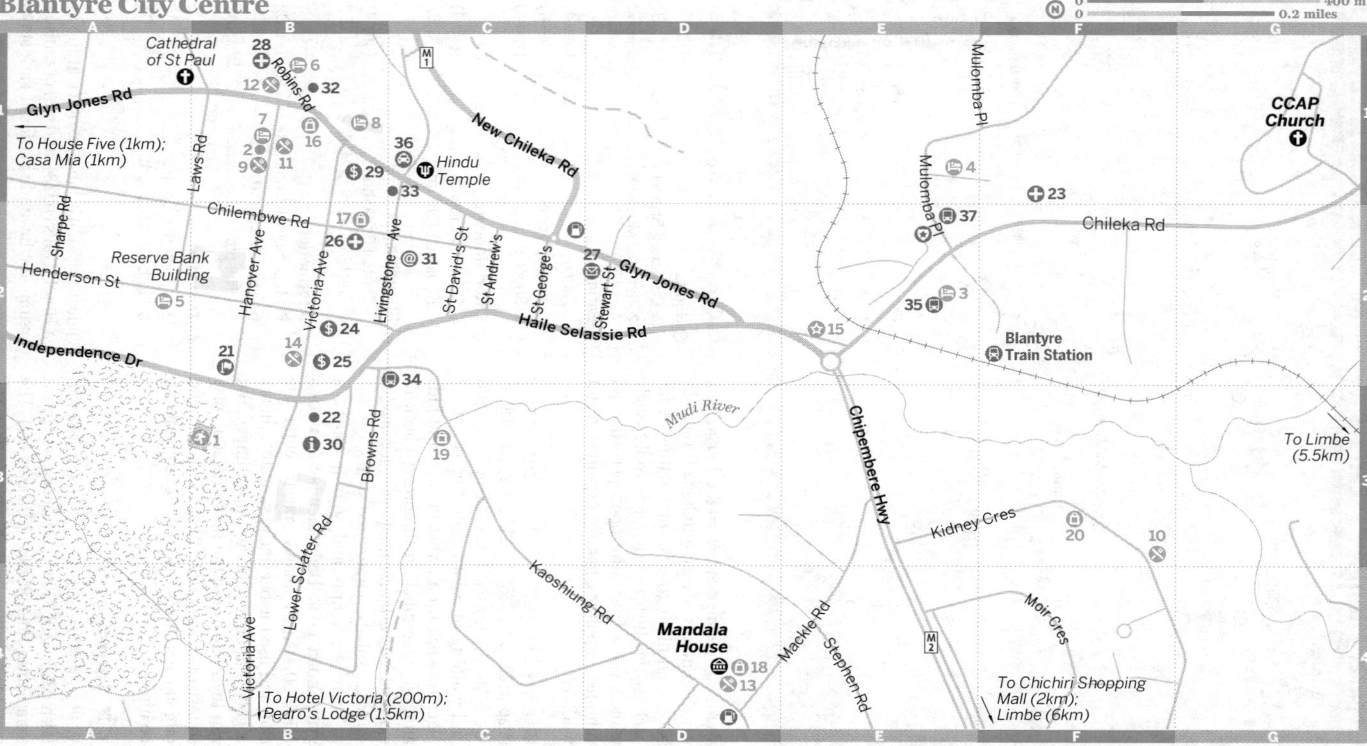

Blantyre City Centre

at its magical Mvuu Camp (p319), as well as safaris further north.

Responsible Safari Company ADVENTURE TOUR
(☎01-602407; www.responsiblesafaricompany.com) With solid green ecocredentials, this safari tour operator has myriad different trips up its sleeve from three-day tours to Lake Malawi, to three-day hiking adventures on Mt Mulanje. Beyond this there are culture vulture two-week tours, specialised tours of southern or northern Malawi and much more. Call Kate for more information.

Sleeping

There are a couple of decent options for budget travellers as well as an excellent choice of midrange and top-end accommodation. Most are located near the city centre, though a couple of the budget options are near the main bus station.

TOP CHOICE **House Five** GUESTHOUSE $$$
(☎0888-901762; www.housefivemw.com; Kabula Hill Rd; s/d incl breakfast US$100/120; P 🛜 ❄) This hillside accommodation sits in a lush garden and brims with charm, from its outdoor bistro serving up pizza and pasta, to its friendly staff. Individualistic rooms excel with parquet floors, walls decked in impressionist paintings, and antique furniture. Romantic and peaceful, this may be the city's most charming place to get away from the hubbub.

Protea Hotel Ryalls HOTEL $$$
(Map p326; 01-820955; ryalls@proteamalawi.com; 2 Hanover Ave; s/d US$215/245;) This stately monolith is the oldest established hotel in Malawi; opened in 1922 it was a legendary stop for travellers on the Cape-to-Cairo route. With its wood-panelled lobby, elegant restaurant, pool and gym and bar, it remains the premier choice of business people.

Rooms deserve the four-star rating with stylish fittings, huge beds and sumptuous decor. Ryalls also runs the superb 21 Grill on Hanover next door. There's also a Wilderness Safaris (p325) office here to help you arrange trips to nearby Liwonde National Park.

Sunbird Mount Soche Hotel HOTEL $$$
(Map p326; 01-820071; www.sunbirdmalawi.com; Glyn Jones Rd; s/d US$185/210;) Another spotless addition to the Sunbird portfolio, Mount Soche boasts spick-and-span, international-style rooms – somewhat on the small side – in the centre of town; think thick carpets, DSTV, mustard walls, darkwood furniture, desk and air-con. There's an internet cafe here too, as well as **Pablo's Lounge** (Map p326; Mount Soche Hotel, Glyn Jones Rd), a new sports bar that was being finished as we passed. Quality.

Hostellerie de France GUESTHOUSE $$$
(01-669626; www.hostellerie-de-france.com; cnr Chilomoni Ring Rd & Kazuni Close; standard d/tr/f from US$60/70/100;) You'll find everything you need here, from standard rooms, to executive doubles, apartments and family suites, and there are discounts for long stayers.

The swimming pool (and attached Jacuzzi!) looks out across the valley to Mt Ndirande and there's a restaurant with a pretty sophisticated menu (garlic mussels, goose-liver pâte, rabbit in white wine and mustard) and excellent French wines. Staff can also organise great-value car rental.

Malawi Sun Hotel HOTEL $$$
(Map p326; 01-824808; www.malawisunhotel.com; Robins Rd; s/d from US$126/160;) This comfortable hotel has an imposing African-style lounge with great mountain views. There's a tempting swimming pool, internet area, plus the flavoursome Deepend Grill, a chic spot for Western fare, ice cream and cocktails. Rooms are decent and very fresh with DSTV, comfy beds, bathrooms and air-con.

Choose from the main building or chalets. Also on-site, the Aamari restaurant serves everything from pasta and curries to beef stew and *nshima* (mains MK1000) and there's also a fast-food court nearby.

Kabula Lodge LODGE $$
(01-821216; www.kabulalodge.co.mw; off Michiru Rd, Kabula Hill; dm/s/d with shared bathroom US$10/15/30, r US$40;) Hidden down an exclusive street on the crest of a hill, northwest of the city centre, Kabula enjoys peace aplenty and scenic mountain views on both sides. The rooms are equally pleasing with wrought-iron beds, minimal decor, DSTV and fans and bathrooms. Dinner can be requested; alternatively there's a TV lounge and a self-catering kitchen. Rates include breakfast.

Pedro's Lodge LODGE $$$
(01-833430; www.pedroslodge.com; 9 Smythe Rd, Sunnyside; s/d US$75/105;) There are eight rooms in this large house set in leafy gardens. Rooms have homy interiors and tasteful fresh linen, DSTV and restful views. Best of all it's peaceful. There's even a large and very soppy dog to keep you company.

Hotel Victoria HOTEL $$$
(01-823500; www.hotelvictoriamw.com; Victoria Ave; s/d MK25,000/35,000;) Upscale Victoria attracts corporate types thanks to its pool, marble lobby and inviting restaurant dishing up tasty local fare. Rooms enjoy plump pillows, armoires, thick carpets, DSTV, desks and fridges. Ask for one away from the road.

Doogles GUESTHOUSE, CAMPGROUND $$
(Map p326; 0999-186512, 01-821128; www.dooglesl odge.com; Mulomba Pl; campsite/dm MK1250/MK2000, chalets with/without bathroom US$35/25;) Magnetising backpackers to it like iron filings, with its fresh-white courtyard and centrepiece pool, huge bar and lush gardens, Doogles is a good place to stay and it's right near the bus station. It has superfresh rooms with mustard-hued walls, clean dorms and chalets.

It also has bikes for hire and internet and wi-fi. Finally, you can pitch your tent here. But if you want somewhere peaceful you'd better try elsewhere, as it can get a little noisy.

Henderson Street Guest House GUESTHOUSE $
(Map p326; ☎01-794572, 01-823474; 19 Henderson St; s/d MK5500/6000; P 📶) Five minutes' walk from the centre, this old-fashioned place sits in a leafy garden and has cosy – if tired – rooms with bathrooms and DSTV. There's a welcoming verandah for drinks and breakfast, and the lady who runs the place glitters with charm. Price includes a huge breakfast.

Careful though of walking back here at night as there has been the odd mugging in the grounds.

Limbe Country Club CAMPGROUND $
(☎01-841145; Livingstone Ave; campsite per person MK2000; P 📶) An alternative for those with wheels. Here you can park and camp on the edge of the playing fields. Rates include club membership, so you can use the showers and restaurant inside.

Eating

TOP CHOICE **21 Grill on Hanover** STEAKHOUSE $
(Map p326; ☎01-820955; Hanover Ave, Protea Hotel Ryalls; mains around MK3000; ⏲noon-2pm & 6.30-10pm; P ❄ 📶) Fit for a senator, this fine restaurant opened in '69 is showing no signs of fatigue. Sit at the granite-topped bar, or get sucked into a comfy Chesterfield before you tuck into a salad, flame-grilled steak or the signature '21 spare ribs dipped in bourbon sauce'. Complete the hedonism with a slice of their excellent chocolate gateau.

Casa Mia INTERNATIONAL $$
(☎01-915559; casamia@africa-online.net; Kabula Hill Rd; mains MK2500-5000; P ❄ 📶) One of the classiest dining options in the city, you'll need your smarts on to visit this lovely restaurant. Within its wine-stacked interior are antique Cinzano prints, white-cloth tables, and an exclusive clientele feasting on dishes such as grilled chambo, smoked salmon and risotto. Eat in or outside.

Mandala Cafe CAFE $
(Map p326; Mandala House, Mackie Rd; mains MK1200; ⏲8.30am-4.30pm Mon-Fri, 8.30am-12.30pm Sat; P 📶) Sit on a breezy stone terrace in the grounds of Mandala House, or inside at this chilled cafe within the old house itself. There are swings and a see-saw to keep the kids happy, a selection of tourist leaflets and magazines to browse, and a speedy wi-fi hotspot. Regulars love the Italian cuisine, fillet steak, thai chicken, freshly brewed coffee, iced tea and homemade 'cakes of the day'. A real oasis.

Hong Kong Restaurant CHINESE $
(Map p326; ☎01-820859; Robins Rd; mains MK1000; ⏲noon-2pm & 6-10pm Tue-Sun; P ❄ 📶) Like a slice of '50s Shanghai, Hong Kong is an atmospheric pagoda-style building with a red wooden ceiling festooned in red lanterns, and walls dancing with twisting dragon murals. Food is good, and comes in generous portions – alongside the usual sweet and sour and spring rolls you'll find chicken with peanuts and whole chillies, and fried chicken gizzards.

Hostaria ITALIAN $
(Map p326; Kidney Cres, Uta Waleza Centre; mains from MK1200; ⏲noon-2pm & 6.30-9pm Mon-Sat; P ❄ 📶) Welcoming Hostaria has red-checked-cloth tables, lemon walls, a buzzing ambience and hearty menu of wood-fired pizzas and delicious homemade pasta dishes. There's a mezzanine lounge upstairs, Coke chandeliers and daily specials on the chalkboard.

Bombay Palace INDIAN $
(Map p326; ☎0888-600600, 0888-400400; Hanover Ave; mains MK2300; ⏲noon-1.45pm Tue-Sun, 6.30-10pm daily; ❄ 📶) Approaching its 10th birthday, this classy Indian restaurant with mushroom-grey walls and vivid artwork spans chicken tikka massala to tandoori, prawns and sizzling mutton dishes to plenty of veggie choices.

Blue Elephant STEAKHOUSE $
(Map p326; ☎01-915559, 0999-965850; Kidney Cres, Ginnery Cnr; mains from MK1250; ⏲noon-late; P ❄ 📶) Choose from booths inside or tables alfresco beneath an awning. This is a great watering hole for German beers and carb-heavy grub such as chargrilled burgers and steaks. The meatballs are particularly memorable. Come weekend, it's packed with a lively local and expat crowd who come for the thumping disco and live music.

Food Court FAST FOOD $
(Map p326; Robins Rd, Malawi Sun Hotel; dishes around MK700; ⏲10am-10pm) With striking views of the mountains, this breezy alfresco courtyard is surrounded by a fried chicken joint (Blue Savannah), an ice cream parlour (Scoops) and cafe (Shakes) where can get your favourite chocolate bar whizzed into a milkshake. It's a nice spot for kids and an alcohol-free zone.

Jungle Pepper FAST FOOD $
(Map p325; ☎0999-826229, 0888-826229; www.junglepepperpizza.com; pizzas MK1100-1400; ⏰10.30am-2.30pm & 4.30-8.30pm) This popular takeaway pizza shop shares a big shaded courtyard at the Chichiri Shopping Mall with a number of other fast-food joints. Toppings veer toward the exotic, such as peri peri and mango chicken. You can also buy pizza by the slice for MK600, and get a decent cappuccino here.

Self-Catering

The main **Peoples** (Map p326; Victoria Ave) supermarket sells food and other goods, much of it imported from South Africa or Europe and sold at similar prices. There are also huge **Shoprite** (Map p325; Kamuzu Hwy, Chichiri Shopping Cente) and **Game** (Map p325; Kamuzu Hwy, Chichiri Shopping Cente) supermarkets a few kilometres out of town.

Drinking

Garden Terrace Bar BAR
(Map p326; Sunbird Mount Soche Hotel, Glyn Jones Rd) Catering to a more sophisticated market, its tranquil surrounds are appealing. At the same hotel, the Sportsman's Bar is favoured by local business people and other movers and shakers.

Entertainment

Both the Blantyre Sports Club (p325) and the Limbe Country Club (p329) feature regular live music. Occasional live music is played at both the Sunbird Mount Soche Hotel (p328) and Protea Hotel Ryalls (p328).

Blantyre's main sports venue is the **Kamuzu Stadium** (Map p325; off Makata Rd) between the city centre and Limbe. This is also Malawi's national stadium; international football and other events are held here. There's no regular program but matches are advertised in the newspaper and on billboards around town.

Warehouse Cultural Centre THEATRE
(Map p326; www.thewarehouse-malawi.net) Wedged between the railway line and a major roundabout, this former depot now consists of a soundproofed theatre, cafe and bar. It's one of the country's most exciting venues and a staunch supporter of Malawian music, art, dance, theatre and literature. The owners organise a diverse timetable including regular poetry readings, comedy shows, screenings, writing workshops and live-music events featuring the best Malawian music has to offer.

Cine City Cinema CINEMA
(Map p325; ☎01-912873; Kamuzu Hwy, Chichiri Shopping Mall; Mon-Thu, MK1200 Fri-Sun; ⏰closed Tue) Big-name films are shown at 5.30pm and 8.30pm daily (except Tuesdays) with an extra 2.30pm showing at the weekend. It's in the basement of the Chichiri Shopping Mall, underneath Game supermarket.

Shopping

There are a number of **craft stalls** (Map p326; Chilembwe Rd), where the work on sale is excellent and browsing is refreshingly hassle-free. The more chaotic **Municipal Market** (Map p326; Kaoshiung Rd) is also worth a visit. For high-end craft hunters, **African Habitat** (Map p326; ☎01-873642; Uta Waleza Shopping Centre, Kidney Cres; ⏰7.30am-4.30pm Mon-Fri, 8am-noon Sat) is a good bet – it's a cavernous boutique full of furniture, jewellery, sculpture, art, textiles and books. Two kilometres out of town is the **Chichiri Shopping Mall** (Map p325; Kamuzu Hwy), which has bookshops, pharmacies, boutiques and two large supermarkets.

For buying print film, getting digital photos printed or passport photos taken, there is **CES Photo Express** (Map p326; Glyn Jones Rd; ⏰7.30am-5pm Mon-Fri, 8am-1pm Sat).

La Galleria ARTS & CRAFTS
(Map p326; Mandala House; ⏰9am-5.30pm Mon-Sun) Situated in the oldest colonial dame in the city, Mandala House, this eclectic gallery features vividly coloured, contemporary artwork by local artists, as well as sculpture, bedspreads, curtains and huge, carved wood thrones.

Central Africana Bookshop BOOKSHOP
(Map p326; centralafricana@africa-online.net; Uta Waleza Centre, Kidney Cres) This old established bookshop is on two levels and is an excellent spot for picking up pictorials of the lake and wildlife as souvenirs of your stay. There are also charming old prints and maps.

Central Bookshop BOOKSHOP
(Map p325; Chichiri Shopping Mall) There's a wide selection of fiction, kids illustrated books, potboilers, biographies and motivational self-help titles.

Information

Dangers & Annoyances

It's not safe to walk around the city alone at night; in particular, there have been reports of muggings of travellers walking in between Doogles and the city after dark. Always use a taxi at night. Also watch your valuables when around the busy bus and minibus stations at Blantyre and Limbe. Bag snatcing occasionally happens in daylight.

Emergency

Ambulance (☎998)

Fire (☎01-871999)

Police Station (☎01-823333)

Rapid Response Unit (☎997) Emergency wing.

Internet Access

You will find plenty of internet cafes in Blantyre. Skyband and Globe wi-fi hotspots are available throughout the city.

Tusa Internet Café (Map p326; off Livingstone Ave; per min MK6) High-speed internet access.

Medical Services

One Stop Pharmacy (Map p326; Chilembwe Rd; ⏲8am-6pm Mon-Fri, 9am-2pm Sat) This well-stocked pharmacy sells bilharzia tablets (if you've been swimming in the lake), as well as malaria prophylaxis.

Mwaiwathu Private Hospital (Map p326; ☎01-834989, 01-822999; Chileka Rd; ⏲24hr) For private medical consultations or blood tests, this hospital, east of the city centre, is good. A consultation is US$10; all drugs and treatment are extra.

Queen Elizabeth Central Hospital (Map p325; ☎01-874333; ⏲24hr) The malaria test centre at this government-run hospital, off Chipembere Hwy, charges US$10 for a malaria test. Ask for directions as the test centre is hard to find.

Seventh Day Adventist Clinic (Map p326; ☎01-820399; Robins Rd) For medical or dental problems, this clinic charges US$10 for a doctor's consultation and US$10 for a malaria test.

Money

There are a couple of branches of the **National Bank of Malawi** (Map p326; Victoria Ave) and one branch of **Standard Bank** (Map p326; Victoria Ave) on Victoria Ave. They all change cash and travellers cheques and have 24-hour ATMs.

Post

Post Office (Map p326; Glyn Jones Rd; ⏲7.30am-4.30pm Mon-Fri, 8-10am Sat) Has poste restante and EMS express mail.

Tourist Information

Immigration Office (Map p326; Government Complex, Victoria Ave) If you need to extend your visa, Blantyre has an immigration office.

Tourist Office (Map p326; ☎regional tourism officer 0888-304362; Government Complex, Victoria Ave; ⏲7.30am-5pm Mon-Fri) This small office in the Department of Tourism stocks a few leaflets, sells maps of Malawi (MK500) and can offer enthusiastic, though not always that helpful, advice. It's on the 2nd floor.

Travel Agencies

Jambo Africa (Map p326; ☎01-835356; www.jambo-africa.com; SS Rent A Car building, Glyn Jones Rd) Now relocated beside the Hindu temple, this is a great one-stop shop for travel tickets, car hire and accommodation. It also has package trips to Nyala Lodge (p341) in Lengwe National Park among other excursions. Speak to Max.

Getting There & Away

Air

Blantyre's Chileka airport is about 15km north of the city centre.

Air Malawi (Map p326; ☎01-820811; Robins Rd; ⏲7.30am-4.30pm Mon-Fri, 8am-noon Sat)

British Airways (Map p326; ☎01-820811; www.britishairways.com; Livingstone Towers, Glyn Jones Rd)

KLM & Kenya Airways (Map p326; ☎01-824524; Protea Hotel Ryalls, 2 Hanover Ave)

South African Airways (Map p326; ☎01-820627; Livingstone Towers, Glyn Jones Rd)

Bus & Minibus

Blantyre's main bus station for long-distance buses is **Wenela Bus Station** (Map p326; Mulomba Pl), east of the centre. National Bus Company and AXA City Trouper buses run from here to Lilongwe (MK1800, four hours), Mzuzu (MK4000, nine to 10 hours), Monkey Bay (MK1800, five to six hours) via Zomba (MK750, 1½ to two hours) and Mangochi (MK1500, four to five hours), Mulanje (MK1000, 1½ hours) and Karonga (MK5500, 14 hours, change at Mzuzu).

AXA Executive buses depart from the **Automotive Centre** (Map p325; Ginnery Cnr), where you'll also find its ticket office, and call at the Chichiri Shopping Mall and the car park outside Blantyre Lodge (near the main bus station) before departing the city. They leave twice daily to Lilongwe (MK1800, four hours).

Long-distance minibuses go from the **Limbe Bus Station** (Map p325); most leave on a fill-up-and-go basis. It's often quicker to get a local minibus to Limbe bus station and then a long-distance bus or 'half-bus' from there rather than wait for AXA or other bus services in Blantyre. Routes include Zomba (MK1000, one hour), Mulanje (MK1500, 1¼ hours), Mangochi (MK2000) and the border at Muloza (MK2200, 1½ hours).

Long-distance minibuses to the Lower Shire including Nchalo (MK1000, two hours) and Nsanje (MK2000, four hours) leave from the **City Bus Station** (Map p326) near Victoria Ave in Blantyre, between 8am and 5pm.

The car park next to Blantyre Lodge is the pick-up and drop-off point for long- distance bus companies headed for Jo'burg. **Intercape** (Map p326; ☎0999-403398) goes to Jo'burg at 8.30am on Tuesday, Thursday, Saturday and Sunday (MK27,000, 25 hours). **KJ Transways** (Map p326; ☎01-877738, 01-914017) leaves for Lilongwe every morning at 7.30am (MK2000).

Getting Around

To/From the Airport

A taxi from the airport to the city costs around MK8000, but agree on a price with the driver first. The price can be negotiated down a bit if you're going from the city to the airport. If your budget doesn't include taxis, frequent local buses between the City Bus Station and Chileka Township pass the airport gate. The fare is MK800.

Bus

Blantyre is a compact city, so it's unlikely you'll need to use public transport to get around, apart from the minibuses that shuttle along Chipembere Hwy between Blantyre City Bus Station and Limbe Bus Station.

Taxi

You can find private-hire taxis at the Sunbird Mount Soche Hotel or at the bus stations. A taxi across the city centre costs around MK800; between the centre and the main bus station costs from MK1000; and from Blantyre to Limbe costs around MK2000.

Around Blantyre

Blantyre is surrounded by three 'mountains' (Michiru, Soche and Ndirande), all actually large hills that can be hiked to the summit. Some hikers have been attacked on Mt Ndirande, so you should only go here with a guide. You should be able to arrange this at your accommodation for around MK1000 per day. The path up Mt Soche starts at Soche Secondary School.

MT MICHIRU CONSERVATION AREA

If you have a day to spare you could head for the nature trails at **Mt Michiru** (admission per person/car MK50/200), 8km northwest of the city. It's good for birdwatching, with more than 400 species recorded here, and resident animals include monkeys, klipspringers and even leopards, though you're unlikely to see any of them. It's still a pleasant place to spend a few hours, however, with beautiful views all around. Particularly lovely is the picnic area overlooking the city, with seats carved out of the rock on a bluff at the edge of the mountain. You might also notice a huge cross on the side of the hill – the Way of the Cross Roman Catholics march up the mountain on a pilgrimage every Easter.

To reach the **visitor centre** (where the trails start), take Kabula Hill Rd from the city and Michiru Rd through a select suburb and then a township. At the end of the sealed road (3km from Blantyre) a dirt road leads along the eastern foot of the mountain. Take the left turn signposted 'nature trails', which leads you to a green gate from where you'll be directed to the reception further up the hill. After you've paid the entry fees staff can give you a map or will arrange a guide for you at no extra charge (though a tip of about MK200 is appropriate). There's no public transport, but you could get a taxi as far as the driver is prepared to go along the dirt road – that won't get you very far though – the road is terrible, especially after the rains, and much better attempted in a 4WD. What's more, there are very few visitors so you'd have trouble getting a lift back.

FISHERMAN'S REST

Fisherman's Rest (☎0888-836753; www.fishermansrest.net; P 🚸) is a nature reserve, lodge and tea house, and makes a good place to stop off on the way down to the Lower Shire or as a day trip from Blantyre. The reserve is open from sunrise to sunset and has several attractive nature trails; although you're not likely to see many animals other than a few antelopes, the surroundings are beautiful and the views out over the Rift Valley awesome. The three chalets have verandahs and wicker chairs, comfy beds and mozzie nets, while the tea house and gift shop sells locally grown coffee, teas and serves English breakfast and Malawian fare. Fisherman's Rest accepts volunteers at its primary school to help with its literacy program. Information Technology teachers are particularly welcome.

Sleeping & Eating

If you want to stay the night there's a cosy **lodge** (☎0888-836753; sleeps 6 people, per night for hire of lodge incl breakfast US$375, plus each additional guest $40; P @ 📶) that can be rented out in its entirety with three bedrooms, a farmhouse-style kitchen and a fantastic lounge area complete with huge stone fireplace. It's set in an acre of gardens. Inside the reserve itself is the **Woodland Cottage** (☎0888-836753; s/d incl breakfast US$80/115; P) with en suite rooms and a family apart-

MALAWI'S CUP OF TEA

South and east of Blantyre, on the rolling hills of the Shire Highlands, the climate is ideal for growing tea, and the area is covered with plantations (or 'estates'). The first tea bushes were imported from India during the early days of the Nyasaland colony, and the tea production quickly became a major industry. It's now a major export crop (along with tobacco and sugar), providing thousands of people with jobs.

As you travel along the main road between Limbe and Mulanje, the hills on either side are covered with a patchwork of vibrant-green tea fields dotted with dense pockets of deep-green pine and palms. The tea-pickers (men and women) work methodically through the lines of bushes, picking just a few leaves and a bud from the top of each and throwing them into large baskets on their backs. The leaves are then transported to a tea factory where they are trimmed and dried before being packed in bags and boxes ready for export.

It may be possible to arrange a tour of an estate and factory; simply call the estate and ask a senior manager if it's possible to visit. The best place to start with is **Satemwa Tea Estate** (☎01-473500, 01-473233; www.satemwa.com) near the small town of Thyolo (*cho*-low) on the main road between Limbe and Mulanje. Otherwise the Mulanje Infocentre (p333) at the Chitakale Trading Centre can organise tours of local estates.

ment opening out onto a verandah. For those with a more rustic bent, hidden deep in the bush are wooden stilted **bushcamp hides** (☎0888-836753; s/d US$80/115) with twin beds, private bathroom facilities and stunning views over the valley from their verandahs.

Below the lodge is the **Old Mill Tea House** (meals from MK1000; ⏱9am-6pm). You can sit on the cafe's verandah and soak up the view between sampling delicious homemade soups and cakes, as well as substantial meals such as Thai curries and lasagne. Entry to the nature reserve is free for customers, and homy accommodation is available at the Tea House for US$40 per person per night including breakfast (though, unfortunately, none of the rooms have views).

Mulanje

POP 17,000

Mulanje is famous for both its infinity of emerald-green tea plantations, and the achingly pretty Mt Mulanje – a massif of some 20 peaks reaching over 2500m. The town has an ATM, a bus station and little else but a few guesthouses. There are two parts to Mulanje. If coming from the direction of Blantyre, which most travellers are, you'll first hit the **Chitakale Trading Centre** (where the dirt road to Likhubula turns off the main sealed Blantyre–Mulanje road). Here you'll find the **Mulanje Infocentre** (☎01-466506, 01-466466; infomulanje@malawi.net), a PTC and two petrol stations. Continue for 2km to Mulanje town where the main bus station, hotels and banks are all located.

Sleeping & Eating

TOP CHOICE **Kara O' Mula** LODGE $$$
(☎01-466515; www.karaomula.com; s/d US$50/65; P@☜≋) Hidden up a dirt track, this delightful eyrie clothed in lush vegetation is right under Mt Mulanje and has a swimming pool (fed by fresh water from a small waterfall), lively bar, and, up at the house, a romantic verandah to drink up the elevated views.

Rooms (choose between the lodge or chalets up the hill) are fresh, with tiled floors, vaulted thatch ceilings, attractive linen, quirky homemade furniture and bathrooms. They're also equipped with fans. Outside, the garden brims with banana and blue gum trees. Very good meals are available too from MK1300. Homy, welcoming and the perfect base from which to hike.

Mulanje Motel MOTEL $
(☎01-466245; r with/without bathroom MK3000/2500; P) Heading closer to Likhubula on the main road, Mulanje Motel has clean rooms with thick blankets on sturdy beds, fresh white walls and bathrooms. There's also a cafe-bar.

Mulanje View GUESTHOUSE $

(☎01-466348; s/d with shared bathroom MK1050/3000; Ⓟ) In the skirts of Mt Mulanje this old red-brick trusty has basic rooms with amazing views of the towering massif. There are no en suite bathrooms. There is a bar-restaurant (serving plates of the usual *nshima* and meat for around MK600) and the garden is dotted with little thatched gazebos for chilling out in.

Getting There & Away

AXA buses go to/from Blantyre (MK850, 1½ hours), as do minibuses (MK700, 1¼ hours). If you're heading for the border with Mozambique, minibuses and *matolas* run to Muloza (MK400, 30 minutes).

Mt Mulanje

A huge hulk of twisted granite rising majestically from the surrounding plains, Mt Mulanje towers over 3000m high. All over the mountain are dense green valleys and rivers that drop from sheer cliffs to form dazzling waterfalls. The locals call it the 'Island in the Sky' and on misty days (and there are many of those) it's easy to see why – the mountain is shrouded in a cotton-wool haze, and its highest peaks burst through the cloud to touch the heavens.

PINES ON MULANJE

The pine plantations on Mulanje were first established by the colonial government in the early 1950s, mainly around Chambe. The sides of the entire massif are too steep for a road so all timber is cut by hand and then carried down on a cableway (called the skyline) or on the heads of forest labourers. As you're going up the Chambe Plateau Path you'll see these incredibly hardy guys walking downhill, sometimes running, with huge planks of wood balanced on their heads.

The plantations provide employment for local people and wood for the whole of southern Malawi. A bad side effect is the pine trees tend to spread slowly across the natural grassland as seeds are blown by the wind. These introduced trees disturb the established vegetation balance – which is always precarious in highland areas.

Mulanje measures about 30km from west to east and 25km from north to south, with an area of at least 600 sq km. On its northeastern corner is the outlier Mchese Mountain, separated from the main massif by the Fort Lister Gap. The massif is composed of several bowl-shaped river basins, separated by rocky peaks and ridges. The highest peak is Sapitwa (3001m), the highest point in Malawi and in all Southern Africa north of the Drakensberg. There are other peaks on the massif above 2500m and you can reach most of the summits without technical climbing.

Of particular note is the endemic Mulanje cedar, which can grow up to 40m high. There's plenty of wildlife on the mountain too – klipspringers, vervet monkeys and rock hyraxes are all seen regularly, and birdlife includes black eagles, buzzards and kestrels.

Some people come to the base of the mountain just for a day visit, but the stunning scenery, easy access, clear paths and well-maintained huts make Mulanje a fine hiking area and many travellers spend at least three days here.

GUIDEBOOKS & MAPS

The *Guide to Mulanje Massif,* by Frank Eastwood, has information on ascent routes and main peaks plus a large section on rock climbing, but nothing on the routes between huts.

If you need detailed maps, the Department of Surveys prints a map of the mountain at 1:40,000, which shows most of the paths and huts. The 1:30,000 *Tourist Map of Mulanje* covers a similar area, overprinted with extra information for hikers. Both these maps cost MK650 and are usually available from the **Department of Surveys Map Sales Offices** in Lilongwe and Blantyre, but stocks occasionally run dry.

GUIDES & PORTERS

Porters are not obligatory but they make the hiking easier, especially for the first day's steep hike from the Likhubula Forestry Office (p337). Guides are definitely recommended to help you through the maze of paths.

Arrange guides and porters only at Likhubula, as the forest station keeps a registered list, which works on a rotation system.

There is a standard charge of around MK2000 per day per porter and MK2500 per guide (regardless of group size). The total fee for the whole trip should be agreed

A MULANJE TRAVERSE

The route described here, from Likhubula to Fort Lister Gap, is the most popular of several options. It can be done in four days.

Likhubula Forestry Office to Chambe Hut

There are two options: the Chambe Plateau Path, which is short and steep (two to four hours), and the Chapaluka Path (3½ to five hours), which is less steep and more scenic. From the hut verandah, there are good views of the southeastern face of Chambe Peak (2557m), but if you fancy reaching the summit of this spectacular peak, from Chambe Hut it will take you five to seven hours to get to the top and back. The ascent is stiff and the paths are vague, so you may need a guide. About two to 2½ hours from the hut, you reach a large cairn on a broad, level part of the ridge at the foot of the main face. You might be happy with reaching this point, which offers excellent views over the Chambe Basin to the escarpment edge and the plains far below.

Chambe Hut to Chisepo Hut or Thuchila Hut

This route is 12km (five to six hours). About two hours from Chambe, you reach Chisepo Junction, where a path leads up to the summit of Sapitwa Peak (3001m). You can hike to the summit of Sapitwa but it's a toughie and the upper section involves some tricky scrambling among large boulders and dense vegetation. From Chisepo Junction you should allow three to five hours for the ascent, plus two to four for the descent.

You can then either spend the night at Chisepo Hut or push on through to either Chambe or Thuchila Hut. If you're short of time, you can do a shorter loop by descending from Thuchila Hut to Lukulezi Mission, then hiking or catching a *matola* back to Likhubula.

Thuchila Hut to Sombani Hut

This stage (12km, four to five hours) takes you across a small col and down into the Ruo Basin. About two hours from Thuchila Hut, you reach Chinzama Hut, where you can stop if you want an easy day. The large mountain directly opposite Sombani Hut is Namasile (2687m), which takes about three hours to ascend, plus two hours on the descent. The path is steep and strenuous in places, spiralling round the northern side of the mountain to approach the summit from the west. A guide is recommended unless you're competent on vague paths in bad weather.

Sombani Hut to Fort Lister Gap

This stage (5km, three hours) is all downhill, with great views over the surrounding plains. There are a lot of forks, so a guide is useful to show you the way; otherwise, at every fork keep going down. For the last section you follow a dirt track, past Fort Lister Forest Station, from where it's another 8km along the dirt road to Phalombe village. There's little or no traffic, so you'll have to hike (about two hours), but it's pleasant enough. Most porters include this stretch in the fee you pay for the final day.

From Phalombe there are one or two buses a day back to Likhubula or Mulanje (MK200, one hour) and there should be plenty of *matola* (MK250).

before departure and put in writing. Fees are paid at the end of the trip but porters are expected to provide their own food, so about 25% may be required in advance. You may want to tip your porters and guides if the service has been good; a rule of thumb is to pay something around an extra day's wage for every three to five days. The maximum weight each porter can carry is 18kg.

HIKING ROUTES

The three main ascent routes go from Likhubula: the **Chambe Plateau Path** (also called the Skyline Path), the **Chapaluka Path** and the **Lichenya Path**. Other routes, more often used for the descent: **Thuchila Hut to Lukulezi Mission**; **Sombani Hut to Fort Lister Gap**; and **Minunu Hut to Lujeri Tea Estate**.

Mt Mulanje

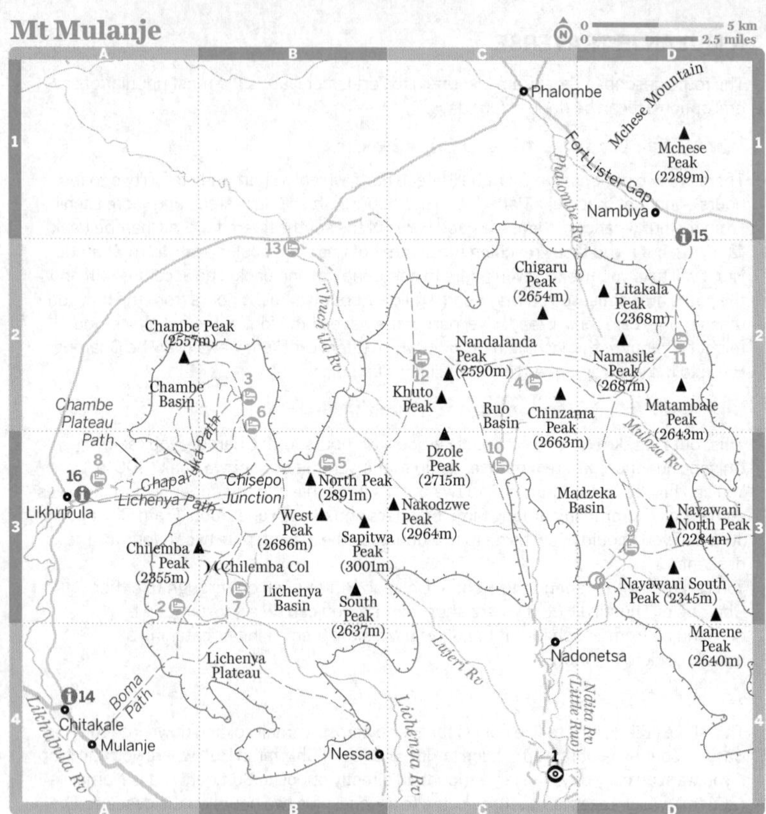

Once you're on the massif, a network of paths links the huts and peaks, and many different permutations are possible. Be warned that some of the routes are impassable or otherwise dangerous. The route from Madzeka Hut to Lujeri is very steep, for example, as are the Boma Path and the path from Lichenya to Nessa on the southwestern side of Mulanje.

As a rough guide, it takes anything from two to six hours to hike between one hut and the next, which means you can walk in the morning, dump your kit, then go out to explore a nearby peak or valley in the afternoon.

Sleeping

BELOW THE MOUNTAIN

Likhubula Forest Lodge LODGE $$
(☎01-467737, 0999-220560; campsite per person US$6, s/d without bathroom incl breakfast US$25/31, s/d incl breakfast US$31/37, whole lodge US$240; P@) This faded but lovely old colonial house has lots of character; a homey kitchen, five clean rooms (two with their own bathrooms) and a communal lounge with rocking chairs, and a nightly fire crackling. The food comes highly recommended and the easy charm of the staff make it a memorable place to overnight.

Thuchila Tourist Lodge LODGE $
(☎0881-103353; thuchilatlodge@africa-online.net; r from MK6500, r with TV from MK7500; P@) Twenty kilomentres past Likhubula on the road to Phalombe, you reach a rocky turn off to Thuchila. The place has an edge-of-the-world feel to it (maybe it's the caged baboons outside), its lush gardens nestled in the shadow of the massif. There's a clean restaurant dishing up stews, fish and chicken.

There are passable rooms with a shared bathroom, though preferable are the red-brick chalets further up the hill each with

Mt Mulanje

Sights

1 Lujeri Tea Estate....C4

Sleeping

2 CCAP Cottage....A3
3 Chambe Hut....B2
4 Chinzama Hut....C2
5 Chisepo Hut....B3
6 France's Cottage....B2
7 Lichenya Hut....B3
8 Likhubula Forest Lodge....A3
Lujeri Guest House....(see 1)
Lujeri Lodge....(see 1)
9 Madzeka Hut....D3
10 Minunu Hut....C3
11 Sombani Hut....D2
12 Thuchila Hut....C2
13 Thuchila Tourist Lodge....B2

Eating

Pizzeria Basilico....(see 14)

Information

14 Chitakale Trading Centre....A4
15 Fort Lister Forestry Office....D1
16 Likhubula Forestry Office....A3
Mulanje Infocentre....(see 14)

their own bathroom. Convenient for walkers, the lodge is at the base of the path to Thuchila Hut.

ON THE MOUNTAIN

Forestry Huts CHALET $

(campsite per adult/child MK400/200, huts per adult/child MK700/350) On Mulanje are eight forestry huts: **Chambe**, **Chisepo**, **Lichenya**, **Thuchila**, **Chinzama**, **Minunu**, **Madzeka** and **Sombani**. Each is equipped with benches, tables and open fires with plenty of wood. Some have sleeping platforms (no mattresses); in others you just sleep on the floor. You provide your own food, cooking gear, candles, sleeping bag and stove (although you can cook on the fire). A caretaker chops wood, lights fires and brings water, for which a small tip should be paid.

Payments must be made at Likhubula Forestry Office – show your receipt to the hut caretaker. Camping is permitted near the huts when there are no more beds.

CCAP Cottage CHALET $

(dm MK700) On the Lichenya Plateau, this is similar to the forestry huts but there are utensils in the kitchen, plus mattresses and blankets. You can make reservations at the CCAP Mission in Likhubula.

France's Cottage CHALET $

(dm MK700) A more comfortable option than the huts, this small two-bedroom cottage sleeps six and comes with a living room complete with cooking fireplace. There are two single beds and two bunk beds. It's in the Chambe Basin near the Chambe Hut. Ask at the Likhubula Forestry Office or contact the Mountain Club of Malawi for further information.

Eating

BELOW THE MOUNTAIN

Pizzeria Basilico PIZZERIA $

(☎0888-878830; small/large pizzas from MK700/1050) Underneath Mulanje Infocentre this place has a breezy terrace overlooking the street and serves an excellent selection of wood-fired pizzas (you can see them rolling the dough before your very eyes), as well as a range of pastas and grills.

Information

Hiking on Mt Mulanje is controlled by the **Likhubula Forestry Office** (PO Box 50, Mulanje; 7.30am-noon & 1-5pm), at the small village of Likhubula, about 15km north of Mulanje town. Entry fees are MK100 per person; vehicle entry fee costs MK200 and the forestry office car park is MK100 a day. The friendly and helpful staff can arrange guides and porters from an official list. You must register here and make reservations

MALAWI'S ADVENTURE SPORT

Taking place July each year, the **Mt Mulanje Porters' Race** follows a gruelling, rocky route over the country's highest peak. When it started more than 10 years ago it was only open to porters and guides, but these days anyone can take part. Starting at the **Likhubula Forestry Office**, participants run up 25km of rugged terrain to the Chambe and Lichenya Plateaus and back, reaching 2500m above sea level at the highest point. If you think you can handle it, see www.mountmulanje.org.mw. Fast runners can expect to finish in around three hours. We recommend you arrive in Mulanje at least a day or two before the race to acclimatise to the elevation.

for the mountain huts (you can also call or write in advance). Camping is permitted only near huts and only when they're full. Open fires are not allowed – this is especially important during the latter part of the dry season when there is a serious fire risk. The collecting of plants and animals is forbidden.

Also good for information is the Mulanje Infocentre (p333; speak to Richard), based at Chitakale Trading Centre, on the corner of Phalombe Rd. It's set up to give travellers all pertinent information about hiking on the mountain and carries a good selection of books and maps. It rents out sleeping bags (per day MK800), and tents (eight-man/two-man per day MK2500/1500), and can also arrange mountain guides and porters. Tours to the nearby Dziwe la Nkhalamba waterfall (MK2500) and to the Lujeri and Mulli Brothers tea estates (per person US$25) are also arranged.

There have long been plans to develop rock climbing and abseiling tours on the mountain in the near future, but currently there's a shortage of gear. Contact the **Mountain Club of Malawi** (☎01-821269; www.mcm.org.mw) to get more information on joining its organisation and hooking up with other climbers.

There is nowhere to buy food on Mt Mulanje so you must carry all you need. At Likhubula there's a small market, but you're better off getting supplies at Chitakale, which has shops, stalls and a small supermarket, or in Blantyre.

Dangers & Annoyances

Hikers should remember that Mulanje is a big mountain with notoriously unpredictable weather. After periods of heavy rain, streams can become swollen and impassable – do not try to cross them! Wait until the flood subsides or adjust your route to cross in safety further upstream. Also, be aware that much of the mountain's granite surface can become very slippery and dangerous when wet. Even during the dry season, it's not uncommon to get rain, cold winds and thick mists, which make it easy to get lost. Between May and August, periods of low cloud and drizzle (called *chiperone*) can last several days, and temperatures drop below freezing. Always carry a map, a compass and warm and waterproof clothing should the weather change, or you risk suffering from severe exposure. Never set out on a climb alone and always tell someone where you're going and when you plan to return.

Getting There & Away

There are bus services that run between Blantyre and Mulanje town. The dirt road to Likhubula turns off the main sealed Blantyre–Mulanje road at Chitakale, about 2km west of the centre of Mulanje town – follow the signpost to Phalombe. If you're coming from Blantyre on the bus, ask to be dropped at Chitakale. From here, irregular *matola* run to Likhubula (MK300). If you're in a group, you can hire the whole *matola* to Likhubula for around MK2000. Alternatively, you can walk (10km, two to three hours); it's a pleasant hike with good views of the southwestern face of Mulanje on your right.

Lower Shire

A baking stretch of flat plains, swampland, sugar cane and maize fields, this is where the Shire River makes its final journey before plunging into the great Zambezi. Coming from the north, the main road spirals sharp-

CHAMBE–LICHENYA LOOP

This short but beautiful route is great for a taste of Mulanje. It starts and finishes at Likhubula Forestry Office, and takes three days and two nights (staying at the spacious Lichenya Hut, and cosy Chambe Hut with a crackling fire), but it could be shortened to two days.

Likhubula Forestry Office to Chambe Hut

This stage is the same as the first stage of the Mulanje Traverse (p335).

Chambe Hut to Lichenya Basin

This stage is four to five hours. Heading east from Chambe Hut (towards Thuchila), turn right at a junction about 1½ hours from Chambe Hut to reach the Lichenya Basin, and either the CCAP Cottage or Lichenya Hut.

Lichenya Basin to Likhubula Forestry Office

This stage is four to five hours. Go across a col to the east of Chilemba Peak (you could sidetrack up here for fine views – allow two hours to return) then descend through beautiful forest to eventually reach Likhubula.

LIVING LIKE A PLANTER

A couple of days sinking G&Ts on the verandah of a beautiful old planter's home makes an atmospheric start (or end) to a hike up Mt Mulanje. Following are some of our suggestions.

The **Lujeri Tea Estate** (☎01-460243, 01-460266) sits at the base of Mt Mulanje between Mulanje town and Muloza and is reached by a winding dirt road that makes its way up past estate workers' houses, avenues of tall pines and acres of bright-green tea. After the main gates you'll reach the **Lujeri Guest House** (s/d US$60/80, whole house US$190, sleeps 10;), a quaint old planters' home with high ceilings, a wide cool verandah, chintzy central lounge with fireplace, and a small swimming pool shaded by trees and moss-covered rocks. A stay at neighbouring **Lujeri Lodge** (whole house US$200, sleeps 10;), a larger and grander version of the Guest House, is like stepping back in time. It's a classic colonial tin-roofed affair; you can almost hear the tinkling of laughter and jazz piano as you're lounging on the enormous wraparound verandah. The gardens are an explosion of lush plants and flowers and there's a large swimming pool and miniature tennis court should you wish to be active. The staff at both lodges can direct you to beautiful walks in the shadow of the mountain.

Stunning **Huntingdon House** (☎01-794555; www.satemwa.com; r incl breakfast/full board from US$105/175; P) sits on the Satemwa Tea Estate (p333) near the small town of Thyolo. Built in 1936 by Scottish planters with Francophile tendencies, this one-storey dame exudes charm and elegance, from its doric columns and porticoes, to its stone fireplaces and silver candlebra. Stepping inside is like passing into an old French chateau, and add to this the finely calibrated service and it really does feel as if you've travelled back to colonial days. The house is operated by Ulendo Travel Group (p278) and the original family who first settled here, and bedrooms are individually finished with four-posters, comfy couches, step-through mozzie nets, rain showers and roaring fires. Our favourite room was the exquisitely chandeliered dining room. Outside, the garden is an Eden of silvery oaks, poplar and gum trees, and home to some 60 species of birds. Within the 2000-hectare plantation coffee, tea, blue gum and Guatemala grass all grow, and cattle are farmed; the best way to see it is by borrowing one of the lodge's bikes. Horse riding and walking trails are also available.

ly downwards – affording breathtakingly beautiful views out towards Mozambique – to meet the dense heat of the valley below. A small strip of territory it may be, but there's a lot to see here, including three wilderness areas, one of which is the excellent Majete.

MAJETE WILDLIFE RESERVE

Majete Wildlife Reserve (www.majete.org; adult/child MK2000/1000, vehicle MK200, maps MK100) is a rugged wilderness of hilly *miombo* woodland and savannah, hugging the west bank of the Shire River. Poaching in the 1980s and 1990s left the park utterly depleted and dilapidated, but since it was taken over by **African Parks** (www.africanparks-conservation.com) in 2003, things have really been looking up. A perimeter fence has been erected around the whole reserve (the only completely fenced park in Malawi) and is patrolled constantly by guards, while accommodation and roads have been massively upgraded. With journalists flocking from top international magazines and newspapers to cover its lion reintroduction program, and the establishment of the sumptuous Mkulumadzi Lodge, Majete may soon be the top park in Malawi .

There are now more than 3000 animals in Majete, most translocated from other parks in Malawi and elsewhere in Southern Africa, including hyenas, sables, nyalas, bushbucks, impalas, servals, civets, zebras, antelopes, 10 black rhinos, 300 buffaloes, more than 300 elephants, 200 hippos and leopards.

As Malawi's first Big Five park, Majete is leading the way for the rest of the country. African Parks' objective is to restore natural areas and make them financially self-reliant; so when this particular park is handed back to Malawi's Department of National Parks, it will be fully self-supporting.

Sights & Activities

Mkulumadzi Lodge has a 7000-hectare slice of the 7000-sq-km park, which is literally bursting with animals. There are 250km of tracks in the park, and you'll need a high-

LION REINTRODUCTION: THE RETURN OF THE KING

The return of the King begins in Majete Wildlife Reserve. Lions, due to poaching, have not been seen here since the '80s, so four lions being donated by South Africa (two males from Pilanesberg National Park and two females from Madikwe Game Reserve) are big news. Translocation will cost a hefty US$50,000, funded by Robin Pope Safaris (p278). Majete meanwhile, has been preparing for this moment over the last nine years, with US$12 million dollars spent on upgrading its roads, improving infrastructure, ring-fencing the park and restocking it with thousands of animals (including leopards in 2011). Local poachers have even performed a *volte-face* and become wardens.

In June 2012, veterinarians set out to capture the lions and place them in the *boma* (holding pen) at the same time, so that they began their 30-day quarantine together. On arrival in Malawi one of the female lions died of hypertension. Remaining lions Shire, Sapitwa and Chimwala, were officially released on 1st September, from their *boma*, and began to explore, form a pride and make their first kills. It's hoped that they'll breed and have cubs within the next three to nine months. Watch this space.

clearance car to get around – especially during the wet season. The two main routes here are the Mkurlmadzi Rd, which runs parallel to the Shire River (although not near enough for you to see it from the track) and Namitsempha Rd, heading west from the entrance. Along Mkulumadzi Rd, just past the park entrance, are the grand Kapichira Falls, which David Livingstone failed to cross on one of his expeditions back in 1859; further on is Mvuu Spot, a small hide from where you can watch hippos frolicking in the river.

If you'd rather your activities were organised there is plenty on offer, including bush walks (per person US$20), wildlife drives (per person US$25), and night wildlife drives (US$35). You can also opt to have a scout join you in your own car (US$15). Hiking Majete Hill is also possible (US$40), as are boat rides past hippos on the Shire River (US$20).

At the entrance to the park is a small open-air **heritage centre** and **gift shop** featuring a display of art and craftwork made in and around Majete by local people. There's also a little **museum** with displays on the region's heritage as well as information on local conservation projects.

Sleeping

There are currently three places to stay in the reserve: an upmarket bushcamp, a community campsite, and one of the newest and most exquisite boutique lodges in the country.

TOP CHOICE **Mkulumadzi Lodge** LODGE $$$
(☎01-794491; www.mkulumadzi.com; high/mid-season per night per person incl 2 wildlife drives & full board US$378/337; P❄@🛜≋) The first reason Majete is the brightening star in Malawi's firmament is the introduction of lions; the second is this extraordinary lodge romantically reached by a suspension bridge over a croc-lathered river. Opened in 2012, Mkulumadzi is a fusion of African tradition and boutique chic.

Imagine a high thatched ceiling strung with contemporary lights and ballasted by columns of leadwood trunks, driftwood art installations, and a kidney-shaped pool outside – not that you'll be doing much swimming given the friendliness of local elephants who wander into the lodge.

Food is eaten communally at night and glorious it is too. The chalets themselves are artfully blended with the bush with grass roofs, and look out on to the Shire River; think step-in rain showers and windows that give you widescreen views of the river as you flop in a sunken, candlelit bath. Run with warmth and efficiency, the camp offers morning walks to a hide close to the river (it's well situated for spotting black rhinos coming for a dawn drink); or night drives to see hippos rising from the bank in the moonlight. Also expect to see civets, bushbucks, lots of elephants and the blazing red eyes of crocodiles. All wildlife drives are included, as is food and drink. If you're getting here by bus, free transfers are available from Chikwawa village.

Community Campsite CAMPGROUND $
(campsite s/d US$10/15, tent hire US$25; P) Enabling visitors on a budget to stay in the park and fully immerse themselves in the park's wildlife-viewing activities, this campground has shady places to pitch up, park or sleep on a stilted deck under the stars. There's also drinkable water, clean ablution blocks and hot showers, as well as cooking facilities for barbecuing. You do need to bring your own food though.

Profits are ploughed directly back into the wellbeing of the park. To get here turn left just before the heritage centre.

Thawale Camp CAMPGROUND $$$
(☎0999-521741; www.african-parks.org; luxury tent per person incl full board from US$170; P@) Situated around a floodlit watering-hole, this upmarket bushcamp is about 3km from the reserve's main entrance. There are six double and twin tented chalets on raised wooden platforms, and each has its own verandah overlooking the watering-hole. There are gorgeous bathrooms out back, complete with deep baths, stone sinks and loos with a view! They're also well spaced out so you really get the sense that you're in the middle of nowhere.

There's a central lodge for meals (the food is excellent) with plenty of comfortable chairs to sink into, safari books for browsing and a stone terrace with outdoor fire pit. Dinner can be combined with an 'under the stars boma night' with entertainment from the local Gule Wamkulu dancers. The camp isn't fenced so expect regular visits from elephants, buffaloes and other creatures. One hundred percent of the camp's revenue is ploughed straight back into conserving and protecting Majete.

Getting There & Away

Majete lies west of the Shire River, some 70km southwest of Blantyre. Follow the road to Chikwawa from where signs will direct you to the reserve. By public transport, the nearest you can get is Chikwawa.

LENGWE NATIONAL PARK

Lengwe (admission per person US$10, per car US$3) is Malawi's southernmost park. It's flat and arid with plenty of driveable tracks among mixed woodland and grassy *dambo* (wetlands). The sparse vegetation means that animal viewing is good here; in the dry season animals congregate around the park's few permanent watering holes. Mammals include nyalas (at the northern limit of their distribution in Africa), bushbucks, impalas, duikers, kudus, warthogs and buffaloes, as well as hyenas and leopards and the occasional elephant (last seen 2009). There's also a large and varied bird population. The park has several walking trails and hides overlooking the watering holes, where you can watch the animals come and graze. There's one within five minutes' walk of the lodge.

Activities

Nyala Lodge can organise a wide range of activities in the park such as wildlife drives (per person US$20), walking safaris (per person US$12) and evening tours to **Ndankwera Cultural Village** where you'll be fed and entertained for US$45 per person (minimum four people). It also arranges a number of boat trips including fishing trips and full-day excursions to Elephant Marsh (per person US$200).

At the park entrance is a **museum** and a small **gift shop** selling woven rugs and bags as well as locally made produce such as Lengwe peanut butter and baobab jam.

Sleeping

Nyala Lodge LODGE $$$
(☎01-823709, 01-835356; www.jambo-africa.com; s/d incl breakfast per person US$72/103, s/d with half board per person US$85/150, campsite per person US$6, basic chalets with shared bathroom $US40; P❄@) Managed by Jambo Africa, there's a stylish bar and restaurant in the central lodge, and high-ceilinged rooms in clay-pink *rondavels* boasting fresh white walls, wicker chairs, polished stone floors and choice African art.

Nyala lacks the geographical drama of say Mkulumadzi, Tongole or Mvuu Camp for there's no elevation, no river flowing by, nor are the animals particularly exotic. For those on a budget there is a separate campsite and basic chalets for self-caterers.

Getting There & Away

By car, take the main road from Blantyre south towards Nsanje. By public transport, take a bus from Blantyre to Nchalo or Nsanje. About 20km from the Shire Bridge a signpost indicates Lengwe National Park to the right. The park entrance is another 10km to the west through sugarcane plantations.

ELEPHANT MARSH

The Elephant Marsh is a large area of seasonally flooded plain on the Shire River about 30km downstream from Chikwawa, just south of the vast Ilovo Sugar Estate. Despite the name, there are no elephants here any more, although vast herds inhabited the area fewer than 100 years ago. Some hippos and crocodiles occur in quiet areas, but the main draw is the spectacular selection of birds. This is one of the best **birdwatching** areas in Malawi; you'll see a number of rare waders here. Even if you're not a fan of our feathered friends, it's worth considering a visit here simply to sample this peaceful and very unusual landscape, and spend a morning or so floating on the lily-studded waters past baobabs and stately palm trees.

As mornings and evenings are the best times to see birds (it's also not so hot), travellers without wheels may find it convenient to stay overnight in the village of Bangula, which has a council rest house. If you have a car, you could stay in Nchalo.

Getting There & Around

The only way to see the marsh properly is by boat. The usual way of doing this is to hire a boatman and his dugout canoe at a small village called Mchacha James on the east side of the marsh, about 7km from Makhanga.

If you're driving, head southwest of Blantyre for 30km and turn left (east) at Thabwa (the bottom of the escarpment). Makhanga is another 65km or so further south, following the Thyolo Escarpment. From Makhanga, head north towards Muona village. After 2.5km a dirt track leads west for 4.5km through villages and small fields to Mchacha James. This route is not signposted so ask for directions – it may be worth arranging a local guide in Makhanga. During the rains it sometimes isn't possible to cross the bridge to Mchacha James. You can probably get a boat across and then walk but you might not want to leave your car unattended.

If you're without wheels, take the bus from Blantyre that travels to Nchalo and Nsanje. You can get a *matola* from either of these towns to Makhanga. Alternatively, you can get off this bus at Bangula and then take a *matola* through Chiromo to Makhanga. From Makhanga, you can walk (it's a good hour), take a bicycle-taxi or charter a *matola* to Mchacha James.

Nyala Lodge (p341) arranges day trips to the Elephant Marsh, as does Jambo Africa (p331) in Blantyre.

MWABVI WILDLIFE RESERVE

Sitting at the country's southernmost tip, **Mwabvi** (admission per person/car MK750/300) is the smallest, most remote and least accessible of Malawi's wildlife reserves. As with many of the country's other wilderness areas, Mwabvi has been severely hit by poachers in the past, and wildlife stocks have been diminished, though species here do include buffaloes, kudus, sable antelopes, bushpigs, bushbucks and a handful of leopards. In Mwabvi, though, it doesn't seem to matter. The magic of coming here is its very isolation and its untouched wilderness atmosphere. The scenery is gorgeous too – gentle wooded hills sit alongside sweeping boulders and clear streams tumble though steep rocky gorges. Get up high and you'll be rewarded with spectacular views over the Shire and Zambezi Rivers.

Getting There & Away

Access is possible only with a 4WD. The reserve office is reached from the main road between Chikwawa and Nsanje, 8km off the main road just east of the village of Sorgin and about 10km west of Bangula. To get here it's a pleasant drive through fields and past villages. Note: there's no public transport here.

MWABVI: WHAT'S IN A NAME?

Mwabvi Wildlife Reserve is named after the river that runs through it and also after the endangered Mwabvi tree, only one of which remains in the park (ask one of the wardens to direct you to it – it's clearly marked). The root and bark of the tree is poisonous and, as the story goes, in olden days was used as a measure against witchcraft. If suspicious, supernatural events were taking place in the local village, the elders would pound up the roots of a Mwabvi tree, make it into a powerful drink, line up the villagers and force them one by one to drink... The innocent would instantly regurgitate the concoction, but the perpetrators of the dastardly deeds would suffer a painful death.

UNDERSTAND MALAWI

Malawi Today

The last couple of years in Malawi have been colourful to say the least, with the reign of its controversial president, Bingu wa Mutharika, coming to an end amid an economic fiasco. In April 2012, when Mutharika's heart gave out, fresh blood was pumped into the political system in the form of its new premier – women's rights activist and former vice president, Dr Joyce Banda.

As Banda came to power the country was in the grip of a fuel crisis, and nepotism and corruption in the ruling elite were rife. More worryingly, confidential files revealed by the *Sunday Times* in November 2012 proved that her predecessor had tried to have her killed to block her becoming prime minister (as vice president she would have automatically succeeded him in the event of his demise). A truck had been arranged to crash into her car; fortunately for Banda, she switched vehicles at the last moment.

Banda has other challenges on her hands: Malawi remains one of the world's poorest countries (with a per capita GNP of less than US$250), nearly half the population is chronically malnourished and life expectancy is only 53 years (owing in large part to the HIV/AIDS infection rate in Malawi, which is estimated to run at almost 12%). Increased immunisation and improved access to running water have helped reduce the infant mortality rate, though according to UNICEF it still sits at about one in eight children under five years old dying of preventable causes such as neonatal conditions, pneumonia, diarrhoea, malaria, HIV-related diseases and, of course, malnutrition. Malawi is urbanising rapidly and the rate of population growth in the cities is far higher than that in rural areas. The burgeoning population is straining natural resources, and schools, hospitals and other social institutions are overflowing.

According to the CIA World Factbook, Malawi's total population is around 16.3 million and is growing at an unsustainable 2.8% a year. Because the country is so small, this creates one of the highest population densities in Africa. About 85% of Malawians live in rural areas and are engaged in subsistence farming or fishing, or working on commercial farms and plantations. Around half the population is under 15 years of age. Against this backdrop, Banda continues to achieve as much as she can in the event her reforms do not get her elected for a second term in 2014.

Economy & Diplomacy

Malawi is one of the world's poorest and least developed countries. Its economy depends on agriculture, which accounts for some 35% of GDP and 90% of export revenues. Tobacco is the main cash crop, accounting for over 70% of exports. Also important are tea, sugar and coffee. And while agriculture is the main economic driver, mining and construction are increasingly important to the nation's economy.

After Mutharika set the rate of Malawi's currency, the kwacha, at an unrealistically high level on the international markets, and banned foreign exchange, international investment and liquidity quickly evaporated (the latter falling in 2009 by 23%). This in turn hamstrung Malawi's ability to pay for imported goods like fuel, which ground the country to a halt on every level. Economic growth in 2011 slowed to 5.8% from 6.7% in 2010 due to reduced donor inflows, and vital shortages of foreign exchange and fuel. Riots broke out in July 2011 over decreasing living standards and by 2012 British and US funding had been suspended following the leader's increasingly despotic outbursts.

Enter Joyce Banda, who, when she came to power after Mutharika's death in early 2012, set about repairing the bridges burnt by her predecessor, inviting the British High Commisioner back and forging a new friendship with Hillary Clinton. Banda has highlighted the need for Malawi's economy to be self sufficient from funding in the near future, and the International Monetary Fund (IMF) has pledged a donation of US$157 million in 2012 to help her achieve this end. Confidence has been further bolstered by the new president reaching out to neighbouring African countries like Nigeria, who will import Malawi's rice and give seasoned advice on the extraction of Malawi's oil reserves.

Banda quickly began addressing the fuel crisis, striking a deal with PTA Bank to borrow funds to boost fuel supply, which is expected to normalise sometime in 2013, setting Malawi's farms and factories back on track.

Further brave steps by Banda have included devaluing the kwacha by 40%, promising to repeal Malawi's ban on homosexuality, taking an immediate 30% personal pay cut, and attempting to sell the US$8.4m presidential jet, instead travelling internationally by commercial carrier. As one of only two female African leaders, Banda has the world's attention, and while she has it she is doing what she can to effect massive internal change.

History

Roots

Hominids existed in the area now known as Malawi as long as 2.5 million years ago, evidenced by the discovery of a jawbone in Karonga in 1993.

The first major influx of humans were hunter gatherers, around 3000 years ago; the second wave began in the 1st century AD with the Bantu people. A further wave of Bantu-speaking peoples arrived around the 14th century AD, and soon coalesced into the Maravi kingdom (late-15th to late-18th century), centred in the Shire River Valley.

But let's rewind a little. By the first century AD, eastern Africa had started trading with the ever-intrepid Phoenicians. This contact with the outside world was to steadily increase through trade with the Persians, and by AD 1300 the trading city of Kilwa was established on an island 2km off modern-day Tanzania. Gold filtered through from the powerful Shona Kingdom in what was known as Great Zimbabwe, and trade occurred between the Shona, the Swahili and the Persians. Then the Portuguese arrived, and under the pretext of protecting the region from the spread of Islam, proceeded to monopolise the gold trade.

By 1596 Portugal controlled the Zambezi River and the flow of gold from the Shona kingdom by instituting their own puppet ruler in the Zambezi Valley. Ivory had by this time joined gold as a much-sought-after commodity by traders, and the Portuguese were understandably respectful and more than a little fearful of the dynastic king Chief Masula who ruled much of what is today southern and central Malawi, known then as Maravi.

Migration into the area of Malawi stepped up with the arrival of the Maravi people (from whom the modern-day Chewa are descended), who established a large and powerful kingdom in the south in the late 15th century, and the Tumbuka and Phoka groups, who settled around the highlands of Nyika and Viphya during the 17th century. The early 19th century brought with it two more significant migrations. The Yao invaded southern Malawi from western Mozambique, displacing the Maravi, while groups of Zulu migrated northward from southern Africa to settle in central and northern Malawi.

The Difaqane ('The Crushing')

Also known as the *Mfecane*, meaning the 'crushing' or 'scattering', the period between 1815 to about 1840 saw indigenous tribes in southern Africa involved in internecine bloody struggles. Much of this can be attributed to one man, Shaka, king of the Zulu tribe. In the early 19th century there were three centralised kingdoms: the Ngwane, Mdwandwe and Mthethwe. Shaka, ruler of the latter, revolutionised military warfare by replacing the throwing spear with a stabbing spear and surrounding his enemy in a tight horseshoe then closing in on them. Very soon widespread massacre spread like a plague of locusts across Southern Africa, depopulating countries and killing some two million people.

Among those that fled were the Mdwandwe clan, who headed for Mozambique, coercing the local Tonga people to form a co-operative army with them – the Jere-Ngoni. By 1825, blazing their own trail of carnage, the Jere-Ngoni entered Malawi, terrorising the Yao people near the lake and the Tumbuka people to the north, raiding villages, butchering old men and forcibly enlisting young men. The army settled on Lake Malawi and were to remain there until the Mdwandwe chief's death in 1845. This bloody period is remembered as 'The Killing'.

The Dark Days of Slavery

The story of slavery in Malawi begins in the 16th century when Omani Arab traders, with the aid of Yao tribesmen, sold slaves from non-Yao tribes to the Portuguese, who sent them to work on plantations in Mozambique or Brazil. Portuguese interests were effectively stemmed in 1824 by the arrival of Sultan Said of Muscat, who captured Mombasa. The demand for ivory and slaves in markets – Zanzibar, Kilwa, Mombasa and Quelimane – was by then huge, and to meet the demand, the sultan's traders made deeper incursions into the African interior. While America and Great Britiain were moving to abolish the slave trade, the sultan accelerated it; by 1839 over 40,000 slaves were being sold through the Zanzibar slave market.

Malawi's coastal trading centres included Karonga, Nkhotakota, and Salima on Lake Malawi. Of particular infamy was the slave port of Nkhotakota, where slave trader, Salim-bin Abdullah (Jumbe) set up his headquarters in the 1840s. From here about 20,000 slaves were annually transported across the lake where they were forced to walk the three- to four-month journey to Kilwa to be sold. The journey across the lake might see as few as 20 out of 300 surviving the heinously cramped conditions. And on the march, slackers or the sick were beheaded to make swift use of their neck brace harnesses.

The Yao people were complicit with the Arab traders, converting to Islam and working for them to find slaves. The marauding Yao moved north, killing and capturing the local Chewa and Maganja by the hundreds.

The Colonial Era & National Resistance

By the 1880s the competition among European powers in the area was fierce. Colonial rule brought with it an end to slave-traders and interethnic conflicts, but it also brought a whole new set of problems. As more and more European settlers arrived, the demand for land grew, and the local inhabitants found themselves labelled as 'squatters' or tenants of a new landlord. The 'hut tax' (a levy per household paid to the British administration with grain, labour or money) was introduced here too and traditional methods of agriculture were discouraged. Increasing numbers of Africans were forced to seek work on the white-settler plantations or to become migrant workers in Northern and Southern Rhodesia (present-day Zambia and Zimbabwe) and South Africa. By the start of the 19th century some 6000 Africans were leaving the country every year. (The trend continued throughout the colonial period: by the 1950s this number had grown to 150,000.)

Fomented by Scottish missionaries, protest against British colonial rule bubbled to the surface shortly before WWI. Sparks of revolt initially erupted in Nyasaland (the British name for Malawi) out of the Laws Mission School in Blantyre. Edward Kamwana organised the first protests against forced taxation. Then John Chilembwe, another student from the mission school, entered the fray, and the protest movement gained momentum. On 23 January 1915, three armed raiding parties set out from Chilembwe's 'Provident Industry Mission' to attack European-owned estates in the Shire Highlands, killing a number of Europeans before Chilembwe was hunted down and shot. But for black Malawians, the movement towards self-government had begun.

Further protests were to erupt with the idea of 'federating' Nyasaland with Southern and Northern Rhodesia. After WWII, white

DR LIVINGSTONE, ANTI-SLAVERY CRUSADER

The three 'Cs' – Christianity, colonisation and commerce – were the watchwords of Dr David Livingstone, Scottish explorer and missionary. With the convergence of all three, he hoped he could put an end to the plague of African slavery, what he was to refer to in the case of Nkhotakota as 'bloodshed and lawlessness'. Indeed, as his paddlesteamer headed up the Shire River the sight of bloated bodies – victims of rampant butchering – was a daily occurrence, and Livingstone would later publish accounts of the atrocities he'd witnessed that would sensitise and heighten public disgust in the West.

In 1878 the Livingstonia Central African Mission Company (later renamed the African Lakes Corporation) was formed, and it built a trading centre in Blantyre. The company then established a commercial network along the Shire River and the shores of Lake Nyasa, which due to its vigilance and presence had a serious effect on the slave trade in the region; after several clashes many slave traders were forced to leave.

Missions were established at Cape Maclear (1874), but due to malaria the mission was forced to relocate to Bandawe (1881) and then to the chilly heights of Livingstonia (1894). The most important base, however, was on Likoma Island, where the remarkable St Peter's Cathedral can still be seen today. In many ways the influence of the Scottish missionaries was to shape the future fabric of the country, bringing with it literacy, carpentry skills, farming methods, new crops, and altruism, in sharp contrast to the self-serving interests of many other colonialists. Furthermore, unlike missions from other churches, the Scottish missionaries never used violence to convert people and they risked their own lives to stop slavery, end local internecine wars and even oppose the cruelty of colonialism. In 1895, twenty-one years after Livingstone's death, slavery was finally abolished; his benign presence still looms large even today.

southern Rhodesians were keen to pursue this. Malawi's future leader, Dr Hastings Banda, was quick to point out that colonialism offered an unequal prison-and-warder relationship to the African, but under Rhodesian rule it would be a return to slavery. The Nyasaland African Congress (NAC) voiced its opposition most loudly, aided by Banda (now in London and practising as a doctor, but a politically active spokesperson for the NAC in the UK). Despite this, British assent was given to federation and in 1953 Nyasaland came under Rhodesian authority.

By the time Banda returned to his home country in 1958 there were 60,000 members in the NAC. The first riot against federation took place in 1959 in Zomba; following this there was another riot in Nkhata Bay, and shortly thereafter a state of emergency was declared. Banda and 1000 of his supporters were arrested but, illustrating a sea change in London's perspective on Nyasaland, he was shortly released. In 1962 Britain agreed to a plan of self-government in the country, and by February 1963, Banda was sworn in as the prime minister of Nyasaland. The country was granted full independence, and was restored to its original name, Malawi, on 6 July, 1964.

Banda: Hero to Villain

After being made president of Malawi in 1966, Banda began consolidating his position, and demanded that several ministers declare their allegiance to him. Many resigned rather than do so and took to opposition. Banda forced them into exile and banned other political parties. He continued to increase his power by becoming 'president for life' in 1971, and banning the foreign press. He established Press Holdings, effectively his personal conglomerate, and the Agricultural Development & Marketing Corporation, to which all agricultural produce was sold at fixed rates, and thus gained total economic control, accruing an estimated fortune of some US$445 million. Miniskirts, women in trousers, long hair for men and other such signs of Western debauchery were outlawed.

Throughout this move towards dictatorship Banda remained politically conservative, giving political support to apartheid South Africa, which, in turn, rewarded Malawi with aid and trade. This angered the Organisation of African Unity (OAU), which was furious at Banda's refusal to ostracise the apartheid regime.

Banda had a bizarre range of habits. He was fond of wearing jaunty gangster-style hats and carrying an African fly-whisk; and at public appearances he was often accompanied by a group of women who danced and chanted words of praise, clad in customised outfits with his face printed all over them.

With the end of the Cold War in the 1990s, things began to get dicey for Banda. South Africa and the West no longer needed to support him, and inside the country opposition was swelling. In 1992 the Catholic bishops of Malawi condemned the regime and called for change, and demonstrations, both peaceful and violent, added their weight to the bishops' move. As a final blow, donor countries restricted aid until Banda agreed to relinquish total control.

In June 1993 a referendum was held for the people to choose between a multiparty political system and Banda's autocratic rule. Over 80% of eligible voters took part; those voting for a new system won easily, and Banda accepted the result.

The 1990s: Fresh Hope

At Malawi's first full multiparty election in May 1994, the victor was the United Democratic Front (UDF), led by Bakili Muluzi. On becoming president, Muluzi moved quickly – political prisons were closed, freedom of speech and print was permitted, and free primary school education was to be provided. The unofficial night curfew that had existed during Banda's time was lifted. For travellers, the most tangible change was the repeal of that notorious dress code.

The Muluzi Government also made several economic reforms with the help of the World Bank and the IMF; these included the withdrawal of state subsidies and the liberalisation of foreign-exchange laws.

In April 1995 former president Banda was brought to trial, accused of ordering the murder of three government ministers who died in a mysterious car accident in 1983. He was acquitted and the result was greeted with general approval, especially when Banda went on to apologise publicly for any harm caused unwittingly or intentionally by members of his government. As the population warmed once more to Banda, it became clear that the UDF's honeymoon period was well and truly over.

By 1996 the economic reforms were hitting the average Malawian citizen very hard.

Food prices and unemployment soared. There were reports of increased malnutrition, and crime, particularly robbery, increased in urban areas. Matters were made worse by a slow resumption of international aid, after it had been frozen in the final years of Banda's rule.

In November 1997 Dr Banda finally died. His age was unknown, but he was certainly over 90.

Mutharika: Malawi's New Dictator

In July 2002 Muluzi attempted to change the constitution by proposing an Open Terms Bill to parliament, which would have given him life presidency. When it was defeated, Muluzi chose Bingu wa Mutharika as his successor, and in 2004 he duly won the election. Many thought he would simply follow in Muluzi's footsteps, but Mutharika soon declared his independence by quitting the UDF and setting up his own party, the Democratic Progressive Party (DPP). Controversially, he set about restoring Banda's reputation as a great African hero.

The massive famine in 2005 put the pressure on, with Malawi bearing the brunt of crop failure and drought in the region – in 2006, under the Highly Indebted Poor Country Initiative, Malawi qualified for debt relief.

The 2004 re-election victory for President Mutharika kicked off a tumultuous second term; in 2010, Mutharika expelled his deputy Joyce Banda (no relation to Hastings Banda) from the party, but had no choice but to retain her as vice president since she was elected in 2009 as his running mate. In response, the indomitable Banda formed her own People's Party. Then in 2011 a diplomatic spat erupted between Mutharika and Great Britain, after a leaked document accused him of being 'autocratic'. Mutharika responded by expelling the British high commisioner, and Britain – Malawi's biggest donor – immediately froze millions of dollars of aid.

The consequences were profound, and by the end of 2011 Malawi was crippled by fuel prices that soared by up to 150% – and terrible fuel shortages that ground the country's already ailing industry to a halt. Foreign exchange was also banned as Mutharika took the further inflammatory measure of inflating Malawi's currency to a highly unrealistic value on the international markets. And in July 2011 the US shelved a $350 million overhaul of the dilapidated power grid after police killed 20 protestors in a crackdown on an unprecedented wave of antigovernment protests. Not surprisingly, up to 40% of the country's expats prepared to leave Malawi for good.

Then in April 2012, in a sudden reversal of fortunes for the country, President Mutharika's heart stopped. The army placed a cordon around Joyce Banda's house to assist her succession to power (lest Mutharika's cronies enacted a coup), and she was sworn in – to great relief – in the same month.

Malawi Way of Life

Population

Although Malawi might be made up of a patchwork of different tribes, there is one commonality that has earned the country

THE CHEWA

The Chewa are the largest ethnic group in Malawi. During the first millennium AD, they migrated through Zambia and then on to central Malawi, conquering local tribes as they went and eventually establishing a powerful kingdom in 1480 that covered southern Malawi as well as swaths of Mozambique and Zambia. During the 17th century, Malawi experienced an influx of diverse cultures and dynasties, but the Chewa kept their ethnicity distinct through language, tattoos and secret societies.

The Chewa believe that god (Chiuta or Chautu) created all living things during a thunderstorm, at a mountain range that straddles the Malawi and Mozambique border. They also believe that contact between spirits and the living is achieved through a dance called *Gule Wamkulu*. Today, however, Chewa culture is a mixture of traditional beliefs and European influences; although Christianity is the dominant religion, it's common practice to consult a witch doctor in times of trouble.

To really experience Chewa culture, it's best to immerse yourself in a village. There is a cultural village offering overnight stays (p319) near Liwonde National Park.

SPORT

Football (soccer) is the nation's favourite sport; from kids in backstreets kicking around a ball of compacted paper, to Sunday league hopefuls and the millions who listen to soccer matches on the radio, everyone loves it. The national team, nicknamed The Flames, were recently dropped from FIFA's top 100 countries due to a lack of funding and an inability to play many international matches, but local passion for them continues unabated.

Another more gentle sport you're likely to encounter is *bawo*, an equivalent to checkers. Boxing is also a minor sport and Malawi has one very effective professional pugilist on the world stage in the form of heavyweight Isaac Chilemba. At the 2012 Olympics the country was represented in the athletics stadium by two of its athletes, and by one in the pool. Meanwhile more elitist games like golf, tennis, squash and rugby flourish within the expat community at a number of country clubs.

the enviable moniker 'The Warm Heart of Africa': Malawians are super friendly – perhaps the friendliest folk of the whole African continent.

Malawi's main ethnic groups are the Chewa, dominant in the central and southern parts of the country, the Yao in the south, and the Tumbuka in the north. Other groups include the Ngoni (also spelled Angoni), inhabiting parts of the central and northern provinces, the Chipoka (or Phoka) in the central area, the Lambya and the Ngonde (also called the Nyakyusa) in the northern region, and the Tonga, mostly along the lake shore.

There are small populations of Asian and European people living mainly in the cities and involved in commerce, farming (mainly tea plantations) or tourism.

Malawi's small Indian population first came to the country when they were brought in by the British in the early 1900s to help construct a railway line between Malawi and Mozambique. During the Banda regime they were not allowed to participate in politics and certain sections of the economic sector, and many were forced to leave the country.

Most expats in Malawi are here on a short-term basis and involved in business, aid or the diplomatic service.

Religion

Not surprisingly, given the determination of Scottish missionaries in the late 19th century, Malawi has a high Christian population; Christianity accounts for some 82.7% of the religious pie. Dating back to the conversion of the Yao people during the days of Arab slave traders, Muslims account for around 13%. Traditional religions comprise most of the remainder.

Women in Malawi

Despite the fact that women constitute 52% of the country's population, serious gender disparities still exist in terms of employment opportunities and social standing. Men have a higher literacy rate than women because more girls than boys are forced to drop out of school.

Until 1994, under the rule of Hastings Banda, women were banned from wearing miniskirts or trousers. A spate of attacks on women for not wearing traditional dress in early 2012 made it feel as if the clocks were being turned back again. This time, however, hundreds of women took to the streets of Blantyre and Lilongwe in protest. However, Malawi's progressive new incumbent, Joyce Banda, comes from a background of female civil rights empowerment; so perhaps things may soon begin to change in the favour of women.

The Arts

Music & Dance

Traditional music and dance in Malawi, as elsewhere in Africa, are closely linked and often fulfil an important social function, beyond entertainment. In Malawi there are some traditions that spread country-wide, as well as regional specialities in which local ethnic groups have their own tunes and dances.

Malawian musical instruments are similar to those found in other parts of East and Southern Africa, with local names and special features. These include various drums, from the small hand-held *ulimba*, made from a gourd, to ceremonial giants carved from tree-trunks, and the *mambilira*, which is similar to the Western xylophone, but with wooden keys, and sometimes played over hollow gourds to produce a more resonant sound.

Modern home-grown contemporary music is not a major force in Malawi as it is in, say, Zimbabwe or South Africa. However, it has increased in popularity, due largely to influential and popular musicians such as Lucius Banda, who performs soft 'Malawian-style' reggae, and the late Evison Matafale. Other reggae names to look out for are the Black Missionaries and Billy Kaunda.

Literature

Like most countries in Africa, Malawi has a very rich tradition of oral literature. Since independence, a new school of writers has emerged, although thanks to former president Hastings Banda's sensitivity to criticism, many were under threat of imprisonment and lived abroad until the mid-1990s. Oppression, corruption, deceit and the abuse of power are common themes in their writing.

Poetry is very popular. Steve Chimombo is a leading poet whose collections include *Napolo Poems*. His most highly acclaimed work is a complex poetic drama, *The Rainmaker*. Jack Mapanje's first poetry collection, *Of Chameleons and Gods,* was published in 1981. Much of its symbolism was obscure for outsiders, but not for Hastings Banda – in 1987 Mapanje was arrested and imprisoned without charge; he was eventually released in 1991.

Most critics agree that Malawi's leading novelist is Legson Kayira, whose semi-autobiographical *I Will Try* and *The Looming Shadow* earned him acclaim in the 1970s. A later work is *The Detainee*. Another novelist is Sam Mpasu. His *Nobody's Friend* was a comment on the secrecy of Malawian politics – it earned him a 2½-year prison sentence. After his release he wrote *Prisoner 3/75* and later became minister for education in the new UDF government.

A more modern success story is Samson Kambalu, whose autobiography *The Jive Talker: or, how to get a British Passport* tells of his transition from schoolboy at the Kamuzu Academy to conceptual artist in London.

Malawi's Natural Environment

The Land

Pint-sized Malawi is no larger than the US state of Pennsylvania. It's wedged between Zambia, Tanzania and Mozambique, measuring roughly 900km long and between

MUST READ: *THE BOY WHO HARNESSED THE WIND,* BY WILLIAM KAMKWAMBA & BRYAN MEALER (2009)

William Kamkwamba was one of seven children born to a family of subsistence farmers. When the drought of 2001 brought famine the following year, and terrible floods destroyed their crops, 14-year-old William was told they couldn't afford to continue his education; worse still, they were running out of food. Thirsty for a better future, William educated himself, devouring books at his former primary school. He read physics; his natural curiosity had always driven him to try and understand the mechanics of things like cars and radios. One particular book was about energy and electricity generation through windmills.

Reading this book, William had a light-bulb moment – with electricity his family could plant three times a year, not just once. In a country where only 2% had access to the coveted energy, this would be an amazing coup – if he could succeed. Ridiculed by those around him, and exhausted from his work in the fields every day, William picked around for scrap – found a shock absorber, extractor fan, bike parts and piping – and painstakingly began his creation; a four-bladed windmill. Soon, neighbours were coming to see him to charge their phones on his windmill. His next windmill was used to pump water.

When news of William's invention spread, people from across the globe offered to help him. Soon he was re-enrolled in college and travelling to America to visit wind farms. *The Boy Who Harnessed the Wind* charts his incredible story. Since his book's success, William has been mentoring kids, teaching them how to create their own independent electricity sources – which in turn are powering computers in their primary schools.

THE MANE STORY

At around the same time (mid-2012) as Joyce Banda was making her first seismic changes to the fortunes of the economy, a buzz was building in the West about the reintroduction of lions into Malawi's Majete Wildlife Reserve. It may sound insignificant, but for a country with such abundant natural beauty so long overlooked in favour of neighbouring countries with greater wildlife stocks, a lion injection was just what was needed to bring it back to the fore. As we write, major magazines and newspapers – from *Wanderlust* to *The Sunday Times* – are covering this story, reintroducing Malawi to the world as Africa's next big thing.

80km and 150km wide, with an area of 118,484 sq km.

Almost one-fifth of the country is covered by that great 'inland sea', Lake Malawi. Lying in a trough formed by the Rift Valley, it makes up over 75% of Malawi's eastern boundary. A strip of low ground runs along the western lakeshore, sometimes 10km wide, sometimes so narrow there's only room for a precipitous footpath between the lake and the steep wall of the valley. The lakeshore is sandy in many places, with natural beaches, particularly in the south. Beyond the lake, escarpments rise to high, rolling plateaux covering much of the country.

Malawi's main highland areas are the Nyika and Viphya Plateaux in the north and Mt Mulanje in the south, and the country's highest point is the summit of Sapitwa (3002m) at the centre of Mt Mulanje. There are also several isolated hills and smaller mountains dotted around, the largest being the Zomba Plateau, near the town of the same name.

Malawi's main river is the Shire (pronounced *shir*-ee); it flows out of the southern end of Lake Malawi to flow into the Zambezi River in Mozambique.

Wildlife

Animals

Until 2012 Malawi was considered a mere also-ran among other African big-game safari destinations, but that all changed with the reintroduction of lions in Majete Wildlife Reserve. For those less concerned with ticking off the 'Big Five' (lions, leopards, buffaloes, elephants and rhinos), the country has plenty to offer; in Nkhotakota Wildlife Reserve for instance, you can now kayak past crocodiles at Tongole Wilderness Lodge. Many people head for Liwonde National Park, noted for its herds of elephants and myriad hippos (as well as impalas, bushbucks and kudus). Liwonde and Majete are the only parks in the country where you might see rhinos.

Elephants are regularly seen in Nkhotakota Wildlife Reserve, Majete and Nyika National Park, and the latter is renowned for roan antelopes and reedbucks, zebras, warthogs and jackals. It also has the country's largest population of leopards – around 100 of them. Nearby Vwaza Marsh is known for its hippos as well as elephants, buffaloes, waterbucks and other antelopes, but is currently in poor shape.

Lake Malawi has more fish species than any other inland body of water in the world, with a total of over 600, of which more than 350 are endemic. The largest family of fish in the lake is the *Cichlidae* (cichlids). Other fish families in the lake include *usipa*, or lake whitebait, *mpasa* (lake salmon) and *kampango* (catfish), which you'll see on quite a few menus.

Malawi is rewarding for birdwatchers: over 600 species have been recorded and birds rarely spotted elsewhere in Southern Africa are easily seen here, including the African skimmer, Böhm's bee-eater and the wattled crane.

Plants

Miombo woodland is the dominant vegetation in Malawi. The dominant trees of the open-canopy *miombo* are *Julbernadia globiflora* and several types of *Brachystegia*. Mopane woodland occurs in hot lowland areas that have relatively low rainfall, including the Shire Valley, the plains along the southern shores of Lake Malawi and some of the smaller lakes. The iconic baobab tree, which favours the same dry conditions, frequently occurs in mopane woodland areas. There isn't much forest left in Malawi (most has been cleared), but areas do exist that are thought to be remnants of the extensive evergreen forests that once grew all over the country, as well as in southern Tanzania, northern Zambia, and Mozambique. There are two main types – montane evergreen forest and semi-evergreen forest. Montane grassland occurs above 1800m and is predominantly found on the Nyika Plateau in northern Malawi, where the rolling hills are covered in grass.

National Parks

Malawi has five national parks. These are (from north to south) Nyika, Kasungu, Lake Malawi (around Cape Maclear), Liwonde and Lengwe. There are also four wildlife reserves – Vwaza Marsh, Nkhotakota, Mwabvi and Majete. Over 16% of Malawi's land is protected.

Traditionally the wildlife reserves have been less developed than the national parks, but this is changing with the likes of Nkhotakota and Majete, both of which have new, upscale lodges and improved roads and animal stocks.

All national parks and reserves have accommodation; this ranges from simple campsites and rustic rest houses to self-catering chalets and extremely comfortable lodges. In most parks and reserves, accommodation – lodges, chalets and campsites – is run by private companies like Wilderness Safaris and Robin Pope Safaris.

As well as national parks and wildlife reserves, Malawi has almost 70 forest reserves across the country. The largest forest reserves, and the most famous for tourists, include Mt Mulanje, the Zomba Plateau, Ntchisi and Dzalanyama. On Mulanje there's a series of huts especially for hikers and trekkers.

All parks and reserves generally cost US$10 per person per day (each 24-hour period), plus US$3 per car per day. Citizens and residents pay less. All fees are payable in kwacha or dollars.

Environmental Issues

Environmental issues for Malawi include population growth, air and water degradation, industrial pollution, deforestation, soil erosion, urban encroachment, habitat and wildlife destruction and the conservation of resources.

Malawi's population is growing rapidly, putting ever-increasing demands on the land and other natural resources – the vast

MALAWI'S MOST IMPORTANT NATIONAL PARKS & WILDLIFE RESERVES

PARK	SIZE	FEATURES	ACTIVITIES	BEST TIME TO VISIT
Majete Wildlife Reserve	700 sq km	*Miombo* woodland, marshes; elephants, hippos, zebras, buffaloes, lions, rhinos, crocs	Wildlife drives, walking safaris, birdwatching, boat safaris	May-Oct
Lake Malawi National Park	94 sq km	Glittering waters; over 1000 species of colourful fish	Snorkelling, kayaking, scuba diving, sailing	May-Oct
Nkhotakota National Park	1800 sq km	*Miombo* forest, bush; nyalas, warthogs, buffaloes, elephants, leopards, crocodiles	Croc & elephant spotting, birdwatching, kayaking, fishing	Jul-Nov, Dec-Jan for birdwatching
Liwonde National Park	580 sq km	Marshes, mopane woodland; elephants, rhinos, hippos, crocodile-filled Shire River	Wildlife drives, walking safaris, boat safaris, birdwatching, rhino sanctuary	Sep-Dec
Nyika National Park	3200 sq km	Sweeping highland grasslands; antelopes, zebras, leopards, hyenas, elephants	Hiking, cycling, trekking, birdwatching	Sep-Oct for mammals, Oct-Apr for birds
Vwaza Marsh Wildlife Reserve	1000 sq km	Wetlands; buffaloes, elephants, hippos, antelopes, crocodiles	Wildlife walks & drives	Jun-Nov for mammals, year-round for birdwatching

majority of Malawians live without electricity and therefore the use of wood as a source of fuel in Malawi is very high. It's estimated that 30% of the country's forests have disappeared over the past 10 years, with over 500 sq km being cleared each year, mostly for fuel. Although some replanting is taking place, at the current rate the woodlands and forests will eventually disappear.

Another environmental challenge faced by Malawi is overfishing. Population growth has increased the demand for fish to an extent that stocks are now taken from the lake at an unsustainable level. An initiative launched by the government in early 2009 and funded by the African Development Bank hopes to discourage fishermen from fishing in shallow waters – the breeding ground where many fish lay their eggs – by providing them with the necessary equipment to fish in deeper waters.

To learn more about environmental issues facing Malawi, or to find out about volunteering opportunities, get in touch with **Project African Wilderness** (☎01-11945455, 0884-024925; www.projectafricanwilderness.org), the **Wildlife Action Group of Malawi** (www.wag-malawi.org) or **Ripple Africa** (www.rippleafrica.org).

SURVIVAL GUIDE

Directory A–Z

Accommodation

BUDGET

In national parks and along the lakeshore, many places offer camping as well as self-catering chalets or cabins. Camping costs from around US$3 to US$10, depending on whether you're presented with long-drop toilets and bucket showers, or well-equipped affairs with hot showers and power points. You'll also find some very welcoming backpacker hostels all over the country, in the major cities as well as at popular lakeshore destinations such as Cape Maclear and Nkhata Bay. Prices range from US$5 to US$10 for a dorm up to about US$10 to US$20 per person for a double or triple with shared facilities and around US$30 for an en suite room. Ordinary guesthouses are less inspiring.

PRICE RANGES

The following price ranges refer to a double room in high season.

$ Less than US$20

$$ US$20 to US$50

$$$ More than US$50

MIDRANGE

Midrange hotels and lodges range from about US$20 up to US$50 for a double, including taxes, usually with private bathroom and breakfast, sometimes with air-con. Additionally, some backpackers' lodges have stylish en suite options for around US$30 to US$50 for a double.

TOP END

Standard top-end hotels in the big cities and at beach resorts range from US$50 to US$250 for a double room, with in-room facilities such as private bathrooms, TVs, air-con and telephones, and hotel facilities such as swimming pools, tennis courts and organised activities. The price normally includes taxes and breakfast. Then there are the exclusive beach hotels and safari lodges, which charge anything from US$100 to US$450 per person, per night, though this usually includes all meals and some activities.

Activities

Malawi provides a hugely exciting range of activities for travellers. Lake Malawi is the main destination, so diving and snorkelling are particularly popular.

BIRDWATCHING

Malawi is a great destination for birding with more than 600 species recorded here. The best place to start is the national parks. Liwonde is an excellent spot, with particularly good birdlife along the river, and the forests in Nyika are also good. For water birds, Elephant Marsh in Malawi's far south is your surest bet. Land & Lake Safaris in Lilongwe can organise birdwatching tours around the country.

DIVING, SNORKELLING & OTHER WATERSPORTS

Lake Malawi's population of colourful fish attracts travellers to come scuba diving. The lake is reckoned by experts to be among the best freshwater diving areas in the world, and one of the cheapest places to learn how to dive. The water is warm and (depending on season) visibility and weather conditions are usually good. Places where you can hire scuba gear and take a PADI Open Water course include Nkhata Bay, Cape Maclear, Likoma Island and Senga Bay. If you don't want to dive you can still have fun with the fish. Gear for snorkelling can be hired from most dive centres, and most lakeside hotels rent snorkelling equipment.

Upmarket places along the lake have facilities for water-skiing or windsurfing. You can also go sailing, or join luxurious 'sail safaris' where everything is done for you – Danforth Yachting and Pumulani, based in Cape Maclear on the southern lakeshore, can organise this for you. Kayaking is available at Cape Maclear and Nkhata Bay and at many of the lodges that dot the lakeshore.

FISHING

You can go fishing in Lake Malawi for *mpasa* (also called lake salmon), *ncheni* (lake tiger), *sungwa* (a type of perch), *kampango* or *vundu* (both catfish). There are trout in streams on the Nyika, Zomba and Mulanje Plateaux, and tigerfish can be hooked in the Lower Shire River. Anglers can contact the **Angling Society of Malawi** (www.anglingmalawi.com) for further details. Great salmon fishing can also be had at Tongole Wilderness Lodge on the Bua River in Nkhotakota Wildlife Reserve.

HIKING

The main areas for hiking are Nyika and Mulanje. Other areas include Zomba, and various smaller peaks around Blantyre. Mulanje is Malawi's main rock-climbing area, with some spectacular routes, although local climbers also visit smaller crags and outcrops. Rock climbing can also be arranged in Livingstonia and in the Viphya Plateau.

The **Mountain Club of Malawi** (☎01-821269; www.mcm.org.mw) provides a wealth of information about hiking on Mt Mulanje.

HORSE RIDING

There's a stables on the Zomba Plateau that can arrange short rides, and horse riding is also popular at Kande Beach near Chintheche.

CYCLING

Several of the lakeshore lodges hire out mountain bikes, usually for about US$10 a day. Areas that are great for mountain biking include Nyika National Park (through Chelinda Camp), with its hilly landscape and good network of dirt tracks, and the Viphya Plateau (through Luwawa Forest Lodge). Both offer hire bikes.

Business Hours

Offices and shops in the main towns are usually open from 8am to 5pm weekdays, with an hour for lunch between noon and 1pm. Many shops are also open Saturday morning. In smaller towns, shops and stalls are open most days, but keep informal hours. Bank hours are usually from 8am to 3.30pm weekdays. Post and telephone offices are generally open from 7.30am to 5pm weekdays, sometimes with a break for lunch. In Blantyre and Lilongwe, they also open Saturday morning.

Children

There are few formal facilities for children in Malawi; however, Malawi is generally a safe and friendly place for children to visit. Older kids will love the many outdoor activities that Malawi has to offer and many of the lodges in Malawi's wilderness areas and beaches are geared towards families.

Most of the big international hotels in Blantyre and Lilongwe can provide babysitting services, family rooms and cots for babies, as can several of the tourist lodges up and down the coast. Similarly, many of the big city restaurants frequented by expats and tourists will be able to provide high chairs. Disposable nappies and formula are widely available in supermarkets and speciality shops in Lilongwe, Blantyre and Mzuzu, but they can be difficult to find elsewhere.

One caveat – never let your children swim in Lake Malawi just before (and after) dusk; tragic stories about kids who outstayed their welcome and got taken by crocs and hippos (who come out at this time) are many.

PRACTICALITIES

» Malawi's main **newspapers** are *the Daily Times*, *The Malawi News* and *The Nation*. Watch out too for *The Eye*, a quarterly portable glossy detailing the best things to see and do, as well as an indispensable directory.

» **TV Malawi** was launched in 1999 and consists mostly of imported programs, news, regional music videos and religious programs. International satellite channels are available in most midrange and top-end hotels.

Climate

Malawi has a tropical climate with a number of regional variations. The country's steamiest areas are the Shire Valley and Lake Malawi. Malawi's highland regions include Nyika, Mulanje and Dedza and can be very cold at certain times of the year, especially at night. The hot rainy season kicks in between November and March.

Customs Regulations

Like any country, Malawi doesn't allow travellers to import weapons, explosives or narcotics. Plants and seeds, livestock and live insects or snails are also prohibited. It is illegal to take products made from endangered animals or plants out of the country. A yellow-fever certificate is required from people arriving from an infected area.

Electricity

Electricity supply is 220V to 240V/50Hz and plugs are of the British three-prong variety.

Embassies & Consulates

German Embassy (☎01-772555; Convention Dr, City Centre, Lilongwe)

Mozambican Embassy (Map p270; ☎01-774100; Convention Dr, City Centre) Consulate (Map p325; ☎01-843189; Rayner Ave, 1st fl, Celtel Bldg)

South African Embassy (☎01-773722; sahe@malawi.net; Kang'ombe Bldg, City Centre, Lilongwe)

UK High Commission (☎01-772400; off Kenyatta Rd, City Centre) Consulate (Hanover Ave, Blantyre)

US Embassy (Map p270; ☎01-773166; Convention Dr, City Centre, Lilongwe)

Zambian Embassy (☎01-772590; Convention Dr, City Centre, Lilongwe)

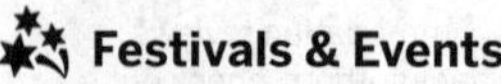

Festivals & Events

The Malawi **Lake of Stars Music Festival** (www.lakeofstarsfestival.co.uk) takes place each October in Senga Bay and attracts live music acts from around Africa and the UK. It lasts for three days and proceeds go to charity.

Food

Nshima is Malawi's staple diet. Made from ground corn, it's ubiquitous and served with a sauce or alongside meat and vegetables. Despite the fact Malawi has no sea it has a wealth of fish from Lake Malawi with favourites like *chambo* (similar to bream) and *mpasa* (like salmon) and *usipa* (like sardines). You'll often find seafood presented in curry, or with a plate of fries.

For dessert you can expect tasty *mbatata* (cinnamon and sweet potato) cookies, as well as *nthochi* (banana bread). As well as this typically Malawian fare you can expect great steaks at reasonable prices in the cities, and hearty western style cuisine in safari lodges.

PRICE RANGES

In this chapter, the following price ranges refer to a standard main course.

$ Less than US$10

$$ US$10 to US$20

$$$ More than US$20

Gay & Lesbian Travellers

Male and female homosexuality is illegal in Malawi. On top of this, the people of Malawi are conservative in their attitudes towards gays and lesbians, and gay sexual relationships are culturally taboo.

Insurance

When buying your travel insurance, always check the small print – some policies specifically exclude 'dangerous activities' that could be anything from scuba diving to horse riding. You should check whether the medical coverage is on a pay first, claim later basis, and more importantly, ensure that your medical coverage includes the cost of medical evacuation.

Internet Access

You'll find several internet cafes in Lilongwe, Blantyre and Mzuzu and most towns.

The introduction of wireless broadband by Skyband means most hotels and restaurants in Lilongwe, Blantyre and Mzuzu have wi-fi, as do myriad hotels around the country. To get online, buy prepaid Skyband vouchers – the cost is MK600 for one hour, MK2400 for five hours.

Legal Matters

Marijuana or cannabis is also known locally as 'Malawi gold', or *chamba*. Being caught buying, selling, or in possession of it, can incur anything from a high fine (several thousand dollars), to a maximum penalty of life imprisonment. Beware too that some dealers are police informers. These days most hostels and campsites will not allow you to smoke openly.

Maps

Useful maps, available in local bookshops, include the government-produced *Malawi* (1:1,000,000), showing shaded relief features and most roads, and the *Malawi Road & Tourist Map* (same scale), showing all main roads, some minor roads and national parks (but no relief) plus street maps of the main towns.

For more detail, government survey maps (1:50,000 and 1:250,000) of Malawi and some of its cities are available from the Department of Surveys Map Sales Offices in Blantyre and Lilongwe. Regional and city maps cost MK650; survey maps covering the whole of Malawi cost MK3500.

Money

Malawi's unit of currency is the Malawi kwacha (MK). This is divided into 100 tambala (t).

Bank notes include MK200, MK100, MK50, MK20, MK10 and MK5. Coins are MK1, 50t, 20t, 10t, 5t and 1t, although the small tambala coins are virtually worthless.

At big hotels and other places that actually quote in US dollars you can pay in hard currency or kwacha at the prevailing exchange rate. At present there is limited foreign exchange in the country.

ATMS

Standard and National Banks are the best bet for foreigners wishing to withdraw cash, and accept Visa, MasterCard, Cirrus and Maestro cards at their ATMs. ATMs are found in most cities and towns including Lilongwe, Blantyre, Mzuzu, Karonga, Liwonde, Salima, Mangochi, Kasungu and Zomba, as well as a couple in Nkhata Bay and Monkey Bay.

CREDIT CARDS & TRAVELLERS CHEQUES

You can use Visa cards at some but not all of the large hotels and top-end restaurants (be warned that this may add a 5% to 10% surcharge to your bill). It seems even harder to use a MasterCard.

You can change travellers cheques at most major banks and bureaux de change, although you will need to show them the original purchase receipt. You can sometimes use travellers cheques to pay at large hotels and lodges.

TIPPING

Tipping is not generally expected in Malawi, as many restaurants and services will add on a service charge to your bill.

Photography & Video

The usual sensitivity rules apply for photographing people; don't push cameras into people's faces and ask beforehand if they mind having their photo taken. In rural areas you will often find children keen to get in front of the lens and see themselves displayed on your LCD screen.

Post

Some letters get from Lilongwe to London in three days, others take three weeks, while in rural areas, the post can be very slow. Post offices in Blantyre and Lilongwe have *poste restante* services.

To African destinations, letters less than 10g and postcards cost MK80. To Europe, India, Pakistan and the Middle East it's MK150 and to the Americas, Japan or Australasia postage is MK200. It's quicker (and probably more reliable) to use the EMS Speedpost service at post offices. Letters up to 500g cost MK750 to Europe and MK1000 to Australia and the USA.

Airmail parcels now cost about MK2000 plus MK500 per kilo to send items outside Africa. Surface mail is cheaper.

Public Holidays

When one of these dates falls on a weekend, normally the following Monday is a public holiday. Islamic holidays are also observed throughout Malawi by the Muslim population.

New Year's Day 1 January
John Chilembwe Day 15 January
Martyrs' Day 3 March
Easter March/April – Good Friday, Holy Saturday and Easter Monday
Labour Day 1 May
Freedom Day 14 June
Republic Day 6 July
Mother's Day October – second Monday
Christmas Day 25 December
Boxing Day 26 December

Safe Travel

CRIME & PUNISHMENT

Times are hard in Malawi, and desperate people will do desperate things; in recent years incidences of robberies or muggings have increased. Avoid walking alone at night in Blantyre and Lilongwe.

Road blocks are frequent throughout the country, though most police who'll stop you just want to say hello rather than breathalyse you. Drivers caught drink driving or speeding can have their vehicles confiscated on the spot, and face a fine and/or imprisonment. Also beware of driving at night where the road becomes an obstacle course of cows, goats, potholes, villagers, cyclists and abandoned cars – all of which have no lights on!

WILDLIFE

Potential dangers at Lake Malawi include encountering a hippo or crocodile after dusk when they come up on to beaches. The Shire River is aflood with crocodiles and locals disappear in dugouts on a regular basis, so be careful of dipping your hand in the water if on a river safari. Popular tourist beaches are safe, although, just to be sure, you should seek local advice before diving in. The most dangerous animals in Malawi are the mosquitoes that transmit malaria.

Shopping

You can find all kinds of curios and souvenirs for sale, including animals and figures carved from wood, bowls and chess-sets, and the very popular 'chief's chair', which is a three-legged stool made from two pieces of wood, with a high back decorated with pictures.

There are craft stalls aimed at tourists in both Blantyre and Lilongwe as well as in the country's more popular tourist areas. Prices are usually not fixed, so you have to bargain, but if you prefer not to, there are craft shops in Blantyre and Lilongwe that use price-tags, though they're generally more expensive.

BARGAINING

At craft and curio stalls, where items are specifically for tourists, bargaining is expected. Some vendors might initially ask for double the price they're willing to accept; haggle until you arrive at a mutually agreeable price. Try not to have the attitude that people are trying to rip you off. If the price seems fair and affordable to you, there's no point in bargaining someone down just for the sake of it.

Solo Travellers

Solo travellers might attract a little attention in rural areas, especially a woman, but other than that people will barely notice you. Of course, solo travellers should be extremely careful at busy bus stations, and avoid walking around isolated areas, or at night (especially women).

A single room is usually more than half the price of a double or twin room, and many of the more upmarket, full-board lodges and safari companies apply a single person supplement.

Telephone & Mobile Phones

The international code for Malawi if you're dialling from abroad is 265. Telephone calls within Malawi are inexpensive, around MK50 per minute depending on the distance, and the network between main cities is reliable, although the lines to outlying areas are often not working. Calls to mobiles within Malawi cost around MK70 per minute.

Mobile-phone coverage is extensive in Malawi. Mobile-phone prefixes are 0888 or 0999 and the major network is Airtel. Sim cards are readily available from street vendors for around MK1500 and include a small amount of airtime. You can buy top-up cards from supermarkets, internet cafes and petrol stations.

PHONE CODES

Malawi does not have area codes, but all landline numbers begin with 01, so whatever number you dial within the country will have eight digits. Numbers starting with 7 are on the Lilongwe exchange; those starting with 8 are in Blantyre; 5 is around Zomba; 4 is the south; 3 is the north; and 2 is the Salima area.

GOVERNMENT TRAVEL ADVICE

Some government websites offer travel advisories and information on current hot spots.

Australian Department of Foreign Affairs (www.smarttraveller.gov.au)

British Foreign Office (☎0845-850-2829; www.fco.gov.uk)

Canadian Department of Foreign Affairs (☎800-267 6788; www.voyage.gc.ca)

US State Department (☎888-407 4747; http://travel.state.gov)

Time

Malawi is two hours ahead of Greenwich Mean Time (GMT/UTC). The country does not have daylight saving time. When it's noon in Malawi, it's 2am in Los Angeles, 5am in New York, 10am in London, 8pm in Sydney and 10pm in Auckland.

Toilets

There are two main types of toilet in Malawi: the Western style, with a toilet bowl and seat; and the African style, which is a hole in the floor, over which you squat. In towns and cities, especially in cafes, restaurants and hotels frequented by foreigners, toilets are generally of the Western variety. Bus stations are another story!

Tourist Information

There are tourist information offices in Blantyre and Lilongwe but you're much better off asking for advice from your hostel or hotel, or from a travel agency. Outside Malawi, tourism promotion is handled by UK-based **Malawi Tourism** (☎0115-982 1903; www.malawitourism.com), which responds to inquiries from all over the world.

Travellers with Disabilities

Even though there are more disabled people per head of population here than in the West, there are very few facilities. A few official buildings are constructed with ramps and lifts – but not many, and probably not the ones you want to visit. Some major hotels in the cities also have ramps and/or lifts, but again, not many.

Visas

Visas are not required by citizens of Commonwealth countries, the USA and most European nations. On entering the country you'll be granted a 30-day entry stamp, which can easily be extended at immigration offices in Blantyre or Lilongwe; however, the next month requires a fee of MK5000.

Volunteering

There are numerous volunteer opportunities in Malawi. A good initial contact is **Volunteer Abroad** (www.volunteerabroad.com), which has listings of current volunteer options in Malawi. Otherwise, local grassroots opportunities include the following ones:

Billy Riordan Memorial Trust (www.billysmalawiproject.org) Has an established clinic in Cape Maclear and provides medical care in the area. The trust needs medical volunteers (doctors, dentists, nurses, lab technicians).

Butterfly Space (www.butterfly-space.com) Involved in a number of projects in Nkhata Bay, including a nursery and a community resource centre. It encourages volunteers who can devote more than a few weeks and get involved with the local community.

Cool Runnings (☎0999-915173, 01-263398; coolrunnings@malawi.net) Involved in a variety of projects, including local education, in the Senga Bay area.

Panda Garden (☎0999-140905; www.heedmalawi.net; Main St, Chembe village) Based in Cape Maclear, Panda Garden is always on the lookout for divers (to help with bilharzia research in the lake) and art teachers.

Ripple Africa (☎0044 (0)1525 216346; www.rippleafrica.org) Recruits volunteer teachers, doctors, nurses and environmental workers for a number of projects based in Nkhata Bay district.

Wildlife Action Group (www.wag-malawi.org) Uses volunteers to assist in the management and maintenance of the Thuma Forest Reserve.

Women Travellers

Malawi is generally a safe destination for women travelling alone or with other women and you can anticipate few problems. In fact, many women travellers report that, compared to North Africa, South America and numerous Western countries, Malawi feels relatively safe and unthreatening.

If you do receive hassle from men, firmly decline their advances and you'll usually be left alone. If you want to go out at night apply the same common sense that you would at home.

Malawian women dress conservatively, in traditional or Western clothes, so when a visitor wears something significantly different from the norm, she will draw attention. In the minds of some men, revealing too much flesh will be seen as provocative. Wearing short shorts or a bikini might be acceptable on the beach in tourist areas but elsewhere it will meet with disapproval.

Getting There & Away

The main way to get to Malawi is by land or air. Overland, travellers might enter the country from Zambia, Mozambique or Tanzania. Boats also bring travellers over Lake Malawi from Mozambique. There are no direct flights to Malawi from Europe or the United States. The easiest way to reach the country by air is via Kenya, Ethiopia or South Africa. Flights, tours and rail tickets can be booked online at www.lonelyplanet.com/travel_services.

Entering Malawi

Entering Malawi you must present a passport with at least six months of validity remaining, and should be in possession of an onward or return ticket, though this is seldom checked. Tourists are generally given a 30-day stay, extendable once you're in the country.

Air

AIRPORTS & AIRLINES

Kamuzu International Airport (LLW; ☎01-700766), 19km north of Lilongwe city centre, handles the majority of international flights. Flights from South Africa, Kenya, Zambia and Tanzania also land in Blantyre at **Chileka International Airport** (BLZ; ☎01-694244). The country's national carrier is **Air Malawi** (www.flyairmalawi.com), which operates one internal (Lilongwe to Blantyre) and several regional flights. **Ulendo Airlink** (www.ulendo.net/flyer), the aviation wing of Ulendo Travel Group, operates safe twin-prop planes to domestic locations including Likoma Island and a number of safari parks.

AIRLINES FLYING TO/FROM MALAWI

Air Malawi (☎01-773680, 01-820811; www.flyairmalawi.com) has a decent regional network, with flights heading to Dar es Salaam, Johannesburg, Nairobi, Lusaka and Harare from Blantyre and Lilongwe.

South African Airways (☎01-772242, 01-620617; www.flysaa.com) flies twice weekly between Blantyre and Johannesburg, and five times weekly between Lilongwe and Johannesburg (with connections to Durban, Cape Town etc).

Kenya Airways (☎01-774524, 01-774624, 01-774227; www.kenya-airways.com) flies four times a week to/from Nairobi and six times a week to/from Lusaka.

Ethiopian Airways (☎01-771308, 01-771002; www.flyethiopian.com) flies four times a week from Addis Ababa.

Land

BORDER CROSSINGS

Mozambique

SOUTH

Take a minibus to the Mozambican border crossing at Zóbuè (*zob*-way; MK500) and then a minibus to Tete (US$6), from where buses go to Beira and Maputo. You could also get a Blantyre–Harare bus to drop you at Tete and then get a bus to Beira or Maputo.

CENTRAL

For central Mozambique, there are several buses per day from Blantyre to Nsanje (MK850), or all the way to the Malawian border at Marka (pronounced '*ma*-ra-ka'; MK900). It's a few kilometres between the border crossings – you can walk or take a bicycle taxi – and you can change money on the Mozambique side. From here pick-ups go to Mutarara and Vila de Sena.

NORTH

There are three border crossings from Malawi into northern Mozambique: Muloza, from where you can reach Mocuba in Mozambique, and Nayuchi and Chiponde, both of which lead to Cuamba in Mozambique.

Regular buses run from Blantyre, via Mulanje, to Muloza (MK750). From here, you walk 1km to the Mozambican border crossing at Melosa, from where it's another few kilometres into Milange. From Milange there's usually a *chapa* (pick-up or converted minibus) or truck about every other day in the dry season to Mocuba, where

CLIMATE CHANGE & TRAVEL

Every form of transport that relies on carbon-based fuel generates CO_2, the main cause of human-induced climate change. Modern travel is dependent on aeroplanes, which might use less fuel per kilometre per person than most cars but travel much greater distances. The altitude at which aircraft emit gases (including CO_2) and particles also contributes to their climate change impact. Many websites offer 'carbon calculators' that allow people to estimate the carbon emissions generated by their journey and, for those who wish to do so, to offset the impact of the greenhouse gases emitted with contributions to portfolios of climate-friendly initiatives throughout the world. Lonely Planet offsets the carbon footprint of all staff and author travel.

you can find transport on to Quelimane or Nampula.

Further north, minibuses and *matolas* run a few times per day between Mangochi and the border crossing at Chiponde (MK800). It's then 7km to the Mozambican border crossing at Mandimba and the best way to get there is by bicycle taxi (US$2). Mandimba has a couple of *pensãos,* and there's at least one vehicle daily, usually a truck, between here and Cuamba (US$10).

The third option is to go by minibus or passenger train from Liwonde to the border at Nayuchi (MK850). You can then take a *chapa* from the Mozambican side of the border to Cuamba.

South Africa

There are a number of bus companies running services from Lilongwe and Blantyre to Johannesburg. **Intercape Mainline** (☎0999-403398; www.intercape.co.za) operates a service between Lilongwe and Johannesburg on Tuesday, Wednesday, Saturday and Sunday for US$78, leaving at 6am; as does **Chiwale Bus Co** (☎0999-034014) who are cheaper at US$68 and leave from the same location at 6am on Saturday only. From Blantyre, try **Ingwe Coach** (☎01-822313). Buses from Lilongwe leave from outside the petrol station on Paul Kagame Rd in Old Town. In Blantyre, most Johannesburg-bound buses depart from the car park outside Blantyre Lodge.

Tanzania

If you want to go the whole way between Lilongwe and Dar es Salaam, there are five Taqwa buses per week (Tuesday, Wednesday, Saturday and Sunday, US$50) that depart from Devil St in Lilongwe. These buses also pick up and drop off in Mzuzu (US$30) leaving at midnight and arriving in Dar es Salaam around 2.10pm the next day. Mbeya (Tanzania) is handy for going between northern Malawi and southern Tanzania.

If you're going in stages, buses and minibuses run between Mzuzu and Karonga (MK2000, three to four hours), from where you can get a taxi to the Songwe border crossing (MK1200). It's 200m across the bridge to the Tanzanian border crossing.

Once on the Tanzanian side of the border, minibuses travel to Kyela (7km) and on to Mbeya, where you will need to overnight before continuing on the next morning to Dar es Salaam. You can change money with the bicycle-taxi boys, but beware of scams.

Zambia

There are four direct buses per week (two on Tuesday and two on Friday) between Lilongwe and Lusaka (MK6000), also departing from Devil St – the journey takes at least 12 hours. Regular minibuses run between Lilongwe and Mchinji (MK400). From here, it's 12km to the border. Local shared taxis shuttle between Mchinji and the border crossing for around MK200 per person, or MK1000 for the whole car.

From the Zambian side of the border crossing, shared taxis run to Chipata (US$2), which is about 30km west of the border, from where you can reach Lusaka or South Luangwa National Park.

If you've got a 4WD you can cross into northern Zambia via Chitipa in northern Malawi. It's four hours from Karonga to Chitipa on a rough dirt road, and then the Malawian border crossing is 5km out of town. After going through customs it is another 80km or four hours' drive to the Zambian border crossing at Nakonde.

BUS

It is possible to cross into Malawi by bus from Tanzania, Zambia and South Africa, and there are direct services from Johannesburg, Dar es Salaam, Nairobi and Lusaka to Blantyre and Lilongwe. When crossing the border you will have to get off the bus to pass through customs and pay for your visa.

BOAT

The Lake Malawi ferry *Ilala* stops at Metangula on the Mozambican mainland. If you're planning a visit you must get a visa in advance and make sure to get your passport stamped at Malawian immigration on Likoma Island or in Nkhata Bay. The *Ilala* was out of service for repairs at the time of research but will hopefully be back on the water shortly.

CAR & MOTORCYCLE

You will need a valid *carnet de passage* for your car, which will require entry/exit stamps when entering/leaving the country, as well as full car registration details and insurance documents, and you will have to pay US$20 road tax. If you don't have a *carnet* you will need to purchase a temporary import permit for US$3 and compulsory third-party insurance costs US$25 for a month. You won't find fuel or supplies at the borders themselves so take enough to continue to the nearest town.

TRAIN

If you're heading to northern Mozambique, a freight train *sometimes* departs from Limbe on Wednesdays at 7am, travelling via Balaka and Liwonde to the border at Nayuchi. From Nayuchi (where there are moneychangers) you can walk to Entre Lagos, and then get a *chapa* to Cuamba. That said, this is an unreliable mode of transport and you're better off taking the bus.

Getting Around

You can travel around Malawi by air, road, rail or boat. Compared to other countries in the region, distances between major centres are quite short, and generally roads and public transport systems are quite good, making independent travel fairly straightforward.

Air

For domestic flights, departure tax is US$5.

AIRLINES IN MALAWI

The domestic schedule of **Air Malawi** (☎01-788415, 01-753181, 01-772123; www.flyairmalawi.com) has diminished somewhat and the airline currently only operates regular flights between Lilongwe and Blantyre (one way MK43,000). Air Malawi's booking system is not always reliable, so be prepared for lost reservations or double bookings.

Bicycle

Bicycles are available for hire at many lodges throughout Malawi at a cost of around US$10 per day. You can also hire bicycles or arrange mountain-bike tours through Land & Lake Safaris in Lilongwe.

Boat

The **Ilala ferry** (☎01-587311; ilala@malawi.net) chugs passengers and cargo up and down Lake Malawi once a week in each direction. Travelling between Monkey Bay in the south and Chilumba in the north, it makes 12 stops at lakeside villages and towns in between. (You can get to the Mozambican mainland via the *Ilala*.) Many travellers rate this journey as a highlight of the country, although there are occasionally nasty storms. If you're unlucky, be prepared for some pitching and rolling.

The whole trip, from one end of the line to the other, takes about three days. The official schedules are detailed in the table below (only selected ports are shown).

NORTHBOUND

PORT	ARRIVAL	DEPARTURE
Monkey Bay	–	10am (Fri)
Chipoka	1pm (Fri)	4pm (Fri)
Nkhotakota	12am (Sat)	2am (Sat)
Metangula	6am (Sat)	8am (Sat)
Likoma Island	1.30pm (Sat)	6pm (Sat)
Nkhata Bay	1am (Sun)	5am (Sun)
Ruarwe	10.15am (Sun)	11.15am (Sun)
Chilumba	5pm (Sun)	

SOUTHBOUND

PORT	ARRIVAL	DEPARTURE
Chilumba	–	1am (Mon)
Ruarwe	6.45am (Mon)	8am (Mon)
Nkhata Bay	12.45pm (Mon)	8pm (Mon)
Likoma Island	3.15am (Tue)	6.15am (Tue)
Metangula	noon (Tue)	2.00pm (Tue)
Nkhotakota	5.30pm (Tue)	7.30pm (Tue)
Chipoka	3.30am (Wed)	7.30am (Wed)
Monkey Bay	10.30am (Wed)	–

The *Ilala* has three classes. Cabin Class was once luxurious and the cabins are still in reasonable condition. The spacious 1st Class deck is most popular with travellers, due largely to the sociable bar. There are also seats, a shaded area and mattresses for hire (MK500) in case you're doing the long-haul journey. Economy covers the entire lower deck and is dark and crowded, and engine fumes permeate from below.

Cabin Class and First Class passengers can dine in the ferry's restaurant, where a beef curry, *peri-peri* chicken or meal of similar standard costs about MK800. Food is also served from a galley on the Economy deck; a meal of beans, rice and vegetables costs under MK150.

Reservations are usually required for Cabin Class. For other classes, tickets are sold only when the boat is sighted.

SAMPLE ROUTES & FARES

All of the following sample fares are from Nkhata Bay.

DESTINATION	CABIN (MK)	1ST CLASS (MK)	ECONOMY (MK)
Nkhotakota	14,900	6820	1190
Monkey Bay	28,240	16,110	2710

When the *Ilala* stops at lakeside towns or villages, the water is too shallow for it to come close; the lifeboat is used to ferry passengers ashore. On its southbound journey, the *Ilala* docks at Nkhata Bay for seven hours and traders come aboard, selling food, drinks and newspapers.

Bus & Minibus

Malawi's main bus company is **AXA Coach Services** (☎01-876000; agma@agmaholdings.net). AXA operates three different classes. Coaches are the best and the most expensive. It's a luxury nonstop service with air con, toilet, comfortable AXA Executive reclining seats, snacks and fresh coffee, good drivers and even an on-board magazine. Services operate between Blantyre and Lilongwe twice a day from special departure points in each city (not the main bus stations).

AXA Luxury Coach and City Trouper services are the next in line. These buses have air con and reclining seats as well as TVs, but don't have toilets. They ply the route between Blantyre and Karonga, stopping at all the main towns with limited stops elsewhere.

Lastly, there are the country commuter buses, handy for backpackers as they cover the lakeshore route.

If you're headed for Mzuzu another alternative is the comfortable Super Sink Bus between Lilongwe and Mzuzu.

There are also local minibus services which operate on a fill-up-and-go basis.

In rural areas, the frequency of buses and minibuses drops dramatically – sometimes to nothing. In cases like this, the 'bus' is often a truck or pick-up, with people just piled in the back. In Malawi this is called a *matola*.

RESERVATIONS

You can buy a ticket in advance for AXA Executive, Luxury Coach and City Trouper services, all of which have set departure times. They have offices at the main bus stations and departure points or you can also buy tickets at branches of Postdotnet (post, internet and business centres found in Malawi's major towns). A week's notice is sometimes needed for the Executive coach, particularly for Friday and Sunday services.

Car & Motorcycle

The majority of main routes are mostly quality sealed roads, though off the main routes roads are rutted and potholed, making driving slow and dangerous. Secondary roads are usually graded dirt. Some are well maintained and easy to drive on in a normal car; others are bad, especially after rain, and slow even with a 4WD. Rural routes are not so good, and after heavy rain are often impassable. Several lodges along the lakeshore have poor access roads that need a 4WD. The same goes for the country's national parks and wildlife reserves.

BRING YOUR OWN VEHICLE & DRIVING LICENCE

If you're bringing a car into Malawi from any other country without a *carnet*, a temporary import permit costs US$3 (payable in kwacha) and compulsory third-party insurance is US$25 for one month. There's also a US$20 road tax fee – you must produce the documentation for this if you are driving the car out. When you leave Malawi, a permit handling fee of US$5 is payable. Receipts are issued.

You need a full driving licence (international driving licence is not necessary), and are normally required to be at least 23 years old and have two years' driving experience.

FUEL & SPARE PARTS

Fuel costs around US$1.54 per litre of diesel. Supplies are often limited so always keep your tank no lower than half full (how's that for optimism!). Spare parts are available in Lilongwe, Blantyre and Mzuzu.

HIRE

Most car-hire companies are based in Blantyre and Lilongwe and can arrange pick-up-drop-off deals. International names include Avis, and there are several independent outfits like Crossroads Car Hire. Check the tyres: bald tread will not get you up the mountain to Livingstonia.

Self-drive rates for a small car with unlimited mileage start at around US$50 per day. For a 4WD you're looking at around US$150 per day. To this add 17.5% government tax, plus another US$3 to US$7 a day for insurance. There will usually be a fee of about 5% for using a credit card. Also, most companies will quote you in dollars but if you pay by card they'll have to exchange this into kwacha first – usually at a hugely unfavourable rate.

If you'd rather not drive yourself, most companies will arrange a driver for you at a cost of around US$45 a day.

Avis (☎in Blantyre 01-692368, in Lilongwe 01-756105, 01-756103) Also has offices at Lilongwe and Blantyre airports and at some large hotels.

Crossroads Car Hire (☎01-750333; Crossroads Mall, next to the Crossroads Hotel; saloon/4WD with fully comprehensive insurance per day US$100/149; ⏰9am-5pm Mon-Fri) Solid 4WD vehicles, and fully comprehensive insurance, allowing you to self-drive on the toughest roads the country's parks can throw at you.

Sputnik Car Hire (☎01-761563; www.sputnik-car-hire.mw; Lilongwe)

SS Rent A Car (☎in Blantyre 01-822836, in Lilongwe 01-751478; www.ssrentacar.com)

INSURANCE

Third-party insurance is a requirement for all drivers, but this can be arranged through car-hire companies or purchased at border crossings.

ROAD RULES

Malawians drive on the left. Seat belts are compulsory. Speed limits are 80km per hour on main roads and 60km in built-up areas.

Tour & Safari Companies

Several companies organise tours around the country, ranging from a few days to three weeks. Trips into Zambia or Mozambique are also available. Most safaris are vehicle based, although some outfits also organise walking trips, or boating on the lake. Tours normally include transport, accommodation and food.

Survival Guide

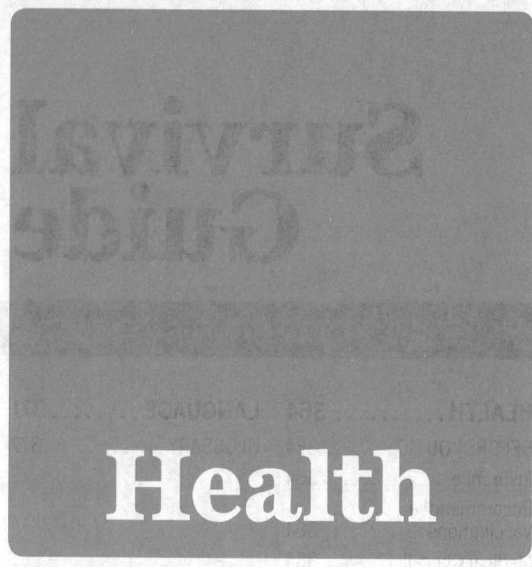

Health

While Africa has an impressive selection of tropical diseases, it's more likely you'll get a bout of diarrhoea or a cold than a more exotic malady. Stay up to date with your vaccinations and take basic preventive measures, and you'll be unlikely to succumb to any of the serious health hazards.

BEFORE YOU GO

» Get a check-up from your dentist and your doctor if you take any regular medication or have a chronic illness, such as high blood pressure or asthma.

» Organise spare contact lenses and glasses (and take your optical prescription with you).

» Get a first-aid and medical kit together and arrange necessary vaccinations.

» Consider registering with the **International Association for Medical Advice to Travellers** (IAMAT; www.iamat.org), which provides directories of certified doctors.

» If you'll be spending much time in remote areas (ie anywhere away from capitals and major cities or tourist centres), consider doing a first-aid course (contact the Red Cross or St John Ambulance) or attending a remote medicine first-aid course, such as that offered by the **Royal Geographical Society** (www.wildernessmedicaltraining.co.uk).

» Carry medications in their original (labelled) containers. A signed and dated letter from your physician describing all medical conditions and medications, including generic names, is also a good idea.

» If carrying syringes or needles, be sure to have a physician's letter documenting their medical necessity.

Insurance

Find out in advance whether your insurance plan will make payments directly to providers or will reimburse you later for overseas health expenditures. Most doctors and clinics in the region expect up-front payment in cash.

It's vital to ensure that your travel insurance will cover any emergency transport required to get you at least to Johannesburg (South Africa), or all the way home, by air and with a medical attendant if necessary.

If your policy requires you to pay first and claim later for medical treatment, be sure to keep all documentation. Some policies ask you to call back (reverse charges) to a centre in your home country where an immediate assessment of your problem is made. Since reverse-charge calls aren't possible in many parts of the region, contact the insurance company before setting off to confirm how best to contact them in an emergency.

Recommended Vaccinations

The **World Health Organization** (www.who.int/en/) recommends that all travellers be covered for diphtheria, tetanus, measles, mumps, rubella and polio, as well as for hepatitis B, regardless of their destination.

According to the **Centers for Disease Control & Prevention** (www.cdc.gov), the following vaccinations are recommended for the region: hepatitis A, hepatitis B, rabies and typhoid, and boosters for tetanus, diphtheria and measles. While a yellow-fever vaccination certificate is not officially required to enter any of the three countries unless you are entering from a yellow-fever infected area, carrying one is advised, and is often requested.

Medical Checklist

Carry a medical and first aid kit, to help yourself in the case of minor illness or injury. Possible items to include:

» Antibiotics (prescription only), eg ciprofloxacin (Ciproxin) or norfloxacin (Utinor)

» Antidiarrhoeal drugs (eg loperamide)

» Acetaminophen (paracetamol) or aspirin

» Antibacterial ointment (eg Bactroban) for cuts and abrasions (prescription only)
» Anti-inflammatory drugs (eg ibuprofen)
» Antihistamines (for hayfever and allergic reactions)
» Antimalaria pills
» Steroid cream, such as hydrocortisone (for allergic rashes)
» Bandages, gauze, gauze rolls
» Adhesive or paper tape
» Scissors, safety pins, tweezers
» Thermometer
» Pocket knife
» Insect repellent containing DEET for the skin
» Insect spray containing Permethrin for clothing, tents and bed nets
» Sun block
» Oral rehydration salts
» Iodine tablets (for water purification)
» Syringes and sterile needles
» Sterile needles, syringes and fluids if travelling to remote areas
» Self-diagnostic kit that can identify malaria in the blood from a finger prick, and emergency treatment

Internet Resources

General information:

Lonely Planet (www.lonelyplanet.com)

MD Travel Health (www.mdtravelhealth.com)

Fit for Travel (www.fitfortravel.scot.nhs.uk)

International Travel and Health (www.who.int/ith) A free, online publication of the World Health Organisation.

Government travel-health websites:

Australia (www.smartraveller.gov.au)

Canada (www.phac-aspc.gc.ca/tmp-pmv/index.html)

UK (www.nhs.uk/nhsengland/Healthcareabroad/pages/Healthcareabroad.aspx)

USA (www.cdc.gov/travel)

Further Reading

» *A Comprehensive Guide to Wilderness and Travel Medicine* by Eric A Weiss (1998)
» *Healthy Travel* by Jane Wilson-Howarth (1999)
» *Healthy Travel Africa* by Isabelle Young (2000)
» *How to Stay Healthy Abroad* by Richard Dawood (2002)
» *Travel with Children* by Cathy Lanigan (2004)

IN AFRICA

Availability & Cost of Health Care

Throughout much of the region, capital cities are the only places with good emergency medical service. For Western standards, expect to pay Western prices.

If you become seriously ill, seek treatment in the capital city or in South Africa or return home. If you fall ill in an unfamiliar area, ask staff at a top-end hotel or resident expatriates where the best nearby medical facilities are. In an emergency contact your embassy.

Well-stocked pharmacies are found in capital cities and some major towns. These will invariably carry chloroquine and sometimes Fansidar (both for malaria) and other basics, though it's best to bring whatever you think you may need from home.

Always check the expiry date before buying medications, especially in smaller towns. We've given some suggested dosages, but they are for emergency use only. Correct diagnosis is vital.

There is a high risk of contracting HIV from infected blood transfusions. The **BloodCare Foundation** (www.bloodcare.org.uk) is a useful source of safe, screened blood, which can be transported to any part of the world within 24 hours.

Infectious Diseases

Following are some of the diseases that are found in the region, although with a few basic preventive measures, it's unlikely that you'll succumb to any of these.

Cholera

Cholera is usually only a problem during natural or artificial disasters (eg war, floods or earthquakes), although small outbreaks can possibly occur at other times. Travellers are rarely affected. Cholera is caused by a bacteria and spread via contaminated drinking water. The main symptom is profuse watery diarrhoea, which causes debilitation if fluids are not replaced quickly. An oral cholera vaccine is available in the USA, but it is not particularly effective. Most cases of cholera can be avoided by careful selection of good drinking water and by avoiding potentially contaminated food. Treatment is by fluid replacement (orally or via a drip), but sometimes antibiotics are needed. Self-treatment is not advised.

Dengue Fever (Break-Bone Fever)

Dengue fever is spread through the bite of the mosquito. It causes a feverish illness with headache and muscle pains similar to those experienced with a bad, prolonged attack of influenza. There might be a rash. Self-treatment: paracetamol and rest.

Diphtheria

Diphtheria is spread through close respiratory contact. It usually causes a temperature and a severe sore throat.

Sometimes a membrane forms across the throat resulting in the need for a tracheostomy to prevent suffocation. Vaccination is recommended for those likely to be in close contact with the local population in infected areas. More important for long stays than for short-term trips.

Filariasis

Tiny worms migrating in the lymphatic system cause filariasis. The bite from an infected mosquito spreads the infection. Symptoms include localised itching and swelling of the legs and/or genitalia. Treatment is available.

Hepatitis A

Hepatitis A is spread through contaminated food (particularly shellfish) and water. It causes jaundice and, although it is rarely fatal, it can cause prolonged lethargy and delayed recovery. If you've had hepatitis A, you shouldn't drink alcohol for up to six months afterwards, but once you've recovered, there won't be any long-term problems. The first symptoms include dark urine and a yellow colour to the whites of the eyes. Sometimes a fever and abdominal pain might be present. Hepatitis A vaccine (Avaxim, VAQTA, Havrix) is given as an injection: a single dose will give protection for up to a year, and a booster after a year gives protection for 10 years. Hepatitis A and typhoid vaccines can also be given as a single dose vaccine, Hepatyrix or ViATIM.

Hepatitis B

Hepatitis B is spread through infected blood, contaminated needles and sexual intercourse. It can also be spread from an infected mother to the baby during childbirth. It affects the liver, causing jaundice and occasionally liver failure. Most people recover completely, but some people might be chronic carriers of the virus, which could lead eventually to cirrhosis or liver cancer. Those visiting high-risk areas for long periods or those with increased social or occupational risk should be immunised. Many countries now routinely give hepatitis B as part of the routine childhood vaccination. It is given singly or can be given at the same time as hepatitis A (hepatyrix).

A course will give protection for at least five years. It can be given over four weeks or six months.

HIV

Human immuno-deficiency virus (HIV), the virus that causes acquired immune deficiency syndrome (AIDS), is a significant problem in the region. The virus is spread through infected blood and blood products, by sexual intercourse with an infected partner and from an infected mother to her baby during childbirth and breastfeeding. It can be spread through 'blood to blood' contacts, such as with contaminated instruments during medical, dental, acupuncture and other body-piercing procedures, and through sharing used intravenous needles. At present there is no cure; medication that might keep the disease under control is available, but these drugs are often unavailable for most locals and not readily available for travellers, either. If you think you might have been infected with HIV, a blood test is necessary; a three-month gap after exposure and before testing is required to allow antibodies to appear in the blood.

Malaria

Malaria is prevalent in all three countries, and is especially a risk in Mozambique. Taking prophylaxis or otherwise protecting yourself from bites is very important. Infection rates are higher during the rainy season, but the risk exists year-round and it is extremely important to take preventative measures, even if you will just be travelling for a short time.

Malaria is caused by a parasite in the bloodstream spread via the bite of the female Anopheles mosquito. There are several types of malaria, falciparum malaria being the most dangerous type and the predominant form in parts of the region. Infection rates vary with season and climate, so check out the situation before departure. Unlike most other diseases regularly encountered by travellers, there is no vaccination against malaria. However, several different drugs are used to prevent malaria and new ones are in the pipeline. Up-to-date advice from a travel-health clinic is essential as some medication is more suitable for some travellers than others. The pattern of drug-resistant malaria is changing rapidly, so what was advised several years ago might no longer be the case.

Malaria can present in several ways. The early stages include headaches, fevers, generalised aches and pains, and malaise, which could be mistaken for flu. Other symptoms can include abdominal pain, diarrhoea and a cough. Anyone who develops a fever in a malarial area should assume malarial infection until a blood test proves negative, even if you have been taking antimalarial medication. If not treated, the next stage could develop within 24 hours, particularly if falciparum malaria is the parasite: jaundice, then reduced consciousness and coma (also known as cerebral malaria) followed by death. Treatment in hospital is essential and the death rate might still be as high as 10% even in the best intensive-care facilities.

Many travellers are under the impression that malaria is a mild illness, that treatment is always easy and successful, and that taking antimalarial drugs causes more illness through side effects than actually getting malaria. This is unfortunately not true. Side effects of the medication depend on the drug being taken. Doxycycline can cause heartburn and indigestion; mefloquine (Larium) can cause anxiety attacks, insomnia and nightmares, and (rarely) severe psychiatric disorders; chloroquine can cause nausea and hair loss; proguanil can cause mouth ulcers; and Malarone is expensive. The side effects are not universal and can be minimised by taking medication correctly (eg with food). Also, some people should not take a particular antimalarial drug (eg people with epilepsy should avoid mefloquine, and doxycycline should not be taken by pregnant women or children younger than 12).

If you decide that you really do not wish to take antimalarial drugs, you must understand the risks and be obsessive about avoiding mosquito bites. Use nets and insect repellent, and report any fever or flu-like symptoms to a doctor as soon as possible. Some people advocate homeopathic preparations against malaria, such as Demal200, but as yet there is no conclusive evidence that this is effective and many homeopaths do not recommend their use.

People of all ages can contract malaria and falciparum causes the most severe illness. Repeated infections might result eventually in less serious illness. Malaria in pregnancy frequently results in miscarriage or premature labour. Adults who have survived childhood malaria have developed immunity and usually only develop mild cases of malaria; most Western travellers have no immunity at all. Immunity wanes after 18 months of non-exposure, so even if you have had malaria in the past and used to live in a malaria-prone area, you might no longer be immune.

If you will be away from major towns, it's worth considering taking standby treatment, although this should be seen as emergency treatment only and not as routine self-medication. It should be used only if you will be far from medical facilities and have been advised about the symptoms of malaria and how to use the medication. If you do resort to emergency self-treatment, medical advice should be sought as soon as possible to confirm whether the treatment has been successful. In particular you want to avoid contracting cerebral malaria, which can be fatal in 24 hours. Self-diagnostic kits, which can identify malaria in the blood from a finger prick, are available in the West and are a worthwhile investment.

The risks from malaria to both mother and foetus during pregnancy are considerable. Unless good medical care can be guaranteed, travel in malarial areas while pregnant should be discouraged unless essential.

Meningococcal Meningitis

Meningococcal infection is spread through close respiratory contact and is more likely in crowded situations, such as dormitories, buses and clubs. Infection is uncommon in travellers. Vaccination is recommended for long stays and is especially important towards the end of the dry season. Symptoms include a fever, severe headache, neck stiffness and a red rash. Immediate medical treatment is necessary.

The ACWY vaccine is recommended for all travellers in sub-Saharan Africa. This vaccine is different from the meningococcal meningitis C

ANTIMALARIAL A TO D

A Awareness of the risk. No medication is totally effective, but protection of up to 95% is achievable with most drugs, as long as other measures have been taken.

B Bites - avoid at all costs:

» Sleep in a screened room, use a mosquito spray or coils and sleep under a permethrin-impregnated net at night. Light-weight travel-style nets are not readily available in the region, so buy one before leaving home.

» Cover up in the evenings and at night with long trousers and long sleeves, preferably with permethrin-treated clothing. Light-coloured clothing is best.

» Apply appropriate repellent to all areas of exposed skin in the evenings. While prolonged overuse of DEET-containing repellents may be harmful, especially to children, its use is considered preferable to being bitten by disease-transmitting mosquitoes.

» Avoid perfumes, aftershave and heavily scented soaps.

C Chemical prevention (ie antimalarial drugs) is usually needed in malarial areas. Expert advice is needed as resistance patterns can change, and new drugs are in development. Not all antimalarial drugs are suitable for everyone. Most antimalarial drugs need to be started at least a week in advance and continued for four weeks after the last possible exposure to malaria.

D Diagnosis. If you have a fever or flu-like illness within a year of travel to a malarial area, malaria is a possibility, and immediate medical attention is necessary.

vaccine given to children and adolescents in some countries; it is safe to be given both types of vaccine.

Poliomyelitis

Generally spread through contaminated food and water. It is one of the vaccines given in childhood and should be boosted every 10 years, either orally (a drop on the tongue) or as an injection. Polio can be carried asymptomatically (ie showing no symptoms) and could cause a transient fever. In rare cases it causes weakness or paralysis of one or more muscles, which might be permanent.

Rabies

Rabies is spread by receiving the bites or licks of an infected animal on broken skin. It is always fatal once the clinical symptoms start (which might be up to several months after an infected bite), so postbite vaccination should be given as soon as possible. Postbite vaccination (whether or not you've been vaccinated before the bite) prevents the virus from spreading to the central nervous system. Animal handlers should be vaccinated, as should those travelling to remote areas where a reliable source of postbite vaccine is not available within 24 hours. Three preventive injections are needed over a month. If you are infected and have not been vaccinated, you will need a course of five injections starting 24 hours, or as soon as possible, after the injury. If you have been vaccinated, you will need fewer postbite injections and have more time to seek medical help.

Schistosomiasis (Bilharzia)

This disease is spread by flukes (minute worms) that are carried by a species of freshwater snail. The flukes are carried inside the snail, which then sheds them into slow-moving or still water. The parasites penetrate human skin during paddling or swimming and then migrate to the bladder or bowel. They are passed out via stool or urine and could contaminate fresh water, where the cycle starts again.

Paddling or swimming in suspect freshwater lakes (including many parts of Lake Malawi) or slow-running rivers should be avoided. Although parts of Lake Malawi might be low risk, other areas (including some popular tourist destinations) bring a risk of contracting bilharzia.

In some cases there may be no symptoms, with others there might be a transient fever and rash. Advanced cases might have blood in the stool or urine. Long-term effects can be very harmful; it is essential that you have a check-up for the disease when you get home or reach a place with good medical services.

Be sure your doctor is familiar with bilharzia, and be aware that the disease may have a long incubation period and may not be initially apparent, so you might need more than one test. A blood test can detect antibodies if you might have been exposed and treatment is then possible in specialist travel or infectious-disease clinics. If not treated the infection can cause kidney failure or permanent bowel damage. It is not possible for you to directly infect others.

Trypanosomiasis (Sleeping Sickness)

Spread via the bite of the tsetse fly. It causes a headache, fever and eventually coma. There is an effective treatment.

Tuberculosis (TB)

Tuberculosis is spread through close respiratory contact and occasionally through infected milk or milk products. BCG vaccination is recommended for those likely to be mixing closely with the local population, although it gives only moderate protection against TB. It is more important for long stays than for short-term stays. Inoculation with the BCG vaccine is not available in all countries. It is given routinely to many children in developing countries. The vaccination causes a small permanent scar at the site of injection, and is usually given in a specialist chest clinic. It is a live vaccine and should not be given to pregnant women or immunocompromised individuals.

TB can be asymptomatic, only being picked up on a routine chest X-ray. Alternatively, it can cause a cough, weight loss or fever, sometimes months or even years after exposure.

Typhoid

This is spread through food or water contaminated by infected human faeces. The first symptom is usually a fever or a pink rash on the abdomen. Sometimes septicaemia (blood poisoning) can occur. A typhoid vaccine (typhim Vi, typherix) will give protection for three years. In some countries, the oral vaccine Vivotif is also available. Antibiotics are usually given as treatment and death is rare unless septicaemia occurs.

Yellow Fever

Zambia, Mozambique and Malawi all require you to carry a certificate of yellow-fever vaccination only if you are arriving from an infected area (a requirement which is vigilantly enforced, and which includes travellers coming from Tanzania into Mozambique, and applies also to those going from Zambia into South Africa). However, it is still often requested at points of entry, and is recommended for almost all visitors by the **Centers for Disease Control & Prevention** (www.cdc.gov).

Yellow fever is spread by infected mosquitoes. Symptoms range from a flu-like illness to severe hepatitis (liver inflammation), jaundice and death. The yellow-fever vaccination must be given at a designated clinic and is valid for 10 years. It is a live vaccine and must not be given to immuno-compromised or pregnant travellers.

Travellers' Diarrhoea

Although it's not inevitable that you will get diarrhoea while travelling in the region, it's certainly likely. Diarrhoea is the most common travel-related illness and sometimes can be triggered by simple dietary changes.

To help prevent diarrhoea, avoid tap water, only eat fresh fruits and vegetables if cooked or peeled, and be wary of dairy products that might contain unpasteurised milk. The small plastic bags of water sold on street corners are best avoided. Take care with fruit juice, particularly if water may have been added. Milk in many smaller restaurants is made from reconstituted milk powder, which is safe if it's been made with boiled or mineral water.

With freshly cooked food, plates or serving utensils might be dirty, so be selective when eating food from street vendors and make sure that cooked food is piping hot all the way through.

If you develop diarrhoea, drink plenty of fluids, preferably an oral rehydration solution containing water (lots), and some salt and sugar. A few loose stools don't require treatment, but if you start having more than four or five stools a day, start taking an antibiotic (usually a quinoline drug, such as ciprofloxacin or norfloxacin), and an anti-diarrhoeal agent (such as loperamide) if you are not within easy reach of a toilet. If diarrhoea is bloody, persists for more than 72 hours or is accompanied by fever, shaking chills or severe abdominal pain, seek medical attention.

DRINKING WATER

Don't drink tap water unless it has been boiled, filtered or chemically disinfected (such as with iodine tablets). Don't drink from streams, rivers and lakes. It's also best to avoid drinking from pumps and wells; some bring pure water to the surface, but the presence of animals can contaminate supplies. Bottled water is widely available, except in very remote areas, where you should carry a filter or purification tablets.

Amoebic Dysentery

Contracted by eating contaminated food and water, amoebic dysentery causes blood and mucus in the faeces. It can be relatively mild and tends to come on gradually, but seek medical advice if you think you have the illness as it won't clear up without treatment (which is with specific antibiotics).

Giardiasis

This, like amoebic dysentery, is also caused by ingesting contaminated food or water. The illness usually appears a week or more after you have been exposed to the offending parasite. Giardiasis might cause only a short-lived bout of typical travellers' diarrhoea, but it can also cause persistent diarrhoea. Ideally, seek medical advice if you suspect you have giardiasis, but if you are in a remote area you could start a course of antibiotics.

Environmental Hazards

Heat Exhaustion

This condition occurs following heavy sweating and excessive fluid loss with inadequate replacement of fluids and salt, and is particularly common in hot climates when taking unaccustomed exercise before full acclimatisation. Symptoms include headache, dizziness and tiredness. Dehydration is already happening by the time you feel thirsty; aim to drink sufficient water to produce pale, diluted urine. Self-treatment: fluid replacement with water and/or fruit juice, and cooling by cold water and fans. The treatment of the salt-loss component consists of consuming salty fluids, as in soup, and adding a little more table salt to foods than usual.

Heatstroke

Heat exhaustion is a precursor to the much more serious condition of heatstroke. In this case there is damage to the sweating mechanism, with an excessive rise in body temperature; irrational and hyperactive behaviour; and eventually loss of consciousness then death. Rapid cooling by spraying the body with water and fanning is ideal. Emergency fluid and electrolyte replacement is usually also required by intravenous drip.

Insect Bites & Stings

Mosquitoes might not always carry malaria or dengue fever, but they (and other insects) can cause irritation and infected bites. To avoid these, take the same precautions as you would for avoiding malaria. Use DEET-based insect repellents. Excellent clothing treatments are also available; mosquitoes that land on treated clothing will die.

Bee and wasp stings cause real problems only to those who have a severe allergy to the stings (anaphylaxis). If you are one of these people, carry an 'epipen' (an adrenaline (epinephrine) injection), which you can give yourself. This could save your life.

Sandflies are found in some areas. They usually only cause a nasty, itchy bite, but they can carry a rare skin disorder called cutaneous leishmaniasis. Prevention of bites with DEET-based repellents is sensible.

Bed bugs are often found in hostels and cheap hotels. They lead to very itchy, lumpy bites. Spraying the mattress with crawling-insect killer after changing bedding will get rid of them.

Scabies is also frequently found in cheap accommodation. These tiny mites live in the skin, particularly between the fingers. They cause an intensely itchy rash. The itch is easily treated with malathion and permethrin lotion from a pharmacy; other members of the household also need treating to avoid spreading scabies, even if they do not show any symptoms.

Snake & Scorpion Bites

Don't walk barefoot, or stick your hand into holes or cracks. However, 50% of people bitten by venomous snakes are not actually injected with poison (envenomed). If bitten by a snake, don't panic. Immobilise the bitten limb with a splint (such as a stick) and apply a bandage over the site, with firm pressure (similar to bandaging a sprain). Do not apply a tourniquet, or cut or suck the bite. Get medical help as soon as possible so antivenene can be given if needed.

Scorpions are frequently found in arid areas. They can cause a painful bite that is sometimes life-threatening. If bitten, take a painkiller. Seek medical treatment if collapse occurs.

Traditional Medicine

At least 80% of the African population relies on traditional medicine, often because conventional Western-style medicine is too expensive, because of prevailing cultural attitudes and beliefs, or simply because in some cases it works. Although some African remedies seem to work on malaria, sickle cell anaemia, high blood pressure and some AIDS symptoms, most African healers learn their art by apprenticeship, so education is inconsistent and unregulated.

Language

WANT MORE?

For in-depth language information and handy phrases, check out Lonely Planet's *Africa Phrasebook* and *Portuguese Phrasebook*. You'll find them at **shop.lonelyplanet.com**, or you can buy Lonely Planet's iPhone phrasebooks at the Apple App Store.

English is the official language in Malawi and is widely spoken. Chichewa, one of the many languages in Malawi, is used throughout the country as a lingua franca.

Portuguese is the official language of Mozambique. It is widely spoken in larger towns, less so in rural areas. Mozambique's numerous African languages, all of which belong to the Bantu family, can be divided into three groups: Makhuwa-Lomwe languages, spoken by more than 33% of the population, primarily in the north; Sena-Nyanja languages in the centre and near Lake Niassa; and Tsonga languages in the south. The exact number of languages spoken in Mozambique has not been established, but it is estimated that there are at least nine, and perhaps as many as 16. Outside southern resorts and the areas bordering Zimbabwe and Malawi, English is not widely spoken. In northern Cabo Delgado and Niassa provinces near the Tanzanian border, Swahili is frequently heard and may be more useful than Portuguese.

In Zambia, English is the official language and is widely spoken. Of the scores of local languages spoken in Zambia, the main four are covered in this chapter: Bemba, Lozi, Nyanja and Tonga. Zambians place much emphasis on the relationship between speakers and it's very important to use the correct forms of address, particularly with the Lozi. There are often two different ways to say 'you' and to greet people, depending on their social status. The informal mode is used for children, friends and peers. The polite mode is used for strangers, elders and adults of equal or higher status. In this chapter the abbreviations 'inf' for informal and 'pol' for polite are included where required.

BEMBA

Bemba is spoken very widely in Lusaka and in the Copperbelt, Luapula, Central and Northern Provinces of Zambia. When addressing elders, add *bashikulu* (grandfather) for a man and *bamama* (grandmother) for a woman. You can generally get by using English numbers for prices and times.

Basics

Hello.	*Muli shani.*
Greetings!	*Uli shani?* (inf) *Mwapolenipo mukwai!* (pol)
Goodbye.	*Shalapo.* (inf) *Shalenipo mukwai.* (pol)
Good morning.	*Wabuka shani?* (inf) *Mwashibukeni?/* *Mwabuka shani?* (pol)
Good evening.	*Icungulupo/* *Mwatushenipo mukwai.*
Good night.	*Icungulopo.*
Please.	*Mukwai.*
Thank you./ Excuse me.	*Natasha./Natotela./* *Banjeleleko.*
Yes.	*Ee (mukwai).*
No.	*Awe./Teifyo.*
How are you?	*Uli shani?* (inf)/ *Muli shani?* (pol)
I'm fine.	*Ndifye bwino.*
Good./Fine./OK.	*Chawama./Chilifye./* *Chisuma./Chilifye bwino.*
I don't understand.	*Nshumfwile bwino.*

What's your name?	*Niwe nani ishina?* (inf) *Nimwe banani ishina?* (pol)
My name is ...	*Ishina lyandi ni ne ...*
How much?	*Shinga?/Nishinga?*
toilets	*ifimbusu*
men	*baume*
women	*banakashi*
today	*lelo*
tomorrow	*mailo*
tomorrow (early)	*mailo ulucelo*
yesterday	*mailo yafumineko*

Eating & Drinking

Please bring me ...	*Ndetele niko ...*
bananas	*nkonde*
beans	*cilemba*
beer	*bwalwa*
bread	*umukate*
cassava	*kalundwe*
chicken	*inkoko*
coffee	*kofi*
eggs	*amani*
fish	*isabi*
fruit	*icisabo/ifisabo* (sg/pl)
meat	*inama*
milk	*umukaka*
mushrooms	*ubowa*
oranges	*amachungwa*
peanuts	*mbalala*
potatoes	*ifyumbu*
tea	*chai*
vegetables	*umusalu*
(drinking) water	*amenshi (yakunwa)*

CHICHEWA

The most common Chichewa translations are given here, but keep in mind when using this that you may not be speaking 'proper' Chichewa. Importantly, though, you'll be understood, and locals in Malawi will be pleased to hear a visitor using their language.

Basics

Mazungu means 'white person', but is not a derogatory term. *Bambo* literally means 'father' but is a polite way to address any Malawian man. The female equivalent is *Amai* or *Mai*. Chichewa speakers talking together will normally use English for numbers, prices and expressing time.

Hello.	*Moni.*
Goodbye.	*Tsala bwino.* (if leaving) *Pitani bwino.* (if staying)
Good night.	*Gonani bwino.*
Please.	*Chonde.*
Thank you.	*Zikomo.*
Excuse me.	*Zikomo.*
Yes./No.	*Inde./Iyayi.*
How are you?	*Muli bwanji?*
I'm fine.	*Ndili bwino.*
Good./Fine./OK.	*Chabwino.*
What's your name?	*Dzina lako ndani?*
I don't understand.	*Sindikunva.*
How much?	*Ntengo bwanji?*
I want ...	*Ndifuna ...*
I don't want ...	*Sindifuna ...*
to buy	*kugula*
to sleep	*kugona*
men	*akuma*
women	*akazi*
today	*lero*
tomorrow	*mara*
tomorrow (early)	*m'mara*
yesterday	*dzulo*

Eating & Drinking

Please bring me ...	*Mundi passe ...*
to eat	*kudya*
bread	*buledi*
chicken	*nkhuku*
coffee	*khofi*
eggs	*mazira*
fish	*somba*
fruit	*chipasso/zipasso* (sg/pl)
lake perch	*chambo*
meat	*nyama*
milk	*mkaka*
potatoes	*batata*
tea	*ti*
vegetables	*mquani*
water	*mazi*

LOZI

Lozi is spoken mainly in Zambia's Western Province. If greeting royalty or aristocrats, use *Ba lumele Malozi, sha*. English numbers are usually used to express time.

Basics

Hello.	*Eeni, sha.* (general) *Lumela.* (inf) *Mu lumeleng' sha.* (pol)
Goodbye.	*Siala (foo/hande/ sinde).* (inf) *Musiale (foo/hande/ sinde).* (pol)
Good morning.	*U zuhile.* (inf) *Mu zuhile.* (pol)
Good afternoon/ evening.	*Ki manzibuana./ U tozi.* (inf) *Mu tozi.* (pol)
Good night.	*Ki busihu.*
Please.	*Sha.*
Thank you (very much).	*N'itumezi (hahulu).*
Excuse me.	*Ni swalele.* (inf) *Mu ni swalele.* (pol)
Yes.	*Ee.* (inf) *Eeni.* (pol)
No.	*Awa.* (inf) *Batili.* (pol)
How are you?	*U cwang'?/W'a pila?/ W'a zuha?* (inf) *Mu cwang'?/Mw'a pila?/ Mw'a zuha?* (pol)
I'm fine.	*N'i teng'./N'a pila./ N'a zuha.*
Good./Fine.	*Ki hande.*
OK.	*Ku lukile.*
I don't understand.	*Ha ni utwi.*
What's your name?	*Libizo la hao ki wena mang'?* (inf) *Libizo la mina ki mina bo mang'?* (pol)
My name is ...	*K'i na ...*
How much?	*Ki bukai?*
toilets	*bimbuzi/limbuzi*
men	*banna*
women	*basali*
today	*kachenu*
tomorrow	*kamuso*
tomorrow (early)	*kamuso kakusasasa/ ka mamiso*
yesterday	*mabani*

Eating & Drinking

Use *Ndate* (sir) or *Ma* (madam) to denote 'please'.

Numbers – Lozi

1	*il'ingw'i*
2	*z'e peli or bubeli*
3	*z'e t'alu or bulalu*
4	*z'e ne or bune*
5	*z'e keta-lizoho*

Please bring me ...	*Ndate/Ma, ha mu ni fe ...*
banana	*likonde/makonde* (sg/pl)
beans	*manawa*
beef	*nama ya komu*
beer	*bucwala/mutoho* (sg/pl)
bread	*sinkwa*
chicken	*kuhu*
coffee	*kofi*
egg	*lii/mai* (sg/pl)
fish	*tapi*
food	*licho/sicho*
freshwater bream	*papati*
fruit	*tolwana/litolwana* (sg/pl)
gravy	*mulo*
meat	*nama*
milk	*mabisi*
mushrooms	*mbowa*
peanuts/cashews	*ndongo*
pork	*nama ya kulube*
potatoes	*makwili*
rice	*raisi*
salt	*lizwai*
sweet	*munati*
tea	*tii*
vegetable	*miloho/muloho* (sg/pl)
(drinking) water	*mezi (a kunwa)*

NYANJA

Nyanja is widely spoken in Lusaka and in the Central and Eastern Provinces of Zambia. You can generally get by using English numbers for prices and times.

Basics

Hello.	*Bwanji.*
Good morning.	*Mwauka bwanji.*
Good afternoon.	*Mwachoma bwanji.*
Good night.	*Gonani bwino.*
Goodbye.	*Pitani bwino/salani bwino.*
Thank you./ Excuse me.	*Zikomo.*

Thank you very much.	*Zikomo kwambiri.*
Yes./No.	*Inde./Iyai.*
How are you?	*Uli bwanji?* (inf) *Muli bwanji?* (pol)
I'm fine.	*Ndili bwino.*
Good./Fine./OK.	*Chabwino.*
I don't understand.	*Sindimvera.*
What's your name?	*Dzina ianu ndani?*
My name is ...	*Dzina ianga ndine ...*
How much?	*Ndizingati?*
toilets	*chimbuzi*
men	*amuna*
women	*akazi*
today	*lelo*
tomorrow	*mawa*
tomorrow (early)	*m'mawa*
yesterday	*dzulo*

Eating & Drinking

Please bring me ...	*Ndifuna kukhala ndi ...*
beans	*kaela*
beef	*nyama ya ng'ombe*
beer	*mowa*
bread	*buledi*
chicken	*nkuku*
coffee	*khofi*
eggs	*ma egesi*
fish	*nsomba*
fruit	*cipatso/zipatso* (sg/pl)
meat	*nyama*
milk	*mukaka*
pork	*nyama ya nkumba*
potatoes	*mapotato*
sweet potato	*kandolo*
tea	*tiyi*
vegetables	*mbeu zaziwisi*
(drinking) water	*mandzi (yo kumwa)*

PORTUGUESE

Most sounds in Portuguese are also found in English. The exceptions are the nasal vowels (represented in our pronunciation guides by ng after the vowel), which are pronounced 'through the nose'; and the strongly rolled *r* (rr in our pronunciation guides). Also note that the symbol zh sounds like the 's' in 'pleasure'. The stressed syllables are indicated with italics. Masculine and feminine forms of nouns and adjectives are provided in the following phrases where necessary, indicated with 'm' and 'f' respectively.

Basics

Hello.	*Olá.*	o·*laa*
Goodbye.	*Adeus.*	a·de·*oosh*
How are you?	*Como está?*	*ko*·moo shtaa
Fine, and you?	*Bem, e você?*	beng e vo·*se*
Excuse me.	*Faz favor.*	faash fa·*vor*
Sorry.	*Desculpe.*	desh·*kool*·pe
Yes./No.	*Sim./Não.*	seeng/nowng
Please.	*Por favor.*	poor fa·*vor*
Thank you.	*Obrigado.* *Obrigada.*	o·bree·*gaa*·doo (m) o·bree·*gaa*·da (f)
You're welcome.	*De nada.*	de *naa*·da

What's your name?
Qual é o seu nome? — kwaal e oo *se*·oo *no*·me

My name is ...
O meu nome é ... — oo *me*·oo *no*·me e ...

Do you speak English?
Fala inglês? — *faa*·la eeng·*glesh*

I don't understand.
Não entendo. — nowng eng·*teng*·doo

Directions

Where's (the station)?
Onde é (a estação)? — *ong*·de e (a shta·*sowng*)

What's the address?
Qual é o endereço? — kwaal e oo eng·de·*re*·soo

Could you please write it down?
Podia escrever isso, por favor? — poo·*dee*·a shkre·*ver* ee·soo poor fa·*vor*

Can you show me (on the map)?
Pode-me mostrar (no mapa)? — *po*·de·me moosh·*traar* (noo *maa*·pa)

Eating & Drinking

What would you recommend?
O que é que recomenda? — oo ke e ke rre·koo·*meng*·da

I don't eat ...
Eu não como ... — e·oo nowng *ko*·moo ...

I'd like (the menu).
Queria (um menu). — ke·*ree*·a (oong me·*noo*)

Cheers!
Saúde! — sa·*oo*·de

That was delicious.
Isto estava delicioso. — *eesh*·too *shtaa*·va de·lee·see·*o*·zoo

Please bring the bill.
Pode-me trazer a conta. — *po*·de·me tra·*zer* a *kong*·ta

MOZAMBIQUE'S LOCAL LANGUAGES

While Portuguese will greatly facilitate your travels in Mozambique, a few greetings and basic phrases in one of the local languages will be warmly received. Changana (also called Tsonga) is one of the most useful languages in Maputo and southern Mozambique.

Good morning.	*lixile* ('li-*shee*-le')	**Good afternoon.**	*lipelile*
Goodbye.	*salani*	**Thank you.**	*kanimambo*

In the far north near Lake Niassa, most people speak Nyanja.

Good morning.	*mwaka bwanji*	**Good afternoon.**	*mwalongedza*
Goodbye.	*ine de likupita*	**Thank you very much.**	*zikomo kwambile*

The main languages in central Mozambique are Sena and Ndau. To greet someone in Sena, say *magerwa*. In Ndau, it's *mawata*. In and around Chimoio, you will also hear Manyika with the greeting *mangwanani*.

In much of Nampula and Cabo Delgado provinces, where major languages include Makonde and Makhuwa, the most useful greeting is *salaam'a*.

In northern Cabo Delgado Swahili is useful; here are some basic phrases in Swahili.

Hello.	*Jambo./Salama.*	**1**	*moja*
Goodbye.	*Kwa heri.*	**2**	*mbili*
How are you?	*Habari?*	**3**	*tatu*
I'm fine, thanks.	*Nzuri.*	**4**	*nne*
Yes.	*Ndiyo.*	**5**	*tano*
No.	*Hapana.*	**6**	*sita*
Please.	*Tafadhali.*	**7**	*saba*
Thank you (very much).	*Asante (sana).*	**8**	*nane*
You're welcome.	*Karibu.*	**9**	*tisa*
Excuse me.	*Samahani.*	**10**	*kumi*

Emergencies

Help!	*Socorro!*	soo·*ko*·rroo
Go away!	*Vá-se embora!*	*vaa*·se eng·*bo*·ra
Call ...!	*Chame ...!*	*shaa*·me ...
a doctor	*um médico*	oong *me*·dee·koo
the police	*a polícia*	a poo·*lee*·sya

I'm lost.
Estou perdido. shtoh per·*dee*·doo (m)
Estou perdida. shtoh per·*dee*·da (f)

I'm ill.
Estou doente. shtoh doo·*eng*·te

Where is the toilet?
Onde é a casa de banho? *ong*·de e a *kaa*·za de *ba*·nyoo

Shopping & Services

I'd like to buy ...
Queria comprar ... ke·*ree*·a kong·*praar* ...

How much is it?
Quanto custa? *kwang*·too *koosh*·ta

It's too expensive.
Está muito caro. shtaa *mweeng*·too *kaa*·roo

There's a mistake in the bill.
Há um erro na conta. aa oong *e*·rroo na *kong*·ta

Time & Numbers

What time is it?
Que horas são? kee *o*·rash sowng

It's (10) o'clock.
São (dez) horas. sowng (desh) *o*·rash

Half past (10).
(Dez) e meia. (desh) e *may*·a

morning	*manhã*	ma·*nyang*
afternoon	*tarde*	*taar*·de
evening	*noite*	*noy*·te
yesterday	*ontem*	*ong*·teng
today	*hoje*	*o*·zhe
tomorrow	*amanhã*	aa·ma·*nyang*

1	*um*	oong
2	*dois*	doysh
3	*três*	tresh
4	*quatro*	*kwaa*·troo
5	*cinco*	*seeng*·koo
6	*seis*	saysh
7	*sete*	se·te
8	*oito*	oy·too
9	*nove*	no·ve
10	*dez*	desh
20	*vinte*	*veeng*·te
30	*trinta*	*treeng*·ta
40	*quarenta*	kwa·*reng*·ta
50	*cinquenta*	seeng·*kweng*·ta
60	*sessenta*	se·*seng*·ta
70	*setenta*	se·*teng*·ta
80	*oitenta*	oy·*teng*·ta
90	*noventa*	no·*veng*·ta
100	*cem*	seng
1000	*mil*	meel

Transport

boat	*barco*	*baar*·koo
bus	*autocarro*	ow·to·*kaa*·roo
plane	*avião*	a·vee·*owng*
train	*comboio*	kong·*boy*·oo
... ticket	*um bilhete de ...*	oong bee·*lye*·te de ...
one-way	*ida*	*ee*·da
return	*ida e volta*	*ee*·da ee *vol*·ta

I want to go to ...
Queria ir a ... ke·*ree*·a eer a ...

What time does it leave/arrive?
A que horas sai/chega? a ke *o*·rash sai/*she*·ga

TONGA

Tonga is spoken mainly in Zambia's Southern Province. You can generally get by using English numbers for prices and time.

Basics

Hello.	*Wabonwa/Wapona.* (inf) *Mwabonwa/Mwpona.* (pol)
Goodbye.	*Muchale kabotu.*
Good morning.	*Mwabuka kabotu.*
Good evening.	*Kwa siya.*
Good night.	*Kusiye kabotu.*
Please.	*Ndalomba.*
Thank you./Excuse me.	*Amuninjatile.*
Thank you very much.	*Twalumba kapati.*
Yes.	*Ee.*
No.	*Pepe.*
How are you?	*Muli buti?*
I'm fine.	*Ndi kabotu.*
Good./Fine./OK.	*Mbubo.*
What's your name?	*Ndiweni izyina?*
My name is ...	*Izyina iyangu ndime ...*
I don't understand.	*Tandileteleli.*
How much?	*Mali nzi?*
toilets	*chimbuzi*
men	*ba lumi/mulombwana*
women	*ba kaintu*
today	*tunu*
tomorrow	*chifumo*
yesterday	*ijilo*

Numbers – Tonga

1	*komwe*
2	*tobilo*
3	*totatwe*
4	*tone*
5	*tosanwe*

Eating & Drinking

Please bring me ...	*Mu ndetele ...*
beans	*bunyanga*
beef	*nyama ya ng'ombe*
beer	*bukoko*
bread	*chinkwa*
chicken	*nkuku*
coffee	*nofi*
eggs	*ma gee*
fish	*inswi*
meat	*nyama*
milk	*mukupa*
onion	*hangisi*
potatoes	*mapotato*
pumpkin leaves	*lungu*
rice	*laisi*
sweet potato	*chibwali*
tea	*tii*
tomatoes	*lunkomba*
vegetables	*cisu mani*
(drinking) water	*menda (a kumwa)*

GLOSSARY

4WD – four-wheel drive; locally called 4x4

ablutions block – found at camping grounds and caravan parks: a building that contains toilets, showers and washing-up area; also known as an amenities block
aldeamento – fortified village complex (Mo)
ANC – African National Congress
animist – a system of belief in the existence of the human soul, and in spirits that inhabit or are represented by natural objects and phenomena, which have the power to influence human life for good or ill
assimilados – a colonial-era population classification, referring to those Mozambicans who adopted Portuguese customs and ways (Mo)

baía – bay (Mo)
bairro – neighbourhood, area or section of town (Mo)
baixa – the lower-lying area of a city or town; in coastal Mozambique this often means the part of the city near the port, and the baixa is frequently synonymous with 'commercial district' (Mo)
bakkie – utility or pick-up truck (pronounced 'bucky')
barraca – market stall or food stall; also a thatched shelter at camping grounds, often with plug points (Mo)
bilharzia – water-borne disease caused by blood flukes (parasitic flatworms) that are transmitted by freshwater snails
biltong – a chewy dried meat that can be anything from beef to kudu or ostrich
BIM – Banco Internacional de Moçambique
boma – town (Ma, Z)
braai – a barbecue
buck or **bok** – any kind of antelope
buhobe – staple made from maize, millet or cassava flour (Lozi) (Z)
bushcamp – a small and exclusive place to stay deep in a national park, usually dismantled in the wet season, then rebuilt next dry season
busunso – any sauce used with buhobe (Z)

camião, camiões – truck(s) (Mo)
camp (noun) – a place to stay, but not necessarily one that entails 'camping', or even budget accommodation; throughout Africa, many places with 'Camp' in the name are upmarket establishments – effectively small hotels in or near national parks but retaining the feel of being out in the bush
capitania – port authority (Mo)
capulana – a colourful cloth worn by women around their waist (Mo)
casa de cultura – literally, 'house of culture'; cultural centre found in each provincial capital. The *casas de cultura* exist to promote traditional culture and are good sources of information on traditional music and dance performances in the area (Mo)
casal – room with a double bed (Mo)
cascata – waterfall (Mo)
casita – bungalow (Mo)
CBD – Central Business District; city centre or downtown area
cell phone – mobile phone (wireless)
cerveja – beer (Mo)
chambo – a fish of the tilapia family, commonly eaten in Malawi
chapa – any public transport that is not a bus or truck; usually refers to converted minivans or pick-ups
chibuku – local style mass-produced beer, stored in tanks and served in buckets, or available in takeaway cartons (mostly in Malawi) and plastic bottles known as *scuds* (Ma, Z)
chiperone – damp misty weather that affects southern Malawi (Ma)
chitenje – multicoloured piece of material used as a scarf and sarong
correios – post office (Mo)

dagaa – small, sardine-like fish (Ma, Mo)
dagga – (pronounced dakha) Southern African term for marijuana, not to be confused with *dagaa*
dambo – area of grass, reeds or swamp alongside a river course (Z, Ma)
dassies – herbivorous gopher-like mammals of two species: *Procavia capensis*, also called the rock hyrax, and *Dendrohyrax arborea* or tree hyrax; these are not rodents but thought to be the closest living relatives of the elephant
dhow – Arabic sailing vessel that dates from ancient times
dia da cidade – city or town day; a holiday commemorating the town's founding, often celebrated with parades and song and dance performances (Mo)
difaqane – forced migration by several Southern African tribes in the face of Zulu aggression; also known as *mfecane*
djembe – a type of hand drum
donga – steep-sided gully caused by soil erosion
donkey boiler – a water tank positioned over a fire and used to heat water for showers and other purposes

drift – a river ford; most are normally dry

duplo – room with two twin beds; see also casal

EN1 – Estrada Nacional 1; the main south-north highway in Mozambique; also often N1.

EN6 – Estrada Nacional 6; the highway running from Beira west towards Chimoio and the Mozambique–Zimbabwe border; also often N6.

estrada – road, highway (Mo)

euphorbia – several species of cactus-like succulents that are endemic in Southern Africa

feira – trading fair (Mo)

flotty – a hat for canoe safaris, with a chin-strap and a bit of cork in a zippered pocket to ensure that it floats in case of a capsize

fortaleza – fort (Mo)

Frelimo (Frente da Libertação de Moçambique) – Mozambique Liberation Front

fynbos – fine bush, primarily proteas, heaths and ericas

galabiyya – man's full-length robe

game – formerly used for any animal hunted, now applied to all large, four-footed creatures

GMA – Game Management Area

igini – magic charm used by witches; other magic charms are also known as *inkuwa* (Z, Ma)

ilha – island (Mo)

ilya – a delicacy of very thin corn porridge mixed with yogurt and sugar (Lozi) (Z)

indígenas – literally, 'indigenous people', refers to a colonial-era population classification (Mo)

inselberg – isolated ranges and hills; literally 'island mountains'

Izzit? – rhetorical question that most closely translates as 'Really?' and used without regard to gender, person or number of subjects; therefore, may also mean 'Is it?', 'Are you?', 'Is he?', 'Are they?', 'Is she?', 'Are we?' , etc; also 'How izzit?', for 'How's it going?'

jesse – dense, thorny scrub, normally impenetrable to humans

just now – refers to some time in the future but implies a certain degree of imminence; it could be half an hour from now or two days from now

kalindula – modern Zambian style of music involving a blend of Congolese rumba and more gentle indigenous sounds (Z)

kampango – catfish (Ma)

kankobele – thumb piano; consists of narrow iron keys mounted in rows on a wooden sound board (Ma)

kapenta – an anchovy-like fish (*Limnothrissa mioda*) caught in Lake Kariba

KK – popular nickname for Kenneth Kaunda (not derogatory) (Z)

kotu – king's court (Z)

kwacha – Zambian and Malawian currency

kwasa kwasa – Congo-style rhumba music

lago – lake (Mo)

LAM – Linhas Aéreas de Moçambique; Mozambique's national airline

litunga – king (Z)

LMS – London Missionary Society

lupembe – wind instrument made from animal horn

lutindzi – type of grass

mabele – sorghum (Z, Ma)

machamba – small farm plot (Mo)

machibombo – bus (Mo)

makishi – a dance performed in Zambia featuring male dancers wearing masks of stylised human faces and with grass skirts and anklets (Z)

makwaela – a type of dance characterised by *a cappella* singing accompanied by foot percussion

Malawi shandy – non-alcoholic drink made from ginger beer, Angostura bitters, orange or lemon slices, soda and ice

mapiko – masked dance of the Makonde people; also refers to the wooden masks worn by the dancer (Mo)

marginal – beach road (Mo)

marimba – African xylophone, made from strips of resonant wood with various-sized gourds for sound boxes

marrabenta – Mozambique's national music, with an upbeat style and distinctive beat

matola – pick-up or van carrying passengers (Ma)

mbira – thumb piano; consists of five to 24 narrow iron keys mounted in rows on a wooden sound board

mealie meal or **mielie pap** – maize porridge, a dietary staple throughout the region; known as *xima* in Mozambique (Z, Ma)

mercado – market (Mo)

metical, meticais – Mozambican currency

mielies – cobs of maize

migração – immigration (Mo)

minas (minas de terra) – land mines (Mo)

mfecane – see *difaqane*

miombo – moist open woodland, also called *Brachystegia* woodland; comprises mainly mopane and acacia *bushveld*

monte(s) – mountain(s) (Mo)

mopane worms – the caterpillar of the moth *Gonimbrasia belina*, eaten as a local delicacy throughout the region

mpasa – lake salmon (Ma)
murunge – see *mzungu*
muti – traditional medicine
mzungu – white person, especially in Zambia and Malawi

nganga – fortune teller
nalikwanda – huge wooden canoe that is painted with black and white stripes and carries the *litunga* (Z)
ncheni – lake tiger fish (Ma)
now now – definitely not now, but sometime sooner than *just now*
nshima – filling maize porridge-like substance eaten in Zambia; known as nsima in Malawi and *xima* in Mozambique
nyanga – panpipes; also the name of a dance in which the dancer plays the panpipes (Mo)

pan – dry flat area of grassland or salt, often a seasonal lake-bed
parque nacional – national park (Mo)
participation safari – an inexpensive safari in which clients pitch their own tents, pack the vehicle and share cooking duties
pastelaria – shop selling pastries, cakes and often light meals as well (Mo)
Pedicle, the – the tongue of Democratic Republic of Congo territory that almost divides Zambia into two
peg – milepost
pensão, pensões – inexpensive hotel(s) (Mo)
photographic safari – safari in which participants carry cameras rather than guns
pint – small bottle of beer or can of oil (or similar), usually around 300ml to 375ml (not necessarily equal to a British or US pint)
piri-piri or **peri-peri**– hot pepper sauce (Mo)
potjie – (*poy*-kee) a three-legged pot used to make stew over an open fire; also refers both to the stew itself and to a gathering at which the stew forms the main dish
pousada – hotel or inn, usually a step up from a *pensão* (Mo)
praça – square (Mo)
praia – beach (Mo)
prazeiro – prazo holder (Mo)
prazo – privately owned agricultural estates allocated by the Portuguese crown; the prazo system was used by the Portuguese between the 17th and early-20th centuries in an attempt to strengthen their control in Mozambique (Mo)

refresco – soda, soft drink (Mo)
régulo – chief, traditional leader (Mo)
relish – sauce of meat, vegetables, beans etc eaten with boiled *mielie* meal (*nsima*, *nshima* etc)
Renamo (Resistência Nacional Moçambicana/ Mozambican National Resistance) – the main opposition party in Mozambique
reserva – reserve (Mo)
robot – traffic light
rondavel – round, African-style hut
rooibos – literally 'red bush' in Afrikaans; herbal tea that reputedly has therapeutic qualities
rua – street (Mo)

sangoma – witchdoctor; herbalist
slasher – hand tool with a curved blade used to cut grass or crops, hence 'to slash' means 'to cut grass'
sungwa – a type of perch (Ma)

tackies – trainers, tennis shoes, gym shoes
tambo – fermented millet and sugar drink
TDM (Telecomunicações de Moçambique) – the national telecommunications company
timbila (plural of mbila) – type of marimba or xylophone used by the Chopi people (Mo)
toasties – toasted sandwiches
township – indigenous suburb, typically a high-density black residential area
tufo – a dance of Arabic origin, common on Mozambique Island and along the northern Mozambican coast (Mo)

UTC – Universal Time Coordinate (formerly GMT); the time at the prime meridian at Greenwich, UK

veld – open grassland (pronounced 'felt'), normally in plateau regions; lowveld, highveld, bushveld, strandveld, panveld
vlei – (pronounced 'flay') any low open landscape, sometimes marshy
watu – dugout canoe used in western Zambia (Z)

xima – maize- or cassava-based staple, usually served with a sauce of beans, vegetables or fish; also known as upshwa in some areas (Mo)

zol – see *dagga*

behind the scenes

SEND US YOUR FEEDBACK

We love to hear from travellers – your comments keep us on our toes and help make our books better. Our well-travelled team reads every word on what you loved or loathed about this book. Although we cannot reply individually to postal submissions, we always guarantee that your feedback goes straight to the appropriate authors, in time for the next edition. Each person who sends us information is thanked in the next edition – the most useful submissions are rewarded with a selection of digital PDF chapters.

Visit **lonelyplanet.com/contact** to submit your updates and suggestions or to ask for help. Our award-winning website also features inspirational travel stories, news and discussions.

Note: We may edit, reproduce and incorporate your comments in Lonely Planet products such as guidebooks, websites and digital products, so let us know if you don't want your comments reproduced or your name acknowledged. For a copy of our privacy policy visit lonelyplanet.com/privacy.

OUR READERS

Many thanks to the travellers who used the last edition and wrote to us with helpful hints, useful advice and interesting anecdotes:

Marco Addino, Courtney Alev, Catherine Bartlett, Caroline Bell, George & Diane Bowden, Werner Bruyninx, Jonathan Cassels, Emilie Cuq & Romain Girault, Lieke De Jong, Paul Dobson, Judith Fisher, Sarah Foster, Wolfgang Gehring, L.j.a. Gerringa, Clare Goodey, Luke Goss, Hugo Grote, Milena Guarino, Anna Gueorguieva, Simone Gunkel, Craig Hardie, Cecilia Harlitz, Martin Heinrich, Roz Hughes, Jackie Jeong, Tamara Kahn, Dirlk Kruse-etzbach, Sarah Lahti, Zach Leigh, Sara Lindquist, Andrew Lockyer, Karen Martin, Megan Mcclintock, Pete Morrison, Mike Orr, Martina Osterndorff, Floor Oudshoorn, Aristea Parissi, Kate Parkes, Peter Pichler, Rochelle Pincini, Anneliese Pretorius, Richard Purser, Charlie Radclyffe, Paul Retzlaff, Anton Rijsdijk, Anja Roza, Meriwether Schmid, Søren Schou, Marije Schouten, Emanuela Tasinato, Kimon Theodossis, Kelly Thompson, Maria Toczek, Janine Van Wilgen, Maina Van Der Zwan, Remco Van Hees, Kim Verheul, Per Vilhelmsson, Cecily Vincent, Leela Voss, Beatrice Wienand, Marcus Wood.

AUTHOR THANKS

Mary Fitzpatrick

I'd like especially to thank my coauthors (Richard, Michael and Nick), Andrew Johnson in northern Mozambique, Drew Garland in Vilankulo, Andrew Kingman and Zach O'Donnell in Chimoio, the countless Mozambicans who helped along the way, and Will, Glenn, Brigitte, Adrian and the rest of the team at Lonely Planet. My biggest thanks goes to Rick, Christopher, Dominic and Gabriel for their company, patience and good humour while this book was being researched and written.

Michael Grosberg

Thanks to all those who welcomed me with open arms and shared their insight, experience and knowledge of Zambia: Amy Waldman, Oli Dreike, Andy Hogg, Jess and Ade Salmon, Alec Cole and Emma Wood, Tyrone McKeith, Linda van Heerden, Greg Heltzer, Riccardo Garbaccio, Meegan Treen, Natalie Clark, Adrian Penny, Lynda and Rick Schulz, Glenn Evans, Sheila Donnelly, Ian Stevenson (who let me 'co-spot' on an anti-poaching flight over the Lower Zambezi), Mindy Roberts, Nathalie Zanoli and Samrat Datta.

Trent Holden & Kate Morgan

There are some HUGE thank yous to give out for the help we received while researching. First up thanks to Joy in Vic Falls and Kim in Livingstone for all your assistance in getting some of the nitty gritty stuff down pat. The Seremwe brothers, James and George, for all their guidance and assistance. Sally Wynn for her unparalleled knowledge of Kariba and around, Choice Mushunje from Zimbabwe Parks, Gordon Adams, Ann Bruce and Jane High from the east, and Val from Bulawayo. Thanks also to all the travellers we met, including John and Linda Hutton for all the suggestions. Finally, huge thanks to the production team, particularly Will Gourlay and Glenn van der Knijff.

Nick Ray

Biggest thanks are reserved for my lovely wife Kulikar Sotho, and to our young children Julian and Belle, for accommodating my occasional long-distance road trips. In Zambia, thanks to Sam, Heather and Team Kasanka, to Mark and Mel at Kapishya Hot Springs, to Craig and Elise at Ndole Bay, to Vic at Nkamba Bay, to Mike and Lari at Mutinondo and to all the super-friendly Zambians I encountered along the way who are such great ambassadors for their country.

Richard Waters

My special thanks to Rob and Lindsay McConaghy and their excellent team who provided specialist advice every step of the way; Chris Badger, Zane, and Emma and Chris; Gaye Russell, Kate Webb and my Malawian pal Gareth Watson for keeping me company. Thanks also to James Lightfoot for his valuable help. Finally my gratitude to the people of Malawi who remain in adversity among the most decent I've ever met.

ACKNOWLEDGMENTS

Climate map data adapted from Peel MC, Finlayson BL & McMahon TA (2007) 'Updated World Map of the Köppen-Geiger Climate Classification', *Hydrology and Earth System Sciences*, 11, 163344.

Cover photograph: Hippopptamus (Hippopotamus amphibius) Zambia, Ian Murphy/ Getty Images.

This Book

This 2nd edition of Lonely Planet's *Zambia, Malawi & Mozambique* guidebook was researched and written by Mary Fitzpatrick, Michael Grosberg, Trent Holden, Kate Morgan, Nick Ray and Richard Waters. The previous edition of *Zambia & Malawi* was written by Alan Murphy, Nana Luckham and Nicola Simmonds, and the previous edition of *Mozambique* was written by Mary Fitzpatrick. This guidebook was commissioned in Lonely Planet's Melbourne office, and produced by the following:

Commissioning Editors William Gourlay, Glenn van der Knijff

Coordinating Editor Kate Whitfield

Coordinating Cartographer Jolyon Philcox

Coordinating Layout Designers Frank Deim, Lauren Egan

Managing Editors Brigitte Ellemor, Martine Power

Managing Cartographers Alison Lyall, Adrian Persoglia

Managing Layout Designer Chris Girdler

Assisting Editors Kate Evans, Elizabeth Harvey, Lauren Hunt, Gabrielle Innes, Pat Kinsella, Rosie Nicholson, Sam Trafford

Cover Research Naomi Parker

Internal Image Research Kylie McLaughlin

Language Content Branislava Vladisavljevic

Thanks to Dan Austin, Imogen Bannister, Penny Cordner, Ryan Evans, Justin Flynn, Larissa Frost, Genesys India, Jouve India, Asha Ioculari, Kate Mathews, Annelies Mertens, Trent Paton, Raphael Richards, Averil Robertson, Angela Tinson, Gerard Walker

index

ABBREVIATIONS

Ma	Malawi
Mo	Mozambique
Z	Zambia

000 Map pages
000 Photo pages

D

000 Map pages
000 Photo pages

E

F

000 Map pages
000 Photo pages

000 Map pages
000 Photo pages

X

Y

Z